Modern Real Estate Principles

William M. Shenkel

Professor, Department of Real Estate
and Urban Development
College of Business Administration
University of Georgia

Modern Real Estate Principles

1977

Business Publications, Inc. Dallas, Texas, 75243
IRWIN-DORSEY LIMITED Georgetown, Ontario L7G 4B3

First Printing, April 1977
Second Printing, November 1977

ISBN 0–256–01965–7
Library of Congress Catalog Card No. 76–57334
Printed in the United States of America

Preface

EVEN THE casual observer will agree that real estate, its development, management, ownership, and control, is undergoing rapid change. Accordingly, this text has been written to expose the student to current issues believed most relevant. The book will have special appeal to instructors and students alike because of four main features.

First, the beginning seven chapters explain the new institutional environment facing the real estate industry. The first chapter should be of particular interest since it explains the economic role of real estate. The next chapter introduces real estate characteristics, while the following two chapters examine public land-use controls and the new environmental controls. The treatment of these topics gives the student new insights into the increasing restrictions on real estate ownership. This new material has been introduced without sacrificing background chapters common to real estate text books: namely, the legal aspects of real estate, ownership interests, and real estate instruments. Another chapter on legal descriptions provides practical examples. Since few persons over their life fail to encounter mistakes in legal descriptions, these chapters are developed in more than usual detail.

Second, four chapters cover the leading methods of analyzing real estate. Here again, these chapters are developed in some detail. These chapters provide students with practical tools since most students anticipate using methods of valuation and real estate analysis.

Third, four chapters cover new real estate financing procedures. Because this area has undergone considerable change over the last few years, each chapter deals with up-to-date real estate financing methods, including mortgage credit sources. In addition, this part of the book covers the secondary mortgage market and the new real estate financing techniques. A discussion of leasehold financing and new mortgage repayment arrangements give these chapters special appeal. By placing the chapter on investment analysis after the appraisal and financing chapters, the student is shown how investment analysis is affected by methods of valuation and different financing methods. Explanations of the more advanced cash flow analysis, mortgage equity capitalization, and feasibility analysis go beyond the conventional treatment of real estate finance in introductory texts.

Fourth, the chapters on real estate operations, for example, the chapter on real estate brokerage and title closing, will be of particular interest to career-minded students and individuals desiring a background in real estate for other personal reasons. The growing importance of real estate management warrants emphasis on the management function, the management agreement, and the growing importance of tenant laws—all of which are in the chapter on Real Estate Management. The Institute of Real Estate Management has provided the author with materials that make this chapter particularly significant.

Note also that the chapter on home ownership analysis provides sufficient examples and explanations to enable a student to cope with the rent versus owning decision. And since investment in real estate now extends over international boundaries, a special effort has been taken to present the main issues of the international real estate market.

The author is deeply indebted to four persons who reviewed the manuscript and made numerous helpful suggestions. The four reviewers responsible for improving manuscript quality are Cecilia A. Hopkins, College of San Mateo, California; John Kokus, The American University, Washington, D.C.; Bruce P. Kebbekus, Aetna Life and Casualty, Hartford, Connecticut; and Patricia Garland, Northeast Louisiana University, Monroe, Louisiana.

In addition, selected chapters were submitted to numerous others for their suggestions which proved invaluable in writing the final text. The author is especially grateful to Leonard P. Vidger, San Francisco State University; James H. Boykin, Virginia Commonwealth University, Richmond, Virginia; B. E. Tsagris, California State University, Fullerton, California; Don R. Epley, University of Arkansas, Fayetteville, Arkansas; Sydney C. Reagan, Southern Methodist University, Dallas, Texas; and James P. Gaines, Kent State University, Kent, Ohio.

Attorneys Edward J. Hardiman, Lansdale, Pennsylvania; Perrin C. Hamilton, Philadelphia, Pennsylvania; and Gaylord A. Wood, Jr., Fort Lauderdale, Florida, furnished useful illustrated material. My colleagues in the Department of Real Estate and Urban Development, namely, Richard C. Haney, Hans R. Isakson, James B. Kau, and Charles F. Floyd, Department Chairman, also reviewed selected chapters and offered many worthy suggestions. The conscientious work of Clay Weibel, my graduate student assistant, is also sincerely appreciated.

My personal thanks are extended to my secretary, who was responsible for manuscript preparation, Suzanne F. Hoy. Her meticulous attention to detail immeasurably improved the quality of the text. While this work benefited from the assistance of many persons, the author accepts final responsibility for possible omissions and errors.

March 1977   WILLIAM M. SHENKEL

Contents

Ownership: *Single Ownership. Concurrent Ownership.* Multiple Ownership: *Tenancy in Partnership. Real Estate Syndicates. Real Estate Investment Trusts. Real Estate Corporations. Condominium Ownership. Cooperative Ownership.*

Home Purchase Decision: *Determining Family Housing Needs. Evaluating a Proposed Purchase. Title Closing.*

Modern Real Estate Principles

1

The Real Estate Industry and the Economy

After reading this chapter, you should be familiar with the following points:

1 The structure of the real estate industry.
2 The objectives of the National Association of Realtors® and its affiliate members.
3 The objectives and general requirements of real estate license laws.
4 The relative importance of real estate in terms of total national wealth.
5 The significance of real estate investment, housing expenditures, and real estate debt in the national economy.

REAL ESTATE ACTIVITIES cover more than the buying and selling of real estate. Consider the houses, stores, shopping centers, high-rise office buildings and apartments, factories, and even schools, streets, and public buildings. Each land development, each building, and each real estate project at some time requires the services of many real estate specialists. Real estate specialists concentrate on developing investments, property management, land development, mortgage financing, counseling, appraisal, and related tasks.

THE REAL ESTATE INDUSTRY

Experts trained in real estate may be found in government, private industry, and in the many operations of real estate professional and trade associations. Because of the growing specialization in real estate, real estate personnel are found in large organizations and in the small offices offering professional services to the public. Figure 1–1 summarizes the role of private industry, the professional and trade associations, and government real estate activities.

FIGURE 1–1

Organization of Real Estate Activities

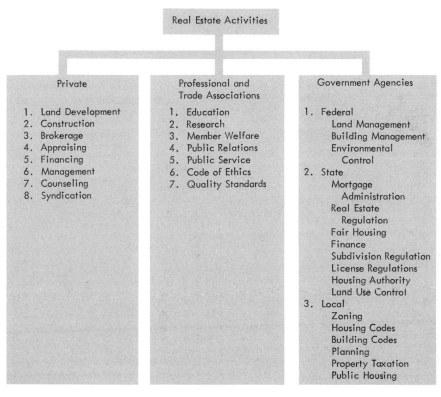

The Private Role

Private industry, concentrating in real estate, serves numerous functions, ranging from offering brokerage services to the more analytic tasks of appraising, counseling, and making feasibility studies. Within the categories of Figure 1–1 are companies that offer the full range of real estate services and companies that specialize in single operations, such as developing residential property or developing shopping centers. Other firms and individuals offer only real estate management or appraising, counseling, or other special tasks for their clients.

There is a growing interest in the employment of real estate specialists by industrial corporations. Corporations functioning on a national basis must employ management representatives to guide decisions in planning business locations. Some of the larger manufacturing firms engage personnel to negotiate leases, to acquire sites, and to construct new branch offices or plants. Other corporations that own real estate as incidental to their main business also function as real estate development organizations. In this list would be included timber companies that own millions of acres, some of which are suitable for urban or recreational development. Oil, mining and paper companies that own timber acreage are among the organizations that include trained staffs of real estate personnel.

It should be added that corporations that own real estate as a necessary part of their operation have an equal interest in an organized real estate department. The American Telegraph & Telephone Company is reputed to administer some 15,000 properties covering office buildings, industrial sites, and real estate necessary for telephone plant, equipment and personnel. Similarly, industrial firms that operate branch plants require personnel to negotiate leases, construct new plants, acquire new sites, and dispose of surplus real estate assets. Corporate real estate operations seem to be an expanding field, especially with the development of franchise motel, restaurant, and retail businesses.

Trade Associations

The real estate industry is characterized by highly organized professional and trade associations. The National Association of Realtors® includes affiliates that specialize in marketing real estate, appraising, guiding foreign real estate investment, and undertaking other technical tasks. The Building Owners and Managers Association and the National Association of Homebuilders are representative of other associations that sponsor research and issue publications for the benefit of members. Real estate organizations actively support educational programs and establish qualifications for professional designations of their membership.

Government Agencies

Government agencies employ numerous trained real estate personnel. Indeed, federal, state, and local agencies have broad responsibilities in the valuation, management, acquisition, and disposition of real estate on a large scale.

Federal Operations. For instance, the Post Office Department has responsibility for managing 44,000 real estate parcels which are under lease or ownership. Such government offices must be staffed with real estate personnel familiar with brokerage operations, property financing, management, and the negotiation, execution, and administration of long-term leases.

The Department of the Interior probably represents one of the more outstanding real estate operations among public or private organizations. Among the Department of the Interior agencies involved in complex real estate operations is the Bureau of Indian Affairs, which acts as trustee for some 51 million acres of Indian-owned real estate. To administer the trusteeship, the Bureau employs land planners, farm agents, appraisers, property managers, and other professional real estate experts. The National Park Service, the Fish and Wildlife Service, and the Bureau of Land Management are other Department of the Interior agencies that employ persons trained in real estate.

The Bureau of Public Roads, with its staff of appraisers, planners, and real estate economists, is another office with an impressive volume of real estate activity. Most persons are aware that the Department of Housing and Urban Development administers numerous housing programs. Again, its staff includes a full range of professionally trained real estate personnel.

State Agencies. State agencies are active in real estate planning, appraising, leasing, property management, and housing operations. In particular, state highway departments have appraisal staffs, relocation experts, negotiators, and personnel of many related disciplines drawn from the real estate industry. Some states need staffs to administer housing authorities, industrial development offices, tourist operations, and redevelopment functions. Some of the state offices with responsibility for property taxes employ large staffs of appraisers and other real estate technicians.

Local Government. In many respects local government offices parallel those of federal and state agencies. Virtually every county needs staff for administering the local property tax. Local agencies frequently support industrial development programs, urban renewal operations, and housing development corporations that provide housing for low-income groups. Clearly, these government operations provide opportunities and employment for the person who wants to be actively engaged in real estate.

In sum, government agencies at all levels play leading roles that affect real estate decisions. The federal government dominates in many areas, namely, in financing real estate developments through mortgage insurance and guarantee programs, in enforcing environmental laws, and in managing federally owned land and buildings. The states administer housing development programs, regulate the licensing of real estate salespersons and brokers, and in many instances actively supervise the property tax functions of local government. They enforce regulations on new subdivisions, and they usually administer certain state laws on environmental and land use controls.

Local government concentrates on land use controls, namely, zoning ordinances, building codes, housing codes, local planning, public housing, and property tax administration. Through these functions, local government influences the direction and growth of real estate activity. In this environment a highly organized real estate industry has developed.

REAL ESTATE SPECIALIZATION

Compared to other fields of knowledge, professional education in real estate subjects is relatively new. Real estate as an organized industry was encouraged by (1) the enactment of state real estate license laws that regulate and qualify real estate brokers and salespersons and (2) the formation of real estate trade associations. With the enactment of laws that required real estate agents to pass qualifying examinations to act as real estate brokers, standards and qualifications were raised considerably.

The first such licensing act, enacted by California, was upheld in 1919 by the state Supreme Court. It stated that an agent "should have in a particular degree the qualifications of honesty, truthfulness and good reputation." Today the 50 states and the District of Columbia not only require a qualifying examination for real estate brokers and salespersons but in many instances require specialized real estate courses.

Though practices among the states vary, the educational requirements prevailing in the state of Georgia indicate the national trend toward higher educational standards for the industry. The requirements for a Georgia real estate license include the following:

1. At least 18 years of age.
2. U.S. citizen.
3. High school graduate or holder of a certificate of equivalency.
4. Twenty-four class hours of a course of study approved by the Real Estate Commission or five credit hours in a real estate subject at an accredited university or college.
5. Successful completion of a written three-hour examination.

An applicant for a real estate broker's license must serve three years as a licensed salesperson, complete 60 class hours in a course approved by the Real Estate Commission, or substitute 15 credit hours in real estate subjects at an accredited university or college. To illustrate further, in the state of Indiana a person must have a bachelor of arts degree in order to qualify as a real estate broker. Colorado and Wyoming, on the other hand, permit an applicant for a real estate broker's license to substitute a bachelor of arts degree for two years of required real estate sales experience.

It will be appreciated that license requirements provide minimum standards. The individual who qualifies as a real estate salesperson or broker is not necessarily an expert in the field. To be successful in the industry, a person must know more than regulations governing real estate agents or the requirements of real estate forms, listing agreements, and real estate arithmetic. To gain expertise, some prospective members of the real estate industry pursue college courses leading to a bachelor's, master's or Ph.D. degree with real estate as the major course of study.

For the practitioner, organized real estate affiliates sponsor fairly formal educational programs which, if successfully completed, lead to industry-recognized designations, such as the Certified Property Manager (CPM) of the Institute of Real Estate Management. Junior colleges, centers of continuing education, and other adult educational programs provide specialized courses to increase the competence of persons hoping to work in real estate finance, appraising, management, construction, sales, and in numerous other real estate fields.

The extent of real estate brokerage activity is indicated by the number of individuals who have qualified for real estate brokers' and salespersons' licenses. The latest report from the National Association of License Law Officials lists 999,757 licensed real estate salespersons and 553,313 licensed real estate brokers. The greatest number of licensees are in the more populous and developing states, namely, California, Florida, Texas, New York, Illinois, and Michigan. While these numbers are impressive, they cover only part of the real estate activity. To engage in most other real estate specialties, a state license is not required.

Organized Real Estate

Real estate organizations active in promoting education and advancing the status of their members professionally are members of the National Association of Realtors®. This organization started in Chicago in 1908 with an organizational meeting attended by representatives of local organizations of real estate brokers from 13 states. Formerly known as the National Association of Real Estate Boards, the present organization includes a number of affiliated organizations covering specific areas of real estate specialization.

To gain membership in the National Association of Realtors®, an individual must join the local real estate board organized within the communities of each state. Each local board is a member of a state Realtors® association. Only members of the National Association of Realtors® are allowed to use the copyrighted name Realtor®. Members of the organization must subscribe to the 24 articles of the Code of Ethics. Each local Board of Realtors® has the power to enforce the Code of Ethics among its membership. Thus the members must observe not only state laws and regulations governing real estate agents but also the Code of Ethics enforced by the local Board of Realtors®.

The Code of Ethics.[1]   Although it is not feasible to cover each article of the Code of Ethics, selected examples show how membership as a Realtor® adds to the services a broker renders to the public. The full text of the Code of Ethics is included in the appendix to this chapter. It should be added that not all licensed real estate brokers and salespersons are members of the National Association of Realtors®. There is no compulsion on nonmember licensees to follow the Code of Ethics. However, a number of states have adopted the Code of Ethics as part of the state salesperson's and broker's license regulations. A salesperson's or broker's license may be revoked or suspended for violation of regulations similar to those of the Code of Ethics.

Realtors® are in violation of the Code of Ethics if they commit fraud, misrepresentation, or unethical practices in real estate transactions. Article 3 requires that "[the Realtor®] should endeavor to eliminate in his community any practices which could be damaging to the public or bring discredit to the real estate profession." While fraud and misrepresentation serve as grounds for revocation and for other legal action against a licensed real estate salesperson or broker, Article 3 includes unethical practices which may not specifically be stated in real estate laws and regulations. For example, unethical practices may come under Article 7, which states:

> In accepting employment as an agent, the Realtor® pledges himself to protect and promote the interests of the client. This obligation of absolute fidelity to the client's interest is primary, but it does not relieve the Realtor® of the obligation to treat fairly all parties to the transaction.

Legally the broker serves as agent for his employing principal, the seller in the case of property listed for sale through a real estate broker. Article 7 requires that the broker treat both the buyer and the seller fairly in negotiating a real estate transaction, though legally the broker serves only the principal.

Further, the Code of Ethics follows state and federal laws dealing with discrimination. Article 10 prohibits Realtors® from denying equal professional services to any person for reasons of race, creed, sex, or country of national origin. Moreover, under Article 16 the Realtor® must not accept any commission, rebate, or profit on expenditures made for his principal,

---

[1] The National Association of Realtors® reserves exclusively unto itself the right to comment on and interpret the Code and particular provisions thereof. For the National Association's official interpretations of the Code, see *Interpretations of the Code of Ethics, National Association of Realtors®*.

without the principal's knowledge and consent. In this context the principal refers to the party employing the Realtor®, typically a seller who lists property for sale through a Realtor®.

Other articles of the Code of Ethics cover relations of the real estate broker in dealing with the public, government agencies, and other member-Realtors®. Controversies and disputes over commissions are referred to local boards according to the Code of Ethics.

Affiliated Member Organizations. Table 1–1 lists nine affiliates of the National Association of Realtors®. Each of these affiliates holds educational conferences, offers courses, and sponsors publications in its subject area for member education. To encourage higher membership qualifications, several of the affiliates require experience, education, and demonstrated competence as a condition of membership. For example, the Institute of Real Estate Management requires that prospective members pass two examinations, submit a management survey report for evaluation, and acquire a minimum of three years of management experience. Other

TABLE 1–1

Affiliated Organizations of the National Association of Realtors®

Organization	Total Membership	Professional Designation*
Realtors® National Marketing Institute	37,309	CCIM, 620; CRB, 675
Women's Council of Realtors®	12,180	None
American Institute of Real Estate Appraisers	7,844	MAI, 3,991; RM, 663 (plus 3,190 candidates)
Farm and Land Institute	5,286	AFLM, 319
Institute of Real Estate Management	6,224	CPM, 3,183; AMO, 406; ARM, 335 (plus just short of 2,300 candidates)
American Chapter, International Real Estate Federation	1,373	None
Society of Industrial Realtors®	1,215	SIR, 802 Active, 134 Salesman Affiliate, 279 Associate
Real Estate Securities and Syndication Institute	987	CRSM, 2; CRSS, 19
American Society of Real Estate Counselors	441	CRE, 441

* Designations:

AFLB—Accredited Farm and Land Broker (recently changed to AFLM).
AFLM—Accredited Farm and Land Member.
AMO—Accredited Management Organization
ARM—Accredited Resident Manager.
CCIM—Certified Commercial Investment Member.
CPM—Certified Property Manager.

CRB—Certified Residential Broker.
CRE—Counselor of Real Estate.
CRSM—Certified Real Estate Securities Marketer.
CRSS—Certified Real Estate Securities Sponsor.
MAI—Member Appraisal Institute.
RM—Residential Member.
SIR—Society of Industrial Realtors®

Source: Latest figures available reported in letter dated November 5, 1976, from Mrs. Beverly F. Dordick, Librarian, National Association of Realtors®.

affiliates of the National Association of Realtors® have similar requirements for membership which usually call for qualifying examinations and
experience in the particular specialty.

The largest group, affiliated with the National Association of Realtors®,
the Realtors® National Marketing Institute (formerly the National Institute
of Real Estate Brokers), numbers some 37,309 members. To encourage
members to increase their qualifications, this group permits members to
earn the Certified Commercial Investment Member or the Certified Residential Broker designation by taking special courses. Over 1,200 of its
members hold these types of membership.

Clearly the trend is toward higher professional standards in the real
estate industry. The standards are being raised by real estate licensing
agencies that require more education to qualify for a salesperson's or
broker's license. At the same time, the trade associations, especially affiliates of the National Association of Realtors®, are constantly introducing
new courses and higher qualifications for their listed designations. A review
of the many specialties in real estate illustrates why these higher standards
are introduced.

Real Estate Specialties

Virtually every community requires services from members of the real
estate industry. Houses, retail stores, office buildings, industrial property,
shopping centers, and public buildings are developed, managed, and
operated by individuals familiar with real estate. The more popular specialties require several areas of training. The main areas of specialization are
shown in Table 1–2.

Real Estate Brokerage. In a sense the real estate salesman or broker
serves as the central marketplace for buyers and sellers. Legally the
broker usually represents the seller who agrees to pay a commission if the
broker secures a buyer. Even here, as suggested by Table 1–2, some
brokers specialize by property type.

1. *Residential Brokers.* The residential agent must know the legal
responsibilities of an agent to his principal, the selling owner. To be effective, the broker must know the current demand for the property offered
for sale. With respect to the buyer, the broker requires a detailed knowledge of neighborhoods and their characteristics. The many problems associated with home ownership, for example, property taxes, utility costs,
and zoning restrictions, are examples of details which the broker must
learn. Local real estate regulations, mortgage financing, appraising, and
income tax aspects of home ownership are other subjects which the real
estate broker must acquire to serve buyers and sellers.

2. *Commercial Real Estate Brokers.* The commercial real estate
broker deals with sophisticated investor-buyers. Apartments, office buildings, and retail stores call for a thorough knowledge of the supply and

TABLE 1–2

Functional Division of the Real Estate Business

Function	Main Subject Activity
Real estate brokerage	Residential Commercial Industrial Farmland
Real estate appraising	Residential Commercial Industrial Farms Appraising for condemnation
Real estate management	Apartments Shopping centers Office buildings
Real estate finance	Land development Residential Commercial Industrial Farms
Real estate counseling	Income property Capital gains Real estate investment portfolio Feasibility studies
Real estate syndication	Limited partnerships Investment corporations
Construction	Land acquisition Development planning Construction management Marketing projects
Ancillary functions	Title insurance Planning Surveying Architecture

demand for these specialized properties. Because of the complexities of these properties, some brokers specialize exclusively in commercial property. Maintaining a personal contact with institutional investors and mortgage lenders is an important part of the broker's responsibilities.

3. *Industrial Brokerage.* Industrial real estate brokers deal with a highly specialized type of real estate and with knowledgeable clients who are quite specific in their requirements. The industrial broker handles three types of industrial sites: industrial acreage, sites in organized industrial districts, and redeveloped industrial land in central areas. The industrial broker must be familiar with the technical requirements of industry that are most adapted to each of these land use types. For example, the prospect who wants a 100-acre industrial site with railroad trackage and

limited-access highway frontage has needs quite different from those of a prospect who requires 100,000 square feet of warehouse space in an organized industrial district. Special industrial site requirements, industrial construction, industrial utilities, and industrial land use regulations represent additional details required of industrial brokers.

Since industrial brokers sell real estate not only in their local area but in regional and national markets, they must be experienced in estimating industrial site utility. For each plant or site listed by the industrial broker, he must be ready to report physical details of the site, including soil characteristics, topography, zoning, the availability of utilities and transportation, location advantages, and convenience to a labor supply, raw materials, and industrial markets. Clients who frequently deal with properties priced at over $1 million deserve a careful review of the amenities of the area for industrial purposes.

4. *Farmland Brokers.* Besides having the knowledge held by a licensed real estate broker, the farm specialist must know the details of farm operation and must have some knowledge of farm economics. To communicate with farm operators who buy and sell farm real estate, the latter type of knowledge is a necessity. In addition the farm broker actively solicits listings for agricultural property which is in transition from rural to urban use. In this case the broker must be familiar with the market for urban land.

Real Estate Appraising. To gain recognition as a real estate appraiser, membership is required in one of the associations specializing in appraising activity. The appraisal organizations include:

   The American Institute of Real Estate Appraisers
   The Society of Real Estate Appraisers
   The American Society of Farm Managers and Rural Appraisers
   The International Association of Assessing Officers
   The National Association of Independent Fee Appraisers
   The American Right of Way Association
   The American Society of Appraisers

Each of these organizations sponsors educational courses and requires a combination of experience, passing grades on examinations, and a demonstration of appraisal competence. Each organization issues a "designation" to members who qualify by education and experience for such recognition.

Like other real estate specialists, the real estate appraiser may engage in the appraisal of all property types or may specialize in a particular property type. Table 1–2 indicates that some real estate appraisers confine their work to single-family dwellings. In the large metropolitan areas other appraisers develop a specialization in appraising certain commercial properties, such as shopping centers and apartment dwellings. Some real estate appraisers develop reputations for their expertise in valuing industrial property and farms. Condemnation appraising refers to valuations for the taking of private property for public purposes, such as roads, pipelines, easements, and electric transmission rights-of-way.

Real Estate Management. Real estate managers do more than collect rent. Their primary task is to operate real estate to earn the highest possible financial return over the longest time period. Managers control tenant relations and work toward an efficient property operation. Managers also represent owners by protecting their investment and suggesting alternative measures to increase their income through programs of remodernization or remodeling. The property manager is responsible for advertising and merchandising to attract suitable tenants. Responsibility for maintenance, such as heating, lighting, decorating, building repairs, and building services, is delegated to the manager.

In the case of commercial property, property managers select the most suitable tenants, particularly for office buildings and shopping centers. For the income from a building is dependent not only on a high level of occupancy but on the selection of compatible tenants. An incompatible mix of tenants reduces income. Corporations, trust departments of banks, and individual investors employ the specialized services of real estate managers.

Real Estate Finance. Because of the capital required for real estate, including houses, most purchases and new construction are financed. Savings and loan institutions, life insurance companies, and banks, among others, have specialists who deal with mortgage financing. Mortgage specialists must be familiar with government programs, state lending regulations, and real estate appraisal techniques. In addition to a knowledge of finance and real estate, the mortgage specialist must learn the legal requirements of mortgages and learn how to evaluate the borrower's credit. For instance, the Mortgage Bankers Association, the American Bankers Association, and the U.S. League of Savings Association's sponsor a series of educational courses to train personnel in this specialty.

Real Estate Counseling. Members of the Society of Real Estate Counselors specialize in giving businesses and individuals advice about real estate. Counselors should know virtually every phase of the real estate business. They must know trends in income-producing property, and they must deal in many types of property. Their services are demanded by buyers, sellers, developers, and investors, including individuals and corporations proposing to complete a real estate transaction.

Real Estate Syndication. The changing money market and tax aspects of real estate investment have encouraged this new, increasingly important area of real estate specialization. The specialist here develops and offers real estate in limited partnerships for investment purposes, of which some are private and others publicly registered. The innovation introduced by the syndicator is the act of organizing people to invest in real estate as a group. In this way individuals are encouraged to make relatively small investments in large-scale property. The client does not become personally involved in managing property operations, and the investor benefits from the limited liability provided by the syndicator. The services of the real estate security dealer increase the amount of capital available for income-producing properties in expanding urban areas.

Construction. While the construction industry is not a direct part of the real estate industry, it clearly overlaps various real estate disciplines. For instance, contractors engaged in constructing single-family dwellings vary from the small speculative builder who constructs fewer than ten houses a year on scattered lots to the contractor-developer who develops the land, constructs the houses, and markets the finished houses to the first buyers. The small speculative builder ordinarily purchases lots in an existing subdivision and builds a speculative house with construction financing secured through local banks. Normally he would not construct or build a house for speculation unless there appeared to be a ready market for the finished house. This type of contractor may also build custom houses to order. Construction is not started until the site has been selected, plans have been prepared, and the buyer has made a firm commitment to buy the finished house, ordinarily with a long-term mortgage arranged in advance of the sale.

Large-scale developers may create residential neighborhoods by converting agricultural or vacant land to subdivisions and then building houses under a restricted number of floor plans. In such instances the contractor must have personnel familiar with subdivision regulations, subdivision planning, construction, financing, and real estate brokerage.

These operations contrast with the operations of the commercial or industrial contractor who operates over a regional area. Such contractors construct buildings to the order of the developer or client who contracts locally for new construction. Contractors in this category specialize in the construction of motels, shopping centers, public buildings, and the like. Frequently they have limited real estate experience, depending on their clients to provide other real estate services.

Ancillary Functions. Certain other functions, while closely related to real estate, are sufficiently specialized to call for their own education, training, and experience requirements. Normally lawyers work in the title insurance field and planners pursue a special course of study unrelated to real estate activities. Similarly, surveying and architecture are related disciplines calling for technical education and degree requirements apart from those of other real estate disciplines. Some authorities would list these ancillary functions as part of the real estate business, though operating as separate disciplines. To this list could be added other private businesses dependent on the growth of real estate markets and their efficient operation.

REAL ESTATE AND THE ECONOMY

The degree of specialization and the growth of real estate organizations suggest the relative importance of real estate as a scarce resource. Indeed, real estate accounts for a substantial share of the gross national product; it serves as a significant source of investment and as an important source of consumption expenditures. Before explaining the relative importance of real estate as a scarce economic resource, it is appropriate to explore how the anticipated population growth will accelerate the relative importance of land and buildings.

Population Growth

The current population of 214.435 million[2] is expected to increase to 223 million by 1980 and to 262 million by the year 2000. These projections, as reported by the Bureau of the Census, assume a slight increase in the average life span, an annual net immigration of 400,000 persons per year, and that each group of 1,000 women will bear an average of 2,100 children during their lifetime.[3] If these projections are fairly realistic, resources invested in land developments, housing, industrial plants, shopping centers, and the like assume even more critical importance.

Even more significant is the change in the number of households that has occurred over the last generation. The number of households determines the national demand for housing. Table 1–3 on page 16 lists the number of households by states according to the 1950 and 1970 census reports. Note that in four states—Nevada, Florida, Arizona, and Alaska—the number of households increased over 100 percent from 1950 to 1970. An increase of less than 10 percent was shown by only two states—South Dakota (9.8 percent) and West Virginia (5.4 percent). Nationally the number of households increased almost 50 percent between 1950 and 1970. It is anticipated that the census of 1980 will show the same trends. For one thing, the number of single households is increasing, which will probably put even greater pressure on real estate resources over the next generation. These trends may be judged with reference to the importance of real estate (1) as a share of national wealth, (2) as a source of investment, (3) as a source of consumption (housing expenditures), and (4) in terms of real estate debt as a proportion of total public and private debt.

Real Estate as a Share of National Wealth

To show the share of real estate in the national wealth, the value of all tangible property in the United States may be classified into land, build-

---

[2] Bureau of the Census, *Population Estimates and Projections* (Washington, D.C.: U.S. Government Printing Office, July 1976), p. 5.

[3] Bureau of the Census, "Projections of the Population of the U.S., 1972 to 2020," *Current Population Reports,* Series P–25, No. 493 (Washington, D.C.: U.S. Government Printing Office, 1972), p. 1.

TABLE 1–3

Number of Households by States (in thousands)

State	1950	1970	Percent of Change, 1950–1970
Alabama...........................	786	1,034	31.6
Alaska............................	31	79	154.8
Arizona...........................	210	539	156.7
Arkansas..........................	525	615	17.1
California.........................	3,336	6,574	97.1
Colorado..........................	392	691	76.3
Connecticut.......................	570	933	63.7
Delaware..........................	90	165	83.3
District of Columbia...............	224	263	17.4
Florida............................	822	2,285	178.0
Georgia...........................	890	1,369	53.8
Hawaii............................	112	203	81.3
Idaho.............................	169	219	29.6
Illinois............................	2,586	3,502	35.4
Indiana...........................	1,169	1,609	37.6
Iowa..............................	781	896	14.7
Kansas............................	588	727	23.6
Kentucky..........................	780	984	26.2
Louisiana..........................	725	1,052	45.1
Maine.............................	255	303	18.8
Maryland..........................	641	1,175	83.3
Massachusetts.....................	1,307	1,760	34.7
Michigan..........................	1,792	2,653	48.0
Minnesota.........................	846	1,154	36.4
Mississippi........................	555	637	14.8
Missouri...........................	1,199	1,521	26.9
Montana...........................	176	217	23.3
Nebraska..........................	395	474	20.0
Nevada............................	50	160	220.0
New Hampshire....................	155	225	45.2
New Jersey........................	1,374	2,218	61.4
New Mexico........................	177	289	63.3
New York..........................	4,330	5,914	36.6
North Carolina....................	994	1,510	51.9
North Dakota......................	162	182	12.3
Ohio..............................	2,315	3,289	42.1
Oklahoma.........................	663	851	28.4
Oregon............................	479	692	44.5
Pennsylvania......................	2,919	3,705	26.9
Rhode Island......................	226	292	29.2
South Carolina....................	515	734	42.5
South Dakota......................	183	201	9.8
Tennessee.........................	871	1,213	39.3
Texas.............................	2,191	3,434	56.7
Utah..............................	188	298	58.5
Vermont...........................	104	132	26.9
Virginia...........................	846	1,391	64.4
Washington........................	737	1,106	50.1
West Virginia......................	519	547	5.4
Wisconsin.........................	968	1,329	37.3
Wyoming..........................	84	105	25.0
Total....................	43,000	63,450	47.6

ings, equipment, and inventories. Intangible wealth, such as stocks and bonds, money, and mortgages, is not included in this tabulation. These figures for tangible wealth are shown in Table 1–4.

In 1968, the latest year for which this information is available, the total value of all buildings represented *almost 50 percent* of the total national wealth. Of this amount, private residential property accounted for almost one half of the value of all buildings. Another 16.7 percent of the total national wealth was invested in public buildings, such as schools, courthouses, and prisons. If the total value of land in the United States is added to these figures, *real estate represented 73.1 percent of the total value of U.S. wealth.* Other tangible wealth, mainly equipment of all sorts and

TABLE 1–4

National Wealth by Type of Property, 1968*

Property Type	Value (in billions)	Percent of Total*
Buildings............................	($1536.9)	(49.9)
Farm.............................	50.0	1.6
Private residential.................	682.7	22.2
Private non-residential............	288.7	9.4
Public............................	515.5	16.7
Land...............................	(715.4)	(23.2)
Private farm......................	152.6	5.0
Private nonfarm...................	418.6	13.5
Public............................	144.2	4.7
Equipment........................	610.8	19.8
Inventories........................	216.2	7.0
Total......................	$3,079.3	99.9

* Totals do not add to 100.0 because of rounding.
Source: *Statistical Abstract, 1975,* 96th ed. (Washington, D.C.: U.S. Government Printing Office, 1975), p. 411.

inventories, accounted for the balance of tangible property in the United States, representing some 26.8 percent of the value of all real and personal property, which totaled $3,079.3 billion.

It should be added that intangible property—stocks, bonds, and money —are not true wealth in the physical sense. Many of these intangible forms of personal property are representative of real assets, such as buildings, land, equipment, and inventory. Duplication is avoided by omitting intangible wealth from these data. It may be expected that with so much of our total national investment in real estate, much of our national income depends on efficient development, management, and investment in real estate.

Annual Investment in Real Estate

The latest figures show that the annual investment in residential and nonresidential buildings constitutes almost 50 percent of gross private

TABLE 1–5

Gross Private Domestic Investment, 1974 (in billions)

Investment	Total	Percent of Total
Nonresidential structures......................	$ 52.0	24.8
Residential structures.........................	46.0	22.0
Producers' durable equipment................	97.1	46.4
Increase in inventories.......................	14.2	6.8
Total...................................	$209.3	100.0

Source: *Statistical Abstract, 1975,* 96th ed. (Washington, D.C.: U.S. Government Printing Office, 1975), p. 381.

domestic investment. Structures amount to 46.8 percent of the annual $209.3 billion of gross private domestic investment. Students of economics will recall the importance of multiplier effects created by changes in gross private domestic investment. Clearly, with building investments equaling the total investment in producers' durable goods, changes in real estate investment, credit, construction, and development have a significant bearing on the national economy. The data for gross private domestic investment are shown in Table 1–5.

Housing Expenditures

Real estate as a consumer good again assumes significance relative to nonhousing expenditures. Table 1–6 shows that consumers spent some

TABLE 1–6

Personal Consumption Expenditures, 1974 (in billions)

Expenditures	Total	Percent of Total
Durable goods		
Automobiles and parts......................	$ 49.7	5.6
Mobile homes.............................	3.5	0.4
Furniture and household		
equipment.............................	58.8	6.7
Other......................................	19.1	2.2
Nondurable goods		
Food and beverages........................	187.7	21.3
Clothing and shoes........................	74.1	8.4
Gasoline and oil...........................	35.9	4.1
Other......................................	82.4	9.4
Services		
Housing....................................	126.4	14.4
Household operation.......................	52.9	6.0
Transportation............................	26.1	3.0
Other......................................	163.6	18.6
Total...................................	$880.2	100.1

Source: *Statistical Abstract, 1975,* 96th ed. (Washington, D.C.: U.S. Government Printing Office, 1975), p. 383.

$126.4 billion on housing during 1974. If housing operating expenses are included in this sum, 20.4 percent of annual personal consumption expenditures were spent on housing and its operation. To be added to this figure are expenditures on furniture and household equipment, which totaled $58.8 billion, or 6.7 percent of annual personal consumption for the same year.

In short, Table 1–6 suggests that over one fourth of personal consumption expenditures are spent on housing, household equipment, and housing operation. This proportion exceeds the amount spent on food and beverages, which accounted for $187.7 billion, or 21.3 percent of total consumption. Note especially that consumers spent considerably more for housing than for automobiles and parts, which accounted for only 5.6 percent of personal consumption.

Real Estate Debt

Most observers are highly critical of the size of the federal debt. At the end of 1974 the federal debt totaled $361 billion. Yet real estate mortgages considerably exceeded this sum: $520 billion, or 18.7 percent of all private and public debt. The amount invested in mortgages was exceeded only by corporate debt, which represented 45.2 percent of total private and public debt in the United States. As Table 1–7 indicates, mortgages absorb a large share of total national savings.

To illustrate this point, consider the total mortgage debt outstanding, classified by type of institution. Much of our national savings flows into the institutions listed in Table 1–8. Note especially that savings and loan associations finance over one third of the value of all the mortgages

TABLE 1–7

Total Public and Private Debt, 1974 (in billions)

Debt	Total	Percent of Total
Public debt		
Federal debt.............................	$ 361	12.9
Federal finance agencies.................	76	2.7
State and local...........................	206	7.4
Total public.........................	($ 643)	(23.0)
Private debt		
Corporate..............................	$1,254	45.2
Farm....................................	87	3.1
Mortgages..............................	520	18.7
Commercial and financial................	83	3.0
Consumer........,..	190	6.8
Total private.........................	($2,134)	(76.8)
Total private and Public.............	$2,777	99.8

Totals may not agree because of rounding.
Source: *Statistical Abstract, 1975,* 96th ed. (Washington, D.C., U.S. Government Printing Office, 1975), p. 473.

financed by the six types of institutions listed in Table 1–8. Commercial banks, federal agencies, life insurance companies, mutual savings banks, and miscellaneous sources follow in importance. The ability of these institutions to attract savings into the mortgage markets determines to an important degree the ability of investors to develop new properties and to enable consumers to purchase new and existing housing.

It is fairly clear that real estate assumes an unusual importance in terms of total national wealth, private investment, and the consumption expenditures of individuals. Real estate serves as an important investment source

TABLE 1–8

Total Mortgage Debt Classified by Type of Institution, 1975
(in millions)

Institution	Total	Percent of Total
Savings and loan associations..............	$286,575	38.0
Commercial banks..........................	137,986	18.3
Federal agencies...........................	91,975	12.2
Life insurance companies..................	89,781	11.9
Mutual savings banks......................	77,738	10.3
Individuals and others.....................	71,072	9.4
Total.................................	$755,127	100.1

Totals do not add to 100.0 because of rounding.
Source: *Federal Reserve Bulletin*, August 1976, p. 42.

for institutions which must invest savings in productive investments, such as mortgages.

SUMMARY

To administer the large volume of economic activity for which it is responsible, the real estate industry has been aided (1) by the enactment of state real estate license laws and (2) by the formation of real estate trade associations. The trend in license law administration is toward raising the standards of persons who are licensed to sell real estate for a commission. Most states require high school graduation or its equivalent, a course of specialized study, and successful completion of a written examination. Some states now require a college degree as partial qualification for a real estate broker's license.

The organized real estate industry, centering on the National Association of Realtors®, supports a Code of Ethics which must be observed by the Association's membership. Not all licensed real estate salespersons or brokers are members of the Association. Within the Association, specialists have organized into affiliated groups that offer training and education as a means of qualifying for industry-recognized designations. Real estate specialties include brokerage, appraisal, and other fields requiring technical training and experience, such as real estate management, real estate counseling, dealing in real estate securities, and real estate syndication. Government agencies and corporations regularly employ specialists in these areas.

The total value of buildings represents almost 50 percent of the total U.S. national wealth. If the total land value is added to this figure, real estate amounts to 73.1 percent of the value of all U.S. wealth. The annual investment in structures, in the latest year for which this information is available, constituted almost one half (46.8 percent) of the $209.3 billion of gross private domestic investment. Expenditures on housing, including household equipment and housing operation, have recently totaled 21.3 percent of all consumption expenditures. The latest data show that the volume of outstanding real estate mortgages considerably exceeds the total federal debt. The $520 billion outstanding in mortgages is some 18.9 percent of all total private and public debt. These figures suggest most pointedly that the real estate industry is one of the main contributors to national income, jobs, and investment.

APPENDIX: CODE OF ETHICS, NATIONAL ASSOCIATION OF REALTORS®

ARTICLE 1

The REALTOR® should keep himself informed on matters affecting real estate in his community, the state, and nation so that he may be able to contribute responsibly to public thinking on such matters.

ARTICLE 2

In justice to those who place their interests in his care, the REALTOR® should endeavor always to be informed regarding laws, proposed legislation, governmental regulations, public policies, and current market conditions in order to be in a position to advise his clients properly.

ARTICLE 3

It is the duty of the REALTOR® to protect the public against fraud, misrepresentation, and unethical practices in real estate transactions. He should endeavor to eliminate in his community any practices which could be damaging to the public or bring discredit to the real estate profession. The REALTOR® should assist the governmental agency charged with regulating the practices of brokers and salesmen in his state.

ARTICLE 4

The REALTOR® should seek no unfair advantage over other REALTORS® and should conduct his business so as to avoid controversies with other REALTORS®.

ARTICLE 5

In the best interests of society, of his associates, and his own business, the REALTOR® should willingly share with other REALTORS® the lessons of his experience and study for the benefit of the public, and should be loyal to the BOARD OF REALTORS® of his community and active in its work.

ARTICLE 6

To prevent dissension and misunderstanding and to assure better service to the owner, the REALTOR® should urge the exclusive listing of property unless contrary to the best interest of the owner.

ARTICLE 7

In accepting employment as an agent, the REALTOR® pledges himself to protect and promote the interests of the client. This obligation of absolute fidelity to the client's interests is primary, but it does not relieve the REALTOR® of the obligation to treat fairly all parties to a transaction.

ARTICLE 8

The REALTOR® shall not accept compensation from more than one party, even if permitted by law, without the full knowledge of all parties to the transaction.

ARTICLE 9

The REALTOR® shall avoid exaggeration, misrepresentation, or concealment of pertinent facts. He has an affirmative obligation to discover adverse factors that a reasonably competent and diligent investigation would disclose.

ARTICLE 10

The REALTOR® shall not deny equal professional services to any person for reasons of race, creed, sex, or country of national origin. The REALTOR® shall not be a party to any plan or agreement to discriminate against a person or persons on the basis of race, creed, sex, or country of national origin.

ARTICLE 11

A REALTOR® is expected to provide a level of competent service in keeping with the Standards of Practice in those fields in which the REALTOR® customarily engages.

The REALTOR® shall not undertake to provide specialized professional services concerning a type of property or service that is outside his field of competence unless he engages the assistance of one who is competent on such types of property or service, or unless the facts are fully disclosed to the client. Any person engaged to provide such assistance shall be so identified to the client and his contribution to the assignment should be set forth.

The REALTOR® shall refer to the Standards of Practice of the National Association as to the degree of competence that a client has a right to expect the REALTOR® to possess, taking into consideration the complexity of the problem, the availability of expert assistance, and the opportunities for experience available to the REALTOR.®

ARTICLE 12

The REALTOR® shall not undertake to provide professional services concerning a property or its value where he has a present or contemplated interest unless such interest is specifically disclosed to all affected parties.

ARTICLE 13

The REALTOR® shall not acquire an interest in or buy for himself, any member of his immediate family, his firm or any member thereof, or any entity in which he has a substantial ownership interest, property listed with him, without making the true position known to the listing owner. In selling property owned by himself, or in which he has any interest, the REALTOR® shall reveal the facts of his ownership or interest to the purchaser.

ARTICLE 14

In the event of a controversy between REALTORS® associated with different firms, arising out of their relationship as REALTORS®, the REALTORS® shall submit the dispute to arbitration in accordance with the regulations of their board or boards rather than litigate the matter.

ARTICLE 15

If a REALTOR® is charged with unethical practice or is asked to present evidence in any disciplinary proceeding or investigation, he shall place all pertinent facts before the proper tribunal of the member board or affiliated institute, society, or council of which he is a member.

ARTICLE 16

When acting as agent, the REALTOR® shall not accept any commission, rebate, or profit on expenditures made for his principal-owner, without the principal's knowledge and consent.

ARTICLE 17

The REALTOR® shall not engage in activities that constitute the unauthorized practice of law and shall recommend that legal counsel be obtained when the interest of any party to the transaction requires it.

ARTICLE 18

The REALTOR® shall keep in a special account in an appropriate financial institution, separated from his own funds, monies coming into his possession in trust for other persons, such as escrows, trust funds, clients' monies, and other like items.

ARTICLE 19

The REALTOR® shall be careful at all times to present a true picture in his advertising and representations to the public. He shall neither advertise without disclosing his name nor permit any person associated with him to use individual names or telephone numbers, unless such person's connection with the REALTOR® is obvious in the advertisement.

ARTICLE 20

The REALTOR®, for the protection of all parties, shall see that financial obligations and commitments regarding real estate transactions are in writing, expressing the exact agreement of the parties. A copy of each agreement shall be furnished to each party upon his signing such agreement.

ARTICLE 21

The REALTOR® shall not engage in any practice or take any action inconsistent with the agency of another REALTOR®.

ARTICLE 22

In the sale of property which is exclusively listed with a REALTOR®, the REALTOR® shall utilize the services of other brokers upon mutually agreed upon terms when it is in the best interests of the client.

Negotiations concerning property which is listed exclusively shall be carried on with the listing broker, not with the owner, except with the consent of the listing broker.

ARTICLE 23

The REALTOR® shall not publicly disparage the business practice of a competitor nor volunteer an opinion of a competitor's transaction. If his opinion is sought and if the REALTOR® deems it appropriate to respond, such opinion shall be rendered with strict professional integrity and courtesy.

ARTICLE 24

The REALTOR® shall not directly or indirectly solicit the services or affiliation of an employee or independent contractor in the organization of another REALTOR® without prior notice to said REALTOR®.

Note: Where the word REALTOR® is used in this Code and Preamble, it shall be deemed to include REALTOR®-ASSOCIATE. Pronouns shall be considered to include REALTORS® and REALTOR®-ASSOCIATES of both genders.

The Code of Ethics was adopted in 1913. Amended at the Annual Convention in 1924, 1928, 1950, 1951, 1952, 1955, 1956, 1961, 1962, and 1974.

Published with the consent of the NATIONAL ASSOCIATION OF REALTORS®, author of and owner of all rights in the Code of Ethics of the NATIONAL ASSOCIATION OF REALTORS®, ©NATIONAL ASSOCIATION OF REALTORS® 1974—all rights reserved. REALTOR® is a registered collective membership mark which may be used only by real estate professionals who are members of the NATIONAL ASSOCIATION OF REALTORS® and subscribe to its strict Code of Ethics.

REVIEW QUESTIONS

1. What is the purpose of state real estate license laws?
2. In your view, are the minimum requirements to qualify as a real estate salesman sufficiently rigid? Give reasons for your answer.
3. What are the main topics covered by the Code of Ethics observed by members of the National Association of Realtors®?
4. What are the general requirements to qualify as a member of the Institute of Real Estate Managers? In your view, are these minimum qualifications adequate standards for the management industry?
5. In reviewing the various real estate specialties, what educational and experience requirements would you recommend for qualification?
6. In your view, what is the significance of real estate judged in terms of total national wealth?

7. What consequences to the national economy would you expect as real estate activity declines? Explain fully. In your answer, include the effect upon gross private domestic investment, housing expenditures, and mortgage debt.

SELECTED REFERENCES

Hoagland, Henry E. *Real Estate Principles,* chap. 4. 3d ed. New York: McGraw-Hill Book Co., 1968.

Pearson, Karl G. *Real Estate: Principles and Practices,* chap. 1. Columbus: Grid, Inc., 1973.

Ring, Alfred A., and Dasso, Jerome. *Real Estate Principles and Practices,* chap. 1. 8th ed. Englewood Cliffs, N.J.: Prentice-Hall, Inc., 1977.

Weimer, Arthur M.; Hoyt, Homer; and Bloom, George F. *Real Estate,* chaps. 1 and 3. 6th ed. New York: Ronald Press Co., 1972.

2

Real Estate Characteristics

After reading this chapter you should be familiar with the following points:

1 The allodial system of land tenure in the United States.

2 The technical definition of real estate and real property.

3 The concept of land as a commodity, as space, and as an economic resource.

4 The distinction between personal property and fixtures.

5 How five economic characteristics of land affect real estate decisions.

6 The main physical characteristics of different land uses.

7 The allocation of land among competing uses through the interaction of supply and demand.

LAYPERSONS frequently do not understand the difference between real estate and personal property. The unskilled practitioner may fail to distinguish between the *physical* aspects of real estate and the property *rights* associated with real estate ownership. Others confuse the economic characteristics of real estate with its physical characteristics. In addition, most persons would agree that the transfer of real estate involves a series of exceedingly complicated steps which are not widely known.

Accordingly, the terms associated with real estate, real property, land, personal property, and fixtures should be defined before the unique features of real estate are covered. This leads to a discussion of real estate as a scarce resource to be allocated among competing uses.

REAL AND PERSONAL PROPERTY

The laws and customs covering real estate depart markedly from the laws affecting the ownership of personal property. To convey personal property from Mary Smith to John Jones, only a properly executed bill of sale is required. In real estate, however, special legal documents, procedures unique to real estate, and strict rules prevail. In part, these procedures arise from the difficulty of transferring real estate ownership. That is, you cannot physically hand over a 1,500-square-foot house and lot to a buyer. Instead, a highly formal procedure and a set of legal documents apply in the transfer of real estate interests.

Real Estate Ownership

Our system of landownership, referred to as the *allodial,* or *alodial, system,* consists of private ownership without the payment of money or services to other persons. Such payments or services were required under the *feudal system* of ownership. Among the 50 states, real estate laws tend to conform to colonial practices. Accordingly, most of our land titles conform to English law. However, in the southwestern states certain elements of Spanish law are still evident. Louisiana is the only state that bases landownership on Napoleonic law. For the most part, land titles in the United States may be traced to land grants from the king of the ruling country. For instance, a portion of Florida was granted by the King of Spain in 1817 by the following proclamation:

> On November 12, 1816, the Grantees herein memorialized the King of Spain for a Grant of land in Florida, for colonization purposes about 36 miles West of the St. Johns River and about 52 miles West of St. Augustine, which said lands extended four leagues to the East Point of the compass in a rectilinear figure taking for the center a place called Alachua formerly inhabited by Seminole Indians . . . provided, however, that the said land had been abandoned by the Indians and also provided that the same was settled within three years by two hundred families.

Even today certain estates in the Southwest may be traced to Mexican land grants or to grants from the Spanish crown. Although the land tenure system in the United States descended directly from the feudal tenures, the feudal land system was rejected in favor of a system of private ownership. In colonial times it was believed that the acquisition, possession, and protection of property was an essential, natural, and inalienable right. Under the allodial land system, it is necessary to distinguish among five terms: *real estate, real property, land, personal property, and fixtures.* See Table 2–1 for a summary of definitions for these terms.

TABLE 2–1

A Summary of Ownership Terms

Ownership Terms	Definition
Real estate	Land and its attachments.
Real property	The legal rights associated with land-ownership: the interests, benefits, and rights inherent in the ownership of the physical real estate.
Land	Economic concept: The surface with all of its characteristics—water, soil, mineral deposits, and climate. Land as space: Ownership of property gives possession and control of a limited space. Land as a resource: Land is a scarce resource that should be maximized and allocated to the most efficient use.
Personal property	Movable items that are not permanently affixed to land or buildings.
Fixtures	An article (formerly personal property) installed or attached to land or buildings in a permanent way so that it becomes part of the real estate.

Real Estate. In practice, the terms *land, real estate,* and *realty* are interchangeable. Real estate refers to the physical property, technically defined as *land and its attachments.* For example, a house permanently affixed to the land becomes part of the land and is conveyed with the land—the land and building are viewed as real estate. The distinction is important where the building may be constructed by a tenant on leased land. A default on the lease may mean that the tenant forfeits his interest in the building since the landowner acquires full use, possession, and rights to the land and its attachments in the event of a default by the tenant.

In other instances property not attached to the land is not part of the real estate—for example, a mobile home trailer on wheels and not affixed to the land. If, however, the mobile home is permanently connected to sewer, water, gas, and electricity and is supported by a permanent foundation (even though the wheels are present), the mobile home would be considered part of the land in most jurisdictions. Conveyance of the land would include the mobile home.

Legally the term *land* refers to the surface, the subsurface, and the space above the land. A land parcel, which is described on a flat plane, extends to the center of the earth and continues above the land to some point in which public rights prevail. (See Figure 2–1.) It will be recog-

FIGURE 2–1

Property Rights Associated with Fee Ownership

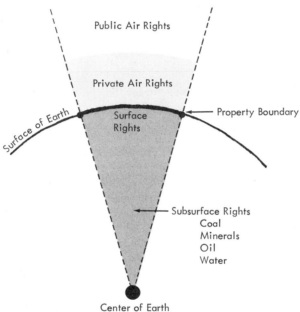

nized that space above the land may reach a height where public rights prevail over private rights—for example, the right of the public to fly airplanes over the land. International rights begin at some point above the earth, allowing nations to launch satellites that travel high above the earth's surface.

In some instances the physical properties of the land below the surface may be more valuable than the surface rights. In fact the surface may have nominal value relative to subsurface rights in the case of oil, minerals, rock quarries, and other deposits of considerable value. The same reasoning holds true of urban space in which the right to use the airspace (over railroad tracks, for instance) to build high-rise office buildings may be more valuable than the surface rights. Indeed, the purchaser of a condominium acquires the right to use the airspace occupied by his condominium in addition to the right to use common areas, such as the parking lot, hallways, and other facilities held in common with other condominium occupants.

Real Property. Real property refers to the legal rights associated with landownership. The term has been defined as "the interests, benefits, and rights inherent in the ownership of the physical real estate."[1] Real property rights are highly divisible. Legally the ownership of property rights consists of a bundle of rights like a bundle of sticks that may be conveyed individually or in groups, according to the owner's wish. Thus, real property refers to *interests held in land and its attachments.* Absolute ownership—the full bundle of rights—gives the owner exclusive rights of possession, use, and enjoyment. In addition, absolute ownership includes the right to dispose of the property by sale, will, or gift. Some of the more common ways to divide property rights include the conveyance of:

Subsurface rights independently of surface rights.

The airspace above the surface.

Possession for a limited time (a lease).

Use rights for a limited purpose (a right-of-way easement).

A mortgage that pledges an interest in real estate as security for a loan.

Many other means of dividing property rights give real estate owners considerable flexibility in acquiring, financing, and disposing of property interests. In some instances the conveyance of these partial interests may be combined to serve the special needs of parties to a real estate transaction.

The Concept of Land. A developer looks at land as capital, whereas the planner views land more in terms of space. Others refer to land only in the physical sense, such as a farmer who considers the physical characteristics and productivity of the soil. For the present purpose it is convenient to emphasize (1) the economic concept of land, (2) land as space, and (3) land as a capital resource.

1. *The Economic Concept.* In this sense land is defined broadly to include the surface with all of its characteristics—water, soil, mineral deposits, and other natural phenomena, including climate, that is, the wind, rainfall, ice, and snow. Besides referring to these *natural* characteristics, the economic concept refers to all *man-made improvements,* such as irrigation ditches, waterways, highways, and streets. In other words land is considered to be a part of nature which is identified with the geography of an area: mountains, lakes, forests, soil, and other resources. In sum, the economic concept views land as all natural and man-made structures subject to use, possession, and control.

---

[1] Byrl N. Boyce (ed.), *Real Estate Terminology* (Cambridge, Mass.: Ballinger Publishing Co., 1975), p. 172.

2. *Land as Space.*   Ownership of property gives possession and control to a limited space. Some view the characteristics of space as the controlling element in landownership. In analyzing the feasibility of a subdivision, judgments must be made with respect to the space proposed for conversion from, say, agricultural to residential purposes.

The essential problem in considering land as space is to provide for a system of harmonious, mutually attractive land uses. Owners and planners attempt to separate incompatible uses of space, for example, commercial districts and single-family dwellings. At the same time, land must be allocated to the less desirable land uses, for example, sanitary landfills. In still other cases there is an economic advantage in grouping land uses according to their mutual attraction. Apartment house neighborhoods, industrial parks, and medical-hospital areas are cases in point. Much of our legislation regulating and controlling land use leads to the most acceptable, efficient use of space.

3. *Land as a Resource.*   The real estate economist views land as a scarce resource that should be maximized and allocated to the most efficient use. In considering a multiple-family housing project, questions arise as to the number of the apartments which would ideally be placed on a given tract. If population density is too high, traffic congestion and the utility of multiple-family space would be lowered by overcrowded facilities, which decreases the enjoyment of property. On the other hand, if too few units are allowed, land is not utilized in its most efficient manner. Low-density land use, on sites in which high-density land use would be preferred, increases housing costs per unit, raises per unit utility expenses, lowers the local property tax base, and thus represents economic waste.

In another sense, developers add capital to land in order to produce an income property. There is some optimum land investment appropriate to an office building, a new apartment project, or a residential subdivision. "Overinvestment" in land may lead to uneconomic operation and an eventual mortgage foreclosure. Even farmers and timber companies view land as an economic resource necessary for the production of income.

Personal Property

Personal property, legally known as chattel, is sold by a bill of sale. If the price is less than $500, the sale of a chattel does not need to be in writing. Under our concept of ownership, property is either real estate or personal property. As a rule, personal property refers to movable items that are not permanently affixed to land or buildings. For example, lumber delivered to a site remains personal property until it is incorporated into the building and is permanently attached to the land. In some cases items that would normally be regarded as personal property may be conveyed with the land like other real estate. In these cases, the items in question are classified as fixtures.

Fixtures

An article which was originally personal property is classified as a fixture if it is installed or attached to the land or building in a permanent way so that it becomes part of the real estate. Chandeliers adapted to a dining room ordinarily would be considered fixtures. Even a stereo high-fidelity music system or a television set may be fixtures if they are specially fitted into wall cabinets or attached to the building so as to be inseparable and permanently affixed. The legal determination of a fixture rests on four tests:

1. The way in which the item is attached to the building.
2. The character of the item.
3. The intent of the parties.
4. The relation of the parties.

In the first case, if the article is attached and cannot be removed without damage or without limiting the utility of the building it would be regarded as a fixture. Built-in ovens and ranges and built-in furniture would be cases in point. Custom-made windows and air conditioner units especially fitted to the house would fall into the second category. If the parties act as if their intent were to make items of personal property a permanent part of the building, most courts would hold that the intent of the parties governs the definition of such personal property as fixtures. On the other hand, refrigerators, washing machines, and dryers which are normally taken by the owner to his next residence are not generally intended to serve as fixtures.

ECONOMIC CHARACTERISTICS OF LAND

Land serves as both a consumption and an investment good. In this regard land is subject to the laws of supply and demand, as are other consumer or producer goods. However, the unique economic characteristics of land complicate the allocation of land resources to the best possible use. The uniqueness of land governs land use controls and the complex manner in which land is conveyed, modified, and adapted to the needs of the population.

Immobility

Because land is fixed in place, a shortage of land in one location may not be compensated by a surplus in another area. A subdivision of single-family dwellings in St. Petersburg, Florida, does not satisfy a shortage of houses in Palm Springs, California. In contrast, personal property, for example, machinery and raw materials, may be easily transferred to areas in short supply.

Consider the consequences of immobility. A builder who has over-estimated the demand for housing in St. Petersburg, Florida, faces substantial loss if the dwellings are not sold within a reasonable time. On the other hand, a landowner holding land for subdivision development in an area of extreme housing shortages may experience unusual capital gains. The immobility of land and buildings places a premium on feasibility studies and analytic techniques that suggest the ideal land use, given the local demand.

Durability

Land and buildings are relatively long-lasting assets. It is claimed that a building may last virtually indefinitely if it is properly maintained and protected from wear and tear and action of the elements. The durability of buildings is both an advantage and a disadvantage. The advantage lies in the fact that the relatively long durability of building encourages relatively long-term credit, which may extend up to 50 years. Thus a lender who believes that an asset has an estimated economic life of 50 years may be inclined to advance funds over, say, 30 years.

However, the durability of buildings is also partly the cause of slum and blight. As areas decline in importance because of shifts in population or the loss of economic opportunity, poorly maintained properties tend to create neighborhoods of dilapidated structures that in themselves are relatively long lasting. If properties had a shorter economic life, neighborhoods would be less affected by substandard buildings that are beyond their economic usefulness but remain physically usable.

Durability also means that an oversupply of real estate, say, single-family dwellings, cannot be withdrawn from the market. New construction must therefore stop until existing buildings are sold. In other businesses an oversupply leads to the withdrawal of products from the market. Because of the durability of real estate, mistaken judgments of the amount demanded aggravate the problem of adjusting supply and demand.

Divisibility

Because the physical asset, land and building, is not transferred physically from one buyer to another, the rights to possession, use, and enjoyment may be divisible into rights that meet special needs of consumers and investors. In some circumstances, the right to use real estate under a lease is more economically feasible than absolute ownership. In other instances, it is unnecessary to acquire absolute ownership but only the right to use the property for a limited and special purpose. This latter device is used by power companies, for example, in acquiring an easement for electric transmission lines over private property. Rather than acquire the absolute ownership of land under the transmission lines, these companies would acquire only the right to use the property for transmission lines. Owners may continue to use land covered by such an easement if the use is not incompatible with the electric transmission lines, for example, grazing, farming, and recreational use. The divisibility of real estate enables owners to adapt real estate to special needs of the public.

Land Modification

While land is a relatively scarce resource, it is equally true that land may be modified considerably. In fact, it is such modification that permits alternative uses of land as economic conditions change. Thus a low-rise retail building gives way to a high-rise office building, land used for pasture assumes greater importance as a shopping center, or, more dramatically, as population expands, low-density residences are replaced by multiple-family structures. In the last illustration, note that although the land is relatively fixed it is modified in such a way that the land space per dwelling unit decreases. While a single-family dwelling may support one residential unit per 10,000 square feet, land use succession to multiple-family use may change this ratio to one apartment unit per 1,000 square feet of land use.

So while it is true that land is fixed in supply, its modification effectively increases the relative supply of land. The same principle holds true for a change in access. Land which was formerly suited only for agricultural use may succeed to dwelling use with the construction of a new limited-access highway. Such highways tend to increase the availability of space for urban purposes. Limited-access highways may decrease driving time to the point that outlying locations are demanded for residential use. Again the modification of land, in this instance by improved access, effectively increases the supply of subdivision property.

The principle of modification enables owners to change property uses to succeeding uses in accordance with urban needs. As the character of surrounding properties changes, single-family dwellings in the downtown fringe area tend to be adapted to professional use. A multiple-story frame dwelling may be transformed into a modern office building. So while land is durable, immobile, and divisible, it is also subject to considerable modification that allows owners to adapt property to changing needs.

High Capital Value

The high value of land accounts for other market imperfections. Buyers and sellers are not as free to enter and leave the real estate market as they are markets for other goods. The high cost of housing, which is probably the most expensive single purchase of the typical family, restricts the number of families entering the buyer's market. Though new housing may be urgently demanded, buyers in the market for real estate are highly dependent not only on the cost of credit but on its availability. Consequently real estate sales vary with the cost of credit and the availability of mortgage money. In short, the marketability of real estate and its efficient use may be adversely affected by monetary conditions, since buyers are dependent on long-term credit.

PHYSICAL CHARACTERISTICS OF LAND

The utility of land depends not only on economic characteristics but on physical attributes. The question of the best land use may turn on the importance attached to physical characteristics versus economic characteristics. For example, certain types of land are ideally suited to the raising of specialized crops. Thus the availability of irrigation water makes the desert sands near Indio, California, one of the few areas in the United States which have the combination of soil, water, and temperature required for commercial date production. Yet some date groves have been converted to single-family dwellings. Economically, the area is suitable for residential subdivisions; physically, the land is especially well adapted to a particular crop.

Because of such conflicts, it is appropriate to review the physical characteristics of land in their relation to land use. For the present purpose, the physical characteristics may be classified according to the main land use types: (1) agriculture, (2) residential, (3) commercial, (4) industrial, and (5) recreational.

Agricultural Land

Probably few land areas are not adapted to some form of agriculture. The main determinants of agricultural use relate to the soil and its features, topography, temperature, rainfall, and location. The physical characteristics of agricultural land vary by type of crop production.

Irrigated Land. Irrigation calls for relatively intensive production. Besides the required physical characteristics of irrigated land, its location must be within economical transportation distance for the crops under production. Given this requirement, the physical characteristics relate primarily to the soil. A highly sandy soil is unsuitable for irrigation because of the loss of water. Sprinkler irrigation does not require the strictly level land necessary for ditch irrigation, but the topography must not be unusually steep. Moreover, the quality of the water used to irrigate land must not be toxic to commercial crop production. Because of the high cost of production, irrigated land is generally intensively developed for row crops, though pasture, rice, and other crops are irrigated on a more extensive basis.

Dry-Land Farms. The vast corn, wheat, oats, and barley acreage of the Middle West is largely devoted to cereal grains. Such land is usually equally adapted to grazing purposes. The more productive soils with favorable rainfall (and more accessibility) tend to succeed to dry-land farming as a more profitable endeavor. Like irrigated land, dry-land farms require suitable soil, drainage, temperature, and rainfall.

Grazing Lands. Grazing lands range from marginal property in desert or mountainous areas to subirrigated land of high production, for example, in central Florida and Klamath, Oregon. For the most part, grazing represents an extensive type of land use, covering land which is remote or unproductive because of limited soils, unfavorable topography, and limited rainfall. The intensity of the grazing depends on the carrying capacity of the soil, that is, the quality of pasture grasses.

Timber Production. Timberland must be physically adapted to timber reproduction, and it must be accessible. The more productive timber areas have combinations of soil and moisture that produce a high annual volume of new timber growth. The less costly the access to growing timber, the more suitable the land is for timber production. Foresters are inclined to view timber as a crop which may take 20 or more years to mature. Soil, climate, and location must be favorable for commercial timber operations.

Residential

A combination of economic and physical characteristics causes land to succeed from agricultural to residential use. Even here physical attributes of land dictate the type of residential development. While residential property may be found in areas of mixed land uses, ideally urban residential land must include a fairly common set of characteristics.

The residential subdivision must have access such that each site fronts on an all-weather road. This single requirement eliminates the selling of lots in remote subdivisions on the side of a mountain with no access, which is illegal in most states. Each site must be physically adapted to a residence; it must be fairly level, well drained, and not subject to unusual hazards, such as high winds or frequent flooding. Other characteristics of the lot depend on the residential development, ranging from low-income to luxury houses. In most instances certain amenities are associated with residential site utility: schools, recreation, employment opportunity, convenience shopping, and the like.

In the case of multiple-family projects, land characteristics may be adapted to the low-rise garden court apartment showing relatively low-density land uses to the high-rise elevator building in central locations. In the first instance, an open landscaped layout on a rolling site with convenient means of transportation or ready access to limited-access highways is most suitable. In the case of the high-rise building, the physical characteristics would include proximity to entertainment centers and cultural facilities, shopping within walking distance, and the availability of public transportation. High-rise buildings vary from specialized structures adapted to retirees and the elderly to luxury units in prestige urban apartment districts.

Commercial Land

Generally speaking, commercial land is more highly developed than residential property. As population expands, there is a tendency to convert former residential property to commercial use. In more outlying areas agricultural property may be converted to commercial shopping center use.

As a general observation, commercial property includes arterially oriented land uses by businesses that must locate on commercial street frontage, such as new car agencies, building supply stores, fast-food restaurants, and a range of other operations that depend on auto transportation. Commercial frontages adapted to such businesses are termed strip shopping centers in contrast to the more centralized shopping centers and downtown areas.

Certain businesses are adapted to central locations. Here the physical characteristics are to be differentiated from other types of commercial space. The availability of paved streets, sidewalks, and utilities and proximity to government offices and financial institutions mark these sites from other commercial space. Because of the central orientation of downtown property, certain businesses must locate in these areas, such as budget furniture stores, secondhand stores, and offices dependent on locations near the courthouse (for example, real estate offices, insurance companies, title companies, lawyers, accountants, and small loan companies). The central location, therefore, is characterized by good access, transportation facilities, and intensive land use. Probably no other land in the urban area is as adequately served by utilities as central commercial space.

The number of shopping centers, including the neighborhood centers with typically 10 to 15 stores, the larger community centers, and the air-conditioned regional centers of as many as 100 stores, continue to increase. The shopping center must be within convenient driving time of residential districts. It must have a site which is readily identified from main traffic arterials. Level land adapted to building construction on a site of adequate area and shape dictates the minimum utility requirements of shopping center space.

Industrial Land

To qualify as industrial land, the site must have soil of proper load-bearing capacity. For the greatest utility, the site should lead to low-cost transportation to the market or from raw material sources. Firms that process raw materials that lose weight in manufacturing tend to require a site near the source of raw materials. This places a premium on locations served by transportation facilities: rail, truck, air, or water. Those industries that gain weight in production, for example, the bottling of beverages, tend to require a site reasonably near centers of population and with excellent truck access. On the other hand, firms that produce highly valuable products of low weight are more independent of locational requirements. They emphasize the attractiveness of the community's amenities and the availability of professional and skilled labor.

It is convenient to classify industrial land on the basis of main locational characteristics: *industrial acreage*—usually in suburban and outlying locations; *redeveloped land* in urban renewal areas, usually in downtown fringe areas; and the *organized industrial district*. Within these classifications are industrial sites intermixed with other competing land uses of our major cities.

Industrial Acreage.   Industries that seek industrial acreage are sufficiently capitalized to acquire relatively large sites for current and later plant expansion. They are prepared to invest in land leveling, site preparation, and water, waste disposal, and other utility systems. A site with suitable transportation, protected from surrounding encroachments, and sufficiently level for economic industrial use falls into this category. Raw material processors and manufacturing plants with typically 500 to 1,000 square feet of building area per employee prefer industrial acreage.

Centrally Located Industrial Land.   Industries adapted to central locations capitalize on the proximity to low-cost labor. Certain other industries must maintain close contact with centrally located customers. Food processors, wholesale florists, and printers are frequent examples. While centrally located space is intensively used, much of the land is suited for reuse by small industries demanding low-cost space. Rehabilitated industrial buildings near the older downtown districts conform to this requirement.

Organized Industrial Districts.   Special emphasis should be given to the organized industrial districts. These are areas that are subdivided and especially adapted to industrial purposes. These sites are arranged to maximize rail transportation, truck transportation, and in some instances, airfreight. Land use restrictions encourage a compatible grouping of industries and at the same time control architectural standards to maintain a pleasing, attractive industrial community. Off-street parking and truck loading space help preserve the utility of industrial space and prevent neighborhood deterioration and traffic congestion. Usually industries in the more highly developed districts must be operated so as not to cause nuisances, pollution, and noise, or to impair site appearance in ways that might detract from the utility of industrial space.

Recreational Land

Recreational land ranges from property privately developed and operated for profit to public areas reserved for parks and multiple uses, such as the national forests. For the most part recreational land is especially adapted to outdoor activities, such as skiing, water sports, winter sports, hunting, fishing, and camping. With an expanding population and the trend toward increasing leisure time, it may be anticipated that a premium will be placed on land with characteristics that fit social and recreational needs. In this regard the trend seems to be toward land developments that encourage multiple use. The combining of timber and agricultural production with hunting and of flood control with water sports are cases in point.

LAND USE ALLOCATION

In the broadest sense land tends to assume the use most urgently needed. In the United States land is allocated to different purposes largely by the operation of the real estate market. Since land is a relatively scarce resource, owners tend to maximize their return by devoting land to its most profitable use.

While the dependence on the market as a means of determining land use dominates our system, the public has been reluctant to let the market exercise exclusive control over land use. Increasingly, government regulations guide land use development according to public standards. On the local level, zoning districts that set aside land for specific purposes restrict complete reliance on the market mechanism. If the zoning code is insufficient to bring about the desired allocation, private developers establish specialized land use projects. The organized industrial district which may be publicly or privately owned is an example of space specifically reserved for a selected group of compatible industries. The operation of the industrial park, the selection of occupants, and aesthetic controls dealing with landscaping, utility layouts, design, and management are directed to a particular kind of land use. Developers have introduced other controls that restrict the free market to produce, for example, harmonious residential districts or an attractive shopping center.

Environmental controls imposing strict rules on land use prohibit operations and distractions that have an unfavorable impact on coastal waters or clean air, or that adversely affect the natural environment in other ways. These restraints administered on the federal, state, and local levels are additional evidence that the market process is not accepted as the sole means of allocating land.

Apart from these qualifications, however, landowners are relatively free to devote land to that use which produces the greatest economic return. To illustrate, buyers in the market for agricultural land that is adapted to multiple-family projects will bid the price up so that farmers have an inducement to abandon agricultural use to the new owners, who then devote the land to a more intensive, urban use.

Even here individual property rights may be exercised so that an owner may devote land to an uneconomic use. Such is the case of a farmer operating an irrigated cotton farm in the suburban fringe of Phoenix, Arizona. Though the adjoining land may be devoted to low-density residential use, the individual may prefer to operate a farm. However, even if there is no direct compulsion against owners to devote their land to alternative uses, the market encourages more intensive use by variations in rent and land prices. So while the market is highly imperfect, the forces of supply and demand tend to prevail.

Supply Characteristics

As a general rule the market for real estate is local. In the case of a single-family dwelling, it will be appreciated that a three-bedroom brick house in the northern part of a city is not a perfect substitute for a three-bedroom brick dwelling in the southern part of the city. Since the supply is relevant to a fairly local area, real estate prices may vary solely because of unique conditions of supply prevailing in a local market.

A neighborhood in popular demand and expanding in the direction of growth illustrates a short-run restriction on the supply of available dwellings. Buyers who seek dwellings in this neighborhood must compete in the open market for the preferred location. The price will tend to increase because houses in other, less preferred neighborhoods are not perfect substitutes. The supply of real estate tends to be centered in a small, localized market.

It will be recognized further that unlike other goods, the supply of real estate may not increase materially in any one year. The lag between the inception of a subdivision and the final sale of the first dwelling usually extends over one year or more. Even in the construction of nonresidential buildings, delays in site preparation, building, planning, construction, and financing seriously restrict the adjustment of supply to the demand for real estate.

Consider also the site selection process of an industrial firm. A firm that is capital intensive, relatively free of labor shortages, and manufactures highly valuable products with low transportation costs normally has a wide range of sites to select from—even over a region covering several states. Such a relationship produces a highly elastic demand curve with a relatively large supply of available space.

The converse is true for the retailer who must locate near a traffic generator, such as a shopping center supermarket. To retail shoes, for example, the retailer must locate near an important source of pedestrian traffic, which is ideally found in an appropriately developed shopping center. The demand for such space is relatively inelastic; the retailer has few alternative sites among which to choose.

The Demand for Space

It is generally conceded that the demand for commercial space is a *derived demand*. A site in which annual rents are relatively high tends toward high-density development with correspondingly high site values. This point may be illustrated by assuming two sites: A, a high-rent site, and B, a relatively low-rent site. To earn income to pay the higher ground rent of site A, the developer will invest in a more costly building than he would for site B. For example, the higher ground rent of site A might justify a 12-story, high-rise apartment building while site B might only call for a 2-story walk-up. These relationships are shown in Figure 2–2. The density of development, the building investment, and the land price will be greater for site A than for site B. The annual ground rent tends to dictate the degree and density of development.

It should be observed that the demand for retail and office space tends to be highly localized. Firms and businesses that must locate near cus-

FIGURE 2–2

Building Investments under Relatively
High and Low Ground Rents

Site A: Two Acres	
Annual ground rent................	$ 10,000
Site value.........................	$ 100,000
Total building investment..........	1,000,000

Site B: Two Acres	
Annual ground rent................	$ 5,000
Site value.........................	50,000
Total building investment..........	500,000

tomers or that much locate within a fairly narrow range of choices tend to bid competitively for the short and fairly fixed supply. The result is to increase office rents and rent for commercial space in prime areas. In a declining district, the relative oversupply of space goes unused at any price. Vacant buildings of long-standing abandoned property are the result of the declining utility of property. Low productivity and therefore low rents indicate a falling demand and decreasing property values.

SUMMARY

Our land tenure system generally follows English law based on the allodial land tenure system. This system provides for private landownership without payment of money or service to other persons The terms *real* estate, *realty,* and *land use* generally refer to the physical property. Technically real estate includes land and its attachments, such as buildings and other man-made structures. Real property covers the range of legal rights associated with landownership, which are highly divisible. Real property ownership implies the right to buy and sell partial rights in real estate, such as subsurface rights, surface rights, and air rights.

The concept of land includes the view that land is the surface with all its characteristics and other natural phenomena, including climate and the surrounding environment. In some respects property ownership is viewed as control over a space. Economists are more inclined to view land as an economic resource that must be allocated to the most efficient use. Goods which would normally be regarded as personal property become fixtures and a part of the land if they are installed or attached in such a manner as to become part of the real estate. The four tests of a fixture usually determine whether the property is classified as personal property or a fixture: the interest of the parties, the character of the item, the method of attachment, and the relationship of the parties.

Economically real estate is mobile, durable, divisible, subject to modification, and of relatively high capital value. The physical attributes of land vary according to land use types: agricultural, residential, commercial, industrial, recreational, and other, less common types.

Subject to market imperfections and government regulations, land tends to be allocated according to the market: the interaction of supply and demand. In this respect the supply of real estate is usually confined to a local market whose characteristics differ according to whether the property is residential, commercial, or industrial. The demand for nonresidential space is a derived demand. The demand for a site depends on its utility for residential use and on its income-producing capacity.

REVIEW QUESTIONS

1. Explain fully the difference between real estate and personal property.
2. What specific rights does a property owner have under an absolute form of ownership?
3. Discuss land as a right to the possession and control of space.
4. Differentiate between personal property and fixtures.
5. Explain how the immobility of land affects real estate decisions.
6. Why is the divisibility of land an important economic advantage?
7. How does the fact of land modification help to adjust the supply of land to the most urgent use? Give an example.
8. If land is physically suitable for residential use, why do owners continue to use land for agricultural production?
9. What are the main classifications and physical characteristics of industrial land? Explain fully.
10. Give examples showing why land is not always allocated to the most efficient use.
11. In what sense is the demand for commercial space a derived demand?

SELECTED REFERENCES

Barlowe, Raleigh. *Land Resource Economics,* chap. 2. 2d ed. Englewood Cliffs, N.J.: Prentice-Hall, Inc., 1972.

Brown, Robert Kevin. *Real Estate Economics,* chap. 5. Boston: Houghton Mifflin Co., 1965.

Ring, Alfred A., and Dasso, Jerome. *Real Estate Principles and Practices,* chap. 3. 8th ed. Englewood Cliffs, N.J.: Prentice-Hall, Inc., 1977.

Smith, Wallace F. *Urban Development,* chap. 7. Berkeley: University of California Press, 1975.

3

Public Land Use Controls

After reading this chapter, you should be familiar with the following points:

1 The four public rights over the private ownership of real property.
2 The main differences between the exercise of the police power and the right of eminent domain.
3 The way in which the property tax discriminates among taxpayers.
4 The three main elements of zoning ordinances.
5 Zoning innovations that overcome limitations of early zoning practices.
6 The content of local subdivision regulations and the means of gaining subdivision approval.
7 The objective of building, housing, and other regulatory codes.
8 The purpose of state and federal regulations in the sale of subdivision property.

IT IS in the public interest to enforce certain restrictions on the private use of land. Even under common law, land could not be used in such a way as to cause a nuisance or harm neighbors. For instance, a property owner may not excavate land in such a manner as to endanger the proper support of buildings on adjoining land. It is also a fairly well-accepted doctrine that land uses must not disturb the peace and enjoyment of other property owners. Loud noises from an adjoining commercial or industrial property near residential districts or even loud music in the early hours of the morning gives rise to legitimate and enforceable complaints. Over time, these restrictions on the use of private property have led to a series of laws and regulations under the inherent powers of government.

PUBLIC RIGHTS OVER REAL PROPERTY

Under our system, it is held that government has four inherent rights over private property: the police power, the right of eminent domain, the right of taxation, and the right of escheat. (See Figure 3–1.) These public

FIGURE 3–1

Public Rights over Private Property

Public Rights	Qualifications
Police power	Right to regulate private property for the public interest, convenience, and necessity
Eminent domain	Right to take private property in the public interest upon payment of just compensation
Taxation	Right to tax private property according to constitutional and statutory law
Escheat	Right of the state to acquire title of the property of a deceased person who dies without a will or legal heirs

rights over private property are justified in the public interest. Although their exercise may cause economic losses to individuals, such losses are viewed as one of the limitations of private ownership. Although government has certain inherent rights, a question arises as to the fairness and reasonableness of their exercise. A separate discussion of the four inherent rights shows the degree to which private rights are restricted.

The Police Power

Government has an inherent right to exercise the police power for regulatory purposes. The federal and state governments have this right, but in practice it is delegated to local governments for implementation. In the United States the exercise of the police power on land use is largely vested in the counties and in the cities and other municipalities. Under the inherent right of the police power, cities may enact *zoning codes* that regulate property use, *housing codes* that affect the use and occupancy of residential property, *building codes* that insure safe, habitable buildings, *subdivision controls* that provide for the conformity of subdivisions with local requirements, and numerous other regulatory measures.

If the police power is exercised, normally the property owner gains no offsetting compensation or payments from local agencies. For example, a property owner may feel aggrieved and even suffer economic loss if his residentially zoned acreage is denied commercial zoning. In this respect, the property owner stands in much the same position as an automobile driver who is compelled to operate only a safe vehicle and who must observe traffic rules no matter how unreasonable, onerous, and inconvenient the driver considers such rules to be.

Consider a community that zones land as a conservation area, preventing the construction of permanent buildings. Or consider an airport zoning regulation that prohibits the construction of buildings over a certain height under designated landing glide paths. In each case the owner receives no compensation. The regulation is justified in the public interest, convenience, or necessity.

The Right of Eminent Domain

Like the police power, the power of eminent domain belongs to the states independent of the Constitution. The power belongs to the states because they are sovereign entities; it is one of the necessities of government. The Constitution, statutes, and common law only limit the right of eminent domain. Again, the right of eminent domain is justified on the grounds of protection of the public health, safety, convenience, and general welfare.

Eminent Domain Limitations. The power of eminent domain, which must be exercised in the public interest, requires the payment of *just compensation* for the private property taken. Formerly, the right was generally limited to taking private property for public purposes. However, the Housing Act of 1949 provided for the exercise of eminent domain in urban renewal efforts in which private property was acquired, assembled, redeveloped, and offered for sale to private owners—usually at a considerable financial loss. In essence this represents the exercise of eminent domain for private purposes. In this instance the redevelopment of slum and blight through the power of eminent domain was justified in the public interest.

Another point to remember is that just compensation is guaranteed and protected by the federal and state constitutions, statutory law, and common law. This provision may be traced to the Magna Charta, which established the rule that "no freeman shall be disseized, or divested, of his freehold . . . , but by the judgment of his peers, or by the law of the land."

The federal Constitution under the Fifth Amendment specifies that private property shall not be taken without the payment of just compensation. Virtually every state has a similar provision in its constitution. Even so, the 14th Amendment, ratified in 1868, extended provisions of the 5th Amendment to all the states. Therefore, it is a well-established rule that a private property owner subject to the exercise of eminent domain is entitled to just compensation, meaning market value in most jurisdictions.

Certain other qualifications apply to eminent domain. First, the right is extended to licensed public utilities whose prices or rates are regulated by government. These include railroads, electric power companies, natural gas companies, telephone companies, and the like. Since such companies operate under a system of regulated rates, it would be unfair to allow private property owners to withhold the use of their land for public utility purposes. In this sense public utilities are regarded as quasi-public agencies.

Just Compensation. At this point, it should be recognized that local government agencies may have the option of proceeding under either the police power or the power of eminent domain to accomplish a given purpose. In contrast to the zoning of private property for conservation purposes in a floodplain area, the local agency may acquire a *flowage easement,* giving the public the right to flood and maintain the property for flood control purposes. The property owner will then be given compensation for giving up part of his bundle of rights, though he would retain title to the property subject to the right of flooding.

If the right is exercised under police power, no compensation is paid; if the right is acquired under eminent domain, the property owner will receive just compensation. A similar condition would occur in acquiring an avigation easement over private property at the end of airports, thus preventing owners from erecting structures under the glide path. Avigation easements would be acquired by a public agency under eminent domain and upon payment of just compensation. If buildings are prohibited under the glide path under the exercise of police power, no compensation is paid.

Exercising the right of eminent domain does not necessarily mean that the property owner would be deprived of the title and use of his property. To construct an electric transmission line or a natural gas pipeline, only the right to use the property for this specific purpose would be required. In these circumstances an easement—the right to use property for a limited purpose—would be acquired, giving the owner the right to use the property in ways consistent with the easement. Such restrictions would probably prohibit the construction of buildings under the transmission line or over the pipeline or prevent property uses that would interfere with the maintenance of the utility. If an easement is acquired, the land remains in private ownership and may be used for multiple purposes.

The Right to Taxation

This right is another inherent right of the sovereign state. Local governments typically operate under delegated powers of the state to impose a system of local taxes for the support of local government. For the present purpose, this right is especially important with respect to the administration of the local real property tax.

The Property Tax System. An individual pays property taxes according to the assessed value of his property and the annual tax rate or tax levy. To illustrate how the tax rate is determined by a local government agency, consider the simplest possible case in which the annual tax rate is derived from the total tax base and the proposed operating budget of the agency.

The total value of property assessments in the district is termed the tax base. Suppose, for instance, that the tax base totaled $10 million for a given city—the sum of all property values subject to the local property tax. If it is decided that the city requires $100,000 to operate in the next fiscal year, the city would impose a tax of 10 mills. A mill represents one tenth of one cent. The tax rate of 10 mills is determined by dividing the required budget of $100,000 by the tax base of $10 million:

$$\frac{\$100,000}{\$10,000,000} = \$0.01, \text{ or 10 mills}$$

Thus a homeowner with a house valued by the tax assessor at $40,000 would pay an annual property tax of $400.

In practice the states impose numerous restrictions on this process. Some states require special property tax elections to approve certain property tax levies. The state constitutions and statutes may further restrict local agencies in the amount of the property tax levy or in the amount a levy may increase in a single year.

The above illustration demonstrates two separate operations common to the property tax: (1) the determination of the just and fair assessed value and (2) the determination of the tax rate. The assessing operation is undertaken by the county tax assessor or a comparable official. His function is confined to valuation. In setting their budgets, the governing agency, the city council, the county commission, the school board, and the like assume responsibility for the annual tax.

Yet the general taxpayer tends to assign responsibility for his property tax to the assessing officer since an increase in the assessed value, with no offsetting decrease in the millage rate, increases property taxes. Clearly the tax base is the responsibility of the assessor, who has no control over budgets or the tax rate.

Assessment Uniformity. As a general rule, local taxing jurisdictions— the office of the county assessor, the office of the city assessor, or another like agency—are directed to assess all property on a uniform basis. An owner's home must be uniformly valued for property tax purposes; the assessor must value each dwelling fairly and uniformly. Generally each property must be assessed according to a market value standard. Some states, such as Florida, require the assessor to find a true 100 percent market value of the property in his jurisdiction. In other states, such as Washington, a fractional system of assessment applies. Here the assessor must assess each property owner 25 percent of the true and fair value. True and fair value ordinarily would be regarded as the current market value.

While the objective of uniformity is a worthy goal, assessors are unable to examine each property often enough to insure ideal assessment uniformity. As a result property assessments tend to show considerable individual deviation.

As a test of uniformity, individual sales of houses may be compared to their respective assessed values. Ideally a house selling for $40,000 would be assessed for $40,000 in a state that requires a 100 percent assessment. On the other hand, if the same dwelling were assessed at $60,000 the property owner would pay property taxes 50 percent higher—an unjustified, discriminating assessment. The ratio of assessed value to sales price in this case is 150 percent ($60,000/$40,000).

To illustrate further, note Table 3–1, which arranges the assessed values of 4,877 dwellings by their assessment ratios in groups of two percentage points. Note that the median assessment ratio of the 4,877 dwellings is 16.1 percent. Note also that some 12.0 percent of the assessments are less than 10 percent of true market value. Forty dwellings have assessments of 90 percent or more of the market value. If property assessments were uniform, all the dwellings in Table 3–1 would be assessed at the same uniform percent of sales price. The property tax payments vary among individual dwellings according to the variation in their assessed ratios (assuming the same tax rate).

Although this analysis deals with the nonuniformity of individual assessments, in practice assessors may discriminate among property types. Typically single-family dwellings have a lower assessed value than does commercial or industrial property. This is an example of extralegal assessments in which the assessor has applied different standards of value to different property types.

In other cases the same assessing officer may assess city property higher than rural property; high-valued property may be assessed improperly with lower relative assessed values than the assessed values placed on low-valued property. Typically newer houses have higher relative assessed values than do older dwellings of the same value. These and other wide variations in assessed values are a common feature of the property tax.[1]

---

[1] For additional discussion, see Theodore R. Smith, "Sales Ratios and Property Tax Regressivity," *Assessors Journal,* vol. 7, no. 3 (October 1972), pp. 25–42; and William M. Shenkel, "Property Tax Assessment Ratios: A Critical Review," ibid., pp. 3–19.

TABLE 3–1

The Range of Sales Assessment Ratios by Intervals of 2 Percent, Montgomery, Pennsylvania*

Assessment Ratio Intervals	Number of Sales	Percent of Total Number	Assessment Ratio Intervals	Number of Sales	Percent of Total Number
Under 6.0.........	339	5.5	54.0–55.9...........	3	0.0
6.0– 7.9.........	197	3.2	56.0–57.9...........	6	0.1
8.0– 9.9.........	202	3.3	58.0–59.9...........	1	0.0
10.0–11.9.........	405	6.6	60.0–61.9...........	5	0.1
12.0–13.9.........	861	14.1	62.0–63.9...........	6	0.1
14.0–15.9.........	1,043	17.1	64.0–65.9...........	0	0.0
16.0–17.9.........	875	14.3	66.0–67.9...........	3	0.0
18.0–19.9.........	749	12.2	68.0–69.9...........	2	0.0
20.0–21.9.........	528	8.6	70.0–71.9...........	4	0.1
22.0–23.9.........	308	5.0	72.0–73.9...........	3	0.0
24.0–25.9.........	212	3.5	74.0–75.9...........	3	0.0
26.0–27.9.........	67	1.1	76.0–77.9...........	4	0.1
28.0–29.9.........	63	1.0	78.0–79.9...........	1	0.0
30.0–31.9.........	33	0.5	80.0–81.9...........	7	0.1
32.0–33.9.........	24	0.4	82.0–83.9...........	2	0.0
34.0–35.9.........	22	0.4	84.0–85.9...........	5	0.1
36.0–37.9.........	16	0.3	86.0–87.9...........	4	0.1
38.0–39.9.........	11	0.2	88.0–89.9...........	0	0.0
40.0–41.9.........	19	0.3	90.0–91.9...........	2	0.0
42.0–43.9.........	14	0.2	92.0–93.9...........	0	0.0
44.0–45.9.........	3	0.0	94.0–95.9...........	0	0.0
46.0–47.9.........	7	0.1	96.0–97.9...........	3	0.0
48.0–49.9.........	7	0.1	98.0–99.9...........	0	0.0
50.0–51.9.........	8	0.1	100 and over.......	35	0.6
52.0–53.9.........	5	0.1	Total.........	6,117	100.0

* The arithmetic mean is 17.9 percent. The median is 16.0 percent. In part, the sales assessment ratios below 6.0 percent and above 50.0 percent may be explained by imperfect data, for example, assessments on unfinished buildings and non-bona fide sales.
    Source: Calculated by the author from data supplied by Montgomery County, Pennsylvania.

Tax Capitalization. The assessment discrepancies cause the property tax to discriminate among individual taxpayers. Since these distorted assessed values may pass unnoticed, certain property owners are subsidized at the expense of less favored taxpayers. Or, tax favoritism may be capitalized in higher market values. Consider, for example, a $5 million assessed value applied to an apartment building. If the tax rate is 50 mills, the annual tax would be $250,000. Suppose, however, that the assessed value is only $2½ million. With the same millage rate the annual tax would be $125,000. In dollar terms this difference results in an annual tax discrepancy of $125,000. If this tax difference between like properties is capitalized at 10 percent, the result would be a tax discrimination of $1,250,000 against the higher assessed property ($125,000/0.10 = $1,250,000).

In short, while local governments, through state delegation of the right of taxation, have the power to assess and levy taxes on real property, this power may discriminate against individual property owners if it is not competently exercised. Thus a system of nonuniform assessments distorts the real estate market, causes economic loss, and seriously limits home ownership and property investments.

The Power of Escheat

The land tenure system of the United States requires that each property be owned by an individual, company, government agency, or other entity. What happens, then, if a property owner dies without a will or known heirs? In these circumstances, an attempt will be made to locate qualified heirs under state law. If no heirs are found, then the property reverts to the state. While this is a nominal right of the state, it does provide for the ownership of property which temporarily assumes an ownerless state. As a result of the right of escheat, all property eventually ends in the hands of an owner.

LOCAL LAND USE CONTROLS

Local land use controls regulate the use of property in the public interest. For the present purpose, zoning ordinances, the general plan, subdivision controls, and the various building, housing, and other regulatory codes deserve added explanation.

Zoning Ordinances

Local zoning ordinances rest upon the delegated power of the state to regulate property. The right to zone property and otherwise regulate private property uses is relatively new. Under common law, property owners were prohibited from using property for noxious, inharmonious uses. In colonial times, the colony of Massachusetts prohibited gunpowder mills and powder houses in residential districts. Similarly, a Wisconsin act of 1899 authorized cities to designate zones for buildings and structures according to fire risks. Los Angeles was credited in 1916 with enacting the ordinance that protected its residential areas from commercial and industrial encroachment.[2] Most zoning codes today are based on land use districts, building height and bulk controls, and density regulations. This type of zoning regulation was enacted by the city of Euclid in New York State in 1916 and was declared constitutional in 1921. From this time, the right to establish a system of land use classifications by districts, the right

---

[2] See William M. Shenkel, "The Economic Consequences of Industrial Zoning," *Land Economics,* vol. 40, no. 3. August 1964, pp. 180–93.

to control building bulk, and the right to establish minimum building standards developed from numerous court tests of the local power to regulate property use.

For example, the preamble to the New York City zoning resolution states:

> This resolution was adopted in order to promote and protect public health, safety, and general welfare. These general goals include, among others, the specific purposes set forth in the statements of legislative intent for the respective districts and groups of districts.

Officially the title of the zoning suggests the comprehensive nature of zoning regulations:

> A resolution regulating the *height and bulk* of buildings and other structures, regulating and *determining the area* of yards, courts, and other open spaces, and the *density* of population, and *regulating and redistricting* the *location of trades and industries and the location of buildings* designed for specific uses within the City of New York, and for such purposes *dividing the city into districts*. (Emphasis supplied)

To administer zoning regulations most codes establish a well-defined set of land use districts.

Land Use Districts. Property owners must rigidly observe zoning regulations controlling land use. Typically land use districts begin with the single-family detached residential district (usually termed an "R-1 district"). They progress from single-family dwellings to various multiple-family, high-density residential districts. Commercial districts are outlined in numerous categories ranging from the neighborhood retail area to regional shopping centers. The last main use districts defined by the typical ordinance include manufacturing districts. Figure 3–2 shows 12 types of zoning districts established by ordinance in the city of Madison, Wisconsin. A brief review of district zoning shows how zoning regulations control property uses.

1. *Residential Districts.* The single-family dwelling district tends to be fairly exclusive. Uses permitted in the residential district are usually described as one-family dwellings and accessory buildings and uses incidental to each one-family dwelling, including private garages and noncommercial greenhouses when placed upon the same lot or parcel of ground. Usually the single-family residential district provides for limited home occupations with limitations on the size and placement of business signs. Rooming houses and boardinghouses may be excluded, depending on the restrictiveness of the particular zoning ordinance. Schools, playgrounds, parks, recreational areas, churches, and certain types of public buildings may be allowed. Normally the district would prohibit property uses regarded as encroaching on single-family dwelling use—for example, farming or livestock ownership for commercial purposes or on a scale that would be objectionable to the occupants of surrounding properties because of noise,

FIGURE 3–2

Zoning Districts Established by the Zoning Ordinances of the City of Madison, Wisconsin

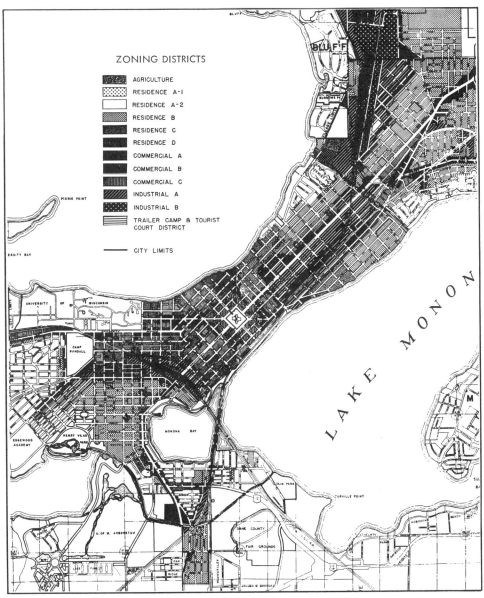

Zoning ordinances establish land use districts that regulate land use in each district.

dust, or odor. Residential districts typically define the minimum allowable square feet of land area, side yard building setbacks, and front and rear yards.

Provision will also be made for other residential categories: duplexes, quadruplexes, low-rise garden court apartments, high-rise apartment buildings, and the like. Normally only restricted commercial uses would be allowed in such residential areas.

2. *Commercial and Industrial Districts.* Similar arrangements prevail for commercial and manufacturing districts. But here there is an important difference. Recall that the single-family detached dwelling district provided for exclusively residential land uses. As additional districts are considered, they tend to be *progressively inclusive.* For instance, in a residential zone permitting two-family dwellings, it may be provided that uses in the preceding district (as listed in the zoning ordinance) are allowed. Therefore, while two-family dwellings are not permitted in a single-family dwelling district, because of the progressively inclusive feature, single-family dwellings are allowed in duplex or two-family dwelling districts. This principle as it extends to commercial and manufacturing districts allows mixed property uses, even to the point of allowing a mixture of inharmonious property uses.

For example, a zoning ordinance setting aside a district for office-institutional uses may state that uses permitted in multiple-residence districts are allowed. Similarly, in manufacturing districts that allow fabrication, assembly, distribution, and storage operations, uses allowed in the wholesale business district may also be permitted. For example, in an industrial district that allowed stockyards, bulk storage of petroleum, and slaughterhouses, the uses in the preceding industrial district were permitted.

The final effect of progressively inclusive districts is to permit the development of mixed, inharmonious land uses. An owner of land in a heavy industrial district that permits the uses of the preceding district may dispose of his property to a nonheavy industrial user. Over time, competing property uses develop into a district of commercial, industrial, and sometimes residential uses. Much of the slum and blight surrounding downtown fringe areas has resulted from incompatible property uses.

Bulk and Height Restrictions. With respect to residential areas, bulk regulations protect against congestion and lead to more desirable and stable residential neighborhoods. To accomplish these aims, the allowable density and physical volume of buildings are specified by the usual zoning ordinance. Such restrictions protect residential property in the right to the light, air, and space provided by the minimum standard for open space.

Bulk regulation may impose a floor area ratio, which is defined as the total floor area divided by the lot area. A building of 20,000 square feet of floor area on a lot of 10,000 square feet has a floor area ratio of 2.0. In addition the height is generally regulated by establishing a maximum allowable building height. In residential areas, a 1½-story height limita-tion is not unusual. To illustrate, New York City controls density in a residential area by providing for an open space ratio of 150 percent. The open space ratio is the open space of the zoning lot expressed as a percent of the floor area. With an open space ratio of 150 percent, a building of 20,000 square feet of floor area must have an open space of 30,000 square feet. Besides these regulations, zoning ordinances provide for minimum front, rear, and side yards. For example, a minimum lot area of 9,500 square feet and a minimum lot width of 100 feet may be required in a single-family dwelling detached area. A 20-foot minimum depth may be required for front yards, and a 15-foot minimum width for side yards.

Other Minimum Standards. Certain minimum standards prevailing for the respective land use districts tend to preserve neighborhood characteris-tics. For example, a single-family dwelling of less than 600 square feet may be prohibited in a residential district. Or a minimum lot area may be specified, for example, 6,000 square feet. As these minimum standards are applied in the respective districts, a tendency toward conformity and the grouping of harmonious land uses would result.

Zoning Code Provisions. Though zoning ordinances vary, they gen-erally include the following topics:

Establishment of Land Use Districts	Zoning Board of Appeals
Rules for the Interpretation of District Boundaries	Powers and Duties of the Board of Appeals
Application of District Regulations	Appeals from the Board of Appeals
Nonconforming Uses	Duties of Administrative Officials
Schedule of District Regulations	Schedule of Fees and Charges
Administration and Enforcement	Amendments
Administration of Violation Complaints	Penalties for Violations
	Definitions

The details covered by these sections vary with the complexity of the local ordinance problems. Note that virtually every ordinance makes pro-vision for nonconforming uses. These are defined as structures that would not be permitted under the existing zoning ordinance. Although the uses may have been lawful prior to the adoption of the current zoning ordi-nance, they become nonconforming under the current ordinance. Most zoning codes provide that a nonconforming use may not be enlarged or increased or altered in any way that increases its nonconformity. If a non-conforming building is abandoned or destroyed by fire or other natural causes, the use may not be continued. This provision is necessary to gradually eliminate nonconforming structures. Without this provision, non-conforming uses would be continued indefinitely.

Nonconforming uses contrast with zoning variances. A variance is a relaxation of the terms of the zoning ordinance where the variance will not be contrary to the public interest. Ideally a variance is allowed owing to conditions peculiar to the property and not the result of the applicant's actions. The variance is allowed where literal enforcement of the ordinance would result in unnecessary and undue hardship. Usually a variance would be authorized only for height, area, and size of structure or a relaxation of side yard and open spaces. Note also that zoning ordinances provide procedures for the appeal of the administration and enforcement provisions.

Zoning Innovations.   Traditionally the zoning codes have followed the concept established in 1916 by the village of Euclid, New York. The central idea was that zoning regulations must control the purchase, development, and use of individual subdivision lots. While at the time this approach may have been a satisfactory means of controlling scattered developments, such controls lack flexibility for planning larger scale developments. Other changes have revised the controls, some of which are still applied, that relate to industrial land use. Some of the leading trends affecting urban land use warrant further mention.

1. *Planned Unit Developments.*   The planned unit development gives developers more flexibility in arranging space for maximum utility. The system of land use districts specified in the zoning ordinance is based on the separation of different types of land use in discrete districts. But in planning an integrated large-scale development, certain retail, residential, and industrial uses may be combined in a pleasing and attractive working and living environment. Planned unit zoning is based on the following objectives:

1. To provide variety and flexibility in land development.
2. To allocate land efficiently, providing for private maintenance and common open spaces.
3. To promote the more efficient use of public facilities for residential and ancillary purposes.

In providing for residential development, planned unit developments allow for flexibility in lot frontage and lot area and permit mixed property uses where the effect contributes to a more desirable community.

This philosophy is expressed in the new town developments which provide for a system of mixed land uses. Typical examples include Reston, Virginia, a new town of 7,180 acres; Laguna Niguel, California, 7,100 acres; El Dorado Hills, California, 9,800 acres; and Irvine Ranch, California, 93,000 acres. Columbia, Maryland, a new town of some 15,000 acres, is another example of a development in which site planning provides for shopping, employment, and other community facilities. In each of these examples, the planning integrates property uses into a functioning community.

2. *Industrial Performance Standards.* Industrial land use has been handicapped by long lists of prohibited industries. Prohibited lists have been criticized on the ground that they assume an industry is guilty of creating a nuisance. Observers have noted that it is not the industry that is guilty but its operation. To illustrate the impact of prohibited lists, consider the following list, which is typical of such a zoning ordinance:

Alcohol distillation	Pickle manufacture
Ammonia, bleaching, or chlorine manufacture	Piled rubber goods manufacture
Arsenal	Planing mills
Bag cleaning	Potash works
Boiler works	Rolling mills
Central mixing plant for cement, mortar, plaster, or housing material	Saltworks
	Sauerkraut manufacture
	Smelting of tin, copper, zinc, or iron ores
Cotton oil manufacture	Soap manufacture
Dog pound	Soda and compound manufacture
Dyestuff manufacture	Stove polish manufacture
Emery cloth or sandpaper manufacture	Tallow, grease, or lard manufacture or refining from or of animal fat
Extermination or insect poison manufacture	Tanning, curing, or storage of rawhides or skins
Feed mills	Tar distillation or manufacture
Fertilizer manufacture	Tar roofing or waterproofing manufacture
Forge plant	
Glue, size, or gelatin manufacture	Tobacco manufacture or treatment
Iron, steel, brass, or copper foundry or fabrication	Vinegar manufacture
Paint, oil, shellac, turpentine, or varnish manufacture	Wool pulling or scouring
	Yeast plant
Paper and pulp manufacture	

Surely, with proper controls a glue manufacturer or a maker of sauerkraut could conduct operations in an attractive building on a landscaped lot with off-street parking and truck-maneuvering space that would add to the local property tax base and employment. To accomplish such ends, *performance standards* substitute for lists of prohibited industries.

Performance standards control the operation of industry. That is, industry is considered acceptable if it is operated in conformity with standards that control noise, air pollution, fire, and explosive hazards. For instance, an industry would be acceptable if it were operated so as not to cause a noise level above 90 decibels at the property line. Performance standards, though difficult to administer, are directed at industry operation without assuming that industries are a nuisance that must be eliminated regardless of the way in which they are operated.

Land Use Planning

Ideally, a community would develop a land use plan in which the sum of land values would be the maximum as determined by market forces. This result would be realized if each parcel were employed at its optimum use. The general plan is directed to this task.

Sometimes called the comprehensive or master plan, the general plan is a statement of community goals covering the physical development of the community with respect to its social, economic, and political objectives. As accepted by the local community, the plan allocates public and private land for recreational, public, commercial, residential, and industrial uses. The general or comprehensive plan, which is required in some states for every organized community, is controlled by government policy, coordinates public and private agencies, and provides for a continual review of land use and related planning issues. Figure 3–3 illustrates the General Plan that has guided the development of Palm Springs, California, since 1959.

Because land planning tends to maximize community goals, it varies with the community. Some experts direct the master plan to promoting the local economic bases: for example, tourism in Miami Beach, Florida, and Palm Springs, California; prefabricated metal manufacturing in New Britain, Connecticut, and the farm implement industry in the Quad Cities of Illinois and Iowa (Rock Island, Moline, and East Moline, Illinois, and Davenport, Iowa).

To reach these goals the general plan will include a detailed survey of the *physical characteristics* of the community. Natural resources, topography, climate, present land use, and other physical characteristics will suggest the best land development plan for maximum use. The master plan survey also includes *a study of the economic base:* those activities in which people earn their living. The main sources of employment, the local labor skills, the transportation system, the state and local tax system, and other economic data would be relevant to an economic analysis. The last part of the general plan, the *social survey,* covers population characteristics: education, age level, household size, per capita income, and the like.

Such a study leads to the tentative allocation of major land use areas. The general plan is used to guide public and private investments in buildings, recreational centers, streets, and different property uses. In short, the master plan encourages the type of land use development that best meets local needs. In a sense the general plan sets the stage for other land use controls that implement it. Indeed, zoning regulations, subdivision regula-

FIGURE 3-3

The Original General Plan That Has Guided the Present Development of Palm Springs, California

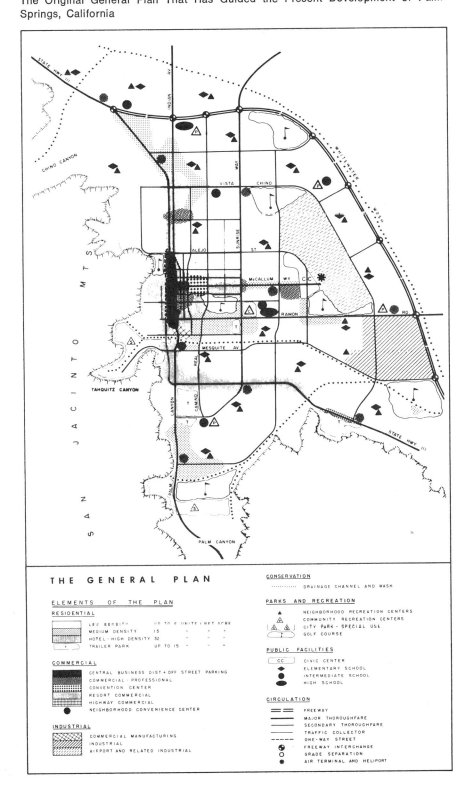

tions, and building and other codes are among the devices that help expedite objectives of the general plan.

Local Subdivision Regulations

Many of the problems of older neighborhoods may be traced to inadequate local subdivision regulations. The central problem arises among subdivisions that have substandard streets of too narrow width or streets that are poorly placed with respect to the existing traffic pattern and that include a subdivision plan poorly adapted to modern housing. To insure that subdivisions conform to local regulations, most organized communities require local approval of a subdivision before land may be subdivided and sold as individual lots.

Local Subdivision Approval.   A typical subdivision is defined as "the division of a parcel of land into five or more lots or parcels for the purpose of transfer of ownership or building development. . . ." While the number of lots defining a subdivision varies, the legal definition of a subdivision is directed to controlling residential development. Toward this end, land used in agriculture, defined as parcels of five acres or more that do not involve new street construction, is normally exempt. In other respects, subdivision regulations require approval by numerous city, township, county, or other local offices. Because subdivisions must conform to the local plan, the zoning ordinance, and safety regulations, a number of offices must be consulted for approval. The main issues relate to street access, lot layout, and minimum standards covering street construction and paving, water, sewage, and other utility installations.

While the states and federal government have placed various other controls on subdivision development, for the most part their interest is in preventing fraud and misrepresentation in the sale of subdivision land. These provisions are in addition to the environmental controls administered on the state and federal levels. With these qualifications, subdivision approval requires consultation with local government agencies. Although the names of the agencies vary among jurisdictions, the function of each office is fairly common to the subdivision approval process.

1. *The Planning Commission.*   In those communities which have adopted a general plan, subdivision developers must gain the approval of the planning commission, which coordinates subdivision review by local officials to the end that the proposed subdivision conforms with the zoning ordinance, building codes, and other regulations that affect lot sale and development. The planning commission has the ultimate responsibility for approving subdivision design. The layout of roads and public spaces and the minimum lot area must conform to the existing street pattern and utility layout.

2. *The County Engineer.*   The local office which has responsibility for municipal water, sewerage, and drainage must approve the planned utility

system. If this office is responsible for the construction of streets, roads, and sidewalks and their location, these must also be reviewed by the county engineer. Since the subdivider will dedicate approved streets to the city or county, their future maintenance becomes a city-county expense. Hence the county engineer is responsible for seeing that physical construction meets minimum local construction standards.

3. *Fire and Police Protection.*   Subdivisions have been disapproved by fire departments because the street plan did not provide for the convenient access of fire-fighting equipment. Approval of the subdivision by the fire department insures that streets and utilities will permit the movement of emergency equipment. Likewise, the water supply must be available at appropriate access points at proper pressures. Similarly, the traffic division of the police department examines the street plan with respect to traffic control, school patrols, and pedestrian, auto, and truck traffic.

4. *Local School Boards.*   The local school board has responsibility for future school planning. An unanticipated new subdivision could shift the demand for school space substantially. Subdivision approval by local school agencies permits school officials to anticipate the need for new school facilities and the space requirements of those facilities.

5. *Parks and Recreation.*   If a municipality has an organized park and recreational program, new subdivisions must contribute to the health, stability, and welfare of neighborhoods. Planning for parks requires a balance of land use to meet the recreational needs of children, other age groups, and the community as a whole. The park department may negotiate with the subdivider for the preservation or dedication of space for playground and other recreational needs.

6. *Other Agencies.*   In some communities a potential subdivider may be required to coordinate the subdivision with mass transportation officials. There may be a need to minimize the volume of traffic or to reserve space for off-street parking or to provide for mass transit facilities. Similarly, though not directly involved in local operations, the property tax assessor must be consulted with respect to records, plans, and the assessment of proposed subdivision land.

Given these approvals, the county recorder or clerk of the court may only accept subdivisions that conform to legal descriptions showing the exact boundaries and clear title. The recording of the proposed plat must be in accordance with state law and county ordinances. A review of typical subdivision procedures demonstrates the need to closely observe local subdivision regulations.

The Preliminary Plan.   Subdivision approval starts with the submission of the preliminary plan to the local planning office. At this step the agency only grants conditional approval. A favorable report means that the agency will grant conditional approval if the plan generally conforms to local subdivision standards. The approval is conditional on making recommended changes that conform to the requirements of the planning agency.

FIGURE 3–4

A Portion of the Woodlands Subdivision of Fort Lauderdale, Florida, Showing a List of the Requirements for Final Approval

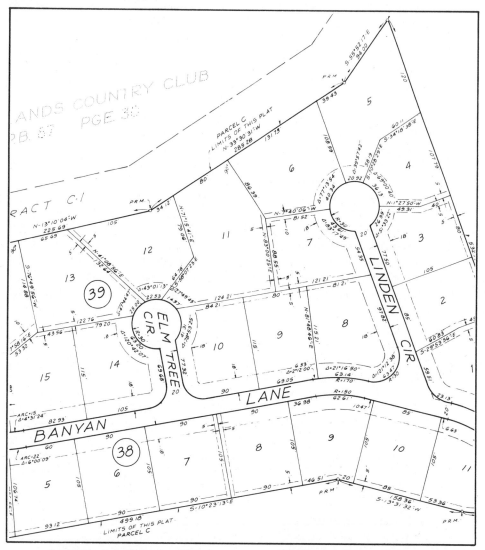

1. Right-of-way lines of streets, easements and other rights-of-way, and property lines of residential lots and other sites, with accurate dimensions, bearings and curve data.
2. Name and right-of-way width of each street or other right-of-way.
3. Location, dimensions and purpose of any easements.
4. Number to identify each lot or site.
5. Purpose for which sites, other than residential lots, are dedicated or reserved.
6. Minimum building setback line on all lots and other sites.
7. Location and description of monuments.
8. Names of record owners of adjoining unplatted land.
9. Reference to recorded subdivision plats of adjoining platted land by record name, date and number.
10. Certification by surveyor or engineer.
11. Statement by owner dedicating streets, rights-of-way and any sites for public uses.
12. Approval by local authorities.
13. Title, scale, north arrow and date.

Source: *Suggested Land Subdivision Regulations* (Washington, D.C.: U.S. Government Printing Office, 1960), p. 53.

Conditional approval does not constitute final approval of the subdivision plan.

Preparation of the Final Plat. After conditional approval, the subdivider is allowed to stake out the plat in accordance with the survey proposed in the preliminary plan. At this stage a final map is prepared which is submitted together with a bond certifying that improvements will be completed as specified. The final plat is approved after the survey and the final map have been accepted. The survey is reviewed by a registered engineer or a licensed land surveyor to determine whether it meets the technical requirements of state and local law.

Approval of the final plat will be granted if the streets are laid out to conform with adjoining streets in their general direction and construction. The name of the plat must agree with planning rules governing subdivision designations, and all taxes and special assessments must be paid by the date of approval. Figure 3–4 shows the detail required on a subdivision map. Note the list of requirements for final approval.

Recording Subdivision Plats. After final approval of the subdivision by the designated planning official, the subdivision will be accepted for recording. Recording allows the subdivider to describe property by lots and blocks such that the map will be filed with the complete legal description for every property. The recording will be accepted if it carries with it an affidavit from a licensed surveyor that the survey is correct with regard to the required surveying monuments and that it meets other local and state laws. While the act of recording a subdivision constitutes a public dedication of streets, playgrounds, and public areas, it does not necessarily signify final approval. The developer will usually be required to post a performance bond or a certified check in sufficient amount to insure the completion of all required streets and utilities.

Building and Other Regulatory Codes

Building codes, housing codes, electrical codes, and plumbing codes represent an exercise of the police power—they are directed to the protection of the public health, safety, and welfare. At the same time they must not violate constitutional provisions that protect persons against the deprivation of life, liberty, and property without due process of law.

Building Codes. Building codes seek to insure the safety of buildings used by the public by regulating the construction materials used and the standards of construction. A separate section of such codes relates to the type of permitted plumbing materials and the minimum construction requirements for sewerage systems. Similarly, electrical codes define acceptable electrical materials and their manner of connection and insulation. The purpose of building codes is described by the International Conference of Building Officials in the following terms:

> To provide minimum standards to safeguard life or limb, health, property and public welfare by regulating and controlling the design, construction,

quality of materials, use and occupancy, location and maintenance of all buildings and structures within the city and certain equipment specifically regulated herein.

Where building codes are effective, they apply to the construction, alteration, moving, demolition, and repair of all nonpublic structures. Enforcement is provided by the permit system. New construction is legally permitted only after a permit has been issued by the designated official. The applicant must demonstrate that the proposed building complies with local building code requirements. Inspectors are required to approve the construction before occupancy will be permitted. Failure to secure a permit before construction subjects the offender to heavy fines and possible loss of the structure.

Housing Codes. Housing codes maintain minimum housing standards: they restrict the number of persons legally permitted in dwellings; they require that housing be kept in proper repair; they provide for the maintenance of sanitary housing conditions; and they establish minimum ventilation and lighting standards. Most housing codes require adequate protection against fire, minimum hot and cold running water, and a heating system that complies with the code.

The model housing code developed by the state of New York goes even farther in regulating the construction of mobile homes and mobile home courts. The model housing ordinance for mobile homes covers detailed regulations on (1) general requirements, (2) design and construction, (3) space requirements, (4) light and ventilation, (5) mechanical systems and equipment, and (6) minimum maintenance. Figure 3–5 lists the minimum standards of the model code for general requirements, design and construction.

FIGURE 3–5

Model Housing Code Covering General Requirements, Design and Construction, and Space Requirements

---

GENERAL REQUIREMENTS

a.—Mobile home design and construction shall conform to generally accepted standards of the mobile home industry.

b.—Materials, assemblies, and equipment shall conform to generally accepted standards with respect to strength, durability, corrosion and fire resistance, and other qualities recognized under such standards.

c.—Habitable and nonhabitable space shall be arranged, located, lighted, and ventilated so as to be appropriate for the intended use.

d.—Mechanical systems and equipment shall be designed, installed, and located so that under normal conditions of use such systems and equipment shall be capable of functioning safely and efficiently without being forced to operate beyond the designed capacity.

e.—Equipment requiring operation, inspection, or maintenance shall be located so that easy access to it is provided.

FIGURE 3–5 (*continued*)

f.—Plumbing, heating and electrical systems shall be properly connected to approved sources of supply when a mobile home is in a fixed location and occupied for living purposes.

g.—Mobile home units, including mechanical systems and equipment shall be maintained and operated so as to be free of conditions conducive to personal injury or detrimental to health or welfare.

DESIGN AND CONSTRUCTION

Mobile homes shall be structurally sound, effectively insulated, and capable of sustaining designed dynamic loading.

Body and Body Framing

a.—Body frames shall be designed and constructed as complete units. Wall and floor surfaces shall be firmly attached to body framing members. Doors and windows shall be securely framed in place. Framing and exterior skin shall be surface treated or painted to prevent deterioration.

b.—Roofs shall be pitched for proper drainage and shall be weathertight. Roof decks shall be of metal or noncombustible materials.

c.—Wood body framing shall be of seasoned lumber and shall provide adequate support and rigidity. Members shall be joined so as to insure permanent attachment to each other.

d.—Metal body framing shall be of structural formed sections, riveted, bolted or welded together. Where different metals are joined precaution shall be taken to prevent electrolytic action.

e.—Insulation of floors, roof, and exterior walls shall consist of noncombustible materials.

f.—Ventilation shall be provided to minimize deterioration of structural members from condensation or other causes.

Chassis

a.—Chassis shall extend substantially the length of the body and shall be capable of supporting the live and dead loads to which subjected.

b.—Tongue or drawbar shall be secured to the chassis and shall be capable of supporting the weight of the forward end of the mobile home. If designed to support gas cylinders, the tongue shall be of sufficient strength and shall permit secure attachment.

c.—Hitch shall be securely attached to the tongue so as to become an integral part of the tongue.

d.—Axles, spring assemblies, and wheels shall be capable of supporting the calculated loads.

Placement

Placement of mobile home on mobile home stand by jacks or supports shall be such as to insure the retention of the mobile home in a fixed position.

Source: *Housing Codes*, vol. 2: *Model Housing Code* (New York: Division of Housing, State of New York, 1960), pp. 42–44.

Some states, such as Connecticut, Iowa, Massachusetts, Michigan, Minnesota, New Jersey, and Pennsylvania, have enacted state housing codes that apply throughout the state or to selected cities. Some states have enacted housing codes and allow municipalities to adopt other codes not inconsistent with state law. Approximately 30 percent of some 13,000 local governments have enacted housing codes. The general direction of a housing code is suggested by the Uniform Housing Code issued by the International Conference of Building Officials:

> Housing codes provide minimum requirements for the protection of life, limb, health, property, safety and welfare of the general public and the owners and occupants of residential buildings. The provisions of this code shall apply to all buildings or portions thereof used, or intended to be used for human habitation.

Housing inspectors bring both administrative and judicial pressures to bear against violating owners. In some cases the municipality has the right to remedy the deficiency and charge the cost to the owner. Rigid and area-wide enforcement of the housing code is virtually impossible because low-income families cannot afford the necessary repairs to bring houses in compliance with the code.

Code Evaluation.   Although directed to a worthy purpose, building codes have been criticized on the grounds that they prevent the introduction of new materials and mass-produced housing. Codes that require specific types of materials, such as cast-iron pipe, effectively bar satisfactory substitutes, such as plastic piping, that meet or surpass required performance tests.

In addition communities that adopt their own codes vary in the types of materials and building standards that they permit. Widely varying codes make it difficult for producers of mass housing and manufactured homes to comply with the myriad provisions of local codes. Such manufacturers would like to be treated on a regulatory basis, as safety standards in automobiles are treated. The mass production of automobiles would be virtually impossible if every local community regulated auto safety standards. Consequently it is held that the mass production of housing is limited by a system of local building codes that substitute for state or federal standards.

STATE AND FEDERAL REGULATIONS

Generally speaking, state subdivision controls protect the public from misrepresentation, deceit, and fraud in the sale of subdivision lots. Before these laws were enacted, unscrupulous developers would sell residential lots which were impossible to utilize for residential purposes: lots inaccessible by road, lots underwater (the Florida Everglades), and lots with topographical features that made residential use highly questionable. Many states provide for state investigators who review each proposed subdivision. State officials ensure that the published facts, which are often required to be given to each proposed purchaser, are complete and truly represent the property offered for sale. Some states require that out-of-state land be subject to the same review. The point of sale governs the jurisdiction of state subdivision laws, not the location of the subdivision.

State Subdivision Regulations

These regulations are based on the premise that if the buyer is informed of the relevant facts there can be no fraud or basis for complaint. Therefore, subdivision regulations provide for giving adequate and accurate information to the buyer. In states that enforce subdivision regulations, brokers and salespersons who sell subdivision lots without giving the purchaser full information or who misrepresent facts are in violation of the state law. Usually their state real estate licenses are subject to revocation or suspension.

A typical state subdivision law is illustrated by California's requirement that notice of a proposed subdivision be filed with the state. The subdivider must fill out a questionnaire providing minimum information for state review:

The name and address of the title owner.
The name and address of the subdivision.
The legal description of the acreage or subdivision map.
A statement of title, including encumbrances and unpaid taxes.
A statement covering the provisions for sewerage disposal and public utilities.
Evidence of conformity to local regulations.

Based on these preliminary statements, a public report is eventually issued by the investigation agency. In California the report must be delivered to the prospective purchaser on the state-approved form. In some instances, subdividers must furnish copies of advertising materials, brochures, radio transcripts, and other promotional material for review.

The public report is conditional upon completion of the subdivision as advertised. The stricter subdivision regulations require a completion bond and arrangements for the satisfaction of outstanding liens on subdivision land. Buyers must be assured that improvements will be completed free of construction liens. Conveyance instruments, terms of sales, and instruments of assignment must be adequate for purchaser protection.

For example, subdivisions may be constructed with a blanket mortgage covering individual lots. Individual lots then must be sold free of the blanket mortgage in states imposing these restrictions. Lot sales subject to a blanket mortgage or encumbrance are allowed only if the developer (1) agrees to impound sufficient monies to protect the interest of the purchaser, (2) places title to the subdivision in trust under an agreement providing for the release of each lot from the blanket encumbrance upon the sale of the lot, and (3) furnishes a bond to the state in the amount and form approved by the state real estate commissioner. The terms of the bond provide for the return of monies paid or advanced by the purchaser if a proper release from the blanket encumbrance is not forthcoming.

The Interstate Land Sales Full Disclosure Act

The various states do not uniformly regulate sales of subdivided land. With the growing interest in purchasing lots in the Southwest and in the southeastern states, many buyers purchase unseen land sites. To control the growing abuses in this area, Public Law 90–48, enacted August 1, 1968, prohibits fraud, misrepresentation, and deceit in the sale of subdivision lots over interstate boundaries. The act applies to subdivisions divided into 50 or more lots offered for sale or lease as part of a common promotional plan. Under the act, it is unlawful for a developer or agent to use any means of transportation or communication (such as the U.S. mails) in interstate commerce unless he conforms to the act.

Since the act is intended to control the interstate sale of subdivided lots to the public, certain exclusions are provided: sales to contractors for the purpose of constructing buildings, sales of mortgages or deeds of trust, real estate sold under court order, sales of real estate owned by the government, and sales of lots which are free of all encumbrances if the purchaser has inspected the lots which he proposes to purchase. In addition, lots of five acres or more are exempt from this legislation.

It is now illegal to sell lots subject to the act unless a Statement of Record has been registered with the Secretary of Housing and Urban Development and a copy of the Property Report has been given to the purchaser in advance of the contract agreement. The act defines circumstances in which fraud or deceit results from a lot sale. Moreover, failure to issue the proper report to the purchaser voids the sales contract at the option of the buyer.

The Statement of Record. This statement, which must be filed with the Secretary of Housing and Urban Development, includes the name and address of each person having an interest in the lots of the subdivision. In addition, the statement of record must include data of interest to purchasers:

1. The legal description of the subdivision and a description of the topography, including a map showing lot dimensions and streets.
2. A statement of the condition of title.
3. A statement of the present condition of access, taxes, sewerage facilities, and the precise location of the subdivision with respect to nearby municipalities.

4. A statement of the consequences of a failure of the developer to satisfy an outstanding blanket encumbrance.
5. Details on the corporation and copies of the articles of partnership and related papers showing ownership.
6. Copies of the original deed establishing title to the subdivision and copies of all forms of conveyances used to sell lots, including easements or other restrictions.
7. A statement of the selling terms, conditions, prices, and grants and the financial statement, certified as required by the Secretary.

The Property Report.   This report gives information that the Secretary believes important to the purchaser. The report may not be used for promotional purposes, nor may the seller represent that the Secretary approves or recommends the subdivision. The Secretary has the right to issue a permanent or temporary injunction or restraining order to enjoin acts or practices considered deceitful or a misrepresentation. To achieve this objective the Secretary has the power to subpoena witnesses, books, and papers. A violation of the act is subject to a fine of not more than $5,000 and imprisonment of up to five years, or both.

In practice the Property Report tends to be fairly complete. Besides the minimum information listed, developers must cite unusual conditions relating to the subdivision location, for example, subdivision limitations, such as jet aircraft noise, air pollution from local plants, and the possibility of floods. The Property Report must provide information on the availability of water and other utilities.

The Secretary may add certain observations, such as "The future value of this land is very uncertain" or "Do not count on appreciation." Other precautions are noted covering financial obligations that might endanger title.

These and other restrictions relate to full disclosure as a means of preventing fraud and misrepresentation. It is believed that if the buyer is given reasonable information, no fraud or misrepresentation will occur. It should be added that the federal government does not inspect, investigate, appraise, or endorse subdivision offerings. The federal agency relies only on information provided by the developers; federal officials do not check the authenticity of the developers' statements.

SUMMARY

Though ownership of real estate gives the owner exclusive rights of enjoyment, possession, and use, these rights are subject to certain public rights, namely, the police power, the right of eminent domain, the right of taxation, and the right of escheat. Local land use controls are an exercise of the police power which gives the state an inherent right to regulate property in the public interest, convenience, welfare, safety, and necessity.

No compensation is paid to property owners for use restrictions falling under an exercise of the police power.

Under eminent domain, property owners may be compelled to transfer rights to the state and its administrative agencies upon payment of just compensation—meaning market value. While the right of taxation affects all property owners, the improper administration of this right materially affects property values. Over- or underassessing a property relative to like properties discriminates against property owners.

Zoning ordinances provide for land use districts, control the height and bulk of buildings, and set forth minimum property standards. A limitation of zoning codes, the progressively inclusive district, allows mixed property uses and leads to inharmonious and incompatible land use. Prohibited industry lists are another leading limitation; however, these are being replaced by performance standards that control the operation of an industry according to acceptable criteria as stated in the zoning ordinance.

The master or general plan is based on surveys of physical characteristics and the economic base and on a social survey. The land use plan allows a community to guide land use according to community goals. Regulations administered locally provide for subdivisions that conform to local planning and zoning standards. Building codes, another exercise of the police power, provide for buildings that promote the public health, safety, and welfare. Building codes that are inflexible and control construction to the extent of banning new techniques limit the mass production of housing. State and federal subdivision regulations are directed to the prevention of fraud and misrepresentation in the sale of subdivided land.

REVIEW QUESTIONS

1. Indicate why the state has an inherent right of regulation under the police power.
2. Differentiate between the right of eminent domain and the police power.
3. In what way does the property tax arbitrarily discriminate among taxpayers?
4. Give an example of each of the three main property uses controlled by local zoning ordinances.
5. What are the arguments in favor of performance standards in local zoning ordinances? What other zoning innovations overcome common limitations of local zoning practices?
6. Why are local subdivision regulations enacted?
7. Describe the three-part procedure in seeking subdivision approval.
8. Explain the differences in objectives between building codes and housing codes.
9. What are the main objections voiced against building and housing codes?
10. What objectives justify state regulation of subdivisions? How are these objectives accomplished?

11. Explain the rationale and the methods of administering the sale of sub-divided land over interstate boundaries.

SELECTED REFERENCES

Atteberry, William; Pearson, Karl; and Litka, Michael. *Real Estate Law,* chap. 9. Columbus: Grid, Inc., 1974.

Babcock, Richard F. *The Zoning Game,* chaps. 7 and 8. Madison: University of Wisconsin Press, 1966.

Barlowe, Raleigh. *Land Resource Economics,* chap. 18. 2d ed. Englewood Cliffs, N.J.: Prentice-Hall, Inc., 1972.

Bosselman, Fred; Callies, David; and Banta, John. *The Taking Issue,* chaps. 10 and 13. Washington, D.C.: U.S. Government Printing Office, 1973.

Harris, Marshall. "Private Interest in Private Lands: Intra- and Inter-Private," in Howard W. Ottoson (ed.), *Land Use Policy and Problems in the United States.* Lincoln: University of Nebraska Press, 1963.

Kristjanson, Kris, and Penn, Raymond J. "Public Interest in Private Land: Private and Public Conflicts," in Howard W. Ottoson (ed.), *Land Use Policy and Problems in the United States.* Lincoln: University of Nebraska Press, 1963.

4

Environmental Controls

After reading this chapter, you should be familiar with the following points:

1 The trend away from preregulation land use controls to a case-by-case review of land use projects.
2 Zoning and planning deficiencies that have led to environmental controls.
3 The extent of federal support for measures that improve air quality.
4 The main elements of water pollution controls as they affect land use.
5 How coastal zone controls affect proposed land use projects.
6 The purposes of the National Environmental Policy Act.
7 The main elements of an environmental impact statement.
8 How no growth–limited growth policies have been introduced by local communities.

FEDERAL, LOCAL, AND STATE CONTROLS that guide environmental objectives have revolutionized land use practices. The achievement of good land use is regarded by many as the most fundamental of our social and economic objectives since land is the basic source of food, fiber, shelter, water, and oxygen. Sound land use practices help control pollution and help preserve the political, social, and economic structure.

In the past, land use controls have been administered largely by local government officials. More recently, the public has shown an intense interest in how land use affects the environment and the quality of life. Accordingly it is no longer possible in most communities to construct an industrial plant without making detailed provisions for noise abatement, adequate waste disposal, off-street parking and truck maneuvering space, and mitigating adverse impacts on the environment. It is no longer possible to embark on a major project armed only with a zoning variance and a building permit. Through new environmental legislation, the public has approved—and even demanded—that land use practices comply with acceptable environmental standards.

The increasing concern over land use arises from the concentration of 70 percent of the population in metropolitan areas, with over half of this population in suburbs. This shift of population from city centers to the suburbs resulted in the daily conversion of 2,000 acres from rural to urban use from 1960 to 1970. The urban area now involves some 35 million acres. These trends have led to new techniques to control air and water pollution and limit development in coastal areas. Our system of land use controls, centered as it is in local communities, has proven inadequate to deal with these environmental issues. As a consequence, federal and state legislation has introduced a set of detailed, complex procedures for the approval of land use projects.

LAND USE AND THE ENVIRONMENT

The growing concern over land use practices that affect the environment led to the passage of the National Environmental Policy Act of 1969. Related laws include the Clean Air Act Amendment of 1970 and the Federal Water Pollution Control Act Amendments of 1972. In addition, the Coastal Zone Management Act of 1972 provides assistance to 34 coastal states and territories desiring to guide resource management in coastal areas. According to the Council on Environmental Quality, at the present writing 48 states have enacted legislation or proposed programs to expand the role of state government in land use regulation.

On the local level, the International City Managers Association reports that 36 percent of all counties with populations of over 400,000 have created citizen and environmental commissions to evaluate the effects of land use development on the local environment.

This revolution has changed the emphasis on land use controls from the *preregulation type of controls* found in subdivision regulations, zoning codes, and housing codes to a *case-by-case review* of land use projects. The review method of control enables the regulating agency to maintain a constant monitoring of community and environmental impacts. As a result, federal, state, and local laws provide for environmental impact statements and project plans that include an evaluation of the total effect of land development.

Zoning Code Deficiencies

The change in emphasis from preregulation to project review arises from certain inherent deficiencies in traditional land use controls. It is held that the land allocation process, at least in the past, has largely followed the free-market principle to the extent that land developers have capitalized on certain economic incentives that work against preferred development patterns.

Consider a site zoned for single-family use that is economically suited for multiple-family use. A potential developer is often advised to buy a less expensive single-family site and to apply for rezoning to multiple-family use. Spot zoning of this type creates land use islands that conflict with the preferred land use planning. The tendency to approve *spot zoning* applications (sometimes under considerable pressure from developers) constitutes a significant limitation of the preregulation type of land use controls.

Note also that traditional zoning assumes that marked differences in land use should be segregated—single-family districts from commercial districts, industrial districts from multiple-family districts, and so on. Yet there are certain advantages in placing convenient shopping facilities in a residential area. Examples are cited in which planned industrial parks complement—not detract from—adjoining residential areas. Typically, zoning districts prohibit such a convenient, compatible intermingling of uses. In the view of some authorities, *segregated zoning districts* have adversely affected the environment.

A related issue deals with the question of whether a community should establish criteria for land uses that are expected to remain unchanged over the life of a neighborhood. The record shows that it is undesirable not to anticipate changes. In contrast, zoning regulations accommodate changes by introducing amendments and variances which are intended to be used rarely and then only for hardship cases. Yet in the face of neighborhood change, zoning variances, zoning amendments, and spot zoning do not provide stability of neighborhood land use or a logical mechanism for changing neighborhood land use. Zoning regulations are *poorly adapted to accommodate change* as compared to a case-by-case review system.

In still other instances communities have provided for "snob" zoning districts which intentionally bar low- and even middle-income housing. These ordinances establish unusual lot areas, for example, five acres, or provide for minimum frontage and side yards common to upper-income housing. Such so-called *large lot zoning ordinances* increase the per unit and per resident costs of sewers, electricity, water, and street paving. Zoning ordinances of this kind are seldom justified on the grounds that they preserve open space and slow community growth. These and other deficiencies of local zoning ordinances have created a need for additional controls that are more directly related to the environmental effects of real estate developments.

Planning Limitations

Environmental controls have developed partly because of four recognized deficiencies in land use planning. Their importance deserves a brief explanation.

1. The general plan, which designates a proposed land use plan, has in itself encouraged suburban sprawl and retarded the rehabilitation of older neighborhoods. Weaknesses of the general plan are aggravated by the property tax and by an income tax that favors the development of new projects in the suburbs. Capital gains taxes and higher depreciation allowances on projects with comparatively low land values and high building values favor new projects at the expense of neighborhood rehabilitation. In a sense, the extension of public services into newly developed areas has been undertaken by sacrificing the older, established areas. The combination of planning oriented to growth and tax policies—local, state, and federal—has encouraged outward sprawl, increased the cost of local government, and discouraged land use rehabilitation in established, developed areas.

2. The planning of land uses by districts contributes to excessive travel. Shopping centers that require considerable driving substitute for neighborhood centers which could be harmoniously planned in residential districts. In short the separation of land use into districts has not helped to reduce the amount of travel of either people or goods.

3. Moreover, individuals faced with undesirable social change have reacted by migrating to nonproblem areas. The individual owner typically reacts not by accommodating to change and improving the neighborhood but by leaving a declining area for more compatible districts. This individual reaction accelerates environmental problems. The planning process emphasizes new developments at the expense of neighborhood rehabilitation. New developments with all of their sprawl affect the environment more intensively than does guiding growth into rehabilitated neighborhoods.

4. It may be observed that highway transportation has been heavily subsidized. Apparently the planners and the community favor automobile and truck transportation over mass transportation. Government programs have contributed to this preference, with the result that a premium is placed

on fossil fuels, adding to air pollution from exhaust gas emission. Clearly the dependence on conventional zoning and planning procedures to guide the land use practices desired today has proven inadequate. A review of new environmental land use laws shows how the public is seeking new solutions to the problems of land use.

AIR POLLUTION CONTROLS

With the enactment of the Clean Air Amendments of 1970 (Public Law 91–604, December 31, 1970), each state was given the primary responsibility for controlling air quality within its boundaries. To support this program, grants are available to air pollution control agencies of up to two thirds of the cost of planning, developing, establishing, or improving programs for the prevention or control of air pollution. The act further required the publication of a list of air pollutants

a. which in the judgment of the administrator have an effect on public health or welfare;
b. the presence of which in the ambient air results from numerous or diverse mobile or stationary sources; and
c. for which air quality criteria had not been issued before the enactment of the Clean Air Amendments of 1970.

National primary and secondary ambient air quality standards for each air pollutant were further prescribed by the act.

At present five programs dealing with air pollution are administered by the Environmental Protection Agency. (See Figure 4–1.) Note that the National Aerometric Data Bank analyzes air quality data at 247 Air Quality Control Regions. The data system includes an analysis of emission data from some 900 sources covering 3,300 areas and 65,000 points.

The program concentrates on emissions of particulate matter, some of which are *uncontrollable,* from erosion, forest fires, volcanoes, and other natural phenomena. The volume of *controllable* emissions is mostly caused by burning fuels, chemical dust, and spray-producing activities. These controllable emissions have increased approximately 15 percent over the last three decades. Remedies for controlling air pollution have concentrated on shifting fuel from oil to gas; applying technological controls, such as filtering, scrubbing, and electrostatic precipitation to reduce stack emissions; and outright prohibition of the burning of solid waste. Despite these measures, at the end of 1973 Los Angeles, Denver, Washington, D.C., Chicago, St. Louis, Philadelphia, and New York City, among other cities, exceeded the average ambient concentration of particulate matter at the primary standard (75 micrograms per cubic meter, annual average).

The concern about air pollution is partly related to land use practices. To some extent cities influence their own climate since local atmospheric conditions are affected by buildings and other structures arranged in vari-

FIGURE 4-1

EPA's Major Air Quality and Emissions Monitoring Networks and Data Banks

---

National Aerometric Data Bank (NADB)

Compiles and analyzes air quality data collected primarily by state and local agencies (but also from federal monitoring programs) at monitoring sites located in 247 Air Quality Control Regions across the country. Data are submitted by the states to EPA on a quarterly basis. Considerable time (several months) is presently required for transmittal, authentication, assimilation, and analysis of state data. Until recent years, submission of state data was on a voluntary basis, so the historic record is severely limited by incompleteness, inadequacies, and inconsistencies in the available data.

National Emissions Data System (NEDS)

Compiles and analyzes emissions data for each Air Quality Control Region and emissions source category, submitted semiannually by the states. Approximately 900 source categories, 3,300 area sources, and 65,000 point sources are described nationwide. Emissions estimates for each region are calculated on the basis of emissions factors and control efficiencies for each source.

National Air Surveillance Network (NASN)

The principal federal air quality monitoring network, begun in the mid-1950s and presently including more than 200 monitoring sites operated with state and local cooperation. Limited for the most part one monitoring site (usually center-city) per major urban area, so frequently unable to characterize air quality influences of outlying industrial sources. Best available long-term historic nationwide record for TSP and SO_2, although decentralization efforts since 1973 have produced some apparent disruption and delays.

Continuous Air Monitoring Program (CAMP)

Federal system for continuous monitoring of gaseous air pollutants, initiated by U.S. Public Health Service in 1962 to provide a historic trends record and to investigate effects of short-term fluctuations in source strengths, winds, temperature, and precipitation on measured ambient pollutant concentrations. Operated by EPA, cooperatively with city agencies, in Chicago, Cincinnati, Denver, Philadelphia, St. Louis, and Washington, D.C. Generally limited to one center-city site per urban area. Presently being decentralized.

Other Programs

Conducted for special purposes. These include EPA's Particle-Size Network, Membrane Filter Network, Precipitation Network, and Community Health and Environmental Surveillance System (CHESS), as well as many state and local monitoring programs and special studies, addressed to regional and local air quality assessment needs.

Source: *Environmental Quality*, The 5th Annual Report of the Council on Environmental Quality, Wash., D.C.: Government Printing Office, 1974, p. 260.

ous heights and patterns. The properties of building materials and the paved areas around buildings influence the sunlight, temperature, humidity, and other variables affecting air pollutants.

Further, considerable attention has been given to air pollutants produced by the automobile, namely, carbon monoxide, hydrocarbons, and nitrogen oxide. The emission controls on new vehicles, according to the Commission on Environmental Quality, have led to a progressive reduction of the average emission of carbon monoxide and hydrocarbons: from an average of 89 grams per vehicle-mile traveled in 1965 to an average of 62 grams per vehicle-mile traveled in 1973. Despite these favorable trends, controllable emissions of hydrocarbons roughly doubled between 1940 and 1970, primarily from motor vehicles, refineries, and petroleum storage and processing facilities.

The more recent shift to the use of fuels with high sulfur content has increased the amount of sulfur dioxide in such cities as Philadelphia, which showed a higher level in 1974 than in 1973. Similar experiences were recorded in New York City and the northern New Jersey area. The record reveals, most pointedly, that land use activities that add to air pollution will be subject to land use and environmental restrictions. Highway location, mass transportation projects, and industrial developments will be subjected to more intensive case-by-case reviews with respect to potential air pollution.

PROTECTING WATER QUALITY

Environmental controls relate to the restoration and maintenance of the national water system. At present the main impetus for controlling water pollution lies in provisions of the Federal Water Pollution Control Act Amendments of 1972 and the Coastal Zone Management Act of 1972. The former is directed to controlling the chemical, physical, and biological quality of water supplies. The latter relates to developments that are located in the coastal zones as defined by the act.

Water Pollution Controls

According to the water pollution control amendments of 1972, it is the national goal that:

1. the *discharge of pollutants* into the navigable waters be eliminated by 1985;
2. wherever attainable, an interim goal of water quality which provided for the *protection and propagation of fish, shellfish, and wildlife* and provided for recreation in and on the water be achieved by July 1, 1983;
3. the discharge of *toxic pollutants in toxic amounts be prohibited;*
4. Federal *financial assistance* be provided to construct *publicly owned waste treatment works;*

5. *areawide waste treatment management planning processes* be developed and implemented to assure adequate control of sources of pollutants in each State; and
6. a *major research and demonstration effort* be made to develop technology necessary to eliminate the discharge of pollutants into the navigable waters, waters of the contiguous zone, and the oceans.[1] (Emphasis supplied.)

The 1972 amendments to the Water Pollution Control Act require that every discharger of pollutants obtain a permit that specifies the allowable amount and constituents of his effluent. The permit contains a schedule specifying the date on which the discharger will be in full compliance. The states issue the permits as established by the administrator of the Environmental Protection Agency (EPA). States that do not administer a permit program are administered by the EPA permit system. The act establishes a water quality standard to determine whether additional pollution reduction is necessary for a particular stretch of water. As the act reads, ". . . by 1977 municipal treatment plants must provide secondary treatment and all industrial plant discharges must meet standards based on the best practicable means currently available." The standards for 1983 are tighter. Some 207 industrial categories are covered by the EPA.

It should be added that the 1972 amendments broadened federal responsibility for all navigable waters. The act encompasses standards that protect aquatic life and permit recreational activities, such as boating and fishing. Water quality, under the standards set forth, is generally sufficient to protect the public water supply for agricultural, navigational, and industrial uses.

Building codes increase the federal share of treatment plants to 75 percent of cost. Municipal construction increased public sewerage services to a population of *163 million* by 1973—a considerable increase from the 140 million people benefiting from sewers in 1968. Surveys estimate that by 1977 the total cost of secondary treatment standards will be some $60.7 billion.

The importance of this legislation for land use lies in other new requirements of the 1972 amendments:

1. In the planning process, alternative techniques for providing municipal treatment, including land treatment, must be considered.
2. The cost effectiveness of treatment facilities must be assured.
3. Industrial plants discharging wastes into municipal treatment plants must pretreat the wastes so as not to undermine the normal operations of the municipal plants.
4. Industries must contribute their share of the cost of constructing and operating municipal treatment plants.

---

[1] Federal Water Pollution Control Act Amendments of 1972.

5. Environmental impact statements must be prepared for waste treatment plants.

Regulations controlling federal construction grants require industries, businesses, federal installations, and private citizens to pay a user charge, depending on the cost of service. Volume discounts to larger industrial firms are prohibited.

The Management of Coastal Zones

Congress has defined a coastal zone as an area measured from a shoreline in to a point necessary to control shorelands for uses that have a direct and significant impact on coastal waters. Coastal waters are defined to include the area of the Great Lakes and their connecting waters, harbors, bays, and marshes, as well as areas that include a measurable quantity of seawater. In the Coastal Zone Management Act of 1972, Congress reported:

> . . . the increasing and competing demands upon the lands and waters of our coastal zone occasioned by population growth and economic development, including requirements for industry, commerce, residential development, recreation, extraction of mineral resources and fossil fuels, transportation and navigation, waste disposal, and harvesting of fish, shell fish, and other living marine resources, have resulted in a loss of living marine resources, wild life, nutrient-rich areas, permanent and adverse changes to the ecological systems, decreasing open space for public use, and shore line erosion. . . .

Accordingly, Congress seeks to preserve and restore the resources of the nation's coastal zone and to encourage states to exercise their responsibilities in the coastal zone by implementing management programs to achieve wise land use.

Under the law, all federal agencies and programs affecting the coastal zone must cooperate and participate with state and local governments in accomplishing the purposes of this act. The states are encouraged to prepare management programs under grants authorized by the act. The law makes annual grants to any coastal state to assist in the development and management program. Programs must include:

1. An identification of the boundaries of the coastal zone subject to the management program.
2. A definition of what shall constitute permissible land and water uses within the coastal zone which have a direct and significant impact on the coastal waters.
3. An inventory and designation of areas of particular concern within the coastal zone.
4. An identification of the means by which the state proposes to exert control over the land and water uses referred to in item 2 above, in-

cluding a listing of relevant constitutional provisions, legislative enact-
ments, regulations, and judicial decisions.

5. Broad guidelines on the priority of uses in particular areas, including
specifically those uses of lowest priority.

6. A description of the organizational structure proposed to implement
the management program, including the responsibilities and interrelationships of local, area-wide, state, regional, and interstate agencies in
the management process.

Federal grants are not to exceed two thirds of the cost of the management programs available to the respective states. Programs developed
under state sponsorship must be submitted for federal approval. Up to two
thirds of the annual cost of administering a state management program
may be subsidized by the federal government. Federal approval of management programs is authorized only for states that have adopted rules
and regulations to manage the coastal zone with federal approval and with
the full participation of other local, state, and regional organizations.

Each state must coordinate its management program with local, area-
wide, and interstate plans and must establish an effective mechanism for
continuing consultation and coordination with other related agencies.
Management programs are approved only after a public hearing, a review,
and approval by the governor. Each management program must make provision for the preservation or restoration of designated areas for their conservation, recreational, ecological, and aesthetic values. In each plan, the
national interest must be given adequate consideration in preserving facilities which are more than local in nature.

In some instances state legislation has been more restrictive. The California Coastal Zone Conservation Act of 1973 defines the coastal zone as
extending seaward to the outer limit of the state jurisdiction and inland to
the highest elevation of the nearest coastal mountain range. In the more
populous counties the inland boundary extends to the highest elevation of
the nearest coastal mountain range or five miles, whichever is less. The
California act creates a Coastal Zone Conservation Commission and six
regional commissions to administer the act. The main thrust of the legislation requires the implementation of a coastal zone conservation plan. Such
a plan must define the public interest and apply ecological planning principles. The comprehensiveness of the plan is indicated by its required
components, which include:

1. A land use element.
2. A transportation element.
3. A conservation element for the preservation and management of the
scenic and other natural resources of the coastal zone.
4. A public access element for maximum visual and physical use and
enjoyment of the coastal zone by the public.
5. A recreation element.

6. A public services and facilities element for the general location, scale, and provision in the least environmentally destructive manner of public services and facilities in the coastal zone. This element includes a power plant siting study.
7. An ocean mineral and living resources element.
8. A population element for the establishment of maximum desirable population densities.
9. An educational or scientific use element.
10. Reservations of land or water in the coastal zone for certain uses, or the prohibition of certain uses in specific areas.

With the preparation of the coastal zone plan, developments must be undertaken within the coastal zone only after obtaining a permit authorizing such development from one of the coastal zone regional commissions and any other permits required from city, county, state, regional, or other local agencies. No permit will be issued without a two-thirds vote of a regional commission for operations calling for dredging or altering marshes, rivers, lagoons, or bays, or for any other development that reduces the size of a beach usable for public recreation. A two-thirds vote is also required for developments that would substantially interfere with the ocean view from state highways near the coast or adversely affect areas of open water free of visible structures.

NATIONAL ENVIRONMENTAL POLICY

Much of the activity in environmental controls has been initiated as a consequence of the National Environmental Policy Act of 1969. The purpose of the act is defined as follows:

> To declare a national policy which will encourage productive and enjoyable harmony between man and his environment; to promote efforts which will prevent or eliminate damage to the environment and biosphere and stimulate the health and welfare of man; to enrich the understanding of the ecological systems and natural resources important to the Nation; and to establish a Council on Environmental Quality.

The Council on Environmental Quality is composed of three members appointed by the president with the advice and consent of the Senate. The act requires that each member shall be qualified by his training, experience, and attainments to analyze and interpret environmental trends and information of all kinds, and to appraise programs and activities of the federal government in the light of the policy set forth in the act. The members of the council must prepare an annual environmental quality report, review and appraise various programs and activities of the federal government, and make recommendations, investigations, studies, and surveys consistent with the requirements of environmental legislation.

In short the National Environmental Policy Act (NEPA) has incorporated an environmental perspective into land use decisions. Though the act relates only to the federal government, to date some 48 states have either proposed or enacted similar acts. The Council on Environmental Quality has issued guidelines for the preparation of environmental impact studies and has issued a set of recommendations on the content of these statements and on procedures for their preparation.

Early History

The first test of the act related to an interpretation by the Secretary of the Interior concerning the application of the act to permits for construction of the Trans-Alaskan Pipeline. The court ruled that the Secretary of the Interior could not grant permits without meeting the requirements of NEPA.

In another leading decision, the *Calvert Cliffs* case, the U.S. Court of Appeals for the District of Columbia ruled that the Atomic Energy Commission (AEC) procedures for licensing nuclear power plants were unacceptable. The nuclear power plant was considered a major federal action that significantly affected the quality of the environment and therefore required an impact statement. The controversy turned on acceptance by the AEC of state or regional water quality agency statements as adequate evidence that there would be no adverse effect on the environment. After the court ruling, the AEC was directed to make an independent evaluation and to balance a variety of environmental factors, such as the thermal effects of power plant discharge of cooling water, even if other federal or state agencies had certified that their own environmental requirements would be satisfied. The court decision indicated that an impact statement could not be properly made and later ignored. The court ruled that environmental information was to be secured, reported, and used in making agency environmental decisions.

As a result of this decision, the applications of 110 nuclear power plants and 10 nuclear facilities required an expanded or new environmental review. Subsequently the AEC introduced new procedures to program impact statements as part of its administrative activities.

Now federal agencies must make, first, a full disclosure of all information necessary for environmental decision makers, and, second, must engage in balanced decision making. The duty of full disclosure involves both research—the accumulation and analysis of data—and the presentation of data in the impact statement. Federal agencies are responsible for developing the necessary information if adequate information is not available for decision making.

In this regard Section 102 of NEPA requires an agency to "utilize a systemic, interdisciplinary approach [to] insure the integrated use of the natural and social sciences and the environmental design arts in planning and decision-making which may have an impact on man's environment."

Each agency is directed to make every effort to bring together a wide variety of relevant professional viewpoints and backgrounds in the preparation of an impact statement. In the final analysis full disclosure depends on whether the statement fulfills the purpose of an impact statement: to provide a basis for (1) the agency's decisions, (2) an independent evaluation, and (3) a judicial review.

In the first 4½ years after NEPA was approved, impact statements were prepared for 5,430 federal agency actions. The largest number of statements were filed by the Department of Transportation, covering mostly significant actions by the Federal Highway Administration and the Federal Aviation Administration. The Army Corps of Engineers accounted for approximately 21 percent of all new statements filed in the most recent year.

Current Developments

Currently some 35 states require environmental impact statements (EIS) similar to those required by the federal law. Such statements are required for major actions or projects undertaken directly by state agencies. The laws governing the application of impact statements to local government actions vary among the states. Although impact statements may not be required for private actions administered by localities, federal law requires an impact statement for any action involving a federal lease, permit, license, certificate, or other entitlement. This means that private projects requiring a federal permit, such as the Trans-Alaska Pipeline, also require an EIS. For example, California has accepted some 6,000 impact statements each year on private actions and actions of local governments. This volume of activity arises from an interpretation that an EIS is required for *a private project which requires the approval of any government entity.* Similarly, the Massachusetts act applies to "any work, project or activity of any person, firm or corporation which may cause damage to the environment."

Community Environmental Objectives

It seems clear that environmental impact statements are required for virtually all significant land use projects. Some authorities are suggesting impact statements for developments that require rezoning, zoning variances, subdivision approval, shopping centers, planned unit developments, or any significant development over which local, state, and federal officials have control. The Urban Land Institute has suggested that community objectives underlying an EIS should deal with five topics:

1. The local economy.
2. The natural environment.
3. Aesthetic and cultural values.
4. Public and private services.
5. Housing and social conditions.

The Local Economy. Land developments change the net revenue flow (tax revenues less government expenditures), local employment, and wealth. For instance, local projects may increase the local property tax base and increase local revenue from income, sales, and utility taxes. Certain miscellaneous revenues from licenses and other charges may also increase. Expenses related to households tend to increase as a result of new housing projects: educational costs, health and welfare costs, and expenditures for recreation, libraries, streets, and public utilities. The impact statement will show how land use projects will affect the local economy with respect to local revenue, expenditures, personal income, and the general level of wealth.

The Natural Environment. An impact study relating to changes in the natural environment must be directed to local objectives in controlling pollution, protecting wildlife, preserving the natural environment, and conserving scarce resources. Pollution relates to the quality of air, visual aesthetics, unpleasant odors, and the emission of smoke and particulate matter. Engineering studies for EIS purposes normally deal with water and noise pollution and with the effect of the development on open space programs, wildlife, vegetation, and the consumption of scarce resources, such as surface water, electric power, and fuels.

Aesthetic and Cultural Values. These values depend on the views of the local community. Through ratings by experts and citizen surveys, an effort is made to evaluate the general appeal of the notable appearance of a proposed development. The EIS will correct hearsay information and the prejudices of outspoken citizens. Architectural plans, artists' sketches, and aerial and street-level photographs are preferred in the EIS.

Public and Private Services. This section measures the impact of the development on major government services, primarily health and safety, recreation, education, local transportation, and shopping. The issue of health and safety may relate to the changes that are likely to occur in the rate of water shortage incidences and to index studies of the quality of drinking water. If the project will increase population, it is relevant to show the expected change in the number of people who will be served by hospital facilities, crime control, and fire protection, including fire hazards from new developments.

For example, the educational level, age distribution, and attitudes of new entrants into the community may have a bearing on arson, false alarms, and accidental fires. Recreation is important with respect to the number of people within a reasonable distance of recreational facilities, changes in the usage rates of these facilities, waiting times, facility space per resident, and estimates of how the project will change the perceived pleasantness of the recreational experience. Similar data relate to the effect on education and on access to adequate community service facilities and employment. Shopping is measured in terms of the estimated change in the number of stores and services, by type, within an average distance of residential concentration.

FIGURE 4-2

Illustrative Display of Impact Measure Data—Hypothetical Proposal: 20-Story Office Building with Shopping Plaza Replacing Tenement Housing

Impact Area	Measure	Impact on Clientele Groups			Compliance with Comprehensive Plans
		A. Local Jurisdiction (50,000 people)	B. Immediate Neighborhood (500 people)	C. Low-Income Families in the Jurisdiction (5,000 people)	
Local economy	Change in net fiscal flow	+$200,000 to $300,000	N/A	N/A	N/A
	Net number of new jobs	+200 to 300 jobs	+10 to 20 jobs	+50 to 70 jobs	Yes
Aesthetics	Number of people whose views will be blocked	300 to 400 people	250 to 300 people	250 to 300 people	N/A
	Percent people (in random survey) finding development attractive	75% (of sample)	40% (of sample)	N/A	Partly yes, partly no (general opinion is in compliance, local opinion is not)
Air pollution	Number of additional people expected to be exposed to x ppm for over y hours more than z times a year	+4,000 to 8,000 people	+300 to 500 people	N/A	No
Local transportation	Change in average auto travel time to reach destination x in neighborhood	+3 to 5 minutes	+3 to 5 minutes	N/A	No
Housing stock	Change in number of housing	−50 substandard units	−50 substandard units	−50 substandard units	Partly yes (removal of substandard housing); partly no (accommodations for displaced families)
Neighborhood stability	Number of residents displaced	150	150	130	Yes

Source: Philip S. Schaenman and Thomas Muller, *Measuring Impacts of Land Development* (Washington, D.C.: Urban Institute, 1975). p. 34.

Housing and Social Conditions. Community objectives must deal with the potential number of people displaced or relocated as a result of the project. For example, how will the proposed project change attitudes toward the neighborhood in terms of its attractiveness, friendliness, crowdedness, and overall desirability as a place in which to live and work? The project may change the type of housing demanded and revise the population distribution by age, income, or religion to the point of adversely affecting the community's population density, sociability, and friendliness.

Groups Affected by Land Development

An example of the type of data required for a 20-story office building that will replace tenement housing is shown in Figure 4–2. Note that the six elements listed show the impact on the local jurisdiction of 50,000 people, the immediate neighborhood, and low-income families. While this example relates to a relatively small group, it is clear that impact statements of this type will probably be required in the main metropolitan areas. It should be emphasized further that the groups potentially affected by a development will vary. The following list, prepared by the Urban Land Institute, shows what groups may be affected by land use projects.

Physical Proximity

Persons living or working on the land proposed for development.

Persons living or working immediately adjacent to the proposed development.

Persons in neighborhoods surrounding the proposed development.

Persons within commuting distance (one hour by public transit, for example) from proposed commercial and industrial developments.

Business Relationship

Builders, Realtors, bankers, and others directly involved in the development.

Owners and managers of businesses or property in the neighborhood.

Political Jurisdiction

Citizens of the local jurisdiction containing the development.

Citizens of immediately adjacent jurisdictions and of the entire metropolitan area.

Citizens of the state and nation.

Socioeconomic and Demographic

Age groups.

Racial and ethnic groups.

Persons of various income levels, from poor to affluent.

Other Interest Groups

Tourists.

Landowners.

Others.

The Long-Term Public Interest

All present groupings over time.

Future generations.

Criticism of Environmental Policy

NEPA has been subjected to considerable criticism. Since more than 70 federal agencies have incorporated impact studies into their administrative procedures, it is not surprising that considerable criticisms have been raised by all interested parties. Agencies have been accused of complying with the legislation in letter but not in spirit.

Noncompliance. The more prominent claims warrant mention. The balancing–decision-making process rests on stated priorities, preferences, and weights placed on specific factors; decisions proceed with great uncertainty, causing agencies to fall back on data supporting the established agency missions. As a result some agencies have canceled some projects and modified others to implement the national environmental policy. It is held that agencies must reconcile conflicts and arrange compromises, not elect *either* to carry out a development *or* to protect the environment.

Overlapping Jurisdictions. The act has failed to eliminate clashes among agencies with overlapping or conflicting responsibilities. Such clashes arise, for example, among agencies responsible for regulating steam electric power generation. Because of the vast amounts of water needed for cooling, steam power generating plants locate near large bodies of water. The water discharged into the lake, river, or bay may increase the natural water temperature to the point of materially affecting the marine aquatic life. In these circumstances it is not always clear which agency must do the balancing under NEPA, trading off competing factors and undertaking an overall analysis of the project's impact.

New Environmental Policies. Another issue concerns the question of whether an agency can initiate a new environmental policy under the NEPA umbrella. Critics have questioned whether an agency may use NEPA authority to overly protect the environment. Most observers would argue that NEPA has limited powers for agencies to initiate new environmental programs and extend their domain.

Industry Criticisms. New environmental laws have been criticized for the delays resulting from development approval. Development firms have borne added costs of planning and preparing impact studies. In Sacramento, California, the preparation of an environmental impact study relating to a 500-unit, single-family subdivision costs over $25,000. The cost is based on a formula related to the type of project and its size, topography, vegetation, and effects on watercourses. To cope with these added expenses, leading California firms, such as the Irvine Company of Newport Beach, which is developing 82,000 acres, have prepared a checklist covering environmental impact procedures. The checklist provides a test of whether the project is likely to succeed or would be halted because of planning or legal oversights. Present indications are that such a procedure will be fairly standard among property developers.

ELEMENTS OF AN ENVIRONMENTAL IMPACT STATEMENT

Section 102 of the 1969 National Environmental Policy Act requires the coverage of five topics in addition to the descriptions of present conditions and of the proposed project:

1. The probable environmental impact of the proposed action.
2. Any adverse environmental effects which cannot be avoided upon approval of the proposal.
3. Alternatives to the proposed action.
4. The relationship between local short-term uses of the environment and the maintenance and enhancement of long-term activity.
5. Any irreversible and irretrievable commitments of resources which would be involved in the proposed action, should it be implemented.

Both the Council on Environmental Quality and the Department of Housing and Urban Development have provided outlines guiding EIS preparation. In addition numerous consultants and state and local agencies have developed their own interpretations of EIS content and format. For example, the California environmental law requires a discussion of mitigation measures and the growth-inducing impacts of a proposed project.

Jens Sorensen and Mitchell Moss of the University of California recommend that the EIS deal with three points: (1) identification of the environmental, social, and economic conditions that may be changed by the project; (2) prediction of the intensity and spatial dimensions of the changes likely to occur; and (3) evaluation of the costs and benefits to different groups in society. To date no single format for preparing environmental impact statements has been universally accepted. Indeed, leading experts prefer a highly flexible format. In fact it is unlikely that a single format and content would be universally acceptable for all agencies.

Probably the leading reference for the preparation of an environmental impact statement is the NEPA format shown in Figure 4–3. A brief explanation of this format indicates the procedural steps required in real estate projects subject to NEPA.

1. *Present Conditions.* The description of present conditions includes the physical features of the site and area. Also included are the area's

FIGURE 4–3

Basic NEPA EIS Framework

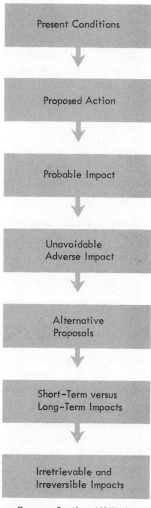

Source: Section 102(2) (c) of
the 1969 National Environmental
Policy Act.

social and aesthetic characteristics, its general location, present land uses, and a legal description of the project.

2. *The Proposed Action.* The proposed project is described, including its purpose, status, and location. A 500-unit apartment project financed by HUD would detail the number of apartments and rooms, the construction layout, and the like.

3. *The Probable Impact.* Probably the largest section of the impact statement, this portion of the report relates to the effect of the project on local residents and users, including the impact on the physical, social, and

aesthetic environment. Project sponsors must discuss precisely the nature of the impact and what will be affected in terms of the source and its severity, duration, and scope. Included are quantitative measures, such as population densities, data on the projected emission of particulate matter, and the relative importance of environmental factors according to local environmental standards. Steps to be taken by the developer and others to minimize these effects must be described in relation to the environmental impact.

4. *The Unavoidable Adverse Impact.* Assuming that a project is implemented, this section describes adverse environmental effects which cannot be avoided. The description should include physical, social, and aesthetic impacts. Steps to be taken by the developer or agencies which will tend to negate the environmental damage are outlined. Some analysts recommend that the environmental impact should include adverse effects

which could be avoided if an alternative proposal were adopted;
which could not be avoided by any alternative and which could be avoided by choosing the recommended proposal.

5. *Alternative Proposals.* Alternative proposals might include limited or reduced construction, more conventional development, or construction on some other site.

6. *Short-Term versus Long-Term Impacts.* The anticipated effects during construction and the short- and long-term impacts of construction are covered in this portion of the EIS. The statement describes the relationship between local, short-term uses of the environment and the maintenance and enhancement of long-term productivity. Consider, for example, large-scale subdivision development in central Florida. To some extent residential development may restrict the flow of water which regularly proceeds from the Appalachian Mountains to the Florida Everglades. Increased subdivision activity in central Florida would absorb considerable groundwater, which may further limit the water required for the sustenance of the Florida Everglades. The long-term effect of approving unlimited subdivision activity would produce harmful and irreversible long-term impacts on the ecological balance of the Everglades. Such information provides the reviewer data with which to exercise the balanced decision making required under NEPA.

7. *Irretrievable and Irreversible Impacts.* If the view is taken that a project commences a chain of events which, once started, may not be broken, then certain resources will be exhausted and unrecoverable. The construction of buildings absorbs resources which will be irreversibly committed. Every project creates ultimate consequences relating to population distribution and pressures on natural resources and public services. While some of these factors relate to growth-induced impact, they create long-range changes that absorb capital outlays for public facilities, and they affect the physical, social, and aesthetic environment. Data in this

section relate to private and public capital outlays and to the anticipated permanent changes in the natural environment.

NO GROWTH–LIMITED GROWTH POLICIES

Land use controls have been adopted by local and state agencies as a means of limiting population growth. Doubts about the "growth is good" ethic have encouraged certain communities to restrict growth. Such states as Oregon, Delaware, California, and Colorado have questioned the advisability of further population growth beyond the carrying capacity of the community. Certain land use controls have been specifically directed to limiting growth, namely, (1) large lot regulations, (2) zoning density controls, and (3) building moratoriums.

Large Lot Zoning

In New Jersey the Superior Court struck down a zoning ordinance that provided for a minimum lot size of 40,000 square feet in a residential district where typical lots were from 9,000 to 25,000 square feet in area. The court held that the ordinance was a deliberate attempt to reserve land for use by affluent members of the population and to discourage its use by low-income families. The large lot requirement was held to be unreasonable and therefore invalid.

In another case the large lot requirement provided for a minimum three-acre residential site, a minimum floor area, and a minimum cubic building content. The ordinance was held invalid as a means of preserving the aesthetics of the community. In Washington, D.C., population density has been indirectly controlled—since 1910—by limiting the height of buildings to 130 feet. Voters have approved a resolution to limit the height of buildings to 55 feet in Boulder, Colorado. In the town of Sanbornton, New Hampshire, a U.S. Court of Appeals upheld a decision holding a six-acre minimum lot to be a valid zoning regulation. The court found that the six-acre minimum lot size promoted the general welfare by preventing the construction of new houses that would have an irreversible effect on the area's ecological balance, destroy scenic values, and significantly damage the rural character of the small town. While the law on large lot minima is uncertain, it seems clear that large lot zoning may not be used to exclude certain racial or economic groups.

Zoning Density Controls

Zoning density regulations have long been an integral part of the zoning code. Recently, communities have adapted this feature to limit population growth. The township of Madison, New Jersey, enacted a zoning ordinance that restricted apartment construction to 500–700 units, presumably to promote a reasonably balanced community. In the same state the township of Mount Laurel prohibited multifamily construction. Both ordinances were declared invalid by the state Superior Court. The first decision held that the restriction failed to promote a balanced community in accordance with the general welfare; the second decision held that the ordinance discriminated against the poor and deprived them of adequate housing.

Similarly zoning ordinances that exclude multiple-family housing (exclusionary zoning) have been held invalid if their effect is to prohibit low- and moderate-income housing. The court in Pennsylvania ruled that a zoning ordinance cannot be held valid if its primary purpose is to prevent the entrance of newcomers in order to avoid future burdens on public services and facilities (*National Land and Investment Company* v. *Kohn,* 419 Pa. 504, 215 A2d 597, 612, 1966).

To be sure, communities have different capacities to accommodate growth. In desert areas, water is scarce and must be obtained by irrigation projects at the expense of another geographic area. In communities in Florida, both water and sewage disposal have practical limits of expansion. Most observers would agree that eventually a community must have the right to prevent its own destruction by balancing available resources with population growth. Apparently zoning density controls directed to limiting population growth must apply to all developments equally rather than be discriminatory on racial or economic grounds.

Building Moratoriums

Under the police power, communities have the right to withhold subdivision approval, building permits, and the right to connect with municipal sewers and water supplies. By withholding these privileges, population growth may be effectively and directly controlled. As a temporary device, pending study of environmental implications, Boulder, Colorado, declared a building moratorium. Restricting applications for sewer connections was a device used in Fairfax County, Virginia, to limit population growth. In Dade County, Florida, voters approved a building moratorium permitting county commissioners to declare a halt in certain areas while environmental studies were being made. Moratorium declarations have been used as a temporary device pending the study of growth problems. To date, limiting population by withholding building rights has been approved provided that the moratorium is temporary. Usually these temporary restrictions permit the community to develop a plan for orderly, controlled growth.

SUMMARY

The trend in land use regulation is away from *preregulation controls* to a system of *case-by-case reviews*. The inherent limitations of conventional land use controls have been largely responsible for this change. Zoning code deficiencies, primarily spot zoning, limitations of segregated zoning districts, the inability of inflexible zoning ordinances to accommodate change, and large lot zoning ordinances, handicap orderly community development. The general plan administered by urban communities has also encouraged urban sprawl, contributed to excessive travel, encouraged individuals to migrate to nonproblem areas, and contributed to the subsidy of highway transportation.

The concern over environmental impact has led to federal legislation controlling air quality. Today land use projects, locally administered, must meet the requirements of such federal legislation. Similarly federal water pollution legislation requires municipal treatment plants to provide secondary treatment of all industrial plant discharges to meet new standards by 1977. The coastal zones, as controlled by the Coastal Zone Management Act of 1972 and various state laws, must be developed under a management program prepared under grants authorized by federal legislation. Land use projects are authorized only if they conform to environmental restrictions placed on coastal zone areas.

The National Environmental Policy Act requires the preparation of environmental impact studies for projects involving a federal action which significantly affect the environment. These studies must identify community objectives and the various groups affected by land development. Criticisms of environmental policy center on the noncompliance of government agencies, the overlapping jurisdictions of regulatory agencies, and the initiation of new environmental policies not coming under federal policy. Industry has criticized environmental policy on the grounds that the procedures are costly, uncertain, and subject to much delay.

The elements of an impact statement center on a description of seven components: present conditions, the proposed action, the probable impact, the unavoidable adverse impact, alternative proposals, short-term versus long-term impacts, and irretrievable and irreversible impacts.

These environmental issues, which seem insurmountable, have led to local no growth–limited growth policies. Among the more common techniques falling under the police power are large lot zoning ordinances, zoning density controls, and building moratoriums.

REVIEW QUESTIONS

1. Distinguish between preregulation land use control and a case-by-case review of land use projects. Give an example to illustrate your answer.
2. Explain four deficiencies of zoning ordinances that have led to environmental controls.
3. What planning limitations have encouraged a case-by-case review of land use projects?

4. In what way has the Clean Air Amendments of 1970 improved air quality?
5. In general, how would you describe the national goal with respect to water pollution?
6. How are land use projects affected by federal water pollution legislation?
7. What is the purpose of the Coastal Zone Management Act of 1972?
8. What is included in management programs controlling land in the coastal zone area?
9. In your view, what effect will coastal zone conservation plans, illustrated by California, have on a land use project? Explain fully.
10. Explain the National Environmental Policy Act in your own words.
11. What environmental issues were resolved in the early history of the National Environmental Policy Act of 1969?
12. What community objectives should be addressed by an environmental impact study?
13. List groups that would be affected by the development of a 500-unit apartment project in your community.
14. What are the main criticisms voiced against the National Environment Policy Act?
15. Explain the main parts of the basic NEPA EIS framework.

SELECTED REFERENCES

Burchell, Robert W., and Listokin, David. *The Environmental Handbook.* New Brunswick, N.J.: Center for Urban Policy Research, Rutgers— The State University, 1975.

Caroll, Thomas E. "Environmental Controls and Their Relation to the Financial Community," *Journal of Commercial Bank Lending,* vol. 54 (April 1972), pp. 36–41.

Clark, Robert A. "Developers Struggle to Meet Environmental Demands," *Mortgage Banker,* vol. 33 (August 1973), pp. 10–17.

Clawson, Marion. "Environment and Land Use," *Planning,* vol. 41 (June 1975), pp. 26–28.

Environmental Quality, Fifth Annual Report of the Council on Environmental Quality. Washington, D.C.: U.S. Government Printing Office, 1974.

Fisher, Anthony C., and Krutilla, John V. "Valuing Long Run Ecological Consequences and Irreversibilities," *Journal of Environmental Economics and Management,* vol. 1 (August 1974), pp. 96–108.

Lamm, Richard D., and Davison, Steven A. G. "The Legal Control of Population Growth and Distribution in a Quality Environment: The Land Use Alternatives," *Denver Law Journal,* vol. 49, no. 4 (1973), pp. 1–51.

McGee, David L., and Smith, Gerald H. "Environmental Diseconomies in Suburban Expansion," *American Journal of Economics and Sociology,* vol. 31 (April 1972), pp. 181–88.

5

Real Estate Interests and Ownership

After reading this chapter, you should be familiar with the following points:

1 The property rights associated with freehold estates of inheritance.

2 The main differences between the three forms of fee ownership.

3 The main elements of two estates not of inheritance: the ordinary life estate and legal life estates.

4 How community property estates differ from property rights associated with curtesy, dower, and tenancy by the entireties.

5 The four estates associated with less than freehold estates.

6 How easements appurtenant and easements in gross apply to the acquisition of property rights for a specific purpose.

7 How tenancy in common varies from joint tenancy.

8 The main elements of multiple ownership, primarily tenancy in partnership, syndicates, corporations, real estate investment trusts, corporations, condominiums, and cooperatives.

IN REAL ESTATE TRANSACTIONS, two issues must be resolved: first, what interest is conveyed, and second, how is ownership to be held? In resolving the first issue, a partial interest may be acquired more economically than the purchase of a full interest. A department store, for example, may prefer to acquire retail space with a 15-year lease. As a tenant, the store acquires the right of possession over the lease term. In this case, a partial interest substitutes for the purchase of a full interest.

The ownership to be held is the next issue. Again it may be more prudent to acquire a joint interest or to hold the property in a partnership, corporation, joint venture, or syndicate rather than acquire sole ownership. In fact, real estate experts attempt to combine the best type of interest to be acquired—depending on the needs of the parties—with the most legally acceptable and economical type of ownership.

Because of the critical importance of these two questions, the chapter describes the interests commonly available to property owners and the manner in which ownership may be held. Virtually all parties to a real estate transaction must reach decisions on these two points.

REAL ESTATE INTERESTS

Real estate interests fall into two main categories: *freehold estates* and *less than freehold estates*. The freehold designation originated under the English feudal system. Today freehold estates usually refer to interests in land. Less than freehold estates cover leases, easements, and other interests which are regarded as personal property. It should be emphasized that real estate may be subject to combinations of these different estates and types of ownership. Further, the many ways of owning estates apply to most of the freehold and less than freehold estates.

Freehold Estates

Freehold estates are estates of uncertain duration. The most common division of freehold estates include *estates of inheritance* giving the owner rights which prevail over his life and which pass to his heirs. Freehold estates *not of inheritance* continue only during the life of the person whose life determines the duration of the estate. Suppose that A transfers title to B during B's life. On B's death the title or estate reverts to C. The estate held by B is not an estate of inheritance.

Estates of Inheritance. Estates of inheritance incorporate variations of the fee simple estate which may be traced to early English law. Under the feudal system, a fief, which later became known as a fee, was a grant from the king to tenants who usually held the grant or fief over their lifetime. At the discretion of the king, a fee was later conveyed to the tenant "and his heirs and assigns forever," converting the estate into one that could be inherited.

The ownership of land involves three rights associated with an estate or an interest in real estate:

1.   The right of exclusive possession.
2.   The right of quiet enjoyment.
3.   The right of disposition.

The highest form of ownership includes these rights associated with real property ownership. In holding the right of exclusive possession, an owner may borrow, control entry onto his land, and may even collect damages because of trespass. The exclusive right of possession gives the owner complete control of his land. Other parties must seek permission to enter the land of an owner holding this right.

The right of quiet enjoyment is unrelated to noise or other disturbances. It refers to the legal right of holding possession without disturbance because of defects in title. Holding the right of quiet enjoyment gives the owner the right to use his land in any manner consistent with local laws. The owner is entitled to the proceeds of the land; the land may be devoted to his own personal use; the owner benefits from the produce of the land or from rents received from tenants.

The right of disposition permits the owner to use the property over his life or to sell all or part of his interest. Provided that statutes prohibiting discrimination against others are observed, the owner may sell to others by any means available under the law. When holding the right of disposition, the owner may transfer an interest by will upon death. Only by operation of the law may the owner lose his ownership, for example, as a result of the owner's failure to pay property taxes or other debts or of the government's exercise of eminent domain.

1. *Fee Simple Absolute.*   Under the allodial ownership system of the United States, the fee refers to an absolute ownership for "life, his heirs and assigns forever." Under English law a fee simple absolute conveyed title over the life of the owner which could be inherited without restrictions. It was called "simple" to indicate that the title was held without restrictions. This is the maximum title which may be acquired in real estate.

While rights of the owner of the fee are paramount, the rights are subject to land use restrictions coming under the police power, the right of eminent domain, the right of taxation, and the power of escheat. Public rights exercised under these four limitations of ownership are justified on grounds of public welfare. These public rights, some statutory and some exercised under common law, mean that the property owner must use his property in conformity with local zoning codes, building regulations, and similar laws.

Further, it is well recognized that owners may not use property so as to cause a nuisance to their neighbors. This rule may be applied to prevent unsanitary conditions, an unusual number of pets or animals, or the storage of materials constituting exceptionally dangerous explosive or fire hazards.

The unauthorized commercial or industrial use of property zoned for residential use is another case in point.

Even with these restrictions, the owner of the fee simple estate has considerable latitude in conveying rights of absolute ownership. The owner may develop part of the property subject to a mortgage for construction of a neighborhood shopping center. With the completed building, the owner may lease commercial space to tenants for a limited period, say, 5, 10, or 15 years. Or the owner may grant rights to use portions of the property for sewer lines, storm drains, or electric transmission lines. An owner is free to sell the right to use the airspace above the surface, to rent parking spaces on the surface, and if appropriate, to convey subsurface rights, namely, the right to extract oils or other mineral deposits. If these rights are not in conflict, they may be exercised concurrently.

2. *Fee Simple Determinable.* This estate refers to a fee simple estate that terminates upon the occurrence of a known event. The conveyance usually includes language that specifies the fee "so long as, until, or during" an event. For instance, a property owner may convey a fee simple determinable *so long as* the land is used for public school purposes. Assume that a property owner conveys land to a church as long as the property is used as a church site. The event that automatically terminates the estate is the abandonment of church use. If the church decides to vacate the site for a new location, under a fee simple determinable, title automatically reverts to the original owner.

3. *Fee Subject to Condition Subsequent.* In operation a fee simple subject to a condition subsequent incorporates virtually the same possessory and use rights of the fee simple determinable. The language associated with this estate qualifies the estate in conveyance language stating "on the condition that" with an added statement that the original owner may repossess the premises.

In other words, the fee simple conditional continues until the owner takes affirmative action to repossess the premises. Hence, in this estate two conditions are necessary for termination: (1) the stated event must occur, that is, church use has been abandoned; and (2) the original owner must take steps to reenter and repossess the property. Without reentry and repossession, the fee simple subject to a condition subsequent continues even though the terms of the conveyance have been broken. However, the granting owner maintains the right to recover the fee simple estate. In contrast to the fee simple determinable, which ends immediately upon the occurrence of the stated event, the fee simple subject to a condition subsequent requires overt steps by the granting owner to terminate the estate.

Estates Not of Inheritance. To complicate matters further, owners are confronted with various forms of life contracts and certain legal estates provided by statute. Statutory law governs the rights of married persons and the interests of the surviving spouse. To distinguish between estates not of inheritance, it is customary to refer to conventional life contracts and legal life estates: those estates treated by statute that cover the interests of a surviving spouse.

1. *The Ordinary Life Estate.* The ordinary life estate is created by an act of the granting owner. The conveyance transfers the estate, giving all rights of use, enjoyment, and possession to some person for the life of the person receiving the estate or some other person. Upon the death of the person whose life measures the estate the life estate automatically terminates. To create this estate the owner must express his intention by deed or by will. If A transfers a life estate to B during B's life with the provision that the estate is to revert to the original owner upon B's death, A holds the *remainder*—which is an estate in fee simple. Accordingly, A is known as the *remainderman.*

In the typical case an *ordinary life estate* is illustrated by the transfer of a life estate from A to B during B's life. In other instances the owner may wish to grant an estate to B for the life of C. Here the life estate measured by the life of a party other than the grantee creates an estate *pur autre vie.* The life of C serves as a time clock which measures the duration of the estate.

In either case the life estate is generally regarded as the smallest estate to be acquired. In sum, a life estate gives to the life tenant the exclusive right to possess, enjoy, and use the estate provided that he observes limitations common to life estates. The remainderman holds only a future estate that turns to a fee ownership upon the termination of the life estate. Because of the interest of the remainderman, the life tenant must observe certain limitations not found in the unrestricted fee simple estate.

The life tenant must not commit undue waste. The property may not be subject to permanent injury, such as the cutting of timber or subjecting the property to a use which prevents the remainderman from accepting the property in an unchanged condition at the termination of the life estate. Ordinarily the life tenant may not change the nature of the present land use or destroy land improvements. Moreover, the life tenant must pay taxes, maintain the property, and undertake repairs or other steps necessary to preserve the value of the property.

State statutes often limit the right of the life tenant to mortgage the life estate. Further, if the life tenant elects to lease the premises, the lease terminates as the life tenant's interest expires. The leasing tenant may not legally hold over after expiration of the life estate without the permission of the remainderman. In some states a life estate is automatically terminated if the life tenant violates life tenant restrictions, such as committing undue waste or failure to pay taxes or keep the property in repair.

A formal life contract peculiar to certain states provides for a *homestead right* giving limited protection of the family home from creditors. Though the homestead is technically a legal life estate created by statute, it usually requires a formal declaration on a specified form which must be filed for record by the head of the family. The family, as defined by statute, is usually identified as two or more persons, with the head of the household responsible for family support. Provided that the head of the family has an ownership interest, the homestead law variously protects the home from a forced sale to satisfy debtors. For most property, limits stated in dollars (or in number of acres) are usually placed on the exemption. For instance, the homestead right applies to a maximum of 160 acres on rural property in the state of Florida.

The original justification of the homestead right was to protect the family from losing its home under a forced sale to satisfy creditors. The homestead right attempts to protect the wife and family from indigent husbands and from creditors of a decreased husband. Though there are exceptions, local real estate taxes generally have priority over homestead rights.

2. *Legal Life Estates.* The conventional life estate is created by express acts of the owner. In the case of legal life estates, the interest is created by operation of the law. State law establishes various classifications arising from legal marriages. The most common provisions deal with *curtesy, dower, tenancy by the entireties,* and *community property.*

Though the state law varies, several states, among others, Alabama, Arkansas, Hawaii, and North Carolina, provide for life estates for the husband in all real estate owned by the wife during marriage. Commonly, *curtesy* requires a valid marriage and the birth of a living child during marriage. The estate is terminated by divorce or the death of the husband. In states providing for curtesy, the husband should sign all conveyance documents with the wife to extinguish the right of curtesy.

Dower rights refer to the interest of a surviving wife in land acquired by the husband during marriage. Under common law, the surviving widow was entitled to a life estate in one third of land held as a freehold estate of inheritance during marriage. States providing for dower provide for an *inchoate* or *consummate* dower interest.

The inchoate dower refers to the anticipated interest the wife has in land of the husband which cannot be defeated by the husband or by will. Thus, during the life of the husband, the wife holds a contingent interest of an inchoate dower.

Upon the husband's death some states provide for the division of one third of the land to which the wife's dower is attached if she so elects. The completed dower of the surviving wife is considered a tenant in dower with a life estate. At the husband's death, the surviving wife assumes all rights and obligations of a conventional life estate tenant. Some states grant the surviving wife the right to take a portion of her husband's entire estate, including realty and personalty, in place of the dower interest. Like the curtesy interest, a dower may be released by joining with the husband in executing conveyance instruments.

On the death of the husband, the widow has a consummate interest not only in all realty owned by the husband at the time of death but in all realty that he owned during marriage in which she did not release her dower right. The dower right is released by signing conveyance instruments with the husband. Similarly, a dower estate terminates by divorce, death of the wife, or election of the wife to accept other parts of the husband's estate in lieu of the dower interest.

States that provide for *tenancy by entirety* treat ownership by husband and wife as ownership by one person. In effect, each party assumes ownership of the entire property. As tenants by the entirety, neither the husband nor the wife may convey property or force a partition of the property during the lifetime of the other spouse. On the death of either party, the estate is solely owned by the survivor.

Community property, a heritage from Spanish law, prevails in the states of Arizona, California, Hawaii, Idaho, Louisiana, Michigan, Nebraska, Nevada, New Mexico, Oklahoma, Oregon, Texas, and Washington. Community property states recognize two types of property owned by married persons: separate property and community property. Separate property is owned by the husband or the wife at the time of marriage or is acquired by either during marriage by inheritance, will, or gift. Property in this category is owned independently from any interest of the other spouse.

Property acquired by either spouse during marriage becomes community property, belonging to both parties as co-owners. It is assumed that husband and wife should share equally all property acquired during marriage. The law assumes that each spouse owns an undivided one-half interest of all that is earned or gained by both, regardless of the share contributed by the other spouse. Community property rights prevail even though a deed may recite the name of only the husband or the wife. To extinguish community property interests, the husband and wife must both sign documents transferring property held as community property. No conveyance instrument or contract is valid without the separate signatures of the husband and wife with a community property interest.

Note, however, that there is no survivorship in community property which is common to a tenancy by the entireties. Each spouse is assumed to own an undivided interest; the surviving spouse takes his or her one-half interest, with the heirs of the deceased taking the other half. To vest the other spouse in his or her one-half interest requires that community property interests be transferred by will. Like other legal estates, community property interests terminate on death, divorce, or the voluntary agreement of husband and wife to divide property equally.

Less Than Freehold Estates

Less than freehold estates refer to leases that convey the right to possession, use, and enjoyment for a limited time. The person holding a less than freehold estate acquires the *leasehold* estate or interest. While the time of possession is definite, leasehold estates may extend over several generations. The instrument creating a leasehold estate is termed a lease and may be oral or written. Most states require a lease of one year or more to be in written form to be enforceable.

Technically the owner of the fee granting the lease holds the leased fee interest. (See Figure 5–1.) The owner who executes a lease becomes the *lessor* who grants possession to the tenant, or *lessee*. The tenant agrees to pay rent and observe other terms of the lease in return for use and possession, as required by the lease instrument. At the end of the lease the leasehold interest terminates; use, possession, and other attributes of

FIGURE 5–1

The Creation of a Leased Fee and Leasehold Interest

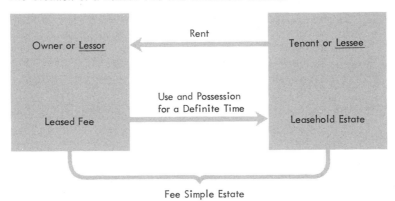

property ownership revert to the fee owner. The leased fee or leasehold estate may be conveyed to others, mortgaged, and assigned as other interests in real estate. The four legal variations of leasehold estates cover the estate for years, periodic tenancies, tenancies at will, and tenancies by sufferance.

Estates for Years. Leasehold estates that continue for a definite period of time are known as estates for years. The time may be highly variable —one month, one year, or conceivably, 99 years. Subject to the lease agreement, the lessee (tenant) has the exclusive right to possess and use the leased property, provided that he observes the terms of the lease. To qualify as an estate for years, a lease must have a definite term, a beginning date and an ending date, at which time the lessee must vacate the premises. By custom, leases seldom extend beyond a maximum of 99 years. The custom was established after the state of Massachusetts enacted a statute specifying that all leases for terms exceeding 100 years would be held as freehold estates. This led lawyers to prepare leases with a maximum 99-year term.

Periodic Tenancies.   These leases, also known as leases from year to year, continue until one of the parties to the lease gives notice of termination. Typically the parties agree to leases by the week, month, or year. Such tenancies may continue for an indefinite period; they tend to be renewed indefinitely unless either party gives notice of termination. A statutory 30-day written notice is not an unusual requirement for the termination of a month-to-month tenancy. Much variation in the laws covering estates for years prevails among the 50 states.

Tenancy at Will.   An estate created lawfully with the consent of owner and tenant that may be terminated at the will of either party constitutes a tenancy at will. Although the term of the tenancy is uncertain, the tenant continues in possession with the express approval of the owner. Statutes generally require that the termination be exercised by the giving of proper legal notice (30 days for a month-to-month tenancy is not uncommon). Most states specify the requirements of statutory notice—the time, form of notice, and method of service. The estate is terminated by the death of the owner or the tenant.

Tenancy at Sufferance.   In a sense tenancy at sufferance is a misnomer. A tenant who enters the premises lawfully under an existing lease and holds over without permission of the owner at the termination of the lease illustrates a tenancy at sufferance. In effect, the tenant has no stated rights in realty since he continues to use the premises without the express consent of the owner. This type of tenancy continues until the owner either consents to the sitting tenant or takes action to repossess the premises. Such a tenant differs from a trespasser because the tenant at sufferance gained lawful possession with the consent of the owner. A tenancy at sufferance becomes a tenancy at will or a periodic tenancy at the time the owner consents to the continued occupancy. Because the tenant holds no interest in the premises, most states require no notice to terminate a tenancy at sufferance. The tenant occupying premises under this tenancy has no economic interest to mortgage, convey, or assign to others.

EASEMENT RIGHTS

Though not an estate in land, an easement represents a nonpossessory interest in real estate. In the simplest terms, an easement is the right to use land for a specific purpose. Easements are conveyed by written instruments which may not be terminated by the will of the owner. The holder of an easement right is governed by the terms of the easement giving him limited use of land, typically for right-of-way purposes—the right to use land for the construction and maintenance of electric transmission lines, irrigation ditches, pipelines, and the like. Easements are administered according to whether they are easements appurtenant or easements in gross.

Easements Appurtenant

Suppose the owner of tract A in Figure 5–2 grants a 50-foot-wide access easement to B, allowing B to gain access to lake frontage. In this instance, A grants an easement appurtenant for the benefit of B. The person benefited by an easement holds the *dominant estate,* while the person granting the easement has the *servient estate.* An easement appurtenant is said to run with the land. In the former example, A in conveying his property to

FIGURE 5–2

Illustration of the Servient and Dominant Estate Created by a Right-of-Way Easement

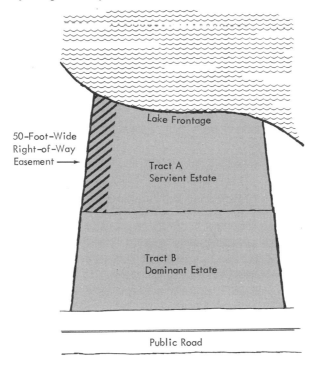

C conveys the land subject to B's right of access over the right-of-way easement. The easement appurtenant is not sold separately, but is transferred with title to the property of A and his successors.

Easements in Gross

An easement in gross is personal. It does not run with the land; it does not create a dominant and servient estate. Because this easement is personal, it cannot be assigned, conveyed, or inherited, though it gives the right to use the land of another for a specific purpose. Easements in gross are commonly used for signs, billboards, and other special purposes.

The special merit of an easement is that the owner may continue to own property in fee, conveying only the right to use property for a specific purpose. The person acquiring an easement generally needs only a limited use of the property which does not require fee ownership. For some purposes, such an easement for an electric transmission line, the owner may continue to use the property for agricultural purposes and yet convey the right-of-way for high-voltage transmission lines.

License

With a license an owner may grant permission for the temporary use and possession of real estate. The holder of a license has no interest in the land; it is merely a personal privilege granted by the owner. Ordinarily the license may be written or oral, and it cannot be assigned or inherited. The purchase of a theater ticket—a form of license—gives the holder the right to attend an event which may be revoked without reason at the discretion of the owner. Without a license, entry on the land of another would constitute trespass, for example, hunting on land without the permission of the owner.

REAL ESTATE OWNERSHIP

For the present purpose, it is convenient to explain single ownership, concurrent ownership, and multiple ownership. Concurrent ownership includes joint ownership with two or more persons. The latter term describes various business organizations adapted to real estate ownership. To illustrate, A may be ill-advised to invest his total investment capital of $500,000 in a single apartment house project. It may be more prudent to invest $250,000 as a joint owner in two apartment house projects. The diversification of risks may justify joint ownership in two projects as an alternative to single ownership in one project. Similarly, there are distinct financial advantages in converting $100,000 into corporate shares which are invested in real estate as opposed to purchasing $100,000 of real estate directly as a sole owner. An understanding of ownership interests guides decisions on these issues.

Single Ownership

Ownership of real estate by one individual is known technically as *ownership in severalty*. The term refers to a single ownership "severed" from other real estate. The word *several* has no association with ownership in severalty. While the ownership may be centered in one individual, who enjoys all property rights associated with the ownership, there are certain legal differences between owning land as the sole owner and owning it jointly with others or in some form of multiple ownership. The main differences relate to sharing liabilities, separating responsibilities, and allocating benefits under alternative forms of ownership. The variations of concurrent ownership significantly change the property rights of joint owners.

Concurrent Ownership

Joint ownership by two or more persons normally assumes one of two forms: tenancy in common or joint tenancy.

Tenancy in Common.   Two or more owners holding a tenancy in common have an undivided interest in real estate that:

1.   Permits ownership in unequal shares of interest.
2.   Provides no right of survivorship.
3.   May be created at different points in time.
4.   Includes the right to partition individual interests.

Unlike joint tenancy, a tenancy in common allows joint owners to hold varying shares of interest. For example, a surviving wife, son, and daughter may inherit an apartment building as tenants in common. The undivided interest may be divided by conveying a 50 percent undivided interest to the widow and a 25 percent undivided interest to each child. There is no requirement that an interest in a tenancy in common be equal among co-owners. Moreover, each owner has the right to sell part or all of his tenancy in common interest or to pass his respective interest to heirs.

This latter feature is common to all tenancies in common. At the death of a tenant in common, the interest of the deceased may be willed or passed on to heirs under state law. In contrast to other types of ownership, the interest does not automatically revert to the surviving joint owners. Moreover, individual shares of ownership may be merged, divided, or sold at different points in time. A party holding a 25 percent interest as a tenant in common may transfer part or all of his interest to his own children or to others in smaller shares, independently of the other tenants in common.

In some states, a tenant in common may force partition of the property to convert an individual interest to cash or to a divided share in real estate equal to the ownership interest. If the interest is held in an apartment dwelling which is difficult to divide physically into shares, the owner may force a sale to gain his share. On the other hand, if a tenancy in common is in land, an individual tenant may force physical partition of the property to acquire sole ownership in proportion to the interest held. In case of a dispute arising over the right of partition, the parties may resolve the conflict by seeking remedy in court.

Joint Tenancy.   The right of survivorship is the main distinguishing feature of joint tenancy. If A owns a joint tenancy with B, B acquires sole ownership upon the death of A. To establish this type of relationship, joint tenancy requires four conditions, referred to as the four unities:

1. Unity of interest.
2. Unity of time.
3. Unity of title.
4. Unity of possession.

In the absence of any one of the four requirements, no joint tenancy is created. In contrast to tenancy in common, joint tenants always own equal shares. A joint tenancy of five ownerships would vest a 20 percent undivided interest in each of the joint tenants. In addition, the tenants must have acquired title at the same time under the same document. For this reason it is impossible for a sole owner to convey a joint tenancy with another party. By conveying an interest back to himself, he would violate the requirement that both joint tenants acquire title under the same document at the same time. In these circumstances, the owner must convey property to a third party who in turn conveys back a joint tenancy. Each tenant has the same right of possession and identical rights in the undivided interest.

The trend is away from holding title in joint tenancies. Some states have abandoned joint tenancy, while others require definite language to create joint tenancy. To differentiate between joint tenancy and tenancy in common, some states require that the joint tenancy include language that conveys title, such as "joint tenants with right of survivorship and not as tenants in common." In the more restrictive states, deeds that do not specifically include reference to the right of survivorship have been held to create a tenancy in common. It should be added that a joint tenant may convey his interest to another, who then holds a tenancy in common with respect to the remaining joint tenants. If A holds a joint tenancy with B and C and conveys his undivided interest to D, D would hold a tenancy in common with B and C, who remain as joint tenants with respect to each other.

MULTIPLE OWNERSHIP

The main options available under multiple ownership include partnerships, corporations, syndications, real estate investment trusts (REIT), condominiums, and cooperatives. In each instance the legal form of ownership is adapted to the needs of specialized real estate investments and to the peculiar requirements of property owners.

Tenancy in Partnership

Ownership in a partnership is controlled by the Uniform Partnership Act, which has been adopted in 48 states. A variation of the partnership form of ownership is provided by states that recognize *limited* and *general* partners. This form of ownership separates the investor function from management operations.

Partnership Rights in Real Estate. Where the Uniform Partnership Act applies, partners share equal rights of possession and use of real estate held for partnership purposes. A partnership interest may not be conveyed to others without the consent of the other partners. Property held by the partnership is exempt from rights of dower and curtesy, and may not be partitioned among the partners unless the claims of creditors are satisfied.

Other details are controlled by the partnership agreement, which defines the partnership as an association of two or more persons who carry on business for a profit. The terms of the partnership generally require the consent of all partners for the addition of other partners or the sale of a partnership interest. If a general partnership is formed, ownership may be taken and conveyed in the names of individual partners. The agreement may designate individuals to take title in partnership property and to act for the partnership. In the conveyance of real estate interests, partners can act only within the authority designated by the partnership agreement. Upon the death of a partner, normally the agreement provides for the transfer of a partnership interest to the remaining partners, with reimbursement to the estate according to the value of the partnership share.

Limited Partnerships. Two financial advantages accrue to a limited partnership: limited liability and income tax advantages. In this type of ownership, the limited partner has no voice in management, though he is entitled to information on financial and other operative details. The limited partner can be held liable only for the amount of his capital investment. In the event of a $500,000 mortgage default, a limited partner with a $100,000 investment can be held personally liable only for his $100,000 partnership interest.

Though title to real estate is taken in the name of the partnership, only the general partner has the right to execute deeds, mortgages, or other real estate conveyances. Real estate developers and managers form limited partnerships to acquire equity capital for real estate investment purposes.

Since the limited partner is liable only for his investment, this type of ownership retains the limited liability of a corporation without incurring liability for corporate net income taxes. To qualify for this tax treatment, limited partners must remain passive, act as investors, and not take part in management.

Further, limited partners gain from partnership losses. Under the Tax Reform Act of 1969, investors in new residential real estate, for example, apartment buildings, may use a rate of depreciation on that real estate which is double the straight-line rate. Suppose that a $1,000,000 apartment building is depreciated for income tax purposes at 2 percent a year, or $20,000. If the building is a new apartment dwelling, $40,000 would be allowed for depreciation during the first year. Suppose further that in a high income tax bracket a taxpayer must pay a 70 percent income tax on additional income. Thus, if an additional income of $40,000 is subject to a 70 percent tax, the taxpayer would owe $28,000 in income taxes. If, however, he has a depreciation deduction as a limited partner, and if his share of the loss (because of the high depreciation allowance) reported by the partnership is $40,000, he would save $28,000 in personal income taxes. In other words, a taxpayer in a high income tax bracket gains in a limited partnership by (1) limiting personal liability and (2) offsetting personal income taxes with losses of the partnership.

Real Estate Syndicates

Real estate syndicates refer to organizations formed to gain from an interest in real property, including its sale, exchange, trade, or development. The organization usually consists of a limited partnership but may also represent other ownership forms. The parties to the syndicate are bound to a syndication agreement governing the rights, duties, and liabilities of syndicate owners.

In the trade, syndicators are individuals who form the syndicate and who typically manage the syndicate as general partners. Syndications may be (1) limited partnerships, interests in which are sold to private individuals, or (2) formal offerings sold interstate and requiring the approval of the Securities and Exchange Commission. The advantages of a syndicate are described in the standards of practice published by the real estate syndication division of the California Real Estate Association:

> By bringing together individuals for the purpose of group investment in real estate, the Realtor Member is providing an opportunity for individuals to invest in larger properties for profit without personal involvement in management operations and without exposure to unlimited liability.
>
> In so doing, the Realtor Member expands investment opportunities in real estate, making real property investments available to individuals who may otherwise be denied the benefits of such ownership. The Realtor Member is making available increased capital for the expansion of the real estate industry; for the creation of income producing properties; the building of cities and the development of industry and productive farms.
>
> Many individual investors do not have the training or experience of the Realtor Member, or the time to acquire investment skills, and must rely on the Realtor Member's professional skills in making real estate investments. The Realtor Member is therefore zealous in maintaining and improving the standards of his calling and shares with his fellow members of the CREA Syndication Division of common responsibility of competence, integrity and honor.
>
> In the interpretation of his obligations, the Realtor Member endeavors,

to the best of his ability, in his syndication activities, both public and private, to meet the standard of being Fair, Just and Equitable to all concerned.

Accepting this standard as his own, the Realtor Member pledges himself to observe its spirit in his syndication activities and to conduct those activities in accordance with the following Standards of Practice.[1]

In organizing a syndicate, the syndicator faces operations not found in the usual real estate transaction, namely, marketing the syndicate, acquiring property suitable for syndication, managing syndication property, and reselling syndication property.

Acquisition. Before acquiring property, the syndicator selects property suitable for syndication, makes a market feasibility analysis, and negotiates purchase terms. A statement of the allowable building depreciation and the probable tax treatment of the property will be prepared for properties finally selected for syndication. The general partners will select those properties showing the highest return, the maximum cash flow available under favorable financing terms. The cash flow refers to net income after mortgage and income tax payments.

Marketing. A certain amount of market research underlies syndication. Assuming that the property is economically feasible for syndication, it must be determined whether the proposed marketing plan conforms to state and federal laws governing the registration and sale of securities. At this point the partnership agreement is drawn to expedite the initial methods of financing the syndicate. The proposed general partner will prepare a full summary of estimated operations, showing operating income, operating expenses, and net income before provisions for depreciation and mortgage payments. The marketing plan will estimate the proposed distribution to limited partners, based on their respective shares.

Management. The syndicator assumes responsibility for property management, including the location of tenants, the negotiation of leases, and the supervision of custodial services for residential properties. The general partner must maintain books and records for monthly, quarterly, and annual reports according to the syndication agreement. If this is a new property, the syndicator must supervise construction and negotiate with local governments in securing the necessary permits and project approval.

Resale. At some point it is appropriate for the parties to the syndication to convert their interests to a capital gain—especially if the depreciation and mortgage interest deductions have reached fairly substantial proportions. Some plan of marketing the property at the most advantageous time serves the interest of the syndication.

---

[1] Source: Burton E. Smith, "The California Experience—A Model for National Commitment," in Stephen E. Roulac (ed), *Real Estate Securities and Syndication* (Chicago, Illinois: National Association of Real Estate Boards, 1973), pp. 21–22.

Real Estate Investment Trusts

First authorized in 1960, real estate investment trusts include some 210 organizations with total assets of over $20 billion. It is claimed that over 500,000 people own shares in real estate investment trusts. The rationale of these trusts lies in giving small investors a means of obtaining a share in professionally managed real estate properties or mortgages. Shares in a real estate investment trust may be sold in the same way as other stocks or bonds.

Provided that real estate investment trusts comply with tax regulations, they are exempt from federal corporate net income taxes on income paid to shareholders. To qualify they must distribute at least 90 percent of net income to shareholders. They are organized as corporations and are operated by trustees who are elected by shareholders. The trustees are organized in much the same way as the boards of directors of other private corporations. Some trusts specialize in loans and investments on a nationwide basis while others invest in regional projects. Some REITs may prefer investments in first mortgages, including construction loans to builders; development loans to finance site improvements; long-term mortgage loans on improved real estate; or short-term mortgages, generally less than ten years, on completed buildings held by developers. A few real estate investment trusts engage in second or junior mortgages. About 18 percent of the total assets held by REITs are invested in equities.

Real Estate Corporations

Real estate corporations are chartered under the laws of each state limiting the financial liability of real estate developers to the assets of the corporation. Suppose that a real estate developer proposes to develop a shopping center on 40 acres. The developer would be advised to form a corporation which would allow participation by other investors without endangering their personal assets. Shares in the corporation may be exchanged without affecting the ownership of real estate assets. If the corporation has limited assets, lenders may require the pledge of personal assets before approving a first mortgage. By and large, corporate ownership of real estate conforms to the procedures and requirements governing corporate operations for other business purposes.

Condominium Ownership

Condominium ownership, which is especially common in multiple-family dwellings, retains the advantages of a multiple-family unit but provides the ownership rights that characterize single-family dwellings. Ownership of a condominium apartment gives exclusive possession and use of an apartment unit with an undivided interest in the common elements. The term *common elements* refers to the apartment house site, the elevator, the hallway space, and all other facilities of the apartment building which the condominium owner shares with other owners. In reality the owner acquires the right to use the airspace occupied by his particular apartment. In buying a condominium interest, the owner arranges his own financing and title insurance, and with few restrictions he is free to sell his ownership in the open market. Ownership rights turn on three documents: the declaration, the condominium bylaws, and the management agreement.

The Declaration.　The condominium declaration commits a property to the condominium form of ownership. The most important legal document affecting property rights, it provides for the administration of condominium property. It defines the rights of individual owners with regard to the maintenance of each condominium unit, and it defines the responsibilities of individual owners. Declarations, with their required exhibits, may number over 100 legal-size pages. The declaration provides a legal description of each ownership as a space in contrast to legal descriptions that describe a land area common to other ownerships.

In the declaration, the maximum liability of individual owners for maintenance and expenses is equal to the share that the individual condominium bears to the total property value. A \$30,000 condominium in a \$3 million project would have a maximum share of 1 percent in the maintenance charges and other liabilities of the condominium. The proportion of liabilities that each condominium owner will bear is stated in the declaration.

Corporation Bylaws.　While the declaration establishes a condominium, the bylaws relate to the administration of condominium affairs. Ordinarily each condominium owner has one vote in the management of condominium affairs. A board of directors is vested with the right to levy and collect assessments against member units and to expend funds for the maintenance, repair, replacement, improvement, and management of the condominium. Rules and regulations which must be observed by the condominium owners will be prepared by the board of directors. Rules commonly used by voluntary associations, such as those governing the election of officers, amendments to the bylaws, and accounting for funds, are also contained in the bylaws of the condominium.

The Management Agreement.　In a new condominium project the sponsor initially assumes control under a management agreement. At some point, when all or some stipulated proportion of the condominium units are sold, the responsibility for hiring employees and contracting for services, maintenance, and repairs is transferred to an association of condominium owners. Normally the association hires a management firm to undertake these tasks. The management agreement defines the authority of the managing agent and specifies the maximum expenditures for maintenance and repairs that may be made without approval of the members or their elected board.

With these three documents—the declaration, the corporation bylaws, and the management agreement—a legal framework exists to give owners property rights in a single condominium unit that may be mortgaged, sold, and assigned to others, subject only to legislation and regulations governing condominiums. An evaluation of condominium ownership is provided in Chapter 20.

Cooperative Ownership

Cooperative apartments have been popular in large urban centers because they give purchasers certain advantages not gained by renters. The owner of a cooperative apartment lacks certain ownership rights associated with a condominium. Briefly stated, the cooperative, usually a nonprofit corporation, acquires or sponsors the development of an apartment house project. Prospective purchasers acquire ownership *shares* in the cooperative equal in value to a given apartment unit. With the ownership of cooperative shares, the purchaser is given a *proprietary lease* granting him the use and occupancy of the selected apartment.

The main differences between cooperative ownership and condominium ownership may be summarized as follows:

1. A cooperative apartment project is financed with a single mortgage; a co-op apartment purchaser finances his purchase according to his prorated share of an existing mortgage on the entire project. Cooperative apartment owners do not have the financing flexibility of condominium purchasers.
2. Cooperative owners have virtually unlimited liability for repair, maintenance, and other expenses. Recall that condominiums may levy no more than a specified percentage of expenses and other liabilities against each owner. Cooperative owners do not have this protection; they are jointly responsible for liabilities and the expenses of operation.
3. In some cooperatives, the purchaser must resell the unit back to the cooperative at the original purchase price.

The current trend favors condominium ownership over cooperative ownership. Condominium owners may sell their interest on the open market, though sometimes the board of directors must approve the sale; a condominium owner may finance his purchase in terms suited to his needs; his liability for expenses of operation is limited to a stated percentage. The economic aspects of condominium and cooperative ownerships are treated more fully in Chapter 20.

SUMMARY

Prospective buyers of real estate have the choice of buying partial interests in real estate. Freehold estates, divided between estates of inheritance and estates not of inheritance, include property interests representing the maximum form of ownership: the fee simple absolute. The buyer of such an estate acquires the right of exclusive possession, the right of quiet enjoyment (a legal right to hold possession without disturbance because of defects in title), and the right to dispose of the property by sale, will, or other means.

Alternatively, the fee simple estate may be granted so as to terminate upon the occurrence of a known event. For example, land may be granted for public school purposes *so long as* it is used for such purposes (a fee simple determinable). The estate terminates if the property is used for other purposes. A fee simple subject to condition subsequent terminates upon the occurrence of some stated event *if* the owner takes affirmative steps to repossess his interest.

Estates not of inheritance are ordinary life estates which terminate upon the death of a designated person. The holder of the life estate, known as a life tenant, must preserve the property for the remainderman, who acquires title upon the termination of the life estate.

These estates contrast with legal life estates created by statute. Curtesy rights give the husband a life estate in all real estate owned by the wife during marriage. A dower right gives the surviving wife an interest in land acquired by the husband during marriage. Tenancy by the entireties considers the husband and wife as owning property in a single ownership. Many of the western states are known as community property states because in these states the husband and wife share equally in property acquired during marriage.

The leasehold estate, or the interest of the tenant or lessee, and the leased fee, or the interest of the owner or lessor, are both less than freehold estates. Such estates may be an *estate for years*—a lease that continues for a definite period of time; a *periodic tenancy*—a lease that continues until one of the parties to the lease gives legal notice of termination; or a *tenancy at will,* in which the tenant continues in possession with the express approval of the owner and which may be terminated at the will of either party. A *tenancy at sufferance* grants no legal right to the tenant, who merely holds possession without the permission of the owner—typically the tenant holds over without the consent of the owner at the time a written lease expires.

Easements appurtenant, which run with the land, are partial interests in real estate covering the right to use property for a special purpose. Easements in gross are personal and do not run with the land. A license is a temporary grant by the owner to use and possess real estate. It creates no interest in land, and is merely a personal privilege granted by the owner.

Real estate may be under sole ownership (ownership in severalty) or under concurrent ownership: either as a tenant in common or as a joint tenant. A joint tenancy requires four unities: interest, time, title, and possession.

In exploring the possibility of multiple ownership, an investor may consider limited partnerships which grant no voice in management to the limited partner and limit the partner's liability to the amount of his capital investment. Under this arrangement, the general partner assumes responsibility for the operation, management, and control of the partnership according to the limited partnership agreement.

Real estate syndicates, real estate investment trusts, and corporations are other devices to convert the ownership of real estate into marketable interests that allow relatively small investors to participate in expensive real estate projects. A condominium interest constitutes an interest in real estate which is described as space (for example, apartment 103) plus an undivided interest in common elements. A condominium is formed by a declaration and is operated under corporation bylaws and the condominium management agreement.

Cooperative ownership provides for the purchase of a cooperative share with the right to use and possession granted under a proprietary lease. As compared to condominiums, cooperative ownerships have less flexibility in financing and have unlimited liability rather than a fixed proportion of liability for property operation and maintenance.

REVIEW QUESTIONS

1. What three rights are associated with an ownership of real estate?
2. Give an illustration showing how you would recommend conveyance of a fee simple determinable.
3. Distinguish between a fee simple absolute and a fee subject to condition subsequent.
4. Explain the ownership rights and responsibilities of a life tenant.
5. How do rights of dower and curtesy affect the transfer of real estate interests?
6. Explain the main differences between tenancy by the entirety and community property.
7. Define the following terms: *lessor, lessee, leased fee,* and *leasehold estate.*
8. Generally speaking, which of the less than freehold estates has the highest value? Which is the least valuable?
9. Give an example of an easement appurtenant, identifying the dominant and servient estate.
10. Show four ways in which a tenancy in common varies from a joint tenancy.
11. What is the role of limited and general partners?
12. In what ways do syndications appeal to investors?
13. Briefly explain four main operations of a syndicator.
14. What is the main rationale lying behind real estate investment trusts?
15. Why weren't real estate investment trusts feasible before 1960?

16. Property rights in condominiums are largely governed by three documents. Explain fully.

17. What are the advantages of condominium ownership over a cooperative ownership?

SELECTED REFERENCES

Atteberry, William; Pearson, Karl G.; and Litka, Michael P. *Real Estate Law,* chap. 3. Columbus: Grid, Inc., 1974.

Ellis, Donald H. "Basic Elements of Syndication," in Stephen E. Roulac (ed.). *Real Estate Securities and Syndication,* chap. 2. Chicago: National Association of Real Estate Boards, 1973.

Hebard, Edna L., and Meisel, Gerald S. *Principles of Real Estate Law,* chap. 6. Cambridge, Mass.: Schenkman Publishing Company, Inc., 1967.

Hoagland, Henry E. *Real Estate Principles,* chap. 3. 3d ed. New York: McGraw-Hill Book Co., 1955.

MacElhenny, Bernard J., Jr. "Organizing the Broker's Office for Syndication," in Stephen E. Roulac (ed.), *Real Estate Securities and Syndication,* chap. 4. Chicago: National Association of Real Estate Boards, 1973.

Ring, Alfred A., and Dasso, Jerome. *Real Estate Principles and Practices,* chap. 4. 8th ed. Englewood Cliffs, N.J.: Prentice-Hall, Inc., 1977.

6

Real Estate Instruments

After reading this chapter, you should be familiar with the following points:

1 The legal requirements of an enforceable contract: the special meanings attached to *valid*, *void*, *voidable*, and *unenforceable* contracts.
2 The remedies available if a contract is in default.
3 The features of an installment contract.
4 Option contracts.
5 An understanding of warranty deed covenants.
6 The distinguishing feature of a special warranty deed.
7 The manner in which quitclaim and bargain and sale deeds vary from warranty deeds.
8 Deeds for special purposes.
9 The requirements of an enforceable deed.
10 The effect of recording deeds.
11 The requirements of an enforceable lease.
12 The differences in leases classified by rental terms.
13 The more common features of a long-term development lease.

CERTAIN REAL ESTATE INSTRUMENTS are so commonly used that it is difficult to deal in real estate without knowledge of their characteristics. The special instruments that have been developed for conveying and leasing real estate vary considerably in their legal and economic effects. In addition, the importance of other contracts warrants explanation—the installment land contract, options, and leases.

It should be emphasized that in negotiating, developing, and managing real estate, lay members of the real estate industry are careful not to engage in the unlicensed practice of law. The law requires that only attorneys offer legal advice and prepare legal instruments. Yet it is important to acquaint the real estate practitioner with the main elements of real estate instruments commonly used in the trade. It is virtually impossible to communicate on real estate matters without at least a summary knowledge of the differences among specialized real estate documents. It is deemed worthwhile, further, to indicate situations in which special real estate documents are commonly used. For this reason, the chapter concentrates on real estate contracts, deeds, and leases.

REAL ESTATE CONTRACTS

Some forms of real estate contracts are encountered in real estate transactions. In the normal course of events, if an owner lists property with a real estate broker, between the time of listing and the title transfer many contracts will control the transactions involving the seller, the buyer, the broker, the lender, the title insurance company, and the closing agent.

Indeed, some of the instruments used in real estate are specialized forms of contracts. Standardized agreements are available to cover deposit receipts or earnest money receipts, contracts for sale, and listing agreements. Because these contracts are closely related to the closing of the sale, their discussion is deferred to the chapter on real estate brokerage (Chapter 16). In this chapter emphasis is given to the basic contract document, real estate options, and real estate installment contracts.

The Basic Contract Document

Most real estate contracts conform to the definition of a basic contract document: *a voluntary agreement between two or more competent parties who, for a consideration, agree to do or refrain from doing some particular legal act*. To acquire status as an enforceable agreement, real estate contracts, like other contracts, must meet the legal requirements of enforceable contracts.

Legal Requirements

When the main elements of a contract leading to its enforceability are explained, the vocabulary associated with a contract must be borne in mind throughout the discussion. Care must be taken to distinguish among contracts which are (1) valid, (2) void, (3) voidable, and (4) unenforceable.

In the present context, a *valid contract* refers to an instrument that satisfies all legal requirements. A valid contract contains all the essential elements required by law.

A *void contract* has no legal effect. The parties to the contract have no legal agreement; they have no legal obligation that can be either ratified or enforced. A void contract is for practical purposes no contract. Any contract for an illegal purpose would conform to this definition.

A *voidable contract* may be enforced or rejected at the option of one of the parties. It is also unenforceable against the same party. The case arises in a contract involving a minor. The minor has the option of holding the adult to the contract, yet the adult may not enforce the contract against the minor. The contract is voidable by the minor.

An *unenforceable contract* in the case of real estate would be an oral contract conveying an interest in real estate. Although the contract might be valid between the parties, it would be unenforceable if either party elected not to perform under his or her oral agreement.

Elements of a Contract

In real estate, contracting parties may create contracts which are *express* or *implied*. Most real estate contracts are express in that the parties declare terms, conditions, and their intent by written or oral statements. An implied contract is an agreement evidenced by acts and conduct. Suppose that in the absence of a written agreement a managing agent arranges for the replacement of a broken window in a rented dwelling. Suppose further that the owner inspects the work in progress but offers no comment. If he offers no objection to the work, it is implied that the owner consents to the repair; he would be responsible for an implied contract to pay for the work performed.

Persons in real estate use two other types of contracts: *bilateral* and *unilateral* contracts. The former refers to a promise that is exchanged for a promise: "I will pay you $1,000 to reroof my house." The latter is a promise that is exchanged for an act: "I will pay you a commission of 5 percent if you sell my house during the next 90 days." To administer the various contracts in real estate, you must have the elements of an enforceable contract.

1. In writing.
2. Parties competent to contract.
3. A lawful object.
4. A consideration.
5. An offer and an acceptance.
6. A legal description.
7. Proper signatures.

Contract in Writing. If the contract conveys an interest in real estate, it must be in writing. Only leases of less than one year are severally exempt from this rule. Moreover, the written document must be sufficiently complete and definite to establish intent. Although the contract may be amended by mutual consent, the written terms of the contract may not be changed by oral agreement. Even witnesses to an oral agreement are immaterial if the law requires that the contract be in writing.

The requirements are sufficiently broad to invalidate any unwritten agreement requiring a buyer to pay an indebtedness on an outstanding mortgage or other indebtedness made to the seller. With few exceptions most states apply the parol evidence rule which prohibits oral agreements as admissible evidence in contract disputes. It is presumed that the contract as written is complete and finalized with certainty.

Parties Competent to Contract. For a contract to be valid the parties to the contract must be legally competent to enter into a contract. Minors, persons judged legally insane, and certain other persons without the legal power to contract would not qualify. American Indians owning property under the Allotment Act of 1887 have no right to convey an interest in real estate without the written authorization of the Bureau of Indian Affairs, which acts as trustee for land held in trust for American Indians. Though Indians are competent in other matters, legally they have no power to convey an interest in allotted lands. An act of Congress is generally required to convey or alienate tribally owned Indian property which is held in trust. Persons acting for corporations, partnerships, and charitable organizations must show that they are legally empowered to execute real estate contracts according to the organization's charter or bylaws or by resolution of the board of directors or a similar governing entity. Without proof of competency, no contract could be held valid.

Lawful Object. A real estate contract to purchase or sell property for an illegal purpose would be void and unenforceable. Acts forbidden under local or state law—for example, the sale of spirituous beverages, the operation of a house of ill repute, or illegal gambling—are often-cited examples.

Consideration. Consideration, which is usually paid in money, is defined to include the receipt of a benefit or sacrifice by either or both of the contracting parties. A promise may constitute a valid consideration if each party is obligated to do something not required without the contract. Generally only a sufficient consideration is required, which is not necessarily adequate. It is reasoned that the seller has the right to convey real estate for any price, and he is presumed to act with full knowledge of the facts.

Offer and Acceptance. Parties to a contract must evidence their willingness to contract by words or acts. There must be evidence of the offer (by the offeror) and of its acceptance by the offeree. The contract is binding when the offer is properly accepted. In real estate, complications arise in that the first offer is seldom accepted; a buyer may counter the offer with another proposal, which becomes an offer to the seller. In fact, a series of offers by one party may be rejected by the other party, who submits revised proposals or offers. No contract prevails until an offer is accepted by the offeree. During negotiations, either party may withdraw an offer before its acceptance.

Legal Description. In some contracts the legal description consists of only the street address. Contracts of sale may identify the property in this way. In installment land contracts, the property conveyed should be described by a proper legal description showing boundaries and property lines with absolute certainty. A contract conveying an interest would be held invalid if the property is described with such indefiniteness that the land conveyed could not be accurately determined. If the intent of the parties is readily determinable, mistakes in legal descriptions do not necessarily invalidate a contract.

Proper Signatures. Unlike other conveyances, a contract must be signed by all parties to it. In this regard it should be noted that a contract may only be enforced against the parties who sign it. The wife who fails to join her husband in signing a real estate contract or a promise to convey real estate may not be forced to execute the deed. A buyer would have an action against the husband for damages, but he could not force conveyance of the property against the wife who in effect holds an interest as co-owner.

Contract Default

If a real estate contract covers the sale of real estate, both the seller and the buyer have a number of remedies in the event of default by the other party. The circumstances of each transaction determine the best legal action.

Default by the Buyer. If the sale is a long-term contract giving the purchaser possession before the seller issues the deed, the seller must extinguish all interest of the buyer, including eviction of the buyer from occupied premises and any interest of the buyer in the property (his equity), and must clear any title defects which may have been recorded by the buyer.

Subject to the contract agreement, the seller may ordinarily exercise three options: terminate the contract, keeping installments as damages; sue for damages; or bring action against the buyer for specific performance under the contract. These remedies may be restricted by state statute—the buyer is not always required to forfeit his payments where installments represent a substantial proportion of the purchase price. The contract language details the right to declare forfeiture in the event of default by the buyer. In the absence of further showing, damages will ordinarily be limited to the difference between the amount paid by the buyer and the market value of the property at the time of default.

Default by the Seller. The remedies available to the buyer are substantially the same as those available to the seller: in the event of seller default, the buyer may elect to sue for specific performance or damages or may terminate the contract and recover payments as damages. In some respects the buyer assumes an added risk in the real estate contract. The seller, though acting in good faith, may be unable to deliver title as specified under the contract. Meanwhile, a buyer who enters possession with the prospect of gaining title at the end of the installment period may have added expensive improvements to the land. These improvements generally become the property of the seller; the buyer usually recovers only his payments and costs.

INSTALLMENT LAND CONTRACTS

Installment land contracts provide for the conveyance of real estate under terms which are generally unavailable under deeds and mortgage arrangements. In effect, the seller promises to deliver title when the installment payments are completed and if the buyer has observed the other purchase terms. The seller retains title as security, and the buyer enjoys use and possession while the contract is in force.

The installment contract is a popular substitute if either the property or the buyer do not qualify for long-term mortgage credit. Savings and loan associations, commercial banks, mortgage bankers, and others may consider certain properties as poor security risks by reason of their location, construction, or other deficiencies. For example, a single-family dwelling within one mile of a major airport runway may not qualify for mortgage financing. This might also hold true for a dwelling in a remote country location 30 miles from the nearest city; or for a dwelling with construction deficiencies (a weak foundation, an unusually awkward floor plan); or for a dwelling that lacks salability (for example, a $50,000 dwelling in a neighborhood of $20,000 dwellings). In such instances, the seller may elect to sell with unusually favorable terms: a very low down payment and installment payments over 15 or 20 years with interest. In these circumstances the seller assumes the risks of a lender.

In other instances, the property may be ineligible for a mortgage because of the poor credit risk of the buyer—an inadequate or uncertain income, insufficient savings for a minimum down payment. Again the seller may elect to take a nominal down payment and assume financing risks. Vacant land is commonly sold in this way since historically vacant land has not been legally eligible for a first mortgage among the main savings institutions.

Land Contract Provisions

Installment contracts provide that the seller convey title when all installments have been paid. Some sellers arrange to convey title when a certain portion of the purchase price has been paid in installments, giving the buyer title subject to a mortgage for the balance of the purchase price. Although no particular form is required, the contract must have elements of an enforceable real estate instrument. The contract describes terms of the sale and the type of deed to be delivered, for example, a warranty deed with a release of dower and homestead. It is implied that the seller conveys a marketable title free of defects other than those specified in the contract. Though the seller may be required to give evidence of a marketable title at the time the contract is executed, the buyer assumes certain risks in the installment land contract.

Buyer Risks

A seller who dies before a contract is fulfilled subjects the buyer to possible claims against the estate. Other risks are largely associated with the fact that the seller, not the buyer, has the title of record. The chief risks may be summarized in three points:

1.   The buyer is restricted in assigning or transferring an interest under a land contract. Because contracts can be quickly terminated, investors and others are reluctant to assume the risks of land installment contracts.
2.   Even with full performance, the buyer is not guaranteed clear title. Claims against the seller often prevent the seller from performing. Though the title is marketable at the beginning of the contract, the buyer assumes the risk of claims arising during the installment period.
3.   The death of the seller before the contract is fulfilled may subject the buyer to extensive litigation in protecting his interest.

To protect the buyers in land installment contracts used in the interstate sale of lots, real estate developers and agents must observe the provisions of the Interstate Land Sales Full Disclosure Act. The act requires the seller or his agent to make full disclosure of property characteristics and sale terms to the buyer. These details are explained in the chapter on real estate brokerage (Chapter 16).

OPTION CONTRACTS

The option contract is an agreement that gives the buyer the right to purchase property at a fixed price within a given time in return for a consideration. If the option is exercised within the stated time, the consideration usually becomes part of the purchase price. Within the option period, the buyer has the option of complying with all the terms of the agreement or he or she may be relieved from the terms of the agreement without being sued for damages or specific performance. The buyer purchases the right to demand performance of the seller within the stated time but does not bind himself to any contract or performance.

By making property available at a known price and on known sale terms, the option contract enables the buyer to negotiate for other properties, to secure financing, or to organize a syndicate. Without the option, by which the price is determined before the decision to buy is made, the buyer would have difficulty in arranging complicated legal and financial details. To be enforceable, the option contract must include the legal elements of a valid contract.

DEEDS

When private property was first recognized, a real estate transfer was accomplished by physically exchanging a clump of ground before witnesses. As the practice spread, such transfers were documented by written statements. These written statements evolved as deeds, which are defined as *written instruments that convey an interest in real estate*. The interest conveyed depends largely on the type of deed used for conveyance.

Type of Deeds

Among the deeds available to transfer real estate interests, the·warranty deed is preferred by the buyer since it contains certain promises of the seller that protect title. Special warranty deeds, quitclaim deeds, and bargain and sale deeds give the buyer less protection. Other purposes are served by certain other deeds—for example, the trust deed, the executor's deed, and the sheriff's deed.

Warranty Deeds. In the warranty deed the seller makes certain promises or covenants to the buyer. These covenants are included only in warranty deeds:

1. The covenant of seizin.
2. The covenant of quiet enjoyment.
3. The covenant against encumbrances.
4. The covenant of further assurances.
5. The covenant of warranty of title.

Under the first covenant, the seller promises that he or she is seized or possessed of the real estate described in the deed and that as owner the seller has the right to transfer title. This covenant is violated if the land is subject to a 40-foot right-of-way easement across the property which *was not noted* in the deed. Or suppose that the seller did not have a valid title at the time the deed was executed. The buyer could then sue the seller under the warranty deed for violation of the *covenant of seizin.*

The *covenant of quiet enjoyment* means that the seller warrants that ownership provides for the peaceful use of the property, free of claims by other persons lawfully claiming a superior title to the same property. The practical effect of this covenant protects the holder from claims falling under a mortgage which was not mentioned at the time of transfer. If the buyer loses title because of foreclosure of an undisclosed mortgage, the buyer could sue the seller for damages because this covenant was broken.

The *covenant against encumbrances* protects the buyer from any lien or debt against the property, known or unknown to the buyer and seller at the time of conveyance, which was not reported in the deed. Claims or other debts known at the time of conveyance should be identified in the deed. Failure to observe this rule gives the buyer the right to sue under the covenant against encumbrances.

The *covenant of further assurances* adds to the validity of title since the grantor promises to obtain any further documents necessary to give the seller title as stated in the warranty deed. Violations of this covenant would include failure to obtain the wife's signature where it is needed to extinguish dower, joint tenancy, or community property rights. In other words any defect in title which may be remedied by executing other conveyances would be required by this covenant.

The *covenant of warranty* provides that the seller will defend title against claims of persons contesting title even after execution of the deed. The seller must pay the expenses of defending the buyer's title, for example, the expenses of defending a title against a minor who has not released his claim and who later brings a title action against the buyer.

The five covenants are not explicitly stated in warranty deeds. They are implied under the statute governing the warranty deeds of each state. To qualify as a warranty deed, the conveyance must include specific words that imply a warranty deed with all of its covenants. Typical language identifying a warranty deed usually includes such expressions as "grant and convey," "convey and warrant," or "grant and release." Provided that the intent is to execute a warranty deed and that the required statutory language is included in the deed of conveyance, the five covenants remain in force. Figure 6–1 illustrates the warranty deed used in Florida. Note the granting clause approved in that state.

Special Warranty Deeds.   Understandably the seller may be reluctant to execute a warranty deed and make promises to enforce covenants for acts committed before his ownership. With a special warranty deed, the seller may restrict his liability to title defects occurring after the seller acquired title. Although the special warranty deed includes the covenants of a warranty deed, the buyer's remedy is restricted to covenants that were broken because of events that took place during the seller's ownership.

Suppose that a company engaged in timber operations wants to sell 1,000 acres of land poorly suited to timber reproduction. If the company has reason to suspect that the title may be contested by unknown heirs or former married parties who have not released their claim, a special warranty deed would be advised. The company would accept title responsibility only for acts committed during its ownership. With incomplete knowledge of title before its ownership was acquired, the company would minimize risks by conveying under a special warranty deed.

FIGURE 6–1

Statutory Warranty Deed Used in the State of Florida

Printed for Lawyers' Title Guaranty Fund, Orlando, Florida

This instrument was prepared by:

GAYLORD A. WOOD, JR.
603 Court House Square Building
200 Southeast Sixth Street
FORT LAUDERDALE, FLORIDA 33301

Warranty Deed (STATUTORY FORM — SECTION 689.02 F.S.)

This Indenture, Made this   day of   19   , **Between**

of the County of   , State of   , grantor°, and

whose post office address is

of the County of   , State of   , grantee°,

Witnesseth, That said grantor, for and in consideration of the sum of

Dollars,

and other good and valuable considerations to said grantor in hand paid by said grantee, the receipt whereof is hereby acknowledged, has granted, bargained and sold to the said grantee, and grantee's heirs and assigns forever, the following described land, situate, lying and being in   County, Florida, to-wit:

and said grantor does hereby fully warrant the title to said land, and will defend the same against the lawful claims of all persons whomsoever.

° "Grantor" and "grantee" are used for singular or plural, as context requires.

In Witness Whereof, Grantor has hereunto set grantor's hand and seal the day and year first above written. Signed, sealed and delivered in our presence:

_____   _____(Seal)

_____   _____(Seal)

_____   _____(Seal)

_____   _____(Seal)

STATE OF
COUNTY OF
I HEREBY CERTIFY that on this day before me, an officer duly qualified to take acknowledgments, personally appeared

to me known to be the person described in and who executed the foregoing instrument and acknowledged before me that   he   executed the same.
WITNESS my hand and official seal in the County and State last aforesaid this   day of
19

My commission expires: Notary Public

FIGURE 6–2

Quitclaim Deed Form Used in the State of Pennsylvania

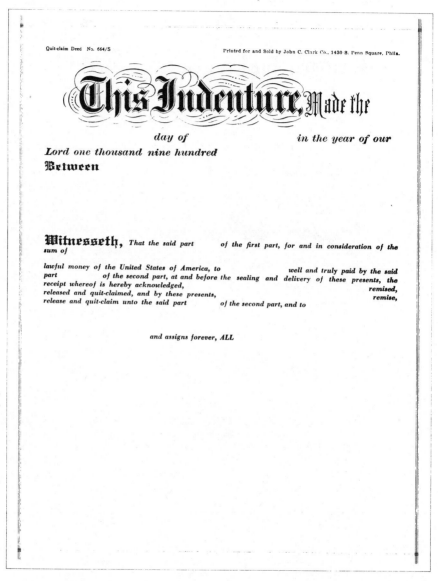

Quitclaim Deeds. Among the deeds of conveyance the quitclaim deed gives the buyer the least amount of title protection. No covenants are stipulated in this deed. The conveyance language of a quitclaim deed typically reads, "remise, release, and forever quit claim." Under this language the seller transfers only the interest that he holds in the real estate described. If it is established that the seller had no interest, the buyer has

FIGURE 6-2 (continued)

Together *with all and singular, the tenements, hereditaments and appurtenances thereunto belonging, or in any wise appertaining, and the reversions, remainders, rents, issues and profits thereof:* **And** *also, all the estate, right, title, interest,*
property, claim and demand whatsoever, as well in law as in equity, *of the said part   of the first part, of, in, or to the above-described premises, and every part and parcel thereof, with the appurtenances.*
To have and to hold *all and singular the above-mentioned and described premises, together with the appurtenances, unto the said part   of the second part,*

and assigns forever.

In Witness Whereof,

Sealed and Delivered
IN THE PRESENCE OF US:

Commonwealth of Pennsylvania } SS.
County of

On this, the   *day of*   *, 19   , before me, the undersigned*
Officer,
                              , personally appeared

known to me (satisfactorily proven) to be the *person   whose name   is (are) subscribed to the within instrument, and acknowledged that   he executed the same for the purposes therein contained.*
In Witness Whereof, *I hereunto set my hand and official seal.*

acquired no interest. On the other hand, if the title is legally enforceable and without defects, the quitclaim deed may give the buyer title as good as that obtained under a warranty deed. With a quitclaim deed, the seller makes no covenants or warranties of title. Figure 6-2 illustrates the quitclaim deed form applied in the state of Pennsylvania.

The quitclaim deed is most useful in releasing defects in title. A wife who fails to release her dower interest or a minor coming of age may be

FIGURE 6–2 *(concluded)*

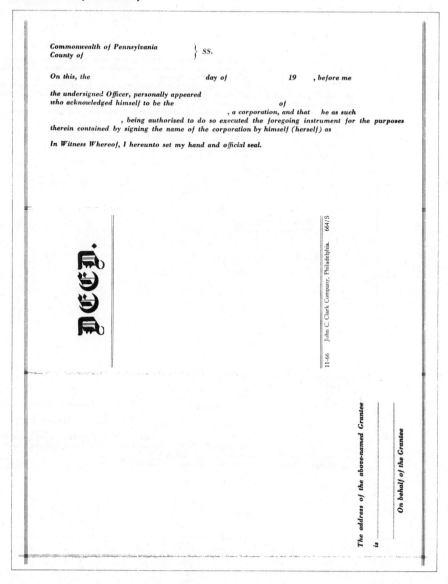

Commonwealth of Pennsylvania
County of   } SS.

On this, the   *day of*   *19*   *, before me*

the undersigned Officer, personally appeared
who acknowledged himself to be the   *of*
                                                             , a corporation, and that   he as such
              , being authorized to do so executed the foregoing instrument for the purposes
therein contained by signing the name of the corporation by himself (herself) as

In Witness Whereof, I hereunto set my hand and official seal.

11-66   John C. Clark Company, Philadelphia.   664/S

The address of the above-named Grantee

is

On behalf of the Grantee

asked to execute a quitclaim deed to release any claims against property conveyed. Similarly a corporation that conveyed title without proper signatures to a deed may relinquish any subsequent claims with a quitclaim deed. For this reason most authorities recommend the quitclaim deed to clear up questionable titles.

Bargain and Sale Deeds. Such deeds fall between the warranty and the quitclaim deed. In a bargain and sale deed the key words required by statute typically read "grant, bargain, and sell." The particular state statute identifies the required conveyance words. Here the seller conveys the land and not an interest in the land, as in a quitclaim deed. The deed includes no warranties of title. However, the deed is somewhat superior to a quitclaim deed in that there is an implied assumption that the seller has possession and title.

Deeds for Specific Purposes. Numerous deeds have developed to cover particular legal purposes. The more common deeds include the executor's deed, the sheriff's deed, correction deeds, and trust deeds. Note also that many states have defined deeds in a special way. Thus, a grant deed in California conforms to a special warranty deed. In Georgia, similarly, a security deed substitutes for the warranty deed and mortgage. That is, the security deed is a conveyance by a warranty deed that secures a debt. The deed transfers the power of attorney to a lender who is authorized to sell the property upon default of a debt. This arrangement enables the lender to exercise the power of sale in the event of default without proceeding under more time-consuming and costly mortgage foreclosure procedures.

1. *Executor's Deeds.* The executor operates under the direction of the court. Title to the real estate of a deceased person who dies without a will or with a will which contains no power of sale, will be sold under an executor's deed. In this type of deed the full sales price must be stated and the executor warrants title only against his acts. No other warranties are extended by the executor who executes the deed under court approval.

2. *Correction Deeds.* In preparing deeds, the misspelling of names, errors in legal descriptions, or important omissions are not unusual. If corrections are made on the original document, questions may be raised about their authenticity. It is usually impractical to make erasures on or additions to an executed deed.

The best alternative is to execute a correction deed that states something like the following: "This deed is to correct the deed dated between the grantor [seller] _____ and the grantee [buyer] _____ and recorded in deed book _____, page _____, in King County, Washington." The correction deed must conform to the requirements of an enforceable deed and establish the proper chain of title. The reference to recording refers to a public file containing deeds of record in the county recorder's or other office designated for this purpose.

3. *Sheriff's Deeds.* Lenders foreclosing on a mortgage must follow statutory requirements that lead to the eventual public sale of foreclosed property. A foreclosure action may require that the property be sold at a public sale for the benefit of the lender. Conveyance at a public sale upon foreclosure will be under a sheriff's deed or its equivalent. Since the sheriff acts for the public, no warranty or representations may be made on the title. Buyers must assume risks for title defects.

4. *Trust Deeds.* In the states of California and Arizona, among others, the trust deed substitutes for a mortgage. In effect, a deed of trust conveys title to a trustee, a third party who holds the title for the benefit of the lender or the beneficiary. The borrower (trustor) executes the trust deed in return for a long-term mortgage. If the borrower defaults on monthly payments, then the terms of the deed of trust direct the trustee to transfer title to the lender in satisfaction of the debt. This procedure sidesteps the lengthier foreclosure procedures that are common to statutes regulating mortgages. In California, a creditor may secure clear title under a trust deed after 3 months and 21 days, whereas mortgage foreclosure actions require more than a year. Actually the deed of trust is a financing instrument rather than a conveyance of title.

Deed Requirements

Because the deed is a contract, it must be executed with the same formality that is required for an enforceable contract. In addition, deeds must follow stricter requirements because of the inherent problems of conveying real estate. Unlike the conveyance of personal property, the conveyance of an interest in real estate must be in *writing*. Statutes governing this requirement follow practices established by the Statute of Frauds, an English law first enacted in 1676 which stated that no estate or interest could ". . . be assigned, granted or surrendered, unless it be by Deed or Note in Writing, signed by the Party for assigning, granting or surrendering the same, or their Agents thereunto lawfully authorized by Writing. . . ."[1]

In addition to the requirement for a written instrument, a valid deed must cover seven other essential requirements:

1. A legally competent grantor.
2. A consideration.
3. A grantee.
4. A granting clause.
5. A legal description.
6. Execution by the grantor.
7. Delivery and acceptance.

The Legally Competent Grantor. A valid deed must have a grantor who has authority to convey title. The issue arises in the case of minors, owners declared legally insane, and corporate officers transferring corporate realty. If the grantor is a married person, the marital status should be indicated. Both married persons should join in the deed as grantors. A deed with a grantor who is a legal minor or who is proven insane at the time of conveyance is generally voidable but not necessarily void. Corporate officers must usually submit evidence of their capacity to act for the corporation in conveying corporate real estate.

---

[1] *Great Britain's Statutes,* vol. 3: *1603–1698,* pp. 384–87.

The Grantee.   The grantee is the party named in the deed to receive the real estate interest conveyed. To be enforceable the deed must name a grantee capable of owning title. Thus a deed that conveys an estate to a nonexistent person is void and a deed conveying an estate to a deceased person, a fictitious being, or an unborn person is ineffective. There must not only be a person or entity qualified to convey title but also a person or entity legally invested with the right to acquire title in real estate.

The Consideration.   An enforceable deed must have a *good* or *valuable* consideration. As with other enforceable contracts, the consideration is evidence that something of value was paid for the interest conveyed. A good consideration, which is valid between the grantor and the grantee, is considered an adequate substitute for money. Thus, title may be conveyed in return for love and affection or other considerations not measured in money.

A valuable consideration constitutes the purchase price in money or other things of value measurable in dollars. Generally it is not necessary to specify the amount of consideration for a deed to be enforceable. In most cases the custom is to recite the consideration in nominal terms: "$10 and other good and valuable consideration." Only in deeds executed by guardians or an executor and in certain other statutorily defined deeds must the actual price be stated. It is usually sufficient to merely indicate that a nominal consideration was paid for the interest conveyed.

The Granting Clause.   Words of conveyance must indicate the grantor's intent to convey an interest in real estate. While no specific technical words are required, care must be taken to use the appropriate words as defined by statute that conform to the type of conveyance intended, for example, a warranty deed, a quitclaim deed, or a bargain and sale deed. The granting clause indicates the intentions of the grantor.

The Legal Description.   An enforceable deed must describe the land conveyed so that it can be located and identified. A deed with an indefinite description is void. While the law does not specify the type of legal description used, the recorded lot number of subdivisions and designations identified by the U.S. Government Rectangular Survey or by a metes and bounds description are among the available alternatives. While an address may be sufficient, in practice a street address or other general statement describing land is too indefinite for practical use. The importance of descriptions in real estate conveyances justifies the explanation of legal descriptions contained in the following chapter.

Execution by the Grantor.   The grantor must execute the deed by signing the instrument with appropriate witnesses as required. The signature should conform to the name appearing as grantor. When the deed is executed, the grantor's name should appear in the form that he used when he accepted title.

Witnesses to the deed must conform to state law, which may require one or, more commonly, two witnesses. Witnesses merely confirm the authenticity of the grantor's signature. It is common practice to acknowledge signatures on deeds before a notary public. While acknowledgment is not required for enforceability as between the grantor and the grantee, some states require it before the deed is accepted for recording.

The act of recording refers to filing the deed for record with the government agency designated to accept real estate and other documents for record-keeping purposes. Usually this will be an office in the local county courthouse—for example, the registry of deeds, the county recorder, or the clerk of the court.

Delivery and Acceptance.   The grantor must do more than execute the properly prepared deed with all the required signatures. Title is not conveyed until the deed is delivered and accepted by the grantee. Delivery does not necessarily require that the grantor physically hand over the document to the grantee. In this regard the grantor must act with the intent of passing title; the delivery must be voluntary.

In some states recording the deed is a presumption of valid delivery. In other states the deed is placed with a third party who holds the deed until the buyer has met the terms of the sale, at which time the deed is delivered by an agent of the grantor. There must be a mutual intent to convey title at the time the deed is delivered by the grantor and accepted by the grantee.

Deed Recording

A deed does not have to be recorded in order to be effective between the grantor and the grantee. However, it is also true that an unrecorded deed is void with respect to subsequent buyers. For example, if A conveys land to B and A dies before the deed is recorded, there is a possibility that the heirs of A, not knowing of the sale to B, will convey the same land to C. If the land was not occupied by B, C would have no way of knowing of the sale to B. If C recorded before B, C would prevail over B.

The purpose of the recording procedure is to protect parties who act in ignorance of earlier unrecorded conveyances. Legally the act of recording serves as *constructive notice* to the public of the existence of such a conveyance or other instrument. In real estate the public is charged with notice of recorded deeds and real estate instruments. In this respect constructive notice substitutes for actual notice. It is presumed that the parties engaged in real estate transactions have the duty to examine public records. Usually the recording statutes provide for the recording of deeds, mortgages, and other instruments relating to land title.

Deed Restrictions

The owner has the right to dispose of land in any manner that is not contrary to public policy. To protect adjoining property, the owner may place restrictions on the use of the property conveyed. For instance, the grantor may add a restrictive covenant in a deed that states:

The use of this land is restricted to the construction of a single-family residence, not exceeding one story in height.

In further illustration, the grantor may restrict the grantee to buildings constructed of brick veneer or bar commercial use or require that a single-family dwelling have a minimum area of 1,500 square feet.

Provided that the restriction is reasonable, it may be enforced by parties to the agreement and by other persons who benefit. For example, in a subdivision restrictions may be part of a general plan for a residential development. Presumably restrictions benefit all owners of real estate in the subdivision and may be enforced by any owner who purchased with knowledge of the restrictions.

LEASES

The lease is a contract between the owner (lessor) and the tenant (lessee). It is also a conveyance transferring exclusive use and possession to the tenant under the terms of the lease in return for rent or other consideration. It is not uncommon to encounter a commercial lease of 50 pages or more outlining the duties and responsibilities of the owner and the tenant. Historically the tenant was given exclusive rights of use and possession as limited by the terms of the lease. An enforceable lease, at a minimum, must contain elements common to the requirements of a valid contract:

1. A beginning and ending date.
2. Identification of the lessor and the lessee.
3. A legal description of the property leased.
4. The rental terms, including the time and place of payment.
5. Signatures of the parties to the lease.

These points cover only the minimum legal requirements. In practice a lease extending for more than one year will generally detail the rights and responsibilities of the parties at considerable length. The prominent features of leases used in commercial development deserve further explanation. In this discussion the relations between tenants and apartment owners are omitted, since these are a separate subject.

Types of Leases

The most common method of classifying leases relates to the method of paying rent. In this respect leases fall into one of five classifications or their combinations: (1) fixed rent leases, (2) graduated leases, (3) price index leases, (4) revaluation leases, and (5) percentage leases.

Fixed Rent Leases. Lenders financing property subject to a lease prefer fixed rent leases. In the event that the tenant defaults on a long-term mortgage, the lender is subject only to a known fixed liability. With this qualification, fixed rent leases are generally limited to relatively short terms, for example, three, five, or ten years. Under continuing inflation, owners are reluctant to commit property over a long term in the face of expected price increases. Indeed, a fixed rent over a relatively short term gives the owner the option of negotiating rent to a current level. Moreover, the tenant has less risk under a fixed rent schedule over a short term in that he does not face the risk of paying increasing rent with a decreasing ability to pay.

Graduated Rent Leases. It is not unusual for parties to negotiate fixed rents which vary over the leased term. For example:

Year	Annual Rent
First two years..............	$1,000
Next three years...........	2,000
Next five years.............	5,000

A graduated rent schedule is adapted to numerous situations, such as a situation involving a commercial tenant who has a newly developing business or one involving a location in the direction of growth in an expanding area. In such situations both the owner and the tenant anticipate that the business of the tenant and the value of the location will improve over the succeeding years.

For relatively short terms, a graduated rent schedule represents a subsidy to the tenant who, it is presumed, will have greater ability to pay market rent in later years. On the other hand, as the term increases there is greater danger that the step rate increase may rise *above* market rents to the point of endangering the solvency of the tenant. For this reason step rate rents are seldom adaptable to relatively long-term leases, say, more than ten years. The uncertainty of future income argues against this form of rent payment. However, graduated rents seem to be a useful device to adjust rents to the low earning capacity of property undergoing development.

Price Index Leases. The owner and tenant may have a mutual interest in adjusting rent to changes in the general price level. That is, if prices increase 10 percent, it seems reasonable to adjust rents upward by the same amount. The justification of a price index lease is that it maintains the economic position of the owner and the tenant; neither party gains an advantage under a price index lease.

Yet it will be appreciated that market rents may not always change at the same rate as changes in the general price level. The best that may be said for price index leases is that they preserve the purchasing power of the owner in terms of the relative prices of goods and services. Further, much depends on the selection of the price index.

In practice, most leases are probably tied to the consumer price index, which measures the purchasing power of urban workers in selected cities. Others have used the implicit price deflator (reported monthly by the Department of Commerce) or the wholesale price index as an alternative price deflator. The implicit price deflator has the advantage of measuring price changes in all goods and services produced in the economy—not merely the goods and services purchased by urban workers.

Revaluation Leases. Revaluation leases call for rental reappraisals at specified times over the lease term. For example, the lease may require reappraisals at five-year intervals by a board of three appraisers—one selected by the owner, another selected by the tenant, and the third selected by the two appointed appraisers.

This procedure rests on the willingness of the owner and the tenant to accept the findings of the reappraisal board. The recommended rents are not compulsory on the parties to the lease. Further, the tenant may think that he is being penalized for his superior management of a business. In opposition, the owner may reason that rent increases not because of the tenant's operations but because of the location's inherent advantages. Failure to resolve these attitudes may lead to expensive litigation. The chances of litigation increase with increases in the frequency of revaluation periods.

Percentage Leases. Rents based on gross sales tend to be favored for downtown and shopping center tenants. In a newly developed shopping center, a tenant may offer to pay a minimum rent, which provides a minimum rate of return on the owner's investment, with the provision that as gross sales reach a certain level, the owner will be paid a percentage of the gross sales: say, 1½ percent of annual gross sales over $1,500,000 for a supermarket chain store in a community shopping center. As a general rule, tenants with a relatively large volume of low-markup sales (supermarket chains) pay relatively low percentage rents, whereas high-markup, low-turnover retail businesses (jewelry stores) pay higher percentage rents. Periodical surveys of percentage rents are undertaken by the Urban Land Institute and the National Association of Realtors®.

While percentage rents have the general appeal that they base the rent on the tenant's ability to pay—as his gross receipts increase, rents increase—they are inappropriate for certain tenants. They are difficult to enforce against relatively small tenants with poor accounting systems; they cannot be applied to businesses based on personal services, for example, dentists, doctors, or accountants; and they are inapplicable to many industrial operations—warehousing, industrial plants, and other nonretail operations.

Elements of a Development Lease

In a long-term lease, the rights of the parties deserve detailed attention, for, in effect, the owner typically commits property over one or two generations. Hence parties to the lease must anticipate considerable detail covering the future duties of the owner and the tenant. Accordingly it is not uncommon to find leases containing 50 or more pages of contract terms. See Figure 6–3 for a standard lease form prepared for use in Phila-

FIGURE 6-3

Standard Lease Form of 29 Charges for the State of Pennsylvania

Uniform Lease No. 50
Revised June 1970

Printed by John C. Clark Co., 1326 Walnut St., Phila.

Lease Agreement

1—Parties

This Agreement, MADE THE————————————————————day of—————
one thousand nine hundred and————————————————(19————), by and between——————

(hereinafter called Lessor), of the one part, and—————————————————

2—Premises

(hereinafter called Lessee), of the other part.
    WITNESSETH THAT: Lessor does hereby demise and let unto Lessee all that certain——————

in the————————————————of————————————State of Pennsylvania, to be used and occupied as

————————————————————————————————and for no other purpose,

3—Term

for the term of————————————————beginning the————————day of——————,
one thousand nine hundred and————————(19————), and ending the————————day of——————,

4—Minimum Rent

one thousand nine hundred and————————(19————), for the minimum————————rental of——————

————————————————(Dollars) ($————————), lawful money of the United States of America, payable
in monthly installments in advance during the said term of this lease, or any renewal hereof, in sums of——————

Dollars ($————————) on the————————————day of each month, rent to begin from the————————day of
————————, 19————, the first installment to be paid at the time of signing this lease.

5—Inability to give Possession

    If Lessor is unable to give Lessee possession of the demised premises, as herein provided, by reason of the holding over of a previous occupant, or by reason of any cause beyond the control of the Lessor, the Lessor shall not be liable in damages to the Lessee therefor, and during the period that the Lessor is unable to give possession, all rights and remedies of both parties hereunder shall be suspended.

6—Additional Rent
(a) Damages for Default

    (a) Lessee agrees to pay as rent in addition to the minimum rental herein reserved any and all sums which may become due by reason of the failure of Lessee to comply with all the covenants of this lease and pay any and all damages, costs and expenses which the Lessor may suffer or incur by reason of any default of the Lessee or failure on his part to comply with the covenants of this lease, and each of them, and also any and all damages of the demised premises caused by any act or neglect of the Lessee.

(b) Taxes

    (b) Lessee further agrees to pay as rent in addition to the minimum rental herein reserved all taxes assessed or imposed upon the demised premises and/or the building of which the demised premises is a part during the term of this lease. in excess of and over and above those assessed or imposed at the time of making this lease. The amount due hereunder on account of such taxes shall be apportioned for that part of the first and last calendar years covered by the term hereof. The same shall be paid by Lessee to Lessor on or before the first day of July of each and every year.

(c) Fire Insurance Premiums

    (c) Lessee further agrees to pay to Lessor as additional rent all increase or increases in fire insurance premiums upon the demised premises and/or the building of which the demised premises is a part, due to an increase in the rate of fire insurance in excess of the rate on the demised premises at the time of making this lease, if said increase is caused by any act or neglect of the Lessee or the nature of the Lessee's business.

(d) Water Rent

    (d) Lessee further agrees to pay as additional rent, if there is a metered water connection to the said premises, all charges for water consumed upon the demised premises in excess of the yearly minimum meter charge and all charges for repairs to the water pipes or meters on the premises, whether such repairs are made necessary by ordinary wear and tear, freezing, hot water, accident or other causes, immediately when the same become due.

(e) Sewer Rent

    (e) Lessee further agrees to pay as additional rent, if there is a metered water connection to said premises, all sewer rental or charges for use of sewers, sewage system, and sewage treatment works servicing the demised premises in excess of the yearly minimum of such sewer charges, immediately when the same become due.
    All rents shall be payable without prior notice or demand at the office of Lessor in——————

7—Place of Payment

or at such other place as Lessor may from time to time designate by notice in writing.

8—Affirmative Covenants of Lessee
(a) Payment of Rent

    Lessee covenants and agrees that he will without demand
    (a) Pay the rent and all other charges herein reserved as rent on the days and times and at the place that the same are made payable, without fail, and if Lessor shall at any time or times accept said rent or rent charges after the same shall have become due and payable, such acceptance shall not excuse delay upon subsequent occasions, or constitute or be construed as a waiver of any of Lessor's rights. Lessee agrees that any charge or payment herein reserved, included or agreed to be treated or collected as rent and/or any other charges or taxes, expenses, or costs herein agreed to be paid by the Lessee may be proceeded for and recovered by the Lessor by distraint or other process in the same manner as rent due and in arrears.

(b) Cleaning, Repairing, etc.

    (b) Keep the demised premises clean and free from all ashes, dirt and other refuse matter; replace all glass windows, doors, etc., broken; keep all waste and drain pipes open; repair all damage to plumbing and to the premises in general; keep the same in good order and repair as they now are, reasonable wear and tear and damage by accidental fire or other casualty not occurring through negligence of Lessee or those employed by or acting for Lessee alone excepted. The Lessee agrees to surrender the demised premises in the same condition in which Lessee has herein agreed to keep the same during the continuance of this lease.

(c) Requirements of Public Authorities

    (c) Comply with any requirements of any of the constituted public authorities, and with the terms of any State or Federal statute or local ordinance or regulation applicable to Lessee or his use of the demised premises, and save Lessor harmless from penalties, fines, costs or damages resulting from failure to do so.

(d) Fire

    (d) Use every reasonable precaution against fire.

(e) Rules and Regulations

    (e) Comply with rules and regulations of Lessor promulgated as hereinafter provided.

(f) Surrender of Possession

    (f) Peaceably deliver up and surrender possession of the demised premises to the Lessor at the expiration or sooner termination of this lease, promptly delivering to Lessor at his office all keys for the demised premises.

(g) Notice of Fire, etc.

    (g) Give to Lessor prompt written notice of any accident, fire, or damage occurring on or to the demised premises.

(h) Condition of Pavement

    (h) Lessee shall be responsible for the condition of the pavement, curb, cellar doors, awnings and other erections in the pavement during the term of this lease; shall keep the pavement free from snow and ice; and shall be and hereby agrees that Lessee is solely liable for any accidents, due or alleged to be due to their defective condition, or to any accumulations of snow and ice.

(i) Agency on Removal

    (i) The Lessee agrees that if, with the permission in writing of Lessor, Lessee shall vacate or decide at any time during the term of this lease, or any renewal thereof, to vacate the herein demised premises prior to the expiration of this lease, or any renewal hereof, Lessee will not cause or allow any other agent to represent Lessee in any sub-letting or reletting of the demised premises other than an agent approved by the Lessor————————————————————and that should Lessee do so or attempt to do so, the Lessor————————————————————may remove any signs that may be placed on or about the demised premises by such other agent without any liability to Lessor or to said agent, the Lessee assuming all responsibility for such action.

9—Negative Covenants of Lessee
(a) Use of Premises

    Lessee covenants and agrees that he will do none of the following things without the consent in writing of Lessor first had and obtained:
    (a) Occupy the demised premises in any other manner or for any other purpose than as above set forth.

(b) Assignment and Sub-letting

    (b) Assign, mortgage or pledge this lease or under-let or sub-lease the demised premises, or any part thereof, or permit any other person, firm or corporation to occupy the demised premises, or any part thereof; nor shall any assignee or sub-lessee assign, mortgage or pledge this lease or such sub-lease, without an additional written consent by the Lessor, and without such consent no such assignment, mortgage or pledge shall be valid. If the Lessee becomes embarrassed or insolvent, or makes an assignment for the benefit of creditors, or if a petition in bankruptcy is filed by or against the Lessee or a bill in equity or other proceeding for the appointment of a receiver for the Lessee is filed, or if the real or personal property of the Lessee shall be sold or levied upon by any Sheriff, Marshal or Constable, the same shall be a violation of this covenant.

FIGURE 6–3 (continued)

(c) Signs *(c)* Place or allow to be placed any stand, booth, sign or show case upon the doorsteps, vestibules or outside walls or pavements of said premises, or paint, place, erect or cause to be painted, placed or erected any sign, projection or device on or in any part of the premises. Lessee shall remove any sign, projection or device painted, placed or erected, if permission has been granted and restore the walls, etc., to their former conditions, at or prior to the expiration of this lease. In case of the breach of this covenant (in addition to all other remedies given to Lessor in case of breach of any conditions or covenants of this lease) Lessor shall have the privilege of removing said stand, booth, sign, show case, projection or device, and restoring said walls, etc., to their former condition, and Lessee, at Lessor's option, shall be liable to Lessor for any and all expenses so incurred by Lessor.

(d) Alterations, Improvements *(d)* Make any alterations, improvements, or additions to the demised premises. All alterations, improvements, additions or fixtures, whether installed before or after the execution of this lease, shall remain upon the premises at the expiration or sooner determination of this lease and become the property of Lessor, unless Lessor shall, prior to the determination of this lease, have given written notice to Lessee to remove the same, in which event Lessee will remove such alterations, improvements and additions and restore the premises to the same good order and condition in which they now are. Should Lessee fail so to do, Lessor may do so, collecting, at Lessor's option, the cost and expense thereof from Lessee as additional rent.

(e) Machinery *(e)* Use or operate any machinery that, in Lessor's opinion, is harmful to the building or disturbing to other tenants occupying other parts thereof.

(f) Weights *(f)* Place any weights in any portion of the demised premises beyond the safe carrying capacity of the structure.

(g) Fire Insurance *(g)* Do or suffer to be done, any act, matter or thing objectionable to the fire insurance companies whereby the fire insurance or any other insurance now in force or hereafter to be placed on the demised premises, or any part thereof, or on the building of which the demised premises may be a part, shall become void or suspended, or whereby the same shall be rated as a more hazardous risk than at the date of execution of this lease, or employ any person or persons objectionable to the fire insurance companies or carry or have any benzine or explosive matter of any kind in and about the demised premises. In case of a breach of this covenant (in addition to all other remedies given to Lessor in case of the breach of any of the conditions or covenants of this lease) Lessee agrees to pay to Lessor as additional rent any and all increase or increases of premiums on insurance carried by Lessor on the demised premises, or any part thereof, or on the building of which the demised premises may be a part, caused in any way by the occupancy of Lessee.

(h) Removal of Goods *(h)* Remove, attempt to remove or manifest an intention to remove Lessee's goods or property from or out of the demised premises otherwise than in the ordinary and usual course of business, without having first paid and satisfied Lessor for all rent which may become due during the entire term of this lease.

(i) Vacate Premises *(i)* Vacate or desert said premises during the term of this lease, or permit the same to be empty and unoccupied.

10—Lessor's Rights Lessee covenants and agrees that Lessor shall have the right to do the following things and matters in and about the demised premises:

(a) Inspection of Premises *(a)* At all reasonable times by himself or his duly authorized agents to go upon and inspect the demised premises and every part thereof, and/or at his option to make repairs, alterations and additions to the demised premises or the building of which the demised premises is a part.

(b) Rules and Regulations *(b)* At any time or times and from time to time to make such rules and regulations as in his judgment may from time to time be necessary for the safety, care and cleanliness of the premises, and for the preservation of good order therein. Such rules and regulations shall, when notice thereof is given to Lessee, form a part of this lease.

(c) Sale or Rent Sign Prospective Purchasers or Tenants *(c)* To display a "For Sale" sign at any time, and also, after notice from either party of intention to determine this lease, or at any time within three months prior to the expiration of this lease, a "For Rent" sign, or both "For Rent" and "For Sale" signs; and all of said signs shall be placed upon such part of the premises as Lessor may elect and may contain such matter as Lessor shall require. Prospective purchasers or tenants authorized by Lessor may inspect the premises at reasonable hours at any time.

(d) Discontinue Facilities and Service *(d)* The Lessor may discontinue all facilities furnished and services rendered, or any of them, by Lessor, not expressly covenanted for herein, it being understood that they constitute no part of the consideration for this lease.

11—Responsibility of Lessee *(a)* Lessee agrees to be responsible for and to relieve and hereby relieves the Lessor from all liability by reason of any injury or damage to any person or property in the demised premises, whether belonging to the Lessee or any other person, caused by any fire, breakage or leakage in any part or portion of the demised premises, or any part or portion of the building of which the demised premises is a part, or from water, rain or snow that may leak into, issue or flow from any part of the said premises, or of the building of which the demised premises is a part, or from the drains, pipes, or plumbing work of the same, or from any place or quarter, whether such breakage, leakage, injury or damage be caused by or result from the negligence of Lessor or his servants or agents or any person or persons whatsoever.

(b) Lessee also agrees to be responsible for and to relieve and hereby relieves Lessor from all liability by reason of any damage or injury to any person or thing which may arise from or be due to the use, misuse or abuse of all or any of the elevators, hatches, openings, stairways, hallways, of any kind whatsoever, which may exist or hereafter be erected or constructed on the said premises, or from any kind of injury which may arise from any other cause whatsoever on the said premises or the building of which the demised premises is a part, whether such damage, injury, use, misuse or abuse be caused by or result from the negligence of Lessor, his servants or agents or any other person or persons whatsoever.

12—Responsibility of Lessor

(a) Total Destruction of Premises *(a)* In the event that the demised premises is totally destroyed or so damaged by fire or other casualty not occurring through fault or negligence of the Lessee or those employed by or acting for him, that the same cannot be repaired or restored within a reasonable time, this lease shall absolutely cease and determine, and the rent shall abate for the balance of the term.

(b) Partial Destruction of Premises *(b)* If the damage caused as above be only partial and such that the premises can be restored to their then condition within a reasonable time, the Lessor may, at his option, restore the same with reasonable promptness, reserving the right to enter upon the demised premises for that purpose. The Lessor also reserves the right to enter upon the demised premises whenever necessary to repair damage caused by fire or other casualty to the building of which the demised premises is a part, even though the effect of such entry be to render the demised premises or a part thereof untenantable. In either event the rent shall be apportioned and suspended during the time the Lessor is in possession, taking into account the proportion of the demised premises rendered untenantable and the duration of the Lessor's possession. If a dispute arises as to the amount of rent due under this clause, Lessee agrees to pay the full amount claimed by Lessor. Lessee shall, however, have the right to proceed by law to recover the excess payment, if any.

(c) Repairs by Lessor *(c)* Lessor shall make such election to repair the premises or terminate this lease by giving notice thereof to Lessee at the leased premises within thirty days from the day Lessor received notice that the demised premises had been destroyed or damaged by fire or other casualty.

(d) Damage for Interruption of Use *(d)* Lessor shall not be liable for any damage, compensation or claim by reason of inconvenience or annoyance arising from the necessity of repairing any portion of the building, the interruption in the use of the premises, or the termination of this lease by reason of the destruction of the premises.

(e) Representation of Condition of Premises *(e)* The Lessor has let the demised premises in their present condition and without any representations on the part of the Lessor, his officers, employees, servants and/or agents. It is understood and agreed that Lessor is under no duty to make repairs or alterations at the time of letting or at any time thereafter.

(f) Zoning *(f)* It is understood and agreed that the Lessor hereof does not warrant or undertake that the Lessee shall be able to obtain a permit under any Zoning Ordinance or Regulation for such use as Lessee intends to make of the said premises, and nothing in this lease contained shall obligate the Lessor to assist Lessee in obtaining said permits; the Lessee further agrees that in the event a permit cannot be obtained by Lessee under any Zoning Ordinance or Regulation, this lease shall not terminate without Lessor's consent, and the Lessee shall use the premises only in a manner permitted under such Zoning Ordinance or Regulation.

13—Miscellaneous Agreements and Conditions

(a) Effect of Repairs on Rental *(a)* No contract entered into or that may be subsequently entered into by Lessor with Lessee, relative to any alterations, additions, improvements or repairs, nor the failure of Lessor to make such alterations, additions, improvements or repairs as required by any such contract, nor the making by Lessor or his agents or contractors of such alterations, additions, improvements or repairs shall in any way affect the payment of the rent or said other charges at the time specified in this lease.

(b) Agency *(b)* It is hereby expressly agreed and understood that the said .... is acting as agent only and shall not in any event be held liable to the owner or to Lessee for the fulfillment or non-fulfillment of any of the terms or conditions of this lease, or for any action or proceedings that may be taken by the owner against Lessee, or by Lessee against the owner.

(c) Waiver of Custom *(c)* It is hereby covenanted and agreed, any law, usage or custom to the contrary notwithstanding, that Lessor shall have the right at all times to enforce the covenants and provisions of this lease in strict accordance with the terms hereof, notwithstanding any conduct or custom on the part of the Lessor in refraining from so doing at any time or times; and, further, that the failure of Lessor at any time or times to enforce his rights under said covenants and provisions strictly in accordance with the same shall not be construed as having created a custom in any way or manner contrary to the specific terms, provisions and covenants of this lease or as having in any way or manner modified the same.

(d) Conduct of Lessee *(d)* This lease is granted upon the express condition that Lessee and/or the occupants of the premises herein leased, shall not conduct themselves in a manner which the Lessor in his sole opinion may deem improper or objectionable, and that if at any time during the term of this lease or any extension or continuation thereof, Lessee or any occupier of the said premises shall have conducted himself, herself or themselves in a manner which Lessor in his sole opinion deems improper or objectionable, Lessee shall be taken to have broken the covenants and conditions of this lease, and Lessor will be entitled to all of the rights and remedies granted and reserved herein for the Lessee's failure to observe any of the covenants and conditions of this lease.

(e) Failure of Lessee to Repair *(e)* In the event of the failure of Lessee promptly to perform the covenants of Section 8*(b)* hereof, Lessor may go upon the demised premises and perform such covenants, the cost thereof, at the sole option of Lessor, to be charged to Lessee as additional and delinquent rent.

14—Remedies of Lessor If the Lessee

(a) Does not pay in full when due any and all installments of rent and/or any other charge or payment herein reserved, included, or agreed to be treated or collected as rent and/or any other charge, expense, or cost herein agreed to be paid by the Lessee, or

(b) Violates or fails to perform or otherwise breaks any covenant or agreement herein contained; or

(c) Vacates the demised premises or removes or attempts to remove or manifests an intention to remove any goods or property therefrom otherwise than in the ordinary and usual course of business without having first paid and satisfied the Lessor in full for all rent and other charges then due or that may thereafter become due until the expiration of the then current term, above mentioned; or

(d) Becomes embarrassed or insolvent, or makes an assignment for the benefit of creditors, or if a petition in bankruptcy is filed by or against the Lessee, or a bill in equity or other proceeding for the appointment of a receiver for the Lessee is filed, or if proceedings for reorganization or for composition with creditors under any State or Federal law be instituted by or against Lessee, or if the real or personal property of the Lessee shall be sold or levied upon by any Sheriff, Marshal or Constable; ....

then and in any or either of said events, there shall be deemed to be a breach of this lease, and thereupon ipso facto and without entry or other action by Lessor:

(1) The rent for the entire unexpired balance of the term of this lease, as well as all other charges, payments, costs and expenses herein agreed to be paid by the Lessee, or at the option of Lessor any part thereof, and also all costs and officers' commissions including watchmen's wages and further including the five percent chargeable by Act of Assembly to the Lessor, shall, in addition to any and all installments of rent already due and payable and in arrears and/or any other charge or payment herein reserved, included or agreed to be treated or collected as rent, and/or any other charge, expense or cost herein agreed to be paid by the Lessee which may be due and payable and in arrears, be taken to be due and payable and in arrears as if by the terms and provisions of this lease, the whole balance of unpaid rent and other charges, payments, taxes, costs and expenses were on that date payable in advance; and if this lease or any part thereof is assigned, or if the premises or any part thereof is sub-let, Lessee hereby irrevocably constitutes and appoints Lessor Lessee's agent to collect the rents due by such assignee or sub-lessee and apply the same to the rent due hereunder without in any way affecting Lessee's obligation to pay any unpaid balance of rent due hereunder;

FIGURE 6–3 (*continued*)

(2) This lease and the term hereby created shall determine and become absolutely void without any right on the part of the Lessee to save the forfeiture by payment of any sum due or by other performance of any condition, term or covenant broken; whereupon, Lessor shall be entitled to recover damages for such breach in an amount equal to the amount of rent reserved for the balance of the term of this lease, less the fair rental value of the said demised premises, for the residue of said term.

15—Further Remedies of Lessor In the event of any default as above set forth in Section 14, the Lessor, or anyone acting on Lessor's behalf, at Lessor's option:

(a) may without notice or demand enter the demised premises, breaking open locked doors if necessary to effect entrance, without liability to action for prosecution or damages for such entry or for the manner thereof, for the purpose of distraining or levying and for any other purposes, and take possession of and sell all goods and chattels at auction, on three days' notice served in person on the Lessee or left on the premises, and pay the said Lessor out of the proceeds, and even if the rent be not due and unpaid, should the Lessee at any time remove or attempt to remove goods and chattels from the premises without leaving enough thereon to meet the next periodical payment, Lessee authorizes the Lessor to follow for a period of ninety days after such removal, take possession of and sell at auction, upon like notice, sufficient of such goods to meet the proportion of rent accrued at the time of such removal; and the Lessee hereby releases and discharges the Lessor, and his agents, from all claims, actions, suits, damages, and penalties, for or by reason or on account of any entry, distraint, levy, appraisement or sale; and/or

(b) may enter the premises, and without demand proceed by distress and sale of the goods there found to levy the rent and/or other charges herein payable as rent, and all costs and officers' commissions, including watchmen's wages and sums chargeable to Lessor, and further including a sum equal to 5% of the amount of the levy as commissions to the constable or other person making the levy, shall be paid by the Lessee, and in such case all costs, officers' commission and other charges shall immediately attach and become part of the claim of Lessor for rent, and any tender of rent without said costs, commission and charges made after the issue of a warrant of distress shall not be sufficient to satisfy the claim of the Lessor. Lessee hereby expressly waives in favor of Lessor the benefit of all laws now made or which may hereafter be made regarding any limitation as to the goods upon which, or the time within which, distress is to be made after removal of goods, and further relieves the Lessor of the obligations of proving or identifying such goods, it being the purpose and intent of this provision that all goods of Lessee, whether upon the demised premises or not, shall be liable to distress for rent. Lessee waives in favor of Lessor all rights under the Act of Assembly of April 6, 1951, P. L. 69, and all supplements and amendments thereto that have been or may hereafter be passed, and authorizes the sale of any goods distrained for rent at any time after five days from said distraint without any appraisement and/or condemnation thereof.

(c) The Lessee further waives the right to issue a Writ of Replevin under the Pennsylvania Rules of Civil Procedure, No. 1071 &c. and Laws of the Commonwealth of Pennsylvania, or under any other law previously enacted and now in force, or which may be hereafter enacted, for the recovery of any articles, household goods, furniture, etc., seized under a distress for rent or levy upon an execution for rent, damages or otherwise; all waivers hereinbefore mentioned are hereby extended to apply to any such action; and/or

(d) may lease said premises or any part or parts thereof to such person or persons as may in Lessor's discretion seem best and the Lessee shall be liable for any loss of rent for the balance of the then current term.

16—Confession of Judgment If rent and/or any charges hereby reserved as rent shall remain unpaid on any day when the same ought to be paid, Lessee hereby empowers any Prothonotary, Clerk of Court or attorney of any Court of Record to appear for Lessee in any and all actions which may be brought for rent and/or the charges, payments, costs and expenses reserved as rent, or agreed to be paid by the Lessee and/or to sign for Lessee an agreement for entering in any competent Court an amicable action or actions for the recovery of rent or other charges, payments, costs and expenses, and in said suits or in said amicable action or actions to confess judgment against Lessee for all or any part of the rent specified in this lease and then unpaid including, at Lessor's option, the rent for the entire unexpired balance of the term of this lease, and/or other charges, payments, costs and expenses reserved as rent or agreed to be paid by the Lessee, and for interest and costs together with an attorney's commission of 5%. Such authority shall not be exhausted by one exercise thereof, but judgment may be confessed as aforesaid from time to time as often as any of said rent and/or other charges, payments, costs and expenses, reserved as rent shall fall due or be in arrears, and such powers may be exercised as well after the expiration of the original term and/or during any extension or renewal of this lease.

17—Ejectment When this lease shall be determined by condition broken, either during the original term of this lease or any renewal or extension thereof, and also when and as soon as the term hereby created or any extension thereof shall have expired, it shall be lawful for any attorney as attorney for Lessee to file an agreement for entering in any competent Court an amicable action and judgment in ejectment against Lessee and all persons claiming under Lessee for the recovery by Lessor of possession of the herein demised premises, for which this lease shall be his sufficient warrant, whereupon, if Lessor so desires, a writ of Execution or of Possession may issue forthwith, without any prior writ or proceedings whatsoever, and provided that if for any reason after such action shall have been commenced the same shall be determined and the possession of the premises hereby demised remain in or be restored to Lessee, Lessor shall have the right upon any subsequent default or defaults, or upon the termination of this lease as hereinbefore set forth, to bring one or more amicable action or actions as hereinbefore set forth to recover possession of the said premises.

18—Affidavit of Default In any amicable action of ejectment and/or for rent in arrears, Lessor shall first cause to be filed in such action an affidavit made by him or someone acting for him setting forth the facts necessary to authorize the entry of judgment, of which facts such affidavit shall be conclusive evidence, and if a true copy of this lease (and of the truth of the copy such affidavit shall be sufficient evidence) be filed in such action, it shall not be necessary to file the original as a warrant of attorney, any rule of Court, custom or practice to the contrary notwithstanding.

19—Waivers by Lessee of Errors, Right of Appeal, Stay, Exemption, Inquisition Lessee expressly agrees that any judgment, order or decree entered against him by or in any Court or Magistrate by virtue of the powers of attorney contained in this lease, or otherwise, shall be final, and that he will not take an appeal, certiorari, writ of error, exception or objection to the same, or file a motion or rule to strike off or open or to stay execution of the same, and releases to Lessor and to any and all attorneys who may appear for Lessee all errors in the said proceedings, and all liability therefor. Lessee expressly waives the benefits of all laws, now or hereafter in force, exempting any goods on the demised premises, or elsewhere from distraint, levy or sale in any legal proceedings taken by the Lessor to enforce any rights under this lease. Lessee further waives the right of inquisition on any real estate that may be levied upon to collect any amount which may become due under the terms and conditions of this lease, and does hereby voluntarily condemn the same and authorizes the Prothonotary or Clerk of Court to issue a Writ of Execution or other process upon Lessee's voluntary condemnation, and further agrees that the said real estate may be sold on a Writ of Execution or other process. If proceedings shall be commenced by Lessor to recover possession under the Acts of Assembly, either at the end of the term or sooner termination of this lease, or for nonpayment of rent or any other reason Lessee specifically waives the right to the three months' notice and/or the fifteen or thirty days' notice required by the Act of April 6, 1951, P. L. 69, and agrees that five days' notice shall be sufficient in either or any other case.

20—Right of Assignee of Lessor The right to enter judgment against Lessee and to enforce all of the other provisions of this lease hereinabove provided for may, at the option of any assignee of this lease, be exercised by any assignee of the Lessor's right, title and interest in this lease in his, her or their own name, notwithstanding the fact that any or all assignments of the said right, title and interest may not be executed and/or witnessed in accordance with the Act of Assembly of May 28, 1715, 1 Sm. L. 90, and all supplements and amendments thereto that have been or may hereafter be passed and Lessee hereby expressly waives the requirements of said Act of Assembly and any and all laws regulating the manner and/or form in which such assignments shall be executed and witnessed.

21—Remedies Cumulative All of the remedies hereinbefore given to Lessor and all rights and remedies given to him by law and equity shall be cumulative and concurrent. No determination of this lease or the taking or recovering of the premises shall deprive Lessor of any of his remedies or actions against the Lessee for rent due at the time or which, under the terms hereof, would in the future become due as if there has been no determination, or for any and all sums due at the time or which, under the terms hereof, would in the future become due as if there had been no determination, nor shall the bringing of any action for rent or breach of covenant, or the resort to any other remedy herein provided for the recovery of rent be construed as a waiver of the right to obtain possession of the premises.

22—Condemnation In the event that the premises demised or any part thereof is taken or condemned for a public or quasi-public use, this lease shall, as to the part so taken, terminate as of the date title shall vest in the condemnor, and rent shall abate in proportion to the square feet of leased space taken or condemned or shall cease if the entire premises be so taken. In either event the Lessee waives all claims against the Lessor by reason of the complete or partial taking of the demised premises, and it is agreed that the Lessee shall not be entitled to any notice whatsoever of the partial or complete termination of this lease by reason of the aforesaid.

23—Subordination This Agreement of Lease and all its terms, covenants and provisions are and each of them is subject and subordinate to any lease or other arrangement or right to possession, under which the Lessor is in control of the demised premises, to the rights of the owner or owners of the demised premises and of the land or buildings of which the demised premises are a part, to all rights of the Lessor's landlord and to any and all mortgages and other encumbrances now or hereafter placed upon the demised premises or upon the land and/or the buildings containing the same; and Lessee expressly agrees that if Lessor's tenancy, control, or right to possession shall terminate either by expiration, forfeiture or otherwise, then this lease shall thereupon immediately terminate and the Lessee shall, thereupon, give immediate possession; and Lessee hereby waives any and all claims for damages or otherwise by reason of such termination as aforesaid.

24—Termination of Lease It is hereby mutually agreed that either party hereto may determine this lease at the end of said term by giving to the other party written notice thereof at least ______________ prior thereto, but in default of such notice, this lease shall continue upon the same terms and conditions in force immediately prior to the expiration of the term hereof as are herein contained for a further period of ______________ and so on from ______________ to ______________ unless or until terminated by either party hereto, giving the other ______________ written notice for removal previous to expiration of the then current term; PROVIDED, however, that should this lease be continued for a further period under the terms hereinabove mentioned, any allowances given Lessee on the rent during the original term shall not extend beyond such original term, and further provided, however, that if Lessor shall have given such written notice prior to the expiration of any term hereby created, of his intention to change the terms and conditions of this lease, and Lessee shall not within ______________ days from such notice notify Lessor of Lessee's intention to vacate the demised premises at the end of the then current term, Lessee shall be considered as Lessee under the terms and conditions mentioned in such notice for a further term as above provided, or for such further term as may be stated in such notice. In the event that Lessee shall give notice, as stipulated in this lease, of intention to vacate the demised premises at the end of the present term, or any renewal or extension thereof, and shall fail or refuse so to vacate the same on the date designated by such notice, then it is expressly agreed that Lessor shall have the option either (a) to disregard the notice so given as having no effect, in which case all the terms and conditions of this lease shall continue thereafter with full force precisely as if such notice had not been given, or (b) Lessor may, at any time within thirty days after the present term or any renewal or extension thereof, as aforesaid, give the said Lessee ten days' written notice of his intention to terminate the said lease; whereupon the Lessee expressly agrees to vacate said premises at the expiration of the said period of ten days specified in said notice. All powers granted to Lessor by this lease may be exercised and all obligations imposed upon Lessee by this lease shall be performed by Lessee as well during any extension of the original term of this lease as during the original term itself.

25—Notices All notices required to be given by Lessor to Lessee shall be sufficiently given by leaving the same upon the demised premises, but notices given by Lessee to Lessor must be given by registered mail, and as against Lessor the only admissible evidence that notice has been given by Lessee shall be a registry return receipt signed by Lessor or his agent.

26—Lease Contains All Agreements It is expressly understood and agreed by and between the parties hereto that this lease and the riders attached hereto and forming a part hereof set forth all the promises, agreements, conditions and understandings between Lessor or his Agents and Lessee relative to the demised premises, and that there are no promises, agreements, conditions or understandings, either oral or written, between them other than are herein set forth. It is further understood and agreed that, except as herein otherwise provided, no subsequent alteration, amendment, change or addition to this lease shall be binding upon Lessor or Lessee unless reduced to writing and signed by them.

FIGURE 6–3 (concluded)

27—Heirs and Assignees

All rights and liabilities herein given to, or imposed upon, the respective parties hereto shall extend to and bind the several and respective heirs, executors, administrators, successors and assigns of said parties; and if there shall be more than one Lessee, they shall all be bound jointly and severally by the terms, covenants and agreements herein, and the word "Lessee" shall be deemed and taken to mean each and every person or party mentioned as a Lessee herein, be the same one or more; and if there shall be more than one Lessee, any notice required or permitted by the terms of this lease may be given by or to any one thereof, and shall have the same force and effect as if given by or to all thereof. The words "his" and "him" wherever stated herein shall be deemed to refer to the "Lessor" and "Lessee" whether such Lessor or Lessee be singular or plural and irrespective of gender. No rights, however, shall inure to the benefit of any assignee of Lessee unless the assignment to such assignee has been approved by Lessor in writing as aforesaid.

28—Security Deposit

Lessee shall, upon execution hereof, deposit with Lessor as security for the performance of all the terms, covenants, and conditions of this lease, the sum of—————————————————————. This deposit is to be retained by Lessor until the expiration of this lease and shall be returnable to Lessee provided that (1) premises have been vacated; (2) Lessor shall have inspected the premises after such vacation; and (3) Lessee shall have complied with all the terms, covenants and conditions of this lease, in which event the deposit so paid hereunder shall be returned to Lessee; otherwise, said sum deposited hereunder or any part thereof may be retained by Lessor at his option, as liquidated damages, or may be applied by Lessor against any actual loss, damage or injury chargeable to Lessee hereunder or otherwise, if Lessor determines that such loss, damage or injury exceeds said sum deposited. Lessor's determination of the amount, if any, to be returned to Lessee shall be final. It is understood that the said deposit is not to be considered as the last rental due under the lease.

29—Headings No Part of Lease

Any headings preceding the text of the several paragraphs and sub-paragraphs hereof are inserted solely for convenience of reference and shall not constitute a part of this lease, nor shall they affect its meaning, construction or effect.

IN WITNESS WHEREOF, the parties hereto have executed these presents the day and year first above written, and intend to be legally bound thereby.

SEALED AND DELIVERED IN THE PRESENCE OF:

_____   _____ (AGENT)

_____   _____ (SEAL)

_____   _____ (SEAL)

_____   _____ (SEAL)

Lease,

TO

Premises_____

Rent, $_____

Commence_____

Expires_____

1974

John C. Clark Co., Phila.

FOR VALUE RECEIVED————hereby assign, transfer and set over unto ————————————————

Executors, Administrators, Successors and Assigns, all————right, title and interest in the within————— and all benefit and advantages to be derived therefrom.

WITNESS————hand and seal this ——————————day of————————————A. D. 19————

SEALED AND DELIVERED IN PRESENCE OF

delphia. Because each lease is unique attorneys must write modifications to standard lease forms.

While there is no standard order of lease terms, it is convenient to outline the main topics covered by a lease extending over 25 or more years. It is not possible to cover all possible terms since leases vary according to type of property, location, and the complexity of the real estate interest conveyed. For convenience, lease terms are shown by main topic headings, though a given lease may not follow this order of presentation.

A TOPIC OUTLINE OF A TYPICAL LONG-TERM DEVELOPMENT LEASE

Introductory Material
Definitions (gross receipts, refunds, tax receipts).
Land description.

Financial Covenants
Term of lease.
Rental.
Annual accounting.
Rental bond.
Performance bonds.
Bonding companies.
Nonresponsibility notices.
Holding over.

Improvement Clauses
Improvements.
Plans and design.
Construction, maintenance, repair, and alterations.
Completion of development.

Other Rights
Sublease, assignments, and transfers.
Agreements for utility lines and streets.
Encumbrances.
Liens, taxes, assessments, and utility charges.
Lessor's paying claims.

Insurance
Public liability.
Fire and damage insurance.
Unlawful use.

Miscellaneous

Eminent domain.

Arbitration.

Default.

Attorney's fees.

No partnership clause.

Term or trust.

Obligations of lessee.

Status of subleases.

Payments and notices.

SUMMARY

Virtually every real estate transaction requires one or more contracts, that is, voluntary agreements between two or more competent parties who, for a consideration, agree to do or refrain from doing some particular legal act. Contracts may be valid if they satisfy all legal requirements. A contract with no legal effect is a void contract. Voidable contracts may be enforced or reviewed at the option of one of the parties. Certain contracts are unenforceable, for example, an oral contract transferring an interest in real estate.

Real estate contracts must have the seven elements necessary to all valid contracts. Contract default by the buyer gives the seller three options: to terminate, to keep installments as damages, or to sue for damages. If the seller defaults, the buyer may in like manner sue for specific performance or damages or may terminate the contract. In transferring real estate by an installment contract, the buyer risks the possibility that the seller may be unable to convey title when the contract is fulfilled.

Deeds are written instruments that convey an interest in real estate. Among the specialized forms of deeds, the warranty deed usually includes the five covenants of title, giving the buyer the strongest possible title. At the other extreme, the quitclaim deed gives the buyer the least title protection: this deed transfers only the interest held by the seller, if any. To be enforceable, the deed must have the enforceable elements of a contract: the granting clause, the legal description, and the delivery and acceptance and other special requirements of an enforceable deed.

Leases, a specialized form of contract, convey exclusive rights of use and possession as limited by the lease. At the very minimum a lease should have a beginning and ending date, a clear identification of the lessor and lessee, a legal description, rental terms, and proper signatures. Leases are commonly classified by the type of rental payment: (1) fixed rent leases, (2) graduated leases, (3) price index leases, (4) revaluation leases, and (5) percentage leases. Because the long-term lease—a lease of more than

15 years—commits property over one or two generations, it will cover a wide range of topics that require legal counsel for interpretation.

REVIEW QUESTIONS

1. What is the difference between valid, void, voidable, and unenforceable contracts?
2. Explain the seven elements common to an enforceable contract.
3. What remedies are available to the seller if the buyer defaults in a real estate contract?
4. What remedies are available to the buyer if the seller defaults in a real estate contract?
5. What is the main purpose of an installment land contract?
6. What buyer risks are associated with installment land contracts?
7. Explain and illustrate how an option contract is used.
8. Explain the five covenants included in the warranty deed.
9. When would you advise an owner to convey an interest under a special warranty deed? Give reasons for your answer.
10. When would you advise an owner to use a quitclaim deed? Explain why a quitclaim deed would be advised in your example.
11. Differentiate between a bargain and sale and a quitclaim deed.
12. What warranties are included in an executor's deed? A sheriff's deed?
13. Explain how a trust deed substitutes for a mortgage.
14. Explain the requirements of an enforceable deed.
15. What is the significance of deed restrictions? Give an illustration of how deed restrictions are used.
16. Cite five elements of a valid lease contract.
17. Explain the five types of leases classified by rental terms. Give an illustration of how you would use each type of lease.
18. Explain the six main topics covered by a long-term development lease.

SELECTED REFERENCES

Atteberry, William; Pearson, Karl; and Litka, Michael. *Real Estate Law,* chap. 13. Columbus: Grid, Inc., 1974.

Hebard, Edna L., and Meisel, Gerald S. *Principles of Real Estate Law,* chap. 11. Cambridge, Mass.: Schenkman Publishing Company, Inc., 1967.

Ring, Alfred A., and Dasso, Jerome. *Real Estate Principles and Practices,* chaps. 9 and 11. 8th ed. Englewood Cliffs, N.J.: Prentice-Hall, Inc., 1977.

Semenow, Robert W. *Questions and Answers on Real Estate,* chap. 3. 8th ed. Englewood Cliffs, N.J.: Prentice-Hall, Inc., 1975.

Unger, Maurice A. *Real Estate,* chap. 5. 5th ed. Cincinnati: South-Western Publishing Co., 1974.

7

Land Titles and Legal Descriptions

After reading this chapter, you should be familiar with the following points:

1 The origin of the land tenure system.
2 Landownership patterns in colonial times.
3 The significance of legal descriptions to private property ownership.
4 The main features of the government rectangular survey system.
5 The location of land by the rectangular survey system.
6 The main elements of a metes and bounds description.
7 The objective of a recorded subdivision description.
8 The rationale of the state plane coordinate system.

THE DEVELOPMENT of private property correlates closely with social development. Our concept of real estate ownership started with the transition from a country of nomadic hunters to an agrarian society. The communal villages and square field cultivation practices thought to prevail in England from the second century B.C. to the third century A.D. parallel the urban subdivisions and towns of today.[1] The U.S. land tenure system was formed largely from the early feudal practices of England and Western Europe. A brief review of colonial land tenure and the public domain policy shows how our land description systems evolved from these early developments.

Indeed, it is difficult to overemphasize the importance of legal descriptions. Improper legal descriptions—the result of errors on the part of the buyer, seller, broker, public officials, or surveyors—mean that houses may be constructed on the wrong lot, that there may be boundary disputes, and that property owners may have to engage in expensive court litigation. The critical significance of the legal description is suggested by the requirement that a proper legal description must be included in virtually every real estate document.

Familiarity with the four methods of identifying property helps to reduce the possibility of mistakes in legal descriptions. Our system of describing land employs (1) the U.S. Rectangular Survey System, (2) metes and bounds, (3) recorded subdivisions, and (4) the state plane coordinate system. The development of land titles shows how these systems evolved as part of our land tenure system.

ORIGINS OF LAND TITLES

Since the formation of organized society, some rights in land have been granted to all members. Even the penniless pauper has access to public streets and highways. Inherent in our system is the ownership of property subject to rights reserved by society. Early in our colonial period, it was established that a landed right referred to any title or interest in land that was enforceable by law. The system of land tenure emphasized rights and not responsibilities. In this sense, *land tenure* refers to "all the relations established among men, in determining their various rights to the use of land."[2] Most aspects of our present land tenure system may be traced to early English practices.

Land Tenure in England

The practice of dividing land into squares (blocks or miles) was apparently initiated by the Romans during their occupation of Britain. In

---

[1] D. R. Denman, *Origins of Ownership* (London: George Allen and Unwin, Ltd., 1959), p. 14.

[2] Marshall Harris, *Origin of the Land Tenure System in the United States* (Ames: Iowa State College Press, 1970), p. 4.

antiquity, land was apparently laid out in rectangular or square plots according to the average working day of the ploughman. The Roman measure of a day's work related to a land area which was twice the square of a two-oxen plow furrow—an area of approximately 120 feet by 240 feet. Archaeological formations suggest a grid system made up of square land areas of uniform size arranged in groups of two or three squares.[3] In Roman Britain, town planning followed the chessboard principle of laying out lots and blocks in uniform squares—a practice that may be observed in our urban centers today.

The Feudal System of Land Tenure.   The Saxon invasion introduced the feudal system which became part of the English law. Though the land belonged to the people, it was parceled out to individuals. The king, since he spoke for the people, granted certain favored individuals parcels of land called bookland. The book was the instrument setting forth the grant. Under this system military obligations to the king were assigned to every landholder. For example, William the Conqueror, asserting the right of conquest, took title to all land in Great Britain, regranting land to his supporters. Consequently, feudalism has been viewed as a system of government based on the relation of individuals to the land.

Even in modern times, absolute landownership was originally invested in the sovereign—the crown, the state, or the public. It is also true that the sovereign initially held the largest bundle of rights in land. At no time has a sovereign government released all rights of absolute ownership. Governments have retained the police power, eminent domain, taxation, and the power of escheat.[4]

Today, ownership has been accepted as the highest form of land tenure, evidenced by the fee simple title. Under our system the owner holds all rights not reserved by society. Ownership leads to the second most common form of land tenure—the landlord-tenant relationship. The landlord-tenant relationship is based on the requirements that property be held by a superior and that services or payments be rendered by the tenant to the owner.

Right of Inheritance.   These institutions were encouraged by the custom of extending the right of inheritance to owners of titles which were granted by the king. Initially, grants were rights held for a year, then for the life of the grantee, and eventually in perpetuity. Under the feudal system of the Middle Ages, the king granted jurisdiction and finally revenues to leading landowners, thereby creating the great landed estates, that is, a manorial lord system.

The lord held rights of land as possessor which were both political and economic. He held his own courts and administered justice according to his own procedures and customs. The freeholders were farmers who occupied

---

[3] Denman, *Origins of Ownership,* p. 40.
[4] Harris, *Origin of Land Tenure System,* p. 27.

lands on the outskirts of the manor under agreements with the lord, usually in fee form. The freeholders paid lump sums for the original grant and annual charges to the lord.

Thus, the idea of a specific land area belonging to an individual occurred with the transition from a nomadic to an agrarian society. By the ninth and tenth centuries freeholders gained the right to transfer land.

Land Transfer. At first, the transfer was evidenced by a ceremony. The new occupant virtually transferred himself to the land. In other words, the new owner took actual possession of the land and the former owner vacated in a ceremony widely witnessed by neighbors. Later, symbolic deliveries were used in which the seller handed the buyer—in the presence of witnesses—a piece of sod, a few sticks, a latch from the door, or some other appropriate symbol. But this method was only temporarily effective —witnesses would die and, with their death, proof of the transfer.

To overcome this deficiency, parties to the land transfer would place the act of transfer in writing. The writing gradually substituted for transfer of a piece of sod as evidence of the transfer. The transfer was completed by delivery of the charter or a writing that served as permanent evidence of the transaction, much as the delivery of a deed is required today.

Conditions in 16th century Europe added impetus to the European migration to America and help explain our current system of land titles and descriptions. Under the feudal system, the king allotted land to his lords, who were to render certain services to him. In addition, certain areas of land were set aside for free use by the landless serfs as common land on which to grow food, pasture their domestic animals, and secure wood for fuel. The increasing population raised the demand for wool, causing the barons to continually encroach upon the commons by enclosing them for sheep pasture, decreasing the free land allotted to the serfs.

It was widely reported that migration to Virginia was encouraged to decrease the number of unemployed, "diminish begging, vagabondage and crime and thus lessen the cost of poor relief."[5] It has been estimated that by 1696 approximately one fourth of the English population were beggars or otherwise public charges. Indeed, General James Oglethorpe, a member of Parliament, secured a grant of land from George II in 1733 to establish a colony (Savannah, Georgia) to relieve "the distress of many persons of respectable families who were confined in prison in England as insolvent debtors."[6] The state of Georgia was originally formed to aid unfortunates who would also serve as a military outpost against the Spanish. The Georgian colony was the only American colony which did not start from a desire by the promoters for personal profit through landownership.[7]

---

[5] Alfred N. Chandler, *Land Title Origins* (New York: Robert Schalkenbach Foundation, 1945), p. 16.

[6] Ibid., p. 378.

[7] Ibid.

Land Ownership in Colonial Times

American law governing land title is a mixture of policies introduced by the immigrants of Western Europe and England. The English, who were more inclined to immigrate and more tolerant of religious minorities and European ethnic groups, had the greatest influence on the land laws of the United States. Early practices in colonial America helped form the present land tenure system, while the administration of the public domain led to the rectangular system of describing land.

Conflict over Indian Land. It has been claimed that the American colonists looked upon the American Indians as an inferior cultural group to be pushed aside as conditions warranted. The Indians were not believed to hold land titles by anything equivalent to a fee simple estate. While not conceding the Indians' ownership, the American colonies recognized their right of occupancy, a right which was often purchased by the colonists with local government approval. The resulting jurisdictional conflicts, resulting from indeterminate land boundaries, the misunderstanding of alienation by Indians, and squatting by whites on Indian lands, created numerous conflicts which needed federal supervision.

Failure to control the absorption of Indian lands by traders, speculators, and squatters resulted in the Proclamation of 1763, which closed all land west of the crest of the Appalachian Mountains to further settlement. Britain attempted to increase the control over Indian trade and lands by transferring lands north of the Ohio River and west of the Appalachians to the colony of Quebec. This act further damaged relations between England and the 13 colonies.[8] Similarly, in 1775 the Continental Congress attempted to centralize control of Indian land policy by creating three federal departments to regulate the Indian trade and the management of Indian affairs. A policy of federal control of Indian lands, totaling over 51 million acres at present, has continued to the present time.[9]

The Headright System. The headright system was one of the principal means of acquiring land in colonial America. It is not surprising that certain features of this system have become a permanent part of our land title law. To encourage colonization, the headright system awarded land to persons responsible for a new migrant. For example, Virginia allowed 100 acres for each person transported to the colony and remaining in it for three years. Abuses of the headright system led to a 1705 law in Virginia that granted only one headright for the migration of a single party, limited maximum headright grants to 4,000 acres, and reverted to the Crown lands which remained unimproved within three years.[10]

---

[8] Paul W. Gates, *History of Public Land Law Development* (Washington, D.C.: U.S. Government Printing Office, 1968), p. 34.

[9] *Annual Report on Indian Lands,* Bureau of Indian Affairs, Department of the Interior, 1975, p. 1.

[10] Gates, *History of Public Land Law,* p. 35.

Conflicts in title arose over the Virginia practice which entitled an owner to land not claimed or settled upon by others, provided that the Indian title had been surrendered. Because lands were not surveyed, each prospective landowner had to make certain that his 50 or 100 acres was undeveloped and unclaimed before he could begin farm improvements. Virginia was one of the first colonies to recognize squatters' prior rights to land. A squatter could survey the land and outline the location by legal description and file his claim at the local land office. Individuals were allowed to run boundaries as they wished, often leaving no permanent land markers. With no surveys showing permanent monuments, the construction of buildings and other land improvements was virtually the only way private ownership could be determined.

As early as 1642 the courts permitted a person who had mistakenly made improvements on land owned by others to recover the full value of his improvements (as determined by jury) from the rightful owner. If the value of the improvements exceeded the value of the land, the squatter had the option of buying the land at a value determined by jury. Today, this right has developed into the right to gain title by "adverse possession."

New England Township Grants. In contrast to the southern and Middle Atlantic colonies, the New England colonies operated under township grants owned by proprietors who reserved lots for churches and schools, developed roads, and made grants to settlers. Surveyed in advance of settlement, the townships were divided into residential lots and sites for cultivation, pasture, and woodlands. The lots or sections closely resembled the federal township plans adopted for disposition of the public domain.[11]

Problems arising from the indiscriminate method of surveying land raised the price of land and caused much court litigation. Questions of occupancy, adverse possession, escheat, and preemption involved landowners in endless title controversies. By 1774, it was clear that prior surveys and the recording of titles by legal description were needed to guide land selection and settlement.[12] Problems of administering titles and land surveys led to the present system of describing land by government rectangular surveys.

Land Titles and Descriptions in the Public Domain

After the signing of the Treaty of Paris that ended the American Revolution, the problem of administering the public lands was second only to the Indian problem. The public domain, the land owned by the United States outside the original 13 colonies, originated with the cession of land by the colonies to the federal government. Figure 7–1 shows that this land originally extended north of the Ohio River and east of the Mississippi

---

[11] Ibid., p. 44.

[12] Ibid., p. 47.

FIGURE 7-1

Acquisition of the Territory of the United States

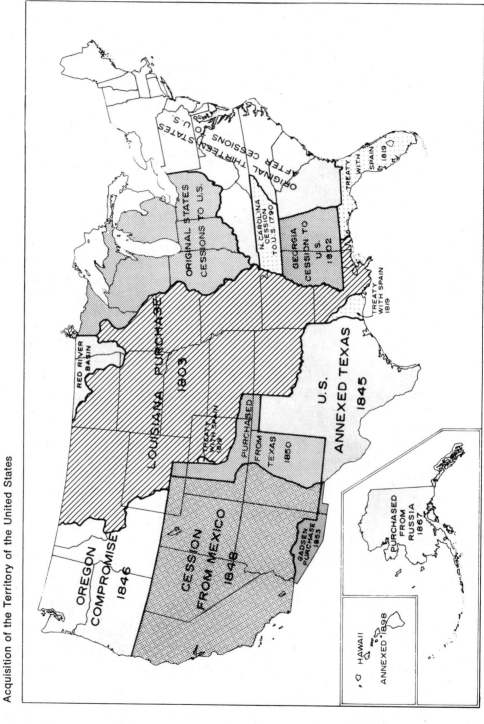

Source: *History of Public Land Law Development* (Washington, D.C.: U.S. Government Printing Office, 1968) p. 76. Prepared by the Bureau of Land Manage-

River. By 1898, with the annexation of the Hawaiian Islands, the territory of the United States was established. The system of describing the public lands by rectangular survey, however, was initially provided by the Land Ordinance of 1785.

The survey system was initiated so that revenues from the sale of the public domain could be used to retire the federal debt. At first, Thomas Jefferson, a strong advocate of the decimal system, proposed a geographic mile of 6,086 feet to establish areas ten miles square divided into 100 lots or sections of one square mile (850 acres).[13] As the law was finally enacted, land was surveyed in six-mile widths running north and south—called ranges—and into townships of six miles running east and west. Early critics feared that survey lines established on a rectangular plan would not be permanent; they would not be easy to relocate, owing to variations in the compass.

Despite these objections, the system was extended by a 1796 law that provided for a surveyor general who was responsible for the rectangular system of surveys consisting of townships of 36 square miles. Each square mile was identified as a "section" of land consisting of 640 acres. Eventually the rectangular survey system was extended to over 2,000,000 square miles of public land, an area covering 92 percent of the total area of the public land in the continental United States.

THE GOVERNMENT RECTANGULAR SURVEY SYSTEM

The comprehensive rectangular survey system provides a simple and definite means of land identification. Land identification under this system provides for:

1. *Principal Meridians and Base Lines.* The principal meridians are designated survey lines running north and south that govern legal descriptions in 30 states. A base line is associated with each principal meridian. The intersection of the principal meridian with the base line is known as the initial point.

2. *Townships and Ranges.* Township lines run in an east-west direction at six-mile intervals from the base line. Townships are 36-square-mile areas. Ranges divide land into six-mile-wide areas running north and south parallel with the principal meridian.

3. *Sections.* Square-mile areas, designated as sections, are established by running parallel lines through each township from south to north and from east to west at one-mile intervals. The sections are numbered from 1 to 36, commencing with number 1 for the northeast section of the township, proceeding west to section 6, south to section 7, east to section 12, and so on, alternately, to number 36 in the southeast corner.

---

[13] Ibid., p. 61.

FIGURE 7–2

A Map Showing the Principal Meridians and Base Lines

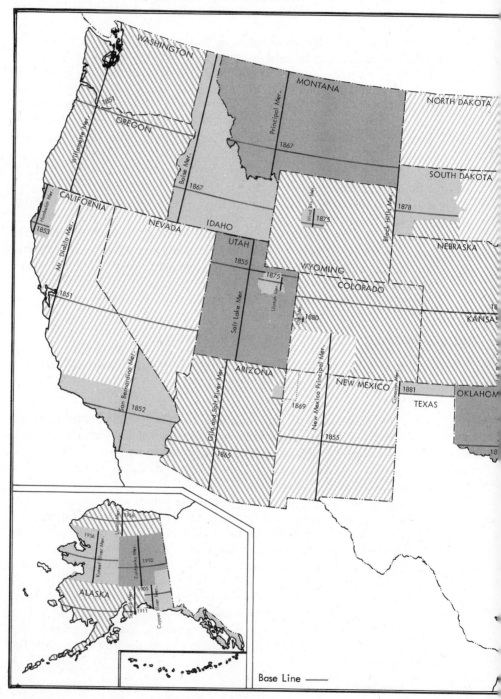

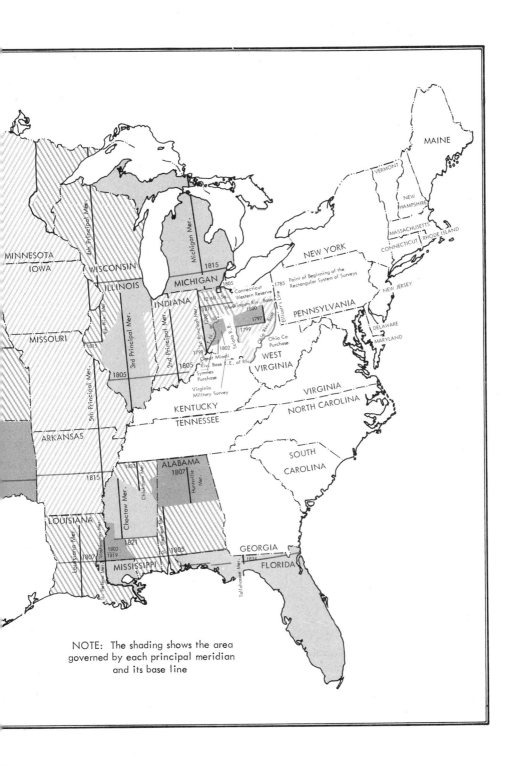

NOTE: The shading shows the area governed by each principal meridian and its base line

4. *Correction Lines.* The system provides for guide meridians and standard parallels at 24-mile intervals which are offset to account for the curvature of the earth. Correction lines are taken up in certain designated sections of a township.[14]

The rectangular survey system is not used in the original 13 states, the other New England and Atlantic coast states, except Florida, and West Virginia, Kentucky, Tennessee, and Texas. The rectangular survey system applies to the following 30 states:

Alabama	Iowa	New Mexico
Alaska	Kansas	North Dakota
Arizona	Louisiana	Ohio
Arkansas	Michigan	Oklahoma
California	Minnesota	Oregon
Colorado	Mississippi	South Dakota
Florida	Missouri	Utah
Idaho	Montana	Washington
Illinois	Nebraska	Wisconsin
Indiana	Nevada	Wyoming

Principal Meridians and Base Lines

A rectangular survey begins with a reference to a north-south line called a meridian and a base line running east and west. To locate a parcel, a legal description, like a street address, must be read backward. The principal meridian serves the same function as the state designation in a street address.

The 33 principal meridian and base lines are shown in Figure 7–2. For example, property descriptions in Florida are governed by the Tallahassee meridian and base line shown in the northwestern part of Florida. Legal descriptions in the states of Washington and Oregon are controlled by the Williamette meridian and the base line which intersect in the Portland, Oregon, area. A legal description for the areas controlled by a rectangular survey must first reference the principal meridian. It should be added that the principal meridians and base lines follow no organized locational principle—they were selected for their expediency for surveying purposes.

Townships and Ranges

Figure 7–3 identifies Township 3 North, Range 1 West of the First Principal Meridian. Note that townships are numbered consecutively north and south of the base line. Ranges divide land into six-mile-wide bands

---

[14] Earl G. Harrington, "Cadastral Surveys for the Public Lands of the United States," in Vernon Carstensen (ed.), *The Public Lands* (Madison: University of Wisconsin Press, 1968), p. 36.

FIGURE 7–3

Township and Range Lines

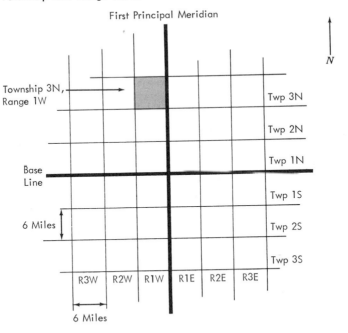

east and west of the principal meridian. Range 1 West shows that the land is located in a six-mile band running north and south, west of the First Principal Meridian. Likewise, Township 3 North is in an area 12 to 18 miles north of the base line. If the 36-mile area were to be described in full, the legal description would read Township 3 North, Range 1 West of the First Principal Meridian.

Sections

Note that the section numbers of Figure 7–4 begin in the upper right-hand corner of the township and are numbered down in a serpentlike manner to section 36. The shaded area shows the location of Section 10, Township 3 North, Range 1 West of the First Principal Meridian. Ideally, every section would measure 5,280 feet on each side, an area of 640 acres. In practice, because the sections are laid out on a horizontal plane without reference to the curvature of the earth, correction lines must be entered to correct for the curvature of the earth.

The system of identifying land by rectangles is continued in describing parts of a section. Figure 7–5 indicates that a section is initially subdivided into quarters of 160 acres. Section quarters theoretically measure 2,640 square feet on each side. Section quarters may be divided into either halves

FIGURE 7–4

Section Lines Showing the Location of Section 10, Township 3
North, Range 1 West of the First Principal Meridian

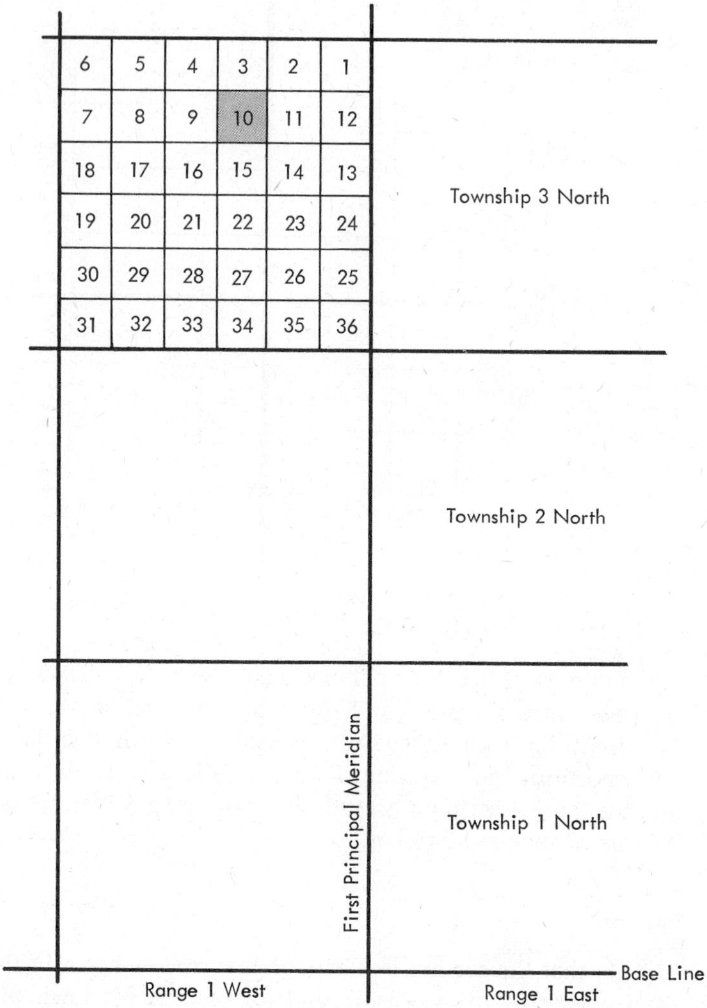

or further quarter sections. For example, Figure 7–5 indicates that the
east half of the northeast quarter consists of an 80-acre parcel measuring
1,320 feet by 2,640 feet.

Even smaller areas may be described by a rectangular survey. A 3.88-
acre parcel in eastern Oregon (Umatilla) was described as: W½ NW¼
SE¼ NE¼ Section 7, T 2 N., R 35 E., W.M., less railroad and highway
rights-of-way, containing 3.88 acres, more or less. The area taken by the
railroad and the highway would be given by the dimensions of the right-
of-way, which together total 1.12 acres. (See Figure 7–6.)

FIGURE 7–5

The Division of a Section, Showing Acreages and Distances

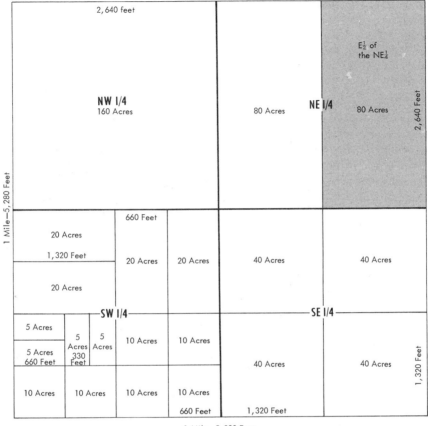

Note: One section = one square mile = 640 acres.
Source: Adapted from *Yearbook of Agriculture, 1958*, p. 210.

Figure 7–7 illustrates a farm area of 120 acres in Yakima County in the state of Washington. Since the parcel extends over more than one section, note that to locate the land described in Figure 7–7, the legal description is read backward. After identifying the range, the township number must be located from the base line. Identification of the section identifies the square mile in which the property is located. Frequently in describing rural property, several sections may be included in a single description. Next, the quarter section of the section must be identified, proceeding backward to the subdivision of the quarter section.

Particular attention must be given to the difference between the words *of* and *and* in reading a rectangular survey. The southeast quarter *of* the southwest quarter of section 1 describes a 40-acre parcel. The southeast

FIGURE 7–6

Area of 3.88 Acres Described by Government Rectangular Survey

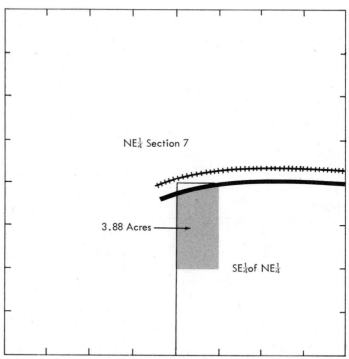

NE¼ Section 7

3.88 Acres ——→

SE¼ of NE¼

W½ NW¼ SE¼ NE¼ Section 7, T 2 N., R 35 E., of the Willamette meridian., less railroad and road rights-of-way, containing 3.88 acres, more or less.

quarter *and* the southwest quarter of section 1 describes 320 acres. Whenever the word *and* is used, it is necessary to refer back to the original section or last-mentioned quarter and again read backward.

Correction Lines

To correct for curvature of the earth, correction lines are introduced
at intervals 24 miles north and south of the base line. These two parallel
correction lines are called standard parallels running east and west from
the principal meridian. Guide meridians are extended north and south of
the base line. They terminate at the points of intersection with standard
parallels and are broken lines which theoretically are 24 miles long. This
is the plan adopted in 1855 which provides for the placement of correction
lines at regular intervals. The procedure is illustrated in Figure 7–8.
Discrepancies caused by the curvature of the earth increase with the
distance from the equator. For example, the convergence between the
six miles from the north and south boundary of a township would be 31.1

FIGURE 7–7

A Farm Area of 120 Acres Described by the Government
Rectangular Survey (Yakima County, State of Washington)

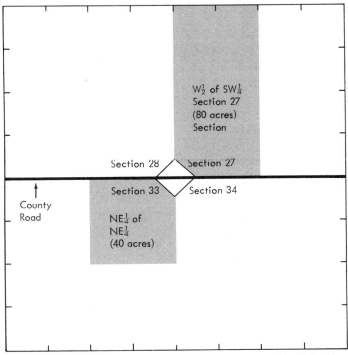

W½ SW¼ Section 27 and NE¼ NE¼ Section 33, Township 12 North,
Range 18 East, Willamette meridian.

feet near the northern boundary of Louisiana and some 47.9 feet near
Minneapolis.[15]

Since the row of sections along the north and west boundaries of the
township contain sections corrected for the curvature of the earth, not
all sections measure precisely 640 acres. Thus sections 1 through 6 on
the north boundary of a township and sections 7, 18, 19, 30, and 31 on
the west boundary may be less than 640 acres, depending on the amount
of correction necessary. To illustrate, if the actual dimension results in an
area of 620 acres—20 acres short—the deficiency will be in the 40-acre
portions along the north boundary of the section.

Moreover, the theoretical dimensions are seldom realized in the field.
There are numerous examples of survey errors permitted under older
survey regulations. The presence of mountain ranges and large bodies of
water greatly modifies the actual area of a section. Figure 7–9 shows the
southwest quarter section of Section 22, Township 4 South, Range 34 East

---

[15] William G. Murray, *Farm Appraisal and Valuation,* 4th ed. Ames: Iowa State
University Press, 1961), p. 55.

FIGURE 7–8

An Illustration of Guide Meridians and Standard Parallels

Source: William G. Murray, *Farm Appraisal and Valuation,* 4th ed. (Ames: Iowa State University Press, 1961), p. 54.

As the rectangular survey system developed, instructions provided for the establishment of guide meridians at 24-mile intervals east and west of the principal meridian, and of standard parallels at 24-mile intervals north and south of the base lines.

of the Boise meridian, which theoretically should measure 2,640 feet on each side, with an area of *160 acres.* The actual acreage is *174.6 acres—* 14.6 acres above the theoretical 160 acre standard. With land of this type suitable for irrigated potato production and currently valued at $1,000 an acre, the land of Figure 7–9 is worth some $14,600 more than it would be if it conformed to the theoretical 160-acre standard.

Fractional Lots

Sections are fractional not only because they are adjacent to the north and west boundaries of a township but because of their proximity to large bodies of water. A section containing a meandering body of water will be divided into government lots numbered in sectional tiers, as shown in Figure 7–10. Lots begin in the northeastern tier, numbered successively toward the western tier, then toward the east and the tier to the south, progressively through the section. With these qualifications, government surveyors have identified section corners and quarter corner sections on

FIGURE 7-9

A Quarter Section Showing Actual Distances and Acreage

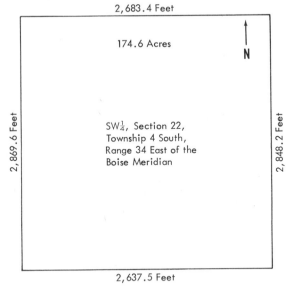

2,683.4 Feet

174.6 Acres

N

2,869.6 Feet

SW¼, Section 22,
Township 4 South,
Range 34 East of the
Boise Meridian

2,848.2 Feet

2,637.5 Feet

FIGURE 7-10

An Illustration of Government Lots of a U.S. Rectangular Survey

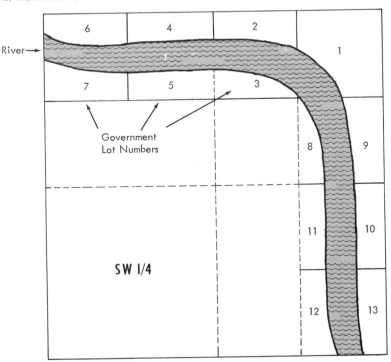

River→

6   4   2

1

7   5   3

Government
Lot Numbers

8   9

11   10

SW I/4

12   13

Section 1, Township 3 North, Range 2 East.

section boundaries. Land described by the U.S. rectangular survey system may be easily identified by locating the appropriate section or quarter corner section marker.

Survey Accuracy

While land may be identified uniquely by this system, land descriptions following the U.S. rectangular survey system have not been without criticism. Initially, rectangular surveys were undertaken by private contractors. In the early years close accuracy was not required. The monuments established at section corners marked the boundaries, regardless of the accuracy of the original survey. Rights were established on the basis of the monuments, and it was soon accepted that surveys made under the direction of the General Land Office, now the Bureau of Land Management, could not be ignored, repudiated, altered, or corrected if they marked the boundaries of lands surveyed by the United States. An 1855 manual of instructions required that survey lines must close within one chain and 50 links (66 feet and 7.92 inches). Surveying instructions issued in 1947 restricted errors to one foot in 3,500 feet for improved or cultivated lands.[16] Since 1910, when the contract system was abolished in favor of government land surveys, section corners have been identified with standard metal posts filled with a core of concrete. These posts are fitted with brass caps marked with steel dies.

METES AND BOUNDS DESCRIPTIONS

Metes and bounds descriptions are universally used. The location and the area of land are defined precisely by describing boundary directions and their turning points. The surveyor starts with a point of beginning (POB) and then indicates the direction of the boundary line and the distance to each turning point or monument around the tract and back to the point of beginning. A metes and bounds description should be sufficiently detailed for a competent surveyor to locate and identify the land parcel. The main components of the legal description depend on the point of beginning, the direction of lines, and monuments.

The Point of Beginning

The point of beginning is a position established by monuments of known position, for example, a point 100 feet west of the intersection of 14th Avenue and Main Street or 'beginning at a point 300 feet north of an iron pin representing the northeast corner of the Johnson tract." The information described as the point of beginning could refer to natural topographical features or man-made structures, such as a railroad right-of-way, a

---

[16] Harrington, "Cadastral Surveys," p. 39.

highway, or some other fixed point. Every metes and bounds description starts with a definite point of beginning.

Direction of Lines

If the property borders on a watercourse or a lake, the direction may be described as a meandering line along some natural geographic feature. Generally, however, the direction would be expressed by degrees within one of four compass quadrants. A compass quadrant is shown in Figure 7–11.

Figure 7–11 shows a line drawn north 60 degrees 20 minutes east. In each instance the surveyor first designates either a *north* or *south* direc-

FIGURE 7–11

Compass Directions for Metes and Bounds Descriptions

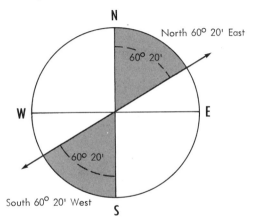

tion. A line going in the opposite direction, as shown in Figure 7–11, would read *south* 60 degrees 20 minutes *west*. After indicating the direction point as either north or south, the surveyor then indicates the number of degrees from a north or south compass point. The direction of the line from the north or south point must proceed either east or west, identifying a quadrant and the direction within the quadrant.

For example, a legal description may read "beginning at a point 100 feet east of the intersection of 14th and Main Streets, north 70 degrees east 120 feet to an iron pin." From the point of beginning the surveyor notes the bearing or direction of the line and the distance to the next monument. By proceeding from the point of beginning to each successive direction and monument, the boundary should end or "close" at the point of beginning. As the boundary changes direction, the surveyor describes each direction by compass degrees and the number of feet to the next monument, proceeding in this way back to the point of beginning.

Monuments

The term *monument* refers to an object that marks a point on the earth's surface. In the original surveys, corner points were typically marked by natural objects, such as trees or large stones. More frequently corner monuments are established by marking points with an iron pipe or bar driven into the ground. Often a concrete or stone monument is marked by permanently attaching a metal plate with identifying numbers. Unfortunately, resurveys have been required because some earlier monuments were established with wooden stakes. Surveyors have been known to mark corners with stones, mounds of stones, or a mound of earth above a buried stone.

An adequate metes and bounds description should include:

1. The name of the surveyor.
2. The survey date.
3. The source of the survey data.
4. The identity of the property.
5. Reference to at least two durable monuments.
6. All dimensions and directions of property lines.
7. Reference to a map recorded in county records.

A metes and bounds description that meets these criteria is shown in Figure 7–12 on page 167. Usually the map will be recorded with the county registry of deeds or some other local office that accepts documents for public record. Generally such maps are filed in plat or deed books which are open to the public and permanently filed for public reference.

In sum, to describe a parcel surveyed by metes and bounds, the length and direction of lines are given in order from the point of beginning; the objects and monuments marking the corner are described; if a boundary follows a prominent feature, the fact is stated in the description; and the area of the parcel is stated. With this information, it is possible to relocate the boundaries of a parcel provided that a surveyor can identify (1) at least one of the original monuments and (2) the true direction of one boundary.

Generally speaking, if an error in the distance occurs, for example, if a tract is described as north 60 degrees 20 minutes west *300 feet* to an iron pin, and the actual distance measures *200 feet,* the actual distance between monuments will generally prevail over the stated distance. In this example, the 200-foot actual distance between the monuments would control.

Recorded Subdivisions

It will be appreciated how awkward it would be to describe city lots and blocks by metes and bounds description. It is much simpler to identify a

FIGURE 7–12

A Metes and Bounds Description, Montgomery County, Pennsylvania

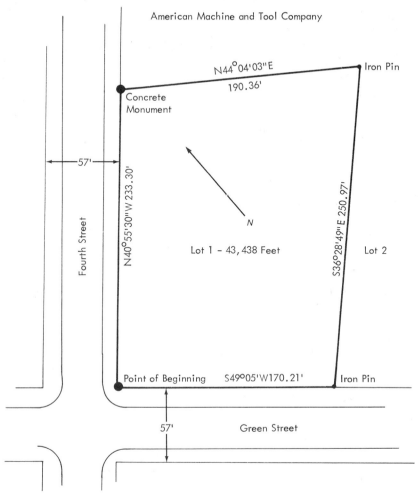

Description of Lot No. 1 shown on plan of subdivision made for Joseph D. Prosser Estate by Urwiler & Walter, Inc., dated November 13, 1975, revised January 26, 1976.

All that certain tract of land situate in the Borough of Royersford, County of Montgomery, Commonwealth of Pennsylvania, bounded and described as follows, to wit:

Beginning at a point on the northeasterly side line of Fourth Street (57 feet wide), said point being the intersection of said side line with the northwesterly side line of Green Street (57 feet wide); thence extending along said side line of Fourth Street North 40 degrees 55 minutes 30 seconds West 233.30 feet to a concrete monument in line of lands of the American Machine & Tool Company; thence extending along said lands North 44 degrees 04 minutes 03 seconds East 190.36 feet to an iron pin in line of Lot No. 2; thence extending along said lot South 36 degrees 28 minutes 49 seconds East 250.97 feet to an iron pin on the aforementioned side line of Green Street; thence extending along said side line South 49 degrees 05 minutes West 170.21 feet to the point and place of beginning.

Containing: 43,438 square feet of land, more or less.

land parcel as lot 3, block 4 of Innis Arden estates, recorded in plat book 20, page 36, King County, Washington. Where a recorded subdivision description prevails, the public may determine the precise location of lots and blocks by turning to the subdivision map on file in the county registry of deeds or with the county recorder, county auditor, or other official accepting documents for public record. Provided that the subdivision meets official approval, the recorded subdivision gives the detailed description of each lot and block by survey so that each lot or land parcel may be precisely located and identified.

Subdivision regulations, administered by local officials, control the standards of the survey and assure that the subdivision meets other local regulations. In some states, including California, the filing of subdivision maps is regulated by state law. Ordinarily the state law is an enabling act; it allows local communities to enact ordinances that regulate the development and recording of subdivisions. The subdivision act is directed to two objectives:

1. To coordinate the subdivision plans and planning—including lot design, street patterns, and rights-of-way for drainage, sewers, and other utilities—with the community pattern and plan, as laid out by the local planning authorities.
2. To insure that the areas dedicated to public purposes by the filing of the subdivision maps, including public streets and other public areas, will be properly improved initially by the subdivider so that in the future they will not become an undue burden on the general taxpayers of the community.[17]

A developer organizing a subdivision must first prepare a tentative map and submit it to agencies of the local government for their approval. Local government officials review the subdivision proposal as regards its compliance with regulations on street improvements and utilities, such as drainage, sewers, water and gas lines, and underground cables. After local government review the subdivider makes whatever changes are necessary and prepares the final map. The final map is reviewed by local agencies and government lending agencies, and if accepted, the map is recorded for permanent record. A recorded subdivision taken from county records is shown in Figure 7–13.

It should be noted that a lot and block description which is not placed on record by recording is not an acceptable legal description. A lot owner of an unrecorded subdivision has no means of identifying and locating his ownership. Generally the laws of most states prohibit the sale of unrecorded lots and blocks.

---

[17] Arthur G. Bowman, *California Real Estate Principles* (Pacific Palisades, Calif.: Goodyear Publishing Company, Inc., 1972), p. 251.

FIGURE 7–13

Lot and Block Descriptions of a Recorded Subdivision, Fort Lauderdale, Florida

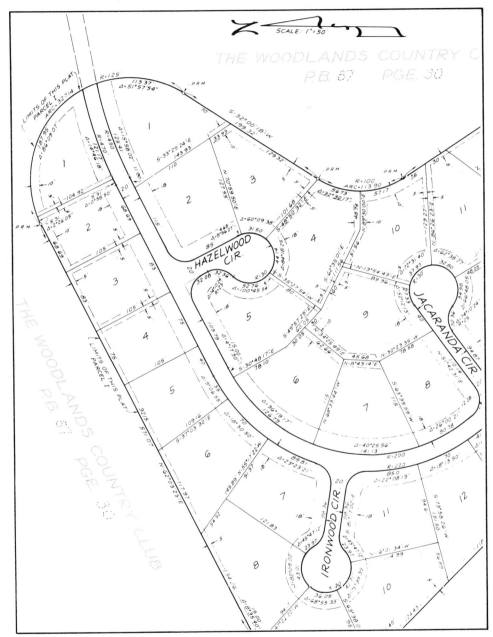

STATE PLANE COORDINATE SYSTEMS

Legal descriptions under government rectangular surveys, metes and bounds, or recorded subdivisions are dependent on marks or monuments which may be destroyed, moved, or otherwise obliterated, willfully or accidentally. The state plane coordinate system provides a permanent method of identifying points. In addition this method minimizes errors arising from the curvature of the earth. A surveying manual prepared by the U.S. Coast and Geodetic Survey advises:

> The use of State coordinates in land descriptions does not mean the abandonment of the older methods of description, either by platted subdivision or fraction of subdivisions, or by metes and bounds. It is intended to supplement either of these methods, and to facilitate the finding, or the checking of the location of, any of the corners implied or described in the older forms of descriptions. It is simply a means of increasing the certainty and facilitating the future field use of the old descriptions, not of superseding them.[18]

In short, a description by government rectangular survey may satisfy the lawyer and the property owner, but it does not ensure that the parcel can be located on the ground. Surveyors have advised that state plane coordinates which are included in a deed are worth the extra work involved in writing a state plane coordinate description.

Longitude and Latitude

Initiated in 1933, the U.S. Coast and Geodetic Survey (now the National Ocean Survey, Department of Commerce) has formed a system of coordinate grids for each state. The system avoids physical landmarks as monuments. Points in the grid are identified by longitude and latitude. Such a system depends on a geodetic survey that employs spherical trigonometry to determine distances and bearings. Because of the high degree of accuracy, the state plane coordinate system has even been used to locate fossilized dinosaur tracks.[19] In short, the system provides a reliable system for describing land and reduces the cost of surveys. The main disadvantage lies in the difficulty of interpretation by lay persons.

In nontechnical terms, the state plane coordinate system relies on monuments arranged in a series of triangles, with coordinates determined precisely by longitude and latitude. In case a monument is lost or destroyed, its location can be found by a geodetic survey. Because of the technical difficulties of a geodetic survey, a grid has been developed for all 50 states.

---

[18] Hugh C. Mitchell and Lansing G. Simmons, *The State Coordinate Systems,* Special Publication No. 235 (Washington, D.C.: U.S. Government Printing Office, 1945), pp. 50–51.

[19] Lyle B. Whittlesey, "New Horizons for a State Coordinate System," *Proceedings,* American Congress on Surveying and Mapping, 1975, p. 204.

To account for the curvature of the earth, each state is divided into zones with a maximum width of 158 miles. Each of the 111 zones is flattened mathematically, with much the same effect as a flattened orange peel. For example, for the three zones of Wisconsin the north-south line is the meridian 90°00′ West longitude. Each zone is divided into a grid with a vertical y axis and a horizontal x axis. Property locations are described according to their xy coordinates.[20]

Coordinate Grids

Note that in Figure 7–14, the location of point B may be expressed as a coordinate of the x and y axes. In the example, point B can be precisely

FIGURE 7–14

Plane-Rectangular Coordinates Illustrating State Coordinate Land Descriptions

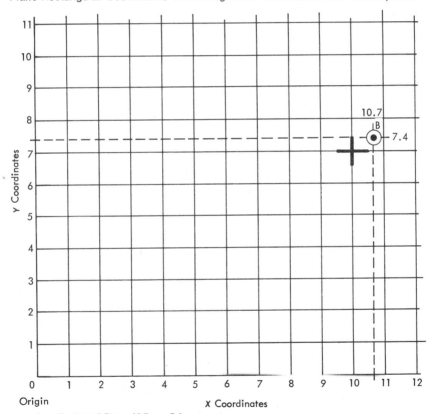

Coordinates of B: $x = 10.7$, $y = 7.4$.
Source: Hugh C. Mitchell and Lancing G. Simmons, *The State Coordinate Systems*, Special Publication No. 235 (Washington, D.C.: U.S. Government Printing Office, 1945), p. 51.

[20] D. David Moyer, and Kenneth Paul Fisher, *Land Parcel Identifiers for Information Systems* (Chicago: American Bar Foundation, 1974), p. 74.

FIGURE 7-15

A One-Acre Parcel Described by a State Plane Coordinate Description, Monroe County, Georgia

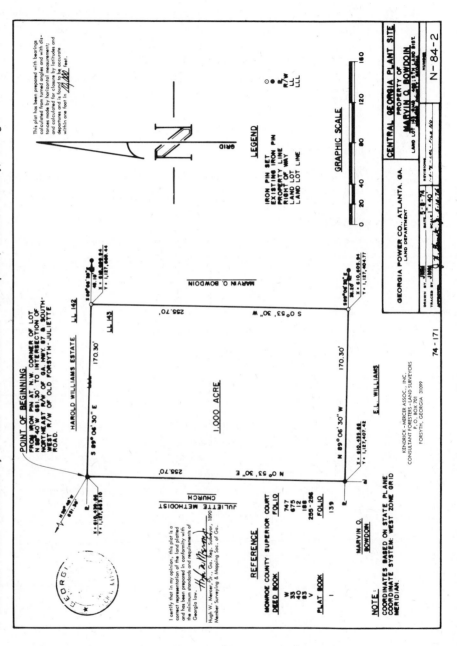

All that tract or parcel of land situate, lying and being in Land Lot 143 of the 466th G. M. D. and the 5th Land District of Monroe County, Georgia and being more particularly described as follows:

To establish the Point of Beginning COMMENCE at the intersection of the Northeast right-of-way line of Georgia State Highway No. 87 and the Southwest right-of-way line of Old Forsyth–Juliette Road; extend thence from said intersection South 58° 40′ East 651.30 feet to an iron pin marking the POINT OF BEGINNING, said POINT OF BEGINNING having a coordinate value of $X = 610,439.66$ and $Y = 1,127,663.10$ (all of the coordinates referred to herein are based on the Georgia State Plane Coordinate System, West Zone Meridian); thence from said POINT OF BEGINNING South 89° 06′ 30″ East along the North line of said Land Lot 143 a distance of 170.30 feet to an iron pin having a coordinate value of $X = 610,609.94$ and $Y = 1,127,660.44$; thence South 00° 53′ 30″ West 255.70 feet to an iron pin and lands now or formerly of E. L. Williams, said iron pin having a coordinate value of $X = 610,605.94$ and $Y = 1,127,404.77$; thence North 89° 06′ 30″ West along the line dividing lands now or formerly of E. L. Williams and lands of Marvin O. Bowdoin a distance of 170.30 feet to an iron pin marking a corner common to lands now or formerly of E. L. Williams, lands of Juliette Methodist Church and lands of Marvin O. Bowdoin, said iron pin having a coordinate value of $X = 610,-435.66$ and $Y = 1,127,407.42$; thence North 00° 53′ 30″ East along the line dividing lands now or formerly of Juliette Methodist Church and lands of Marvin O. Bowdoin a distance of 255.70 feet to the iron pin marking the POINT OF BEGINNING.

The hereinabove described tract of land contains 1.000 acres, more or less, and is shown on a plat dated May 8, 1974 entitled Central Georgia Plant Site, Property of Marvin O. Bowdoin, prepared by Hugh W. Mercer, Jr., Georgia Registered Surveyor No. 1890, designated as Drawing No. N–84–2 and is on record in Plat Book 6, Page 13 in the Office of the Clerk of the Superior Court of Monroe County, Georgia, a copy of which is attached hereto and made a part hereof.

Source: Courtesy of Wade M. Manning, vice president, Georgia Power Company, Atlanta, Georgia.

located by finding 10.7 on the *x* axis and 7.4 on the *y* axis. Thus, a monument tied to the state plane coordinate system may be identified precisely by reference to rectangular coordinates.

Some surveyors use a metes and bounds description with a state plane coordinate survey. Such a procedure is followed by the Tennessee Valley Authority. Note that the iron pins in the description shown in Figure 7–15 are identified precisely by *x–y* coordinates. There would be no danger of being unable to relocate these pins if they were lost or destroyed.

Local surveys are referenced to the state plane coordinates. A surveyor using this system plans a local survey to known points on the state coordinate system. For example, a sphere representing a strip of land surface 158 miles wide can be shown on a single plane so that surveyors will not exceed an error of one foot in 10,000 feet, or almost 2 miles.

In sum, while the system has clear advantages in measuring rights-of-way for highways, utility lines, and public lands, it has not been widely used by lay persons. The system requires considerable technical ability and special training, and it does not tie the location to readily determinable neighborhood points.

SUMMARY

The land titles and legal descriptions used in the United States originated with the institutions of the feudal land system prevailing in medieval England. These institutions, such as written conveyance documents transferring title, the system of recording, the legal description, escheat, and the rules of inheritance, were firmly established during the colonial period. The rights of inheritance, adverse possession, escheat, and other rights associated with private property ownership were accepted before the Revolutionary War.

Colonial experience demonstrated the need for a system of describing land prior to the sale of public lands. The rectangular survey, used in 30 states, depends on a primary reference to principal meridians and base lines. Townships and ranges locate land within a 36-square-mile area. Sections of one square mile include land that may be described in terms of successive quarter divisions. Discrepancies created by the curvature of the earth are compensated by correction lines in designated sections. Fractional sections of odd-shaped parcels resulting from large bodies of water are described by government lots.

A metes and bounds description starts with a point of beginning with the direction of boundary lines, shown first in a north or south direction, and next in the number of degrees toward the east or west. Monuments designate turning points of the boundary; distances between monuments help identify boundary locations. A metes and bounds description must end or close at the point of beginning.

Description by lots and blocks of a recorded subdivision allows the property owner to identify land location by reference to a public recording of the subdivision in a permanent public file—usually a plat book maintained by the county auditor, the registrar of deeds, the county recorder, or some comparable official. As a condition of recording, local and state officials insure that the subdivision meets minimum standards of survey, utility construction, and street and lot layout.

The state plane coordinate system relies on designated points that are determined by longitude and latitude and the formation of a grid. Surveyors then locate points by reference to *xy* coordinates of the state plane coordinates. These descriptions save surveying time and gain extreme accuracy. Lost or destroyed monuments which are identified by the state plane coordinate system may be easily located with precision.

REVIEW QUESTIONS

1. Explain how some rights in land have been granted to all members of society.
2. Under the feudal system of the Middle Ages, who held title to land?
3. Explain how the system of transferring title by written instruments developed from early feudal practices.
4. In what way are the squatter's rights of colonial times similar to the rights of a person claiming under adverse possession?
5. What is the meaning of a principal meridian and a base line?
6. How are townships and ranges used in a government rectangular survey description?
7. How would you describe a 20-acre parcel in a rectangular survey system?
8. How do surveyors compensate for the curvature of the earth in a rectangular survey description?
9. How do surveyors indicate the direction of lines in a metes and bounds description?
10. What is the significance of a monument in a metes and bounds description?
11. What features should an adequate metes and bounds description include?
12. How would a surveyor locate a property corner for land described by lots and blocks of a recorded subdivision?
13. Why do surveyors recommend state plane coordinate legal descriptions?
14. Demonstrate how property would be located under the state plane coordinate system.

SELECTED REFERENCES

Ficek, Edmund F.; Henderson, Thomas P.; and Johnson, Ross H. *Real Estate Principles and Practices,* chap. 2. Columbus: Charles E. Merrill Publishing Co., 1976.

Harris, Marshall. *Origin of the Land Tenure System in the United States.* Westport, Conn.: Greenwood Press, 1953.

Hibbard, Benjamin Horace. *A History of the Public Lands.* Madison: University of Wisconsin Press, 1965.

Mitchell, Hugh C., and Simmons, Lansing G. *The State Coordinate Systems,* pp. 50–51. Special Publication No. 235. Washington, D.C.: U.S. Government Printing Office, 1945.

Ottoson, Howard W. *Land Use Policy and Problems in the United States.* Lincoln: University of Nebraska Press, 1963.

Shenkel, William M. *The Real Estate Professional,* chap. 7. Homewood, Ill.: Dow Jones-Irwin, Inc., 1976.

8

Analyzing Real Estate Markets

After reading this chapter, you should be familiar with the following points:

1 The relation between land use and urban problems.
2 The impact of urban growth.
3 Forces that encourage further population growth in urban areas.
4 The determinants of national housing demand.
5 Elements that affect the supply of housing.
6 Indicators of local housing demand.
7 The concept of housing filtering.
8 An evaluation of rent control.
9 Reasons for the relative decline of central business districts.
10 Shopping center types and techniques of estimating the demand for shopping center space.
11 The main trends observed in office space utilization.
12 Elements of the supply and demand for industrial space.

THE MARKET for real estate is largely an urban market. Even agricultural land use depends on the urban population to consume farm products. Accordingly it seems appropriate to explain the forces which lead to urban growth. Following this introduction, the chapter concentrates on the housing market: the determinants of housing demand and supply and such related issues as the concepts of filtering and rent control. Understanding elements of the commercial real estate market, namely, retail and office buildings, helps minimize investment risks. The chapter closes with a discussion of the industrial real estate market, which is subject to unique market forces.

THE URBAN LAND MARKET

So many social, political, and economic forces affect urban land development that authorities find it difficult to focus on a single issue. Nevertheless, the direction and degree of urban growth closely affect investment decisions of the institutional and individual investor, the speculator, and the home buyer. At the outset it should be noted that urban economists treat the allocation of urban resources as a great social problem that affects everyone. On this point there is little dispute. At the same time the ability to analyze real estate markets minimizes the possibility of capital losses.

The Urban Problem

It has been held that urban life is no longer satisfactory for people. Such a pessimistic view was held by the late Constantinos Doxiadis, an internationally known planner, who regarded the present urban environment as poorly suited to urban populations. According to Doxiadis:

> From the social point of view Man appears to be lost in the big cities, and feels abandoned by progress in many towns and villages. On the political level, new types of societies and new types of people have not yet found their corresponding political institutions. From the technical point of view we see that most settlements do not have the facilities indispensable to their proper functioning, in spite of the technological achievements of our era. And finally, it also holds true aesthetically; we need only look around at the ugliness of human settlements of the present to be convinced of this.[1]

The crisis described by Doxiadis arises from many causes: the increase in population; the tremendous rate of urbanization (which in some areas is increasing by 5 percent per year); the increase in per capita income; unexpected, unforeseen ecological problems; and finally, the sociopolitical impact these forces have had on the lives of human beings. Doxiadis

---

[1] Constantinos A. Doxiadis, *Ekistics: An Introduction to the Science of Human Settlements* (New York: Oxford University Press, 1968), p. 5.

believed that the solution lay in integrating human and natural resources, an unresolved issue because of problems in forecasting social needs. Thus there is a gap between the actual and predicted change in our ability to cope with urban problems. These relationships are diagramed in Figure 8–1.

In his widely quoted book *Megalopolis,* Jean Gottmann, a French geographer, describes the northeastern seaboard of the United States as a continuous urban area which extends from the Atlantic to the Appalachian

FIGURE 8–1

A Comparison between Actual Changes and the Ability to Forecast Changes over Time

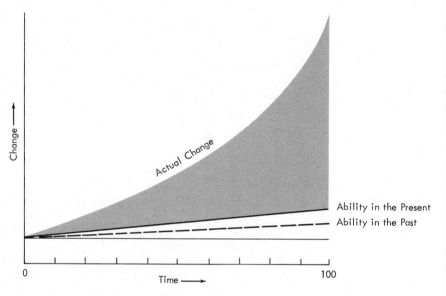

foothills and from southern New Hampshire to northern Virginia. In Gottmann's view, cities have lost their importance to the megalopolis, which nationally has the largest concentrations of population and the highest average density. No comparable area of the world has such a supremacy in politics, economics, and cultural activity.

Developed over some three centuries, the megalopolis, as described by Gottmann, creates new problems for its inhabitants. In his words, "the modern trends in its development and its present degree of crowding provide both examples and warnings for other less urbanized areas in America and abroad and call for a profound revision of many old concepts, such as the usually accepted distinctions between city and country."[2]

[2] Jean Gottmann, *Megalopolis* (New York: Twentieth Century Fund, 1961), p. 4.

The idea of the city as a tightly settled and organized unit must be abandoned. The new patterns of urban regions exert a strong influence on the economic and social foundations of society and directly affect land use. On this point, Gottmann observes further that urbanization owes much to the automobile, which strangles city activity and defeats other means of transportation. For example, "the intense living of megalopolis makes a great deal of waste inescapable, waste of space and time as well as materials."[3] In his view, wealthy and educated people endowed with improved technological means must find ways of avoiding the decline of urban areas.

Urban Concentration

Some 75.2 percent of the people of the United States live in urban communities. This pattern is also observed in other nations; for example, there is an urban population of 83.2 percent in Japan, of 79.1 percent in the United Kingdom, and of 88.5 percent in Australia.[4] The U.S. Census Bureau recognizes 243 standard metropolitan statistical areas, each of which is a county or a group of contiguous counties that include at least one city of 50,000 population. Approximately 69 percent of the U.S. population live in these SMSAs.[5]

The Census Bureau also reports population data by *urbanized areas,* which are generally more inclusive than the SMSAs. The boundaries of an SMSA are determined by political lines, whereas the boundaries of urbanized areas are determined by the patterns of urban land use. The total number of urbanized areas increased from 6,041 in 1960 to 7,062 in 1970. Some 73.5 percent of the total U.S. population are included in urbanized areas.

In addition to these, the Census Bureau recognizes urbanized areas consisting of a central city or cities and the surrounding closely settled territory. Generally speaking, a central city of 50,000 inhabitants or more, or twin cities with contiguous boundaries that economically constitute a single community which has a combined population of at least 50,000, may be classified as an urbanized area. The closely settled territory of an urbanized area includes incorporated places of at least 2,500 inhabitants or more than 100 housing units. Some 248 urban places in the United States hold 58.3 percent of the population.

It is clear that the population of urban areas is increasing. To analyze real estate markets, it is worthwhile to review the forces that encourage

---

[3] Ibid., p. 12.

[4] Wallace F. Smith, *Urban Development* (Berkeley: University of California Press, 1975), p. 1.

[5] U.S. Department of Commerce, 1970 Census of Population, Characteristics of Population, vol. 1, United States Survey, Part 1, Section 1, I-141, I-175.

the urbanization of different land use types. The trends responsible for urbanization may be expected to continue.

Urbanizing Market Forces

Certain economic reasons explain long-run changes in urban communities. The record discloses that the population of the SMSAs is increasing. At the same time the population in central cities has shifted to suburban areas. Heilbrun cites five forces that explain these trends.

1. The trend toward high-density land uses (the overflow effect).
2. Technological innovations.
3. The rise in living standards.
4. Changes in consumer preferences.
5. Public policies favoring urbanization.

The Overflow Effect.   As central cities expand, the price of "relatively" scarce land increases. High-density land uses in the form of high-rise buildings, office towers, and the like compensate for higher land prices. As land prices increase, the metropolitan population is attracted to the lower land prices of the suburbs: the suburban office park, the industrial park, and the garden court apartments and subdivisions of middle- and upper-class housing. In recent times the suburban population has increased at a faster pace than has the population of central cities.[6]

Technological Innovations.   The leading innovation affecting urban growth is the automobile. Some authorities regard the automobile as mainly responsible for shaping the geographic pattern of metropolitan settlements. Over the last two generations, the transportation of goods and people shifted from rail freight and street railways to the truck and the private automobile. Before automobiles, city commuters lived near railroad stations. Manufacturing plants were scattered along railroad lines in multiple-story structures since it was more economic to move goods vertically than horizontally.

With the completion of limited-access highways, economic activities could be dispersed to outlying suburbs. City workers continued to work in central places and moved out to new communities. New suburban shopping centers served growing subdivisions. Hence, the automobile and truck released populations from the need to work and live in central place—railroad-oriented cities.

The Rise in Living Standards.   Families tend to upgrade their housing as income increases. Moreover, higher incomes encourage migration from the city center to the suburbs. At some point families are willing to absorb the higher commuting costs and to accept the additional commuting time

---

[6] James Heilbrun, *Urban Economics and Public Policy* (New York: St. Martin's Press, 1974), p. 34.

associated with the suburbs. Normally such options are not open to relatively low-income families. Rising living standards have led to a dependence on the private automobile, more commuting, and increased migration from high-density central places to low-density suburban areas.

Consumer Preferences. Consumers have preferred the family-centered life of the suburbs to the central place living more common in past generations. Though these trends show signs of reversing, most families still prefer a suburban life-style. The exceptions include the young professionals, the affluent elderly—and the disadvantaged who concentrate in substandardhousing in the central city.

Public Policy. The federal income tax treatment of homeowners adds to the preference for suburban owner-occupancy. The income tax deductibility of mortgage interest and property taxes constitutes a hidden subsidy to homeowners which is not available to renters. Further—though of less importance today—Federal Housing Administration mortgage insurance and Veterans Administration loan guarantees have favored owner-occupied housing. Relatively low down payments, long-term loans, and a system of administered mortgage interest rates are examples of public policies that favor suburban owner-occupancy relative to renting in the central city.

Urban Economics

Economists explain urban formation on the ground that people find it advantageous to carry on various activities in a spatially concentrated fashion.[7] Thus, the urban area serves many functions: it may be a government center, such as a state capital; a goods distribution center, such as Atlanta and Seattle; a financial center, such as downtown Chicago; or a cultural center, such as New York City.

With some exceptions, urban areas are largely a function of market forces. It is held that urban areas create certain economies. To put it differently, it is profitable to site in an urban area. The urban structure is such that it pays a firm to concentrate in an urban area to obtain lower costs of production or a greater sales volume. In addition, the production of industry A benefits by a location near industry B if industry A sells products to industry B. In further illustration, it would be advantageous for employees to live near their source of employment to avoid commuting costs. The resulting competition for land in a high-density area tends to increase land values above land values in low-density areas, thereby giving households and businesses an economic incentive to move from areas of high density to areas of low density.

Urban areas developed partly from an agglomeration of such econo-

---

[7] Edwin S. Mills, *Urban Economics* (Glenview, Ill.: Scott, Foresman and Co., 1972), p. 12.

mies. These economies refer to the lower costs of production that result from locating in an urban area. Thus an industry manufacturing farm implements has an economic advantage in locating near the cities of Rock Island and Davenport in Illinois and Iowa—the center of farm implement manufacturing. The nearness of parts suppliers, ancillary industries, and an adaptable labor supply give industries in farm implement manufacturing a clear advantage in locating in the Quad Cities area—an illustration of an agglomerating economy.

Transportation Economies. Urban size and location interact with the availability of economical interurban transportation. Industries locate near centers of transportation to minimize the cost of loading and unloading. Industries that add weight in manufacturing, industries dependent on a local raw material, and industries producing bulk products congregate in urban areas that have highly developed interurban facilities.

Urban Market Forces. Subject to land use controls, land rent/prices provide for the allocation of land uses. Land that is more productive, for example, land that has greater utility for single-family use or land that produces more income, is bid upward by developers, so that theoretically land is devoted to its maximum use. Defining land rent as the price of the annual services yielded by land, land value is equal to the present worth of the future benefits that can be derived from landownership. Such benefits are measured by the services supplied by land or its annual rental value.

In the simplest competitive model, land value would be equal to the discounted annual rent less transportation costs. This assumes that land centrally located with the same annual rent would be worth more than more distant land by an amount equal to the added transportation costs produced at more distant points. The perfect competitive model would assume the land/rent pattern demonstrated in Figure 8–2.

Consequently, individual firms are assumed to maximize land use by resorting to locations that produce the highest income with the least transportation cost. Similarly, individual households maximize satisfaction by balancing land prices with commuting costs from more distant locations.[8]

In this respect, one urban economist suggests that persons with higher incomes prefer larger land parcels at a lower per unit price which compensates for the added transportation costs of the more distant sites. Conversely, lower income groups pay higher per unit prices for smaller sites which are offset by the lower transportation costs of centrally located land.

Using this technique, it may be shown how rural land tends to be converted to urban land. Again, assuming that the price of land declines with the distance from the center, we may establish a demand for urban land and rural land, as shown in Figure 8–3. In this diagram, land lying be-

---

[8] Mills, *Urban Economics,* p. 59.

FIGURE 8–2

A Diagram of Theoretical Rents Decreasing as Transportation
Costs Increase under Pure Competition

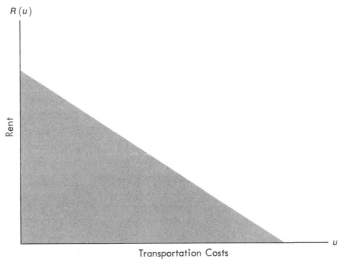

Source: From *Urban Economics* by Edwin S. Mills. Copyright © 1972 by
Scott, Foresman and Company. Reprinted by permission.

FIGURE 8–3

A Diagram Showing the Conversion of Actual Land to Residential
Use as Rents Increase with Decreasing Distance

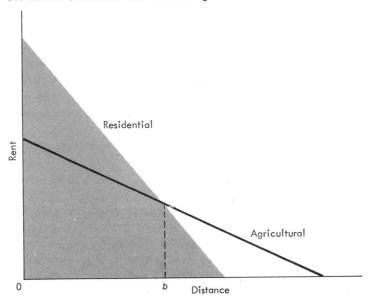

Source: Douglas M. Brown, *Introduction to Urban Economics* (New York:
Academic Press, Inc., 1974), p. 117.

tween point B and point C will be devoted to agricultural uses. From OB, which is closer to the city center, the demand for residential property will cause land to be absorbed for residential purposes. Point B represents the boundary between urban and rural land use.

The illustration demonstrates the concept of land as a productive unit. To the extent that competitive conditions operate, land tends to be used for that purpose which maximizes net income. A separate discussion of residential, commercial, and industrial land indicates how these forces interact among different land uses.

ANALYZING THE HOUSING MARKET

The housing market is highly stratified. It is affected by market imperfections and by public policy, and, more important, it is a local market classified by home occupancy, rental occupancy, type of structure, location, neighborhood age, architectural style, and type of construction. The difficulty of defining the local housing market makes the housing market more complex than the simple concept of the competitive model.

To demonstrate this point, it is necessary to determine demand and supply factors for a national housing market, then to turn to forces important for the owner occupancy and rental occupancy markets. The issue of rent control and a discussion of housing market indicators help to apply techniques of analyzing housing markets.

Elements of the National Housing Market

The forces of supply and demand are partly economic, partly sociological, and partly related to government housing policies.

Determinants of Housing Demand. Most authorities relate housing demand to a set of five variables:

1. Per capita disposable income.
2. Net household formation.
3. Migration of households.
4. Housing demolitions.
5. Relative price of housing services.

Lower per capita disposable incomes have the effect of postponing household formation and causing more families to share space. In periods of declining income, more single persons live with parents, more married persons live with in-laws. As per capita disposable income increases, the number of individuals demanding separate households increases.

As the number of households changes, the demand for new housing changes. The number of households includes a growing number of single retirees, divorced persons, and unmarried singles. While the absolute population may be relatively stable, the increasing number of separate households may create an increasing local demand for residential space. Both the average size of households and the number of households determine how housing sources are allocated. In the last ten years the number of households has increased 23.7 percent. Table 8–1 reveals that the annual rate of household formation has increased over 2 percent over the last two years.

The migration of households from rural areas to urban areas may result in a net increase in the demand for housing. If a family moves from rural substandard housing, which is abandoned, to an urban area, the demand for new housing shows a net increase although the number of households

TABLE 8–1

The Number of Households (in thousands)

Year	Number of Households	Annual Percent of Increase
1967	59,248	—
1968	60,726	2.49
1969	61,805	1.78
1970	63,450	2.66
1971	64,374	1.46
1972	67,132	4.28
1973	68,737	2.39
1974	69,859	1.63
1975	71,769	2.73
1976	73,316 (projected)	2.16
Percent of increase, 1967–1976		23.7

Source: U.S. Department of Commerce, Social and Economic Statistics Administration, Bureau of the Census, *Current Population Reports, Population Estimates and Projections*, Series P–25 and P–20 (Washington, D.C.: U.S. Government Printing Office, July 1, 1967).

remains the same. For a locality, the expected rate of in-migration or out-migration must be considered in projecting the community demand for housing.

The construction of new airports and highways, urban renewal projects, neighborhood clearance programs, and the conversion of property from residential to commercial use decrease the supply of housing and place more households in the housing market. Annually, some new housing merely replaces demolished housing. Not all new construction represents a net addition to the housing stock.

It is reasonable to assume that consumers ration expenditures to maximize satisfaction. As housing prices, that is, construction costs and residential land values, rise above prices for other goods and services, some consumers elect to decrease housing expenditures in favor of food, clothing, and other goods and services. In contrast, an oversupply of housing may depress housing prices/rents relative to other prices.

Supply Determinants. Variables explaining the supply of housing are more complex. The more important variables include factors that affect the flow of savings into housing mortgage markets, federal monetary policy, lender policies on real estate housing finance, and changes in construction costs. The interaction of supply/cost variables is highly complex, involving supply factors that affect (1) single-family dwellings financed with conventional (nongovernmental) mortgages, (2) houses insured by the Federal Housing Administration, (3) houses purchased with Veterans Administration–guaranteed mortgages, (4) multiple-family units, and (5) mobile homes.

As a consequence, the housing supply depends on:

1. New construction.
2. The net change in housing and inventory under construction.
3. The net change in housing vacancies.
4. Less: Demolitions.
    Conversions to nonhousing use.
5. Plus: New public housing construction and new construction of mobile homes.

The latest Census of Housing lists 75.969 million housing units in the United States. However, only 69.337 million units were occupied in 1973 —5.956 million units were year-round vacant units, and less than 1 million units (0.676 million) were seasonal units or vacant units held for migratory labor. Of the total number of units, approximately 68 percent were single-family homes, with about 28 percent in multiunit structures. Some 3.3 million units, or 4 percent of the housing inventory, consisted of occupied mobile homes and trailers.[9]

Of the 69.337 million occupied housing units in the United States, the Bureau of the Census lists 64.4 percent as owner-occupied. Hence, a little over one third of the housing remains in rental status. These figures do not imply that the housing supply is all of adequate quality.

At the end of 1973, some 2.278 million dwellings lacked some or all plumbing facilities, for example, flush toilets or hot and cold running water. The data show further that 47 percent or 13.1 million housing units had rooms that lacked a source of heat. Structural deficiences, such as water leakage, were reported by 7.6 percent of all households surveyed by the Bureau of the Census.[10]

With respect to neighborhoods, 18.3 percent of households reported inadequate transportation, 11.7 percent inadequate shopping facilities, and 6.3 percent inadequate schools. In fact, some 29 percent of the

---

[9] U.S. Department of Commerce, U.S. Bureau of the Census, *Current Housing Reports,* Series H–150–73B, Annual Housing Survey, 1973 (Washington, D.C.: U.S. Government Printing Office, 1975).

[10] Ibid.

households in the central cities of metropolitan areas rated their neighborhoods as only fair or poor.

Estimating the Demand for Owner Occupancy. The potential marketability of new housing construction depends largely on the demand for housing in a given neighborhood, locality, or community. While census data are helpful, these data either apply to large areas or are not sufficiently current. As a consequence, housing consultants tend to measure the demand for local housing from local information. Some of the data indicative of trends in housing demand are given by local population estimates; building permits; new subdivision, mortgage, and deed recordings; and vacancy surveys. Although a historical review of changes in these series indicates the trends in past demand for housing, such data may not always be used as a guide to changing the existing stock of housing. That is, there may be a demand for 500 housing units in a locality, but if five developers try to meet this demand, there would be a temporary surplus of housing since each producer might be unaware of competing projects under construction.

To indicate the potential demand for local housing, refer to local sources to identify trends in housing preferences:

Housing Market Indicators	Data Sources
Population estimates	Local planning commission, local development corporations, state agencies
Building permits	County and city building departments
New subdivision recordings	State real estate commission, county registrar, registry of deeds, or county recorder or auditor
Deed recordings	County recording office
Mortgage recordings	County recording office
Vacancy surveys	Federal Housing Administration reports, local planning commission, local nonprofit housing corporations
Employment data	Unemployment security reports, state labor reports
Retail sales	State sales tax records

These records are complemented by records of local bank deposits, the number of water meters and telephones installed, and the like. Ordinarily, such data complement the more infrequent census data. Data for past years help to project the future demand for housing.

FHA Housing Market Analysis. According to the Federal Housing Administration, local housing demand depends on four factors:

1. The rate of growth in the number of households.
2. Income and employment patterns.
3. Liquid asset holdings (down payment and mortgage term requirements and the availability of mortgage funds).
4. Space, convenience, and style requirements.[11]

The first item, rate of household growth, is determined by the net population growth and certain social forces tending to create smaller households. Households are defined as related or unrelated persons occupying a dwelling unit. Local income and employment patterns affect housing consumption standards. Rising incomes encourage families to seek higher quality housing. Declining employment and incomes encourage households to postpone housing decisions and encourage separate households to join in a single dwelling. The liquid assets available to a household determine its ability to meet housing down payments. Similarly, a shortage of mortgage funds leads to lower loan to value mortgage ratios, higher interest rates, and shorter term mortgages. These unfavorable mortgage terms increase mortgage payments to the point that fewer households are able to meet mortgage payments from current income.

The last item concerns the desire of households to improve living standards and conditions. As family composition and general living customs change, housing also changes, in such terms as the number of rooms, the size of rooms, and the number of persons per room. For instance, housekeeping efficiency and laborsaving devices with today's more modern designs mean that a family now requires fewer rooms than did a family living in 1890. Style changes occurring over the last two generations include modern heating and cooling systems, electricity, ranges, washers, dryers, one or more complete bathrooms, storm windows, and wall and roof insulation.[12]

Housing Filtering.   Because housing is a long-lasting durable good, housing is seldom used up and discarded. More than likely, as a house becomes less desirable because of age, deterioration, or change in the neighborhood, the original occupants move, and the house is sold to a lower income household. To the extent that this process continues, there would appear to be a constant demand for new houses, with an increasing supply of older, used houses available to lower income groups. In this sense the housing market operates in much the same way as the used car market. Hence, filtering has been defined as *a change in occupancy as housing that is occupied by one income group becomes available to the next income group as a result of relatively declining prices or rents.*

Some observers have noted that the filtering process has worked im-

---

[11] *FHA Techniques of Housing Market Analysis* (Washington, D.C.: U.S. Government Printing Office, 1970), p. 157.

[12] Ibid., p. 160.

perfectly. First, the number of newly constructed houses for high-income families is inadequate to supply sufficient houses for middle- or low-income groups. Second, the appeal of some dwellings does not decrease with age; the price of old houses does not always decline. Some owners of existing houses anticipate continuous price increases and are unwilling to accept losses of even normal depreciation. Finally, family ties to local neighborhoods and local institutions prevent families from moving to a new home as anticipated by the filtering theory.

While some houses may be expected to go through the filtering process, the imperfections of the market and the length of time necessary for the filtering process to be effective make it highly uncertain that middle- and low-income groups benefit from new construction that caters exclusively to upper- and upper middle-income groups.

Rent Control. Most authorities agree that rent control tends to decrease the availability of housing.[13] Initially, rent control served as a temporary war emergency measure in both World War I and World War II. The Emergency Price Control Act of 1942 introduced rent controls as part of a system of national wage and price controls. In New York City, rent controls have been administered under enabling legislation of the state of New York, namely, the state Emergency Housing Rent Control Law of 1950. Similarly, the city of Boston has administered rent control under a 1970 state act. Rent control, it is claimed, favors the tenant against arbitrary rent increases exacted by unreasonable dwelling owners. Urban economists, however, have been highly critical of the impact of rent control on both the quality and the quantity of rental housing.

The evidence suggests that rent control leads to *underutilized housing*. Tenants subject to rent control show a reluctance to move to noncontrolled units. Hence, under rent control tenants tend to occupy more housing space over time than they would if rents followed the market standard. Tenants in rent-controlled units make less efficient use of space; they tend to consume more housing compared to housing they would consume under free-market prices.

Further, rent controls without corresponding controls over housing operating expenses encourage *the postponement of repairs and maintenance*. In apartment house operation, most expenses are relatively fixed; for example, property taxes and the cost of utilities and labor are not subject to much variation. In the face of declining net income—resulting from controlled rents and uncontrolled expenses—property owners tend to postpone needed repairs and maintenance. This effect lowers housing standards or results in the abandonment of property.

Rent control *decreases the supply of available housing*. Under rea-

---

[13] See Ira S. Lowry (ed.), *Rental Housing in New York City: Confronting the Crisis,* vol. 1 (New York: New York City Rand Institute, 1970).

sonably competitive conditions the price system largely determines the amount of new housing construction. If net yields on multiple-family operations decline, new rental housing is discouraged. Investors look toward more profitable investment opportunities. Rent controls in the face of variable operating expenses serve as a disincentive to construct new multiple-family housing.

Moreover, institutional *lenders hesitate to finance mortgages on rent-controlled properties.* Since the property owner is restricted in his efforts to recoup rising operating expenses, there is danger that income restrictions will affect the owner's ability to meet mortgage payments. In the face of higher operating costs and lower net yields, property owners find it difficult to finance rent-controlled properties. As a consequence, owners disinvest by postponing repairs and maintenance. Rather than dispose of their investment through normal sale and refinancing, owners may let the property expire naturally.

Rent control *places the burden of inflation on a special group: property owners.* While tenants on fixed incomes have an equitable complaint against rising prices, it is not clear that the living standard of tenants

FIGURE 8–4

Diagram Showing the Effect of Controlled Rents under an Increase in Demand

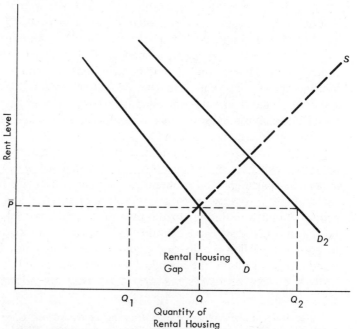

Source: William M. Shenkel, "Rent Control: A Critical Review," *Journal of Property Management,* vol. 39, no. 3 (May–June 1974), p. 105.

should be maintained at the expense of nontenant groups. As property owners face the real burden of rent control, investment in multiple-family housing tends to decline.

These relationships are shown in Figure 8–4. Starting with price P, Q number of units are supplied at the intersection of the supply and demand of rental housing. As demand increases to D_2 under rent control, Q_2 units would be demanded. But the quantity supplied does not increase: it may even decrease. With a withdrawal of housing units, Q_1 units are supplied at rent-controlled price P.

In other words, without rent control and with a fixed supply, Q_2 units would be demanded under free-market conditions, while only Q_1 units would be available. The quantity of housing between Q_1 and Q_2 represents the rental housing gap unsatisfied under controlled rents and an increase in housing demand.

The Demand for Rental Occupancy

Relative to the owner-occupancy market, rental housing is more responsive to changes in demand. As a group, tenants tend to be more informed on the housing rental market compared to the market knowledge of families in the owner-occupancy market. The rental housing market satisfies the demand for housing of a special group whose housing needs are more nearly satisfied by rental units than by owner-occupied units. To predict the potential demand for rental housing, surveys of the potential demand among selected groups must be undertaken. In a given market rental housing especially serves the needs of:

1. Newly married couples.
2. Single households.
3. Mobile workers.
4. Seasonal workers.
5. Corporate executives.
6. Professional groups.
7. Low-income groups.

The low-income groups and newly married couples may have incomes which are relatively insecure, making it difficult for them to undertake the fixed monthly mortgage and household expenses of owner-occupancy. Moreover, they may not have sufficient assets to meet down payments and closing costs. Single households, mobile workers, and seasonal workers tend to prefer rental occupancy because of their personal preferences and their job mobility requirements. Typically these groups favor short-term rental occupancy. Professionals and corporate executives favor the luxury and convenience of urban centers close to entertainment and cultural activities near their source of employment. The potential demand for rental housing would include an estimate of the rents, vacancies, and locations serving these groups.

THE COMMERCIAL REAL ESTATE MARKET

Though there are many types of commercial real estate, office space and retail space dominate. The demand for retail space is a derived demand—a demand derived from the potential volume of retail sales. In turn retail sales are dependent on the buying power of the market area population.

Office space demands are more complex. The demand focuses on space for medical and dental clinics; local service-oriented businesses, such as accounting, real estate, and insurance; and headquarters and branch corporate offices. To a large degree, the demand for retail and office space is largely determined by trends affecting central business districts and suburban development.

Central Business Districts

Historically the central business district (CBD) has played a multiple role. It has operated as a center of city and county government. It has also served as a financial community and an office center for those dependent on financial and government agencies. Originally it was the main retail center, allowing for the greatest amount of comparison shopping—and with high pedestrian traffic, stores selling convenience goods found a ready market. In small towns the CBD was typically the regional marketing center, and in larger cities the CBD showed a high concentration of cultural, entertainment, and recreational facilities.

Since the 1950s, research has disclosed disturbing trends in such cities as New York, Los Angeles, and Chicago. While formerly the central business district served multiple purposes, the dispersion of middle-income groups to the suburbs, with a corresponding movement of industry, shopping centers, and administrative and professional offices, has caused a steady decline in the CBD.[14] On its face, the market for retail space in the CBD has been affected by institutional and economic forces. The main factors limiting the market for CBD space deserve added comment.

1. *Diversified Property Ownership.* Central business districts were subdivided into relatively small lots and blocks to enable each proprietor to build for his particular purpose. Each property was constructed without regard to neighboring lots; buildings followed the architectural preferences

---

[14] Brian G. L. Berry, *Commercial Structure and Commercial Blight* (Chicago: Department of Geography, University of Chicago, 1963), pp. 179–204; and Bernard J. Frieden, *The Future of Old Neighborhoods* (Cambridge, Mass.: MIT Press, 1964), pp. 12–46.

of the owner. Today, divided ownership of buildings that follow no common architectural plan makes it difficult to assemble land for redevelopment.

Retailing, like other businesses, gains from economies of scale: a downtown retailer uses an average square foot floor area today which is much greater than the individual store space required 25 years ago. However, divided ownership makes it difficult to assemble land for expansion or for rebuilding more modern structures. Unwilling owners or owners who demand unreasonable prices encourage relocation to the suburban shopping center.

2. *Inadequate Parking.* The issue is not entirely related to the number of parking spaces. Inadequate parking encompasses traffic congestion, parking space inconvenient to main traffic generators, and parking which is expensive relative to the parking costs of shopping centers. Considered with other handicaps of the downtown area, this factor contributes to the further decline of the CBD.

3. *The Change in Population.* Virtually every city has lost population in central areas over the last generation. Between 1950 and 1970 Chicago lost 7 percent of its population; during the same period Detroit lost 18 percent, Boston 20 percent, and San Francisco 8 percent. As middle- and upper-income groups have abandoned the city, the disadvantaged, minority groups, and the unemployed have increasingly concentrated in central space, further lowering the volume of retail sales.

4. *Poor Land Utilization.* Since downtown blocks were largely developed by single proprietors, the land use pattern follows no integrated planning scheme. While main street frontages are intensively used, the center block and secondary streets are often poorly utilized.

Figure 8–5 shows poor use of space on a retail block in a medium-sized city. In these circumstances, some merchant associations (with the help of city redevelopment offices) have demolished the low-rent, older structures on secondary streets. Demolishing poorly utilized buildings provides space for rear street parking and store entrances. In many instances, retailers have discovered that more people enter from rear street entrances than from front entrances.

5. *Change in Downtown Functions.* The automobile, with its insatiable demands for space and access, has led banks and financial institutions to abandon the CBD for suburban drive-in banking facilities. Professional offices have moved to suburban office parks, and with the transfer of department stores and shopping centers to the suburbs, less pedestrian traffic has lowered the demand for retail space and decreased the number of customers for remaining businesses. Thus, the downtown has lost some of its attraction as a financial center, as an office center, and as a shopping center. Today it is abundantly clear that the downtown is not serving the same functions as it did before World War II or earlier.

FIGURE 8–5

A Downtown Central Business District Block Showing Fractionated Ownership and Poor Space Utilization

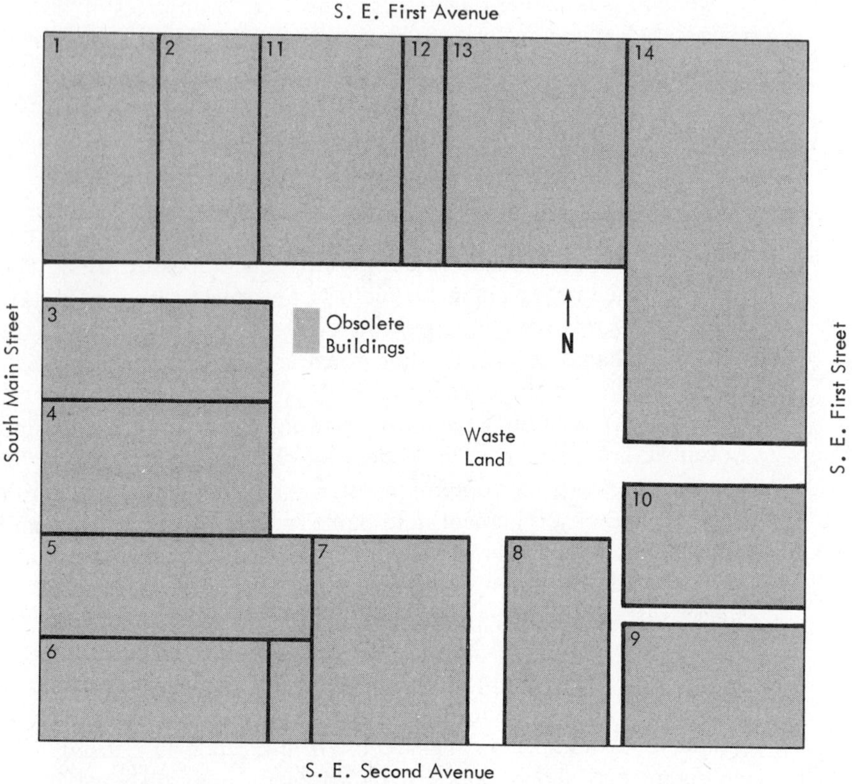

S. E. First Avenue

South Main Street

Obsolete Buildings

Waste Land

N

S. E. First Street

S. E. Second Avenue

1. Men's apparel.
2. Hardware store.
3. Vacant.
4. Billiard parlor.
5. Pawnshop.
6. Welding shop.
7. Warehouse.
8. Warehouse.
9. Bookstore.
10. Piano store.
11. Appliance store.
12. Beauty salon.
13. Women's apparel.
14. Furniture store.

Source: William M. Shenkel, "Opportunities in Downtown Real Estate," *Journal of Property Management,* vol. 27, no. 4 (Summer 1962), p. 198.

The Shopping Center Market

Not all retail operations are adapted to the shopping center. Some retailers still require a highway location, for instance, dealers in building supplies and used and new car dealers. In short, shopping centers represent specially designed retail space identified as regional, community, or neighborhood centers. The new shopping centers feature air-conditioned and heated shopping malls. Each of these shopping centers reveals different operating practices.

Types of Shopping Centers. The *regional shopping center* characteristically has at least one main department store of not less than 100,000 square feet. The total retail space generally ranges from about 300,000 to 800,000 square feet or even more. The regional center is highly comparable to a CBD. It includes stores offering general merchandise, apparel, home furnishings, services, and some recreational facilities. The principal tenants include full and junior department stores, variety stores, supermarkets, and drug stores.

The *community shopping center* depends on a junior department store or a variety store as the main tenant. The center may include apparel, furniture, banking, and professional stores. A typical community center includes retail space of about 160,000 square feet, though such centers generally range from approximately 120,000 square feet to over 200,000 square feet.

The *neighborhood shopping center* specializes in convenience goods—food, drugs, and sundries. In addition, personal service businesses, such as laundries, dry cleaners, barbershops, and shoe repair shops, are found in neighborhood centers. A supermarket usually serves as the main tenant. Typically the space available for stores approximates 50,000 square feet, but it may extend from 36,000 to 70,000 square feet.[15]

The main competitive advantage of shopping centers lies in their proprietary operation. Each store must participate in a merchants' association that sponsors shopping center promotional activities. The architecture and signs of each store must conform to the shopping center design. Space is arranged to maximize convenience and create an attractive appearance. Their more convenient location, parking facilities, and high degree of access account for the popularity of shopping centers in comparison with CBD space.

Estimating the Demand for Commercial Space. Estimating the demand for a shopping center starts, *first,* with identification of the trade market area. Although some empirical data may help identify the geographic area to be served by the proposed shopping center, the estimate turns largely on the intuitive judgment of the researcher. The type of center proposed and its access and physical location with respect to competing shopping areas largely determine the potential trade market area. *Second,* an estimate of the present and projected population helps in gauging the retail sales potential. *Third,* given the population of the trade market area, the per capita income of that population suggests the total amount spent annually on goods and services. Consumer expenditure data contained in *Sales Management Magazine* and the U.S. Retail Census help to establish these projections. *Fourth,* a proportion of the total amount of retail sales in the trade market area is tentatively allocated to the pro-

---

[15] *The Dollars and Cents of Shopping Centers* (Washington, D.C.: Urban Land Institute). 1975.

FIGURE 8–6

A Shopping Mall Trade Area Showing Primary and Secondary Trade Areas

LA CROSSE RETAIL TRADE AREA

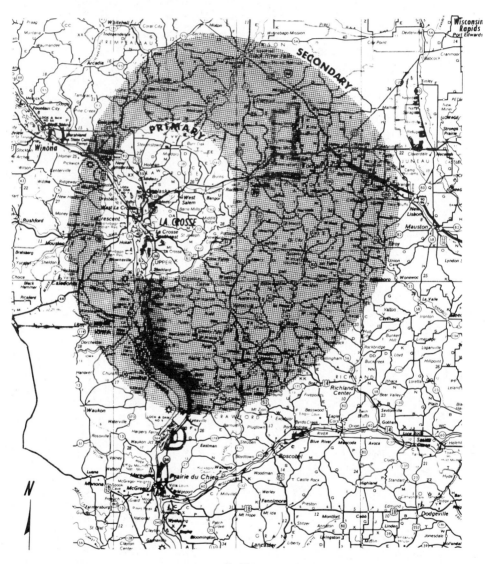

Y - 12

Typically 80 percent of shopping center patronage will come from the estimated primary trade market area.

Source: Map furnished by Mr. Norbert F. Wall, President, Larry Smith & Company, Ltd., Chicago, Illinois, Shopping Center Consultants.

posed center. The estimate, based as it is on personal experience and familiarity with shopping center economics, indicates the potential demand for shopping center space. The end result is to forecast probable retail sales volume by categories for the proposed center. Given the potential sales volume, the estimated annual gross rent and operating expenses indicate the potential annual net income. Figure 8–6 shows an example of a shopping center trade market area estimated for this purpose.

Office Buildings

Like shopping centers and new forms of housing, such as the condominium, office buildings are showing important national trends. At one extreme is the trend toward general-purpose buildings, illustrated by the John Hancock office building in Chicago, which includes retail, office, parking, and residential space. At the other extreme is the growing movement toward executive office parks in the suburbs, strategically located on main limited-access highways. Office structures range from corporate one-tenant buildings, serving as the national or international main office of a corporation, to multiple-tenant buildings which house the offices of a number of concerns and individuals.

In the latter type, the office space is described in terms of the net rentable area. The net rentable area refers to space under lease to tenants. The definition excludes hallways, stairways, the lobby, and other public areas. Some office buildings are highly specialized, for example, medical-dental clinics.

For other office types, the demand and supply of office space relate closely to the local economy. Office buildings constructed in metropolitan areas must be surrounded by compatible buildings with convenient access. Further, federal, state, county, and city offices create a demand for office space for services and businesses that have frequent contact with public agencies. Office districts capitalize on tenants who require frequent person-to-person contacts with other business, financial, and professional offices. Newer buildings depart from the old alphabet shapes in favor of office towers with open landscaped grounds, modern lobbies, elevators, and narrow corridors.

INDUSTRIAL PROPERTY

Unlike commercial establishments, whose demand for real estate is derived from retail sales, industrial firms demand space that decreases production costs and enables them to serve customers better. Accordingly, industry demands space that is:

1.   Near the source of raw materials.
2.   Close to product markets.

3.   In a favorable labor market area, judged in terms of skill, training, and wage rates.
4.   Served with a high degree of amenities.

The Demand for Industrial Space

The first category includes industries that locate near the source of bulky raw materials from mines, oil fields, forests, and the like. For the manufacture of products that lose weight in processing, some industries must seek locations that minimize the cost of transporting bulky, heavy raw materials.

The converse is true for industries that prefer locations near their product market. Breweries, for example, which add weight in manufacturing, reduce transportation costs by locating near centers of high per capita beer consumption. Industries with a high level of customer services—the printing industry, for example—benefit by locating near customers. The competitive advantage of locating near customers is that this enables retailers to reduce inventories.

Prefabricated metal industries capitalize on the availability of highly skilled labor. New Britain, Connecticut, which concentrates on hardware manufacturing, illustrates this type of industry. Similarly, the auto manufacturing companies of Detroit and the aircraft manufacturing and accessory industries found in Wichita, Kansas, Seattle, and the Los Angeles area are labor-oriented firms. The availability of a particular level of skilled labor creates a local demand for space by industries that need specialized labor.

The next category comprises the "footloose" industries that deal in highly valuable, low-weight products, for example, the electronics industry, jewelry manufacturing, and instrument making. Plant owners and managers in this group prefer locations that appeal to scientific, professional, and highly skilled workers. Since such industries are relatively free to select locations that have only nominal differences in transportation costs, or to put it differently, since transportation costs represent such a small proportion of the product cost of these industries, they seek locations with comparative advantages in culture, recreation, and education.

To satisfy the needs of these main categories of industrial land users, the supply of industrial land may be similarly classified into special groups.

The Supply of Industrial Land

Industry established before World War I showed a tendency to site along railroad lines. As a city developed, industries preferred sites in the industrial corridors paralleling the railroad. Constructing multiple-story buildings near the railroad economized on the surface movement of industrial raw materials and products. Today the supply of industrial land is largely concentrated in (1) *centrally located space,* (2) *organized industrial parks,* and (3) *rural acreage.* Within each of these categories land may be stratified into additional subgroups.

While land is subject to much variation, centrally located space is often associated with inadequate parking, a relatively high per unit price, and division into relatively small areas. Such land is ordinarily served with a high level of public utilities and services—municipal water, sewers, police and fire protection, and street maintenance. Centrally located sites quite often have limited parking and are not adapted to future expansion. Truck-maneuvering space is limited, if available. Such central space is utilized by distribution firms, warehouses, and industries that must locate near customers.

Because of the deficiencies of centrally located space, the organized industrial district, which is under proprietary control, has been adapted to a select group of compatible industries. Private developers organizing an industrial district offer land only to industries that are compatible with one another. Many industrial districts favor warehouses, distribution facilities, and "clean" industries.

The buildings in industrial districts are subject to architectural approval, and each site must have adequate space for off-street parking and truck maneuvering. Land uses must conform to standards of the industrial park that minimize noise, smoke emission, outside storage, and any use regarded as incompatible with local industries. The sites are generally restricted to relatively small areas of less than 20 acres; they are expensive, but they dominate the most desirable locations at interstate highway intersections on main routes of transportation.

The popularity of industrial parks lies partly in the services they render to industrial occupants. Zoning, construction, planning, and even convention and recreational facilities are often supplied by the industrial park management.

There remains the industrial acreage in the suburbs and rural areas. Industries that have the resources to develop their own utility systems, that require unusually large acreages for isolation or for later expansion, and that must locate near sources of relatively low-cost labor are in the market for outlying industrial acreage, if the site is reasonably accessible by highway and rail. Industries that require 50 or more acres prefer these locations because the land is available at a relatively low cost per acre.

SUMMARY

Critics of the urban environment contend that urban areas are poorly adapted to human beings. Urban authorities such as Doxiadis believe in integrating human and natural resources to offset population increases, the growing rate of urbanization, and the inevitable ecological problems with their sociopolitical impact on human life. The French geographer Jean Gottmann recommends that the city be abandoned as a unit of planning in favor of regional planning to compensate for the pending decline of urban areas.

The problem arises since 75.2 percent of our population live in urban communities. The U.S. Census Bureau defines 248 urban places that hold 58.3 percent of the population. The urbanizing market forces include the trend toward high-density land usage, technological innovations, rising living standards, changes in consumer preferences, and public policies favoring urbanization.

The economist explains growing urban areas as a function of market forces. Urban locations create economies not realized in nonurban centers. In the view of the economist, land tends to be allocated to its maximum use by buyers who tend to offer land prices equal to the present worth of the future benefits of landownership. Centrally located land assumes a high-density use and a relatively high per unit value which is offset by lower transportation costs. Outlying land tends to assume lower per unit values which move opposite to increased transportation costs.

The national housing market is affected by changes in per capital disposable income, net household formation (which nationally is continuing to increase), the migration of households, housing demolitions, and the price of housing relative to other prices. The demand for housing is related to changes in the housing supply, namely, new construction, vacancies, demolitions, and the conversion of houses to nonhousing use. New public housing construction and mobile homes complete the housing supply equation. Of the 69.337 million dwellings occupied in 1973, 64.4 percent were owner-occupied.

To estimate the demand for local housing, housing consultants refer to local housing market indicators: building permits, the number of new subdivisions, deed recordings, mortgage recordings, and vacancy surveys. These data are supplemented by state and local reports on employment, per capita income, and retail sales.

Housing filtering refers to the tendency of housing to filter downward from one income group to the next lower income group in conjunction with declining prices or rents. The housing filtering process works imperfectly. The supply of houses filtering downward to lower income groups is inadequate for current needs. Moreover, housing prices for older dwellings do not always decline. Finally, the preference for established neighborhoods prevents some occupants from moving to new housing.

Rent control leads to underutilized housing. It encourages owners to postpone needed repairs and maintenance. To the extent that rent control without corresponding control of expenses lowers net income, the construction of new rental housing is discouraged. Lenders are reluctant to finance housing with controlled rents. In short, the burden of inflation is placed on the property owner.

Certain groups show a strong preference for rental occupancy. Among these groups are newly married couples, single households, and low-income households. Certain types of employment also tend to favor rental occupancy.

The demand for commercial space concentrates in central business districts and shopping centers. Most cities show a downward trend in central business district activity—and for several reasons: (1) diversified property ownership, (2) inadequate parking, (3) the change in population, (4) poor land utilization, and (5) the changing role of the CBD.

In contrast, shopping centers—regional, community, and neighborhood —have increased with growing suburbanization. The regional center will have one main department store of not less than 100,000 square feet. The community center includes a junior department store and a typical retail space of about 160,000 square feet. The neighborhood center, specializing in convenience goods, ordinarily includes a supermarket as the main tenant and a typical retail area approximating 50,000 square feet. To estimate the demand for commercial space, identify the trade area, population, per capita income, and potential retail sales of the center.

The office building manager concentrates on marketing the net rentable area—the space under lease to tenants—which excludes hallways, stairways, the lobby, and other public areas.

The demand for industrial property is found among industries that prefer locations near raw materials, the product market, specialized labor, and communities with a high degree of amenities. The space catering to this market includes centrally located space, sites in organized industrial parks, and rural acreage.

REVIEW QUESTIONS

1. In your view, what is "The Urban Problem"?
2. Why do urban economists minimize the importance of city boundaries?
3. Explain why the population tends to concentrate increasingly in urban areas.
4. Discuss five factors that explain long-run changes in urban communities.
5. In what sense are urban areas a function of market forces?
6. Explain the determinants of housing demand in the national market.
7. What are the main supply determinants of housing? Explain thoroughly.
8. What housing market indicators would you study to predict the potential demand for local housing?
9. What factors are considered by the Federal Housing Administration in making a housing market analysis?
10. Why has housing filtering worked imperfectly?
11. Explain the impact of rent control on the quality and quantity of housing.
12. What economic and social groups are attracted to rental occupancy?

13. Describe the main factors that tend to limit the market for central business district space.
14. What are the main characteristics of the different types of shopping centers?
15. What steps would you follow in projecting the demand for a new shopping center?
16. How would you define the net rentable area of an office building?
17. Identify four locational preferences of industry.
18. Describe three main categories of industrial land and their characteristics.

SELECTED REFERENCES

Beaton, William R., and Bond, Robert J. *Real Estate,* chap. 20. Pacific Palisades, Calif.: Goodyear Publishing Company, Inc., 1976.

Brown, Douglas M. *Introduction to Urban Economics,* chap. 11. New York: Academic Press, Inc., 1974.

Doxiadis, Constantinos A. *Ekistics,* introduction. New York: Oxford University Press, 1968.

Gottmann, Jean. *Megalopolis,* chap. 4. New York: Twentieth Century Fund, 1961.

Mills, Edwin S. *Urban Economics,* chap. 6. Glenview, Ill.: Scott, Foresman and Co., 1972.

Smith, Wallace F. *Urban Development,* chap. 7. Berkeley: University of California Press, 1975.

Weimer, Arthur M.; Hoyt, Homer; and Bloom, George F. *Real Estate,* chap. 9. 6th ed. New York: Ronald Press Co., 1972.

9

Real Estate Valuation

After reading this chapter, you should be familiar with the following points:

1 The role of appraisal organizations in qualifying appraisers.
2 The significance of an appraisal code of ethics.
3 The meaning of market value.
4 The elements of the valuation process.
5 The organization of an appraisal report.

THE VALUATION of real estate represents one of the more technical real estate operations. Before 1933, there were virtually no appraisal standards that guided the valuation of real estate for real estate mortgages, the purchase and sale of real estate, and investment or property taxation. The high rate of mortgage foreclosures during the 1930s encouraged the formation of such organizations as the American Institute of Real Estate Appraisers and the Society of Real Estate Appraisers to establish appraisal standards and to teach appraisal techniques. In part, the high rate of mortgage foreclosures was caused by the absence of trained appraisers and a common system of valuation based on market value.

Today, the professional appraiser must have a broad real estate knowledge that includes:

Financial mathematics.	Local real estate markets.
Real estate economics.	Real estate construction.
Real estate market analysis.	Real estate finance.
The characteristics of real estate.	Real estate law.

While appraisers typically are not specialists in all of these subjects, they must have sufficient knowledge of the material in each subject which is relevant to estimating value. In addition, considerable emphasis is placed upon appraisal experience. Typically beginning appraisers work as assistants to experienced appraisers for three years or more before they are recognized as "journeymen" appraisers.

The scope of appraisal activity may be indicated by the number of times a single-family dwelling may be appraised over its economic life. If the dwelling is financed with a loan from a bank or a savings and loan association, it will be appraised by a person trained to value single-family dwellings for mortgage purposes. Moreover, the local property tax assessor must value the property for property tax purposes, using special techniques adapted to mass appraising. The same house may also be valued for several other purposes:

State inheritance taxes.	Purchase or sale.
Federal estate taxes.	Condemnation.
Bankruptcy proceedings.	Personal net income taxes.
FHA or VA loans.	

Similarly commercial, industrial, and farm property will be repeatedly valued for a number of purposes. Add to this list the state, local, and federal agencies that employ appraisers as part of their agency function. Most state highway departments, for instance, employ a staff of appraisers to acquire rights-of-way. Many federal agencies, such as the Department of Housing and Urban Development and the Corps of Engineers, hire appraisers as part of their permanent staff. In further illustration, the Department of the Interior and its many agencies, especially the Fish and Wildlife Service, the National Park Service, and the Bureau of Indian Affairs, maintain a staff of highly trained appraisers. As a result of these demands, both private and public organizations actively sponsor appraisal training programs that concentrate on various appraisal specialties.

APPRAISAL ORGANIZATIONS

The trade associations that offer education and training which lead to various industry-recognized designations, such as the MAI (Member of the American Real Estate Appraisal Institute), include:

The American Institute of Real Estate Appraisers
The Society of Real Estate Appraisers
The National Association of Assessing Officers
The American Right of Way Association
The American Society of Farm Managers and Rural Appraisers
The National Association of Independent Fee Appraisers
The American Society of Appraisers

As their names imply, some of the appraisal organizations tend to concentrate on specialized properties. Members of the American Right of Way Association confine their educational activities to the appraisal of rights-of-way for highways, power lines, pipelines, and other purposes. Appraisal for property tax purposes dominates the activities of members of the National Association of Assessing Officers. Members certified by the American Society of Farm Managers and Rural Appraisers are qualified to appraise farm and rural properties. The American Society of Appraisers includes members who appraise not only real estate but also personal property—gems, coin and stamp collections, furniture, paintings, and the like.

Membership Requirements

Members of these organizations may use designations signifying that they have met certain minimum experience and educational standards of the organization. A member of the Society of Real Estate Appraisers holding the SREA designation

> is a professional member who, in addition to the appraisal of all types of real estate interests and ownerships, has demonstrated his competency in the areas of project feasibility analysis, individual investment analysis and the ability to provide a range of consulting services to clients on a varied number of real estate assignments.

The other appraisal organizations have similar designations representing different specialties and degrees of qualifications established by the membership. While appraisal and experience standards vary among appraisal organizations, generally the membership requirements include the successful completion of examinations, attendance at specified courses, minimum full-time appraisal experience of three to five years, and demonstration of appraisal ability.

Appraisal Code of Ethics

Moreover, membership in an appraisal organization requires that the member observe a code of ethics. The code of ethics guides the professional conduct of the organization's members and protects the public from gross negligence and incompetence. For instance, the code of ethics of the Society of Real Estate Appraisers provides that each member shall:

> . . . Accept only those appraisal and analysis assignments for which he has adequate time, facilities, and technical ability to complete in a competent professional manner, and in which he has no unrevealed present or contemplated future interest.
> . . . Render properly developed, unbiased and objective value opinions, and render properly developed, unbiased and objective analyses.
> . . . Prepare an adequate written appraisal for each real estate appraisal assignment accepted, and prepare an adequate written analysis for each real estate analysis assignment accepted.

The first item ensures that the appraiser accepts only assignments on properties in which he is experienced and in which he has no undisclosed interest. In every instance the appraiser must prepare a written report giving his analysis of market value.

In such states as Florida and Pennsylvania, appraisers must have a state real estate license. For example, to act as an appraiser in Florida, a person must be licensed by the Florida Real Estate Commission. In that state real estate appraisers are included among the persons who must hold a valid real estate license.

> Every person who shall, in this state, for another, and for a compensation or valuable consideration directly or indirectly paid or promised, expressly or impliedly, or with an intent to collect or receive a compensation or valuable consideration therefor, appraise, auction, sell, exchange, buy or rent, or offer, attempt or agree to appraise, auction or negotiate the sale, exchange, purchase, or rental of any real property, or any interest in or concerning the same, including mineral rights or leases. . . .[1]

---

[1] *Florida Real Estate Handbook* (Winter Park, Fla.: Florida Real Estate Commission, 1968), p. 4.

Although a salesperson's or broker's license is required to appraise property in Florida, the qualifying examination does not necessarily insure the minimum knowledge required of a qualified appraiser. Therefore, in Florida appraisers must comply with the real estate license law and also work toward a trade association designation.

MARKET VALUE

The unmodified term *value* means the power of one good to command other goods in exchange. Price is value expressed in money. To have value a commodity must be relatively scarce—not a free good, such as air—and it must have utility. Utility is the quality of a good that creates satisfaction or minimizes dissatisfaction. Hence, real property, assuming utility, is valuable because of its scarcity in relation to effective demand. In one sense, the value of real estate is a function of its utility and its relative supply.

Market Value Defined

The term *market value* has gained a very special meaning for appraisal purposes. A clearer understanding of market value may be gained by reviewing several commonly accepted definitions. For example, one of the more popular definitions states:

> Market value is the highest price in terms of money which a property will bring in a competitive and open market under all conditions requisite to a fair sale, the buyer and seller each acting prudently, knowledgeably and assuming the price is not affected by undue stimulus.[2]

Some authorities prefer a shorter definition:

> Market value is the price at which a willing seller would sell and a willing buyer would buy neither being under pressure.

Market value contemplates (1) value in exchange to persons generally, as distinguished from value in use to a particular person, (2) the marketability of property as a final test of its value, and (3) the value of the highest legal use to which the property may be adapted.

Several assumptions are applied in the term *market value:*

1. Many buyers and sellers, such that the decision to buy or sell on the part of a single buyer or seller does not affect the price.
2. Buyers and sellers who have a reasonable knowledge of the market.
3. A standardized product.
4. Freedom of buyers and sellers to enter and leave the market.

---

[2] Byrl N. Boyce (ed.) *Real Estate Appraisal Terminology* (Cambridge, Mass.: Ballinger Publishing Co., 1975), p. 137.

It is fairly clear that the market value definition forces the appraiser to think in terms of *constructive* value. That is, the appraiser must "construct" a hypothetical value as if the idealized conditions of pure competition prevailed.

Noncompetitive Market

Yet in reality the real estate market does not conform to the criteria for a purely competitive market. For example, buyers and sellers of single-family dwellings are sufficiently few for the sale of a house to affect the offering and asking prices of nearby houses subsequently placed on the market. Since there are relatively few buyers and sellers for a given property, their decisions do affect real estate prices. This situation contrasts to that which prevails in the stock market or in the market for such commodities as wheat and eggs, where the number of buyers and sellers is so large that their individual decisions have little bearing on market price.

It is also apparent that buyers and sellers have a highly imperfect knowledge of the market. The average seller usually enters the market at infrequent periods: five or ten years or more, in the case of single-family dwellings. The familiarity of these buyers and sellers with prices is handicapped by the absence of a central marketplace that reports real estate prices in terms that the average buyer and seller can understand. Moreover, the technical features of real estate, its legal characteristics, construction, and current condition, among other things, call for specialized knowledge that the average buyer and seller do not possess.

In addition real estate is so highly differentiated that it is difficult for buyers and sellers to make price comparisons. Such a problem does not exist for highly standardized products, such as eggs and automobiles, whose prices may be readily compared from one unit to another. The lay person has difficulty in making price comparisons among different parcels of real estate of even the same classification.

Add to this the difficulty of entering and leaving the real estate market. A builder may not withdraw his unsold houses from the market pending a more favorable market for his products. The expensiveness of real estate and the dependence of the buyer on the availability of credit—on terms which he can afford—limit the free entry of the buyer into the market. These factors result in a highly imperfect market that varies considerably from the competitive ideal assumed by the market value definition.

Appraisers facing this dilemma observe the market value definition by appraising property in terms of *the most probable sales price*. In estimating value, it is implicitly understood that the property will be offered for sale on the open market under conventional terms common to the locality. In practice, therefore, the appraiser submits an estimate of value which in his judgment will be realized if the property is offered for sale in a reasonable time under the usual market circumstances. So while the market value standard is followed, in practice it relates closely to the most probable sales price. The assumptions underlying the definition of

FIGURE 9–1

The Concept of Market Value for Appraisal Purposes

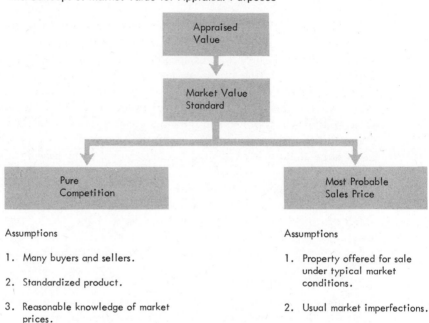

Assumptions

1. Many buyers and sellers.

2. Standardized product.

3. Reasonable knowledge of market prices.

4. Free entry to and exit from the market.

Assumptions

1. Property offered for sale under typical market conditions.

2. Usual market imperfections.

market value and the most probable sales price are illustrated in Figure 9–1.

Other Value Definitions

While appraisers must follow the market value standard, technical terms are used to refer to appraisals undertaken for certain specific purposes. The more common terms include *highest and best use, assessed values, just compensation,* and *insurable value.* The last three terms refer to appraisals undertaken for specific purposes.

The Highest and Best Use. Next to market value, the concept of highest and best use is probably the most important appraisal term. Professional appraisal organizations have defined the term as:

That reasonable and probable use that will support the highest present value, as defined, as of the effective date of the appraisal.

Alternatively, that use, from among reasonably probable and legal alternative uses, found to be physically possible, appropriately supported, financially feasible, and which results in highest land value.[3]

It will be observed that the definition refers to land use and not buildings. For instance, a corner site occupied by a single-family dwelling might more appropriately be improved with a two-story walk-up apartment. In these circumstances the property would not be appraised as a single-family dwelling site with a single-family dwelling but as a walk-up apartment site. If the site is underutilized as a single-family dwelling, the existing building would probably detract from the site value, since the building would have to be torn down for development to the highest and best use.

To follow this valuation principle, it should not be concluded that the highest and best use always means the present use, the use permitted under the present zoning, or the use indicated by the adjoining property. In the first instance, recall that land uses constantly undergo transition. A building appropriate 25 years ago may be inappropriate today. A study of the site must be undertaken to determine the highest and best use under current market conditions.

While zoning controls the legal use, it is also true that zoning may change. Planning and zoning officials frequently allow changes to reflect the present urban market. Although this is a subjective determination, in estimating the highest and best use the appraiser must give his opinion on the probability of a zoning change. Likewise, because adjoining property is used as a pasture, it does not follow that the site under valuation has a similar use. Each appraisal requires a separate determination of the highest and best use.

Assessed Values. In virtually every community real estate is subject to annual property taxes. To calculate the annual property tax, real estate must be valued by a representative of local government who assesses it for local property tax purposes. While state law varies considerably, the assessment is generally based on the concept of true value, just value, just and fair value, or some other term considered equivalent to market value.

In Florida the assessor is required to estimate the *just valuation* of property subject to property taxation. A list of the criteria he or she must follow shows their similarity with the criteria used to estimate market value.

In arriving at just valuation as required under §4, Art. VII of the state constitution, the tax assessor shall take into consideration the following factors:

---

[3] Ibid., p. 107.

1. The present cash value of the property.
2. The highest and best use to which the property can be expected to be put in the immediate future and the present use of the property.
3. The location of said property.
4. The quantity or size of said property.
5. The cost of said property and the present replacement value of any improvements thereon.
6. The condition of said property.
7. The income from said property.
8. The net proceeds of the sale of the property, as received by the seller, after deduction of all of the usual and reasonable fees and costs of the sale, including the costs and expenses of financing.[4]

Assessed values usually vary from market value in some areas because the assessor is directed to base his assessed value on some proportion of market value, say, 50 percent, 40 percent, or 25 percent. Thus, a $30,000 house may have an assessed value of $12,000 in a state that enforces property tax assessments at 40 percent of the market value. As a general rule, the impossibility of reviewing the values of every property each year causes assessed values to lag behind market value.

Just Compensation. Questions over just compensation arise in the taking of private property in the public interest. The acquisition of real estate for public buildings, highways, and other public purposes falls under the Fifth Amendment, which states in part: "Nor shall private property be taken for public use without just compensation." The constitutions of most states have similar provisions. The courts have generally interpreted just compensation as meaning market value. While court interpretations vary, one leading decision defines just compensation as:

> What the property is worth or will sell for as between one who wants to purchase and one who wants to sell. This is what is understood by the words *market value*—what it is worth or what it will sell for in the market.[5]

Under this view, just compensation, although defined in terms of market value, refers to a special type of value encountered in the exercise of eminent domain.

The estimate of just compensation may encompass the other elements of value unique to eminent domain appraising: severance damage and consequential damage. Though state law varies on this point, property owners may be entitled to severance damages only if part of their property is taken for public purposes. Severance damages refer to the loss in value to the remaining property.

---

[4] *Florida Statute Annotated,* vol. 10, secs. 192.01 to 200.

[5] Ross D. Netherton, *Control of Highway Access* (Madison: University of Wisconsin Press, 1963), pp. 315–16.

Assume that a property owner is left with a 30 foot by 40 foot triangular parcel, as shown in Figure 9–2. Severance damages would be calculated as follows:

Value of land *before* the taking............... $20,000
Value of land *after* the taking................. 1,000
Just compensation........................... $19,000
Just compensation is allocated between:
  (1) Value of part taken, determined
     by appraisal........................... $15,000
  (2) Severance damages (just compensa-
     tion, less value of part taken).......... $ 4,000

Because the property remaining has limited use *after* the taking of the right-of-way, the owner is entitled to the loss in value for the 30 foot by 40 foot parcel remaining. Severance values follow because the remaining triangular area is too small and too irregular in shape to have value.

Consequential damages, though defined differently by state law, generally refer to the loss in the value of adjoining property *not a part* of the taking. Airport noise and a change of street grade which leaves a house above the street level are typical examples of consequential damage. These illustrations suggest that while just compensation is defined in terms of market value, various technical and legal points give this type of value a special meaning and application.

Insurable Value. Insurable value refers to value which is ordinarily equal to the value of destructible portions of property that is subject to loss in the case of fire or other catastrophes. Insurable value is stated in the insurance policy and is usually based on the reproduction costs of the structure less physical depreciation and certain exclusions. Ordinarily

FIGURE 9–2

An Illustration of Severance Damages

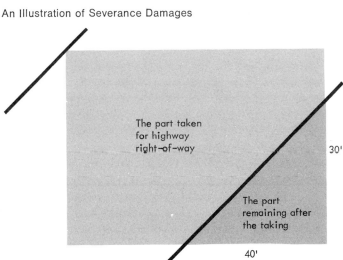

The part taken for highway right-of-way

30'

The part remaining after the taking

40'

the exclusions would include the foundation, the walls, and portions of the property that would not be destroyed by catastrophic events. Again, the concept of insurable value refers to a special-purpose appraisal which must conform to legal and contract requirements. Insurable value is not equal to market value.

The lay person will encounter certain other value terms of questionable merit. Such terms as *sentimental value, value to the owner, use value,* and *historical value* are based on highly subjective criteria. As a consequence, these terms are rarely employed by appraisers. Most of the professional appraisal effort is directed to estimating the market value.

THE VALUATION PROCESS

The valuation process refers to the orderly analysis and presentation of facts to estimate market value. While each appraisal varies according to the property type and the purpose of the appraisal, generally the appraisal will follow five steps, as illustrated in Figure 9–3:

FIGURE 9–3

The Appraisal Process

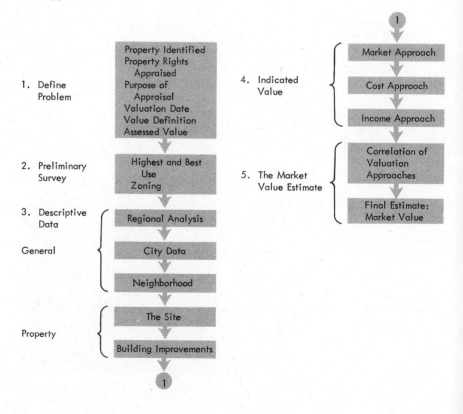

1. Definition of the problem.
2. The preliminary survey.
3. Descriptive data.
4. The indicated value by the market approach, the cost approach, and the income approach.
5. The market value estimate.

Definition of the Problem

Under this step, the appraiser identifies the property appraised by address and legal description. Usually the full legal description is required to identify the property without question.

The property rights appraised refer to the interest to be appraised, such as the fee simple interest, the leasehold interest, the leased fee, or the fee simple, subject to use restrictions, easements, or other limitations on private ownership and use. Since market value may be affected by use restrictions, the interest appraised must be clearly identified. For instance, title to a single-family dwelling may be subject to a 20-foot easement for a pipeline across the front yard. The terms of the easement may affect the placement of trees, landscaping, a garage, or a fence. Or consider a deed restriction that prohibits construction of a building "north of the creek," which is another use restriction that may bear materially on market value. Title documents must often be verified to identify the interest to be valued.

The purpose of the appraisal largely controls the data presented and their organization. If the appraisal is directed to estimating just compensation, the value must follow state or federal eminent domain law. If the problem is to estimate market value for property tax purposes, the appraisal report must include data required by state statutes. In other words the purpose of the appraisal largely controls the selection of evidence offered in support of market value.

The valuation date, the definition of value, and the assessed value complete the part of the appraisal process falling under identification of the problem. The valuation date is especially important. Usually the valuation date will be the date of inspection—not the date the report is signed or delivered. With the specific date of valuation identified, the appraiser is not responsible for subsequent and often unpredictable events unknown at the time of valuation. Legal requirements will often specify a valuation at some earlier date which will restrict the appraisal to the valuation data obtainable at the time of valuation.

The Preliminary Survey

The preliminary survey supports the estimate of the time and effort needed to complete the appraisal assignment. As part of this estimate, the appraiser arrives at his view of the highest and best use. At the date of valuation there will be only one optimum use of the property, which may not be its use or the use of adjoining property at that time.

The preliminary survey will consider the present zoning and other land use restrictions that must be observed. This step helps identify the type of data which will dominate the final estimate of value: the cost of construction in the case of insurable value; probably income data for the appraisal of a 100-unit apartment building; and usually prices of similar property for the valuation of a single-family dwelling appraised for eminent domain purposes.

Descriptive Data

As shown in Figure 9–3, descriptive data include general information about the region, the city, and the neighborhood. With this background the appraiser then considers the site and buildings, describing the main features as they bear on the opinion of value. The descriptive data contribute to the logic of the appraisal process.

General Data. The region varies, depending on the appraisal problem. It may be a multistate area in the case of a valuation report on a 500,000-square-foot industrial plant, or it may be confined to a local community if the appraisal is on a neighborhood shopping center. In covering regional and city data, the appraiser describes data that seem significant to the problem. For an appraisal of an industrial plant that manufactures farm implements, data would be selected to show trends in agriculture, regional population, and employment that bear on the demand for agricultural products. The experience of the appraiser largely determines the content of regional analysis; only points essential to the valuation are described.

The appraiser interprets the data to identify trends favorable or unfavorable to the property value. He or she converts changes in population, income, employment, and other series to percentage changes to show relative growth or decline. In presenting regional and city data, the appraiser avoids unwarranted bias and overstatement of facts. The appraiser does more than merely quote published chamber of commerce data. The analysis includes both favorable and unfavorable factors; the analysis should represent an unbiased interpretation of regional and city appraisal data.

A neighborhood is a community of homogeneous inhabitants or land uses. Neighborhoods may be delineated by streets, highways, or natural boundaries, such as rivers, hills, or other geographic features. The neighborhood description deals with (1) physical characteristics, (2) economic trends, and (3) community facilities. The attention given each item varies according to the appraisal problem.

In covering physical data for an industrial appraisal, surrounding land uses, distance to markets, transportation, and utility systems would be heavily emphasized. In a neighborhood of single-family dwellings, the distance to shopping, employment, recreation, drainage, surrounding property values, and the present age and condition of typical houses would be considered. Indeed the appraiser's interpretation of neighborhood trends may be a controlling factor in his final estimate of value.

Property Data. The preceding material provides a background for the description of the property appraised and the value evidence leading to the final estimate of market value. Appraisal logic next requires a description of the site and of the buildings and other improvements to the site.

The site is considered with all of its features, that is, the topography, soil, area, frontage, drainage, and other factors indicating its suitability for agricultural, commercial, industrial, or residential use. A listing of the factors to consider in the analysis of a commercial site shows the details important to a site description.[6]

1. *Physical attributes*

   Size

   Shape

   Dimensions

   Topography

   Soil and subsoil conditions

   Drainage

   Utilities

   Access

   Man-made improvements

   Proximity of hazards and/or nuisances

2. *Economic factors*

   Prices of comparable sites

   Units of comparison or marketability

   Availability of financing

   Market competition

   Tax burden

   Utilities and services costs

   Rentals

3. *Legal-governmental factors*

   Legal description

   Title data

   Restrictions or easements

---

[6] H. Grady Stebbins, *A Guide to Narrative Appraisal Reporting on Income Producing Properties* (Washington, D.C.: Society of Real Estate Appraisers, 1970), pp. 9–10.

Deed restrictions

Zoning and other public land use and space controls

Taxation and assessment policies

Municipal services

4. *Locational attributes*

Relation to surrounding land-use patterns

Access to and egress from desired and needed facilities

Transportation facilities

Orientation

Compatibility with surrounding uses (including hazards and/or nuisances)

Site analysis will vary considerably according to the property type. In the case of industrial property, for example, the load-bearing quality of the soil, access to transportation, and the availability of industrial utilities are among the factors that would receive more emphasis.

Building Description

In the same manner the description of the building and improvements would be sufficiently detailed to support conclusions on the value of the building. An itemized analysis of the building's structural components, condition, quality of construction, and more significant, functional adequacy would be presented in considerable detail. Again the type of property appraised would govern the form and detail of the report on the structural and equipment components of the building under valuation. In each instance, the report explains the construction and condition of the exterior walls, the foundation, the roof and the interior walls, the floors and ceilings. The detail reported on building equipment and facilities would vary according to the structure.

Indicated Value

The appraisal process rests on the assumption that value is indicated by (1) recent sales of similar property, (2) capitalization of net income, and (3) the cost of production, less depreciation. These three sets of valuation evidence are referred to as the market, income, and cost approaches. Usually, depending on the property appraised and the circumstances of the market, one approach dominates over the others. For example, valuation of a 75-year-old single-family dwelling is best determined by an analysis of comparable sales. The cost and depreciation estimates of such an old building are less reliable than is an analysis of sales of like property. On the other hand, the capitalization of net income would probably be the best means of valuing a ten-year-old, 100-unit apartment building. There are other instances in which the cost approach is preferred: industrial properties, public buildings, and other special structures.

Moreover, in unusual economic circumstances the appraisal process requires that the appraiser apply the valuation approach most relevant under the given circumstances. If he considers recent sales to be depressed because of unusually high local unemployment, which is viewed as temporary, or if costs of production and land values are unusually high because of a temporary shortage of housing, reliance on the three approaches will permit the appraiser to weigh the approach that gives him the most reliable indication of value. A separate discussion of these three valuation approaches shows how the appraiser arrives at his final estimate of value.

The Market Approach. In this instance, it is reasoned that market value is indicated by a comparison of recent sales of like property. It is reasoned further that recent sales of similar properties on the open market are a strong indication of the most probable sales price as of the date of valuation. In making such an analysis, the appraiser considers financing terms, the physical characteristics of the property sold in relation to those of the property appraised, adjustments for the time between the date of sale and the date of valuation, and other factors that bear on current market value. The indicated value reached by the market approach is a derived value; it is derived from prices of similar property sold in the open market.

In practice, an appraiser usually has knowledge of numerous sales of similar property. Suppose, for example, that some 25 recent sales are considered for comparison with a three-bedroom, two-bath dwelling with a double carport. From the 25 sales, three may be selected for inclusion in the report. Ideally the three sales would be three-bedroom, two-bath dwellings with double carports, sold within a few weeks of the appraisal, and similar in age, construction, style, and condition to the property appraised. Actually the appraisal of each transaction calls for some interpretation of how it relates to the value of the property appraised, since properties sold are never identical to the subject property.

The Income Approach. Under the income approach, it is held that market value is equal to the present worth of discounted future income. Hence, the value evidence following this reasoning deals with annual *gross income,* annual *expenses of operation,* and the rate of capitalization. The valuation evidence analyzed in this portion of the report supports the estimate of market value as interpreted from income data.

To illustrate, assume that a parcel of land earns a net rent of $10,000 per year (the annual gross income less property taxes and insurance). If the prevailing rate of capitalization is 8 percent, the land would have an indicated value of $125,000 under the income approach ($10,000/0.08). In other words, the present worth of a future income of $10,000 is $125,000 (assuming a capitalization rate of 8 percent). An investor paying $125,000 for land earning a net income of $10,000 per year would earn 8 percent on the investment.

The Cost Approach. Under the cost approach the appraiser relates value to the cost of constructing the property appraised. The cost of duplicating the property includes the building cost and the cost of land and its preparation for the highest and best use. While this portion of the value estimate relates cost to value, it is important to emphasize that the cost is taken from the recent experience of building contractors, property developers, and others with knowledge of building costs, site sales, and estimates of depreciation.

In a sense the cost approach is a comparative approach—the cost of producing similar buildings is compared to the cost of duplicating the property appraised. While cost is not necessarily value, the cost is used as a further indication of the market value estimate.

The Final Estimate of Value

At this point in the appraisal process the appraiser must weigh the valuation evidence; the appraiser must rely on the appraisal approach which gives the most accurate estimate of market value. In short, the final estimate of value constitutes a judgment on the validity of each valuation approach and a determination of the most accurate evidence of value. The *correlation* constitutes a rational conclusion on the approach that most closely approximates the actual market value.

The *final estimate of value* is a reconciliation of all facts, trends, and observations bearing on market value. Suppose that a ten-year-old apartment building of 100 units reveals the three following value indications:

Approach	Indicated Value
Market	$1,575,000
Cost	1,655,000
Income	1,600,000

Assume further that the sales of apartment buildings used in the market approach dealt with a 250-unit apartment, a 65-unit building, and a 600-unit structure. Further, it might be reasoned that the subjectivity of the cost technique for a ten-year-old structure makes this approach less reliable than the income approach. Thus, the final estimate of market value would probably favor the income approach: $1,600,000.

APPRAISAL REPORTS

The estimate of market value takes the form of a written appraisal report. Such reports may be on standard forms, or they may be presented in a more formal narrative fashion. For mortgage purposes, especially where single-family dwellings are concerned, the form appraisal is more frequently used. For income properties and for appraisal reports prepared for court testimony, for example, in eminent domain proceedings, the narrative appraisal report is a practical necessity.

Form Reports

To illustrate, consider Figure 9–4, which shows one side of a widely used appraisal form for single-family dwellings. Note that the first part of the report identifies the location, date of purchase, original cost, assessed value, annual taxes, and special assessments.

Other portions of the report follow the general format of the appraisal process. The descriptive data include information on the neighborhood and the building improvements. Sufficient room has been given to add descriptive comments that supplement fill-in blanks.

The market and cost approaches both require an indicated value which is correlated with an explanation at the bottom of the form leading to the appraiser's final estimate of the value. The income approach is omitted since the report applies to single-family dwellings.

The reverse side of the form includes space for a floor plan, a photograph, a description of observed depreciation, and extra features of the dwelling or other factors that affect value which are not indicated on the front of the form. In this instance the appraiser is given considerable flexibility in identifying those points most relevant to the valuation estimate. In contrast, the narrative appraisal report requires considerably more detail.

The Narrative Appraisal Report

The narrative appraisal report has been described by the American Institute of Real Estate Appraisers and the Society of Real Estate Appraisers as

> a formal written document which contains (a) the estimate of value, (b) the effective date of the appraisal, (c) the certification and signature of the appraiser, (d) the purpose of the appraisal, (e) the qualifying conditions, (f) an adequate description of the neighborhood and identification of the property and its ownership, (g) the factual data, (h) an analysis and interpretation of the data, (i) the processing of the data by one or more of the three approaches and (j) other descriptive supporting material (maps, plans, charts, photographs).

From this description it will be appreciated that the professional appraiser prepares a formal written statement giving his or her opinion of the value of the property that is identified and described as of the date of valuation, with supporting evidence taken from the three recognized appraisal reports. An outline for the appraisal of single-family dwellings

FIGURE 9–4

Form Appraisal Approved by the Federal Home Loan Mortgage Corporation

RESIDENTIAL APPRAISAL REPORT

File No. _____

To be completed by Lender

Borrower/Client	Census Tract _____ Map Reference _____
Property Address	
City	County _____ State _____ Zip Code _____
Legal Description	
Sale Price $ _____ Date of Sale _____ Property Rights Appraised ☐ Fee ☐ Leasehold ☐ DeMinimis PUD(FNMA only ☐ Condo ☐ PUD)	
Actual Real Estate Taxes $ _____ (yr) Loan charges to be paid by seller $ _____ Other sales concessions	
Lender	Lender's Address
Occupant	Appraiser _____ Instructions to Appraiser

NEIGHBORHOOD

	Urban	Suburban	Rural		Good Avg. Fair Poor
Location	☐ Urban	☐ Suburban	☐ Rural		
Built Up	☐ Over 75%	☐ 25% to 75%	☐ Under 25%	Employment Stability	☐ ☐ ☐ ☐
Growth Rate ☐ Fully Dev.	☐ Rapid	☐ Steady	☐ Slow	Convenience to Employment	☐ ☐ ☐ ☐
Property Values	☐ Increasing	☐ Stable	☐ Declining	Convenience to Shopping	☐ ☐ ☐ ☐
Demand/Supply	☐ Shortage	☐ In Balance	☐ Over Supply	Convenience to Schools	☐ ☐ ☐ ☐
Marketing Time	☐ Under 3 Mos.	☐ 4–6 Mos.	☐ Over 6 Mos.	Quality of Schools	☐ ☐ ☐ ☐
Present Land Use ___% 1 Family ___% 2–4 Family ___% Apts. ___% Condo ___% Commercial				Recreational Facilities	☐ ☐ ☐ ☐
___% Industrial ___% Vacant ___%				Adequacy of Utilities	☐ ☐ ☐ ☐
Change in Present Land Use ☐ Not Likely	☐ Likely (*)		☐ Taking Place (*)	Property Compatibility	☐ ☐ ☐ ☐
(*) From _____ To _____				Protection from Detrimental Conditions	☐ ☐ ☐ ☐
Predominant Occupancy ☐ Owner	☐ Tenant	_____ % Vacant		Police and Fire Protection	☐ ☐ ☐ ☐
Single Family Price Range $ _____ to $ _____ Predominant Value $ _____				General Appearance of Properties	☐ ☐ ☐ ☐
Single Family Age _____ yrs to _____ yrs Predominant Age _____ yrs				Appeal to Market	☐ ☐ ☐ ☐

Note: FHLMC/FNMA do not consider the racial composition of the neighborhood to be a relevant factor and it must not be considered in the appraisal.

Comments (including those factors adversely affecting marketability) _____

SITE

Dimensions _____ = _____ Sq. Ft. or Acres ☐ Corner Lot

Zoning classification _____ Present improvements ☐ do ☐ do not conform to zoning regulations

Highest and best use: ☐ Present use ☐ Other (specify) _____

	Public	Other (Describe)	OFF SITE IMPROVEMENTS	Topo _____
Elec.	☐	_____	Street Access: ☐ Public ☐ Private	Size _____
Gas	☐	_____	Surface _____	Shape _____
Water	☐	_____	Maintenance: ☐ Public ☐ Private	View _____
San.Sewer	☐	_____	☐ Storm Sewer ☐ Curb/Gutter	Drainage _____
	☐ Underground Elect. & Tel		☐ Sidewalk ☐ Street Lights	Is the property located in a HUD identified Flood Hazard Area? ☐ No ☐ Yes

Comments (favorable or unfavorable including any apparent adverse easements, encroachments or other adverse conditions) _____

IMPROVEMENTS

☐ Existing (approx. yr. blt.) 19___ No. Units _____ Type (det, duplex, semi/det, etc.) _____ Design (rambler, split level, etc.) _____ Exterior Walls _____

☐ Proposed ☐ Under Construction No. Stories _____

Roof Material _____ Gutters & Downspouts ☐ None Window (Type): _____ Insulation ☐ None ☐ Floor

☐ Storm Sash ☐ Screens ☐ Combination   ☐ Ceiling ☐ Roof ☐ Walls

Foundation Walls _____ % Basement ☐ Floor Drain Finished Ceiling _____

BSMT   ☐ Outside Entrance ☐ Sump Pump Finished Walls _____

☐ Crawl Space   ☐ Concrete Floor ___% Finished Finished Floor _____

☐ Slab on Grade   Evidence of: ☐ Dampness ☐ Termites ☐ Settlement

Comments _____

ROOM LIST

Room List	Foyer	Living	Dining	Kitchen	Den	Family Rm.	Rec. Rm.	Bedrooms	No. Baths	Laundry	Other
Basement											
1st Level											
2nd Level											

Total _____ Rooms _____ Bedrooms _____ Baths in finished area above grade.

INTERIOR FINISH & EQUIPMENT

Kitchen Equipment: ☐ Refrigerator ☐ Range/Oven ☐ Disposal ☐ Dishwasher ☐ Fan/Hood ☐ Compactor ☐ Washer ☐ Dryer ☐

HEAT: Type _____ Fuel _____ Cond. _____ AIR COND: ☐ Central ☐ Other   ☐ Adequate ☐ Inadequate

				PROPERTY RATING	Good Avg. Fair Poor
Floors	☐ Hardwood	☐ Carpet Over _____		Quality of Construction (Materials & Finish)	☐ ☐ ☐ ☐
Walls	☐ Drywall	☐ Plaster ☐ _____		Condition of Improvements	☐ ☐ ☐ ☐
Trim/Finish	☐ Good	☐ Average ☐ Fair ☐ Poor		Rooms size and layout	☐ ☐ ☐ ☐
Bath Floor	☐ Ceramic	☐ _____		Closets and Storage	☐ ☐ ☐ ☐
Bath Wainscot	☐ Ceramic	☐ _____		Plumbing—adequacy and condition	☐ ☐ ☐ ☐
Special Features (including fireplaces): _____				Electrical—adequacy and condition	☐ ☐ ☐ ☐
				Kitchen Cabinets—adequacy and condition	☐ ☐ ☐ ☐
ATTIC: ☐ Yes ☐ No ☐ Stairway ☐ Drop-stair ☐ Scuttle ☐ Floored				Compatibility to Neighborhood	☐ ☐ ☐ ☐
Finished (Describe) _____ ☐ Heated				Overall Livability	☐ ☐ ☐ ☐
CAR STORAGE: ☐ Garage ☐ Built-in ☐ Attached ☐ Detached ☐ Car Port				Appeal and Marketability	☐ ☐ ☐ ☐
No. Cars _____ ☐ Adequate ☐ Inadequate Condition _____				Effective Age _____ Yrs. Est. Remaining Economic Life _____ Yrs.

PORCHES, PATIOS, POOL, FENCES, etc. (describe) _____

COMMENTS (including functional or physical inadequacies, repairs needed, modernization, etc.) _____

FHLMC Form 70 Rev. 9/75   ATTACH DESCRIPTIVE PHOTOGRAPHS OF SUBJECT PROPERTY AND STREET SCENE   FNMA Form 1004 Rev. 9/75

FIGURE 9–4 *(continued)*

VALUATION SECTION

Purpose of Appraisal is to estimate Market Value as defined in Certification & Statement of Limiting Conditions (FHLMC Form 439/FNMA Form 1004B). If submitted for FNMA, the appraiser must attach (1) sketch or map showing location of subject, street names, distance from nearest intersection, and any detrimental conditions and (2) exterior building sketch of improvements showing dimensions.

COST APPROACH

Measurements	No. Stories	Sq. Ft.
___ x ___	___ x ___	= ___
___ x ___	___ x ___	= ___
___ x ___	___ x ___	= ___
___ x ___	___ x ___	= ___
___ x ___	___ x ___	= ___
___ x ___	___ x ___	= ___

Total Gross Living Area (List in Market Data Analysis below) ___

Comment on functional and economic obsolescence: ___

ESTIMATED REPRODUCTION COST – NEW – OF IMPROVEMENTS:

Dwelling ___ Sq. Ft. @ $ ___ = $ ___
___ Sq. Ft. @ $ ___ = ___
Extras ___ = ___
___ = ___
Porches, Patios, etc. ___ = ___
Garage/Car Port ___ Sq. Ft. @ $ ___ = ___
Site Improvements (driveway, landscaping, etc.) ___
Total Estimated Cost New . . . . = $ ___

	Physical	Functional	Economic
Less Depreciation $	$	$	= $ (___)

Depreciated value of improvements . . . . = $ ___
ESTIMATED LAND VALUE . . . . = $ ___
(If leasehold, show only leasehold value)

INDICATED VALUE BY COST APPROACH . . . . $ ___

The undersigned has recited three recent sales of properties most similar and proximate to subject and has considered these in the market analysis. The description includes a dollar adjustment, reflecting market reaction to those items of significant variation between the subject and comparable properties. If a significant item in the comparable property is superior to, or more favorable than, the subject property, a minus (-) adjustment is made, thus reducing the indicated value of subject; if a significant item in the comparable is inferior to, or less favorable than, the subject property, a plus (+) adjustment is made, thus increasing the indicated value of the subject.

MARKET DATA ANALYSIS

ITEM	Subject Property	COMPARABLE NO. 1		COMPARABLE NO. 2		COMPARABLE NO. 3	
Address							
Proximity to Subj.							
Sales Price	$	$		$		$	
Price/Living area	$	$		$		$	
Data Source							
Date of Sale and Time Adjustment	DESCRIPTION	DESCRIPTION	+(-)$ Adjustment	DESCRIPTION	+(-)$ Adjustment	DESCRIPTION	+(-)$ Adjustment
Location							
Site/View							
Design and Appeal							
Quality of Const.							
Age							
Condition							
Living Area Room Count and Total	Total B-rms Baths	Total B-rms Baths		Total B-rms Baths		Total B-rms Baths	
Gross Living Area	Sq.Ft.	Sq.Ft.		Sq.Ft.		Sq.Ft.	
Basement & Bsmt. Finished Rooms							
Functional Utility							
Air Conditioning							
Garage/Car Port							
Porches, Patio, Pools, etc.							
Other (e.g. fireplaces, kitchen equip., heating, remodeling)							
Sales or Financing Concessions							
Net Adj. (Total)		☐ Plus; ☐ Minus $		☐ Plus; ☐ Minus $		☐ Plus; ☐ Minus $	
Indicated Value of Subject			$		$		$

Comments on Market Data ___

INDICATED VALUE BY MARKET DATA APPROACH . . . . $ ___

INDICATED VALUE BY INCOME APPROACH (If applicable) Economic Market Rent $ ___ /Mo. x Gross Rent Multiplier ___ = $ ___

This appraisal is made ☐ "as is" ☐ subject to the repairs, alterations, or conditions listed below ☐ completion per plans and specifications.

Comments and Conditions of Appraisal: ___

Final Reconciliation: ___

This appraisal is based upon the above requirements, the certification, contingent and limiting conditions, and Market Value definition that are stated in

☐ FHLMC Form 439 (Rev. 9/75)/FNMA Form 1004B filed with client ___ 19 ___ ☐ attached.

If submitted for FNMA, the report has been prepared in compliance with FNMA form instructions.

I ESTIMATE THE MARKET VALUE, AS DEFINED, OF SUBJECT PROPERTY AS OF ___ 19 ___ to be $ ___

Appraiser(s) ___ Review Appraiser (If applicable) ___
☐ Did ☐ Did Not Physically Inspect Property

FHLMC Form 70 Rev. 9/75	REVERSE	FNMA Form 1004 Rev. 9/75

FIGURE 9–4 (*concluded*)

DEFINITION OF MARKET VALUE: The highest price in terms of money which a property will bring in a competitive and open market under all conditions requisite to a fair sale, the buyer and seller, each acting prudently, knowledgeably and assuming the price is not affected by undue stimulus. Implicit in this definition is the consummation of a sale as of a specified date and the passing of title from seller to buyer under conditions whereby: (1) buyer and seller are typically motivated; (2) both parties are well informed or well advised, and each acting in what he considers his own best interest; (3) a reasonable time is allowed for exposure in the open market; (4) payment is made in cash or its equivalent; (5) financing, if any, is on terms generally available in the community at the specified date and typical for the property type in its locale; (6) the price represents a normal consideration for the property sold unaffected by special financing amounts and/or terms, services, fees, costs, or credits incurred in the transaction. ("Real Estate Appraisal Terminology," published 1975.)

CERTIFICATION AND STATEMENT OF LIMITING CONDITIONS

CERTIFICATION: The Appraiser certifies and agrees that:

1. The Appraiser has no present or contemplated future interest in the property appraised; and neither the employment to make the appraisal, nor the compensation for it, is contingent upon the appraised value of the property.

2. The Appraiser has no personal interest in or bias with respect to the subject matter of the appraisal report or the participants to the sale. The "Estimate of Market Value" in the appraisal report is not based in whole or in part upon the race, color, or national origin of the prospective owners or occupants of the property appraised, or upon the race, color or national origin of the present owners or occupants of the properties in the vicinity of the property appraised.

3. The Appraiser has personally inspected the property, both inside and out, and has made an exterior inspection of all comparable sales listed in the report. To the best of the Appraiser's knowledge and belief, all statements and information in this report are true and correct, and the Appraiser has not knowingly withheld any significant information.

4. All contingent and limiting conditions are contained herein (imposed by the terms of the assignment or by the undersigned affecting the analyses, opinions, and conclusions contained in the report).

5. This appraisal report has been made in conformity with and is subject to the requirements of the Code of Professional Ethics and Standards of Professional Conduct of the appraisal organizations with which the Appraiser is affiliated.

6. All conclusions and opinions concerning the real estate that are set forth in the appraisal report were prepared by the Appraiser whose signature appears on the appraisal report, unless indicated as "Review Appraiser." No change of any item in the appraisal report shall be made by anyone other than the Appraiser, and the Appraiser shall have no responsibility for any such unauthorized change.

CONTINGENT AND LIMITING CONDITIONS: The certification of the Appraiser appearing in the appraisal report is subject to the following conditions and to such other specific and limiting conditions as are set forth by the Appraiser in the report.

1. The Appraiser assumes no responsibility for matters of a legal nature affecting the property appraised or the title thereto, nor does the Appraiser render any opinion as to the title, which is assumed to be good and marketable. The property is appraised as though under responsible ownership.

2. Any sketch in the report may show approximate dimensions and is included to assist the reader in visualizing the property. The Appraiser has made no survey of the property.

3. The Appraiser is not required to give testimony or appear in court because of having made the appraisal with reference to the property in question, unless arrangements have been previously made therefor.

4. Any distribution of the valuation in the report between land and improvements applies only under the existing program of utilization. The separate valuations for land and building must not be used in conjunction with any other appraisal and are invalid if so used.

5. The Appraiser assumes that there are no hidden or unapparent conditions of the property, subsoil, or structures, which would render it more or less valuable. The Appraiser assumes no responsibility for such conditions, or for engineering which might be required to discover such factors.

6. Information, estimates, and opinions furnished to the Appraiser, and contained in the report, were obtained from sources considered reliable and believed to be true and correct. However, no responsibility for accuracy of such items furnished the Appraiser can be assumed by the Appraiser.

7. Disclosure of the contents of the appraisal report is governed by the Bylaws and Regulations of the professional appraisal organizations with which the Appraiser is affiliated.

8. Neither all, nor any part of the content of the report, or copy thereof (including conclusions as to the property value, the identity of the Appraiser, professional designations, reference to any professional appraisal organizations, or the firm with which the Appraiser is connected), shall be used for any purposes by anyone but the client specified in the report, the mortgagee or its successors and assigns, mortgage insurers, consultants, professional appraisal organizations, any state or federally approved financial institution, any department, agency, or instrumentality of the United States or any state or the District of Columbia, without the previous written consent of the Appraiser; nor shall it be conveyed by anyone to the public through advertising, public relations, news, sales, or other media, without the written consent and approval of the Appraiser.

9. On all appraisals, subject to satisfactory completion, repairs, or alterations, the appraisal report and value conclusion are contingent upon completion of the improvements in a workmanlike manner.

Date:...................... Appraiser(s)...

FHLMC FORM 439 REV. 9/75

FNMA FORM 1004B

includes the following data, as recommended by the American Institute of Real Estate Appraisers.[7]

Table of Contents:
The Narrative Appraisal Report

Letter of Transmittal
Photograph
Floor Plan
Plot Plan
Identification of Property
Type of Property
Purpose of Appraisal
Definition of Value

Regional Data
City Data
Neighborhood Data
Highest and Best Use
Zoning and Restrictions
Assessed Value and Taxes

Land Description and Value
Comparison of Land Sales
Description of Improvements
Condition of Improvements
Depreciation
Cost Approach
Market Data Approach
Market Data Comparisons
Income Approach
Rental Comparisons

Correlation and Final Estimate of Value
Certificate
Contingent and Limiting Conditions
Qualifications of Appraiser

Addenda

City Map
Neighborhood Map
Market Data Map

Note that the table of contents recommended for the narrative appraisal report closely parallels the appraisal process. The difference lies in the documentation necessary to the narrative report: the letter of transmittal, photograph, floor plan, and plot plan help to identify the property valued. An additional element of the narrative report is the certificate of value in which the appraiser submits his final estimate of value on a signed certifi-

---

[7] *Appraisal Outline for the Appraisal of a Single-Family Residence* (Chicago: American Institute of Real Estate Appraisers, 1966), p. 5.

cate. The contingent and limiting conditions qualify the appraisal report and limit its interpretation and use by the client. A statement of the limiting conditions applying to an apartment house appraisal illustrates the function of this portion of the narrative.

STATEMENT OF LIMITING CONDITIONS

I assume no responsibility for matters legal in character, nor do I render any opinion as to the title, which is assumed to be good. All existing liens and encumbrances have been disregarded and the property is appraised as though free and clear under responsible ownership and competent management.

Further, I have made no survey of the property and assume no responsibility for its accuracy. I am not required to give testimony or attendance in court by reason of this appraisal, with reference to the property in question, unless arrangements have been previously made therefor.

I have no present or contemplated interest in the property appraised.

The distribution of the total valuation in this report between land and improvements applies only under the existing program of utilization. The separate valuations for land and building must not be used in conjunction with any other appraisal and are invalid if so used.

This appraisal has been made in accordance with the Code of Ethics of the Society of Real Estate Appraisers.

The qualifications of the appraiser listed in summary form and maps of the city, neighborhood, and market data complete the documentation. The market data map locates each comparable sale in relation to the subject property for review purposes. Thus, the appraiser not only submits an opinion of value but documents reasons for this opinion in a manner that permits a review of the opinion.

SUMMARY

Real estate valuation is undertaken for numerous reasons, ranging from valuation for various government purposes to valuation for investment and mortgage purposes. To insure uniformity in the valuation process, appraisal organizations have been formed to administer a code of ethics, to qualify designated appraisers, and to further the education of their membership. While some states require real estate licenses to pursue appraisal activity, most appraisers work toward earning an appraisal designation.

The valuation estimate depends largely on the value definition. The technical definition of market value implies that there are many buyers and sellers, such that a single person's decision to buy and sell does not affect the price; that buyers and sellers have a reasonable knowledge of the market; and that the property to be appraised conforms to a standardized product. A free market, implied under the conventional definition of market value, refers to the reasonable freedom of buyers and sellers to enter and leave the market. Alternatively appraisers deal with market value in terms of the most probable sales price.

Certain other definitions important to appraisal activity include the concept of highest and best use—that use which results in the highest land value. Assessed values refer to the statutory definition of value for property tax purposes. While the states vary in their definition, usually the assessed value is defined to mean market value, though it may be legally referred to as true value, just value, just and fair value, or similar terms.

Just compensation arises from constitutional restrictions on the taking of private property for the public interest. The courts define just compensation as market value. Just compensation is reimbursement for the public taking of private property and may include severance damages—damages to the property remaining after part of a property has been taken.

Insurable value is ordinarily equal to the value of the destructible portions of property subject to loss in case of fire or other catastrophes.

For the present purpose the valuation process has been described as a five-part procedure: definition of the problem; the preliminary survey; descriptive data; the indicated value arrived at by the market, income, and cost approaches; and the final market value estimate. The process is more detailed for the lengthier narrative appraisal report but follows the same reasoning as that of the form type of report, which is generally used to value single-family dwellings.

In preparing reports, the appraiser provides a statement of limiting conditions. The statement will say that the appraiser is not responsible for the title or for discrepancies in the legal description. It should include language to the effect that the appraiser has no present or contemplated interest in the property appraised and that the appraisal is made in accordance with a professional code of ethics.

REVIEW QUESTIONS

1. What knowledge would you consider most important to a professional appraiser? Give reasons for your answer.
2. What is the contribution of appraisal organizations?
3. What are the main requirements for membership in the American Institute of Real Estate Appraisers? Do you consider these requirements adequate training and education for a professional appraiser? Why or why not?
4. What is the purpose of an appraisal code of ethics? Give two examples of how a code of ethics protects the public from gross negligence and incompetence.
5. Define value; define market value.
6. Give four reasons why real estate markets depart from the purely competitive market.

7. What is the advantage of defining value in terms of the most probable sales price? Explain thoroughly. Define assessed value, just compensation, and insurable value.

8. What five topics are covered in the valuation process?

9. Explain six features of "defining the problem" in following the appraisal process.

10. To what part of the appraisal process would you assign the highest and best use estimate and present zoning?

11. What is meant by the highest and best use? Give an example illustrating your answer.

12. In the valuation of a single-family dwelling, what data would you include in regional analysis? City analysis? Neighborhood analysis?

13. Explain the five most important features that you would examine in the valuation of a commercial site.

14. What is the rationale of estimating value under three different approaches?

15. Explain the correlation of the three valuation approaches.

16. Explain the main differences between a form appraisal report and a narrative appraisal report in the valuation of a single-family dwelling.

SELECTED REFERENCES

Boyce, Byrl N. *Real Estate Appraisal Terminology*. Cambridge, Mass.: Ballinger Publishing Co., 1975.

Hitchings, T. C., Jr. "The Appraisal Report: Is There a Better Way?" *Appraisal Journal,* vol. 40, no. 2 (April 1972), pp. 217–23.

Klaasen, Romain L. "Brief History of Real Estate Appraisal and Organizations," *Appraisal Journal,* vol. 44, no. 3 (July 1976), pp. 375–92.

Ring, Alfred A. *The Valuation of Real Estate,* chap. 2. 2d ed. Englewood Cliffs, N.J.: Prentice-Hall, Inc., 1970.

Rule, Thomas M. "The Metropolitan Analysis in the Appraisal Report," *Appraisal Journal,* vol. 40, no. 2 (April 1972), pp. 224–30.

Smith, Theodore Reynolds. "New Dimensions in Appraisal Technology," *Appraisal Journal,* vol. 42, no. 1 (January 1974), pp. 47–61.

Spivak, Melton L. "The Future for Computers in Real Estate Valuation," *Appraisal Journal,* vol. 43, no. 1 (January 1975), pp. 80–89.

Tanucci, Katherine Bryan. "Highest and Best Use," *Appraisal Journal,* vol. 42, no. 4 (October 1974), pp. 80–113.

Wendt, Paul F. *Real Estate Appraisal,* chaps. 1 and 9. Athens: University of Georgia Press, 1974.

10

Valuation by the Market and Cost Approaches

After reading this chapter, you should be familiar with the following points:

1 The advantages and disadvantages of the market approach to value.
2 The main sources of real estate sales data.
3 The analysis of real estate sales for appraisal purposes.
4 The calculation of gross income multipliers and their use.
5 The difference between replacement and reproduction costs.
6 Three methods of calculating costs.
7 Methods of estimating depreciation.
8 The advantages and limitations of the cost approach to value.

FOR SOME APPRAISAL PROBLEMS, the market and cost approaches provide the most accurate means of estimating market value. The market approach, which is based on an analysis of recently sold properties, serves as strong evidence of value in the appraisal of vacant land and single-family dwellings. Both types of property are frequently bought and sold in the open market, giving a valid indication of market value.

For properties such as public buildings, churches, and industrial plants —properties that are not commonly sold in the open market—the appraiser relies heavily on the cost approach. Cost data are readily available for new buildings; usually new buildings show little or no depreciation. In these circumstances the cost approach may be equally valid. Special-purpose buildings, which are seldom sold or rented, must be valued by the cost approach. A review of both methods shows that the market and cost approaches depend on the interpretation of widely different data.

First, the special meaning attached to the "market approach" should be noted. Simply stated, the term refers to the ". . . process of analyzing sales of similar recently sold properties in order to derive an indication of the most probable sales price."[1] The approach is also referred to as the market data approach or the sales comparison approach. If you were to appraise a new brick veneer three-bedroom dwelling under this approach, you would search for recently constructed three-bedroom dwellings in the same neighborhood that were sold within the last 12 months or so—the more recent the sale, the more accurate the market indication. Likewise, the greater the similarity between the dwellings sold and the dwelling appraised, the more accurate is the market indication.

In contrast, the cost approach is a method of estimating market value by adding the current land value to the depreciated building cost. To estimate value under this method, the land must be valued separately, usually by sales comparisons. The building value is estimated from costs of recently completed buildings of like design and construction. An allowance for depreciation is deducted from the cost estimate to account for deferred building maintenance and obsolete building features. A separate discussion of the market and cost approaches shows how these two methods differ in their logic.

AN EVALUATION OF THE MARKET COMPARISON APPROACH

The real estate industry relies heavily on the market approach. Here the main problem is to secure representative sales that indicate the prevailing market price. In searching for sales of property similar to the property appraised, the appraiser acts in much the same way as a census taker.

---

[1] Byrl N. Boyce, ed., *Real Estate Appraisal Terminology* (Cambridge, Mass.: Ballinger Publishing Co., 1975).

He or she samples the opinions of many buyers and sellers who have negotiated prices in the free market.

Figure 10–1 illustrates the logic lying behind the market data approach. The example suggests that prices vary for closely comparable properties. Price variation may be explained by differences in the time of sale, location, and physical characteristics, such as the age of the building, its present condition, and its floor area. After studying a sufficient number of sales to support the market value estimate, the appraiser makes the inductive leap, reasoning from repeated observations of the market to the market value estimate—an estimate that is strongly supported by empirical sales evidence. It should be noted that sales prices are *not averaged*. Ap-

FIGURE 10–1

An Illustration of the Market Data Approach

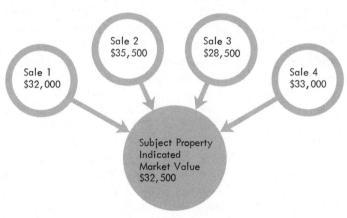

Representative Sales of Similar Property

Sale 2 $35,500

Sale 3 $28,500

Sale 1 $32,000

Sale 4 $33,000

Subject Property Indicated Market Value $32,500

praisers draw their value conclusion from the most representative sales in the light of the best market evidence.

Limitations of the Market Comparison Approach

While on its face this approach seems quite objective, imperfections of the real estate market call for a number of subjective interpretations. Though personal judgments may be minimized, this approach has limitations that may require dependence on the income or cost approach to value.

Time of Sale. In selecting sales, a compromise must be made between a sale selected for its physical comparability and a sale selected for its current indication of value. In the valuation of a 2,500-square-foot *split-level house,* suppose that the house across the street has a similar floor plan and lot size and other highly comparable characteristics. While acceptable in these respects, the sale may have been completed two years ago. Alternatively, another 2,500-square-foot dwelling *one-story* high and differing in other important characteristics may have been sold 30 days ago. In the former case the appraiser must judge how the two-year-old sale covering property of high comparability indicates value today, and how a more current sale of a house with different characteristics indicates the value of a split-level house.

In virtually every application of the market data approach, some allowance must be made for the change in value from the date property was sold to the date of valuation. Because of the general deficiency of sales in some neighborhoods and for some property types, this aspect of the market data approach increases the chance of error.

Dissimilar Property Characteristics. The most casual observation will show that no two real estate properties are exactly alike. Even dwellings with the same floor plan illustrate differences in condition, maintenance, and landscaping. Moreover, each dwelling has a unique location. Houses in the same block show variations in value because the location of each house is unique: a corner lot, an inside lot, a level lot, a steep lot, and the like. Frequently the validity of the market data approach depends largely on how the appraiser "adjusts" for dissimilar characteristics between the property sold and the property appraised. In almost every instance, the estimate of market value must account for physical differences between the property appraised and each comparable sale.

Financing Terms. Buyers shop not only for property suitable for their needs but for favorable credit terms. Indeed, financial difficulties may be such that buyers may be willing to pay more for house A than for house B because house A is available with a smaller down payment or a lower monthly mortgage payment. Furthermore, an owner may be willing to sell for $32,500 if the buyer elects to use an FHA mortgage or for $30,000 if the buyer pays cash. The delay and red tape of FHA financing often encourage sellers to take less for a cash sale. Frequently the analysis of comparable sales requires subjective judgments to offset the effect of sale terms on the price.

Motives of Buyer and Seller. Ideally each comparable sale would result from deliberate negotiations of informed buyers and sellers who are acting under no duress. Suppose, however, that a department store purchases adjoining land for parking space. In this example, there is virtually a one-buyer, one-seller relationship. The retail store has limited alternatives to buy land for parking space. Moreover, the department store may be the only potential buyer for the land. Each party is acting under pressure such that the sales price may not be indicative of the current market values of surrounding land.

Advantages of the Market Comparison Approach

Appraisers may compensate for some of the deficiencies of sales data on the basis of their general familiarity with real estate values. Provided that real estate sales meet minimum standards of acceptance, they offer a fairly objective means of estimating value. In fact, the advantages of the market comparison approach frequently more than compensate for sales data deficiencies.

Current Prices Indicate Market Value. If three 2,000-square-foot houses in the same neighborhood of like construction and features sold for $40,000, $41,000 and $41,500 in the last six months, it is difficult not to concede that a similar property would have a value approximating $41,000 (provided that the properties are in similar condition). Sales prices of like properties are convincing evidence of market value. The public, the courts, and government agencies generally accept qualified market data as market value evidence. This is especially true if prices are independently negotiated by buyers and sellers who have no vested interest in the appraisal of another property.

Personal Bias of the Cost Technique Avoided. While the market approach has certain limitations, it should be judged relative to other approaches. The crucial problem is to rely on that appraisal approach which gives the strongest support to the final value estimate. For on analysis, each approach has inherent limitations. For example, the valuation of a 30-year-old house by the cost approach suffers from the difficulty of acquiring construction costs for a house built with building materials and equipment that are no longer available. The example illustrates the added handicap of estimating the loss in value from poor maintenance, neighborhood decline, and the lack of a modern floor plan and equipment. Comparable sales of similar older buildings would probably give a more accurate indication of value.

Frequently Sold Properties. The market comparison method is ideally adapted to the appraisal of frequently sold properties. In an active real estate market, the large number of available sales gives the market approach a clear advantage over the cost and income approaches. An active market allows the appraiser to select a group of highly comparable sales among different property types and neighborhoods. Such an analysis contributes to the accurate interpretation of current sales prices.

Sources of Comparable Sales Data

Under the market comparison approach, accuracy depends on securing valid real estate sales data. The main object is to obtain only bona fide sales that have been verified as an accurate indication of current market value. To ensure that a sale is bona fide, it is common to eliminate certain transactions which are not considered indicative of market value. Among the real estate sales considered invalid for appraisal purposes are:

1. Sales to or from government agencies.
2. Foreclosure sales or sales completed in anticipation of foreclosure or bankruptcy.

3. Sales between family members.
4. Sales between interrelated corporations.
5. Sales of partial or fractional interests.

Some of the rejections may be made by eliminating sales between parties who have the same name or sales between corporations known to have a common ownership.

With these qualifications, the appraiser has the option of obtaining sales from public, private, or commercial sources. A representative list of places to secure real estate sales information includes:

Public sources

Recorder of deeds
Property tax assessor
State tax commissions

Private sources

Real estate brokers
Multiple-listing services
Financial institutions
Real estate developers
Real estate contractors
Real estate investors

Commercial Sources

Society of Real Estate Appraisers Market Data Centers
Commercial Real Estate Services

The public sources refer to local and state agencies that maintain a file of real estate sales incidental to their function. The recorder of deeds (in some states referred to as the registrar of deeds, the county auditor, or some similar designation) files deeds by book and page number. These are also identified alphabetically in the name of both the seller and the buyer. Since the public file usually includes a facsimile of the deed, deed books represent an excellent place to identify the minimum facts of the sale. Since deed records do not ordinarily show other essential facts, these records must be supplemented by a field inspection and verification of the sales price through interviews with the buyer, the seller, or the broker.

The property tax assessor and the state tax office maintain sales records to assist in the valuation of property for property tax purposes. Quite often the public may use these records to identify real estate sales.

Private sources include real estate brokers, savings and loan associations, and local banks that deal in real estate mortgages. Real estate developers, contractors, and investors who are actively engaged in producing and marketing real estate constitute other sources of sales data. Usually the appraiser must investigate many sources to obtain current information on real estate transactions.

Sales data are also provided for a fee by commercial services. In over 30 cities the Society of Real Estate Appraisers supports market data centers that provide subscribing and cooperating members with lists of single-family dwelling sales, showing property details, sales terms, and other data. In the larger cities, such as Miami, Seattle, and Atlanta, monthly lists of real estate sales classified by location, property type, and other series may be purchased for a fee. In these cases the appraiser must view the property and make further inquiries to gain the necessary appraisal information. The commercial services provide an excellent source for identifying sales which must be researched in greater detail.

Comparable Sales Presentation

The importance of the data source is suggested by the detail required for each comparable sale. Usually it is unlikely that all of this information will be secured from a single source. For example, the appraiser may identify a prospective comparable sale from the local property tax records. Typically additional sales information must be obtained by interviews with the buyer, the seller, or the listing broker. For large-scale income properties, such as a 500-unit apartment or an industrial plant of 100,000 square feet, the sales details would cover physical characteristics of the site and building structure. At a minimum, the market data approach requires the following information:

Name of buyer
Name of seller
Date of sale
Legal description
Deed book and page
Type of conveyance instrument (that is, warranty deed, contract, special warranty deed)
Sales price
 per acre
 per front foot
 per square foot
Terms of sale
Location
Number of square feet, acres, or front feet
Remarks

If the appraisal report is written for the purpose of presenting an appraisal opinion in court, this type of documentation would be required. In addition, lenders who rely on appraisal reports to determine the maximum mortgage loan depend on these data to verify the facts of the sale. Listing the buyer and seller by name, the date of sale, the legal description, and the deed book and page number makes it relatively easy for a third party to verify the transaction. Such documentation proves that the appraiser bases his opinion on actual transactions that may be verified. The price shown on a per unit basis allows the comparison, for example, of a 300-acre land sale with a 100-acre land sale. The same reasoning applies to property improved with buildings. The description of the property—in terms of the square feet, number of acres, or front feet (in the case of a commercial lot) and other details—suggests the relative comparability of the properties sold to the property appraised.

Under the remarks section, it is explained how the property compares to the property under valuation. For instance, it may be noted that real estate prices have increased approximately 10 percent from the date of sale (12 months earlier) to the present time. Under remarks, the appraiser usually notes differences between the property sold and the property appraised and other facts relevant to interpreting the sales price.

Sales Adjustments

It has been pointed out that the appraiser must show how the sale of a property which differs in some important respects from the property appraised leads to the value conclusion. For example, what is the indicated value of a house with *one carport* if a similar house with *two carports* recently sold for $55,000? An analysis of recent sales, let us say, would lead the appraiser to reason that if a house with a *two-car garage* sold for $55,-000, a similar house with a one-car garage would have a value of $54,500. For each important characteristic, the appraiser adjusts the sales price to account for differences between the property sold and the property appraised.

Initially the appraiser must select those features for which each sale must be "adjusted" to show how the price indicated the market value of the property appraised. In the appraisal of single-family dwellings, the more common features subject to adjustment cover:

Terms of sale	Condition of dwelling
Lot area	Location
Lot frontage	Age of building
Square foot floor area	Architectural style
Number of bathrooms	Basements
Carports/garages	Central air conditioning
Type of construction	

There is some practical limit to the number of adjustments that may be made. A practical limit would be six characteristics which would be subject to sales adjustments. For as the number of adjustments increases, the sale gradually loses the required degree of comparability. To cite an extreme example, you would not use the sale of a 3,000-square-foot house to value a 1,000-square-foot house; nor would you ordinarily use the sale of a two-story, 30-year-old wood frame house to appraise a new one-story brick veneer house. Table 10–1 illustrates a typical example of sales adjustments for selected adjustment items.

To illustrate, note that Sale 1, which was made for $37,800 18 months ago, is adjusted upward by $1,600. It is reasoned that a dwelling which sold for $37,800 18 months ago indicates a market value of $39,400. Each sale is adjusted upward to account for the increase in value since the date of sale. Similarly, if the lot of the property under valuation is ten feet wider than the lot of Sale 1 and lots are valued at $50 per front foot, the lot frontage of the property appraised would be worth an additional $500.

TABLE 10–1

Comparable Sales Adjustments for a Single-Family Dwelling

Adjustment Item	Sale Number			
	1	*2*	*3*	*4*
Sales price..............	$37,800	$38,300	$38,000	$41,500
Date of sale (months elapsed).......	18	13	5	3
Time adjustment.........	+1,600	+1,100	+500	0
Lot frontage.............	+500	+600	+1,500	−500
Location.................	−1,000	−400	+500	0
Floor area...............	+300	+500		
Indicated market value of subject...	$39,200	$40,100	$40,500	$41,000

Since the property sold for $37,800 with a lot with ten feet less frontage, the sale indicates a market value of $38,800 with respect to lot frontage. With respect to the location, Sale 1 is adjusted downward by $1,000 since the property appraised has a location regarded as less desirable than that of Sale 1. In this manner each transaction is adjusted upward or downward to account for differences between the property sold and the property appraised.

By accounting for these individual differences, each sale indicates a market value of the subject property (the property appraised). In this instance the indicated values range from $39,200 to $41,000. Next it would be subjectively determined which of these prices would be the most accurate indicator of value. If Sale 4 were believed to be the most comparable property, requiring the least amount of adjustments, the appraiser would probably estimate the market value at $41,000.

Though the market value estimate is highly personal, it should be remembered that the appraiser qualifies his judgment by his experience, his special training, and his general knowledge of market prices. This method of adjusting sales shows how the appraiser arrives at his estimate of value under the market approach and to this extent tends to make the appraisal more objective.

GROSS INCOME MULTIPLIERS

The gross income multiplier (GIM) expresses the relation between gross income and sales price. An apartment house sold for $360,000 with a gross income of $60,000 illustrates an annual gross income multiplier of 6.0 ($360,000/$60,000). The gross income multiplier is established by comparing the sales prices and gross income of numerous income properties of the same type. The gross income multiplier may be used to value property with a known gross income. Assuming a gross income multiplier of 6.0, an apartment dwelling with a gross income of $100,000 would have an estimated market vallue of $600,000.

Annual Gross Income Multipliers Demonstrated

Table 10–2 lists 56 sales of apartment houses showing gross income multipliers arranged by intervals of 1.0. Note that the two intervals 5.00 to 5.99

TABLE 10–2

The Range of Gross Income Multipliers by Intervals of 1.0*

Gross Income Multiplier Intervals	Number of Sales	Percent of Total Number
4.00–4.99.........	6	10.7
5.00–5.99.........	21	37.5
6.00–6.99.........	21	37.5
7.00–7.99.........	4	7.1
8.00–8.99.........	1	1.8
9.00–9.99.........	3	5.4
Total...........	56	100.0

* Median and mean gross income multipliers are 6.04 and 5.19.

and 6.00 to 6.99 have the greatest number of cases among the intervals of Table 10–2. The median gross income multiplier is 6.04. The variation in gross income is accounted for by differences in the expenses of operation. An investor would normally pay more for an apartment showing an annual gross income of $100,000 with a 50 percent expense ratio ($50,000 annual net income) than he would for another apartment with the same gross income but with a 75 percent expense ratio ($25,000 annual net income).

Expenses of operation are related to management efficiency, age of building, type of construction, and apartment type. Generally speaking, it would cost more to operate a 30-year-old, 12-story apartment building than it would to operate a 2-year-old, 2-story garden court apartment project.

Because gross income multipliers vary according to variations in operating expense ratios, care must be taken to use gross income multipliers to value the kind of property typical of the properties used to calculate the gross income multiplier.

To explain further, an older property may be expected to show a relatively high level of annual repair expenses, a fairly high vacancy rate, and an above-average expense ratio. This causes a decrease in the GIM. Hence the GIM assumes a fairly uniform operating expense ratio and vacancy rate. In practice, appraisers select properties recently sold that have a high degree of comparability to the property appraised to calculate the gross income multiplier.

If this condition is met, the gross income multiplier (1) provides another means of estimating value, (2) is easily obtained, (3) avoids the complexities of calculating net income, and (4) is widely used by investors, brokers, and lenders as an initial estimate of market value.

If comparable properties are secured, the gross income multiplier may be used to estimate the overall capitalization rate. This assumes that each example has a representative, typical net income ratio. The net income ratio represents the annual net operating income expressed as a percent of gross possible income. A property showing an annual net operating income of $40,000 and an annual gross possible income of $100,000 would have a net income ratio of 40 percent. Given the net income ratio, the overall capitalization rate may be derived from the formula:

$$\text{Overall capitalization rate} = \frac{\text{Net income ratio}}{\text{Annual gross income multiplier}}$$

If the net income ratio is 0.53 and the annual gross income multiplier is 6.04, the overall capitalization rate is 8.78 percent (0.53/6.04).

Monthly Gross Income Multipliers

In the valuation of single-family dwellings, the estimate of value is based on the monthly gross income multiplier. Sales prices of similar properties are related to the observed monthly rent. Provided that sufficient data are at hand, the relationship between monthly rents and value may be indicated by the market rent. Table 10–3 lists sales prices and their corresponding rents.

For example, a property that sold for $25,000 which was formerly rented for $200 per month indicates a monthly gross income multiplier of 125. To illustrate, assume that the monthly rent on the property appraised is $250. With a multiplier of 125, the estimated market value would be $31,250 (125 × 250).

In using monthly gross income multipliers, certain disadvantages are readily apparent. *First,* the main difficulty lies in securing a sufficient number of properties recently sold that have also been rented. *Second,* the gross income multiplier for a given property varies by the type, age, size, condition, and location of the dwelling. *Third,* subjective adjustments must be made for utilities that the renter may assume. As with the annual gross income multiplier, it is assumed that property taxes, insurance, and other expenses of ownership are comparable to those of the property appraised. Because these conditions are seldom met, large variations in gross monthly

TABLE 10–3

The Derivation of Monthly Gross Income Multipliers for Single-Family Dwellings

Selling Price (1)	Monthly Gross Income (2)	Monthly Gross Income Multipliers (1)/(2)
$25,000.......... $200		125.0
30,000.......... 250		120.0
35,000.......... 280		125.0
40,000.......... 295		135.6
45,000.......... 325		138.5
50,000.......... 350		142.9

rent multipliers call for careful interpretation of the data. A detailed analysis of recent sales usually provides a more accurate indication of value than does the less refined monthly gross income multiplier.

THE COST APPROACH

Also referred to as the summation approach, the cost approach requires (1) an estimate of the building cost of construction, (2) the building depreciation, and (3) the land value. These steps are illustrated in Figure 10–2. The estimated market value is a summation of the land value and the depreciated building value. The method is appropriate for properties that are typically not rented, that is, single-family dwellings, industrial plants, public buildings, and special-purpose properties, such as wharves, piers, and single-purpose manufacturing plants.

It is generally true that the method is more accurate if a property is employed at its highest and best use, if the building is relatively new, if it has suffered little or no depreciation, and if it is constructed like similar

FIGURE 10–2

An Illustration of the Cost Approach

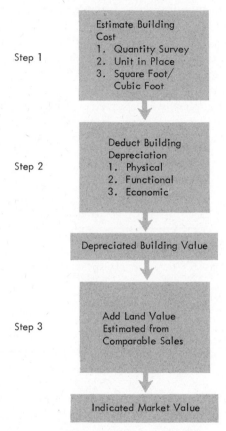

Step 1

Estimate Building
Cost
1. Quantity Survey
2. Unit in Place
3. Square Foot/
Cubic Foot

Step 2

Deduct Building
Depreciation
1. Physical
2. Functional
3. Economic

Depreciated Building Value

Step 3

Add Land Value
Estimated from
Comparable Sales

Indicated Market Value

buildings. For the valuation of older structures, for example, 50-year-old dwellings or old style multiple-story industrial buildings, the cost technique usually lacks the objectivity of the market and income approaches.

Estimating Building Costs

To estimate building costs, you must first identify a reliable source of current costs of construction. Given an adequate source of cost data, it must then be determined whether the costs relate to reproduction or replacement costs. Even if these issues are resolved, a decision must be made on the method of estimating costs: the quantity survey, unit-in-place, or square foot/cubic foot technique. Even assuming that these problems have been solved, appraisers do not always agree on the types of cost data to include in the cost estimation. Indeed, the variations among appraisers in calculating costs of construction indicate that the cost technique is subject to a high degree of personal bias. A separate discussion of these issues illustrates the main problems inherent in the cost technique.

Sources of Cost Data. Local contractors and real estate developers who have constructed recent buildings constitute the best possible source of local cost data. Especially for single-family dwellings, estimates of new construction based on local costs of materials and labor give the most accurate indication of market value. Dividing the contract price by the square foot or cubic foot area of a new building of the same quality of materials and workmanship is a preferred method of securing building costs. Therefore, to estimate building costs, review recently constructed buildings to obtain actual costs of construction for the type of building under valuation.

This data source is not always available for office buildings, public buildings, and other more specialized industrial structures. A local warehouse must often be appraised under the cost approach with little recent warehouse construction to serve as a guide to current local warehouse building costs. Building cost manuals prepared by commercial cost services are the next best alternative. State and local property tax offices and appraisal companies that assess property for property tax purposes develop construction cost manuals that include cost tables showing typical construction costs for different types of buildings and construction.

Published cost data from commercial sources usually include monthly or periodic update services so that published costs are available on a current basis for different cities and regions. The American Appraisal Company of Milwaukee, Wisconsin, and the Marshall and Swift Publishing Company, with offices in leading cities, publish separate cost manuals for single-family dwellings, commercial and industrial properties.

Type of Cost. The valuation of a four-story, 500,000-square-foot industrial building built in 1895 is considerably more complex than estimating the value of a modern, 500,000-square-foot, one-story industrial building. In the former case, a multiple-story building is usually constructed with an outside brick wall, three feet thick at ground level and tapering to 12 inches on the fourth floor. Even if such an industrial building were to be constructed today, it would probably be built with a combination of concrete and steel and constructed like a high-rise apartment or office building. The solid brick wall of 1895 is obsolete; no recent construction of this type would be available to guide the cost estimate. Because of the difficulty of trying to calculate construction for obsolete construction, the appraiser must identify his cost estimate as either a reproduction or a replacement cost estimate.

1. *Reproduction Costs.* Reproduction cost refers to *the cost of reproducing a building identical to the property under valuation.* It is assumed that the cost refers to the same materials, the same architectual design, and the same quality of construction. Accordingly, in applying the cost approach to, say, a five-year-old single-family dwelling, appraisers

would ordinarily estimate the reproduction cost. In appraising an obsolete four-story industrial building constructed in 1895, however, the market value estimate would refer to replacement costs.

2. *Replacement Costs.* For old buildings, because it is difficult to defend the estimated cost of materials which are no longer produced or sold and of workmanship which is no longer available, the appraiser is virtually forced to apply the cost of replacement. The *replacement cost refers to the cost of a building having the same utility as the property appraised.* The American Institute of Real Estate Appraisers defines replacement costs as "the cost of construction at current prices of a new building having utility equivalent to the building being appraised but built with modern materials and according to current standards, design and layout."[2] Hence, for the appraisal of a multiple-story industrial building constructed in 1895, the appraiser must determine the value of an industrial building which would have equal utility. If the four-story industrial building is to be valued under the cost approach, the appraiser must hypothetically assume a similar building which would allow the same type of production to be undertaken but would illustrate modern construction practices.

It will be appreciated that the necessity of basing the value on a hypothetical building having the same utility introduces highly subjective judgments. It would be preferable to supplement such replacement cost estimates by the market or income approach.

Cost Estimating Techniques. The degree of accuracy determines the technique of estimating cost. If the appraisal calls for accuracy comparable to that of a contractor preparing a construction bid, the quantity survey method would be used. If less accuracy is allowable, and if the required estimating skills and data are at hand, unit-in-place estimates substitute for quantity survey methods. In most instances the square foot/cubic foot cost estimate serves the purposes of the appraisal.

1. *Quantity Survey Techniques.* The quantity survey requires a listing of building materials and their costs in addition to the labor required in hours times the hourly labor cost. In summary form the quantity survey estimate would require the separate calculation of the cost of building materials and labor:

$$\text{Quantity of material} \times \text{Price} = \text{Material cost}$$
$$\text{Hours of labor} \times \text{Hourly wage} = \frac{\text{Labor cost}}{\text{Total building cost}}$$

The materials and labor are individually priced for each building component. The necessary detail is illustrated by the building costs of the wood framing of a single-family dwelling. (The costs illustrated are not necessarily current—the data merely illustrate quantity survey detail.)

---

[2] Ibid.

Wood Framing Costs: Quantity Survey Technique

	Reproduction Cost		
	Material	Labor	Total
Wood framing			
Materials			
12 studs 2″ × 4″ × 10′ 80 board feet			
16 joists 2″ × 6″ × 16′ 256 board feet			
20 rafters 2″ × 6″ × 14′ 280 board feet			
616 board feet			
@ $0.27..................... $166.32			
Labor			
20 carpenter hours @ 5.50.....................		$110.00	$276.32
Roof sheathing			
Materials			
864 board feet @ 0.25..................... 216.00			
Labor			
18 carpenter hours @ 5.50.....................		99.00	315.00
Total framing costs, materials, and labor......			$591.32

Printed forms are used to assist in the calculation of the material and labor costs of constructing each building. While the quantity survey is the most accurate cost estimation technique, it requires a detailed list of cost data, time-consuming calculations, and a technical knowledge of construction practices.

2. *Unit-in-Place Estimates.* Costs based on unit in place refer to the combined costs of material and labor to construct a unit of material. The method saves considerable time in estimating costs; it requires less technical knowledge than does the quantity survey estimate. Further, for the most common types of construction, unit-in-place estimates are readily available.

To illustrate, contractors estimate the labor time to construct a brick wall, lay a hardwood floor, or complete a roofing installation. Suppose that a roofer can apply 100 square feet of asphalt shingles in two hours. The cost of the roof would be the labor cost per 100 square feet of roof ($15) and the cost of 100 square feet of roofing shingles ($30). The unit-in-place cost for a new roof would then be expressed as $45 per 100 square feet of roof. Unit-in-place costs are commonly measured in terms of such units as square feet, square yards, lineal feet, and thousand board feet of lumber.

3. *Square Foot/Cubic Foot Estimates.* These estimates are sufficiently accurate for most appraisal purposes. Cubic foot estimates are used to value buildings with varying ceiling heights, such as theaters, auditoriums, and industrial plants. Square or cubic foot building costs are derived from local contractors, the analysis of recently constructed buildings, or cost manuals.

A manual published by the Boeckh Division of the American Appraisal

Company provides cost tables classified by type of residential structure, showing the price per square foot for the base building and lump-sum figures for building fixtures and other building components. The company publishes bimonthly multipliers so that published costs may be maintained on a current basis. For certain types of construction in which suitable market examples are unavailable, cost manuals guide the appraiser's final cost estimate.

Estimating Depreciation

For valuation purposes, depreciation is defined as *a loss in value from any cause.* Appraisers estimate depreciation in terms of physical depreciation and functional and economic obsolescence. In this sense, depreciation represents the difference in value between the building under appraisal and a new, substitute building.

Depreciation, in the sense used here, refers only to the value estimate. The depreciation allowable for income tax purposes is unrelated to depreciation for valuation purposes. The depreciation used in the accounting sense or in income tax accounting follows specific legal rules and financial practices unrelated to the market value. For the present purpose, remember that the estimate of cost is not necessarily equal to market value; usually an allowance must be made to reduce the building cost estimate to market value. Hence the depreciation for appraisal purposes rests on a highly subjective opinion and not on mathematical, legal, or financial rules permissible for nonappraisal purposes.

Physical Depreciation. Buildings lose value because of *normal wear and tear, the action of the elements, and catastrophic events,* such as earthquakes, hurricanes, and fires. The loss in value from these sources represents physical depreciation. Virtually every building shows some evidence of physical depreciation. Consequently, in valuing a building under the cost approach, the cost is reduced by the estimated amount required to correct the physical deficiency (for example, new exterior painting) or by an allowance to account for the aging of the structure at some average rate of decline per year. The latter is highly subjective: a building with an estimated economic life of 50 years would be depreciated by 20 percent at the end of 10 years (2 percent per year).

Functional Obsolescence. The loss in value from *a decrease in functional utility* illustrates functional obsolescence. Building utility decreases because of technological improvements, changes in architecture, new materials, and other innovations that make existing buildings obsolete for their original purpose. Although a house may be physically intact and in excellent condition, functional depreciation may be evident in such forms as a poor floor plan, unusually small rooms, an outmoded heating system, lack of insulation, and limited storage space. The appraiser's familiarity with market preferences and his technical knowledge of building features lead to his estimate of functional obsolescence.

Economic Obsolescence. A new service station would generally decrease the value of a single-family dwelling on an adjoining lot. The owner of the dwelling cannot modify his house or land to minimize the loss in value from this cause. The example illustrates *economic obsolescence: the loss in value from forces external to the property appraised.* The point is that not all depreciation is explained by physical and functional causes. A change in the neighborhood, the unavailability of parking, and the encroachment of such nuisances as noise or smells are factors which lower market value, yet cannot be traced to the property under valuation.

Therefore, after revising the cost estimate and accounting for physical and functional depreciation, experienced appraisers examine the property for losses arising from surrounding environmental factors. For it is quite possible that an undesirable environment will substantially lower the value of a building. In short, economic obsolescence results from factors physically unrelated to the building under appraisal.

To illustrate these concepts, refer to Figure 10–3, which provides examples of depreciation on single-family dwellings. This figure identifies value deficiencies of single-family dwellings. Even if the cost approach is not employed, the recognition of depreciation helps in evaluating real estate sales and gross rent multipliers. If the cost technique is used, these deficiencies would lead to depreciation deductions.

Note that physical depreciation is classified into curable forms that may

FIGURE 10–3

Depreciation Illustrated for Single-Family Dwellings

Types of Depreciation		Illustrative Examples
Physical	Curable	Required exterior painting Wall-to-wall carpets in poor condition Deteriorated asphalt shale roofing Hardwood floors in need of refinishing
	Incurable	Normal wear and tear on wood frame Gradual loss in value due to an aging plumbing system Normal wear and tear to foundation, walls, and support columns
Functional	Curable	Linoleum, kitchen drainboard Old style bathroom plumbing Wood hot air stove 100-ampere electrical service
	Incurable	Bedrooms smaller than 10 feet by 10 feet Awkward floor plan Obsolete architecture
Economic		Encroachment by adjoining incompatible land use Obnoxious smells, air pollution Traffic noise Noise generated by low-flying aircraft

be estimated from the cost required to remedy the deficiency. Such items as the cost of exterior painting and the cost of replacing wall-to-wall carpets or roofing provide a means of estimating the loss in value from new conditions. Physical incurable depreciation concerns losses that are not economically feasible to remedy; yet the examples given indicate that some allowance must be subtracted from replacement or reproduction cost to account for incurable physical depreciation.

Similarly, the functional depreciation examples listed in Figure 10–3 suggest that this type of depreciation is commonly encountered among single-family dwellings. Numerous other examples could be used to supplement this brief list. Like incurable physical depreciation, incurable functional depreciation relates to items that would not be subject to cost analysis. It is much easier to capitalize the rental loss resulting from curable functional depreciation. For example, a poor floor plan would lead to an estimated annual rental loss of $500, which capitalized at 10 percent would indicate a $5,000 loss due to incurable functional depreciation. If the cost technique is to be used, such a procedure, though highly subjective, helps refine that approach.

Note also that economic depreciation is not curable. The examples of Figure 10–3 refer to environmental or neighborhood factors that reduce a dwelling's value. Economic depreciation is not curable since it is difficult to remove these deficiencies by modernization or rehabilitation of the property appraised.

Land Value

In estimating land value under the cost approach, comparable land sales serve as the best evidence of market value. To value the land occupied by a church, an effort would be made to secure data on the sales of vacant land similar in most respects to the site occupied by the church building. Since the cost approach is often relied upon for public buildings, churches, and special-purpose industrial property, considerable difficulty arises in obtaining reasonably comparable land sales. Frequently the sale of similar property which includes a building must be used. The land value of a comparable building is derived by deducting the estimated building value from the sale which includes both land and buildings. Because of the subjectivity involved in obtaining land sales data which are not always very comparable, alternative approaches to value tend to be preferred.

Cost Approach Evaluated

If it is stated that a 2,000-square-foot, single-family dwelling costs $21.50 per square foot to build, it does not follow that the building is worth $43,000, plus the value of a $5,000 lot. First, the cost per square foot may not be typical of local costs. Second, the land value estimate may lack accuracy, and third, the building may be subject to depreciation because of a poor floor plan, an obsolete design, poor workmanship, or inappropriate building materials.

Cost Approach Limitations. The main reasons for inaccurate cost estimates may be summarized in five points:

1. It is not always clear that the cost estimate includes architect's fees, which may vary from 2 percent to 10 percent of the building cost, depending on the services rendered.
2. Selling costs vary widely; the cost estimate may not consistently include normal costs of sale.
3. Costs vary because of differences in the quality of workmanship.
4. Contractors vary widely in their level of efficiency.
5. The cost estimate should include an allowance for overhead and profit, which is highly variable among building contractors.

In addition to these causes of cost variation, variations in the quality of materials cause building costs to vary. A linoleum floor costs less than vinyl tile or wall-to-wall carpets of good quality. A similar generalization may be made with regard to kitchen cabinets, plumbing fixtures, and the many other features of a building. It is also generally true that a contractor who only builds five houses a year would have higher per unit costs than would a contractor who builds 100 houses per year. In the latter case, quantity discounts and the more efficient use of specialized labor lead to lower per unit costs of construction. In using the cost technique, assumptions must be made on these items. Such assumptions vary among appraisers.

The most questionable part of the cost technique relates to the depreciation estimate. Even though depreciation is shown separately by physical, functional, and economic components, in the final analysis the appraiser must make a personal value judgment to reduce the cost new estimate to market value. For these reasons, the cost technique is generally confined to special-purpose properties for which market and income data are unavailable.

This point is illustrated by Table 10–3, which demonstrates the application of the cost approach to an industrial building constructed in 1890. Because the appraisal covers a four-story structure of obsolete construction, the valuation is based on the replacement cost. The depreciation is calculated on percentages which admittedly are highly subjective. To this extent the appraisal depends on the judgment of the appraiser, who presumably has a background in industrial appraising. And even in this instance, the valuation tends to be highly subjective. Personal value judgments on depreciation tend to be supported by the analysis of new and old industrial buildings and by interviews with informed industrial building owners, contractors, and industrial Realtors®. The estimated market

TABLE 10–3

Estimated Market Value of an Industrial Building, Cost Approach

Basic cost per square foot, 12-foot ceiling............... $ 18.56
    Air conditioning.......................................   1.80
    Wet sprinkler system................................   0.42
    Switchgear..   0.50
    Ceiling height..   1.20
        Total estimated cost per square foot............. $ 22.48

Replacement cost
309,657 square feet, @ $22.48......................... $6,961,089

Less depreciation
Physical
    Effective age, 10 years; estimated remaining
    life, 40 years; physical depreciation,
    10/50, or 20%....................................... $1,392,218

Functional obsolescence
    Multiple-story construction (18%)
    Loss of usable space
        Thick walls
        Excess columns
        Stairwells
        Elevator space
        Excess foundation expense
    Loss of production efficiency (10%)
        Poor loading facilities
        Poor layout
        Total functional obsolescence (28%).............. $1,949,105

Economic depreciation
    Encroachments of dilapidated buildings
    Traffic congestion
    Poor site layout (10%)............................. $ 696,108

        Total depreciation...............................   − $4,037,431
Estimated building value.............................. $2,923,658
Land value, 105.7 acres...............................   633,400
        Estimated market value, cost approach....... $3,557,058
                      (rounded) $3,560,000

value of $3,560,000 shown in Table 10–3 includes the estimated land value, which was derived from comparable sales of similar industrial acreage.

Cost Approach Advantages. While the limitations of the cost technique are apparent, frequently it is the only available approach to value. Hence the limitations must be reviewed relative to alternative appraisal approaches. If sales data are deficient and property may not be appraised under the income approach, the cost technique provides the most accurate method of valuation. Certain specific advantages of the cost technique may recommend reliance on this valuation approach.

First, the cost technique tends to be favored for the appraisal of new construction. If the building is designed with typical building features, workmanship, and materials, there is usually a close approximation to new construction cost and market value. The cost approach tends to lose accuracy for buildings showing substantial depreciation.

Second, the cost approach furnishes the best evidence of value for properties having little marketability, namely, public buildings, churches, and highly specialized industrial structures. While the cost technique is highly subjective, in these instances the appraiser has few alternatives to guide his market value estimate.

Third, the cost technique is appropriately used to estimate the cost of building rehabilitation, modernization, or remodeling. Here the capitalization of net income and the market approach supplement the cost approach to value.

Fourth, the cost approach tends to be reasonably accurate if (1) the building shows a minimum of depreciation and (2) the site is developed to its highest and best use. The cost approach to value helps in the decision-making process, for example, in comparing the projected cost of a new apartment building with its capitalized net income value. On the other hand, it would be invalid to appraise a 30-year-old single-family dwelling under the cost approach if a two-story walk-up apartment were believed to be the highest and best use. Therefore, the cost technique is adapted to the valuation of new property which shows little depreciation and represents the highest and best use of the site.

SUMMARY

The market approach refers to the analysis of recently sold property to estimate market value. As a method of valuation this approach is often preferred because sales prices of like property are convincing evidence of market value. The market approach avoids the personal bias of the cost technique and is useful in appraising property frequently sold. Against these advantages are the difficulties of adjusting for the time of sale, for dissimilar property characteristics, for the effect of sales terms on prices, and for the motives of buyer and seller.

Real estate sales involving government, charitable organizations, family members, and interrelated corporations are eliminated as comparable sales. Comparable sales research normally covers public and private sources or commercial services that provide lists of sales data. The recorder of deeds or other official who accepts public documents for the public record is a prime source of information on real estate transfers. Practicing appraisers develop relationships with developers, contractors, investors, and financial institutions that have knowledge of current real estate sales. Sales prices are adjusted to show differences in main valuation features: time of sale, property characteristics, type of financing, location, and the like.

Gross income multipliers express the relation between gross income and sales price. Their reliability depends on the uniformity of ratios, which may not depart from the norm if the gross income multipliers are applied to the appraisal of single-family dwellings.

The cost approach depends on the estimation of cost by one of three techniques. The quantity survey method lists the quantity of materials and labor and their cost to produce a detailed cost estimate. Unit in place refers to the labor and material costs expressed as a per unit value: square foot, lineal foot, board foot, or similar measures. Most appraisers prefer square foot cost estimates.

The cost estimate of a new building is reduced by depreciation in one of three forms: physical depreciation, which is caused by wear and tear, the action of the elements, and catastrophic events; functional obsolescence, which describes a loss in value from changes in design or a loss of building utility; and economic obsolescence, which is a decrease in value that results from forces external to the property appraised. The cost approach is completed by adding the land value (taken from comparable sales analysis) to the depreciated building cost.

The limitations of the cost approach follow from the lack of agreement on cost components. Architectural fees and selling costs, for example, must be assumed for each cost estimate, but the amounts allowed for these vary among appraisers employing this technique. The difficulty is compounded by the differing assumptions of appraisers on the quality of workmanship, contractor efficiency, and the proper allowance for overhead and profit.

Against these limitations may be set certain inherent advantages of the cost approach. The cost technique is appropriate for the appraisal of new construction. It is frequently the best evidence of value for properties having little marketability. It is useful in estimating the cost of building rehabilitation, and it tends to be reasonably accurate if the building appraised has little or no depreciation and if the site is developed to its hightest and best use.

REVIEW QUESTIONS

1. Contrast the logic of the market and cost approaches to value. Explain thoroughly.
2. What are the main limitations of the market approach to value?
3. In view of the advantages of the market comparison approach, what types of property would you appraise by this method?
4. Explain how you would obtain a list of comparable sales.
5. Outline the minimum information necessary for a comparable sales presentation.
6. Show by example how you would adjust real estate sales for appraisal purposes.
7. Demonstrate how you would appraise property by annual gross income multipliers; monthly gross income multipliers.

8. What is the significant difference between reproduction and replacement costs?

9. What estimating techniques would you use to appraise a single-family dwelling under the cost approach? Explain why you would not use other techniques of estimating costs.

10. Define and explain by example the three types of depreciation.

11. Explain four main limitations of the cost approach.

12. In view of the advantages of the cost approach, what types of property would you appraise under this method of valuation?

SELECTED REFERENCES

The Appraisal of Real Estate, chaps. 14 and 16. 6th ed. Chicago: American Institute of Real Estate Appraisers, 1973.

Boeckh Building Valuation Manual, vol. 1: *Residential and Agricultural.* Milwaukee: Boeckh Division, American Appraisal Co., 1972.

Boykin, James H. "Developmental Method of Land Appraisal," *Appraisal Journal,* vol. 44, no. 2 (April 1976), pp. 181–92.

Fredman, Albert J., and White, R. Dean. "A Logical Method of Depreciating Buildings," *Appraisal Journal,* vol. 42, no. 4 (October 1974), pp. 549–64.

Ratcliff, Richard U. *Valuation for Real Estate Decisions,* chaps. 3 and 5. Santa Cruz, Calif.: Democrat Press, 1972.

Sackman, Julius L. "Market Value Approach to Valuation," *Appraisal Journal,* vol. 41, no. 1 (January 1973), pp. 58–74.

Smith, Halbert C. *Real Estate Appraisal,* chap. 7. Columbus: Grid, Inc., 1976.

Wendt, Paul F. *Real Estate Appraisal Review and Outlook,* chaps. 5 and 8. Athens: University of Georgia Press, 1974.

Wesman, Harvey. "Appraising Vacant Land: Current Realities," *Appraisal Journal,* vol. 44, no. 1 (January 1976), pp. 94–97.

11

The Income Approach

After reading this chapter, you should be familiar with the following points:

1 The meaning of contract and economic rent.

2 The reasons for making rental comparisons.

3 Methods of revising annual operating expense statements: the additions, the deletions, and the stabilized expenses.

4 Methods of estimating market rates of capitalization.

5 The use of the present worth of one and the present worth of one per period tables.

6 The residual capitalization techniques.

AT FIRST GLANCE, the valuation of income property would seem fairly simple since it depends on three factors: the annual gross income, the annual expenses of operation, and the capitalization rate. It is reasoned that market value is equivalent to the *present worth of discounted future income.*

Note that it is not the *past* or *present* income that affects value. Consequently, considerable attention is given to the estimate of future gross income, stabilized expenses of operation, and the appropriate capitalization rate that converts net operating income to value. Investors in income property purchase the right to future income which has a present market value. It is this aspect of appraising income property that complicates income property appraisals.

Still another complicated issue concerns the continuing inflation. The general rise in land values, construction costs, and operating expenses in itself creates uncertainty over the future profitability of real estate ownership. Efforts to control inflation and support employment by changes in monetary policy cause unpredictable changes in interest rates. As a result of these trends, appraisers must support their opinion of value with a thorough analysis of the market. The problem of inflation is suggested in Figure 11–1, which shows past trends in the price level.

The consumer price index, based on 1967 prices, measures the relative change in the market basket of goods and services purchased by urban families. Figure 11–1 shows that consumer prices have changed from 94.5 in 1965 to 165.6 in 1975—a 75.2 percent increase. The implicit price deflator, which measures changes in the prices of all goods and services included in the annual gross national product, shows a similar trend. This measure of the price level, based on 1967 prices, has changed from 44.1 in 1940 to 166.8 in 1975, an increase of 278 percent in 35 years.

Note also the change in the index of farm real estate values as determined by the Department of Agriculture. This series shows that farm land values, based again on 1967 prices, have increased by some 82 percent in the last five years. The projections extrapolated in Figure 11–1 may not be realized, but they show how the indexes may change, assuming that past trends continue—which is a mere conjecture at this time. Surely the appraiser operating in this environment must base his estimate on the most careful analysis of gross income, expenses of operation, and the true, market rate of capitalization.

THE GROSS INCOME ESTIMATE

For appraisal purposes considerable care must be taken in evaluating an income statement. Typically the property owner submits an income statement that has been prepared for income tax purposes. If this is the case, certain adjustments must be made. The first difficulty begins with the concept of *contract rent,* which refers to the actual rent collected accord-

FIGURE 11–1

Price Index Trends

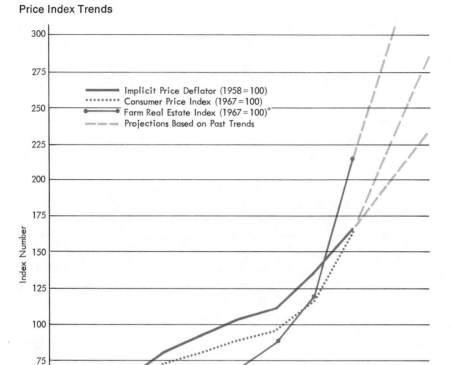

Year

* Index numbers are calculated as of March 1 of each year.

Sources: Implicit price deflator—U.S. Department of Commerce, Bureau of Economic Analysis, *Survey of Current Business,* vol. 55 (July 1975), p. S–2. consumer price index—adapted from *Statistical Abstract of the United States, 1964* (Washington, D.C.: U.S. Government Printing Office, 1965). Farm real estate index—U.S. Department of Agriculture, Economic Research Service, *Farm Real Estate Market Developments,* CD–66 (July 1964), p. 9; CD–78 (July 1973), p. 15; CD–80 (July 1975), p. 10.

ing to either oral or written contract. Since the contract rent may have been determined by past negotiations which are no longer representative of market rent, appraisers must value property according to its *economic rent*. This term refers to the market rent that would be realized at the date of appraisal. Because of the importance of appraising property according to its market rent, an income appraisal includes a comparison of rents on similar properties which indicates the current market rent. The correct interpretation of comparable rents is critical to an accurate valuation.

Rental Comparisons

In making comparisons of rent on similar appraised properties, it is important to think in terms of the *gross possible income* (also known as the potential gross income). Gross possible income, a term used by apartment house managers, is the gross income that would be earned if all apartments were rented, including an imputed rent for apartments occupied by employees. In apartment operations, income will also be realized from other sources: garage and parking fees, store and office rents, laundry equipment, vending machines, and similar charges.

Units of Comparison. Because of the differences in the size of rental properties, gross possible income must be reduced to relative terms, depending on the property appraised. Some of the units of comparison for the more common income properties are shown below:

Property Type	Units of Comparison
Apartment buildings	Apartment unit, per room, per square foot
Shopping centers	Gross leasable area
Office buildings	Net rentable area
Industrial plants	Gross floor area

The gross square feet of an apartment building includes the area of each floor, including cellars, basements, mezzanines, penthouses, corridors, lobbies, stores, offices, and garages within the building—all areas measured from the outside dimensions of exterior walls. The gross square feet excludes unroofed and unenclosed spaces.

Apartment rents may also be compared by the rent per rentable floor area, which is computed by measuring the inside finish of outer walls less the space taken by stairs, elevator shafts, flues, pipe shafts, vertical ducts, air conditioning rooms, fan rooms, janitor closets, balconies, and other areas not available to tenants. The gross possible income, reduced to a square foot basis, provides the best means of comparing market rents with the rent of the property under valuation. Rents shown per room and per apartment may be misleading because these comparisons vary by room size and the number of rooms per apartment.

To analyze the gross income of a shopping center, the Urban Land Institute defines gross leasable area as the total floor area designed for tenant occupancy and exclusive use, including basements, mezzanines, and upper floors measured from the center line of joint partitions and from outside walls. The concept of gross leasable area excludes common areas, such as service areas not rented by individual tenants.

In office buildings, rental data are shown by the net rentable area, which refers to the inside dimensions of office space rented to tenants measured to the center wall of inside partitions. The analysis of rental comparisons allows the market value estimate to be based on the potential market rent and not the contract rent, which may be considerably below current market rent levels.

Tenant Services.   The task of comparing rents is complicated by differences in property types and in the services provided tenants. It would be inaccurate to compare the square foot rents of a 25-unit and a 100-unit garden court apartment to the gross possible income per square foot for a high-rise, 300-unit apartment building. Given the differences in the quality of the space, the services provided tenants, and the locations, this would be like comparing apples with oranges. Similarly, the rents of a neighborhood shopping center occupying a five-acre site should be compared with those of a similar shopping center, not with the rents of an air-conditioned, regional shopping center on 40 or more acres.

The services provided tenants vary widely among apartments. For example, in older buildings utilities may not be individually metered to each unit so that tenants pay for electricity, water, or gas as part of the rent. It would be invalid to compare rents in an apartment building in which the owner pays all utility charges with rents in a building in which utilities are metered and billed separately to each tenant. For the same reason, since an apartment building providing a sauna bath, a swimming pool, and tennis courts would include the expense of these facilities in the rents, those rents could not be compared with the rents of an apartment building without these improvements and services.

In short, considerable appraisal judgment is required in correcting the owner's statement to show the true market rent, considering the quality of space and tenant services. With qualifications accounting for these differences, the valuation opinion starts with an estimate of the gross possible income as if the property were fully rented and rented at the current market rent.

Vacancy and Bad Debt Allowance

It is unlikely that income properties will be fully rented over their economic life. Even in the most favorable rental markets, vacancies occur as a result of the need to rehabilitate, modernize, and redecorate. Hence an estimate providing a "normal" allowance for vacancies and bad debts must be made over the economic life of the property.

Again the estimate will not necessarily agree with the vacancy and bad debt deduction reported by the owner; the estimate will be made after an analysis of the rental market for the property appraised. For this portion of the appraisal, a survey of existing vacancies guides the vacancy projection. Few apartment dwellings are appraised with a vacancy allowance of less than 3 percent. The vacancy allowance may be much higher for properties subject to seasonal occupancy in resort and vacation areas. Before entering annual operating expenses, the appraiser will start with a projection of the gross possible income less vacancy and bad debt allowances, giving an estimate of the *effective gross income.*

```
Gross possible income............... $100,000
Less 6% vacancy and bad
    debt allowances...................  − 6,000
            Effective gross income......... $ 94,000
```

From the effective gross income, annual operating expenses are deducted to give the final figure to be capitalized: the net operating income.

ANNUAL OPERATING EXPENSES

Estimating annual operating expenses represents the second step in appraising property. Annual operating expenses are deducted from effective gross income to estimate net operating income. In the usual case, the appraiser must make a number of revisions to an accounting statement or a property owner's statement prepared for income tax purposes. Actual expenses incurred in the preceding year must be stabilized to agree with average anticipated expenses over the life of the property for capitalization purposes.

In numerous instances, certain expenses allowable for income tax purposes are unrelated to operating expenses and must be deleted. In addition, property owners frequently omit expenses necessary to the operation of income property. These deficiencies result from the fact that income-expense statements prepared for income tax purposes follow income tax law and regulations or are based on actual income and expenses incurred during the year. For appraisal purposes each expense must be reevaluated and adjusted to report operating expenses typically incurred and anticipated over the life of the building.

There is some justification for the complaint that operating expenses are partly related to management efficiency. A poorly supervised property will show a higher level of expenses for supplies and labor and will probably show a higher vacancy rate because of poor owner-tenant relations. In such circumstances, expenses taken from property showing below average man agement efficiency would be inappropriate for valuation purposes. By the same token an unusually efficient management leading to unusually low expenses would distort the estimate of value above current market value. Appraisers assume average, typical management—avoiding the extremes of expenses taken from above or below the average level of management efficiency.

TABLE 11–1

Annual Income and Operating Expenses, 128-Unit Garden Court Apartment

	Total	Per Room	Per Square Foot	Percent of Gross Possible Income
Income				
Gross possible rental income.........	$247,872	462.45	1.95	83.1
Other income........................	50,483	94.18	0.40	16.9
Gross possible income...............	$298,355	$556.63	$2.35	100.0
Less vacancies and bad debts........	−20,885	−38.96	−0.16	−7.0
Effective gross income............	$277,470	$517.67	$2.19	93.0
Expenses				
Payroll...............................	$ 14,918	$ 27.83	$0.12	5.0
Electricity............................	7,757	14.47	0.06	2.6
Gas (less heating fuel)...............	3,879	7.24	0.03	1.3
Water................................	3,282	6.12	0.03	1.1
Heating fuel.........................	298	0.56	0.00	0.1
Management.........................	18,796	35.07	0.15	6.3
Administrative costs..................	6,265	11.69	0.05	2.1
Painting and decorating..............	6,564	12.25	0.05	2.2
Maintenance and repairs.............	17,901	33.40	0.14	6.0
Supplies.............................	1,193	2.23	0.01	0.4
Services.............................	2,984	5.57	0.02	1.0
Miscellaneous operating expenses....	597	1.11	0.00	0.2
Insurance............................	3,282	6.12	0.03	1.1
Real estate taxes....................	27,449	51.21	0.22	9.2
Other taxes.........................	1,492	2.78	0.01	0.5
Reserve for replacements.............	17,901	33.40	0.14	6.0
Total all expenses................	$134,558	$251.05	$1.06	45.1
Net operating income............	$142,912	$266.62	$1.13	47.9

Care must be exercised to present all expenses of operation in a manner that allows comparison with the experiences of other properties. Table 11–1 lists the total expenses of operating an apartment house and the expenses per room, per square foot, and as a percent of gross possible income. This standard format agrees closely with the annual report of income and operating expenses covering apartments, cooperatives, and condominiums prepared by the Institute of Real Estate Management.[1] By following the format of Table 11–1, comparisons may be made between local properties and the average expenses reported in national publications.

Stabilizing Expenses

There are a number of reasons for stabilizing expenses as reported on an income property statement. Actual expenses paid out may not be typical

---

[1] *Income and Expense Analysis: Apartments, Condominiums, and Cooperatives* (Chicago: Institute of Real Estate Management, published annually).

expenses anticipated over the property life. For instance, in a new 100-unit apartment building painting and redecorating expenses would be expected to be minimal in the first two years of operation. Though each apartment would require repainting and redecorating over, say, a five-year life, the actual expenses paid out in the first two years for redecorating would understate the "stabilized" redecorating expense. Therefore, the expenses of redecoration would be based on the cost of redecorating each apartment every five years, for example, to show the true annual expense.

Similarly, property taxes may be changed because of an anticipated increase in assessed values or a projected increase in property tax levies. If an investigation shows these possibilities, the appraiser would be warranted in increasing property taxes above the amount paid in earlier years. In still other cases, expenses may be prepaid, such as insurance paid over a three-year term, requiring an adjustment to show the annual cost. A three-year insurance premium of $1,200 must be reduced to $400 to show the annual insurance expense.

Another point worth considering is the general rise in expenses of operation. Over the last four years, the price of heating fuels has increased by 26.3 percent, according to the Institute of Real Estate Management. While future expenses are unknown, most appraisers would probably base their estimate of stabilized expenses on the past operating experience of the property appraised and on a comparison with typical expenses reported by comparable properties. The preferred procedure is to list expenses in terms of the current and stabilized expenses expected in the immediate future and to account for their uncertainty by capitalizing the anticipated net income by a relatively higher capitalization rate.

Deleting Improper Expenses

Certain expense items allowable for income tax purposes are unrelated to operating expenses. Items commonly entered on operating expense statements that should be omitted include:

Federal income taxes	Personal business expenditures
State income taxes	Mortgage principal payments
Building depreciation	Mortgage interest payments
Capital expenditures	

There are valid reasons for deleting these expenses from an income property statement. Federal and state income taxes have no direct relationship to property operation. They are related to the individual tax liability of the corporation or persons submitting the income tax return. The depreciation allowance for real estate, though an allowable deduction for income taxes, is not entered as an expense of operation. Custom dictates that the provision for capital recovery be accounted for in the capitalization process. In real estate valuation, therefore, depreciation allowances are not entered as an expense. Only the net operating income before depreciation is calculated for appraisal purposes.

Capital expenditures, such as the addition of new carports or garages for an apartment house or the construction of a swimming pool or tennis courts, are *capital expenditures,* not annual expenses of operation. These items would increase the annual recovery of capital and would be amortized over their economic life.

Mortgage principal and interest payments should be deleted. Including mortgage payments for this type of valuation would change net operating income, and therefore the value would vary according to the financing terms. Properties would have a different value according to the mortgage loan ratio, the interest rate, and the term of the mortgage. Extraordinary business expenses atypical of an apartment house operation, such as the use of a private car, attendance at real estate conventions, and other items unique to the owner but not to a typical shopping center or apartment operation, would also be deleted.

Adding Expenses of Operation

The lay person (or an accountant) may omit operating expenses that are not actually paid during the year. Suppose, for example, that a property is owner operated—say, a 20-unit apartment dwelling operated by an owner who lives in one of the units. Ordinarily the owner would not show management as an expense of operation; he contributes his labor to the enterprise. However, if the same property were sold to an investor who elected to employ a professional manager, management expenses would probably amount to some 6 percent of effective gross income. Therefore, management expenses which are omitted from the income statement must be added to show the true annual operating expense.

Furthermore, a nonprofessional investor may not report an allowance for the replacement of short-lived furniture and equipment. If each apartment of a 100-unit building has a $250 refrigerator with an estimated economic life of five years, it follows that each refrigerator (on the average) would be replaced every five years. The annual cost of refrigerators would be $50 ($250/5), or $5,000 per year for all apartments.

Similar adjustments would be made to replace lobby furniture, kitchen range tops and ovens, dishwashers, washing machines and dryers, or furniture. Consequently, the income statement should report the annual cost of replacing building equipment and furniture supplied to tenants.

The same reasoning applies to the allowance for repairs, maintenance, and redecorating. Usually the redecorating allowance will be based on the anticipated cost over a reasonable redecorating cycle. The experience of other property owners in making normal repairs to the building would be helpful in estimating the allowance for annual repair expenses. If the stabilized expenses are valid and improper expenses have been deleted and appropriate expenses added, the deduction of net operating expenses from the effective gross income results in the *net operating income:* that income which is used for capitalization purposes. See Table 11–2 for an illustration of these three adjustments.

First note that the owner's report gives income as the amount actually collected. This figure is adjusted to show the gross possible income less an allowance for vacancy and bad debts. Insurance is stabilized to an annual

TABLE 11–2

Correction of an Annual Income Statement for an Office Building

Owner's Income Statement			*Revised Income Statement*	
Gross income.........		$15,251	Gross possible income, 2,592 square feet	
			@ $6.00.................	$15,552
Less expenses			Less vacancy and bad debt	
Insurance (3 years)...	$ (300)		allowance, 5 percent.....	−778
Property taxes.......	2,150			
Depreciation.........	1,500			
Janitor..............	600		Effective gross income.....	$14,774
Water...............	30			
Car expense........	500		Less expenses	
Power, heat, and light	600		(Insurance).............	$ (100)
Supplies............	180		Management expense,	
			5 percent.............	739
Mortgage payment...	6,026	−11,886	(Property taxes)........	3,000
			Janitor..................	600
Annual income...		$ 3,365	Water..................	30
			Repairs and	
			maintenance..........	300
			Power, heat,	
			and light..............	600
			Supplies...............	180
			Reserve for	
			replacements.........	500 −6,049
			Net operating income	$ 8,725

```
┌────────┐ Items deleted.
──────── Items added.
(        ) Items stabilized.
```

expense; property taxes are increased to show the effect of an increase in assessed value or the annual property tax rate. Three items are deleted, and three other expense items are added. The net operating income of $8,725 is the amount to capitalize, and not the owner's stated income of $3,365.

ESTIMATING CAPITALIZATION RATES

The conversion of annual net operating income to market value is a discounting process: future income is discounted to give the present worth.

An asset earning $10,000 annual income in perpetuity (vacant land), capitalized at 8 percent, has an indicated market value of $125,000 ($10,000/0.08). The sum, $125,000, represents the discounted value of annual income earned in perpetuity. To put it differently, with an investment of $125,000 and annual income of $10,000, the investor earns an 8 percent return.

Four terms are commonly used to describe variations in the capitalization process:[2]

> *The discount rate:* The discount rate is synonymous with the interest rate—the rate of return earned on an investment.
> *The capitalization rate:* The sum of the discount rate and an allowance for capital recapture.
> *The overall rate of return:* The ratio between the annual net operating income and the sales price. It includes capital recapture on the building value.
> *The interest rate:* The rate of return on an investment. It does not include an allowance for capital recovery.

Capitalizing an income of $10,000 gives an indicated market value of $125,000; the 8 percent rate is a *discount rate*. The $125,000 is the amount an investor pays for the right to a future income of $10,000 which results in an 8 percent return on capital.

$$\text{Value} = \$\ 10,000/0.08$$
$$= \$125,000$$

Now assume that an annual net income of $100,000 is earned from the rental of a retail building. Assume further that $80,000 is assigned for the use of the building and that $20,000 represents the rental income from the use of the site. If a discount rate of 8 percent applies, an additional 2 percent must be added to recover the value of a building with a remaining economic life of 50 years ($1/50$th each year equals 2 percent). The resulting 10 percent would be the capitalization rate as shown below.

Starting with the net operating income of $100,000 before depreciation or capital recapture of the building, it is assumed that $20,000 is assigned to the land. Assuming also a remaining building life of 50 years, the income to the building is divided into two parts: the recapture of building capital of $16,000 (0.02 × $80,000) and a return on the building capital of $64,000 (0.08 × $80,000).

The proof of this calculation lies in applying the 8 percent rate of return on capital and the 2 percent rate of capital recapture. Their sum gives a capitalization rate of 10 percent. Therefore, with net income to the building equal to $80,000 and a 10 percent capitalization rate, the building has

---

[2] *Real Estate Appraisal Terminology* (Cambridge, Mass.: Ballinger Publishing Co., 1975).

an indicated value of $800,000 ($80,000/0.10). The capitalization rate includes (1) an annual allowance to *recapture* the building capital (2 percent), straight-line capitalization, and (2) a *return* on capital of 8 percent.

Annual Recapture and Return on Capital

Net operating income
    (before capital recapture)................. $100,000
Assumed income to land.................... −20,000

Income to building
    (50-year building life)..................... $ 80,000
Recapture of capital, straight-line
    (2% of building value).................... −16,000
Return on building capital................. $ 64,000

Proof:
    0.08 rate of *return on capital*
    0.02 *recapture of capital*
    0.10 capitalization rate
    Building value:
      $80,000/0.10............................ $800,000
    Recapture of capital:
      $800,000 × 0.02......................... 16,000
    Return on capital:
      $800,000 × 0.08......................... 64,000
    Net income to building................... $ 80,000

The Market Rate of Capitalization

Errors in market value are magnified by incorrect capitalization rates. A $500,000 net income capitalized at 8 percent has a value of $6,250,000 ($500,000/0.08). The same income capitalized at 10 percent produces a value of $5,000,000. A difference of two percentage points produces a difference of $1,250,000 in market value. For this reason considerable attention is given to the selection of the rate of capitalization.

As a practical matter, appraisers rely on three methods of estimating capitalization rates. Though variations of these techniques may be found, most appraisers apply one of the following methods: market comparison, band of investment, or alternative rates of return.

Market Comparison. The *overall* capitalization rate is given by comparing real estate prices with net operating income. Simply stated, the ratio between income and price gives the overall capitalization rate:

$$\text{Overall capitalization rate} = \frac{\text{Net operating income}}{\text{Sales price}}$$

Following this procedure, the overall capitalization rate is indicated for four apartment buildings sold in Fort Lauderdale, Florida:

Sales Price	Net Operating Income	Indicated Overall Capitalization Rate*
$ 5,395,000..............	$ 443,400	8.2%
3,750,000..............	342,700	9.1
3,641,000..............	310,500	8.5
13,689,000..............	1,196,000	8.7

* Overall capitalization rates vary over time and by location. It is not implied that these rates are applicable to a particular appraisal. Only the method of derivation is emphasized here.

The rationale behind this method rests on its objectivity. It is reasoned that buyers negotiate prices on the expected net income. For example, in the first property, the price of $5,395,000 was paid for the right to earn an expected net annual income of $443,400. In other words, given the net income, a price has been negotiated that results in an overall capitalization rate of 8.2 percent.

The market comparison method has certain limitations: sales prices may be distorted by unusual financial terms, and properties may be operated at high vacancy rates and at varying levels of efficiency. In addition, the overall capitalization rate may vary according to the age and condition of the property and its location. Assuming that the appraiser makes allowances for these factors, he or she selects the capitalization rate that applies most closely to the property appraised. As with comparative sales of property, the appraiser selects the capitalization rate which is appropriate for capitalizing net income.

Band of Investment. The band of investment method weights the return earned on ownership interests held in real estate. Starting with a first mortgage, which is the least risk share, the rate is weighted by the proportion that the first mortgage bears to value. This figure may be readily obtained from mortgages recently negotiated on similar property. The second mortgage, covering a smaller interest in the property, carries a higher interest rate because of the subordinate interest of the second mortgage to the first mortgage. With a 12 percent interest rate and a loan-to-value ratio of 15 percent, the weighted rate of return is 0.01800.

To illustrate, assume that an investigation of local real estate investments reveals a 20 percent rate of return on an equity interest equal to 10 percent of the property value. Hence, if investors require a 20 percent return on a real estate equity of 10 percent, this indicates a weighted return of 2 percent (0.20×0.10). The example below shows how the weighted rate of return produces an indicated capitalization rate of 10.925 percent.

Band of Investment Method of Deriving the Capitalization Rate

Ownership Interest	Interest Rate	Ratio of Ownership Interest to Value	Weighted Value
First mortgage............	0.0950	0.75	0.07125
Second mortgage.........	0.1200	0.15	0.01800
Equity....................	0.2000	0.10	0.02000
Indicated capitalization rate................			0.10925

Provided that reliable information may be secured on first mortgages, second mortgages, and equity shares, and provided that the data are sufficiently consistent and representative, this method gives an accurate indication of the prevailing market capitalization rate.

Alternative Rates of Return. Real estate investments must earn a return competitive with that of other assets of equal risk and certainty of income. On its face this proposition seems reasonable: investors turn to the investment offering the highest rate of return for a given risk. To illustrate this point, consider Table 11–3, which lists returns earned on investments that compete with real estate.

TABLE 11–3

Rates of Return Indicated by Market Interest Rates

	Rate
Federal Reserve Board discount rate..................................	6.00
Prime interest rate.....................	6.48
U.S. five-year bonds—taxable..........	7.65
U.S. ten-year bonds—taxable..........	7.64
Municipal tax exempts (Aaa)..........	6.64
Municipal tax exempts (A).............	7.89
Corporate bonds (Aaa)................	8.78
Corporate bonds (A)..................	9.67
Corporate bonds (Baa)................	10.33
Corporate *new* bonds (Aaa)............	9.37
Corporate *new* bonds (A)..............	9.83
Common stocks—500 (*dividend yields only*)......	4.07
Industrial—425........................	3.72
Railroads—15........................	5.73
Utilities—60.........................	3.24
FHA mortgage rate on dwellings........	9.53

Source: *The Appraiser* (Chicago: American Institute of Real Estate Appraisers, published monthly).

Table 11–3 shows that at a given date, dividend yields ranged from 3.72 percent for 425 industrial stocks to 10.3 percent for corporate bonds. In one respect, reference to dividend yields is misleading since dividend yields do not include the return from capital gains. Though this approach is not used exclusively to select capitalization rates, it provides upper and lower limits for capitalization rates on real estate. This method is highly subjective since the appraiser must account for differences in income characteristics, duration, and the relative risk of each investment.

There are circumstances, however, when the return on real estate would be unusually low. For example, investors may anticipate profits from capital gains which might be considered more important than the annual income. Thus, if investors expect farmland to double in value over the next five years, then they would tend to bid up the price of land to the point that yields fall to nominal levels, say, 2, 3, or 4 percent. In these circumstances, it is more appropriate to derive capitalization rates from the market.

CAPITALIZATION TECHNIQUES

One of two main methods may be selected for capitalization purposes: *straight-line capitalization,* which is an adaptation of capitalization in perpetuity, and *annuity capitalization,* which is a method of capitalizing income for a stated period. If the latter method is used, the appraiser must turn to capitalization tables. The tables most important for appraisal purposes are referred to as the *present worth of one* and the *present worth of one per period.* The first table, for a stated capitalization rate, gives the value of one dollar at a future time. The second table gives the present worth of an income of one dollar payable at the end of a year for a given number of years.[3]

Capitalization in Perpetuity

In capitalizing net income earned on vacant land, it is assumed that land does not depreciate and that it continues to earn income indefinitely. The market value is then indicated by the capitalization in perpetuity formula:

$$MV = I/R$$

Assuming a rate of return of 8 percent and an income of $10,000, the market value would be equal to $125,000:

$$MV = \$\ 10,000/0.08$$
$$= \$125,000$$

---

[3] For a more detailed discussion of capitalization tables consult standard finance references. See, for example, Henry E. Hoagland, Leo D. Stone, and William B. Brueggeman, *Real Estate Finance,* 6th ed. (Homewood, Ill.: Richard D. Irwin, Inc., 1977), chap. 8.

If there is a high degree of risk in earning income, the property will be capitalized at a *higher rate,* for example, 20 percent, which will produce a *lower value.* In contrast, if future income and/or capital gains expectations are favorable (that is, the investor anticipates increasing net income and/ or capital gains), the investor would be typically willing to accept a *lower rate of return,* say, 3, 4, or 5 percent, which would produce a *higher present value.* For the most part, this formula is used only for vacant land since it makes no separate provision for capital recapture of the building value.

Capitalization Tables

A capitalization table is derived from the familiar formula for compound interest:

$$S_1 = P(1 + i)$$

Where:

S_1 = Compound amount of one dollar for one year
i = Rate of interest
P = Principal or amount of money borrowed or invested

Present Worth of One.   This table is derived from the manipulation of the compound of one formula:

$$P = \frac{S}{(1 + i)^n}$$

Therefore, one dollar at the end of a year discounted at 8 percent would be equal to:

$$P = \frac{1.00}{(1 + 0.08)^1}$$
$$= \$0.9259$$

Present worth of one tables are used to value a future sum or reversion at the end of a given period, assuming a stated capitalization. Hence, a dollar postponed to the end of five years, discounted at 8 percent, equals $0.680583. The present worth of one dollar postponed to the end of each year for five years is shown below:

Period	Present Value of $1.00
1	0.925925
2	0.857338
3	0.793832
4	0.735029
5	0.680583

Present Worth of One per Period.   Present worth of one per period tables represent an accumulated form of present worth of one tables. For instance, an income of one dollar payable at the end of the year for five years is equivalent to the present worth of one dollar postponed for each of the five years. That is, an income is merely the present worth of a series of postponed sums as indicated below:

$$\text{Present worth of one per period} = \frac{1}{(1.08)^1} + \frac{1}{(1.08)^2} + \frac{1}{(1.08)^3} + \frac{1}{(1.08)^4} + \frac{1}{(1.08)^5}$$

To find the present worth of one dollar payable at the end of the year for five years, discounted at 8 percent, you would sum the discounted value of a dollar postponed for each year.

$$\begin{aligned}\text{Present worth of one dollar per period, five years, 8 percent discount} &= 0.925925 + 0.857338 + 0.793832 \\ &\quad + 0.735029 + 0.680583 \\ &= \$3.992710\end{aligned}$$

The present worth of one period table is an accumulation of present worth of one factors as indicated below:

Period	Present Worth of One per Period
1...................	0.925925
2...................	1.783264
3...................	2.577096
4...................	3.312126
5...................	3.992710

Table 11–4 shows the present worth of one and the present worth of one per period factors for 100 periods for an 8 percent discount. Consult the appendix for other interest rates and an explanation of other capitalization factors.

To illustrate the use of Table 11–4, suppose that the problem is to calculate the present worth of land worth $100,000 today which reverts to the owner at the expiration of a 50-year lease. Assuming an 8 percent capitalization rate, the land would have a present worth of $100,000 times the present worth of one factor for 50 years.

$$\begin{aligned}\text{Present worth of \$100,000, 50 years, 8\% discount} &= \$100,000 \times 0.021321 \\ &= \$2,132.10\end{aligned}$$

Assume also that the lease provides for an income of $10,000 over 50 years. The present worth of the right to income payable at the end of the year for 50 years, 8 percent discount, would be equal to:

$$\begin{aligned}\text{Present worth of an income, 50 years, 8\% discount} &= \$10,000 \times 12.233485 \\ &= \$122,334.85\end{aligned}$$

TABLE 11-4
Present Worth of One and Present Worth of One per Period Tables: 8%

Periods	Present Worth of One	Present Worth of One per Period	Periods	Present Worth of One	Present Worth of One per Period
1.......	0.925926	0.925926	51......	0.019742	12.253227
2.......	0.857339	1.783265	52......	0.018280	12.271506
3.......	0.793832	2.577097	53......	0.016925	12.288432
4.......	0.735030	3.312127	54......	0.015672	12.304103
5.......	0.680583	3.992710	55......	0.014511	12.318614
6.......	0.630170	4.622880	56......	0.013436	12.332050
7.......	0.583490	5.206370	57......	0.012441	12.344491
8.......	0.540269	5.746639	58......	0.011519	12.356010
9.......	0.500249	6.246888	59......	0.010666	12.366676
10.......	0.463193	6.710081	60......	0.009876	12.376552
11.......	0.428883	7.138964	61......	0.009144	12.385696
12.......	0.397114	7.536078	62......	0.008467	12.394163
13.......	0.367698	7.903776	63......	0.007840	12.402003
14.......	0.340461	8.244237	64......	0.007259	12.409262
15.......	0.315242	8.559479	65......	0.006721	12.415983
16.......	0.291890	8.851369	66......	0.006223	12.422207
17.......	0.270269	9.121638	67......	0.005762	12.427970
18.......	0.250249	9.371887	68......	0.005336	12.433305
19.......	0.231712	9.603599	69......	0.004940	12.438245
20.......	0.214548	9.818147	70......	0.004574	12.442820
21.......	0.198656	10.016803	71......	0.004236	12.447055
22.......	0.183941	10.200744	72......	0.003922	12.450977
23.......	0.170315	10.371059	73......	0.003631	12.454608
24.......	0.157699	10.528758	74......	0.003362	12.457971
25.......	0.146018	10.674776	75......	0.003113	12.461084
26.......	0.135202	10.809978	76......	0.002883	12.463967
27.......	0.125187	10.935165	77......	0.002669	12.466636
28.......	0.115914	11.051078	78......	0.002471	12.469107
29.......	0.107328	11.158406	79......	0.002288	12.471396
30.......	0.099377	11.257783	80......	0.002119	12.473514
31.......	0.092016	11.349799	81......	0.001962	12.475476
32.......	0.085200	11.434999	82......	0.001817	12.477293
33.......	0.078889	11.513888	83......	0.001682	12.478975
34.......	0.073045	11.586934	84......	0.001557	12.480532
35.......	0.067635	11.654568	85......	0.001442	12.481974
36.......	0.062625	11.717193	86......	0.001335	12.483306
37.......	0.057986	11.775179	87......	0.001236	12.484546
38.......	0.053690	11.828869	88......	0.001145	12.485691
39.......	0.049713	11.878582	89......	0.001060	12.486751
40.......	0.046031	11.924613	90......	0.000981	12.487732
41.......	0.042621	11.967235	91......	0.000909	12.488641
42.......	0.039464	12.006699	92......	0.000841	12.489482
43.......	0.036541	12.043240	93......	0.000779	12.490261
44.......	0.033834	12.077074	94......	0.000721	12.490983
45.......	0.031328	12.108402	95......	0.000668	12.491651
46.......	0.029007	12.137409	96......	0.000618	12.492269
47.......	0.026859	12.164267	97......	0.000573	12.492842
48.......	0.024869	12.189136	98......	0.000530	12.493372
49.......	0.023027	12.212163	99......	0.000491	12.493863
50.......	0.021321	12.233485	100......	0.000455	12.494318

Source: William M. Shenkel, *Capitalization Tables for Investment Purposes* (Athens, Ga.: College of Business Administration, University of Georgia, 1972), pp. 64–65.

The value of the owner's interest in holding this lease (the leased fee interest) would be equal to (1) the present worth of the right to the land (reversionary right) at the end of the lease ($2,132.10) and (2) the present worth of the rental income paid over 50 years ($122,334.85). Hence the value of the leased fee would be:

$$
\begin{array}{r}
\$\ \ 2,132.10 \\
\underline{122,334.85} \\
\text{Leased fee value}\quad \$124,466.95 \\
\text{(rounded)}\quad \$124,500.00
\end{array}
$$

The factors in Table 11–4 are also used for the residual capitalization techniques.

Residual Capitalization Techniques

For depreciable buildings, the appraiser has three options in capitalizing net income: the land residual, the building residual, and the property residual capitalization techniques. The type of property appraised and the available data determine the method selected.

Building Residual. In this method, land value is estimated from comparable sales. That portion of net income attributable to land is deducted. The remaining (residual) income to the builder is capitalized by providing for the *return* on building capital and the *recapture* of building capital. The land and building value added give the estimated market value land residual capitalization.

To illustrate, suppose that the property earns a net annual income of $50,000. The land value is independently estimated from comparable sales, say, $300,000. Assuming an 8 percent capitalization, the income attributable to land is $24,000. With a 50-year life, building capital recovery would be equal to 2 percent, straight-line capitalization. Capitalization at 10 percent, adding the 2 percent capital recapture rate and the 8 percent return, indicates a building value of $260,000. Adding the land value of $300,000 gives a market value, building residual, straight-line capitalization of $560,000:

Net operating income......................	$ 50,000
Less income to land $300,000 × 0.08.........	− 24,000
Income to building........................	26,000
Building value $26,000/0.10.................	260,000
Add land value............................	+300,000
Market value, building residual, straight-line capitalization..........	$560,000

Land Residual Capitalization. For a new building showing relatively little depreciation and representing the highest and best use of the land, land residual capitalization is preferred. In this instance, first estimate the building value based on current construction costs. To illustrate, assume a net income of $50,000 and a building value of $260,000 with an estimated 50-year remaining life.

Under an 8 percent return on capital, $26,000 per year would recapture the building investment over 50 years and earn a return of 8 percent. The remaining income of $24,000, attributable to land, would indicate a land value of $300,000 ($24,000/0.08). Land residual, straight-line capitalization is shown below:

Net operating income......................	$ 50,000
Less income to building	
$260,000 × (0.08 + 0.02).....................	−26,000
Income to land.............................	$ 24,000
Land value $24,000/0.08.....................	$300,000
Add building value.........................	260,000
Market value, land residual, straight-line capitalization...........	$560,000

Annuity Capitalization. The two preceding examples assumed straight-line capitalization. It is called straight line because capital recovery is based on a level payment each year, depending on the estimate of the remaining economic life. The amount of straight-line recapture is taken from the reciprocal of the economic life. A building with a 50-year remaining life gives a 2 percent, straight-line recapture rate (1/50); a building with a 40-year remaining life would recapture capital at the rate of 2.5 percent (1/40).

The alternative is to value the property using capitalization tables—a procedure called annuity capitalization. The capitalization is based only on the rate of discount; no separate recapture rate is added. The present worth of one per period tables provide for capital recovery each year, with the rate of return calculated on the declining balance.

Using the preceding example as a case in point, annuity capitalization would be calculated as follows:

Net operating income......................	$ 50,000
Less income to building....................	− 21,253
($260,000/12.233485)	
Income to land.............................	$ 28,747
Land value $28,747/0.08.....................	359,338
Add building value.........................	+260,000
Indicated market value land residual, annuity capitalization.....	$619,000
	(rounded)

Starting with an estimated building value of $260,000, $21,253 is attributable to the building. The factor of 12.233485 is the present worth of the right to an income of one dollar, payable at the end of each year for 50 years, discounted at 8 percent. The income residual to the land, $28,747, is capitalized in perpetuity to give the land value of $359,338. The factor for the present worth of one per period may be used in the building residual method as a substitute for straight-line capitalization.

Property Residual. In the land and building residual techniques, income must initially be divided between land and buildings. In the property residual technique, this problem is avoided. Income from land and building are assumed to be derived from the whole property, land and building.

Therefore, given the net operating income, the first step is to estimate the remaining economic life of the property. If the economic life is estimated to be 25 years, the income is converted to value by the present worth of one per period factor for 25 years at some rate of discount. The next step is to value the reversion: the land value which reverts to the owner at the time the building is assumed to have no value. Suppose a review of local land sales indicates that the site has a current value of $100,000. In this step, it is presumed that land worth $100,000 at present reverts to the owner in 25 years—the end of the economic life of the building. Therefore, the land reversion is discounted to indicate the present worth of the land ($100,000) deferred for 25 years.

The method is illustrated by assuming a net income of $10,000, an 8 percent discount rate, and a land reversionary value of $100,000:

```
Net operating income...................... $ 10,000
Present worth of income
    $10,000 × 10.6747..........................  106,747
Add land reversion
    $100,000 × 0.146018........................   14,601
              Market value, property residual........ $131,348
                                                     $131,500
                                                     (rounded)
```

The factor 10.6747, taken from Table 11–4, represents the present worth of the right of one dollar payable at the end of the year for 25 years, discounted at 8 percent. The present worth of the right to an income of $10,000 for 25 years—the remaining economic life of the building—is $106,747. At the end of the 25 years, only the land has value. The present worth of the land in 25 years is $14,601. Note that errors in estimating the present worth of the land reversion are minimized by the discounting process: A $1,000 error in the current land value is reduced to an error of $146.01 in the final market value. The factor, 0.146018, represents the present worth of one dollar payable in 25 years discounted at 8 percent. The present worth of the income and the land reversionary value indicate a market value, property residual, of $131,500.

It should be noted that these examples assume that the income property is valued independently of financing terms and that the property is held over its economic life. For investment purposes, these are not very realistic assumptions. In practice, investors typically borrow money to purchase real estate, and they may hold the property only for a limited number of years because of income tax aspects of real estate ownership. Methods of treating property by estimating the return on the equity interest and considering the income tax aspects of real estate investment are deferred to the chapter on investment (Chapter 15).

SUMMARY

The income approach rests on the proposition that market value is equal to the present worth of future income. Present income and past income may not be relevant: the approach rests on an estimate of future income. Accordingly, valuation accuracy depends on the estimate of (1) the gross income, (2) the expenses of operation, and (3) the market rate of capitalization.

In estimating gross income, appraisers deal with contract rent—the actual rent collected according to oral or written agreements—and the economic rent, which refers to the current market rent. Ideally the gross income is estimated from a comparison of rents on similar properties. The *gross possible income* or potential gross income refers to rental income, assuming that all components of the property are rented. For an apartment appraisal, gross income comparisons are reduced to rent per apartment, per square foot, and per room, and are adjusted for differences in the level of tenant services and in the quality of the property rented. In each instance, an allowance for vacancy and bad debts is subtracted from gross possible income to give *effective gross income*.

Annual operating expenses must be stabilized (1) to eliminate accounting entries appropriate only for net income tax purposes and (2) to include ordinary operating costs. Operating costs would include an allowance for annual maintenance and repairs, the replacement of equipment, and management expenses (if the property is owner operated). Since the net income estimate relates to future income, past expenses which are expected to increase over the early life of the property would be adjusted upward.

Net operating income resulting from the subtraction of stabilized expenses from effective gross income must be capitalized to show present value. The capitalization rate refers to the discount rate plus an allowance for capital recapture. The capitalization rate is found by the market comparison method, by the band of investment method, and from the rate of return earned on alternative investments.

Straight-line capitalization provides for a constant annual sum for the return of capital. Annuity capitalization employs two capitalization tables: the present worth of one dollar and the present worth of one dollar per period.

In using straight-line or annuity capitalization, three main options are available: the *land residual,* the *building residual,* and the *property residual.* In the first instance, the appraiser estimates building values from recent costs of construction and deducts the amount of income imputed to the building. The remaining income is capitalized to give land value. Adding the building value and the land value produces the indicated market value.

Under the *building* residual technique, the appraiser starts with a market estimate of land value, preferably taken from comparable sales, and de-

ducts the amount of income accruing to the land. The next step provides
for the capitalization of the remaining income to estimate the building
value. Again, adding the land value and the building value gives the market value estimate. In the property residual method, it is assumed that the
income is derived from the use of both land and building, which are capitalized over the economic life of the building. At the end of the building
life, the appraiser estimates the land reversion—the present worth of the
current land value postponed to the end of the building life. The present
worth of one capitalization table is used for this purpose.

REVIEW QUESTIONS

1. Explain the difference between contract and economic rent. Give an
   example to illustrate your answer.
2. Explain how you would make rent comparisons for apartment buildings;
   for shopping centers.
3. Thoroughly explain the significance of the vacancy and bad debt allowance. How would you calculate effective gross income?
4. Why is it necessary to stabilize expenses?
5. Give your reasons for deleting federal income taxes and mortgage payments from a building income statement.
6. Why is it necessary to add management expenses for an owner-operated
   building?
7. Give an example showing the difference between a discount rate and a
   capitalization rate.
8. How would you differentiate between the overall rate of return and the
   interest rate? Give an example showing how you would provide for the
   recapture of capital and the *return* on capital.
9. In your view, what is the best method of estimating the market rate of
   capitalization? Give reasons for your answer; give an example in support of your answer.
10. What is meant by capitalization in perpetuity? Explain thoroughly.
11. What is the difference between the *present worth of one* and the *present
    worth of one per period?* Show how each factor is used.
12. Give an example of building residual, straight-line capitalization.
13. Show how you would apply land residual, annuity capitalization.
14. What is the main reason for using the property residual capitalization?

SELECTED REFERENCES

The Appraisal of Real Estate, chaps. 19 and 20. 6th ed. Chicago: American
    Institute of Real Estate Appraisers, 1973.
Bleck, Erich K. "Real Estate Investments and Rates of Return," *Appraisal
    Journal,* vol. 41, no. 4 (July 1973), pp. 535–47.
Cooper, James R., and Pyhrr, Stephen A. "Forecasting the Rates of Return

on an Apartment Investment: A Case Study," *Appraisal Journal,* vol. 41, no. 3 (July 1973), pp. 312–37.

Erler, Raymond L.   "Rate of Return and Financial Leverage: A Paradigm for Sensitivity Analysis," *Appraisal Journal,* vol. 40, no. 3 (July 1972), pp. 369–77.

Hanford, Lloyd D., Jr.   "Expense Ratios and Their Use," *Appraisal Journal,* vol. 41, no. 1 (January 1973), pp. 100–103.

Kinnard, William N., Jr.   *Income Property Valuation,* chap. 4. Lexington, Mass.: Heath Lexington Books, 1971.

North, Lincoln W.   *Real Estate Investment Analysis and Valuation,* chap. 4. Winnipeg: Saults and Pollard Ltd., 1973.

Paschall, Robert H.   "Stock Market Derivation of Discount Rates," *Appraisal Journal,* vol. 42, no. 2 (April 1974), pp. 236–50.

Wendt, Paul F.   *Real Estate Appraisal Review and Outlook,* chap. 6. Athens: University of Georgia Press, 1974.

12

Real Estate Credit Sources

After reading this chapter, you should be familiar with the following points:

1 How the mortgage market depends on the flow of savings to mortgage investors.

2 The organizational structure of savings and loan associations.

3 The operations of the Federal Home Loan Bank Board System.

4 The mortgage loan policies of savings associations.

5 Federal regulations that limit mortgage loans by commercial banks.

6 The mortgage loan policies of commercial banks.

7 The organizational structure of mutual savings banks.

8 The mortgage loan policies of mutual savings banks.

9 Reasons why life insurance companies invest heavily in mortgages on income property.

10 The role played by mortgage bankers in supplying real estate credit.

11 The real estate mortgage investment policies of real estate investment trusts and pension funds.

WITHOUT FUNDS to finance real estate purchases, housing construction declines and construction employment decreases because purchasers are unable to negotiate mortgage loans on acceptable terms and investors are unable to finance new income-producing developments, such as apartment houses and shopping centers. Opportunities for home ownership, property investments, and employment in the real estate industry depend on the orderly flow of savings into the mortgage market.

The supply of credit for long-term mortgages is divided among a bewildering mixture of institutions. Some are subject only to state regulations. Some are subject to state and federal regulations. Some lenders active in the mortgage market are controlled by different federal agencies, and a few mortgage credit sources are relatively free of federal or state regulation. Added confusion results from mortgage lending policies that meet differing institutional needs of liquidity, yield, and safety of principal. Consequently, a potential borrower—a prospective home purchaser, developer, or corporation—must search for a lender who offers suitable long-term credit with costs commensurate with the type of mortgage offered.

To show how lenders and borrowers adjust to the mortgage market, this chapter explains how savings are allocated to that market. Next, the main sources of real estate credit are distinguished in terms of their mortgage lending activity, regulatory restrictions, and mortgage investment policy.

THE STRUCTURE OF THE MORTGAGE MARKET

The funds invested in mortgages are the second most significant form of private debt. As shown in Table 12–1, private debt, which totaled $2,134 billion at the end of 1974, included mortgages totaling $520 billion, or 24.4 percent of the total private debt. Mortgages outstanding exceed the combined total of commercial and financial, consumer, and farm debt of $360 billion. Mortgage debt is some 1.4 times the size of the present federal debt of $361 billion.

The volume of mortgage activity turns on the amount of the gross national product devoted to savings and the amount of savings annually allocated to the mortgage market. Real estate borrowers must compete for nonmortgage investments, such as government bonds, corporate bonds, and equity funds. Figure 12–1 indicates that savings from the annual gross national product flow through mortgage lenders or financial institutions that finance real estate. Real estate investment creates income that is counted again in the gross national product. If the volume of savings declines, or if mortgage borrowers are unable to compete with other borrowers for savings, mortgage activity declines, with repercussions throughout the real estate and construction industry.

Table 12–2 identifies the total volume of outstanding mortgages by source. The four main financial institutions, *savings and loan associations, commercial banks, life insurance companies,* and *mutual savings banks,*

TABLE 12–1

Total National Private Debt, 1974

Type of Debt	Amount (in billions)	Percent of Total
Corporate debt...........................	$1,254	58.8
Farm debt.............................	87	3.9
Mortgages.............................	520	24.4
Commercial and financial...............	83	3.9
Consumer.............................	190	8.9
Total.............................	$2,134	99.9

Source: U.S. Bureau of the Census, *Statistical Abstract of the United States, 1975,* 96th ed. (Washington, D.C.: U.S. Government Printing Office, 1975), p. 473.

account for 78.5 percent, or almost four fifths, of total mortgages outstanding.

The dependence on personal savings as the main source of mortgage credit is indicated by the volume of mortgage loans held by savings and loan associations. These institutions concentrate on long-term mortgage loans and account for over one third of the total volume of mortgage loans outstanding. Commercial banks hold the second largest mortgage loan portfolio—a share representing 18.3 percent of the total. The two other types of private financial institutions, life insurance companies and mutual savings banks, lend primarily on long-term mortgage credit and account for almost one fourth of the total mortgages outstanding: 22.2 percent.

FIGURE 12–1

The Flow of Savings into the Mortgage Market

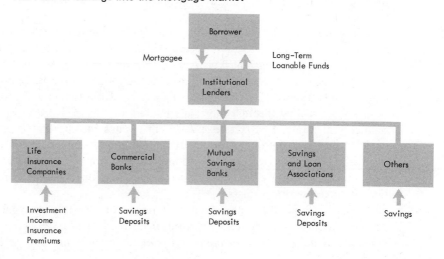

Federal credit agencies include such organizations as the Federal Land Bank, the Federal National Mortgage Association, the Government National Mortgage Association, and the Federal Home Loan Mortgage Corporation. These agencies purchase mortgages from other institutions. The "individuals and others" category of Table 12–2, accounting for almost 10 percent of the total, includes state and local credit agencies, individuals, and other minor sources. Financial institutions within these groups vary widely in the geographic placement of loans, in property type, and

TABLE 12–2

Mortgage Debt Outstanding by Type of Holder

Type of Holder	Mortgage Debt Outstanding (in millions)	Percent of Total
Savings and loan associations.........	$286,575	38.0
Commercial banks....................	137,986	18.3
Life insurance companies.............	89,781	11.9
Mutual savings banks.................	77,738	10.3
Federal and related agencies..........	91,975	12.2
Individuals and others................	71,072	9.4
Total..........................	$755,127	100.1

Source: Adapted from *Federal Reserve Bulletin,* August 1976, p. A42. Data reported are as of the end of the first quarter, 1976.

in type of mortgage loan. A more detailed review of these credit sources shows the degree of mortgage specialization.

SAVINGS AND LOAN ASSOCIATIONS

Savings and loan associations originated from the building societies of England and Germany. These societies were formed to pool the savings of their members and thus enable the members to borrow the funds they needed to build or purchase homes. The purpose of the first U.S. building association, founded in Frankford, Pennsylvania (now part of Philadelphia), in 1831, was to "enable the contributors thereof to build or purchase dwelling houses."[1]

Building associations were organized to allow each member to acquire a home and pay for it in regular installments. When all of the members had achieved this objective, the association was dissolved. From the second and third associations, formed, respectively, in South Carolina in 1843 and in Brooklyn, New York, in 1863, they grew to the point that by 1880 such associations were organized in virtually every state. Their continued growth required some form of government supervision so that by

---

[1] Henry E. Hoagland, Leo D. Stone, and William B. Brueggeman, *Real Estate Finance,* 6th ed. (Homewood, Ill.: Richard D. Irwin, Inc., 1977), p. 394.

1931 46 states controlled savings associations. The assets of savings and loan associations totaled $9 billion in 1930, but declined to $6 billion by 1935. A system of *federally* chartered savings and loan associations was authorized under the Home Owners Loan Act of 1933[2] so that today's savings and loan associations may operate under either federal or state charters. The two main objectives of savings and loan associations are to encourage thrift and to finance home ownership. In meeting these objectives, savings and loan associations face two central problems: (1) they must attract a sufficient volume of savings to meet local home financing needs, and (2) they must keep the cost of home financing at the lowest possible level.

Organization of Savings and Loan Associations

Of the 4,964 savings and loan associations in the United States at the end of 1975, 2,048 were chartered under federal law. State-chartered savings and loan associations, numbering 2,916, represented 58.7 percent of the total number. Of the $295.6 billion held by all associations, 57.7 percent, or $195.4 billion, was held by federal associations. Associations operating under a federal charter are mutually owned, whereas state-chartered institutions may be either mutually owned or owned by private stockholders. The U.S. League of Savings Associations reports that only 709 associations were held under capital stock ownership.[3] The total number of associations has declined approximately 20 percent from 1965 because some associations were unable to compete successfully for savings with other institutions and because of the decreased demand for mortgage loans in some localities.

Insured Deposits.   Federally chartered associations must have deposits insured by the Federal Savings and Loan Insurance Corporation (FSLIC). In 1974 the maximum deposits eligible for insurance were increased from $20,000 on all deposits to

$40,000 on privately owned funds,

$100,000 on public funds invested in the same state, and

$40,000 on public funds invested out of state.

Most state-chartered institutions extend this insurance protection to depositors, though it is voluntary among state-chartered associations. Approximately 97.6 percent of the assets of state and federally chartered associations have deposits insured by the FSLIC. Some states, such as Massachusetts, Ohio, Maryland, and North Carolina, have a state-sponsored system of insuring state-chartered associations. Over the life of FSLIC, approximately 919,710 savers have benefited from deposit in-

---

[2] Leon T. Kendall, *Savings and Loan Business* (Englewood Cliffs, N.J.: Prentice-Hall, Inc., 1962), p. 6.

[3] *1976 Savings and Loan Fact Book* (Chicago: U.S. League of Savings Associations, 1976), p. 52.

FIGURE 12–2

A Map Showing the Location and Jurisdiction of the 12 Regional Federal Home Loan Banks

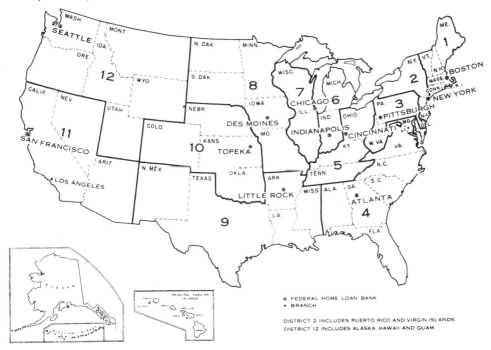

surance. According to data of the U.S. League of Savings Associations, 110 settlement cases have been processed to date. Reserves of the FSLIC grew from $380.9 million in 1960 to over $4.119 billion by the end of 1975.[4]

The Federal Home Loan Bank Board System. Federally chartered associations are supervised by the Federal Home Loan Bank Board, consisting of three members appointed for four-year terms by the president with the consent of the Senate. Expenses of the Board are paid for from assessments against the Federal Savings and Loan Insurance Corporation and member banks. The Board establishes policies, issues regulations, and supervises the operations of the Federal Home Loan Bank System, the Federal Savings and Loan Insurance Corporation, and the Federal Home Loan Mortgage Corporation.

Like the Federal Reserve System, the Federal Home Loan Bank System includes 12 regional banks which are owned by the member banks and do not deal with the public. Each of the 12 regional banks has six public interest directors appointed by the Federal Home Loan Bank Board for four-year terms, while other directors are elected by member institutions for two-year terms. (See Figure 12–2.)

---

[4] Ibid., pp. 106–9.

Regional banks, which also provide statistical and research studies, *serve primarily as a source of credit for member banks.* For example, a savings association typically will have heavy deposit withdrawals during Christmas which may be met with loans from its regional bank. Moreover, when interest rates rise as a result of federal monetary policies, regional banks make loans to members permitting them to meet loan commitments that would be impossible to honor without temporary loans. Membership in the Federal Home Loan Bank System is compulsory for federally chartered associations; state-chartered associations, mutual savings banks, and life insurance companies may join the system if they wish to do so.

Mortgage Loan Policy

The latest data show that savings and loan associations account for almost one half of the conventional first mortgages on one–four-family dwellings. The concentration of residential loans is shown by current reports of the Federal Reserve System.

TABLE 12–3

Mortgage Loans of Savings and Loan Associations
(in billions)

Type of Mortgage	Total Mortgages Outstanding	Percent of Total
1–4-family dwellings	$211.3	84.1
Multiple-family projects	24.4	9.7
Commercial properties	15.6	6.2
Total	$251.3	100.0

Source: *Federal Reserve Bulletin,* November 1975, p. A42.

With a total of $251.3 billion invested in mortgages, 84.1 percent represents loans on one–four-family dwellings. Moreover, in the past savings and loan associations have invested a relatively small proportion of their loans in FHA-insured or VA-guaranteed loans. Of the total assets of savings and loan associations—$295.6 billion—84.3 percent was invested in mortgage loans. If certificates, loans, and notes insured by government-type mortgage investments are included, this proportion increases to 98.7 percent of total assets. The most recent data of the FHLB on 4,078 FSLIC-insured associations indicates that FHA and VA loans outstanding represent about 11.1 percent of their mortgage portfolio.[5]

Consistent with their stated objectives, savings and loan associations concentrate on financing single-family dwellings and specialize in conven-

[5] *1975 Combined Financial Statements: FSLIC Insured Savings and Loan Associations* (Washington, D.C.: Federal Home Loan Bank Board, 1975), p. 6.

tional loans—loans not insured by the Federal Housing Administration or the Veterans Administration. They prefer conventional loans since they secure funds mainly from savings deposits that are lent on local properties. Multiple-family projects and commercial real estate absorb a relatively minor share of total savings and loan mortgages: 9.7 percent and 6.2 percent, respectively. Moreover, savings and loan associations concentrate their investments in the local community—typically loans are restricted to a 100-mile radius.

The Impact of Monetary Policy. As interest rates increase, savings and loan associations lose deposits to investments that pay higher yields. For instance, as short-term interest rates increased in 1973, the net savings flow to savings associations dropped from $32.7 billion in 1972 to $20.5

TABLE 12–4

Home Mortgage Interest Rates and Yields on New Utility and Corporate Bonds for Selected Years

Period	Conventional Loans on New Homes, Effective Interest Rate	New Aaa Utility Issues Yield	Aaa Corporate Bond Yield	Spread between Conventional Loan Rate and	
				Utilities Yield	Corporate Bond Yield
1965	5.81%	4.50%	4.49%	1.31%	1.32%
1970	8.45	8.68	8.04	−0.23	0.41
1971	7.74	7.62	7.39	0.12	0.35
1972	7.60	7.31	7.21	0.29	0.39
1973	7.95	7.74	7.44	0.21	0.51
1974	8.92	9.33	8.57	−0.41	0.35
1975	9.01	9.40	8.83	−0.39	0.18

Source: *1976 Savings and Loan Fact Book* (Chicago: U.S. League of Savings Associations, 1976), p. 35.

billion at the end of 1973. The associations have been unable to increase yields on savings deposits in competition with other financial institutions.

For example, the average yield on savings deposits in 1958 was 1.17 percentage points above comparable rates paid by commercial banks. However, in July 1973 the Federal Reserve Board approved a four-year certificate of deposit with a minimum balance of $1,000 and no interest rate maximum. This increased the share of savings to commercial banks from 43.4 percent in 1972 to 59.2 percent in 1973. The interest ceiling on certificates of deposit was later placed at 7.5 percent by the Federal Reserve Board.

In addition, savings associations must compete with the yields paid on government and corporate bonds. With higher interest rates, yields on bonds increase as the government and corporations bid for the short supply of capital. To illustrate, compare the average interest rate on conventional, new home mortgages with bond yields, as shown in Table 12–4. Note that mortgages paid an interest rate 1.31 points higher than utility bond yields in 1965. In 1970, 1974, and 1975, however, the effective interest rate on conventional mortgages fell below the yield earned on Aaa utility bonds.

Moreover, Regulation Q of the Federal Reserve System establishes a maximum interest rate paid by commercial banks on time and savings deposits. Similar controls are imposed on savings associations by the Federal Home Loan Bank Board. On passbook savings, current regulations allow savings associations to pay an interest rate 0.25 percent higher than the rate paid by commercial banks. Consequently, when market rates of interest rise above Regulation Q ceilings, depositors tend to shift funds from savings deposits to higher yielding investments. This creates considerable instability in the money available for mortgages on singe-family dwellings.

Negotiable Order of Withdrawal (NOW) Accounts.   As an experiment, Congress authorized savings associations to pay up to 5 percent interest on negotiable order of withdrawal accounts in Massachusetts and New Hampshire. Such accounts are actually checking accounts since withdrawals are made transferable by instruments for making payments to a third party. Some states, such as Maine, Vermont, and Connecticut, have extended this privilege to state-chartered associations. Savings banks in New Jersey, Maryland, and Delaware have had this authority for several years. The U.S. League of Savings Associations has favored the extension of interest-bearing checking accounts to savings associations for two main reasons:

1. By offering interest on checking accounts, savings and loan associations may provide such additional services as supermarket units for recording deposits and withdrawals and third-party, automatic bill payment.
2. Savings and loan associations have found that NOW accounts make up 5 to 6 percent of total deposits. A higher level of regular savings deposits has been experienced by associations offering this added service.[6]

The Financial Institutions Act.   Congress has held hearings and considered legislation that would substantially change the role of savings and loan associations. While this legislation has not been approved, the continuing efforts of savings and loan associations and others may eventually lead to the adoption of some of the suggested revisions. The main provisions of the proposed legislation explain the controversy it has created.

1. Depository institutions would be regulated by a single authority which would issue federal charters to mutual savings banks and permit existing institutions to obtain a national bank charter.

---

[6] Norman Strunk, "The Case for NOW Accounts," *Savings and Loan News,* March 1976, pp. 44–48.

2. Regulation Q, controlling deposit interest rate differentials, would be gradually phased out over five years.
3. Savings and loan associations, credit unions, and mutual savings banks would be permitted to issue demand deposits. They would also be allowed to engage in consumer lending, to issue credit cards, and to establish revolving lines of credit.
4. All financial institutions of a given size would be required to maintain the same reserve requirements on deposit liabilities.

The proponents of this legislation argue that it would give savings and loan associations greater flexibility and would decrease their dependence on savings deposits and the residential mortgage market. It is believed that stronger deposit institutions would result if savings institutions were allowed to expand their lending and financial services.[7]

COMMERCIAL BANKS

Mortgage lending by commercial banks has undergone substantial change since the National Banking Act of 1863. A review of the changing philosophy on mortgage lending by commercial banks explains current mortgage practices.

Early Mortgage Policy

Under the National Banking Act of 1863, nationally chartered banks were prohibited from making mortgage loans. The recurring financial crises and land speculation before the Civil War led to numerous bank failures. As a result, Congress attempted to protect national banks from mortgage loans, which were regarded as highly speculative.

With the Federal Reserve Act of 1916, this policy changed to allow a limited amount of mortgage activity. The act allowed nationally chartered banks to grant one-year loans on urban properties. A more dramatic change was introduced by the National Housing Act of 1934, which favored certain types of mortgages.

The National Housing Act allowed nationally chartered banks to exchange defaulted mortgages for government-guaranteed bonds. Mortgages insured by the Federal Housing Administration were exempt from statutory restrictions on loan-to-value ratios and on the maximum maturity of mortgages. At the time, mortgages not insured or guaranteed by a federal agency had a maximum loan-to-value ratio of 75 percent of the appraised value and a maximum 20-year maturity. Mortgage loans could

---

[7] For further discussion of these issues see *Financial Institutions and the Nation's Economy [FINE] Discussion Principles,* Committee on Banking, Currency, and Housing, House of Representatives, 94th Congress, 1st Session, November 1975 (Washington, D.C.: U.S. Government Printing Office, 1975).

not exceed the capital surplus or 50 percent of savings and time deposits, whichever was greater. FHA-insured or VA-guaranteed loans were exempt from these restrictions. With the enactment of the Housing and Community Development Act of 1974, even these restrictions were considerably reduced.

New Loan Authority

A marked change was initiated by the Housing and Community Development Act of 1974, which amended that part of the Federal Reserve Act which controlled mortgage lending. The Housing and Community Development Act (1) broadened the authority of nationally chartered commercial banks to make additional funds available for real estate loans, (2) liberalized regulations controlling loans on buildings under construction, and (3) created loans previously prohibited. The main features of this act may be summarized in eight points. The act

1. Increases the proportion of bank assets that may be invested in mortgages.
2. Permits loans on buildings under construction to be considered commercial loans and not real estate loans under certain circumstances.
3. Exempts mortgages insured by federal agencies from aggregate mortgage loan limitations.
4. Allows loans on second mortgages, provided that they do not exceed 20 percent of capital and surplus.
5. Permits loans on vacant land of up to two thirds of the appraised value.
6. Allows loans on buildings of up to 90 percent of their value and for a term of 30 years.
7. Permits 10 percent of the total mortgages to be granted without restriction as to the length of the mortgage or the loan-to-value ratio.
8. Authorizes long-term loans with no provision for repayment of the principal on one–four-family dwellings, provided that the loans are less than 75 percent of the value of the dwellings.

Of the $135.1 billion mortgage debt outstanding held by commercial banks at the end of 1975, approximately 61.6 percent was invested in residential property. In contrast to savings associations, commercial banks invest in a relatively high proportion of nonfarm, nonresidential mortgages. The record shows that commercial banks have expanded their mortgage holdings in recent years. Commercial banks have invested more heavily in mortgages partly because they have absorbed a greater share of total savings.

Formerly commercial banks held a significant proportion of the residual mortgages in FHA-insured or VA-guaranteed loans. By the end of 1975, government-insured or -guaranteed loans amounted to only 11.4 percent

TABLE 12–5

Mortgage Debt Outstanding Held by Commercial
Banks, December 1975 (in billions)

Type of Mortgage	Amount	Percent of Total
Residential.....................	$ 83.2	61.6
Nonfarm......................	45.5	33.7
Farm.........................	6.4	4.7
Total...................	$135.1	100.0

Source: *Federal Reserve Bulletin*, March 1976, p. A42.

of all residential mortgages held by commercial banks. Since 1960, commercial banks have increased their share of deposits held by all depository institutions (mutual savings banks, commercial banks, savings and loan associations, and credit unions). Their share of savings increased from 39.3 percent in 1960 to 47.9 percent at the end of 1975.[8]

Mortgage Policy

Though commercial banks held only 17.1 percent of the total mortgages outstanding at the end of 1975 on one to four-family dwellings, they are the largest source of construction loans.[9] Since most financial institutions are limited in granting loans on vacant land, construction loans are provided to builders on a short-term basis, generally from 6 months to 60 months for new construction. At the completion of construction, the property is then eligible for a long-term amortized loan. Banks tend to specialize in making these relatively short-term loans at comparatively high interest rates.

MUTUAL SAVINGS BANKS

According to the latest report of the National Association of Mutual Savings Banks, there were 482 mutual savings banks with assets totaling $109 billion. Serving mainly as savings banks, they have directed deposit funds mainly into long-term investments. They do not have as great a variation in deposits as commercial banks since they concentrate in lower turnover time deposits in preference to checking deposits. Virtually all mutual savings banks are insured by the Federal Deposit Insurance Corporation. Nearly all of these banks are located in the Middle Atlantic and New England regions, and approximately seven eighths of them are located

[8] *1976 National Fact Book of Mutual Savings Banking* (New York: National Association of Mutual Savings Banks, 1976).

[9] *Federal Reserve Bulletin,* March 1976, p. A42.

in the states of Massachusetts, New York, Connecticut, Maine, and New Hampshire.

Early Development

Mutual savings banks trace their origin to a Philadelphia savings fund society of 1816 and to the Provident Institution for Savings, which was chartered in Boston in the same year. At first, the charter established a flat rate of interest of 4.8 percent (0.4 percent per month), the surplus to be divided among the depositors every three years.[10] These first savings banks avoided the word *bank,* preferring to be known as societies or institutions. The change in name avoided the controversy surrounding banks in the early 19th century. From their inception mutual savings banks stressed savings as ". . . the most efficient means of decreasing the evils of pauperism."[11]

Mortgage Policies

Concentrated in the northeastern states, mutual savings banks have successfully competed for mortgages by adapting their mortgage investments to their particular needs:

1. They are unregulated by federal agencies, operating instead under state charters.
2. They invest locally and in out-of-state mortgage loans, thus obtaining geographic mobility not found among savings and loan associations.
3. Because of their need for liquidity, they have invested heavily in FHA-insured and VA-guaranteed loans.
4. Their interest rates, fees, and other charges have tended to be relatively low.
5. They depend heavily on the secondary market for mortgages.

To illustrate, in 1975 approximately 64.9 percent of the total assets of mutual savings banks were invested in mortgages. These mortgages account for approximately 10.7 percent of the total mortgages outstanding —a proportion which has been as high as 13.7 percent since 1945. In 1975, 34.7 percent of their mortgage portfolio was in FHA and VA loans. Moreover, they concentrate in residential property; 83.4 percent of the mortgages held by mutual savings banks are in residential mortgages.

Mutual savings banks share problems of disintermediation with savings associations. As deposit interest rates decrease in relation to yields on bonds and government securities, mutual savings banks lose savings de-

---

[10] Weldon Welfling, *Mutual Savings Banks* (Cleveland: Press of Case Western Reserve University, 1968), p. 11.

[11] Ibid., p. 23.

TABLE 12–6

Percentage Distribution of Types of Mortgage
Loans by Mutual Savings Banks, December 31,
1975*

Type of Loan	Percent of Total Number
FHA...............................	18.7
VA................................	16.0
Conventional......................	65.3
	100.0

* Source: *1976 National Fact Book of Mutual Savings Banking* (New York: National Association of Mutual Savings Banks, 1976), p. 54.

posits. They gained deposits in 1971 and 1972 when savings accounts
yielded relatively competitive interest rates. Their deposits declined in
1959, 1965, 1969, and 1973 because of higher yields on competing investments. As a result, mortgage borrowers who depend on mutual savings
banks for loanable funds face recurring shortages as interest rates increase
in response to monetary restraints.

LIFE INSURANCE COMPANIES

Life insurance companies have certain advantages in competing for
long-term mortgage investments. In the first place, life insurance companies may predict their available funds for investment with a high degree
of accuracy. Their income is derived from insurance premiums, which are
highly predictable, and yields on investments. Their expenditures may be
predicted from mortality tables. Second, they are able to make long-term
commitments competitively with banks and savings institutions that have
less predictable sources of funds. Life insurance companies have less need
for liquidity than do commercial and savings banks. And like mutual
savings banks, life insurance companies have considerable flexibility in
placing mortgages geographically. They are controlled only by state regulations and in this respect are free from the restrictions imposed on commercial banks and federally chartered savings and loan associations.

Mortgage Policy

The latest data show that some 30.8 percent of the total investment
portfolio of life insurance companies is placed in mortgages. The types of
mortgages held by these insurance companies are shown in Table 12–7.
Note that over the years 1966–75, the volume of farm mortgages held
by life insurance companies increased each year. The number of mortgages
in FHA-insured loans and VA loans has decreased since 1966. Nonfarm,

TABLE 12–7

Types of Mortgages Owned by U.S. Life Insurance Companies (in millions)

Year	Farm	Nonfarm FHA*	Nonfarm VA	Nonfarm Conventional	Total
1966	$5,240	$12,852	$6,201	$40,316	$64,609
1967	5,569	12,672	6,122	43,153	67,516
1968	5,801	12,469	5,954	45,749	69,973
1969	5,773	12,271	5,701	48,282	72,027
1970	5,649	12,001	5,394	51,331	74,375
1971	5,601	11,336	5,004	53,555	75,496
1972	5,678	10,512	4,660	56,098	76,948
1973	5,996	9,740	4,402	61,231	81,369
1974	6,321	8,600	4,200	67,137	86,258
1975	6,753	8,502	3,903	70,009	89,167

* Includes mortgages insured under the Canadian Housing Act; in 1975 these amounted to $582 million.

Source: *1976 Life Insurance Fact Book* (New York: American Council of Life Insurance, 1976), p. 77.

conventional mortgages, primarily commercial and industrial mortgages, have increased over the same ten-year period. In fact, nonfarm conventional mortgages now total 78.7 percent of the mortgages held by U.S. life insurance companies.

More recently, life insurance companies have decreased their holdings in mortgages on one–four-family dwellings. At the end of 1972, some 29 percent of their mortgages were on one to four-family dwellings. By the end of the first quarter of 1976, this proportion had decreased to 19.4 percent. Current data show the preference of the life insurance companies for mortgages on commercial property—totaling over one half of their mortgage portfolio.[12]

Generally, insurance companies favor borrowers with high credit ratings. The loan-to-value ratio, typically 66⅔ percent to 75 percent of the appraised value, is governed by state law. To offset price inflation, insurance companies often negotiate for a share of the developer's equity

TABLE 12–8

Mortgage Debt Held by Life Insurance Companies, March 31, 1976 (in millions)

Property Type	Total	Percent of Total
1–4-family dwellings	$17,420	19.4
Multifamily dwellings	19,926	22.2
Commercial	45,608	50.7
Farm	6,827	7.6
Total	$89,871	99.9

[12] *Federal Reserve Bulletin,* August 1976, p. A42.

return. For example, an insurance company may charge the market interest rate in addition to a 25 percent share of the owner's equity. In other instances insurance companies have granted mortgage money as a limited partner with a developer who supervises construction and management in return for favorable financing terms.

Loan Correspondents

Insurance companies differ from other sources of mortgage funds in that most of these companies invest through loan correspondents. A loan correspondent is an agent who originates mortgages and collects monthly mortgage payments for an investor, such as a pension fund or an insurance company. Loan correspondents are widely located geographically, enabling insurance companies to make advance commitments on the volume of mortgages that they will accept over a given time for qualified mortgages. Correspondents with an advance commitment then originate loans and document the proposed loans for presentation to and approval by the insurance company. A few of the larger companies staff regional offices to originate and service mortgages. In this way insurance companies allocate mortgage funds geographically by type of loan and, according to their judgment of risk, the need for portfolio diversification.

Because the mortgage policies of insurance companies show major differences from the mortgage policies of other credit sources, the main points deserve added emphasis. Life insurance companies:

1. Invest over state lines.
2. Prefer mortgages on commercial, industrial, and agricultural property.
3. Frequently bargain for a share of the developer's equity return.
4. Restrict loans from 66⅔ percent to 75 percent of the appraised value, depending on state law.
5. Place mortgages through loan correspondents.
6. Do not require the degree of mortgage liquidity required by banks and savings institutions.

There is the added point that since insurance companies are highly *yield-conscious*, they place funds in nonmortgage investments as mortgage yields lag behind those of other investments. In this sense, mortgage funds from insurance companies may vary as monetary policy results in fluctuations in the interest rate.

REAL ESTATE INVESTMENT TRUSTS

Beginning in 1960, amendments to the Internal Revenue Code, Sections 856 to 858, provided for real estate investment trusts (REITs) that enjoyed certain tax advantages common to mutual funds.

Regulatory Restrictions

The REITs give small investors an opportunity to invest in real estate assets which are professionally managed. Diversification, transferability of shares, and the ability to acquire large properties beyond the reach of the individual investor are other advantages of REITs. Investment in the shares of a REIT gives small investors the advantage of the diversified investment portfolio of a large organization.

Under the Real Estate Investment Trust Act, REITs are exempt from corporate net income taxes on net income distributed to shareholders. To be considered a real estate investment trust, the REIT must meet strict financial requirements:

1. Ninety percent or more of earnings must be distributed to shareholders.
2. At the end of each fiscal quarter of its taxable year, at least 75 percent of the value of the total assets of the trust must consist of real estate assets (including interest on loans secured by mortgages on real property and shares in other realty trusts), cash, cash items, and government securities.
3. Beneficial ownership of the trust must be held by 100 or more trust shareholders during at least 335 days of a taxable year of 12 months. More than 50 percent of the outstanding shares may not be owned, directly, indirectly, or constructively, by or for five or fewer individuals, at any time during the last half of the taxable year.
4. The trust may not hold real property primarily for sale in the ordinary course of business.
5. At least 75 percent of the gross income of the trust must be derived from rents, mortgage interest, and gains from the sale of real estate.
6. An additional 15 percent of the gross income of the trust must be derived from the same sources or from dividends or lawful interest or gains from the sale or other disposition of stock or securities, or any combination of the foregoing.
7. Not more than 25 percent of the value of a trust's total assets may be represented by securities.
8. Gross income from sales or other disposition of stock or securities held for less than six months and of real property held for less than four years must be less than 30 percent of gross income.[13]

The National Association of Real Estate Investment Trusts in a 1973 survey reported 210 REITs with assets totaling $20 billion.[14] REITs are

---

[13] See *Public Law 86–799*, Section 10, September 14, 1960, which added Sections 856–58 to chap. 1, subchap. M, of the *Internal Revenue Code of 1954*.

[14] *REIT Fact Book, 1974* (Washington, D.C.: National Association of Real Estate Investment Trusts, 1974), p. 15.

created by a legal document, the Declaration of Trust, which substitutes for a corporate charter. They obtain their initial capital from the sale of stock and additional funds from bank loans. They differ from mutual funds in that REITs do not redeem shares on request. Shareholders must sell shares on the market. Accordingly the market price of a share may go above or below the net asset value per share.

Mortgage Policy

Since they are not subject to federal regulations controlling mortgage investments, REITs have considerable flexibility in investing in real prop-

FIGURE 12–3

Investments and Mortgage Loans of Real Estate Investment Trusts, Year End, 1973

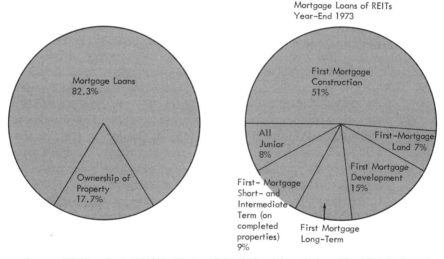

Source: REIT Fact Book, 1974 (Washington, D.C.: National Association of Real Estate Investment Trusts, 1974), p. 28.

erty. Some trusts concentrate on special types of real estate, such as shopping centers, office buildings, or apartments. REITs tend to specialize in (1) short-term construction loans, (2) long-term mortgages, (3) real estate, or (4) a combination of these three types of investments.[15]

Some 82.3 percent of the assets of REITs is invested in mortgages, predominantly first-mortgage loans. Further, REITs have invested heavily in construction loans, which account for 51 percent of their total mortgage investments and generally extend from one to three years. Some REITs

---

[15] *Real Estate Investment Trusts: A Background Analysis and Recent Industry Developments, 1961–1974,* Economic Staff Paper 75–No. 1 (Washington, D.C.: Securities and Exchange Commission, February 1975), p. 6.

have preferred development loans or secondary loans, and others have invested in long-term first-mortgage loans. The range of REIT activity is shown in Figure 12–3. The industry reports a strong preference for construction loans on apartment buildings, followed by condominiums, office buildings, and shopping centers.

Since 1973, the equity shares of a large number of REITs have declined sharply. The market value of REIT shares traded on the New York and American Stock Exchanges fell from $4.800 billion at the end of 1972 to $1.455 billion near the end of 1974.[16] Reasons cited for shareholder losses include delinquent mortgages, high interest rates on borrowed capital, investment in nonearning assets, and the difficulty of acquiring new cash through the sale of securities in the open market. This record has induced some REITs to give up their REIT status so that they may manage a portfolio of foreclosed properties. A REIT is prohibited from acting as a real estate management firm and collecting management fees.

MORTGAGE BANKERS

Before the real estate industry was organized into well-defined trade associations, individuals, say, a lawyer or a real estate broker, arranged real estate loans for a fee. A mortgage loan, which was owed by a farmer, a homeowner, or a businessman, was then sold to an institution which held the mortgage until the loan was paid. Gradually, these individuals developed special techniques to evaluate a mortgage application; they listed borrowers as clients, charging an origination fee for processing the loan; they listed the permanent lender as a client, charging a monthly fee for collecting mortgage payments and performing other loan administrative duties. Mortgage specialists who represented insurance companies that purchased mortgages for long-term investments were called "mortgage correspondents."[17]

These mortgage correspondents formed a trade association in 1914, which is known today as the Mortgage Bankers Association of America. After the Federal Housing Administration was created in 1934, mortgage bankers were active participants in placing FHA-insured mortgages. They collected an annual fee of one half of 1 percent of the mortgage per year paid by the borrower; in addition, they levied an origination fee against the borrower. FHA loans and the development of the secondary market with the Federal National Mortgage Association in 1938, which purchased and sold mortgages from lenders, stimulated the growth of mortgage banking.

---

[16] *Real Estate Investment Trusts,* p. 24.

[17] George Dovenmuehle, "Development of Mortgage Banking," in Robert H. Pease and Lewis O. Kerwood (eds.), *Mortgage Banking* (New York: McGraw-Hill Book Co., 1965), p. 1.

Mortgage Policy

Today, mortgage bankers serve as mortgage loan correspondents to life insurance companies, mutual savings banks, pension funds, and others. They place mortgages on all types of property, including FHA and VA loans. Since they are usually chartered under state corporation laws, they are subject to a minimum of federal supervision. Ordinarily, working capital is secured from commercial banks that advance money against mortgage loans in process and commitments from long-term investors.

A distinction should be made between *mortgage brokers* and *mortgage bankers.* Mortgage brokers do not service loans. They arrange for the purchase and sale of mortgage loans between originators and investors. They operate mostly in the private mortgage market and collect a fee for arranging for the purchase and sale of mortgage loans. Mortgage bankers contribute to the flow of capital from surplus areas of the northeastern part of the United States to deficit areas of the Southeast and the Southwest. They were instrumental in marketing FHA and VA loans that were originated locally and warehoused to financial institutions. Another distinction is that mortgage bankers service collections on mortgages owned by institutional investors.

Mortgage bankers provide three main services:

1. Loan production.
    a. Origination.
    b. Loan application.
    c. Appraisal.
2. Loan supervision.
    a. Loan portfolio administration.
    b. Loan servicing.
    c. Delinquent-loan collection.
3. Other operations.
    a. Loan sales to others.
    b. Real estate management.[18]

The *first task* covers steps to originate a loan for submission to a permanent lender: the evaluation of the applicant's credit and provision of the real estate and other documentation required by a prospective mortgage purchaser. The *second task* relates to the administrative tasks incurred in processing mortgage payments, such as the payment of property taxes and insurance. The mortgage banker accepts payments from the borrower and sends monthly payments to the permanent lender. The mortgage banker also administers delinquent loans and initiates the foreclosure steps for defaulting borrowers. The *third* operation covers the

---

[18] Adapted from Willis R. Bryant, *Mortgage Lending: Fundamentals and Practices,* 2d ed. (New York: McGraw-Hill Book Co., 1962), p. 85.

assembly of mortgages in packages for sale to government agencies or institutional lenders. For loans that are foreclosed, the mortgage banker may continue to manage the foreclosed real estate for the permanent lender.

Loan Commitments

Mortgage bankers operate with advances from commercial banks typically ranging from nine months to two years. Commercial banks furnish operating capital to the mortgage banker because of "commitments" made by permanent investors who agree to buy mortgages of a stated amount during a given time period. In effect, the mortgage banker looks to commercial banks to finance his inventory of mortgages. These funds allow the mortgage banker to document a loan application, assemble mortgages, and transmit a package of mortgages to a permanent investor, say, a New York life insurance company.

The commitment may take one of three forms: the takeout commitment, the allocation commitment, and the standby purchase commitment. The *takeout commitment* is a binding letter of agreement from a permanent lender to a mortgage banker in which the lender agrees to purchase a group of mortgages before a stated time at a given price. The purchase is subject to approval of the borrower's credit and other mortgage loan documentation, such as appraisal reports. A takeout commitment letter serves as security for the commercial bank that advances funds in anticipation of the origination and eventual sale of a block of mortgages to a permanent lender.

The *allocation commitment* states that the permanent lender will purchase, within a specified period of months, a certain volume of mortgages at a given price at a specific location. Although the investor may reject loans because of deficiencies in the property or the borrower's credit or because of the amount or terms of the mortgage, usually the mortgage banker's familiarity with the requirements of the investor is such that the rejection rate tends to be nominal.

The *standby purchase commitment* is an emergency device. It is called standby because it is really not intended to be used unless absolutely required. Suppose that a builder proceeds with an apartment house project during a period of tight money when most lenders have withdrawn from the market. Provided that the project is feasible, the builder may secure a standby commitment from a mortgage company or other source at above-market interest rates for a period longer than the average construction loan—typically three to five years. The builder pays a premium for the commitment letter. With this above-market standby commitment, the builder secures a construction loan to proceed with the project. Here, the builder hopes to secure more reasonable terms from a long-term lender so that he is not required to exercise the standby commitment. If the builder obtains a permanent loan at the market rate, he forfeits his commitment fee of two to four percent of the loan.

OTHER CREDIT SOURCES

Federal credit agencies, pension funds, mortgage investment trusts, and state and local agencies largely account for the balance of mortgage funds. Federal credit agencies that operate in the secondary mortgage market—agencies that buy and sell mortgages from institutional lenders—account for most of the volume from this source. These agencies are discussed in the following chapter. State and local financing agencies deal largely with various subsidized housing programs. They raise capital by the sale of revenue bonds and from repayments of existing loans. The growing importance of pension funds deserves added comment.

PENSION FUNDS

Pension funds accumulate funds over the working life of individuals to provide income for retirement. Managers of pension funds weigh capital security heavily over yields. They have no pressure to maximize yields for their customers, stockholders, or depositors. Moreover, they tend to minimize the costs of administration, leading pension funds to high-grade stocks and bonds. Since pension funds are exempt from federal income taxation, their decisions are based on investment principles independent of tax consequences.

With respect to mortgages, they are free of the lending restraints imposed on banks, insurance companies, and savings and loan associations. Typically a pension fund administrator must follow the "prudent man" rule. This means that the pension trustees must exercise the judgment and care which a reasonable person of intelligence would exercise in his own affairs. They avoid speculation and protect the safety of their capital. Though pension funds account for approximately 1.5 percent of total mortgages outstanding, their assets are expected to increase to $250 billion, which approaches the total assets of $289.3 billion accumulated by life insurance companies at the end of 1975.

Pension funds have not invested heavily in mortgages because: (1) pension fund managers do not have knowledge or administrative experience in judging mortgage investments; (2) there is no daily market quotation on mortgages comparable to the quotations available for stocks and bonds; and (3) monthly mortgage repayments require continual reinvestment of principal, which raises administrative costs.

The reluctance of pension funds to participate in mortgages has been overcome partly by operations of the mortgage banker. The mortgage banker may originate a block of government-insured loans, selling loans to a pension fund and servicing the mortgages for the pension fund purchaser. In addition, the Government National Mortgage Association has originated "pass-through" mortgage-backed securities; that is, the pension fund purchases a security backed by a specific block of loans guaranteed by the United States and underwritten by the Federal Housing Administration or another government agency. By purchasing these securities, pension fund investors are relieved of the administration associated with mortgages. Because of these innovations, observers expect more mortgage money to be available from this source.

SUMMARY

There is no simple explanation of the mortgage market. Real estate loans are originated among different credit sources, each controlled by its own regulatory agencies and mortgage loan policies. Because the volume of mortgages currently represents 24.4 percent of the total private debt, the flow of savings into the mortgage market affects all phases of the real estate industry. Savings and loan associations, commercial banks, life insurance companies, and mutual savings banks account for almost 80 percent of total mortgages outstanding.

Savings and loan associations, which can be federally or state chartered, dominate the mortgage market. To attract depositors, eligible associations insure deposits of up to $40,000 on privately owned funds. The federally chartered savings and loan associations are supervised by the Federal Home Loan Bank Board, much as commercial banks are regulated by the Federal Reserve Board. Savings associations prefer conventional loans to FHA or VA loans; they are heavy investors in mortgages on single-family dwellings. Savings associations direct their policies toward increasing thrift and financing home ownership. Hence their central problem is to attract a sufficient volume of savings to meet local home financing needs, and to be competitive with other mortgage lenders they must keep the cost of financing at the lowest level.

Savings and loan associations are vulnerable to rising interest rates. As yields on competing investments increase, depositors tend to withdraw funds from lower paying savings deposits. One of the innovations used to attract funds, allowable in some states, is the payment of interest on checking accounts—negotiable order of withdrawal accounts.

In the past commercial banks, the second most important source of mortgage credit, have been restricted in their authority to grant mortgage loans. The 1974 Housing and Development Act permitted nationally chartered commercial banks to (1) increase their portfolio of real estate loans, (2) grant more liberal loans on buildings under construction, and (3) approve loans previously prohibited. Junior mortgages and loans on vacant land fall in the last group.

Further, commercial banks have depended heavily on VA and FHA loans because of their lower risk and greater liquidity relative to conventional loans. Commercial banks also tend to specialize in loans on buildings under construction, which are short-term, higher yielding mortgages.

Mutual savings banks emphasize thrift. Concentrated in the northeastern states, they have considerable flexibility in granting loans, and since they are virtually free of federal mortgage regulations they invest both in local and out-of-state mortgages. They have invested heavily in FHA-insured and VA-guaranteed loans, and they depend heavily on the secondary market for mortgages—often buying a package of mortgages from an out-of-state mortgage banker or another source. Like savings and loan associations, they face the risk of deposit withdrawals in periods of high interest rates.

Life insurance companies have certain competitive advantages in the mortgage market: they may predict their available funds for investment with considerable accuracy; they are able to make long-term advance loan commitments which banks and savings institutions are unable to make. Insurance companies do not have the same need for liquidity as deposit institutions, and like mutual savings banks, they are free of federal mortgage regulations and invest over interstate lines. Much of their operation is centered on a system of loan correspondents.

Real estate investment trusts sell shares that give the small investor the advantage of the diversified investment portfolio of a large organization. For the most part their investments center on first mortgages and construction loans. Most of their mortgage portfolio has been placed on income property.

Pension funds have not invested heavily in mortgages because they lack the administrative resources needed to originate and service mortgage loans. Their concern for safety of principal and cost of portfolio administration has further restricted their interest in mortgage investments. The reinvestment of principal repayments introduces other administrative chores discouraging pension funds from increasing mortgage loan portfolios. The availability of marketable securities based on government-backed mortgages encourages the participation of pension funds in real estate finance.

State and local housing corporations concentrate mostly on low- and middle-income housing. In addition federal agencies supply mortgage credit, mostly through the secondary mortgage market—the subject of the next chapter.

REVIEW QUESTIONS

1. Explain the significance of mortgage debt in the national economy.
2. Why is the volume of mortgage activity highly dependent on personal savings?
3. What are the two main objectives of the savings and loan associations? What two central problems must they resolve in meeting these objectives?

4. What is the primary function of the regional banks of the Federal Home Loan Bank Board system? Explain thoroughly.

5. What are the mortgage policies of savings and loan associations? How does monetary policy affect their operation?

6. Why are negotiable order of withdrawal accounts favored for savings associations?

7. In the early history of commercial banks, why were nationally chartered banks prohibited from making mortgage loans?

8. In what three main ways was the authority of nationally chartered commercial banks to make loans increased by 1974 legislation? Give an example of each.

9. Explain how the mortgage policies of commercial banks vary from the mortgage policies of savings associations.

10. Explain the mortgage policies of mutual savings banks.

11. What advantages do life insurance companies have in competing for mortgage investments?

12. What types of mortgage loans are favored by life insurance companies?

13. What is meant by a loan correspondent?

14. What is the rationale of a real estate investment trust?

15. What types of loans have real estate investment trusts preferred?

16. What are three main services of a mortgage banker? Explain fully.

17. What is the difference between a mortgage broker and a mortgage banker?

18. What three types of loan commitments are important to mortgage bankers?

19. Why have pension funds avoided direct participation in mortgage markets?

20. How have securities backed by government-insured mortgages attracted pension funds into the mortgage market?

SELECTED REFERENCES

Beaton, William R. *Real Estate Finance,* chap. 2. Englewood Cliffs, N.J.: Prentice-Hall, Inc., 1975.

Dovenmuehle, George. "Development of Mortgage Banking," in Robert H. Pease (ed.), *Mortgage Banking.* 2d ed. New York: McGraw-Hill Book Co., 1965.

Hoagland, Henry E.; Stone, Leo D.; and Brueggeman, William B. *Real Estate Finance,* chaps. 8 and 15, 6th ed. Homewood, Ill.: Richard D. Irwin, Inc., 1977.

Kendall, Leon T. *The Savings and Loan Business,* chap. 2. Englewood Cliffs, N.J.: Prentice-Hall, Inc., 1962.

Mutual Savings Banking, chap. 6. Englewood Cliffs, N.J.: Prentice-Hall, Inc., 1962.

Shenkel, William M.   *Real Estate Finance,* chaps. 3 and 4. Washington, D.C.: American Bankers Association, 1976.

Wiedemer, John P.   *Real Estate Finance,* chap. 6. Reston, Va.: Reston Publishing Company, Inc., 1974.

Wiggin, Charles E.   "Doing Business in the Secondary Mortgage Market," *Real Estate Review,* vol. 5, no. 2 (Summer 1975), pp. 93–95.

13

The Secondary Mortgage Market

After you have read this chapter, you should be familiar with the following points:

1 The development of national housing policies and the improvement of the mortgage market.

2 The relation between government-insured and -guaranteed mortgages and the operation of the secondary mortgage market.

3 How the secondary mortgage market affects the supply of mortgage money.

4 Reasons for the expanding role of private mortgage insurance.

5 The functions of the Federal National Mortgage Association.

6 The function of the Government National Mortgage Association.

7 The impact of the Federal Home Loan Mortgage Corporation on home mortgages.

8 The purpose of other federal agencies active in rural and agricultural financing.

IT IS DEEMED ESSENTIAL to show how the secondary mortgage market operates before turning to real estate financing techniques; and since the secondary mortgage market follows from mortgages which are insured and conform to nationally applied standards, the chapter starts with an explanation of government-insured and privately insured mortgages. With this information in hand, the differences between the three main agencies active in the secondary market may be emphasized. Their policies significantly affect an individual's ability to finance housing or nonresidential real estate.

It will be recalled that the secondary mortgage market refers to the purchase and sale of mortgages between lenders and public or private agencies. The secondary mortgage market is diagramed in Figure 13–1.

FIGURE 13–1

An Illustration of the Primary and Secondary Mortgage Markets

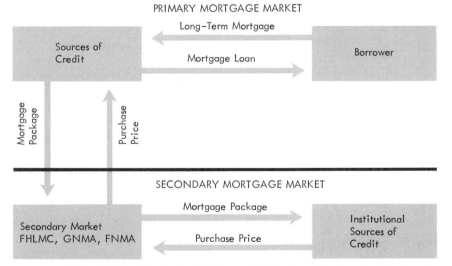

Institutional investors trade in mortgages much as they trade in government bonds. In this market the borrower has no direct participation. Yet borrowers benefit from mortgage funds which are channeled into the primary mortgage market via the secondary mortgage market. The ability of investors to buy mortgages of a known quality and yield through the secondary mortgage market provides funds to institutions that originate loans. An explanation of how mortgage insurance operates demonstrates this point.

GOVERNMENT-INSURED AND -GUARANTEED LOANS

Mutual mortgage insurance was introduced with the formation of the Federal Housing Administration (FHA) in 1934. Mortgages guaranteed by the Veterans Administration (VA loans) for eligible veterans, while not based on insurance, give a degree of safety and liquidity comparable to that of the FHA-insured mortgage. VA loans originated under the Serviceman's Readjustment Act of 1944. The FHA and the VA account for the bulk of federal assistance to mortgage borrowers.

The Federal Housing Administration

The Federal Housing Administration originated with the National Housing Act of 1934. The act was conceived to encourage employment in the building and construction trades. It was believed that insuring mortgage loans would induce lenders to advance money on mortgages and in this way encourage residential construction. New home construction of 93,000 units in 1933 represented only 10 percent of the new homes constructed in 1925.[1] By 1933, approximately one half of all home mortgages were in default.

Mutual Mortgage Insurance. The 1934 Housing Act introduced the housing loan insurance program "to encourage improvement in housing standards and conditions, to provide a system of mutual mortgage insurance and other purposes."[2] While Congress has added numerous programs to the FHA, the agency's main function was to insure mortgages on one- to four-famly dwellings under Section 203 of the Housing Act. The borrower paid a monthly premium equal to one half of 1 percent of the original loan, which was later revised to one half of 1 percent on the unpaid remaining balance. Originally FHA insurance provided for loans on 80 percent of value, 5 to 6 percent interest, and a maximum term of 20 years.

The lender holding a mortgage in default initiated foreclosure proceedings, taking title to the foreclosed property. The title was then transferred to the FHA in return for debentures equal in value to the mortgage and originally paying 3 percent interest (1934). The debentures were guaranteed by the credit of the United States. Under certain circumstances the lender was entitled to the expenses of foreclosure.

The Impact of FHA Insurance. The immediate impact of FHA insurance was to increase the supply of funds to the mortgage market, raise the demand for housing, and stimulate construction employment.

---

[1] *H.R. Report No. 897*, 81st Congress, 2d Session, Committee on Banking and Currency on S.2246, pp. 56–67.

[2] *National Housing Act of 1934*, P.L. 479, 73d Congress, Session 2, chap. 847, June 27, 1934.

1. *Increased Supply of Mortgage Funds.* Lenders were more willing to invest in mortgages because of certain other innovations introduced by the FHA: (1) insurance against mortgage default reduced investment risks; (2) houses insured by the FHA were required to meet minimum property standards; (3) the FHA developed a uniform system of appraising houses for FHA-insured mortgages; and (4) mortgage contracts were standardized.

2. *Increased Demand for Mortgage Funds.* Certain other innovations of the 1934 act increased the demand for home mortgages. First, the FHA introduced the amortized level payment mortgage—in place of the term mortgage; the maturity of the mortgage was gradually increased to the point that 30-year and even 40-year mortgages are now permissible under some housing programs. Second, standardized procedures covering minimum property standards and standard appraisal and mortgage forms allowed the FHA over the years to increase the loan-to-value ratio on residential mortgages. The end result was to lower down payments and reduce monthly mortgage installments, increasing home ownership to middle- and low-income families. To some extent higher interest rates have been offset by higher loan-to-value ratios and longer term mortgages.

In short, FHA-amortized mortgages replaced the 50 to 60 percent term loan of three to five years, often accompanied by second- and third-mortgage financing. Term mortgages provided for interest payments only; the principal was repaid at the end of the term—or the loan was renewed for another term. Today, a borrower may purchase a $45,000 house under FHA terms with a down payment of $3,750—a 91.7 percent loan. Under a Section 203 loan, the maximum loan on FHA houses is graduated downward according to price:

Price Interval	Amount	Percent of Down Payment Required	Minimum Down Payment
First....................	$25,000	3	$ 750
Next....................	10,000	10	1,000
Next....................	10,000	20	2,000
Maximum..............	$45,000	(8.3)	$3,750

The Development of Current FHA Policy. Critical housing shortages experienced after World War II were met by the Housing Act of 1949. The need to increase employment by giving mortgage lenders incentives to finance housing was superseded by policies directed to correcting housing shortages. The 1949 act declared:

> The Congress hereby declares the general welfare and security in the nation and the health and living standards of its people require housing production and related community development sufficient to remedy the

serious housing shortage, the elimination of substandard and other inadequate housing through the clearance of slums and blighted areas, and the realization as soon as feasible of *the goal of a decent home and a suitable living environment for every American family,* thus contributing to the development and redevelopment of communities and to the advancement of the growth, wealth, and security of the nation.[3]

The act stated further that national housing objectives would encourage private enterprise, utilize government assistance to advance private enterprise in meeting housing needs, and encourage local government to assist in well-planned, integrated residential neighborhoods. Governmental assistance was introduced to eliminate substandard and inadequate housing through the clearance of slums and blighted areas. In other words, urban renewal and FHA insurance were used to pursue slum and blight clearance. Urban renewal refers to the program in which the Housing and Home Finance Agency (now the Department of Housing and Urban Development—HUD) gave grants to local communities to purchase slum and blight property. Local agencies redeveloped such areas and sold the "renewed" areas to private investors for the construction of planned developments. Special FHA insurance programs were initiated for this purpose. Mutual mortgage insurance became more than a device to encourage employment in the construction industry; it became a device to promote community redevelopment and other national housing objectives.

This role was reiterated in the Housing Act of 1954, which liberalized the urban renewal features of the 1949 act. The purpose of the Housing Act of 1954 was to

> aid in the provision and improvement of housing, the elimination and prevention of slums, and the conservation and development of urban communities.[4]

Later, responding to the criticism that mutual mortgage insurance had not been directed to low-income families, Congress enacted the Housing and Urban Development Act of 1968. The act introduced various forms of subsidized housing to promote the needs of low-income families. This legislation meant that secondary mortgage operations would be required to support government-assisted programs—a policy that conflicted with leveling out the peaks and valleys in mortgage credit. The 1968 act

> . . . affirms the national goal as set forth in Section 2 of the Housing Act of 1949, of "a decent home and a suitable living environment for every American family."

And further:

> The Congress finds that *this goal has not been fully realized for many of the Nation's lower income families;* that this is a matter of grave na-

---

[3] *Public Law 171,* 81st Congress, 1st Session, chap. 338, July 15, 1949. Emphasis supplied.

[4] *Public Law 560,* 83d Congress, 2d Session, 1954, vol. 68, part 1, August 2, 1954.

tional concern; and that there exist in the public and private sectors of the economy the resources and capabilities necessary to the full realization of this goal.

The Congress declares that in the administration of those housing programs authorized by this Act which are designed to assist families with incomes so low that they could not otherwise decently house themselves, and of other Government programs designed to assist in the provision of housing for such families, the highest priority and emphasis should be given to meeting the housing needs of those families for which the national goal has not become a reality; and in the carrying out of such programs there should be the fullest practicable utilization of the resources and capabilities of private enterprise and of individual self-help techniques.[5]

National policies affecting housing finance were revised by the 1974 act, which terminated some existing programs and added new programs. The comprehensive nature of this act is shown by its eight titles:

Title Number	Topic
I	Community Development
II	Assisted Housing
III	Mortgage Credit Assistance
IV	Comprehensive Planning
V	Rural Housing
VI	Mobile Home Construction and Safety and Standards
VII	Consumer Home Mortgage Association
VIII	Miscellaneous

The policy statement of Title I suggests the new policy on housing. (See Figure 13–2.) The four objectives under Title I are: (1) to improve the social, economic, and environmental conditions in the nation's cities, towns, and small urban communities; (2) to establish and maintain viable urban communities; (3) to provide decent housing, a suitable living environment, and expanding economic opportunities—especially for persons of low and moderate income; and (4) to develop a national urban growth policy.

The main impact of the act on mortgage insurance was covered in Title III, which increased maximum FHA insurance for selected programs administered by the FHA, and by Title VIII, which revised the national housing goals to include the preservation and rehabilitation of housing and neighborhoods. The act provided for assistance to state housing development agencies and for other guarantees and grants to expand local community housing programs.

Therefore, mutual mortgage insurance started out (1) as a means of

---

[5] *Public Law 90–448,* 82 Stat. 476. Emphasis supplied.

FIGURE 13–2

Community Development Policies under the Housing and Community Development Act of 1974

TITLE I—COMMUNITY DEVELOPMENT

Findings and Purpose

Sec. 101. (*a*) The Congress finds and declares that the Nation's cities, towns, and smaller urban communities face critical social, economic, and environmental problems arising in significant measure from—

(1) the growth of population in metropolitan and other urban areas, and the concentration of persons of lower income in central cities; and

(2) inadequate public and private investment and reinvestment in housing and other physical facilities, and related public and social services, resulting in the growth and persistence of urban slums and blight and the marked deterioration of the quality of the urban environment.

(*b*) The Congress further finds and declares that the future welfare of the Nation and the well-being of its citizens depend on the establishment and maintenance of viable urban communities as social, economic, and political entities, and require—

(1) systematic and sustained action by Federal, State, and local governments to eliminate blight, to conserve and renew older urban areas, to improve the living environment of low- and moderate-income families, and to develop new centers of population growth and economic activity;

(2) substantial expansion of and greater continuity in the scope and level of Federal assistance, together with increased private investment in support of community development activities; and

(3) continuing effort at all levels of government to streamline programs and improve the functioning of agencies responsible for planning, implementing, and evaluating community development efforts.

(*c*) The primary objective of this title is the development of viable urban communities, by providing decent housing and a suitable living environment and expanding economic opportunities, principally for persons of low and moderate income. Consistent with this primary objective, the Federal assistance provided in this title is for the support of community development activities which are directed toward the following specific objectives—

(1) the elimination of slums and blight and the prevention of blighting influences and the deterioration of property and neighborhood and community facilities of importance to the welfare of the community, principally persons of low and moderate income;

(2) the elimination of conditions which are detrimental to health, safety, and public welfare, through code enforcement, demolition, interim rehabilitation assistance, and related activities;

(3) the conservation and expansion of the Nation's housing stock in order to provide a decent home and a suitable living environment for all persons, but principally those of low and moderate income;

(4) the expansion and improvement of the quantity and quality of community services, principally for persons of low and moderate income, which

FIGURE 13–2 *(continued)*

are essential for sound community development and for the development of viable urban communities;

(5) a more rational utilization of land and other natural resources and the better arrangement of residential, commercial, industrial, recreational, and other needed activity centers;

(6) the reduction of the isolation of income groups within communities and geographical areas and the promotion of an increase in the diversity and vitality of neighborhoods through the spatial deconcentration of housing opportunities for persons of lower income and the revitalization of deteriorating or deteriorated neighborhoods to attract persons of higher income; and

(7) the restoration and preservation of properties of special value for historic, architectural, or esthetic reasons.

It is the intent of Congress that the Federal assistance made available under this title not be utilized to reduce substantially the amount of local financial support for community development activities below the level of such support prior to the availability of such assistance.

(*d*) It is also the purpose of this title to further the development of a national urban growth policy by consolidating a number of complex and overlapping programs of financial assistance to communities of varying sizes and needs into a consistent system of Federal aid which—

(1) provides assistance on an annual basis, with maximum certainty and minimum delay, upon which communities can rely in their planning;

(2) encourages community development activities which are consistent with comprehensive local and areawide development planning;

(3) furthers achievement of the national housing goal of a decent home and a suitable living environment for every American family; and

(4) fosters the undertaking of housing and community development activities in a coordinated and mutually supportive manner.

attracting investment capital to the housing industry. (2) Next it was to serve the objective of giving every American a decent home. (3) The housing legislation of 1968 concentrated on low-income housing, and (4) by 1974 housing policy encompassed numerous environmental problems and broader issues of urban growth policy. The secondary market for mortgages has been adapted to the changing mortgage market that has developed in response to these trends.

Discount Points. Until 1968, federal home mortgage insurance was directed to middle-income housing. It was not until the Housing and Urban Development Act of 1968 that provision was made for low-income housing. The 1968 act provided for a $200 down payment and for subsidizing interest payments on home loans to a minimum of 1 percent interest and within this restriction stabilizing monthly mortgage payments at 20 percent of the borrower's income. While these programs were being introduced,

Congress established an interest rate ceiling on all FHA loans. While initially the FHA interest rate ceiling was competitive with market rates, after the Korean War the yield on federally insured mortgages fell below market rates.

As a substitute for raising mortgage interest rates, the FHA allows mortgage lenders to charge discount "points," which increases the effective interest rates. Discount points refer to the percentage discount paid the lender as an inducement to make loans at FHA maximum interest rates. A one-point discount means a 1 percent discount. A ten-point discount on a $30,000 loan would be $3,000.

In operation, discount points are paid by the seller to the mortgage lender. To illustrate, suppose that the seller accepts the buyer's offer to purchase a dwelling for $45,000. The buyer obtains an FHA loan for the maximum amount, providing for a down payment of $3,750 for a 25-year loan at 8½ percent interest. Suppose further that the lender requires the market rate of interest, 9½ percent. With a fixed interest rate of 8½ percent, the lender discounts the loan by eight points, giving him an effective interest rate of 9.52 percent if the loan is held to maturity. Under this arrangement, the lender accepts the buyer's promise to repay a loan of $41,250 at 8½ percent over a 25-year term. The lender pays only $37,950 for a loan which is repaid to its face value, $41,250. The 8 percent discount of $3,300 ($3,300/$41,250) is paid by the seller. The seller, who sells the property for $45,000, receives the following sums:

Proceeds to Seller

$37,950 received from lender (the discounted mortgage)
 3,750 received from buyer (down payment)
$41,700 total received by seller
 3,300 discount paid to lender
$45,000 sales price

Under these arrangements, the seller bears the cost of the $3,300 discount. The lender receives payments based on an 8½ percent yield on a mortgage of $41,250 for which he has paid $37,950. If the loan is repaid in eight years, the yield increases to 10.03 percent. Though the seller pays the discount, the final burden may lie with the buyer, who may pay above the market value of the property because it is financed through FHA terms. That is, if the seller anticipates paying the discount, he will attempt to recoup the discount by increasing the sales price.

It should be noted that mutual mortgage insurance provides for a single premium, one half of 1 percent of the unpaid principal balance, for all borrowers. Under a single-premium plan, the preferred risks, that is, good risk borrowers with relatively high, stable incomes and relatively high equities, pay the same premium as poor risk borrowers with equities as low as $200, who buy a low-valued house, have a less stable income, and may borrow under a longer term amortization, that is, a 40-year mortgage term. In one sense preferred risk borrowers subsidize high-risk borrowers. This trend has encouraged borrowers to seek private mortgage insurance which relates the mortgage insurance premium to the degree of assumed risk.

FHA Mortgage Insurance Programs

Today the FHA administers some 50 different mortgage programs, including subsidized and nonsubsidized mortgages. A list of the programs which existed prior to the passage of the 1974 Housing and Community Development Act shows the extent to which FHA mortgage insurance has expanded since its initial emphasis on employment. Though Congress has authorized these programs, funds for their support have not always been available.[6]

Title I

Section 2 (authorized in 1934)
Property Improvements. Insurance of approved lending institutions against loss on loans (usually made without collateral) to alter, repair, improve, or convert existing structures or to build small new nonresidential structures.

Mobile Homes (authorized in 1969)
Insurance of approved lending institutions against loss on loans used to purchase mobile home units by buyers intending to use them as their principal residence.

Title II

Section 203(b) (authorized in 1934)
Insurance of mortgages on proposed, under construction, or existing one–four-family dwellings.

Section 203(h) (authorized in 1954)
Insurance of mortgages to finance the acquisition of proposed, under construction, or existing one family housing by an occupant-mortgagor who is a victim of a major disaster.

Section 203(i) (authorized in 1954)
Insurance of mortgages to finance the purchase of proposed, under construction, or existing one-family housing in outlying areas or farm housing on five or more acres adjacent to a highway.

Section 203(k) (authorized in 1961)
Insurance of loans to finance the alteration, repair, or improvement of existing one–four-family housing located outside urban renewal areas.

Section 207 (authorized in 1934)
Insurance of mortgages used to finance the construction or rehabilitation of rental housing with eight or more units, and on mobile home parks.

---

[6] William M. Shenkel, *Real Estate Finance* (Washington, D.C.: American Bankers Association, 1976), pp. 118–22. Reprinted by permission.

Section 213 (authorized in 1950)

Insurance of mortgages to finance the construction or rehabilitation of cooperative housing projects consisting of five or more units.

Section 220 (authorized in 1954)

Insurance of mortgages to finance the purchase of rehabilitation of 1–11-family housing and multifamily projects of two or more units.

Section 221(d)(2) (authorized in 1954)

Insurance of mortgages to finance the purchase or rehabilitation of low-cost one- to four-family housing for families displaced by governmental action.

Section 221(d)(3) (authorized in 1954)

Insurance of market-rate mortgages on unsubsidized multifamily rental and cooperative housing for low- and moderate-income families and families displaced by governmental action.

Section 221(d)(4) (authorized in 1959)

Insurance of mortgages for general mortgagors (profit motivated) on multifamily rental housing for low- and moderate-income families.

Section 222 (authorized in 1954)

Insurance of mortgages on single-family homes purchased for their own occupancy by persons on active duty with the Armed Forces or the Coast Guard or serving in the U.S. National Oceanic and Atmospheric Administration.

Section 223(a), (b), and (c) (authorized in 1954)

Insurance of miscellaneous-type mortgages, refinancing of existing mortgages, or insurance of mortgages on specified types of permanent housing sold by federal or state governments.

Section 223(d) (authorized in 1961)

Insurance of mortgages to cover the excess of expenses over project gross income incurred during the first two years following the date of completion of the project.

Section 223(e) (authorized in 1968)

Insurance of mortgages used to finance the purchase or rehabilitation of housing located in older, declining urban areas.

Section 223(f) (authorized in 1974)

Insurance of mortgages used to finance the purchase of or to refinance an existing multifamily housing project.

Section 225 (authorized in 1954)

Insurance of additional advances under an open-end provision in a mortgage insured under any section of the National Housing Act on a one–four-family home.

Section 231 (authorized in 1959)

Insurance of mortgages on new or rehabilitated housing projects with eight or more units designed for occupancy by elderly or handicapped individuals.

Section 232 (authorized in 1959)

Insurance of mortgages to finance the construction or rehabilitation of nursing or intermediate care facilities, or a combined nursing home and intermediate care facility.

Section 233 (authorized in 1961)

Insurance of mortgages to finance the construction or rehabilitation of single-family housing and multifamily projects that incorporate new or untried construction concepts designed to reduce housing costs, raise living standards, and improve neighborhood design.

Section 234 (authorized in 1961)
Insurance of project and home mortgages on condominiums.

Section 235 (authorized in 1968)
Insurance of mortgages coupled with interest reduction payments to enable lower income families to purchase new or substantially rehabilitated single-family dwellings or condominium units approved prior to the beginning of construction or beginning of substantial rehabilitation. This program was included in the overall suspension on January 5, 1973, of the subsidized housing programs, and was reactivated, with major revisions, in January 1976.

Section 236 (authorized in 1968)
Insurance of mortgages on rental and cooperative projects coupled with interest reduction payments to make possible lower rents, within the financial reach of low- and moderate-income families, including the elderly or handicapped. This program was included in the overall suspension on January 5, 1973, of the subsidized housing programs. Except as necessary to meet bona fide commitments which cannot be met under the Section 8 Lower Income Housing Assistance program, commitments for additional projects will not be made under the program.

Section 237 (authorized in 1968)
Insurance of mortgages used to finance the purchase of new, existing, or substantially rehabilitated single-family homes by low-income families who, for reasons of credit history, irregular income patterns caused by seasonal employment, or other factors, are unable to meet normal FHA credit requirements.

Rent Supplement Program (authorized in 1965)
Insurance of mortgages on new or substantially rehabilitated rental housing coupled with a rent supplement paid to the private project owner. Assistance covers the difference between the tenant's payment and the market rental, but may not exceed 70 percent of the market rental. This program was included in the overall suspension on January 5, 1973, of the subsidized housing programs. Except as necessary to meet bona fide commitments which cannot be met under the Section 8 Lower Income Housing Assistance program, commitments for additional projects will not be made under this program.

Section 240 (authorized in 1968)
Insurance of mortgages for homeowners to purchase fee simple title to property which is held under long-term leases and on which their homes are located.

Section 241 (authorized in 1968)
Insurance of supplemental loans for alterations, repairs, additions, or improvements to any multifamily housing project financed with an FHA-insured mortgage.

Section 242 (authorized in 1968)
Insurance of mortgages to finance the construction or rehabilitation of private nonprofit and proprietary hospitals, including major movable equipment.

Section 244 (authorized in 1974)
Coinsurance of mortgages by HUD- and FHA-approved private lenders,

whereby losses will be shared in the event of default on a 90 percent–10 percent basis, respectively.

Title VIII

Section 809 (authorized in 1956)
Insurance of mortgages on homes built for sale to civilian employees at or near research or development installations of the Department of Defense, NASA, AEC, or their contractors.

Section 810 (authorized in 1959)
Insurance of mortgages on off-base housing for military or essential civilian personnel of the Armed Services, NASA, or AEC, or employees of contractors thereof.

Title XI (authorized in 1966)

Insurance of mortgages to be used to finance the construction or rehabilitation of group practice facilities, including major movable equipment, for group practice of dentistry, medicine, optometry, osteopathy, or podiatry.

Other Noninsured HUD Programs

Section 8 (authorized in 1974)
Provides housing assistance payments to permit participating owners, developers, and public housing agencies to provide decent, safe, and sanitary housing for lower income families in private accommodations at rents they can afford.

Section 202 (authorized in 1959, amended in 1974)
Provides direct loans which may be used to finance the construction or rehabilitation of rental or cooperative housing.

Indian Housing (authorized in 1937, amended in 1974)
Provides annual contributions to Indian housing authorities to assist in financing the development or acquisition cost of low-income housing projects for Indian families.

Section 518(a) (authorized in 1964)
Authorizes assistance to owners of new one–four-family dwellings approved for mortgage insurance prior to the beginning of construction, where such dwellings are found to have major structural defects or defects which threaten the structural components of the dwellings.

Section 518(b) (authorized in 1970, amended in 1974)
Authorizes assistance to owners of existing one- to four-family dwellings when such housing is determined to require correction of structural or other major defects which so seriously affect the use and livability as to create a serious danger to the life or safety of the inhabitants.

It is fairly clear that the FHA has progressed from an insurance program that initially insured mortgages for the benefit of the lender to more socially oriented programs. From an orientation directed to reducing the lender's risk, the FHA has developed into a series of programs that promote objectives considered beneficial to the community interest, that is, nursing homes, medical clinics, housing for the elderly, subsidized low-income housing, and the like.

Veterans Administration–Guaranteed Mortgages

In contrast to the FHA, the Veterans Administration guarantees loans for eligible veterans. Originally VA loans provided for a 50 percent guarantee of up to $2,000 to the lender in the event of a default, with a maximum mortgage interest rate of 4 percent. Subsequent amendments provide for a maximum guarantee of $17,500, or 60 percent of value, whichever is less.

From the standpoint of the lender, the guarantee changes the effective loan-to-value ratio. For example, a veteran entitled to the full guarantee may negotiate a $50,000 loan with no down payment, giving the lender the equivalent of a 65 percent loan-to-value ratio; a lender limiting the effective loan-to-value ratio to a 75 percent loan could grant a $70,000 loan (no down payment) because of the $17,500 guarantee. The government maximum guarantee of 60 percent applies to loans of $29,167 or less (17,500/29,167 = 60.0 percent); above this amount the $17,500 guarantee applies.

The veteran is prohibited from paying discounts on mortgages. He or she is not required to make a down payment; loan origination fees are limited to 1 percent of the loan; and the veteran is not required to pay closing costs. If the veteran elects to pay the entire loan before maturity, the lender may not levy prepayment penalties. Veterans must hold a certificate of eligibility issued by the Veterans Administration. Eligibility depends on service in the Armed Forces during specified times and on prior use of VA guarantees.

In the event of foreclosure, the VA has the option of paying the guarantee and requiring the lender to dispose of the foreclosed property. In practice, the VA pays the lender the balance of the loan with interest and foreclosure costs. The VA then takes title, reselling through local real estate brokers. Current legislation provides for the purchase of farm homes and mobile homes under similar provisions.

PRIVATE MORTGAGE INSURANCE

Private mortgage insurance (PMI) companies began in 1956 with the Mortgage Guaranty Insurance Corporation (MGIC) in Wisconsin. The assets of the 13 PMI companies grew from $159 million in 1970 to $552 million in 1974—an increase of 347.2 percent in five years.[7]

Insurance Premiums

The main difference between PMI and FHA insurance lies in the insurance premium: in contrast to the FHA's single insurance premium ap-

---

[7] *MGIC Fact Book* (Madison, Wis.: Mortgage Guaranty Insurance Corporation, 1975), p. 5.

plying to all loans, irrespective of their risk, PMI relates the amount of insurance to the degree of risk assumed. Moreover, PMI not only tends to be cheaper for qualified borrowers, but loan-to-value ratios on insured mortgages range upward to 95 percent of the property value. Rates of a private mortgage company are shown in Table 13–1.

Note that insurance premiums are related to the amount of risk. In the case of 20 percent insurance coverage, PMI companies may elect to pay 20 percent of the loss and waive any further interest in the property. In the sale of foreclosed property, the lender may more than recover the loan

TABLE 13–1

Private Mortgage Insurance Premiums

			Insurance Cost as a Percent of the Loan				
			Single-Premium Plans by Years of Coverage				
Insurance Coverage	*Loan-to-Value Ratio*	*Annual Premium Plan*	*4*	*5*	*7*	*10*	*15*
25%	91–95%	1% first year ¼% annually	—	1¾%	2%	2½%	2¾%
	80–90%	¾% first year ¼% annually	1¼%	—	—	2¼%	2½%
20%	91–95%	¾% first year ¼% annually	—	1½%	1¾%	2¼%	2½%
	80–90%	½% first year ¼% annually	1%	—	—	2%	2¼%
	80% and under	¼% first year ¼% annually	—	¾%	1%	1½%	—
10%	80% and under	0.15% first year 0.15% annually	—	0.6%	0.8%	1%	—

Source: Mortgage Guarantee Insurance Corporation.

balance; but if there is a loss above the 20 percent coverage, it is absorbed by the lender. Alternatively, PMI may allow the lender to resell foreclosed real estate before submitting a claim. The insurance payment will be equal to the full extent of loss including foreclosure expenses up to a maximum of a 25 percent loss settlement.

For only 10 percent coverage and for loans limited to 80 percent of the property value, the premium is only 0.15 percent of the loan. Even for 25 percent coverage on a 90–95 percent loan, the premium is limited to 1 percent of the loan the first year and one quarter of 1 percent annually thereafter.

PMI premiums are lower than FHA premiums: one half of 1 percent of the unpaid balance of the loan. Note too that on a $45,000 house under PMI, a borrower would be advanced a 95 percent loan, or $42,750. Under the FHA, the maximum loan would be 91.3 percent, or $41,250.

Borrower Qualification

In part, relatively low premiums are feasible because PMI companies are more restrictive in qualifying the borrowers. A recent report indicated that loans were rejected by one company because of the borrowers' (1) lack of experience in a new business venture, (2) insufficient job and seniority rights, (3) inadequate time on the job, (4) numerous employment changes, (5) unstable sources of secondary income, (6) recent moves into the community, and (7) seasonal employment.

In sum, private mortgage insurance companies:

1. Select the preferred credit risks. They select only qualified, eligible lenders; they regularly review individual loans; they undertake spot checks of local economic factors, lender appraisals, and credit reports; and they insure only approved lenders with demonstrated management ability and a policy of observing high mortgage standards.
2. Process and approve loan applications expeditiously. They avoid the delays that sometimes occur with FHA loans.
3. Insure loans at a relatively high loan-to-value ratio.
4. Provide lower insurance costs for qualified buyers.

With the alternative of private mortgage insurance and the improvement of secondary markets, the real estate industry benefits from a more orderly flow of funds into mortgage markets. This is particularly true for conventional loans which are now eligible for purchase and sale in the secondary mortgage market—and available with the option of private mortgage insurance.

THE SECONDARY MORTGAGE MARKET

Although government-insured loans reduced the risk of the mortgage lender, the housing industry in 1934 still faced major problems centering on four issues:

1. The housing industry required a means of leveling out the peaks and valleys of available home financing.
2. A mechanism was needed to transfer mortgage funds from capital surplus areas to capital shortage areas.
3. A national market for the sale and purchase of home mortgages by institutions was needed.
4. Borrowers required a means of obtaining mortgage funds at rates they could afford.

The secondary market served these functions. It provided liquidity to holders of long-term mortgages and to potential investors seeking higher yields on residential housing mortgages. It provided a means by which long-term investors could convert mortgage loans to cash and help distribute mortgage investment capital to areas of urgent need.

In the absence of an organized secondary market, investors with surplus funds experienced difficulty in obtaining an adequate supply of mortgages during periods of credit ease, and conversely, the housing industry was handicapped by the lack of an efficient market for home mortgages during periods of monetary restraint. The current operations of the secondary mortgage market and current FHA loan policy are closely related to the national housing policy initiated under the Housing Act of 1934 and since materially changed in objectives and in financing techniques.

The Reconstruction Finance Corporation established the RFC Mortgage Company in 1935 "to assist in the reestablishment of a national mortgage market." The agency was authorized to purchase FHA-insured

TABLE 13–2

Mortgage Debt Outstanding by Type of Holder, 1971–1975 (in millions)

Type of Holder	1971	1972	1973	1974	1975
Federal National Mortgage Association......................	$17,791	$19,791	$24,175	$29,578	$31,824
GNMA Pools.......................	3,154	5,815	9,109	13,892	21,257
Government National Mortgage Association......................	5,323	5,113	4,029	4,848	7,438
Federal Home Loan Mortgage Corporation.....................	964	1,789	2,604	4,586	4,987
Farmers Home Administration.....	819	837	1,200	1,600	2,000
Federal Housing and Veterans Administration..................	3,389	3,338	3,476	3,900	5,004
Federal Land Banks (farm only).......................	7,917	9,107	11,071	13,863	16,563
Total.......................	$39,357	$45,790	$55,664	$72,267	$89,073

Source: *Federal Reserve Bulletin*, March 1976, p. A42.

mortgages and, after 1946, VA-guaranteed mortgages. After 1938, this function was assumed by the Federal National Mortgage Association.

In 1968, this agency was converted from a government-owned agency to a government-regulated, privately owned corporation. The Government National Mortgage Association was formed at this time to purchase government-insured, subsidized loans. Under the Emergency Home Finance Act of 1970, the Federal Home Loan Mortgage Corporation was authorized to purchase conventional loans under the supervision of the Federal Home Loan Bank Board. In addition, the Farmers Home Administration and the Federal Land Banks hold mortgages under programs administered by these agencies. The Federal Housing Administration and the Veterans Administration also hold a relatively small volume of mortgages, primarily on foreclosed properties. The extent of mortgage debt held by these organizations is shown in Table 13–2. At the present time, FHA, VA, and conventional loans are bought and sold in the open market, much as government bonds are.

Operations of the Secondary Mortgage Market

To understand the current role of FNMA and other organizations operating in the secondary market, it is worthwhile to review the secondary market under (1) conditions of monetary restraint and (2) conditions of credit ease.

Periods of Tight Credit.   The central problem of the mortgage market arises from cyclical shortages of mortgage funds that affect thrift institutions. That is, in periods of tight credit, savings available for mortgages decline among the main thrift institutions. At the same time, mortgage lenders with considerable portfolio flexibility shift to higher yielding security markets. The secondary market agencies compensate for the shortage of mortgage credit during these periods by offering to *purchase* blocks of mortgages from lenders, giving them additional funds to finance and originate new mortgages.

In addition, by withholding mortgage commitments to lenders, FNMA decreases the flow of funds going into the mortgage market. Without FNMA commitments, rising interest rates would lead to a general withdrawal of funds. Indeed, after 1954 FNMA was reorganized specifically to provide assistance to the secondary market for home mortgages. With a shortage of loanable funds, FNMA purchases mortgages, supplying capital to lenders which may be invested in new mortgages. For instance, in 1975 FNMA sold $1.98 billion of mortgages, but in the same year it also purchased mortgages worth $4.3 billion.[8] During the period of high interest rates in 1973 and 1974, when sales of its mortgage portfolio were fairly nominal ($4.2 million and $70.7 million), FNMA purchased some $7.0 billion and $6.25 billion in mortgages.[9]

Periods of Credit Ease.   The converse holds true in periods of credit ease. At this time secondary market agencies *sell* portions of their portfolio, thus tending to absorb excess funds that lead to overconstruction.

During periods of easy credit, FNMA sells mortgages, absorbing funds that would ordinarily be placed in mortgages. For example, in 1962 FNMA sold $390.6 million from its portfolio, increasing sales to $779.8 million in 1963. Since its purchases for this year were only $181.3 million, FNMA absorbed funds that would ordinarily have been placed in new FHA and VA mortgages.[10]

There is a further contribution of secondary mortgage operations. The demand for mortgage funds tends to be concentrated in developing areas, namely, the South and the West. Yet the supply of long-term capital concentrates in the financial centers of the northeastern states. The discrepancy between capital availability and capital need creates a demand

---

[8] Federal National Mortgage Association, *1975 Annual Report*, p. 8.

[9] Ibid.

[10] *Background and History* (Washington, D.C.: Federal National Mortgage Association, 1973), p. 18.

for the specialized services of mortgage bankers who originate loans in capital shortage areas for out-of-state investors with surplus funds. To accomplish this task, mortgage bankers depend on the secondary mortgage market. They originate loans and sell blocks of mortgages to institutional buyers, creating income from origination and mortgage servicing fees.

In short, with improved secondary markets in conventional FHA and VA loans, large-scale investors buy and sell mortgage funds according to relative yields and the policies of secondary mortgage market agencies. If institutional lenders anticipate increasing interest rates, they tend to withhold investments in fixed interest mortgages. The market value of mortgages with fixed interest rates declines inversely with an increase in the market rate of interest. The possibility of portfolio losses is removed by commitments from FNMA, for example, a commitment to purchase a lender's mortgage portfolio during a stated period at some set figure. Given this commitment, the lender has the option of selling newly originated mortgages to FNMA if interest rates become more attractive on non-mortgage securities.

Private Incorporation. Beginning in 1968, the secondary mortgage market was subjected to two changes: (1) FNMA was reorganized as a privately owned corporation operating under government supervision; and (2) a new government-owned corporation, the Government National Mortgage Corporation (GNMA), was formed. At this time, FNMA was authorized to accept conventional non-government-insured or -guaranteed mortgages. The 1968 legislation freed FNMA from the duty of supporting mortgages on subsidized housing projects. The FNMA charter authorized the sale of preferred stock to the U.S. Treasury and the sale of common stock to private investors, the preferred stock to be retired from capital surplus. Sales of common shares were limited to sellers of mortgages to the association. FNMA was also permitted to raise funds through the sale of certain credit instruments. Under the new organization, FNMA purchases approved mortgages from lenders who qualify as eligible sellers. With a mortgage portfolio totaling $30.79 million at the end of 1975, FNMA is the nation's largest single private purchaser of residential mortgages. An institution that participates in FNMA operations must be:

1. Experienced in making real estate mortgages.
2. A business enterprise that maintains a net worth of not less than $100,000 in assets approved by FNMA.
3. An organization that employs appraisers, underwriters, and attorneys approved by FNMA.

Of the $25.7 million invested in home mortgages, slightly more than 10 percent was invested in conventional loans: $2.5 million.[11] Hence FNMA

---

[11] FNMA, *1975 Annual Report,* p. 8.

has acted as an important source of funds for government-insured and VA mortgages. With the purchase of conventional, noninsured mortgages, it is anticipated that more standardization in mortgage underwriting, appraisal, and administrative procedures will result. The standardization of forms and procedures for conventional loans makes the mortgage market operate even more effectively.

The Government National Mortgage Association

Under 1968 legislation, GNMA was established as a separate government corporation. One of the main responsibilities of the government-owned FNMA assumed by GNMA was the support of mortgages issued for subsidized housing programs, that is, housing for the military, low- and middle-income housing, housing for the elderly, and other national housing programs. Mortgages based on various subsidized housing programs have little appeal to private investors because of limited borrower credit, locations that add to mortgage risk, or mortgages issued under adverse economic conditions.

Pass-through Securities. Probably the main significance of GNMA lies in its authority to issue mortgage-backed securities based on the guarantee of principal and interest on "pass-through" securities which are backed by a pool of mortgages insured by federal agencies or guaranteed by the Veterans Administration. The full faith and credit of the United States guarantee the mortgage-backed securities.

Such securities were created to attract funds from long-term investors who were unwilling or did not have the facilities to service mortgages. In operation, the originating lender applies to GNMA for permission to establish a mortgage pool and issue securities or certificates against the pool of pledged mortgages. Before approval, mortgages must meet GNMA standards with respect to type of property, interest rates, and loan maturity. Mortgages forming the pool must not be issued more than one year before the GNMA commitment. Upon approval, GNMA guarantees the certificates, which are then issued to the original lender in proportion to the share of the mortgage pool purchased. The original issuer of certificates selects eligible loans and passes interest and principal payments to certificate holders.

Holders of certificates may include savings and loan associations, savings banks, credit unions, pension funds, commercial banks, corporations, partnerships, and individuals. The investor is assured of a guaranteed payment of interest and principal on the certificates, which are backed by approved mortgages. At the same time, the holder of the certificate is free from mortgage servicing duties.

The Tandem Plan. This plan combines the operations of GNMA and FNMA for sponsors of nonprofit housing projects. Suppose that a sponsor of a nonprofit housing project secures a commitment from GNMA to buy mortgages at par after construction is completed. At the same time, FNMA agrees to purchase a given amount of mortgages from GNMA at current prices. The mortgages are sold to FNMA at the market price, GNMA paying the difference between the face value of the mortgages and the discounted price.

This plan gives GNMA considerably more leverage. By paying for only the discount, GNMA has more funds available than if it were to hold the entire mortgage in its portfolio. In effect, GNMA guarantees to pay the discount, which sponsors of a specially assisted housing project probably could not afford.

Current FNMA programs cover six types of tandem agreements with GNMA.

Program 16.   This program includes only mortgages insured under the FHA. Programs that subsidize lower income families in buying dwellings or cooperative housing and are authorized under Section 235(*j*) are eligible for FNMA commitments at the same price applying to non-subsidized FHA purchases. GNMA underwrites the loss if the agency has agreed to purchase mortgages at a higher than market price.

Program 17.   Two programs insured by the FHA provide for rent subsidies tied to monthly income (Section 221[*d*]) or mortgage interest rate subsidies (Section 236). The agency processes mortgages according to a price formula which produces the greater of (*a*) prices for a multi-family standby commitment or (*b*) the current over-the-counter price. FNMA has established a preferential price of 2.75 percent above its regular price on the first $1 billion of any such mortgages purchased in any one year.

Program 18.   This program provides an interest subsidy to lower income families purchasing single-family dwellings (Section 235). Prices charged by FNMA in Program 18 mortgages produce yields equivalent to the average yield obtained by FNMA at the current four-month free-market auction.

Program 19.   Programs identified by HUD as part of Operation Breakthrough prototype projects are subject to the same pricing policies as Programs 17 and 18.

Program 20.   This program covers one- to four-family mortgages purchased at market prices from GNMA at regular FHA commitment prices.

Programs 21 and 22.   Starting in 1971, these programs supported FHA–VA housing mortgages. In periods of tight credit, FNMA agrees to support these mortgages above the market commitment prices advanced by GNMA. To encourage private purchase of these mortgages, GNMA agrees to sell commitments to the commitment holder at a price below the price which GNMA has agreed to pay. FNMA serves only as an administrative and warehousing source for price subsidies assumed by GNMA.

The Federal Home Loan Mortgage Corporation (FHLMC)

Legislation enacted in 1970 authorized this corporation, referred to as Freddie Mac, as an agency of the Federal Home Loan Bank Board. The FHLMC operates as a secondary market allowing mortgages to compete for capital on an equal basis with other types of investment. The corporation is authorized to purchase and sell FHA and VA mortgages in addition to conventional mortgages. It concentrates on four types of mortgage packages:

1. Conventional loans.
2. Conventional loans on multiple-family dwellings, fixed constant forward commitment.
3. Participations in conventional mortgages.
   a. Multiple-family dwellings.
   b. Single-family and multiple-family dwellings, with a maximum of 50 percent investment in multiple-family loans.
4. FHA and VA Home Mortgages.

Fixed Mortgage Commitments. The FHLMC introduced a new procedure in making advanced loan commitments. Recall that FNMA works with a fixed interest rate but varies the price of the mortgage. When mortgages of varying prices are purchased at a fixed contract interest rate, the effective yield moves in sympathy with the prevailing market rate of interest. The mortgage holder who sells to FNMA bears the risk of a decline in the value of the mortgage in the event of a higher interest rate. The FHLMC system is based on a fixed mortgage price, allowing the yield to vary and shifting the risk of interest rate increases to the FHLMC. To illustrate, it is necessary to define the *mortgage constant.*

The Mortgage Constant. The mortgage constant refers to annual mortgage and principal payments expressed as a percent of the original mortgage. It is calculated from the monthly mortgage installment required to repay $1 at a given interest rate and mortgage term. For example, a monthly payment of $0.008997 will repay a loan of $1, repayable at 9 percent interest over 240 months. Multiplying the monthly installment necessary to repay a loan of $1 by 12 gives the mortgage constant for a 9 percent, 20-year mortgage, which is 10.8 percent rounded (0.008997 × 12 = 0.107964). In other words, a $100,000 mortgage with a mortgage constant of 10.8 percent would require monthly payments which each year would total 10.8 percent of the mortgage, or approximately $10,800, including principal and interest.

The mortgage constant varies with the length of the mortgage and the interest rate. For example, a mortgage constant of 10 percent applies to a 7 percent, 17-year 3-month mortgage, and to a 9 percent, 25-year 9-month mortgage.[12] In other words, a high interest rate mortgage with a

---

[12] See *Financial Constant and Percent Amortization Tables,* Publication No. 187, rev. (Boston: Financial Publishing Co., 1969).

long maturity may produce the same annual payments that prevail for a shorter term mortgage with a lower interest rate.

Market Interest Rate Changes. The FHLMC bases purchase commitments on a maximum mortgage constant. Even if the market interest rate changes, a developer or borrower using an FHLMC commitment is assured that his mortgage payments will not rise above the stated maximum constant commitment. Using a 22-year amortization period, the FHLMC bases the mortgage constant commitment on the market rate of interest on the date the commitment is issued. When the lender delivers the mortgage, the amortization schedule is increased to 30 years. The FHLMC reserves the right to impose the effective interest rate on the day it accepts the loan up to the point of the maximum constant, based on the 30-year amortization schedule.

In accepting a commitment, a builder knows the exact amount of his loan—it will always be purchased at the agreed face value of the loan— and the maximum monthly payments. If the market interest rate has increased at the time the loan is presented to the FHLMC, the amortization period will be extended to 30 years—producing a constant monthly payment by offsetting higher interest rates with a longer term mortgage. Conversely, if interest rates have decreased, the borrower may extend the amortization rate to 30 years and reduce his monthly payments.

Though showing a current volume below FNMA and GNMA, the Freddie Mac portfolio of almost $5 billion is particularly significant to savings and loan associations, which may convert portfolios to cash for the origination of new mortgages. Thus the three secondary mortgage market institutions benefit borrowers by attracting funds to mortgages which otherwise might flow to more liquid investments.

OTHER FEDERAL MORTGAGE CREDIT AGENCIES

Table 13–2 shows that at the end of 1975 the Federal Land Bank financed $5.4 billion in mortgages. Federal Land Banks originated in 1917 and are organized in 12 regional banks that grant loans on 65 percent of the "normal" value of farms. Loans may be granted to purchase land, construct buildings, or refinance other farm debts. The terms range from 5 to 40 years, with interest subject to the cost of capital, variable over the life of the loan. The loans are serviced through a national farm loan association. The activities of the Federal Land Banks are confined to agricultural property.

The Farmers Home Administration, identified in Table 13–2, absorbs a relatively small amount of mortgages compared to other institutions. The agency, which dates from 1946, is authorized to make direct loans to farmers and others up to 40 years. Such loans are available in rural areas with populations under 2,500. The funds must be used for the construction or repair of dwellings and farm buildings. The Farmers Home Administration is dependent on annual congressional appropriations to fund direct loans in rural areas. The agency makes funds available in rural areas where long-term mortgage funds are largely unavailable. In this sense the program is a form of subsidy for homeowners in rural areas.

SUMMARY

The secondary mortgage market developed as a means of encouraging lenders to invest in FHA mortgages during the depression. The program was instituted primarily to relieve unemployment in the construction industry. Secondary mortgage operations developed from the system of mutual mortgage insurance administered by the Federal Housing Administration. FHA insurance increased the supply of mortgage funds by insuring lenders against default, established minimum property standards, and standardized appraisal methods and mortgage contracts. These measures further increased the demand for mortgages by introducing the amortized repayment plan in which principal repayments were included with each monthly payment.

FHA policy, which started with emergency measures to increase employment, was then directed by 1949 legislation to the national goal of providing a decent home and a suitable living environment for every family. The Housing Act of 1954 liberalized the urban renewal provisions of the 1949 act. With the enactment of the Housing and Urban Development Act of 1968, the FHA introduced subsidized mortgages for low-income families. Finally, the Housing and Community Development Act of 1974 incorporated community development and a broad range of programs, including a system of subsidies and grants for improving housing and other community goals. Thus mutual mortgages underwent substantial transition from their inception in 1934 to the present day.

The secondary mortgage market is dependent on a system of discount points that allows the fixed interest FHA and VA mortgages to meet competitive market rates. A one-point discount is equivalent to a 1 percent discount of the face value of the mortgage. The discount refers to payments made to the lender for accepting a mortgage below the market interest rate—raising the effective yield to the market rate of interest. The FHA mortgage insurance premium applies uniformly to borrowers, regardless of the degree of risk assumed.

Veterans Administration–guaranteed mortgages give lenders the option of granting no-down-payment loans because of the guarantee. A lender who grants a \$50,000 loan in effect holds a 65 percent loan since the \$17,500 (\$17,500/\$50,000 = 35\%) guarantee is viewed as a substitute for a 35 percent down payment.

Private mortgage insurance bases mortgage insurance premiums on the amount of the coverage and the risk assumed. The result is that the premium costs for borrowers are lower than the premium costs offered by FHA. The loan-to-value ratio is higher than that of the FHA, and the time of processing is generally less than the time required for FHA approval.

The secondary mortgage market levels the peaks and valleys of money available for long-term home financing; it provides funds for capital shortage areas and allows a market for sales and purchases of mortgages by financial institutions. Under 1968 legislation the Federal National Mortgage Association became privately owned and government controlled. During periods of tight credit FNMA *purchases* blocks of mortgages; in periods of credit ease it *sells* mortgages on the open market.

The Government National Mortgage Association, established in 1968, mainly supports subsidized housing programs. Moreover, by issuing securities backed by mortgages, it attracts funds from pension funds and other sources which buy securities backed by a pool of mortgages, giving mortgages virtually the same status as other bonds and similar investments. Under the tandem plan, GNMA purchases mortgages issued at below-market interest rates and sells the portfolio to FMNA or the public at the market rate, absorbing the loss as a subsidy to government-assisted mortgages.

The Federal Home Loan Mortgage Corporation, like FNMA, may buy and sell conventional or government-insured and -guaranteed mortgages. The FHLMC makes advance loan commitments by fixing the mortgage price and allowing the yield to vary as the market rate changes. The latter is accomplished by varying the mortgage constant—the annual mortgage principal and interest payments expressed as a percent of the original mortgage. The Federal Land Banks and the Farmers Home Administration concentrate on farm and rural housing loans. The Farmers Home Administration is largely a direct loan program dependent on appropriations from Congress.

REVIEW QUESTIONS

1. Critically evaluate: The FHA was initiated to improve housing standards of low-income families.

2. Describe the impact of FHA insurance on (1) the supply of mortgage funds and (2) the demand for mortgage funds.

3. Describe how FHA policy has changed from the inception of the FHA in 1934 to the current FHA policies pursued under the Housing and Community Development Act of 1974.

4. In your own words, describe how discount points affect (1) the lender, (2) the buyer, and (3) the seller.

5. Calculate the effective loan-to-value ratio for a $40,000 mortgage subject to the maximum VA guarantee.

6. How does private mortgage insurance differ from FHA mutual insurance? Explain thoroughly.

7. What is the function of the secondary mortgage market?
8. Describe how the secondary mortgage operation would function during periods of (1) tight credit and (2) credit ease.
9. What are the separate functions of FNMA and GNMA as provided by 1968 legislation?
10. What is a "pass-through" security?
11. Describe the tandem plan.
12. What is the mortgage constant? Give an example.
13. How do the mortgage commitments of the FHLMC vary from the mortgage commitments of FNMA?

SELECTED REFERENCES

Atteberry, William, *Modern Real Estate Finance,* chaps. 16 and 17. Columbus: Grid, Inc., 1972.

Break, George F., et al. *Federal Credit Agencies.* Englewood Cliffs, N.J.: Prentice-Hall, Inc., 1963.

Ganis, David R. "All about the GNMA Mortgage-Back Securities Market," *Real Estate Review,* vol. 4, no. 2 (Summer 1974), pp. 55–65.

Hines, Mary Alice. *Principles and Practices of Real Estate,* chap. 20. Homewood, Ill.: Richard D. Irwin, Inc., 1976.

Hoagland, Henry E.; Stone, Leo D.; and Brueggeman, William B. *Real Estate Finance,* chap. 21. 6th ed. Homewood, Ill.: Richard D. Irwin, Inc., 1977.

Shenkel, William M. *Real Estate Finance,* chap. 6. Washington, D.C.: American Bankers Association, 1976.

Wiedemer, John P. *Real Estate Finance,* chap. 5. Reston, Va.: Reston Publishing Company, Inc., 1974.

14

Real Estate Financing Techniques

After reading this chapter, you should be familiar with the following points:

1 The legal nature of real estate mortgages.
2 The rights of the lender and borrower under the real estate mortgage.
3 The significance of mortgages ranked by the priority of liens.
4 The manner in which amortization schedules are calculated.
5 The nature of mortgages classified by their purposes.
6 Characteristics of wraparound, variable rate, flexible payment, and partially amortized mortgages.
7 The main features of a trust deed.
8 The main advantages and disadvantages of leasehold financing.
9 Methods of adapting real estate contracts for financing purposes.

To UNDERSTAND real estate finance, it is helpful to review the legal nature of a mortgage instrument. The rights of the lender and borrower vary according to the type of mortgage. For this reason mortgages are explained in terms of their priority of liens, their method of amortization, and their purposes. An explanation is given of the new mortgages that have been introduced to compensate for rising interest rates, namely, wraparound, variable rate, and flexible payment mortgages. The chapter concludes with an explanation of leasehold financing and real estate contracts.

REAL ESTATE MORTGAGES

Mortgages are written instruments that pledge real estate as security for a debt. Without a debt there can be no mortgage. Ordinarily the debt is evidenced by a promissory note, or in some states a bond. Frequently, the mortgage incorporates the promissory note or bond in a single instrument. In executing a long-term mortgage, the borrower typically pledges real estate and his personal credit as security for the debt.

Elements of a Mortgage

To be valid a mortgage must conform to the usual elements of an enforceable contract. Figure 14–1 demonstrates the standard mortgage form used in the state of Florida—referred to as a "mortgage deed' in that state. While state law varies and while certain specialized forms of a mortgage call for different terms and agreements, generally mortgages must include certain common requirements.

1. A mortgage must be in writing.
2. The parties to the mortgage must be legally competent.
3. A clause of the mortgage must pledge real estate as security for the debt.
4. The debt must be identified, with specified terms of repayment.
5. The mortgage must include a valid legal description of the property it covers.
6. The borrower must have a mortgageable interest.
7. The foreclosure conditions should be stated.
8. The mortgage must be properly witnessed or acknowledged according to state law.
9. The mortgage must be delivered and accepted.

Under the Statute of Frauds, enforceable real estate conveyance instruments must be in writing. Oral agreements which are not part of the written instrument are not enforceable. Legal competence refers to the authority of individuals to enter into a contract. Thus, a mortgage executed by a corporate officer acting beyond his delegated authority would not be enforceable. For an instrument to serve as a mortgage, state law requires a

FIGURE 14–1

Standard Mortgage Form for State of Florida

This Mortgage Deed Executed the.................................day of...

A. D. 19........, by

of the County of..., State of...,

hereinafter called Mortgagor; to

of the County of..., State of...,

hereinafter called Mortgagee;

   Witnesseth: That for divers good and valuable considerations, and also in consideration of the aggregate sum named in the promissory note...........of even date herewith, hereinafter described, the said Mortgagor does grant, bargain, sell, alien, remise, release, convey and confirm unto the said Mortgagee, his heirs, legal representatives and assigns, in fee simple, all that certain land of which the said Mortgagor,

is now seized and possessed and in actual possession, situate in...County, State of Florida, described as follows:

   Together With all and singular the ways, easements, riparian and other rights, tenements, hereditaments and appurtenances thereunto belonging or in anywise appertaining, and the rents, issues and profits thereof, and also all the estate, right, title, interest and all claim and demand whatsoever, as well in law as in equity, of the said Mortgagor in and to the same, and every part and parcel thereof, with the appurtenances, and also all buildings, structures and other improvements and all fixtures now on said land or that may hereafter be erected or placed thereon.

   To Have and to Hold the above granted and described premises unto the said Mortgagee and his heirs, legal representatives and assigns, forever.

FIGURE 14–1 (continued)

PROVIDED ALWAYS, and these presents are on this express condition, that if the said Mortgagor or his heirs, legal representatives or assigns shall well and truly pay unto the Mortgagee, or his legal representatives, heirs and assigns, the sums of money herein mentioned, and the interest thereon as it shall become due, together with all costs, charges and expenses, including abstract fees and a reasonable attorney's fee which the Mortgagee may incur or be put to in collecting the same by foreclosure, or otherwise, said indebtedness being generally described as follows:

AND the said Mortgagor, for himself and his heirs, legal representatives or assigns, jointly and severally covenants and agrees to and with the Mortgagee, and his heirs, legal representatives or assigns, that at the time of the ensealing and delivery of these presents he is well seized of said premises in fee simple, and has good right, full power and lawful authority to grant, bargain and sell the same in manner and form aforesaid; that the same are free and clear of all liens and encumbrances whatsoever and that he will forever protect and defend the same against all lawful claims, and that he hereby fully warrants the title to said premises and will defend the same against the lawful claims of all persons whomsoever; that he will permit, commit or suffer no waste, impairment or deterioration of said premises, and will keep the buildings and improvements located thereon in as good condition as they now are, and in the event of damage to or destruction of any of said buildings, to repair, or replace the same forthwith and immediately in as good condition and of the same character of construction as they now are, and to keep all fruit trees, citrus trees and shrubbery that are now or may hereafter be located upon said premises, properly and skillfully pruned, fertilized, watered, sprayed, cultivated and protected, it being specifically stipulated and agreed that the failure and neglect so to do will constitute waste; and will do or permit to be done to said premises nothing that may in any way impair or weaken the security under this mortgage; that he will pay unto the Mortgagee, his heirs, legal representatives or assigns the said promissory note........and the interest on the same as it or they shall become due and payable, past due interest to bear interest at the rate of eight (8) per cent. per annum from its due date until paid, together with all costs, charges, abstract fees and expenses, including attorney's fees, which the said Mortgagee, his heirs, legal representatives or assigns may be put to or incur in collecting the same by foreclosure or otherwise; that the said Mortgagor will in due season pay all taxes, assessments and charges which may be levied upon the said property until the indebtedness aforesaid shall be paid, and that the said Mortgagor, or his heirs, legal representatives or assigns, will promptly satisfy, pay and discharge any and all mechanic's and material-men's liens, and any and all other liens and any and all judgments and decrees which may become liens and charges upon the premises above described, and will keep all buildings that may at any time be on said premises during the continuance of said indebtedness, in good and first-class state of repair, and insured against loss by fire and such other hazards as shall be required by the Mortgagee in such company or companies as the Mortgagee, his heirs, legal representatives or assigns may approve, for at least full insurable value, which policy or policies of insurance are to be issued and maintained in the name of the owner of the fee simple title to said property, and shall contain or have attached thereto as a part thereof a mortgagee clause satisfactory to said Mortgagee, and providing for the payment of any loss payable under any of said policies to and in favor of said Mortgagee, such policy or policies to be held by said Mortgagee, his heirs, legal representatives or assigns, and in the event any sum of money becomes payable under such policy or policies, the Mortgagee, his heirs, legal representatives or assigns, shall have the option to receive and apply the same on account of the indebtedness hereby secured, or to use the same in repairing or replacing said premises to the condition thereof at the time of the execution of this mortgage, or to permit the Mortgagor to receive and use said money or any part thereof for other purposes without thereby waiving or impairing any equity, lien or right under and by virtue of this mortgage.

AND in case of the refusal or neglect of the said Mortgagor, his heirs, legal representatives or assigns to thus repair or replace said premises, or to keep said premises insured as aforesaid, or to pay taxes, assessments or charges or to satisfy and discharge the liens, judgments or decrees above mentioned, then said Mortgagee, his heirs, legal representatives or assigns may, at his option, make such repairs, procure such insurance, or pay such taxes, assessments or charges or pay and discharge such liens, judgments or decrees, and it shall not be obligatory for said Mortgagee, his heirs, legal representatives or assigns to inquire into the validity of tax assessments, tax deeds or special assessments or of sales under such tax or special assessment or to otherwise inquire into the validity of liens or mechanics or material-men, or into the necessity of such repairs, in advancing money in that behalf as above-mentioned, but nothing herein contained shall be construed as requiring the said Mortgagee, his heirs, legal representatives or assigns to advance or expend money for taxes or special assessments or for other purposes aforesaid. All money thus paid shall draw interest at the rate of eight (8) per cent per annum, together with all reasonable attorney's fees, costs, charges, abstract fees and expenses for foreclosure or other pro-

FIGURE 14–1 (*concluded*)

ceedings, and shall be repaid to the Mortgagee, or his heirs, legal representatives or assigns, on demand; and shall become so much additional indebtedness secured by this mortgage, to be paid out of the proceeds of the sale of the mortgaged premises aforesaid, if this mortgage should be foreclosed, and if not otherwise paid by the said Mortgagor, or his heirs, legal representatives or assigns.

AND the said Mortgagor, for himself and his heirs, legal representatives and assigns, severally and jointly, further covenants and agrees to pay all taxes, assessments and charges that may be assessed upon said premises as described above, or upon this mortgage or the indebtedness secured hereby, without regard to any law heretofore enacted, or hereafter to be enacted, imposing payment of the whole or any part thereof upon the Mortgagee, or his heirs, legal representatives or assigns. Upon violation of this understanding or upon the enactment by the State of Florida of any law imposing payment of the whole or any portion of any of the taxes, assessments or charges aforesaid upon the Mortgagee, his heirs, legal representatives or assigns, or upon the rendition by any court of competent jurisdiction of a decision to the effect that the undertaking by the said Mortgagor, as herein provided, to pay all taxes, assessments or charges is legally inoperative or cannot be enforced, then and in either of such events the indebtedness hereby secured, without any deduction shall, at the option of the Mortgagee, or his heirs, legal representatives or assigns, become immediately due and payable, notwithstanding anything contained in this mortgage or any law heretofore or hereafter enacted.

AND it is stipulated and agreed that, in case of default in any of the said payments of principal or interest, according to the tenor or effect of the said note........mentioned above, or breach of any of the covenants or agreements herein contained, then and in any such case the whole of the said principal sum hereby secured and the interest thereon, and any payments made by the Mortgagee, his heirs, legal representatives or assigns, for repairs, insurance, taxes, assessments, liens, judgments, decrees, costs, charges, expenses, abstract fees, attorney's fees or otherwise, shall at the option of the said Mortgagee, or his heirs, legal representatives or assigns, become immediately due and payable without further notice, and this mortgage may be foreclosed in the manner and with the same effect as if the said indebtedness had otherwise matured.

THE proceeds of said foreclosure shall be applied: first, to the expenses incurred hereunder, including a reasonable attorney's fee for such service as may be necessary for the collection of said indebtedness and the foreclosure of this mortgage; second, to the payment of whatever sum or sums the said Mortgagee, or his heirs, legal representatives or assigns may have paid or become liable to pay in carrying out the options, terms and stipulations of this mortgage, together with interest thereon; third, to the payment and satisfaction of said note........and interest.

IT is further expressly stipulated and agreed that the Mortgagee, his heirs, legal representatives or assigns, shall have the privilege, at his option, after the doing of or the omission to do, by the Mortgagor, his heirs, legal representatives or assigns, of any act or thing which will constitute a default in or breach of any of the terms, conditions and covenants herein or in said mortgage note........contained, and upon the commencement, in a court of competent jurisdiction of a suit for the foreclosure of this mortgage, of applying for, either in and by the original bill for foreclosure or otherwise, and shall be entitled, as a matter of right and without regard to the value of the premises, property and estate, or the necessity, reasonableness or expediency therefor, or the solvency or insolvency of the Mortgagee, his heirs, legal representatives or assigns, and without notice to said Mortgagor, his heirs, legal representatives or assigns, to the appointment of some suitable person or corporation as a receiver for the property, premises and estate hereinabove described.

SUCH receiver shall have power to enter upon, receive, recover and take complete, entire and exclusive possession of said property, premises and estate, and the rents, issues and profits thereof; to preserve, maintain, defend and protect such possession and said premises, property and estate; to lease the same for a term to be approved by the Court; to pay all taxes, assessments and levies that are or may become liens thereon; to keep the buildings, furniture and fixtures thereon insured against fire, wind, storm, theft or other disaster; to make reasonable or necessary repairs and he shall have such other powers as may seem proper to the Court. Such receiver, after deducting all charges and expenses attending such receivership, shall apply the residue of such rents, issues and profits to the payment and satisfaction of this mortgage and the note........hereby secured, or to any deficiency that may arise or exist after applying the proceeds of the sale of said premises, property and estate to the amounts due under this mortgage, and the note........hereby secured, including interest, attorney's fees and costs and expenses of said foreclosure.

ALL notes herein described, without preference of one note over another, are equally, ratably and proportionately secured hereby.

THE Mortgagor, or his heirs, legal representatives or assigns further agrees to furnish such other forms of insurance in such amounts as may be required by said Mortgagee, his heirs, legal representatives or assigns, and the provisions relating to fire insurance and policies issued thereunder shall be applicable to such other forms of insurance.

THIS mortgage and the note........and interest secured hereby are to be construed according to the laws of the State of Florida where the same are executed.

IT is covenanted and agreed that the terms "Mortgagor" and "Mortgagee" for convenience herein employed, and any pronouns used in connection therewith, shall be construed to include the plural as well as the singular number, and the masculine, feminine and neuter gender, whenever and wherever the context so admits or requires; and that all covenants and obligations of the respective parties hereto shall extend to and be obligatory upon their heirs, legal representatives, successors and assigns.

IN WITNESS WHEREOF, this mortgage has been executed by the Mortgagor___ in accordance with the laws of the State of Florida, the date first above stated.

Signed, sealed and delivered in the presence of:

....(SEAL)

....

....(SEAL)

statutory clause identifying it as a mortgage. Some states require a mortgage clause that conveys the property with such words as *grants and conveys* or a mortgaging clause that typically includes the word *mortgages*. (Example: John Smith mortgages to the First National Bank.)

Other elements of the mortgage are fairly self-evident. The monthly payment, interest rate, and maturity date of the mortgage must be included as part of the document. The legal description conforming to the requirements of deeds and other legal conveyances identifies the property pledged. Following the legal description would be the estate subject to the mortgage, for example, the leasehold interest (an estate owned by the tenant) or the fee simple estate, and reservations of the estate pledged, such as easements, rights-of-way, and air rights.

Mortgage Covenants

Mortgage covenants are promises of the borrower and lender which are included as part of the mortgage. Typical covenants contain the following items:

1. The borrower shall promptly pay principal and interest when due.
2. The borrower shall pay all taxes, assessments, and other charges.
3. The borrower shall keep the improvements now existing or hereafter erected on the property insured against loss by fire and other hazards.
4. The borrower shall keep the property in good repair and shall not commit waste.
5. The lender may make reasonable inspections of the property.
6. Upon payment of all sums secured by the mortgage, the lender shall release the mortgage without charge to the borrower.

Like other conveyances, mortgages must be signed, witnessed, and acknowledged according to state law. Assuming that the mortgage is properly witnessed and acknowledged it is not enforceable unless it is voluntarily delivered and accepted by the lender. In the usual case, the lender holds the mortgage until the final payment. While the mortgage is an instrument pledging real estate as security, the document itself is personal property which may be bought and sold like other intangible property.

Rights of the Mortgagor

The statutory rights of the mortgagor (borrower) follow from conventions developed under common law. Other rights are stated in the covenants of the instrument. Three rights of the borrower are probably paramount: the equity of redemption, the statutory right of redemption, and prepayment privileges. These rights relate to remedies of the borrower in the event of default and the right to refinance the mortgage.

Equity of Redemption. The borrower has the right to recover the property mortgaged upon payment of the remaining debt due the lender. Most states allow the lender costs and expenses incurred in instituting foreclosure procedures. This right developed as a reaction to the restrictive rules of early common law in which ownership by the lender became absolute if the mortgage was not paid promptly on the due date. Such strict requirements led to state statutes giving the borrower the right to redeem property upon payment of the debt, even if he was unable to meet the exact terms of repayment. At present the right refers to redemption *before the foreclosure sale.* The right begins with the mortgage and continues until legal foreclosure.

Statutory Right of Redemption. Some states grant the right of redemption for a period ranging from six months to two years *after* a foreclosure sale. This right, which becomes effective at the time of the foreclosure sale, refers to the *statutory right of redemption.* The owner of the mortgaged property, on payment of the sale price, interest, and expenses of foreclosure may redeem title to the property at any time during the statutory period.

Where the statutory right of redemption prevails, the purchaser of a foreclosed property stands a good chance of losing title to a borrower protected by the statutory right of redemption. Where the statutory right of redemption prevails, the purchaser usually receives a certificate of sale evidencing an interest which gives the purchaser title only after the statutory period ends. This right discourages lenders from making long-term loans where redemption expenses are lengthy and costly. From the standpoint of the lender, this restrictive feature has encouraged other forms of real estate indebtedness, such as the trust and security deeds discussed below.

Prepayment Privileges. If market interest rates fall below the rate charged under a long-term mortgage, the borrower has an incentive to refinance the property with another lender at a lower interest rate. Suppose that the borrower initially finances the property under a 25-year mortgage at 9.5 percent interest. Suppose further that one year later the market rate falls so that the borrower may obtain an 8.0 percent mortgage. Here, it would be to the borrower's advantage to make the second loan, using the proceeds of the second loan to repay the first loan. To prevent this from occurring, lenders usually impose prepayment penalties over the early life of the loan, say, the first five or ten years. Since the lender expects interest over a long term and absorbs certain expenses in administering a new mortgage, some lenders may impose a penalty of, say, 3 percent on prepayments before the due date. Other lenders prohibit prepayment during the first three years. Still other lenders limit prepayment priviliges to an absolute amount, say, $500 or $1,000 a year, or allow only a certain percentage of the principal to be paid without penalty over the first five years. In sum, prepayment privileges allow the borrower to refinance the property or to sell the property to a third party who desires to purchase free of debt.

Rights of the Mortgagee

The mortgagee (lender) has a right to enforce the terms of the contract calling for payments at a definite time and place and other covenants requiring that the property be maintained in good condition and that tax, insurance, and other obligations of the borrower be satisfied. If through borrower default these covenants are not observed, the most important rights of the lender relate to the right of foreclosure. Associated with this right are acceleration clauses, the right to assign mortgages, and in some instances, the right to levy assumption fees.

The Right of Foreclosure. The right of foreclosure and its detail are governed largely by state statutes. While the time of filing a notice of default, advertising, and foreclosure procedures vary, the right of foreclosure usually falls into one of four categories:

1. Strict foreclosure.
2. Foreclosure by action and sale.
3. Foreclosure by entry and possession (writ of entry).
4. Foreclosure by power of sale.

Strict foreclosure, which is permitted in Connecticut, Illinois, and Vermont, vests title with the lender when the court issues a decree terminating the rights of the borrower. Its use is limited because the borrower has no right to the difference between the market value and the debt, which he would gain under a foreclosure sale. Some states restrict the exercise of foreclosure in these circumstances.

The second method of foreclosure, *by action and sale,* is directed by court order. To foreclose the lender must file a suit for foreclosure which is tried, and if default is proven, the court issues a decree authorizing sale. If the property is sold for less than the debt, the court may issue a deficiency judgment against the borrower. A deficiency judgment attaches to other property of the borrower. Any surplus above the mortgage principal recovered at the foreclosure sale would be paid to other lienholders before the balance is paid to the delinquent borrower.

Foreclosure by *entry and possession,* authorized in Massachusetts, Maine, New Hampshire, and Rhode Island, requires that the lender take possession peaceably, recording and publishing the entry with details. In a sense the lender declares default, and secures a judgment granting the lender possession if the borrower does not satisfy the judgment within a stated time. After the appropriate statutory redemption period, title passes to the lender. In some states, the lender is entitled to deficiency judgments if the amount realized by sale is less than the outstanding mortgage.

Foreclosure by power of sale is usually exercised under a clause in the mortgage granting the lender the power of sale in the event of default—

permitted in some 18 states. Since the power of sale avoids court supervision, lenders favor such clauses. Statutory notice of the sale and sale at public auction are usually required.

Special note must be taken of deficiency judgments. The judgments are authorized in some states and prohibited in others. Recall that the borrower pledges real estate, and makes a personal promise to pay the debt evidenced by the note or bond. The nature of the personal promise is shown by the standard form used for a mortgage in Florida. (See Figure 14–1.) If the foreclosure sale does not satisfy the outstanding debt, some states allow the lender to collect against the personal assets of the borrower —a deficiency judgment. In other states, such deficiency judgments are prohibited or very limited in application.

Acceleration Clauses. Mortgage contracts usually place the borrower in default if he misses a single payment. As a practical matter, lenders may not initiate foreclosure until the loan is 60 or 90 days in default. If default is declared, the acceleration clause gives the lender the right to the *full amount of the principal immediately*. That is, a borrower who has continued payments for three years on a 25-year mortgage and who is declared in default is required to repay the entire principal and not merely the delinquent payments.

Without this clause, lenders could demand only the amount of the defaulted payments, since the balance of the debt is not immediately due and payable. Without acceleration the lender would have to start a series of foreclosure suits to recover each monthly payment. In practice, lenders exhaust all other remedies before instituting foreclosure and exercising the acceleration clause.

Mortgage Assignments. Mortgages are a form of intangible personal property. Hence the lender has the right to assign or sell the mortgage to a third party without consent of the borrower. In fact, the right of assignment makes the mortgage more attractive to lender-investors who may readily convert the mortgage to cash through the secondary market. Thus assignment in no way affects the provisions of the mortgage, note, or bond.

Assumption Fees. An assumption fee is a charge levied against a buyer who assumes an existing loan. For example, the mortgage may read:

> The lender may, at its option, and as a condition of its consent to any transfer of title to the property, subject to this indebtedness, require a fee of not more than one (1) percent of the unpaid balance of the loan.

Under the above clause, a seller who sells a $40,000 dwelling for $10,000 down, with the buyer assuming a $30,000 existing mortgage, would pay the lender a $300 (1 percent) fee.

Frequently it is to the advantage of a borrower to purchase property with a $5,000 down payment, for example, and assume an existing loan of $20,000 that is available at a 7 percent interest rate—a below-market interest rate negotiated ten years earlier. Ordinarily, the lender reserves the right to approve the assumption. Since the lender has lent the money on the personal qualifications of the borrower, it is reasoned that the borrower cannot escape his obligation unless the party assuming the loan has equal or better credit. Assumption fees range from a flat fee of $50 to some percentage of the sale price; some lenders also increase the interest rate.

A buyer may want to continue an existing loan by (1) purchasing "subject to" an existing mortgage or (2) by "assuming" an existing mortgage. A buyer who assumes and agrees to pay the mortgage expresses his intent to assume the mortgage debt; thus, if the mortgage is foreclosed and the proceeds of the sale are insufficient to satisfy the debt, the lender may hold the assuming party personally responsible for the debt. However, state laws vary on this point.

If the borrower elects to buy "subject to" the debt, the borrower is not personally responsible for the unpaid debt. If the lender forecloses, he may not sue the new purchaser under the promissory note. Unless released, the original borrower remains personally liable under the promissory note. The lender has recourse only against the property and not against the person who buys subject to an existing mortgage.

Title and Lien Theory States

Originally, the states followed early English courts that treated mortgages as a lien on real estate pledged as security for a debt. States that still follow this practice are known as *lien theory* states. Title to real estate subject to the mortgage remains with the borrower; the mortgage represents a pledge of real estate as security for a debt. Other states have modified this concept by treating the mortgage as a conveyance of the title to the lender. While the borrower retains the exclusive right of possession, and while on its face the borrower continues as the true owner, his ownership is subject to superior rights of the lender.

Lien Theory States. States following the lien theory require mortgages that typically read "mortgages and warrants." The borrower holds title and remains in possession until the lender exercises his right to foreclose on a defaulted mortgage. Discharge of the debt eliminates the lender's interest in the mortgage in real estate. Among the states treating mortgages as liens are Arizona, California, Colorado, Delaware, Georgia, and Idaho. Some 21 other states follow this practice. In addition, trust deeds and other instruments often substitute for the mortgage. Generally speaking, the lender has no estate in real estate but only the security of a lien. The mortgage is merely collateral held as security for the debt.

Title Theory States. States following this practice—Alabama, Arkansas, Connecticut, Illinois, Pennsylvania, and others—include language in the mortgage that "conveys and warrants." For instance, in the following clause the borrower transfers title to the lender:

> Mortgagor does grant, bargain, sell, alien, remise, release, convey and confirm unto the said Mortgagee, his heirs, legal representatives and as-

signs, in fee simple, all that certain land of which the said Mortgagor is now seized and possessed and in actual possession.

Usually the mortgage gives the borrower the right of possession until default and foreclosure, even though the title is held by the lender. Title is defeated when the borrower pays the mortgage according to the agreed-upon terms. In effect, the lender is the holder of the fee simple estate subject to the right of the borrower to pay the debt and defeat the lender's title. Ordinarily, states require that the lender must take appropriate foreclosure steps to take possession and legally terminate the borrower rights.

TYPES OF MORTGAGES

Needs of the borrower and lender often call for specialized mortgages. To explain, mortgages may be classified according to (1) priority of liens, (2) methods of amortization, and (3) type of property pledged. More recently, because of rising interest rates, relatively new forms of mortgages have been developed. The financial problem resolved by the mortgage dictates the final choice.

Priority of Liens

Up to this point it has been implicitly assumed that a buyer made a down payment, paying the seller by borrowing the balance under a long-term mortgage. To illustrate, assume that the seller conveys title for $35,000. The borrower pays the seller $10,000 at the time of closing, providing for the balance of $25,000 from a lender in return for a 25-year mortgage repayable monthly at 9.5 percent interest per annum and a promissory note for $25,000. The lender owns a first mortgage which has priority over other mortgages and loans executed by the borrower at later dates.

Second-Mortgage Financing.   Suppose, however, that the buyer elects to pay the seller $1,000 down, securing the additional $9,000 under a ten-year mortgage at 12 percent interest. The second lender holds a lien junior to the first mortgage. The second mortgage would usually include a statement that the mortgage is *subordinate* to a prior mortgage which is described according to the amount of indebtedness, the date of recording, the names of the parties, a legal description of the property, and other details.

Such an arrangement is often called *second-mortgage financing* or *junior lien financing.* However, suppose that the borrower defaults on his first mortgage. To protect his loan, the holder of the second mortgage usually requires an agreement providing for the right to pay the first mortgage and add the payment to the second mortgage.

The borrower is advised to include a waiver in the second mortgage stating that the borrower has the right to refinance the first mortgage provided that the refinanced mortgage does not exceed the remaining balance of the first mortgage. This gives the borrower the right to replace the first mortgage with another first mortgage without endangering the priority of the first mortgage. This arrangement allows the borrower to refinance in order to obtain cash or take advantage of more favorable mortgage terms.

Second-mortgage financing is used by borrowers with relatively high incomes but with few assets, for example, a newly licensed physician or a newly graduated engineer. In other cases, borrowers paying on a first mortgage, negotiated, say, 10 years earlier with 15 years remaining, may want to borrow more money, pledging the real estate as security on a long-term loan while maintaining the original mortgage with a below-market interest rate. A second mortgage may be negotiated with a third party at a higher interest rate, say, 12 percent. This may be a cheaper alternative than refinancing the larger first mortgage at current market interest rates.

Purchase Money Mortgages. A mortgage given to a seller as part of the purchase price defines a purchase money mortgage. The seller accepts a purchase money mortgage as a substitute for cash. In the preceding example, the seller might be willing to accept (1) $1,000 cash from the buyer, (2) $25,000 cash, which the buyer obtains from a first mortgage, and (3) a $9,000 purchase money mortgage. In this case, the purchase money mortgage constitutes a second mortgage and in some states does not require a promissory note. Alternatively, the seller could accept a purchase money mortgage for $34,000 and $1,000 cash from the buyer. In this case, the purchase money mortgage would be a first lien. Since the borrower is not personally liable (no note or bond), the seller is only secured by the value of the real estate. Sellers tend to accept purchase money mortgages in lieu of cash only if cash down is sufficient to compensate the seller if default occurs or if the property is sufficiently valuable to serve as security without the personal liability of the borrower.

Mortgages Classified by Repayment Plans

Lenders and borrowers may select from a wide range of amortization plans. In some cases the mortgage repayment plan may be adapted to deferred payment, or to partially amortized plans and their combinations. Probably most amortization plans fall under (1) term mortgages, (2) level payment amortization, (3) variable payment mortgages, (4) flexible payment mortgages, and (5) partially amortized mortgages. Each of these plans may be demonstrated by example.

Term Mortgages. The term mortgage provides for no amortization of principal over the mortgage term. Nationally chartered commercial banks are among the few institutional lenders authorized to grant term mortgages. The use of term mortgages is confined to borrowers with excellent credit, and such mortgages are generally limited to relatively short periods of three to five years.

For instance, suppose that a borrower executes a $10,000 mortgage with a three-year maturity and a 10 percent interest rate. The parties may agree to an annual interest of $1,000 payable monthly, quarterly, semi-annually, or annually. At the end of three years, the principal of $10,000 would be due.

For real estate purposes the term mortgage has inherent limitations. If the mortgage applies to depreciable buildings, the value of the security may decrease over the term; the mortgage provides for no periodic payment of principal, placing an unusual burden on the borrower in requiring a single lump-sum payment. If the principal is not paid on the due date, the borrower's only remedy is to refinance or renew the mortgage for another three years.

Level Payment Amortization. In this case, the mortgage payments are constant; the amount accruing to principal and interest varies with each payment; and interest is calculated against the remaining balance.

For instance, a $30,000 mortgage at 8 percent interest per annum for 25 years would require a monthly payment of $231.61. In the first payment, $200.10 would be paid to interest, while the balance of the payment ($31.51) would retire principal. The interest of $200.10 represents monthly interest on $30,000 ($0.08 \times \frac{1}{12} \times \$30,000$)—rounding errors account for a slightly higher actual interest payment. One twelfth of the annual interest rate of 8 percent is equal to 0.00666. Since the interest is calculated on the remaining balance, interest payments tend to decline over the life of the mortgage; principal payments increase. The amortization schedule for the first 12 months is shown in Table 14–1.

TABLE 14–1

Amortization of a $30,000 Principal, Level Payment, 8 Percent, 25-Years Mortgage (first 12 months)

Month	Total Monthly Payment	Amount Credited to	
		Interest Payment	Principal Payment
1	$231.60	$200.10	$31.50
2	231.60	199.80	31.80
3	231.60	199.50	32.10
4	231.60	199.50	32.10
5	231.60	199.20	32.40
6	231.60	198.90	32.70
7	231.60	198.60	33.10
8	231.60	198.60	33.10
9	231.60	198.30	33.30
10	231.60	198.00	33.60
11	231.60	197.70	33.90
12	231.60	197.70	33.90

The level payment loan allocates a greater proportion of each payment to interest during the early years of the loan. In fact, for the preceding example 49.5 percent of the principal remains unpaid after year 18. The percent of principal repaid each year varies from 1.3 percent to 8.9 percent—years 1 and 25. These figures are summarized in Table 14–2.

From the standpoint of the lender, contributions to principal, ideally, should be greater than the rate of depreciation on the property mortgaged. Under the mortgage assumed for Tables 14–1 and 14–2, payments would total $69,400 over the 25-year loan period. At a 9 percent interest rate, the total payments required to amortize a 25-year, $30,000 loan would total $75,514.

TABLE 14–2

Rate of Principal Repayment, Level Payment Monthly Amortization, 8 Percent, 25-Year Mortgage

End of Year	Amount of Remaining Principal as a Percent of Original Loan	End of Year	Amount of Remaining Principal as a Percent of Original Loan
1.	98.7	14.	67.6
2.	97.3	15.	63.6
3.	95.7	16.	59.3
4.	94.1	17.	54.6
5.	92.3	18.	49.5
6.	90.3	19.	44.0
7.	88.2	20.	38.1
8.	85.9	21.	31.6
9.	83.4	22.	24.6
10.	80.8	23.	17.1
11.	77.9	24.	8.9
12.	74.7	25.	—
13.	71.3		

Variable Payment Amortization. Under this plan, which is less commonly used, the amortization calls for a constant payment to principal. Here the lender and borrower agree to a fixed amount that is applied to principal. With agreement on this point, mortgage payments may be calculated, given the annual interest rate and the frequency of payment. Assuming a principal repayment of $1,000 per year to retire a $5,000 loan and an annual interest rate of 9 percent, the first payment of $1,450 decreases to $1,090 at the end of the fifth year. In this example, principal repayments would total $5,000, and interest would amount to $1,350. These figures are summarized in Table 14–3.

Under this plan, the payments are relatively large during the early years of the mortgage compared to the final years. Because of this feature, the variable payment amortization schedule is less popular.

TABLE 14–3

Amortization under a Variable Payment, $5,000 Mortgage (9 percent interest)

End of Year	Principal Repayment (constant)	Annual Interest	Annual Mortgage Payment	Remaining Balance
1..............................	$1,000	$ 450	$1,450	$4,000
2..............................	1,000	360	1,360	3,000
3..............................	1,000	270	1,270	2,000
4..............................	1,000	180	1,180	1,000
5..............................	1,000	90	1,090	0
Total.....................	$5,000	$1,350	$6,350	—

Partially Amortized Mortgages. Assume a $20,000 loan. An amortization schedule might be based on a 20-year term for only $10,000, with a lump-sum payment for the balance of the mortgage at the end of 10 years. In effect the loan represents a ten-year mortgage with a lump-sum payment of the remaining principal at the date of maturity. The amortization schedule is drawn for less than the principal. In practice, the lump-sum payment, referred to as a balloon payment, is seldom made at maturity since the partial amortization increases equity, qualifying the property for refinancing under a fully amortized first mortgage.

The effect of the balloon mortgage is to reduce the amount of monthly payments without reducing interest rates and without extending loan terms beyond legal maximum limits. The borrower who has excellent credit and is expected to have an increasing income over the life of the mortgage will be accommodated by this type of loan.

Flexible Payment Mortgages. These mortgages allow payments of less than the level amortized mortgage. Development loans and land purchases may call for interest payments only during the initial years of the mortgage with full amortization effective at some stated year. Depending on the maturity of the loan, interest only payments over the initial years may lower monthly payments from 5 to 25 percent below the level payment amortized mortgage.

Some lenders use flexible payment mortgages to reduce risks by providing for split amortization. A 25-year mortgage, could be amortized (1) on the basis of a 15-year payment schedule over the first 5 years, and then (2) at the end of 5 years, the remainder of the loan could be amortized over a 20-year payment schedule. This technique is used to increase a borrower's equity over the initial years of mortgage life. Frequently the plan is used for borrowers approaching retirement age.

Variable Rate Mortgages. Deposit institutions are particularly vulnerable to high interest rates. They face the danger of living with relatively low interest rates earned on outstanding mortgages while they must pay relatively high interest rates to depositors. Unless they pay depositors the market rate of interest paid on other deposits, government bonds, municipal bonds, and similar investments, they lose deposits which may be used for mortgages. With rising interest rates, the *average yield* earned on a mortgage portfolio may fall below the current maximum interest rate paid to depositors.

The variable rate mortgage tends to keep the yield on the mortgage portfolio in close correspondence to market interest rates. Under this plan the borrower and lender agree that mortgage interest may be changed according to some independent index. The index used to revise mortgage interest rates must be available to the public and not under the control of the lender. Some variable rate mortgages are based on interest rates on government bonds, the prime interest rate, or the consumer price index. For instance, some lenders have based mortgage interest on changes in interest on three–five-year Treasury notes, or on the Federal Home Loan Bank Board interest rate series. The Federal Land Bank, which uses variable rate mortgages, bases the rate largely on the changes in the interest rate paid on government bonds. Hence the borrower pays interest which is related to the cost of capital to the Federal Land Bank.

Variable rate mortgages provide for an interest rate that changes in the same proportion as the index adopted as a reference. If interest rates increase, savings institutions are able to pay depositors a higher return within the restrictions of Regulation Q of the Federal Reserve System, which controls the maximum rates that may be paid on savings deposits. In California, variable mortgage interest rates must decrease in the same manner that they are allowed to increase. California restricts interest rate changes under this plan to one quarter of 1 percent semiannually. Further, borrowers have the right to repay the mortgage within 90 days of a change in interest rates without penalty. The latter provision allows the borrower to seek other sources of funds for refinancing if the variable rate rises above the prevailing mortgage interest rate.

Mortgages Classified by Type of Property

Mortgages are adapted to the type of real estate security pledged. The most popular forms of mortgages deserve added comment.

Package Mortgage Financing. Mortgages that include personal property are referred to as package mortgages. A house and lot with a washing machine, a dishwasher, a refrigerator, and other household appliances are included in one mortgage as a single package. Borrowers prefer such mortgages since they minimize the cash required to move into a new dwelling. Expensive household appliances are under long-term payments at mortgage interest rates based on the declining balance. Mortgage financing compares favorably with consumer installment loans, which are at much higher interest rates based on the original loan value and not the declining balance. A typical package mortgage agreement after the legal description would include a broad statement that the mortgage includes buildings, improvements, fixtures or appurtenances including all apparatus, equipment, fixtures and articles which are pledged as part of the mortgage. Some lenders would include the manufacturer, model and serial number of appliances pledged as part of the mortgage.

To illustrate, a $300 appliance included in a 25-year mortgage at 9 percent interest would increase monthly payments by $2.52 per month. While this charge continues over the life of the mortgage, the borrower has use of the machine with virtually no increase in cash requirements. Further, the life of an average loan is approximately seven years, which only slightly exceeds the economic life of the appliance.

Blanket Mortgages. A mortgage covering more than one parcel of real estate represents a blanket mortgage. Usually the blanket mortgage covers subdivided lots in a new subdivision. The owner of potential subdivision land may accept a blanket mortgage as a substitute for cash in return for mortgage payments based on a pro rata share of future lot sales.

In short, the blanket mortgage applies to all subdivided lots. When each house and lot is sold, the seller pays the agreed pro rata portion of the lot sales price to the landowner, who releases the lot from the blanket mortgage. Hence, as each lot is sold, the seller recovers a portion of the blanket mortgage principal—the buyer, in this case the subdivider, agrees to make interest payments over the life of the blanket mortgage. As each new buyer of a house and lot finances his purchase, the landowner holding the blanket mortgage releases his interest on the sold lot. The blanket mortgage continues to be a lien on the remaining unsold property.

Participation Mortgages. On large developments, such as office buildings, shopping centers, and industrial parks, lenders are faced with statutory ceilings on their lending authority on a single property and they may be unwilling to risk financing a large undertaking. The participation mortgage gives several lenders a share in a single mortgage. A participation agreement will assign a proportion of the mortgage to each lender; their risks are diversified by reducing their share. A lender may be willing to invest $300,000 in real estate development under a participation mortgage, and unwilling to invest in a $3 million mortgage on the same project.

Construction Mortgages. Construction loans are special-purpose mortgages to finance new building construction. Construction loans are usually for 18 months but may be approved for up to a 60-month term. Because of the added risk, lenders charge higher interest rates for these loans. Only lenders familiar with building construction make construction loans.

Institutional lenders, especially out-of-state lenders, grant long-term loans only on improved real estate. They do not have the personnel to administer local construction loans. The construction loan agreement is approved only before construction commences. This step prevents unpaid suppliers or workers from establishing a lien that has priority over the construction loan.

Money is advanced to the builder according to some set schedule based on a percent of the building completed. Before scheduled payouts are made to the builder, the lender inspects the building for compliance with building plans, quality of construction, and the like. Sufficient funds are withheld so that if the contractor is unable to finish the building, the lender completes construction according to the building plans. Some lenders, such as local commercial banks, mortgage bankers, and others granting this type of loan, reduce risks further by approving construction loans only if the borrower has arranged permanent financing, conditional upon building completion. Individual borrowers, contractors, subdividers, and developers engaged in new construction must arrange for new construction loans.

Wraparound Mortgages. A wraparound mortgage is a second mortgage that includes an existing mortgage. If a property is subject to an existing mortgage at less than the current mortgage interest rate, and if the borrower wishes additional funds, a new mortgage may be issued to include (1) the existing mortgage and (2) the additional amount lent under the wraparound mortgage. The wraparound mortgage is amortized as if it were the first mortgage.

Wraparound mortgages are frequently used to finance sales of commercial property. Assume that an owner sells a property for $250,000, subject to an outstanding loan of $150,000 at 6 percent for 25 years. The monthly payment on the outstanding loan would total $966.44 principal and interest. Assume further that the buyer pays $50,000 cash and arranges for a wraparound mortgage for $200,000 at 8.5 percent interest for 25 years. The lender of the wraparound mortgage would receive a monthly payment of $1,610.44 from the buyer; from this payment, the lender would make a monthly payment of $966.44 on the existing $150,000 loan. The additional $50,000 would go to the seller. The difference between the two payments is $644 monthly, or $7,728 annually. The lender would maintain the first loan and continue making the $966.44 monthly payments. The lender would, in effect, invest $50,000 and in return would receive a net of $7,728. This is a cash flow of 15.4 percent, including principal, on a $50,000 loan. The borrower benefits from the 8.5 percent interest rate, which is below the 9.5 percent prevailing market interest rate. The lender grants the lower interest rate because of the 6 percent existing mortgage.[1]

A wraparound agreement which refers to the existing mortgage as the *consolidated loan* and subordinates the wraparound mortgage identifies the two mortgages in the following terms:

---

[1] Charles A. Trowbridge, "What Is a Wrap-around Mortgage?" *Real Estate Today*, November/December 1975, p. 46.

1. This mortgage is subject and subordinate to the consolidated mortgage, dated the _____ day of _____, 19___, made between _____ _____, as mortgagor, and _____, as mortgagee, and recorded in the office of the Clerk of the County of _____ on the _____ day of _____, 19___/ in Liber _____

The first mortgage to which the wraparound mortgage is subordinate is clearly identified.

of mortgages at page——and constituting a first-mortgage lien on the premises described in Schedule "A" attached hereto. The said consolidated mortgage is now in the reduced principal amount of _____ dollars ($_____), with interest from the _____ day of _____, 19___, and by its terms, the said consolidated mortgage matures on the _____ day of _____, 19___. (The said consolidated mortgage is hereinafter referred to in this instrument as the "First Mortgage.")

As part of the agreement, the wraparound lender agrees to make payments on the existing mortgage.

2. As to the principal indebtedness of mortgagor to mortgagee in the sum of _____ dollars ($_____) evidenced by the note of even date herewith, made by mortgagor to mortgagee and secured by this mortgage, mortgagee has paid to mortgagor on the execution of this mortgage the sum of _____

The wraparound mortgagee agrees to pay amount due under first mortgage.

dollars ($_____) and mortgagor and mortgagee hereby agree that the balance of said principal indebtedness totaling the sum of _____ dollars ($_____) has been validly incurred by mortgagee hereby agreeing to retain the said balance and pay, as set forth in paragraph _____ of this instrument, to the holder of the First Mortgage the sum of _____ dollars ($_____) being the principal balance remaining unpaid under said First Mortgage.

A wraparound mortgage, which is really a second mortgage, may be used to finance single-family dwellings and other properties.

TRUST DEED FINANCING

Lenders are reluctant to advance funds in states with long redemption periods, often extending over several months, giving borrowers the right to redeem foreclosed property. Consequently, in California, Arizona, and Maryland, among other states, the trust deed substitutes for the two-party relationship created by a mortgage. With a trust deed, lenders using a third-party trustee can acquire title within a much shorter period than would be possible under equity of redemption laws. The minimum period in California is 3 months and 21 days.

Trust Deeds

A trust deed secures a long-term promissory note. Figure 14–2 represents a promissory note approved by FNMA and FHLMC for one- to four-

FIGURE 14–2

A Promissory Note Evidencing a Debt Secured by a Trust Deed

NOTE

US $ . . . .   Washington, D.C.

. . . . , 19 . . . .

FOR VALUE RECEIVED, the undersigned ("Borrower") promise(s) to pay Perpetual Federal Savings and Loan Association, or order, the principal sum of . . . .
. . . . Dollars, with interest on the unpaid principal balance from the date of this Note, until paid, at the rate of . . . .
. . . . percent per annum. Principal and interest shall be payable at the office of said Association in Washington, District of Columbia, or such other place as the Note holder may designate, in consecutive monthly installments of . . . .
. . . . Dollars (US $ . . . .), on the . . . .
. . . . day of each month beginning . . . . , 19 . . . . . Such monthly installments shall continue until the entire indebtedness evidenced by this Note is fully paid, except that any remaining indebtedness, if not sooner paid, shall be due and payable on . . . .
If any monthly installment under this Note is not paid when due and remains unpaid after a date specified by a notice to Borrower, the entire principal amount outstanding and accrued interest thereon shall at once become due and payable at the option of the Note holder. The date specified shall not be less than thirty days from the date such notice is mailed. The Note holder may exercise this option to accelerate during any default by Borrower regardless of any prior forbearance. If suit is brought to collect this Note, the Note holder shall be entitled to collect all reasonable costs and expenses of suit, including, but not limited to, reasonable attorney's fees.
Borrower shall pay to the Note holder a late charge of three (3) percent of any monthly installment not received by the Note holder within fifteen (15) days after the installment is due.
Borrower may prepay the principal amount outstanding in whole or in part. The Note holder may require that any partial prepayments (i) be made on the date monthly installments are due and (ii) be in the amount of that part of one or more monthly installments which would be applicable to principal. Any partial prepayment shall be applied against the principal amount outstanding and shall not postpone the due date of any subsequent monthly installments or change the amount of such installments, unless the Note holder shall otherwise agree in writing. If, within three years from the date of this Note, Borrower make(s) any prepayments in any twelve month period beginning with the date of this Note or anniversary dates thereof ("loan year") with money lent to Borrower by a lender other than the Note holder, Borrower shall pay the Note holder . . . . percent of the amount by which the sum of prepayments made in any such loan year exceeds twenty percent of the original principal amount of this Note.
Presentment, notice of dishonor, and protest are hereby waived by all makers, sureties, guarantors and endorsers hereof. This Note shall be the joint and several obligation of all makers, sureties, guarantors and endorsers, and shall be binding upon them and their successors and assigns.
Any notice to Borrower provided for in this Note shall be given by mailing such notice by certified mail addressed to Borrower at the Property Address stated below, or to such other address as Borrower may designate by notice to the Note holder. Any notice to the Note holder shall be given by mailing such notice by certified mail, return receipt requested, to the Note holder at the address stated in the first paragraph of this Note, or at such other address as may have been designated by notice to Borrower.
The indebtedness evidenced by this Note is secured by a Deed of Trust, dated . . . .
. . . ., and reference is made to the Deed of Trust for rights as to acceleration of the indebtedness evidenced by this Note.

. . . . (Seal)

. . . . (Seal)

. . . . (Seal)
Property Address   *(Execute Original Only)*

DISTRICT OF COLUMBIA—1 to 4 Family—6/75—**FNMA/FHLMC UNIFORM INSTRUMENT**

1M 2/76

family dwellings which evidences a debt secured by a trust deed. The note identifies the principal, the rate of interest, and the terms of repayment. In the last paragraph, the document indicates that the note is secured by a deed of trust.

As shown in Figure 14–3, the trust deed requires a third-party arrangement in which the borrower is the trustor, the lender is the beneficiary, and a third-party is the trustee. In effect, the borrower pledges real estate as security for a long-term loan and transfers title to the trustee which is held "in trust" as security for the lender, the beneficiary of the trust. A trust

FIGURE 14–3

A Diagram of a Trust Deed

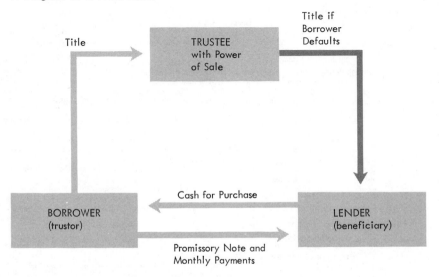

deed approved for Washington, D.C., by FNMA and FHLMC is shown in Figure 14–4.

Note that trust deed covenants closely parallel the covenants of a mortgage. In the trust deed, the borrower grants power of sale to the trustee which is exercised only if the borrower defaults on the promissory note. Paragraph 22 of Figure 14–4 provides for the mortgage release.

> Upon payment of all sums secured by this deed of trust, lender shall request trustee to release this deed of trust and shall surrender all notes evidencing indebtedness secured by this deed of trust to trustee. Trustee shall release this deed of trust without charge to borrower. Borrower shall pay all costs of recordation, if any.

With respect to the administration of the deed of trust, the borrower secures funds and makes payments and otherwise observes practices common to first mortgages.

FIGURE 14–4

Standard Form for a Deed of Trust

DEED OF TRUST

THIS DEED OF TRUST is made this . . . . day of . . . . ,
19 . . . . , among the Grantor, ...
. . . . (herein "Borrower"), ...
. . . . (herein "Trustee"), and the Beneficiary,
. . . . , a corporation organized and
existing under the laws of . . . . , whose address is . . . .
. . . . (herein "Lender").

BORROWER, in consideration of the indebtedness herein recited and the trust herein created, irrevocably grants and conveys to Trustee, in trust, with power of sale, the following described property located in the District of Columbia:

which has the address of . . . . , ... ,

[Street]   [City]
. . . . (herein "Property Address");
[State and Zip Code]

TOGETHER with all the improvements now or hereafter erected on the property, and all easements, rights, appurtenances, rents (subject however to the rights and authorities given herein to Lender to collect and apply such rents), royalties, mineral, oil and gas rights and profits, water, water rights, and water stock, and all fixtures now or hereafter attached to the property, all of which, including replacements and additions thereto, shall be deemed to be and remain a part of the property covered by this Deed of Trust; and all of the foregoing, together with said property (or the leasehold estate if this Deed of Trust is on a leasehold) are herein referred to as the "Property";

To SECURE to Lender (a) the repayment of the indebtedness evidenced by Borrower's note dated . . . .
. . . . (herein "Note"), in the principal sum of . . . .
. . . . Dollars, with interest thereon, providing for monthly installments of principal and interest, with the balance of the indebtedness, if not sooner paid, due and payable on
. . . . ; . . . . ; the payment of all other sums, with interest thereon, advanced in accordance herewith to protect the security of this Deed of Trust; and the performance of the covenants and agreements of Borrower herein contained; and (b) the repayment of any future advances, with interest thereon, made to Borrower by Lender pursuant to paragraph 21 hereof (herein "Future Advances").

Borrower covenants that Borrower is lawfully seised of the estate hereby conveyed and has the right to grant and convey the Property, that the Property is unencumbered, and that Borrower will warrant and defend generally the title to the Property against all claims and demands, subject to any declarations, easements or restrictions listed in a schedule of exceptions to coverage in any title insurance policy insuring Lender's interest in the Property.

DISTRICT OF COLUMBIA—1 to 4 Family—6/75—FNMA/FHLMC UNIFORM INSTRUMENT

FIGURE 14–4 (continued)

UNIFORM COVENANTS. Borrower and Lender covenant and agree as follows:

1. Payment of Principal and Interest. Borrower shall promptly pay when due the principal of and interest on the indebtedness evidenced by the Note, prepayment and late charges as provided in the Note, and the principal of and interest on any Future Advances secured by this Deed of Trust.

2. Funds for Taxes and Insurance. Subject to applicable law or to a written waiver by Lender, Borrower shall pay to Lender on the day monthly installments of principal and interest are payable under the Note, until the Note is paid in full, a sum (herein "Funds") equal to one-twelfth of the yearly taxes and assessments which may attain priority over this Deed of Trust, and ground rents on the Property, if any, plus one-twelfth of yearly premium installments for hazard insurance, plus one-twelfth of yearly premium installments for mortgage insurance, if any, all as reasonably estimated initially and from time to time by Lender on the basis of assessments and bills and reasonable estimates thereof.

The Funds shall be held in an institution the deposits or accounts of which are insured or guaranteed by a Federal or state agency (including Lender if Lender is such an institution). Lender shall apply the Funds to pay said taxes, assessments, insurance premiums and ground rents. Lender may not charge for so holding and applying the Funds, analyzing said account or verifying and compiling said assessments and bills, unless Lender pays Borrower interest on the Funds and applicable law permits Lender to make such a charge. Borrower and Lender may agree in writing at the time of execution of this Deed of Trust that interest on the Funds shall be paid to Borrower, and unless such agreement is made or applicable law requires such interest to be paid, Lender shall not be required to pay Borrower any interest or earnings on the Funds. Lender shall give to Borrower, without charge, an annual accounting of the Funds showing credits and debits to the Funds and the purpose for which each debit to the Funds was made. The Funds are pledged as additional security for the sums secured by this Deed of Trust.

If the amount of the Funds held by Lender, together with the future monthly installments of Funds payable prior to the due dates of taxes, assessments, insurance premiums and ground rents, shall exceed the amount required to pay said taxes, assessments, insurance premiums and ground rents as they fall due, such excess shall be, at Borrower's option, either promptly repaid to Borrower or credited to Borrower on monthly installments of Funds. If the amount of the Funds held by Lender shall not be sufficient to pay taxes, assessments, insurance premiums and ground rents as they fall due, Borrower shall pay to Lender any amount necessary to make up the deficiency within 30 days from the date notice is mailed by Lender to Borrower requesting payment thereof.

Upon payment in full of all sums secured by this Deed of Trust, Lender shall promptly refund to Borrower any Funds held by Lender. If under paragraph 18 hereof the Property is sold or the Property is otherwise acquired by Lender, Lender shall apply, no later than immediately prior to the sale of the Property or its acquisition by Lender, any Funds held by Lender at the time of application as a credit against the sums secured by this Deed of Trust.

3. Application of Payments. Unless applicable law provides otherwise, all payments received by Lender under the Note and paragraphs 1 and 2 hereof shall be applied by Lender first in payment of amounts payable to Lender by Borrower under paragraph 2 hereof, then to interest payable on the Note, then to the principal of the Note, and then to interest and principal on any Future Advances.

4. Charges; Liens. Borrower shall pay all taxes, assessments and other charges, fines and impositions attributable to the Property which may attain a priority over this Deed of Trust, and leasehold payments or ground rents, if any, in the manner provided under paragraph 2 hereof or, if not paid in such manner, by Borrower making payment, when due, directly to the payee thereof. Borrower shall promptly furnish to Lender all notices of amounts due under this paragraph, and in the event Borrower shall make payment directly, Borrower shall promptly furnish to Lender receipts evidencing such payments. Borrower shall promptly discharge any lien which has priority over this Deed of Trust; provided, that Borrower shall not be required to discharge any such lien so long as Borrower shall agree in writing to the payment of the obligation secured by such lien in a manner acceptable to Lender, or shall in good faith contest such lien by, or defend enforcement of such lien in, legal proceedings which operate to prevent the enforcement of the lien or forfeiture of the Property or any part thereof.

5. Hazard Insurance. Borrower shall keep the improvements now existing or hereafter erected on the Property insured against loss by fire, hazards included within the term "extended coverage", and such other hazards as Lender may require and in such amounts and for such periods as Lender may require; provided, that Lender shall not require that the amount of such coverage exceed that amount of coverage required to pay the sums secured by this Deed of Trust.

The insurance carrier providing the insurance shall be chosen by Borrower subject to approval by Lender; provided, that such approval shall not be unreasonably withheld. All premiums on insurance policies shall be paid in the manner provided under paragraph 2 hereof or, if not paid in such manner, by Borrower making payment, when due, directly to the insurance carrier.

All insurance policies and renewals thereof shall be in form acceptable to Lender and shall include a standard mortgage clause in favor of and in form acceptable to Lender. Lender shall have the right to hold the policies and renewals thereof, and Borrower shall promptly furnish to Lender all renewal notices and all receipts of paid premiums. In the event of loss, Borrower shall give prompt notice to the insurance carrier and Lender. Lender may make proof of loss if not made promptly by Borrower.

Unless Lender and Borrower otherwise agree in writing, insurance proceeds shall be applied to restoration or repair of the Property damaged, provided such restoration or repair is economically feasible and the security of this Deed of Trust is not thereby impaired. If such restoration or repair is not economically feasible or if the security of this Deed of Trust would be impaired, the insurance proceeds shall be applied to the sums secured by this Deed of Trust, with the excess, if any, paid to Borrower. If the Property is abandoned by Borrower, or if Borrower fails to respond to Lender within 30 days from the date notice is mailed by Lender to Borrower that the insurance carrier offers to settle a claim for insurance benefits, Lender is authorized to collect and apply the insurance proceeds at Lender's option either to restoration or repair of the Property or to the sums secured by this Deed of Trust.

Unless Lender and Borrower otherwise agree in writing, any such application of proceeds to principal shall not extend or postpone the due date of the monthly installments referred to in paragraphs 1 and 2 hereof or change the amount of such installments. If under paragraph 18 hereof the Property is acquired by Lender, all right, title and interest of Borrower in and to any insurance policies and in and to the proceeds thereof resulting from damage to the Property prior to the sale or acquisition shall pass to Lender to the extent of the sums secured by this Deed of Trust immediately prior to such sale or acquisition.

6. Preservation and Maintenance of Property; Leaseholds; Condominiums; Planned Unit Developments. Borrower shall keep the Property in good repair and shall not commit waste or permit impairment or deterioration of the Property and shall comply with the provisions of any lease if this Deed of Trust is on a leasehold. If this Deed of Trust is on a unit in a condominium or a planned unit development, Borrower shall perform all of Borrower's obligations under the declaration or covenants creating or governing the condominium or planned unit development, the by-laws and regulations of the condominium or planned unit development, and constituent documents. If a condominium or planned unit development rider is executed by Borrower and recorded together with this Deed of Trust, the covenants and agreements of such rider shall be incorporated into and shall amend and supplement the covenants and agreements of this Deed of Trust as if the rider were a part hereof.

7. Protection of Lender's Security. If Borrower fails to perform the covenants and agreements contained in this Deed of Trust, or if any action or proceeding is commenced which materially affects Lender's interest in the Property, including, but not limited to, eminent domain, insolvency, code enforcement, or arrangements or proceedings involving a bankrupt or decedent, then Lender at Lender's option, upon notice to Borrower, may make such appearances, disburse such sums and take such action as is necessary to protect Lender's interest, including, but not limited to, disbursement of reasonable attorney's fees and entry upon the Property to make repairs. If Lender required mortgage insurance as a condition of making the loan secured by this Deed of Trust, Borrower shall pay the premiums required to maintain such insurance in effect until such time as the requirement for such insurance terminates in accordance with Borrower's and Lender's written agreement or applicable law. Borrower shall pay the amount of all mortgage insurance premiums in the manner provided under paragraph 2 hereof.

Any amounts disbursed by Lender pursuant to this paragraph 7, with interest thereon, shall become additional indebtedness of Borrower secured by this Deed of Trust. Unless Borrower and Lender agree to other terms of payment, such amounts shall be payable upon notice from Lender to Borrower requesting payment thereof, and shall bear interest from the date of disbursement at the rate payable from time to time on outstanding principal under the Note unless payment of interest at such rate would be contrary to applicable law, in which event such amounts shall bear interest at the highest rate permissible under applicable law. Nothing contained in this paragraph 7 shall require Lender to incur any expense or take any action hereunder.

8. Inspection. Lender may make or cause to be made reasonable entries upon and inspections of the Property, provided that Lender shall give Borrower notice prior to any such inspection specifying reasonable cause therefor related to Lender's interest in the Property.

FIGURE 14–4 (*continued*)

9. Condemnation. The proceeds of any award or claim for damages, direct or consequential, in connection with any condemnation or other taking of the Property, or part thereof, or for conveyance in lieu of condemnation, are hereby assigned and shall be paid to Lender.

In the event of a total taking of the Property, the proceeds shall be applied to the sums secured by this Deed of Trust, with the excess, if any, paid to Borrower. In the event of a partial taking of the Property, unless Borrower and Lender otherwise agree in writing, there shall be applied to the sums secured by this Deed of Trust such proportion of the proceeds as is equal to that proportion which the amount of the sums secured by this Deed of Trust immediately prior to the date of taking bears to the fair market value of the Property immediately prior to the date of taking, with the balance of the proceeds paid to Borrower.

If the Property is abandoned by Borrower, or if, after notice by Lender to Borrower that the condemnor offers to make an award or settle a claim for damages, Borrower fails to respond to Lender within 30 days after the date such notice is mailed, Lender is authorized to collect and apply the proceeds, at Lender's option, either to restoration or repair of the Property or to the sums secured by this Deed of Trust.

Unless Lender and Borrower otherwise agree in writing, any such application of proceeds to principal shall not extend or postpone the due date of the monthly installments referred to in paragraphs 1 and 2 hereof or change the amount of such installments.

10. Borrower Not Released. Extension of the time for payment or modification of amortization of the sums secured by this Deed of Trust granted by Lender to any successor in interest of Borrower shall not operate to release, in any manner, the liability of the original Borrower and Borrower's successors in interest. Lender shall not be required to commence proceedings against such successor or refuse to extend time for payment or otherwise modify amortization of the sums secured by this Deed of Trust by reason of any demand made by the original Borrower and Borrower's successors in interest.

11. Forbearance by Lender Not a Waiver. Any forbearance by Lender in exercising any right or remedy hereunder, or otherwise afforded by applicable law, shall not be a waiver of or preclude the exercise of any such right or remedy. The procurement of insurance or the payment of taxes or other liens or charges by Lender shall not be a waiver of Lender's right to accelerate the maturity of the indebtedness secured by this Deed of Trust.

12. Remedies Cumulative. All remedies provided in this Deed of Trust are distinct and cumulative to any other right or remedy under this Deed of Trust or afforded by law or equity, and may be exercised concurrently, independently or successively.

13. Successors and Assigns Bound; Joint and Several Liability; Captions. The covenants and agreements herein contained shall bind, and the rights hereunder shall inure to, the respective successors and assigns of Lender and Borrower, subject to the provisions of paragraph 17 hereof. All covenants and agreements of Borrower shall be joint and several. The captions and headings of the paragraphs of this Deed of Trust are for convenience only and are not to be used to interpret or define the provisions hereof.

14. Notice. Except for any notice required under applicable law to be given in another manner, (a) any notice to Borrower provided for in this Deed of Trust shall be given by mailing such notice by certified mail addressed to Borrower at the Property Address or at such other address as Borrower may designate by notice to Lender as provided herein, and (b) any notice to Lender shall be given by certified mail, return receipt requested, to Lender's address stated herein or to such other address as Lender may designate by notice to Borrower as provided herein. Any notice provided for in this Deed of Trust shall be deemed to have been given to Borrower or Lender when given in the manner designated herein.

15. Uniform Deed of Trust; Governing Law; Severability. This form of deed of trust combines uniform covenants for national use and non-uniform covenants with limited variations by jurisdiction to constitute a uniform security instrument covering real property. This Deed of Trust shall be governed by the law of the jurisdiction in which the Property is located. In the event that any provision or clause of this Deed of Trust or the Note conflicts with applicable law, such conflict shall not affect other provisions of this Deed of Trust or the Note which can be given effect without the conflicting provision, and to this end the provisions of the Deed of Trust and the Note are declared to be severable.

16. Borrower's Copy. Borrower shall be furnished a conformed copy of the Note and of this Deed of Trust at the time of execution or after recordation hereof.

17. Transfer of the Property; Assumption. If all or any part of the Property or an interest therein is sold or transferred by Borrower without Lender's prior written consent, excluding (a) the creation of a lien or encumbrance subordinate to this Deed of Trust, (b) the creation of a purchase money security interest for household appliances, (c) a transfer by devise, descent or by operation of law upon the death of a joint tenant or (d) the grant of any leasehold interest of three years or less not containing an option to purchase, Lender may, at Lender's option, declare all the sums secured by this Deed of Trust to be immediately due and payable. Lender shall have waived such option to accelerate if, prior to the sale or transfer, Lender and the person to whom the Property is to be sold or transferred reach agreement in writing that the credit of such person is satisfactory to Lender and that the interest payable on the sums secured by this Deed of Trust shall be at such rate as Lender shall request. If Lender has waived the option to accelerate provided in this paragraph 17, and if Borrower's successor in interest has executed a written assumption agreement accepted in writing by Lender, Lender shall release Borrower from all obligations under this Deed of Trust and the Note.

If Lender exercises such option to accelerate, Lender shall mail Borrower notice of acceleration in accordance with paragraph 14 hereof. Such notice shall provide a period of not less than 30 days from the date the notice is mailed within which Borrower may pay the sums declared due. If Borrower fails to pay such sums prior to the expiration of such period, Lender may, without further notice or demand on Borrower, invoke any remedies permitted by paragraph 18 hereof.

NON-UNIFORM COVENANTS. Borrower and Lender further covenant and agree as follows:

18. Acceleration; Remedies. Except as provided in paragraph 17 hereof, upon Borrower's breach of any covenant or agreement of Borrower in this Deed of Trust, including the covenants to pay when due any sums secured by this Deed of Trust, Lender prior to acceleration shall mail notice to Borrower as provided in paragraph 14 hereof specifying: (1) the breach; (2) the action required to cure such breach; (3) a date, not less than 30 days from the date the notice is mailed to Borrower, by which such breach must be cured; and (4) that failure to cure such breach on or before the date specified in the notice may result in acceleration of the sums secured by this Deed of Trust and sale of the Property. The notice shall further inform Borrower of the right to reinstate after acceleration and the right to bring a court action to assert the non-existence of a default or any other defense of Borrower to acceleration and sale. If the breach is not cured on or before the date specified in the notice, Lender at Lender's option may declare all of the sums secured by this Deed of Trust to be immediately due and payable without further demand and may invoke the power of sale and any other remedies permitted by applicable law. Lender shall be entitled to collect all reasonable costs and expenses incurred in pursuing the remedies provided in this paragraph 18, including, but not limited to, reasonable attorney's fees.

If Lender invokes the power of sale, Lender shall send written notice in the manner prescribed by applicable law to Borrower and to the other persons prescribed by applicable law of the occurrence of an event of default and of Lender's election to cause the Property to be sold. Trustee shall give notice of sale by such public advertisement as Trustee shall deem proper to protect the interests of Borrower and Lender. After the lapse of such time as may be required by applicable law, Trustee, without demand on Borrower, shall sell the Property at public auction to the highest bidder at the time and place and under the terms designated in the notice of sale in one or more parcels and in such order as Trustee may determine. Trustee may postpone sale of all or any parcel of the Property by public announcement at the time and place of any previously scheduled sale. Lender or Lender's designee may purchase the Property at any sale.

Trustee shall deliver to the purchaser Trustee's deed conveying the Property so sold without any covenant or warranty, expressed or implied. The recitals in the Trustee's deed shall be prima facie evidence of the truth of the statements made therein. Trustee shall apply the proceeds of the sale in the following order: (a) to all reasonable costs and expenses of the sale, including but not limited to, Trustee's fees of . . . . % of the gross sale price, reasonable attorney's fees and costs of title evidence; (b) to all sums secured by this Deed of Trust; and (c) the excess, if any, to the person or persons legally entitled thereto.

19. Borrower's Right to Reinstate. Notwithstanding Lender's acceleration of the sums secured by this Deed of Trust, Borrower shall have the right to have any proceedings begun by Lender to enforce this Deed of Trust discontinued at any time prior to the earlier to occur of (i) the fifth day before sale of the Property pursuant to the power of sale contained in this Deed of Trust or (ii) entry of a judgment enforcing this Deed of Trust if: (a) Borrower pays Lender all sums which would be then due under this Deed of Trust, the Note and notes securing Future Advances, if any, had no acceleration occurred; (b) Borrower cures all breaches of any other covenants or agreements of Borrower contained in this Deed of Trust; (c) Borrower pays all reasonable expenses incurred by Lender and Trustee in enforcing the covenants and agreements of Borrower contained in this Deed of Trust and in enforcing Lender's and Trustee's remedies as provided in paragraph 18 hereof, including, but not limited to, reasonable attorney's fees; and (d) Borrower takes such action as Lender may reasonably require to assure that the lien of this Deed of Trust, Lender's interest in the Property and Borrower's obligation to pay the sums secured by this

FIGURE 14–4 (*concluded*)

Deed of Trust shall continue unimpaired. Upon such payment and cure by Borrower, this Deed of Trust and the obligations secured hereby shall remain in full force and effect as if no acceleration had occurred.

20. Assignment of Rents; Appointment of Receiver; Lender in Possession. As additional security hereunder, Borrower hereby assigns to Lender the rents of the Property, provided that Borrower shall, prior to acceleration under paragraph 18 hereof or abandonment of the Property, have the right to collect and retain such rents as they become due and payable.

Upon acceleration under paragraph 18 hereof or abandonment of the Property, Lender, in person, by agent or by judicially appointed receiver, shall be entitled to enter upon, take possession of and manage the Property and to collect the rents of the Property including those past due. All rents collected by Lender or the receiver shall be applied first to payment of the costs of management of the Property and collection of rents, including, but not limited to, receiver's fees, premiums on receiver's bonds and reasonable attorney's fees, and then to the sums secured by this Deed of Trust. Lender and the receiver shall be liable to account only for those rents actually received.

21. Future Advances. Upon request of Borrower, Lender, at Lender's option prior to release of this Deed of Trust, may make Future Advances to Borrower. Such Future Advances, with interest thereon, shall be secured by this Deed of Trust when evidenced by promissory notes stating that said notes are secured hereby.

22. Release. Upon payment of all sums secured by this Deed of Trust, Lender shall request Trustee to release this Deed of Trust and shall surrender all notes evidencing indebtedness secured by this Deed of Trust to Trustee. Trustee shall release this Deed of Trust without charge to Borrower. Borrower shall pay all costs of recordation, if any.

23. Substitute Trustee. Lender, at Lender's option, may from time to time remove Trustee and appoint a successor trustee to any Trustee appointed hereunder by recording a Deed of Appointment. Without conveyance of the Property, the successor trustee shall succeed to all the title, power and duties conferred upon the Trustee herein and by applicable law.

IN WITNESS WHEREOF, Borrower has executed this Deed of Trust.

.... (Seal)
—Borrower

.... (Seal)
—Borrower

DISTRICT OF COLUMBIA, SS:

I, ..., a Notary Public in and for the District of Columbia, do hereby certify that...,
personally known to me as the person(s) who executed the foregoing instrument bearing date of ....
day of..........................., 19...., personally appeared before me in said District and acknowledged said instrument to be........................act and deed, and that........................executed said instrument for the purposes therein contained.

Witness my hand and official seal this.................day of..........................., 19.....

.... (Seal)
Notary Public, D.C.

———————————————— (Space Below This Line Reserved For Lender and Recorder) ————————————————

Security Deeds

Some states have created other instruments that avoid the extensive redemption periods of first mortgages. In Georgia, the security deed substitutes for the warranty deed and mortgage. A security deed transfers title to the lender and (1) provides that the deed secures payment of a debt and (2) grants the lender power of attorney to sell the property upon default of the loan. As with the trust deed, upon full payment of the debt the holder of the security deed cancels the deed or reconveys the property to the borrower. When the debt is paid, the security deed becomes null and void. With the power of sale, the lender avoids the redemption periods of a mortgage.

LEASEHOLD FINANCING

Property owners frequently find it economically advantageous to lease land over a long term. In some cases, property owners are legally prohibited from alienating land titles. Some outstanding developments have been based on long-term lease financing. Dwellings in the Salishan project on the Oregon coast are partly financed under 99-year ground leases. Much of the original 93,000-acre Irvine property south of Los Angeles is based on long-term development leases for residential, industrial, and commercial purposes. Resort developments of the 25,400-acre Agua Caliente Indian Reservation (Palm Springs, California) are based on long-term ground leases.

The long-term lease is one of the main alternatives to acquiring exclusive rights of use. Compared to mortgage financing, the lease gives tenants certain economic advantages: (1) by leasing, tenants gain the equivalent of a 100 percent loan equal to the value of the leased property; (2) rent payable for property used in industry or business is deductible for income tax purposes; and (3) by combining a ground lease with a first mortgage, the tenant reduces the amount required for equity. For the present purpose, consider leases as a means of financing, especially net ground leases and sale leasebacks.

Net Ground Leases

Net ground leases are advised if the land value is relatively high in proportion to the value of buildings. An extreme case is illustrated by a downtown parking lot improved merely with paving which represents a small proportion of the total property value. In these circumstances, the property owner or developer would be unable to deduct landownership costs for income tax purposes. Leasing makes the rent on the land income tax deductible.

Further, if the property owner values the land for lease purposes considerably above the original cost, he may prefer to collect rent in the form of ordinary income for income tax purposes rather than sell the land and pay long-term capital gains taxes. Suppose, for example, that a $100,000 site which originally cost $10,000 is available for lease on a long-term basis for an annual rent of $8,000—an 8 percent return on current value. If the 8 percent rent is lower than the prevailing mortgage interest, say, 9.5 percent, the operator may be well advised to lease rather than buy subject to a mortgage. Moreover, the lease covers the total property value; a mortgage, even if available on vacant land, would cover only part of the property value, depending on the loan-to-value ratio, which might be as low as 50 percent.

By combining mortgage financing with net ground leases, the tenant may reduce the required equity. This point may be illustrated for a single-family dwelling which is constructed on leased land. Consider an example adapted from a net ground lease in Newport Beach, California. Assume that the leased fee value is calculated from a 9 percent capitalization rate, that the ground lease provides for an annual rent of $900, and that the value of the leased land is $36,000. The value of the leased fee (the owner interest) then equals $10,200.

The Value of the Leased Fee (owner or lessor)

2. The present worth of the right to receive contract rent:
    a. The factor for the present worth of $1 per annum for 55 years at 9 percent.. 11.01
    b. The factor, 11.01 times the contract rent of $900................. $ 9,909.00
2. The present worth of the reversion:
    a. The factor for the present worth of the right to use the land in 55 years, discounted at 9 percent.................................... 0.0087
    b. The factor 0.0087 times the current market value of the land, $36,000... +313.21

Value of the leased fee.............................	$10,222.00
(rounded)	$10,200.00

In this instance the tenant would be eligible for a mortgage of $68,640, based on the leasehold interest value:

The Value of the Leasehold Interest (tenant or lessor)

1. Fee simple estate value:
    Market value of land.. $36,000
    Cost of improvement (dwelling)............................... 60,000
    Market value, fee simple estate.............................. $96,000
2. Less the leased fee value..................................... −10,200
3. Value of the leasehold interest.............................. $85,800
4. Less cost of improvement (dwelling).......................... −60,000
5. Leasehold interest in land (lessee interest)................. $25,800
    Maximum loan, 80 percent of the leasehold value of $85,800... $68,640

The loan on the $60,000 proposed building is based on the value of the leasehold interest of $85,800. The lender, granting money on the tenant's interest on an 80 percent loan, would grant a maximum of $68,640 —more than enough to pay for the dwelling construction cost of $60,000. In these circumstances a loan of $60,000 would be approved at the prevailing term and interest rate. The tenant, agreeing to pay ground rent and the mortgage, has no equity interest in either the land or the building. Not all lenders are authorized to make loans on leasehold interests. Others would require that the leased fee interest and rent be subordinate to the interest of the first-mortgage lender.

Sale-Leaseback Financing

A property sale combined with an immediate lease given by the buyer to the seller illustrates a sale-leaseback. The seller continues to possess the property, and he maintains the right of exclusive use according to his lease contract. Industrial and commercial corporations frequently prefer this method of financing since it reduces their real estate investment.

The main advantages to the seller initiating a sale-leaseback are: (1) The seller retains possession of real estate with no capital investment. (2) The seller may deduct rent as an expense of operation. (3) The proceeds of the sale provide capital for business purposes. At the same time the buyer who leases gains a return on his investment from a tenant of his selection.

Because mortgage funds may not be available on the same terms, and because the owner of the property may have exhausted his depreciation allowances for income tax purposes, the lease appeals to a wide range of businesses. Consider Table 14–4 showing rental payments expressed as a percent of the sale price for leases extending from 10 to 55 years, and

TABLE 14–4

Annual Rental Payments Required to Amortize a Sale-Leaseback for Selected Years Based on 7 Percent to 12 Percent Yields*

Lease Term in Years	Yield Rates					
	7%	8%	9%	10%	11%	12%
10.....................	14.24	14.90	15.58	16.27	16.98	17.70
15.....................	10.98	11.68	12.41	13.15	13.91	14.68
20.....................	9.44	10.19	10.95	11.75	12.56	13.39
25.....................	8.58	9.37	10.18	11.02	11.87	12.75
30.....................	8.06	8.88	9.73	10.61	11.50	12.41
35.....................	7.72	8.58	9.46	10.37	11.29	12.23
40.....................	7.50	8.39	9.30	10.23	11.17	12.13
45.....................	7.34	8.26	9.19	10.14	11.10	12.07
50.....................	7.25	8.17	9.12	10.09	11.06	12.04
55.....................	7.17	8.12	9.08	10.05	11.04	12.02

* Percentages are derived from installment of one capitalization tables.

with yields ranging from 7 percent to 12 percent. For example, if the purchaser desires a 9 percent yield, the annual rent under a 30-year lease would be 9.73 percent of the sales price. Thus a $100,000 sale would call for an annual leaseback rent of $9,730 for 30 years.

The feasibility of the sale-leaseback hinges largely on the tax consequences of the transaction. On the sale, for example, the seller is subject to capital gains taxes. Further, the rent on business property is fully deductible for income tax purposes. These advantages must be compared to the depreciation allowances deductible for an owner. Further, the purchase establishes a tax basis according to how much of the sales price may be allocated to depreciable assets, namely, the building and other depreciable improvements. For these reasons, a sale-leaseback is often preferred to conventional mortgage financing.

REAL ESTATE SALES CONTRACTS

As with a purchase money mortgage, the seller assumes all credit risks under a real estate contract. In a contract sale, the seller retains title and grants possessory rights to the buyer. Typically the buyer and seller negotiate the down payment (if any) and installment payments on the contract. The terms are negotiable between the parties. The interest rate usually approaches or exceeds first-mortgage interest rates.

In some instances the seller is virtually forced into a real estate contract if he hopes to sell his property. This situation occurs if the borrower does not qualify for mortgage financing from institutional lenders. Or, alternatively, the real estate offered as security may be poorly located, in poor condition, or deficient in some other respect, resulting in unusual risks to mortgage lenders.

The seller reduces his risk by the terms of the contract: a default on monthly payments usually gives the seller the right to terminate the contract, retaining the contract payments as liquidated damages. State law may limit the right of the seller to retain payments beyond interest rates that exceed statutory interest rate ceilings.

The buyer, in turn, assumes risks in that he is not given title: the buyer has possession only over the life of the contract. If the contract payments are completed as agreed, the contract requires the seller to transfer title under a deed, preferably a warranty deed. Yet over the life of the contract, title is subject to judgment liens, mechanics' liens, and other actions against the seller which may be adverse to the interest of the contract buyer. Property taxes, for example, are levied against the record owner, and if these are unpaid, the property will normally be sold after a specified time. Even with these restrictions, a real estate contract is frequently used for the conveyance of vacant land and rural, remote property since few other financing alternatives are available.

SUMMARY

Mortgages pledge real estate as security for a debt. The debt is evidenced by the promissory note or bond executed by the borrower. Mortgage instruments are executed with all the formality of real estate contracts and include certain covenants or promises of the borrower and the lender. The mortgagor, or borrower, has the right to redeem the property before foreclosure sale: the equity of redemption, or in some states, the statutory right of redemption which allows the borrower to redeem the property during a specified time after a foreclosure sale. The right of the borrower to prepay the mortgage depends on the mortgage contract—usually the lender will impose prepayment penalties over the early years of the mortgage.

The lender has the right to enforce the terms of the mortgage and may foreclose in the event of default. Foreclosure procedures are governed by state law. The acceleration clause is virtually universal among the states, giving lenders the right to the full amount of the principal if the borrower defaults. Moreover, the lender has the right to assign his interest to third parties without affecting the borrower-lender relationship. A borrower, however, who sells his interest to a third party may be required to pay assumption fees—payments to the lender before approval of a third party's assumption of the mortgage. Purchasers buying property *subject to* an existing mortgage are not personally responsible for the mortgage debt.

Classification of mortgages by priority of liens introduces second-mortgage financing, which provides for a second mortgage subordinate to the first mortgage. The holder of the second mortgage usually reserves the right to pay the first mortgage debt if it is in default and to add the payment to the second mortgage. Purchase money mortgages are accepted by the seller as a substitute for cash. They ordinarily do not include a promissory note; accordingly, the buyer assumes no personal liability for the debt.

Classified by repayment plans, mortgages range from the term mortgage, a mortgage that includes no amortization of principal, to the more common level payment amortization, in which mortgage payments are constant over the life of the loan. Here the amount accruing to principal increases and the amount accruing to interest decreases with each payment. Amortization plans also include variable payment mortgages that provide a constant repayment of principal with interest varying on the remaining balance. Partially amortized and flexible payment mortgages allow borrowers to vary principal payments according to financing needs. Variable rate mortgages refer to mortgages in which the interest rate varies according to an independent price (or interest) index.

The package mortgage includes personal property, such as household fixtures, and the blanket mortgage covers more than one parcel of real estate. Participation mortgages, which give lenders a share in a single mortgage, and construction loans, which are short-term obligations to finance new building construction, are frequently used as financial instruments. The wraparound mortgage, actually a second mortgage that includes an existing mortgage, is created if property is subject to an existing mortgage at less than current market interest rates and if the borrower wishes additional money. The wraparound mortgage is amortized as if it were the first mortgage.

Trust deed financing avoids redemption statutes. Under a trust deed, the buyer or trustor conveys title to a third party, the trustee, who holds title for the lender, the beneficiary. If the borrower defaults on the promissory note (which is comparable to a first-mortgage note), the trustee exercises his power of sale and remits the proceeds of the sale to the lender. The security deed is an example of a mortgage that conveys title accompanied by the power of sale, which may be exercised to gain title if the borrower defaults.

Net ground leases provide the tenant with the equivalent of a 100 percent loan equal to the value of leased property. Businesses are attracted to net ground leases since rent is deductible for income tax purposes. By combining a net ground lease with a first mortgage, equity capital may be considerably reduced. Sale-leaseback financing provides for possession of real estate with no capital investment. Again the seller may deduct rent as an income tax expense, and the proceeds of the sale provide capital for business purposes. The feasibility of a sale-leaseback hinges largely on the tax consequences of the transaction—to the seller who leases the property back and to the buyer who collects rent on depreciable property.

Real estate contracts are another form of credit advanced by the seller. If the buyer completes the installment payments called for by the contract, the seller agrees to transfer the title by deed. The risk of the buyer lies in the fact that the seller may not have a marketable title at the time the deed must be executed. The real estate installment contract is usually reserved for properties not eligible for long-term credit, either because of poor borrower credit or a high-risk real estate security.

REVIEW QUESTIONS

1. Explain how the elements of a mortgage include elements of an enforceable contract.
2. Explain three mortgage convenants common to mortgages.
3. Explain the difference between the equity of redemption and the statutory right of redemption.
4. Why do lenders restrict prepayment privileges in a long-term mortgage?
5. Explain the differences among the various ways of foreclosing on a mortgage.
6. What is the rationale supporting acceleration clauses?

7. Do you agree that assumption fees are a legitimate charge by the lender? Why or why not?

8. Explain the advantages and disadvantages in purchasing property *subject to* or *assuming* an existing mortgage. Relate your answer to the interests of the buyer, the seller, and the lender.

9. Explain the difference between title and lien theory states.

10. What is meant by classifying mortgages according to priority of liens?

11. When would you advise a seller to use a purchase money mortgage?

12. Explain why the level payment amortization plan is preferred to a term mortgage.

13. In what circumstances would a lender approve a variable payment or partially amortized mortgage?

14. As a borrower, would you negotiate for a flexible payment mortgage? Why or why not? Explain thoroughly.

15. Critically evaluate: "Variable rate mortgages are fair to both lender and borrower."

16. As a borrower, would you prefer a package mortgage? Explain fully.

17. Explain how a blanket mortgage is used to finance a new subdivision.

18. Why do some lenders avoid making construction mortgages?

19. Explain the circumstances that make a wraparound mortgage attractive to lenders and borrowers.

20. Give an example showing how a trust deed differs from a mortgage.

21. Show how a developer would use a net ground mortgage lease.

22. What are the advantages of sale-leaseback financing to a property owner?

23. When would a borrower be advised to finance a purchase with a real estate contract?

SELECTED REFERENCES

Atteberry, William. *Modern Real Estate Finance,* chaps. 1 and 2, Columbus: Grid, Inc., 1972.

Ficek, Edmund F.; Henderson, Thomas P.; and Johnson, Ross H. *Real Estate Principles and Practices,* chap. 7. Columbus: Charles E. Merrill Publishing Co., 1976.

Hoagland, Henry E. *Real Estate Principles,* chap. 9. 3d ed. New York: McGraw-Hill Book Co., 1955.

Hoagland, Henry E.; Stone, Leo D.; and Brueggeman, William B. *Real Estate Finance,* 6th ed. Homewood, Ill.: Richard D. Irwin, Inc., 1977.

Shenkel, William M. *Real Estate Finance,* chaps. 3 and 6. Washington, D.C.: American Bankers Association, 1977.

Unger, Maurice A. *Real Estate: Principles and Practices,* chap. 6. Cincinnati: South-Western Publishing Co., 1974.

Wiedemer, John P. *Real Estate Finance,* chap. 12. Reston, Va.: Reston Publishing Company, Inc., 1974.

15

Investment Analysis

After reading this chapter, you should be familiar with the following points:

1 The investment objectives pursued by real estate investors.
2 The limitations of rate of return analysis.
3 Investment variables important to mortgage equity capitalization.
4 Methods of calculating cash flow.
5 Techniques of measuring investment feasibility.

NOT ALL INVESTORS seek to maximize net annual income. Investors consider different objectives according to their financial status, their access to credit, and their investment motives. Moreover, real estate varies in its ability to meet these objectives. Consequently, real estate investment may not be approached with simple calculations of the rate of return on invested capital. Real estate investment analysis must consider financing, capital gains, and income tax implications. The fact that real estate may require a relatively large investment in capital, with the prospect of earning income deferred over several years, adds to the difficulty of analyzing real estate investments.

At this point, it is suggested that investment analysis incorporate appraisal and financial techniques presented in earlier chapters. To follow this suggestion, it is important to recognize main investment objectives, then to turn to analysis appropriate for each objective. To pursue this line of thought, the chapter reviews rate of return analysis, mortgage equity capitalization, and cash flow. The chapter ends with a review of techniques of judging investment feasibility, relying on a case study to demonstrate feasibility analysis.

INVESTMENT OBJECTIVES

To select the method of analysis, you must first decide on main investment objectives. Both the type of analysis and the real estate selected will affect the degree to which a given investment meets investor objectives. As a practical matter, investors tend to emphasize seven objectives. This does not mean that one objective is pursued independently of the others. More than likely, investors consider a combination of these objectives: (1) liquidity, (2) maximum current income, (3) future income, (4) protection from inflation, (5) decreased income taxes, (6) capital gains, and (7) safety of principal.

Liquidity

Liquidity is the ability to convert an asset to cash with a minimum loss. Generally speaking, real estate is one of the least liquid investments. For example, it is unlikely that a homeowner could convert his dwelling to cash immediately, that is, if he hopes to sell at the prevailing market value. Under typical market conditions, brokers recommend 60 to 90 days to market a house. This gives sufficient time to expose the property to a reasonable number of buyers and to arrange credit investigations, appraisal reports, and financing for the proposed purchase. If immediate cash is required, the owner could probably find an immediate buyer who would buy at a substantial discount from the market price.

An investor who desires a real estate investment with high liquidity turns to investment in a real estate investment trust share. Liquidity is provided by the ability to sell the share on the stock exchange at the going price. The share is liquid at the current market price. Mortgage pools, a block of mortgages backed by government-guaranteed mortgages, serve a similar purpose. They may be readily converted to cash at a price determined by the market interest rate. Generally, however, real estate investors sacrifice liquidity in favor of other ownership benefits.

Maximum Current Income

Yields on real estate often compare favorably with yields on alternative investments. Investors in real estate may purchase for cash; they prefer not to lower current income by mortgage payments or other obligations. And at one extreme they invest in high-return, risky investments, such as resort properties and improvements capitalizing on the recreation industry. Such investments show yields according to the willingness of the public to engage in leisure-time activities.

Compared to investments in government bonds, real estate may satisfy the objective of maximum current income and certain other investment objectives. In analyzing the ability of real estate to maximize current income, it is judged by its current income and value; the analysis relies heavily on appraisal techniques without regard to the income tax and financing.

Future Income

Some investors prefer to sacrifice current income in anticipation of maximizing future income. Persons in relatively high income brackets facing lower incomes at retirement, or families investing in an estate for their children, are among the groups in this category. Many types of real estate meet this criterion.

Investment in producing orchards—citrus, apple, pecan, and other fruit trees—requires a considerable capital outlay over 10 to 15 years before the yield increases to the point that returns are realized. Investing in timber is another example of a real estate investment earning a deferred income. Investment in land in the path of growth or in shopping centers built in advance of anticipated population growth also meet this requirement. The development of a 500-lot subdivision would probably be made in anticipation of the final sale of lots over several years.

Protection from Inflation

Certainly not all real estate increases in value; not all real estate moves in sympathy with the consumer price index; and not all real estate increases in value at the same rate. Yet historically land values and construction costs have moved upward in correspondence with the declining value of the dollar. For example, the Department of Agriculture reports that from 1936 to 1975 average farm real estate values increased by 230 percent.[1] Because of these trends, some investors place capital in well-protected real estate investments to take advantage of anticipated price increases. Indeed, the chapter on foreign investments explains that some investors include with the rate of return an annual allowance showing the annual rate of increase in property values as a consequence of anticipated inflation.

Decreased Income Taxes

Attractive primarily to individuals subject to high marginal income taxes, real estate has the advantage of accelerated depreciation allowances. Moreover, losses on real estate arising primarily because of the depreciation allowance may be offset against other income—making real estate investment attractive to high-income groups that pay high marginal income tax rates. Indeed, this may serve as the main investment motive, overriding other real estate investment objectives. Cash flow analysis shows the degree to which real estate serves this objective.

Capital Gains

For some taxpayers, paying capital gains taxes, currently at a maximum of 30 percent on long-term capital gains, is a more attractive alternative than paying annual net income taxes at higher marginal rates. Mortgage equity capitalization, illustrated in this chapter, provides a method of basing investment decisions on capital gains opportunities. In fact, some analysts use mortgage equity capitalization as a means of calculating the present worth of earning net income and capital gains. Other experts report that investors may be willing to sacrifice current income in anticipation of earning substantial capital gains.

Safety of Principal

Institutions and individuals charged with preserving capital invest in highly secured real estate. Property developed for long-term lease by the federal government or industrial buildings that are leased to national corporations with the highest credit rating fall into this group. Government agencies and corporations are generally aware of their preferred credit status and the federal net income tax. Consequently, they bargain for the lowest possible rent. Because of the security such use gives their capital, investors are willing to accept relatively low yields.

---

[1] U.S. Department of Agriculture, Economic Research Service, *Farm Real Estate Market Developments,* supplement no. 1 to CD–80, February 1976, p. 3.

RATE OF RETURN ANALYSIS

The rate of return calculation relates net operating income to the capital investment in land and buildings. Table 15–1 is an income statement for a 118-unit apartment showing the net operating income before depreciation and before mortgage payments of $178,010. This was prepared for an estimated project that would cost $1,706,000—a land value

TABLE 15–1

Net Operating Statement, Woodgate Apartments

Annual gross income................................		$308,328
Less vacancy @ 5%................................		−15,418
Effective gross income (EGI)................		$292,910
Less operating expenses		
Taxes...	$23,490	
Insurance ($5/rm/yr)..........................	2,935	
Management (5% EGI).........................	14,645	
Electricity ($12.50/unit/mo)...................	17,700	
Gas ($6.50/unit/mo)..........................	9,200	
Water/sewer ($2.00/unit/mo).................	2,830	
Trash pickup ($1.50/unit/mo)................	2,125	
Maintenance men (2 @ $85).................	8,840	
Air conditioning repair ($10/unit/yr).........	1,180	
Pool maintenance............................	500	
Decorating/repairs ($15/rm/yr)...............	8,805	
Miscellaneous management..................	8,315	
Reserves for replacement		
Carpeting $8,850....................		
Appliances 5,485....................	14,335	$114,900
Net income..............................		$178,010

of $120,000 and construction costs of $1,586,000. The overall rate of return would be calculated as

$$\frac{\$178,010}{\$1,706,000} = 10.4\%$$

On its face, the investor would earn 10.4 percent on the investment. However, while this type of analysis is satisfactory for limited purposes, it has six limitations:

1. It implies that the property is held to the end of its economic life, say, 50 years for an apartment building.
2. It assumes that the property is purchased for cash.
3. It makes no allowance for the effect of net income taxes on investment decisions.
4. It unrealistically calculates net operating income over a 50-year building life.
5. It makes no allowance for the possibility of capital gains or losses.

6.   It assumes that the overall rate of return on invested capital is more important than the rate of return on equity investment.

Investment over Economic Life

In the preceding illustration income was projected over the economic life of the building, which could be 50 or so years. Some investors consider this highly unrealistic. Moreover, it is held that investors are unlikely to consider extremely long-term investments. Because of the operation of our tax laws, investors have incentives to invest over the short run: 5 to 15 years. In addition, if capital gains are experienced, investors prefer to convert ordinary income into capital gains. In short, it is held that investors in income-producing property are unlikely to maintain ownership over the economic life, as the conventional rate of return analysis implicitly assumes.

The Assumption of No Debt

Investors capitalize on opportunities for leverage. Leverage refers to the practice of increasing the yield in invested capital by financing real estate. To make this work, the property yield must be greater than the interest paid on mortgages. For example, consider two investments, one yielding a return on a cash investment, the other earning the same net operating income but financed with a 75 percent loan.

Property A: Cash Investment	Property B: Mortgage Financing
$100,000 investment	$100,000 investment
15,000 net operating income	90,000 mortgage
15 percent yield	$ 10,000 equity investment
($15,000/$100,000)	−8,100 interest (0.09) first year
	$ 6,900 yield after interest
	69 percent yield on equity
	($6,900/$10,000)

In property A, the investor earns a 15 percent yield on a $100,000 cash investment. Suppose now that he executes a $90,000 mortgage requiring a $10,000 cash investment, not $100,000. Assuming a mortgage interest rate of 9 percent, $8,100 interest is paid during the first year, and the investor earns a yield of $6,900 after payment of mortgage interest. The $6,900 return on a $10,000 investment gives a 69 percent yield on equity.

Though the example is based on selected assumptions, it suggests that given favorable opportunities for financing, investors may increase yields on invested capital. Indeed, some authorities consider the yield on equity more significant than the yield on the whole property.

Net Income Tax Factors

The main effect of income tax laws relates to the depreciation allowance on wasting assets (buildings). Since depreciation is an operating expense, property owners may deduct an allowance for depreciation on some properties equal to double the straight-line rate on the declining balance.

Table 15–2 illustrates the effect of depreciation on a 118-unit apartment building. Assuming a building cost of $1,586,000 and a 30-year life for income tax purposes, under the present law the owner could deduct 6.6 percent, or $104,676, as an expense of operation for income tax purposes. In succeeding years, the 6.6 percent depreciation allowance applies to the declining depreciation base. The 6.6 percent rate is double the

TABLE 15–2

Depreciation Allowances for a 118-Unit Apartment Building, Double Declining Balance*

	30-Year Building Life	
Year	Annual Depreciation	Declining Depreciation Base
1	$105,733	$1,480,266
2	98,684	1,381,581
3	92,105	1,289,475
4	85,968	1,203,510
5	80,234	1,123,270
6	74,878	1,048,392
7	65,233	978,499
8	60,884	913,265

*Depreciation base, $1,586,000; land value, $120,000.

3.3 percent straight-line basis deductible over a 30-year economic life (1/30).

Projecting Net Operating Income over the Building Life

It is held that projecting net operating income over a 50-year term is less accurate than projections over 5 or 10 years. Assuming that investments are held for relatively short periods, net operating income projected at the end of the building life is not relevant to an investment decision. Instead, the expected sales price becomes a critical element in the valuation.

Allowance for Capital Gains or Losses

The overall rate of return of 10.4 percent, calculated for the 118-unit apartment building, accounts for no capital gain or loss. In the view of some investors, this approach is inappropriate. In fact, it is held that property is developed and purchased specifically for capital gains opportunities. Because of these approaches to value, the overall rate of return is considered inadequate to deal with the complexities of projecting capital gains or losses. Mortgage equity capitalization deals directly with projected gains or losses; in fact, these projections are important determinants of value.

Return on Equity

To many observers, the overall rate of return on the total property value is less relevant than the rate of return on the actual capital invested— the equity. The overall rate of return implies that the return on equity is not a determinant of investment decisions. An illustration of mortgage equity capitalization explains the reasons for these views.

MORTGAGE EQUITY CAPITALIZATION

Mortgage equity capitalization avoids the weaknesses of the rate of return analysis. To use mortgage equity capitalization, certain assumptions must be accepted. To follow this analysis, it must be assumed that the investor

1. Invests over the short run.
2. Considers capital gains and losses.
3. Finances real estate investments.
4. Invests for a return on equity.

The analysis starts out by assuming the availability of a mortgage with a stated loan-to-value ratio, interest rate, and term. In fact, unfavorable mortgage terms may make an equity investment unattractive. To put it differently, an investor may reject an investment opportunity under a mortgage with a 9.5 percent interest rate, a 15-year term, and a 50 percent loan-to-value ratio. The same project might be highly profitable under a 30-year mortgage with an 8.0 percent interest rate and an 80 percent loan-to-value ratio.

To illustrate this method, the feasibility of a project is indicated by stating the mortgage terms, the projection period, the required yield on equity investment, and a projected sales price at the end of the anticipated investment holding period. Referring again to the 118-unit apartment building, assume the following investment circumstances:

1. A 75 percent loan-to-value ratio mortgage.
2. A 9.5 percent mortgage interest rate.
3. A 25-year mortgage.
4. A required yield on the equity of 15 percent.
5. An investment period of ten years.

6. A projected sales price of $1,616,797 at the end of ten years.
7. An annual net income of $178,010.

In this analysis, only the income remaining after mortgage payments is considered relevant. Assuming that a mortgage of $1,212,598 is available on the above terms, the annual payments on the mortgage would total $127,133.[2]

With an annual net income of $178,010, the investor earns $50,877 on his equity investment. These relationships are shown in Figure 15–1. The

FIGURE 15–1

The Division of Value and Annual Income: Mortgage Equity Capitalization

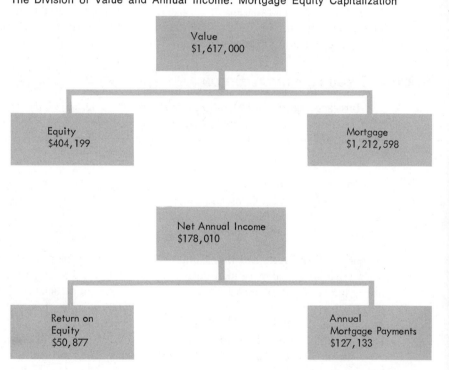

property value of $1,617,000 is divided between the 25 percent equity, $404,199, and the 75 percent mortgage, $1,212,598. In short, the net annual income goes to the return on equity and annual mortgage payments.

Investment Advantages

Given the mortgage and its terms, mortgage equity capitalization gives two investment advantages: the annual return to equity ($50,877) and

---

[2] Calculated from a mortgage constant of 10.48 percent. See an installment of one table, 300 months, 9.5 percent annual interest (0.00873 × 12).

the net value of the sales price, which is deferred ten years. In the former case, the present value of the return to equity equals the present worth of the right to receive the return on equity over ten years. If the investor requires a 15 percent yield, the present worth of one per annum table shows that the right to a dollar income payable at the end of the year over ten years, discounted at 15 percent, is worth $5.01876. Accordingly, $255,339 represents the present worth of the return on equity discounted at 15 percent over ten years ($50,877 × 5.01876).

Capital Gain Discounting

Projecting a sale price of $1,617,000 (rounded) at the end of ten years, the remaining mortgage balance must be deducted. Under the mortgage

TABLE 15–3

Mortgage Equity Capitalization: 15 Percent Yield

Net annual income............................		$178,010
Less mortgage requirement		
0.75 of $1,616,797 × 0.1048....................		−127,133
Annual amount to equity......................		$ 50,877
Present worth of income		
$50,877 × (present worth of one per annum,		
10 years, 15%), 5.01876......................		$255,339
Present worth of reversion		
$1,616,797 deferred 10 years..................	$1,616,797	
Less mortgage balance, after 10 years.......	−1,014,573	
	$ 602,224	
$602,224 deferred 10 years		
(present worth of one, 10 years, 15%) ×		
0.247184......................................		$148,860
Equity value..................................		$404,199
Add original mortgage.........................		$1,212,598
Property value................................		$1,616,797
(rounded)		$1,617,000

terms, the investor would have to pay off the unpaid balance of the mortgage of $1,014,573,[3] giving him cash of $602,224. Since this sum is postponed for ten years, the problem is to calculate its present worth in ten years, discounted at a yield of 15 percent (0.247184). This sum totals $148,860.

Adding the present worth of the return on equity and the present worth

---

[3] See L. W. Ellwood, *Ellwood Tables for Real Estate Appraising and Financing,* 3d ed. (Chicago: American Institute of Real Estate Appraisers, 1972), p. 52. The relevant formula to calculate the percentage of mortgage remaining is $1 - [(f/I - 1) (Sp - 1)]$, where $f =$ mortgage constant, $I =$ mortgage interest rate, and $Sp =$ compound of one at mortgage interest rate over the projection period. For example, $1 - \{[(.1048/0.095) - 1] \ (2.5761 - 1)\} = 0.836694$.

of the reversion produces the equity value of $404,199. In other words, given the required yield of 15 percent, the mortgage terms, an expected holding period of ten years, and an assumed sale price at the end of ten years, the equity is worth $404,199. Adding the mortgage gives a total property value of $1,617,000, rounded. These data are summarized in Table 15–3.

Figure 15–2 indicates that the price the investor pays for the equity interest, given the mortgage, depends (1) on the present worth of the income calculated after mortgage payments, and (2) on the present worth

FIGURE 15–2

The Division of Equity Value under Mortgage Equity Capitalization

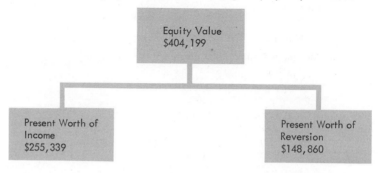

of the reversionary value—the projected sales price less the remaining balance of the mortgage.

Average Yield

Turning to the original assumption of a project cost of $1,706,000 and assuming the same mortgage terms, income, and projection period, what average yield would be realized if the property were sold for its cost at the end of ten years? The answer is shown in Table 15–4. In this case, the mortgage increases to $1,279,500 (a 75 percent loan-to-value ratio) and will require annual mortgage payments of $134,147. At the end of the tenth year, the reversionary value of $635,450 is indicated after paying the remaining balance of the mortgage. Adding the total income for the ten years, $43,863 per year to equity, gives the owner a total return on his investment over the ten years of $1,074,080, or a profit over his investment costs of $647,580. For the ten-year period this results in an average profit of $64,758.00 (647,580/10). Comparing the average profit to the equity investment of $426,500, this shows an *average rate of return* of 15.18 percent ($64,758/$426,500).

In other words, with the income and costs of a 118-unit apartment and

TABLE 15–4

Investment Profit under Mortgage Equity Capitalization

Mortgage	$1,279,500 × 0.105.....................	$ 134,147
Equity	426,500............................	43,863
	1,706,000............................	178,010
Selling price.......................................		1,706,000
$P = [(0.1048/0.0950) - 1] \times 1.5761 = 0.1633$		
Complement; $1 - 0.163306 = 0.836694$		
Subtract mortgage balance $1,279,500 × 0.836694..........		−1,070,550
Equity reversion...		$ 635,450
Income 10 years at $43,863..............................		438,630
Total equity collection..................................		$1,074,080
Investment cost.......................................		−426,500
Profit...		$ 647,580

For assumptions, see text.

the assumptions of a ten-year investment period and a sales price equal to the original cost, the average rate of return is less than that of the earlier example. However, with a required yield of 15 percent, the investor would be advised to pay only $404,199 for the equity interest, assuming a $1,212,598 mortgage.

In these examples, it was assumed that the property would sell at its original investment cost. To account for projected appreciation or depreciation, it is merely necessary to assume some sales price at the end of the holding period. Alternatively, a percent of appreciation or depreciation per year may be assumed to give the same results. In sum, the mortgage equity capitalization technique indicates the value of the equity given some annual rate of appreciation or depreciation—3 percent, 4 percent or whatever.[4]

Financing Trends

Mortgage equity capitalization emphasizes the importance of the mortgage interest rate, the term of the mortgage, and the loan-to-value ratio. Observers have commented that financing methods anticipate continuing inflation. Expectations of continued inflation have led to variable mortgage interest rates, which are tied to the consumer price index, the wholesale price index, or the implicit price deflator (a series prepared by the Department of Commerce to give the gross national product in constant dollars). Under these methods mortgage interest rates vary with the general price level.

Project developers have been confronted with variations in develop-

---

[4] See ibid., pp. 79–102.

ment loans. While the traditional 20-, 25-, or 30-year amortized mortgage may continue, some lenders have granted 30-year amortization loans with the entire principal due at the end of 10 years (a balloon payment).

For example, assuming a 9 percent interest rate and a 25-year term, a loan that required a balloon payment at the end of 10 years would require a lump-sum payment equal to 82.7 percent of the original loan. A $100,000 25-year loan at 9 percent with a balloon payment payable at the end of 10 years would require a lump-sum payment of $82,700, and a 30-year loan would require a lump-sum payment of $89,400. These requirements force the developer to seek new financing at the end of ten years; they permit the lender to renegotiate the loan at current interest rates and to charge additional loan fees.[5]

CASH FLOW ANALYSIS

Cash flow refers to the amount of net cash income remaining after (1) mortgage payments and (2) net income taxes. For commercial real estate, cash flow assumes considerable importance because of the depreciation deduction. Although depreciation is deductible as an expense of operation, money may not actually be spent during the year it is deducted; the depreciation allowance is viewed in part as a form of nontaxable income.

Net Cash Flow

To calculate cash flow as defined here, start with annual net operating income. From this figure, subtract mortgage interest and depreciation. The arithmetic is shown in the example below:

Net operating income......................	$50,000
Less mortgage payments....................	−34,455
Spendable income..........................	$15,545
Add mortgage principal.....................	+5,315
	$20,860
Less depreciation..........................	−10,361
Taxable income............................	$10,499
Less 40% personal income tax...............	−4,200
Aftertax income...........................	$ 6,299
Add depreciation..........................	+10,361
Net cash flow........................	$16,660

Starting with the annual net operating income, mortgage principal and interest payments are deducted to give *spendable income* of $15,545. Be-

---

[5] *Industrial Development Handbook* (Washington, D.C.: Urban Land Institute, 1975), p. 233.

cause mortgage principal repayments are not income tax deductible, they are added back, which, in effect, is the same as deducting mortgage interest in the first year of $29,140. Then by deducting depreciation of $10,361, taxable income amounts to $10,499. Assuming a 40 percent personal income tax, aftertax income amounts to $6,299. And because depreciation is available for spending, depreciation is added, giving a final net cash flow of $16,660.

Property owners in upper income tax brackets may prefer to base decisions on cash flow and not entirely on annual net income. Another way of looking at the problem is to review how the annual net income of $50,000 is distributed in the first year, as shown in this example:

Net Operating Income Allocation	Year 1
1. Mortgage interest....................	$29,140
2. Depreciation allowance..............	10,361
3. Personal income tax.................	4,200
4. Aftertax income.....................	6,299
5. Total net income before taxes........	$50,000
Cash flow: 2 and 4 (after taxes).....	$16,660

Under this analysis, it will be appreciated that cash flow is affected by (1) the financing terms (the mortgage interest) and (2) the amount of depreciation allowed. Indeed, for large-scale investment properties, a depreciation allowance may result in a loss for income tax purposes which under the present law may shelter other income. The individual's income tax rate, a third variable, is unique to each investor. Selected examples illustrate the effect of the first two items.

The Depreciation Allowance

If the objective is to maximize cash flow, the investor seeks that depreciation method which gives the greatest depreciation allowance over the early years of an investment. Table 15–5 compares five depreciation schedules: straight line, 125 percent declining balance, 150 percent declining balance, 200 percent declining balance, and sum-of-the-years'-digit. The table is constructed on the assumption that the building may be depreciated over 40 years, allowing a 2.5 straight-line depreciation rate (1/40). Assuming a depreciable investment of $100,000, the table reveals that for *straight-line depreciation*, 50 percent or more of the depreciation is not recovered until the end of the 20th year. Under *sum-of-the-years'-digit method*, depreciation over the first year totals $4,878; more than 50 percent of the investment is recovered by the end of the 12th year. Sum-of-the-years'-digit depreciation is found by totaling the number of years to establish the denominator and taking as the numerator the maxi-

TABLE 15-5

A Comparison of Depreciation Allowances: 40-Year Life, $100,000 Building

Year	Straight-Line Annual Depreciation	Straight-Line Percent of Depreciable Balance	Declining Balance 1¼ Times Straight Line Annual Depreciation	Declining Balance 1¼ Times Straight Line Percent of Depreciable Balance	Declining Balance 1½ Times Straight Line Annual Depreciation	Declining Balance 1½ Times Straight Line Percent of Depreciable Balance	Declining Balance 2 Times Straight Line Annual Depreciation	Declining Balance 2 Times Straight Line Percent of Depreciable Balance	Sum-of-the-Years'-Digit Annual Depreciation	Sum-of-the-Years'-Digit Percent of Depreciable Balance
1	$2,500	97.5	$3,125	96.88	$3,750	96.25	$5,000	95.00	$4,878	95.12
2	2,500	95.0	3,027	93.85	3,609	92.64	4,750	90.25	4,756	90.37
3	2,500	92.5	2,933	90.91	3,474	89.17	4,513	85.78	4,634	85.73
4	2,500	90.0	2,841	88.07	3,344	85.82	4,287	81.45	4,512	81.22
5	2,500	87.5	2,752	85.32	3,218	82.60	4,073	77.38	4,390	76.29
6	2,500	85.0	2,666	82.66	3,098	79.51	3,869	73.51	4,268	72.56
7	2,500	82.5	2,583	80.07	2,982	76.53	3,675	69.83	4,146	68.41
8	2,500	80.0	2,502	77.57	8,270	73.66	3,492	66.34	4,024	64.39
9	2,500	77.5	2,424	75.15	2,762	70.89	3,317	63.02	3,902	60.49
10	2,500	75.0	2,348	72.80	2,659	68.24	3,151	59.88	3,780	56.71
11	2,500	72.5	2,275	70.52	2,559	65.76	2,999	56.86	3,659	53.05
12	2,500	70.0	2,204	68.32	2,463	63.21	2,844	54.04	3,537	49.51
13	2,500	67.5	2,135	66.18	2,371	60.84	2,702	51.33	3,415	46.09
14	2,500	65.0	2,068	64.12	2,282	58.56	2,567	48.77	3,293	42.80
15	2,500	62.5	2,004	62.11	2,196	56.37	2,438	46.33	3,171	39.63
16	2,500	60.0	1,941	60.17	2,113	54.25	2,316	44.01	3,049	36.59
17	2,500	57.5	1,880	58.29	2,034	52.22	2,201	41.81	2,927	33.66
18	2,500	55.0	1,822	56.47	1,958	50.26	2,091	39.72	2,805	30.85
19	2,500	52.5	1,765	54.70	1,885	48.37	1,986	37.74	2,683	28.17
20	2,500	50.0	1,710	52.99	1,814	46.56	1,887	35.84	2,561	25.61
21	2,500	47.5	1,656	51.34	1,746	44.81	1,792	34.06	2,439	23.17
22	2,500	45.0	1,604	49.73	1,681	43.13	1,703	32.35	2,317	20.85
23	2,500	42.5	1,554	48.18	1,617	41.52	1,617	30.74	2,195	18.66
24	2,500	40.0	1,506	46.67	1,557	39.96	1,537	29.20	2,073	16.59
25	2,500	37.5	1,459	45.22	1,598	38.46	1,460	26.64	1,952	14.63
26	2,500	35.0	1,413	43.80	1,442	37.02	1,387	26.35	1,829	12.80
27	2,500	32.5	1,369	42.43	1,388	35.63	1,318	25.03	1,707	11.10
28	2,500	30.0	1,326	41.11	1,336	34.29	1,252	23.78	1,585	9.51
29	2,500	27.5	1,285	39.42	1,286	33.01	1,189	22.59	1,463	8.05
30	2,500	25.0	1,244	38.58	1,238	31.77	1,130	21.46	1,341	6.71
31	2,500	22.5	1,206	36.36	1,191	30.58	1,073	20.39	1,220	5.49
32	2,500	20.0	1,168	36.21	1,147	29.43	1,020	19.36	1,098	4.39
33	2,500	17.5	1,131	35.07	1,104	28.33	969	18.40	976	3.41
34	2,500	15.0	1,096	33.98	1,062	27.27	920	17.48	854	2.56
35	2,500	12.5	1,062	32.92	1,022	26.24	874	16.61	732	1.83
36	2,500	10.0	1,029	31.89	984	25.26	830	15.78	610	1.22
37	2,500	7.5	996	30.89	947	24.31	789	14.99	487	0.73
38	2,500	5.0	965	29.93	912	23.40	749	14.24	364	0.37
39	2,500	2.5	935	28.99	878	22.52	712	13.53	244	0.12
40	2,500	0.0	906	28.08	845	21.68	676	12.85	122	0.00

mum number of years, decreasing one year each period. For example, a 40-year life produces a total of 820 years, allowing depreciation to be 40/820 of building value (4.878 percent) for the first year, 39/820 for the second year, and decreasing to 1/820 for the last year.

Similarly, in this case declining balance at *double* straight-line rates recovers more than 50 percent of the depreciable base at the end of the 14th year. The table reveals that sum-of-the-years'-digit and declining-balance techniques shift taxable income towards the end of the asset life. Moreover, the greater the depreciation allowance, the greater the amount of cash flow.

Measuring Cash Flow

Table 15–6 illustrates how cash flow changes over a ten-year projection. The data are based on an 83-unit apartment building that cost $855,910, with a land cost of $105,400. Depreciable personal property was $58,848. The building depreciation allowance was 125 percent declining balance, assuming a 50-year building life, resulting in a depreciation of 2.25 percent per year.

Tax Shelter. Federal and state personal income tax rates of 50 percent and 4 percent were assumed for this example. Further, the gross income was projected to increase at a constant rate of 7 percent per year; operating expenses were projected to increase 3 percent per year over the ten years. Note that in this instance the building provides tax shelter over the first three years—for these years, the depreciation allowance exceeds net operating income. Taxable income increases from a negative $21,248 for year 1 to a positive taxable income of $84,840 for year 10.

Percent of Equity. If these assumptions are realized, note that cash flow varies from $1,420 for the first year to $52,485 for the tenth year. The return on an equity investment of $170,158 varies from 42.26 percent in the first year to 71.74 percent for the tenth year. Though cash flow expressed as a percent of the equity investment ranges from 12.04 percent for the fourth year to 22.05 percent for the tenth year, investors attracted by tax shelter would have an incentive to dispose of the property after the third year.

Note also that starting from an equity investment of $170,158, equity buildup from principal mortgage payments increases to $237,994. If the property sells for more than its original cost, equity buildup would be considered a form of income by some investors, especially foreign investors in U.S. real estate. (See Chapter 22 on this point.)

In sum, cash flow starts from net operating income from which mortgage interest payments and depreciation allowances are subtracted to give taxable net income. Assuming some rate of income taxation, aftertax income and the depreciation allowance are added to show net income remaining after mortgage payments and income taxes.

TABLE 15–6

Cash Flow Projections for an 83-Unit Apartment Building

	Year 1	Year 2	Year 3	Year 4	Year 5	Year 6	Year 7	Year 8	Year 9	Year 10
Income after taxes										
Net operating income	$73,867	$81,657	$90,071	$99,154	$108,957	$119,531	$130,935	$143,228	$156,475	$170,746
Debt service—first mortgage:										
Principal	4,614	4,998	5,413	5,863	6,350	6,878	7,449	8,068	8,738	9,464
Interest	67,833	67,449	67,034	66,584	66,097	65,570	64,998	64,379	63,709	62,983
Principal and interest	72,447	72,447	72,447	72,447	72,447	72,447	72,447	72,447	72,447	72,447
Debt service—second mortgage:										
Principal	0	0	0	0	0	0	0	0	0	0
Interest	0	0	0	0	0	0	0	0	0	0
Principal and interest	0	0	0	0	0	0	0	0	0	0
Net spendable income	1,420	9,210	17,623	26,707	36,509	47,084	58,488	70,780	84,027	98,298
Principal—first mortgage	4,615	4,993	5,413	5,863	6,350	6,878	7,449	8,068	8,738	9,464
Principal—second mortgage	0	0	0	0	0	0	0	0	0	0
Depreciation—real	21,398	20,863	20,341	19,833	19,337	18,853	18,382	17,923	17,475	17,038
Depreciation—personal	5,885	5,885	5,885	5,885	5,885	5,885	5,885	5,885	5,885	5,885
Taxable income (or shelter)	−21,248	−12,540	−3,190	6,852	17,638	29,224	41,670	55,041	69,406	84,840
Income tax	0	0	0	3,426	8,819	14,612	20,835	27,520	34,703	42,420
State tax	0	0	0	274	706	1,169	1,667	2,202	2,776	3,394
Income after taxes	−21,248	−12,540	−3,190	3,152	8,113	13,443	19,168	25,319	31,927	39,026
Cash flow										
Income after taxes	−21,248	−12,540	−3,190	3,152	8,113	13,443	19,168	25,319	31,927	39,026
Depreciation—real	21,398	20,863	20,341	19,833	19,337	18,853	18,382	17,923	17,475	17,038
Depreciation—personal	5,885	5,885	5,885	5,885	5,885	5,885	5,885	5,885	5,885	5,885
Principal—first mortgage	4,615	4,998	5,413	5,863	6,350	6,878	7,449	8,068	8,738	9,464
Principal—second mortgage	0	0	0	0	0	0	0	0	0	0
Cash flow	1,420	9,210	17,623	23,006	26,985	31,303	35,986	41,058	46,548	52,485
Equity										
Equity buildup from original equity of $170,158	$174,772	$179,770	$185,184	$191,047	$197,397	$204,275	$211,724	$219,792	$228,530	$237,994
Taxable income/equity	0.0	0.0	0.0	3.59	8.94	14.31	19.68	25.04	30.37	35.65
Cash flow/equity	0.81	5.12	9.52	12.04	13.67	15.32	17.00	18.68	20.37	22.05
Return on equity	42.26	45.42	48.64	51.90	55.20	58.52	61.84	65.17	68.47	71.74

INVESTMENT FEASIBILITY

Real estate investments are not unlike public utilities. Local, state, and federal laws impose restraints on real estate investments. Regulations controlling financial institutions restrict the financing of real estate. The operations of the investor-developer are controlled by regulations governing real estate syndications, interstate land sales, and partnerships and corporations.

Accordingly, real estate investors must overcome special risks common to real estate ownership. These risks bear on projects based on deferred income and on projects in which investment analysis concentrates on income and expense projection. With these qualifications, it seems worthwhile to outline the steps followed in making feasibility studies.

For the present purpose, *a feasibility study may be defined as the reasonable likelihood of satisfying investment objectives.* Thus, an investor compares the anticipated net income—and its discounted present value—to the cost of construction. Presumably, if the project meets investor objectives, it would be feasible if its value exceeds its cost.[6]

Investment Risks

To be sure, real estate investment has risks common to other financial investments. Among these risks, certain real estate investment risks stand out which require more detailed analysis.

Changes in Purchasing Power. An investment of fixed capital value, though showing reasonable yield, declines in purchasing power as the general price level increases (a savings deposit). Ideally, real estate would return market yield rates and still increase in value at least in proportion to changes in the general price level. An investor in real estate must consider the effect of stable or declining values in the face of rising prices that decrease the asset value in terms of constant dollars.

The Interest Rate Risk. Suppose that gross income and expenses are accurately projected over the early years of a proposed investment. There still remains the risk from changes in the market rate of interest. A small change in the interest rate causes large variations in real estate values. Assuming the proposition that present worth is equal to the capitalized value of net income, it may be shown that a small change in interest rates causes substantial changes in value. For example, start with the idea that the present worth of an annual income of $1,000, capitalized at a 10 percent rate, is worth $10,000. Here the interest rate is treated as synonymous with the capitalization rate.

---

[6] For a more detailed explanation, see James A. Graaskamp, *A Guide to Feasibility Analysis* (Chicago: Society of Real Estate Appraisers, 1970), pp. 1–21.

Capitalization Rate	Present Worth of $1,000 per Year
5	$20,000
6	16,667
7	14,286
8	12,500
9	11,111
10	10,000
11	9,090
12	8,333
13	7,692
14	7,143
15	6,667
16	6,250
17	5,882
18	5,556
19	5,263
20	5,000

The presumption in this calculation is that the $1,000 represents annual net income earned in perpetuity. When the capitalization rate is varied from 5 percent to 20 percent, the same income shows a value ranging from $20,000 to $5,000. In sum, interest rates affect capitalization rates; capitalization rates materially change the value of long-term investments.

Liquidity Risk. It is reasonable to anticipate that at some point, investors will convert investments to cash. In this event, there is always the possibility that the conversion will result in a loss. Land investments are especially vulnerable to this risk. An attempt to convert land to immediate cash usually results in substantial losses. Land and other real estate investments are usually converted to cash only after a reasonable time has been taken to expose the properties to the investment market.

Legal Risks. Legal risks start with the risks inherent in acquiring land titles. While warranty deeds, title insurance, and title abstracts minimize these risks, they do not entirely eliminate title risks. Real estate ownership subjects owners to other types of litigation arising from noncompliance with zoning, environmental, and tenant actions, among other recurring legal problems.

Natural Hazards. Catastrophic events from fire, inclement weather, and floods expose property owners to unpredictable risks. In agriculture, risks from agricultural price changes, foreign trade policy, and insect damage must be added. In some instances, these risks are assumed by the investor. He, in turn, invests at a yield rate that compensates him for unusual risks. In a sense, more risky real estate investments are accepted in return for relatively high yields.[7]

---

[7] For an additional discussion of this point, consult Maury Selden, *Land Investment* (Homewood, Ill.: Dow Jones-Irwin, Inc., 1975), pp. 26–36.

Analysis of Deferred Income

Real estate developments requiring unusually heavy capital costs are feasible according to (1) the cost of development and (2) the present worth of net sales realized over the development period. Developers must also anticipate the need for cash at different stages of development. Frequently, the cost of developing a subdivision exceeds the cost of vacant land. In Table 15–7, 67 percent of the projected costs of a 40-acre development represent development costs: the cost of utilities, planning, and engineering surveys. In addition to these costs, the developer absorbs interest on construction loans, legal fees, insurance, property taxes, and bonding expenses. Assuming that the cost projections are reasonably accurate, the project feasibility turns on anticipated annual sales volume.

TABLE 15–7

Estimated Costs of Subdividing 40 Acres

Item	Total
Streets...	$110,055
Sewers...	63,700
Water...	63,860
Underground power...............................	78,000
Underground telephone...........................	58,500
Gas mains..	20,475
Total off-site improvement costs.............	$394,590
Engineering fees.................................	22,372
Total development cost.......................	$416,962
Add land cost....................................	200,000
Total cost of development, 40 acres........	$616,962

Consider, for example, the projection of lot sales on a 3,000-acre development on the west coast of Florida. In this instance approximately 3,600 lots were proposed for development at an average sales price of $20,000. On its face, it would appear that the land had a potential value of $72 million (3,600 × $20,000), less development costs.

However, a comprehensive survey of similar lot sales in the region suggested a potential sales volume limited to 200 lots per year. After development, during the first year, it was anticipated that 200 lots sold at an average price of $20,000 would result in an annual gross income of $4 million. However, the present worth of the 200-lot sales, discounted at 10 percent, would approximate only $3.636 million. This sum is found by multiplying the present worth of $1 discounted at 10 percent (0.909) by $4 million.

Assuming that lot prices remain at $20,000 per lot, an annual sales volume of 200 lots would mean that the subdivision would be developed over 18 years. The present worth of annual gross sales of $4 million, realized over 18 years, would be $32.804 million—considerably less than the potential value, or *undiscounted* potential gross sales, of $72 million.

The point is that income from deferred land sales must be discounted to find the present worth. It would be unrealistic to value the project by multiplying the per unit price by the total number of units available. In dealing with deferred income, the analyst must convert gross sales over time to calculate the present worth less the cost of development. More sophisticated techniques discount net income for each year, to account for varying development costs experienced over the construction period.

Project Analysis

To show the inherent difficulties in estimating project feasibility for income property, it is worthwhile to compare a syndication offer for a proposed apartment project developed under a limited partnership. As stated in the investment offer, the investment objectives were (1) to earn a return from cash flow and (2) to realize yields from tax losses. The projected cash flow and aftertax yield are shown in Table 15–8. With a total equity of investment of $292,000, it was anticipated that investors in a 50 percent income tax bracket would earn an aftertax cash flow ranging from 69.4 percent of their equity after one year to 7.5 percent after eight years. Although these projections seemed reasonable, three years later the project underwent foreclosure. Table 15–9 compares the projected operation for the first year with the actual operating experience at the end of the third year.

These figures show that in the first year projected net operating income of $149,679 would have been more than sufficient to meet annual mortgage payments of $138,987, giving investors considerable benefits from tax shelter. The depreciation of $105,733 over the first year plus interest deductions on construction loans and the first mortgage totaled $129,850. Table 15–9, however, shows that at the end of the third year, net operating income totaled only $64,881. Because the owners had insufficient annual net operating income to make the annual mortgage payments of $138,987, the mortgage was declared in default.

In comparing the *actual* results with the *projections* of the first year, four points stand out. *First,* the estimate of gross possible income was fairly realistic—$342,060 realized, $308,323 projected. *Second,* the vacancy and rent losses greatly exceeded expectations, with the result that effective gross income was some $32,000 lower than projected. *Third,* note also that the projected fixed expenses were fairly reasonable. The results closely approximated the projections. However, a review of the operating expenses—the *fourth* point—shows that utility and payroll expenses were not realistically anticipated. The actual expenses of $195,439 were some $52,213 more than the projected expenses.

Note further that the first year projection of a $149,679 net income ex-

TABLE 15-8

Cash Flow Projections: Apartment Project

Year	Investment	Deductions	Net Income	Interest (management and lease)	Depreciation	Cash Flow	Aftertax Yield (in percent)§
1............	$150,000	$218,758	$ 85,975	$199,000	$105,733*	—	69
2............	81,000	77,543	166,010	144,869‡	98,684	$27,023†	29
3............	61,000	64,533	170,990	143,418	92,105	27,833	20
4............	—	41,685	176,120	131,837	85,968	28,668	17
5............	—	28,944	181,403	130,113	80,234	29,528	15
6............	—	16,270	186,845	123,237	74,878	30,414	13
7............	—	(801)	192,221	126,187	65,223	31,326	10
8............	—	(10,405)	195,244	123,955	60,884	32,266	8

* Assumed 30-year double declining.
† Increased 3 percent per year.
‡ Increased 3 percent per year.
§ Aftertax yield on total investment, assuming a 50 percent bracket.

TABLE 15–9

A Comparison of Projected and Actual Net Operating Income

	Projected 1st Year		Actual 3d Year	
Gross possible income....................		$308,323		$342,060
Less vacancy and rent losses.............		−15,418		−81,740
Effective gross income...................		$292,905		$260,320
Less expenses				
Fixed expenses				
Property tax.........................	$23,490		$21,460	
Insurance...........................	2,935		5,245	
Maintenance and upkeep............	19,325		21,263	
Land lease rental....................	12,000		12,000	
Operating expenses				
Management........................	39,306		40,878	
Payroll expense......................	—		14,960	
Utilities and waste removal...........	31,835		59,272	
Supplies.............................	—		1,354	
Office supplies and telephone........	—		1,834	
Furniture rental......................	—		2,838	
Reserves for replacement				
Carpeting $8,850................				
Appliances 5,485................	14,335	−143,226	14,335	−195,439
Net operating income.............		$149,679		$64,881

ceeded the annual mortgage payments ($138,987) by only $10,692—an amount equal to 3.5 percent of projected gross income. In short, given the projected fixed expenses, net income would be *less* than annual mortgage payments if gross income declined by 3.5 percent ($10,692/$308,323). Most prudent investors would prefer a greater margin of safety.

Therefore, in judging feasibility, considerable care must be taken in estimating (1) the projections of gross income less vacancies and (2) expenses which must conform to the experience of like properties.

Steps in Making a Feasibility Study

Though subject to much qualification, feasibility studies generally follow a fairly uniform procedure. Certainly, they are more complex than the comparison of market value with the cost of development, and certainly, their detail varies for each project. A feasibility study for an organized industrial park would emphasize marketability features not found in a proposed residential subdivision. Generally speaking, however, feasibility studies would follow seven steps:

1. Determine the investment objectives.
2. Select that type of analysis which will show whether the investment objectives will be realized.
3. Undertake a marketability study for the estimation of gross income or sales.

4. Analyze development costs, including planning, legal, and initial financing costs.
5. Project net income from a realistic study of net incomes, vacancies, and expenses of operation.
6. Capitalize net income according to the market rates of capitalization.
7. Present net income and cash flow data according to the investment objectives to be satisfied.

The main difficulty lies in identifying realistic costs of development and projecting net income. If the study relates to income-producing property, the apartment house case suggests that errors in projecting gross income, vacancy rates, and expense allowances are common deficiencies. The discussion revealed further that investment feasibility turns on market capitalization rates and favorable financing.

SUMMARY

Investment objectives encompass more than the maximization of current income. As alternatives, investors may favor liquidity, future income, protection from inflation, decreased income taxes, capital gains, and safety of principal. Moreover, investors may consider a combination of objectives, even though emphasizing a single objective.

Conventional analysis relates the net income to investment cost, giving an annual rate of return. While useful for limited purposes, the rate of return analysis is based on unrealistic assumptions, in the view of some analysts. Among the more questionable assumptions are (1) that the property is held until the end of its economic life, (2) that the property is purchased for cash, (3) that the effect of income taxes on investment decisions is ignored, (4) that the investment calculation makes no allowance for capital gains or losses, and (5) that the rate of return on equity is not considered.

Mortgage equity capitalization includes the financing terms as part of the investment equation, namely, the loan-to-value ratio, the mortgage interest rate, and the length of the mortgage. In addition, this analysis relates the yield to the equity and assumes that the investment is held for a relatively short period. Capital gains or losses are considered in making the final investment decision.

Cash flow is defined as the net income remaining after mortgage payments and net income taxes. In cash flow analysis, the mortgage interest, the depreciation allowance, and the income tax rate control investment prospects. Generally, the greater the depreciation allowance, the greater the cash flow.

Analysis of investment feasibility tends to minimize the risks encountered in real estate. Changes in purchasing power and interest rates and certain legal and natural hazards affect investment feasibility and its attractiveness. In analyzing property showing deferred income, the projection of net income realized over the investment term must be discounted to the present worth. A review of investment projects stresses the importance of accurately gauging gross income and realistically estimating operating expenses. Finally, the capitalization rate, which must agree with required yields of the marketplace, governs investment feasibility.

REVIEW QUESTIONS

1. Explain the main investment objectives. Give an example of each objective to illustrate your answer.
2. Which of the investment objectives are more significant in your opinion? Give reasons for your answer.
3. Illustrate rate of return analysis.
4. What are the objections raised against rate of return analysis for investment purposes? Explain thoroughly.
5. What are the main advantages of selecting a real estate investment to maximize the depreciation allowance?
6. What are the disadvantages of selecting a real estate investment that maximizes cash flow from the depreciation allowance?
7. Illustrate the difference between straight-line and double declining balance depreciation methods.
8. Explain the significance of the seven assumptions common to mortgage equity capitalization.
9. Define cash flow analysis. Give an example.
10. Define a feasibility study.
11. What risks are encountered in making real estate investments?
12. Explain how you would analyze property investments with a deferred income potential.
13. In judging the investment feasibility of an income-producing property, what factors would you review for accuracy?
14. Explain the steps that you would follow in undertaking a feasibility study.

SELECTED REFERENCES

Beaton, William R., and Robertson, Terry. *Real Estate Investment,* rev ed., chap. 1. Englewood Cliffs, N.J.: Prentice-Hall, Inc., 1977.

Maisel, Sherman J., and Roulac, Stephen E. *Real Estate Investment and Finance,* chap 20. New York: McGraw-Hill Book Co., 1976.

Messner, Stephen D.; Schreiber, Irving; and Lyon, Victor L. *Marketing Investment Real Estate,* chap. 12. Chicago: Realtors National Marketing Institute of the National Association of Realtors, 1975.

Seldin, Maury. *Land Investment,* chap. 3. Homewood, Ill.: Dow Jones-Irwin, Inc., 1975.

Seldin, Maury, and Swesnik, Richard H. *Real Estate Investment Strategy,* chap. 3. New York: Wiley-Interscience, a Division of John Wiley & Sons, Inc., 1970.

Smith, Halbert C.; Tschappat, Carl J.; and Racster, Ronald L. *Real Estate and Urban Development,* rev. ed. Homewood, Ill.: Richard D. Irwin, Inc., 1977.

16

Real Estate Brokerage

After reading this chapter, you should be familiar with the following points:

1 The meaning of the term *real estate broker* for state licensing purposes.
2 The content of state real estate license examinations.
3 The trend in educational requirements for real estate salespersons or brokers.
4 Duties of the real estate broker to the principal.
5 Elements of a listing agreement.
6 Differences among listing agreements.
7 Requirements necessary to enforce payment of a real estate commission.
8 Qualifying the prospects and constructing an inventory of single-family dwellings.
9 Techniques for marketing commercial real estate.
10 The main requirements of the National Fair Housing Act.

THOUGH THE TERM *real estate broker* includes persons acting for another in buying or selling real property for a fee or in the expectation of a fee, statutes generally define a broad range of activities that require a real estate license. The model real estate license law prepared by the License Law Committee of the National Association of Realtors® defines a real estate broker as

> . . . any person who for a fee, commission or other valuable consideration, or with the intent or expectation of receiving the same, negotiates or attempts to negotiate the *listing, sale, purchase, exchange* or *lease* of any real estate or of the improvements thereon, or *collects rents* or attempts to collect rents, or who *advertises* or holds himself out as engaged in any of the foregoing activities. The term "broker" also includes any person employed by or on behalf of the owner or owners of real estate to conduct the sale, leasing, or other disposition thereof at a salary or for a fee, commission or any other consideration; it also includes any person who engages in the business of charging an advance fee or contracting for collection of a fee in connection with any contract whereby he undertakes primarily to promote the sale of real estate through its listing in a publication issued primarily for such purpose or for the referral of information concerning such real estate to· brokers, or both.[1]

For administrative purposes, the term *broker* may be defined to include virtually all activities of persons performing a real estate service. The Real Estate License Act prevailing in Texas requires a real estate brokerage license for persons who engage in the following activities:

(*a*) Sells, exchanges, purchases, rents or leases real estate;

(*b*) offers to sell, exchange, purchase, rent or lease real estate;

(*c*) negotiates or attempts to negotiate the listing, sale, exchange, purchase, rental, or leasing of real estate;

(*d*) lists or offers or attempts or agrees to list real estate for sale, rental, lease, exchange, or trade;

(*e*) appraises or offers or attempts or agrees to appraise real estate;

(*f*) auctions, or offers or attempts or agrees to auction, real estate;

(*g*) buys or sells or offers to buy or sell, or otherwise deals in options on real estate;

(*h*) aids, attempts, or offers to aid in locating or obtaining for purchase, rent, or lease any real estate;

(*i*) procures, or assists in the procuring of prospects for the purpose of effecting the sale, exchange, lease, or rental of real estate; or

(*j*) procures or assists in the procuring of properties for the purpose of effecting the sale, exchange, lease, or rental of real estate.

Thus the Texas law defines real estate brokerage to include selling, exchanging, negotiating, leasing, and appraising.[2] Universally in the United

---

[1] See William M. Shenkel, *The Real Estate Professional* (Homewood, Ill.: Dow Jones-Irwin, Inc., 1976), p. 52.

[2] Title 113A, Article 6573a, *Vernon's Annotated Revised Civil Statutes of Texas,* vol. 19.

States, it is unlawful to practice as a real estate broker or to engage in activities defined by the real estate license law without holding a valid real estate sales or brokerage license.

While the activities covered by the state license laws vary, all the laws provide for certain exemptions. For instance, attorneys are generally exempt from state real estate license laws, though some states require a real estate license if the attorney engages in the full-time activity of a real estate broker or salesperson. Persons granted power of attorney who are authorized to engage in real estate transactions are generally exempt. Public officials and court-appointed receivers, trustees, administrators, executors, and guardians are likewise free of real estate license law regulations.

An owner may sell his own property without a license; generally, on-site managers of an apartment complex are exempt even in states that require real estate licenses for property management. Dealings in other specialized property types may be exempt, such as the sale, lease, or transfer of mineral rights, cemetery lots, and business opportunities. In some instances, these latter activities are covered by separate laws.

REAL ESTATE LICENSE REQUIREMENTS

Historically, real estate salespersons and brokers were subject to occupational licenses or taxes under local ordinances. Not until California enacted the first real estate license law in 1917 were real estate brokers required to meet minimum standards of competence. Today real estate license statutes of the 50 states cover these topics: (1) the definition of real estate brokers and salespersons, (2) persons exempt from the license law, (3) the requirements for licensure, (4) the appointment of real estate commissioners, (5) license fees, (6) grounds for refusal, suspension, or revocation of license, (7) license violation penalties, and (8) provision for out-of-state licensees and reciprocity.[3]

License Examinations

At first the early advocates of license laws suggested that an applicant seek the recommendation of five real estate owners in the county in which the applicant resided certifying that he was honest, truthful, and of good moral character. At this time it was feared that competence requirements would be turned down by state legislatures.[4]

Examination Content. From this start, most states came to require that applicants for real estate licenses pass an examination on:

[3] Robert W. Semenow, *Questions and Answers on Real Estate,* 8th ed. (Englewood Cliffs, N.J.: Prentice-Hall, Inc., 1975), p. 472.

[4] Pearl Janet Davies, *Real Estate in American History* (Washington, D.C.: Public Affairs Press, 1958), p. 108.

Real Estate Law	Real Estate Finance
Land Use Controls	Title Closing Procedures
Real Estate Appraisal	Related Real Estate Topics

Related real estate topics include the code of ethics, state license law, property management, and real estate arithmetic.

The real estate license law of Arizona requires a written examination in the English language, demonstrating a knowledge of reading, writing, spelling, and real estate arithmetic. The law further requires an understanding of

(*a*) Principles of real estate conveyances.

(*b*) The general purposes and legal effect of agency contracts, deposit receipts, deeds, mortgages, deeds of trust, security agreements, bills of sale, land contracts of sale and leases.

(*c*) The principles of business and land economics and appraisals.

3.   A general understanding of the obligations between principal and agent, the principles of real estate and business opportunity practice, the applicable canons of business ethics, the provisions of this chapter, and rules and regulations made under this chapter.[5]

Uniform License Examination.   There is some merit in establishing a uniform national examination qualifying real estate salespersons and brokers among the various states. Such an arrangement would expedite the reciprocal licensing of qualified salespersons and brokers among the states. Under this proposal, a licensed person changing residence from, say, California to Florida could be licensed to practice real estate in Florida without having to proceed as a new license applicant under Florida's laws. Toward this goal, on November 8, 1972, the National Association of Real Estate License Law Officials adopted the following motion:

> That the National Association of Real Estate License Law Officials believes it to be in the public interest to stimulate development of real estate license examinations which can be used by more than one state. . . .

In pursuing this objective, the Educational Testing Service of Princeton, New Jersey, initiated steps toward uniform examinations in 1970. At present the Educational Testing Service administers real estate license examinations in 23 states. The uniform license examination developed by the Educational Testing Service covers 14 topic areas. The percent of subjects covered on tests ranges from 2 percent to 26 percent, as shown on p. 394.

In a parallel development, the Real Estate Commission of California offers a similar service to other participating states. Both the Educational Testing Service and the Real Estate Commission of California assist in license preparation, grading, and administration.

---

[5] Section 32–2124, *Arizona Revised Statutes* (*Annotated, 1975 Supplementary Pamphlet*), vol. 10, titles 29–32 (St. Paul: West Publishing Co., 1975).

Examination Topics	Percent of Coverage*
Condominiums...........................	2
Contracts...............................	26
Deeds..................................	6
Fair Housing Act........................	3
Financing instruments...................	10
Financing, means of.....................	10
Interests in real property................	8
Laws of agency..........................	10
Legal property descriptions..............	3
Planning and zoning.....................	3
Property management....................	2
Settlement procedures...................	8
Taxes and assessments..................	3
Valuation of real property...............	6

*Letter dated July 19, 1976, from Joanne Timmins, Associate Program Developer, Educational Testing Service, Princeton, New Jersey.

Educational Requirements

A recent questionnaire survey identified 35 states that provided minimum educational requirements for salespersons and brokers.[6] The educational requirements for qualification as a real estate broker ranged from a college degree (Indiana) to a minimum number of hours in approved real estate classes. The record shows that the states are tightening their educational requirements. In Texas the law provides for increasing educational requirements so that by 1985 the state will require 60 college semester hours or the equivalent to qualify as a broker (salespersons' licenses will be discontinued).

Qualification Date	Salespersons' Educational Requirements
Prior to January 1, 1977	30 classroom hours
Second annual renewal	30 additional classroom hours
Third annual renewal	30 additional classroom hours
After January 1, 1977	6 semester hours of accredited college courses or equivalent
After January 1, 1979	12 semester hours of accredited college courses or equivalent
After January 1, 1981	21 semester hours of accredited college courses or equivalent
After January 1, 1983	36 semester hours of accredited college courses or equivalent
After January 1, 1985	Broker licenses only (60 semester hours of accredited college courses or equivalent)*

*Title 113A, Article 6573a, *Vernon's Annotated Revised Civil Statutes of Texas*, vol. 19.

[6] Author survey, 1975.

California provides an additional example. The California Real Estate Association and other groups have consistently supported legislation raising license standards. The law has been justified by the need to protect the public and to enlarge opportunities for salespersons or brokers to increase their knowledge. The real estate commission has invested $7 million to encourage some 82 community colleges to give real estate courses each semester. Current plans in California call for legislation, effective January 1, 1980, that will require real estate broker applicants to have completed 60 units of college-level courses, including 18 units of real estate specialization. It is proposed by July 1, 1982, to provide only for a Certified Real Property Broker designation and to establish a new Associate Broker category. An Associate Broker's qualifications could be met by a baccalaureate real estate degree. After July 1, 1982, to qualify as a Certified Real Property Broker, the applicant must have a four-year college course with real estate course requirements. Under the proposed plan the Real Estate Commission may accept a combination of two years of college, experience, and examinations as an alternative qualification.[7]

REAL ESTATE AGENCY

Brokers serve in many capacities. They work for a fee on a daily or hourly basis for buyers. They act as consultants on real estate matters. However, most brokers serve as the agent of the seller, who agrees to pay a real estate commission if the broker secures a buyer meeting the seller's terms of sale. In soliciting listings from sellers, the real estate broker develops an inventory of properties for sale. In essence, the broker serves as the marketplace for real estate transactions. This arrangement is shown in Figure 16–1. The buyers are prospects, the sellers are principals. The brokers are the agents who serve the seller-principals.

In practice the real estate broker must find a property that meets buyer requirements, and to this extent the broker serves the buyer-prospect. But the legal relationship between the agent and the principal requires that the broker observe certain duties of the agent to the principal.

Agent Duties to the Principal

A listing seller agrees to pay a commission if the broker completes the purpose of the agency; namely, to find a buyer who meets the terms of sale. The relation between the seller and the broker in this type of agency requires that the broker observe seven duties:

1. The broker must be loyal to his principal.
2. The broker acts as a fiduciary.

---

[7] *Plan for the Professional Development of the Real Estate Industry in California*, California Department of Real Estate, 1975, pp. 13–16.

FIGURE 16–1

Agency-Principal Relationship of a Real Estate Broker

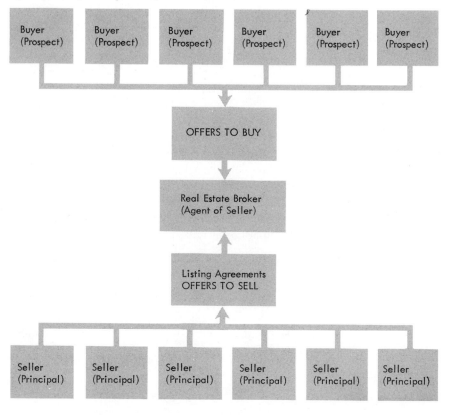

3. The broker must account for money deposits.
4. The broker must obey the instructions of his principal.
5. The broker must act in person.
6. The broker must not have a personal interest in property for which he acts as broker without full disclosure to the principal.
7. The broker is prohibited from acting for both the buyer and the seller without full disclosure.

Loyalty. Active brokers often have access to information that bears on the future value of real estate. Plans for a new shopping center and recent or proposed zoning changes are cases in point. Yet the broker must not gain any advantage over his principal by reason of the agency. The broker must not make misrepresentations and must not conceal facts to the harm of the principal. The broker must not mislead or deceive the principal in any way. In fact, loyalty requires that the broker advise the principal of events that may affect the seller's interest.

Fiduciary.   The fiduciary relationship is formed when good conscience requires that one act at all times for the sole benefit and interest of another. Because of the fiduciary relationship of an agency, the broker has no right to hold an interest adverse to that of his principal. This rule prohibits the broker from buying the seller's property through a third party for resale at a profit.

Deposits.   In serving as an agency, the broker holds monies on deposit pending the closing of the sale, which may take several weeks. Earnest money deposits paid to the broker which accompany an offer to buy remain the property of the buyer until the sale is closed. Similarly, the broker may not withhold funds due the seller. The law of most states requires the broker to keep such trust funds and earnest money deposits in a separate account which must not be commingled with personal funds.

Obey Instructions.   It is equally clear that in offering property for sale through an agency, the seller-principal specifies acceptable terms of sale. If the seller requires a cash down payment, the broker violates the agency in accepting a personal check. If the check is returned for insufficient funds, the agent would be personally responsible—he has not followed instructions of the principal.

Act in Person.   In employing an agent broker, the seller relies on the personal services of the broker. Even if a broker cooperates with another agency in the sale of property, it is presumed that the cooperating broker acts under instructions from the listing agency. Usually this requirement applies to the authority of the agent and not to mechanical, clerical, or bookkeeping duties which may be delegated to other employees. The issue is that the seller enlists the personal services of the broker on the basis of his reputation; consequently, the broker would be in violation of the agency relationship if he delegated his work to others.

No Personal Interest.   If the broker buys property of the principal for whom he acts as broker, the seller must be told that the broker is buying property on his own account. An agent may not gain secret profits from the principal. The broker must not deliberately list the property for an exorbitant price and later secretly buy the property at a lower price in his own name.

Acting for Buyer and Seller.   There are occasions when the broker would represent both the buyer and the seller and collect a commission from both parties. While unusual, this is permissible if both parties are informed and both consent. Without disclosure, the broker is in violation of his agency if he accepts a commission from the principal and third persons. In short, without permission the broker may not serve two masters.

Duties to the Prospect

Common observation of the role of real estate brokers suggests that the broker works diligently with the prospect in satisfying his needs. In this respect, the broker does not earn his commission unless the prospect is satisfied; property must be found that suits the buyer and that may be financed within the limitations of the buyer's income and cash reserves.

In pursuing this objective, the broker must not make any misrepresentations or false promises or commit any fraudulent act. The broker is entitled to "puff his wares" by such statements as "Neighborhood values are going up," "This is a well-built house," or "The house is constructed of only the best-quality materials." Though these statements may be false, they are not actionable. Generally, false statements or promises, on which the buyer relies, and which are known to be false by the broker, are actionable. If the broker states that "I can sell this land for $500 an acre more next year," this would be a false promise; it would violate duties to the prospect, and probably the state license law.

LISTING AGREEMENTS

The listing agreement is a contract employing the real estate broker. The broker agrees to use his best efforts and abilities to find a purchaser. If the broker performs as required by the listing agreement, the seller agrees to pay a stated commission. While some states allow oral listing, good business practice and the laws of some 15 states require that enforceable listings be in writing. Accordingly, listings assume the form of a contract which must observe all the requirements of contract law. To avoid misunderstandings, listing agreements have certain unique elements that describe the rights and duties of the agent and the principal.

Elements of Listing Agreements

The listing agreement should give sufficient facts so that parties to the agreement know definitely when the broker has fulfilled his agency. An adequate listing avoids misunderstanding between buyer and seller on whether certain personal property is included. Since the listing agreement is the first document leading to the closing of the sale, it must be accurate and complete. The minimum information to be included in a listing agreement shows:

1. The names of the parties to the contract, with appropriate signatures.
2. A legal description of the real estate listed, with a street address if applicable.
3. The terms of sale: the sales price; financing terms acceptable to the seller, such as the seller's willingness to accept a second mortgage or a purchase money mortgage as partial payment. The remaining balance of outstanding mortgages, with their terms as of the date of listing, should be stated.
4. A beginning and ending date of the listing agreement.

5. The nature of the listing agreement, for example, the right of the seller to list with other brokers, the right of the seller to sell the property personally without payment of a commission.
6. The agreement to pay a stated commission, usually a percent of the sales price.
7. A description of the personal property to be included in the sale, such as carpets, the TV antenna, draperies, and household appliances.

Although these items are covered in all written listing agreements, variations in listing agreements relate to the right of the seller (1) to sell the property personally without payment of a commission and (2) to list property with other brokers. These rights vary according to the type of listing agreement.

Types of Listing Agreements

The conditions under which a commission will be paid, and even the probability of sale at the highest price, may turn on the type of listing selected by the seller. The different listing arrangements include (1) open listings, (2) net listings, (3) exclusive agency, (4) exclusive right to sell, and (5) multiple listings. Strictly speaking, the last arrangement is not a separate listing type. It is a method of sharing an exclusive right to sell listing with other brokers. An explanation of these listings shows why real estate brokers recommend the exclusive right to sell listing agreement.

Open Listings.   The open listing gives the seller the right to list the property with competing brokers or to sell the property personally without liability for a commission. Some sellers believe that an open listing best serves their interest—that listing with ten brokers produces more prospects than does a single listing.

Real estate brokers recommend against open listings for several reasons. First, the owner may be subjected to commission claims by more than one broker. It is not always possible to definitely determine who was responsible for the sale. Controversy over this point may lead to expensive litigation. Second, brokers complain that because the commission is paid to the broker who first finds the buyer, an open listing does not protect the broker who diligently advertises the property. In fact, because of the possibility that the property may be sold without notice by competing brokers, brokers are unwilling to spend time and effort on a property for which they have no commission protection. Lastly, it is held that under an open listing brokers have an incentive to close the sale quickly and at a lower-than-market price.

Net Listings.   Under such listings the seller establishes a minimum acceptable net price. The real estate broker must add his commission to the required net as part of the sales price. For example, the net listing may state that the price will be such that the seller will realize $40,000. To realize a

$2,000 commission, the broker would list the price of the property at $42,000. In some states, the net listing is unlawful; universally, brokers avoid net listings, primarily because such listings are inconsistent with the agent-principal relationship.

While the agency relationship requires the broker to procure a buyer meeting terms specified by the seller, the net listing may produce a sale in which the broker receives less than the customary commission. Yet if the property is sold at a price considerably higher than is needed to give the broker the customary commission, the broker is not entitled to more than the customary commission. For instance, assume a net listing price of $40,000, a sale for $60,000, and a customary commission rate of 6 percent. The broker would earn only $3,600 from the seller—6 percent of $60,000. The net listing may also encourage sales to third parties friendly to the broker who later resell the property at a higher price to the disadvantage of the seller.

Exclusive Agency.   Although an exclusive agency allows the seller to sell his own property without payment of a commission, the seller agrees to list the property with only one broker during the listing term. The danger in this listing is that the broker risks collusion between his prospect and the seller, who may conspire to avoid the real estate commission. While the seller may sell the property independently through his own efforts, the broker's prospect and the seller may not postpone transfer until the listing agreement expires, intending to avoid the commission. If a sale is consummated after the listing agreement expires, the broker is legally entitled to the commission if the broker was the original and procuring cause of the sale.

Exclusive Right to Sell.   Real estate brokers recommend this listing that grants an exclusive right to sell the property during the listing term. A commission is paid even if the property is sold by the owner; in short, the broker is given exclusive rights to the commission over the listing term.

It is claimed that in return for the exclusive right of sale, brokers are more willing to spend advertising and sales effort to secure the most likely and most qualified buyer. Without legal protection for his commission, less promotional effort will be expended by the broker. If the property is listed at its marketable value, this type of listing probably serves the interest of both parties. Under this plan, the broker has sufficient time to test the market, design an advertising sales campaign, and dispose of the property under the best possible terms.

Such an agreement is especially critical for high-valued property, industrial property, and commercial property. It is not uncommon to grant exclusive right to sell listing agreements for industrial property over a six-month period. The longer period is required to solicit prospects over a regional or national market.

The exclusive right to sell agreement used in Texas is shown in Figure 16–2. Note that from a given date to a given date the seller grants "the ex-

FIGURE 16–2

Exclusive Right to Sell Listing

Multiple Listing Service	COLLIN COUNTY BOARD OF REALTORS *Official form© 1976 COLLIN COUNTY MLS*
	P. O. Box 416
	EXCLUSIVE LISTING AGREEMENT *Plano, Texas 75074*

DATE ON MKT	EXPIRATION DATE		MLS NO.	
AREA	TYPE	ADDRESS	CITY	
			PRICE	REALTOR NO.

COORD: _____ Features   11   12   13   14   15   16   17   18   19   20   21   22   23   24   25
STYLE: (CIRCLE ONE) 1 Trad   2 Col   3 E. Amer   4 Modern or Contp   5 Spanish or Med   6 English   7 French

MLS _____ ADDR _____ CITY _____ $ _____	FOR MLS OFFICE USE ONLY	BOOK
AREA _____ TYPE _____ DESCRIPTION _____ TAXES _____		
LIV. RM. _____ BR 1 _____ STORY _____ EXT. _____		BILL
DIN. RM. _____ BR 2 _____ AGE _____ INT. _____		
BRK. RM. _____ BR 3 _____ GARAGE _____ FNDTN. _____		
KIT. _____ BR 4 _____ HEATG _____ ROOF _____		PIX
DEN _____ BR 5 _____ COOLG. _____ FENCE _____		
LOT SIZE _____		COMP
SCHOOLS _____		
REMARKS: _____		

Measurements Approximate
Financing — Subject to Confirmation by Mortgagee:
1st MORG. _____ UNPD _____ INT. RATE _____ %
YRS _____ DATED _____ LOT _____ BK. _____ ADD. _____
MO. PAY. _____ OWNER _____ PH. _____
REALTOR _____ PH. _____
AGENT _____ PH. _____
COMM. % _____ COMM. SPLIT _____

All Blanks Must Be Filled In.
Any Information Outside Box Will
Not Be Reproduced!

The undersigned Owner represents that the information hereinafter set forth is true and correct according to the best of his knowledge and belief.

To:_____ In consideration of services to be performed by you and/or other members of the Multiple Listing Service of the Collin County Board of Realtors, and your agreement to list the following described real estate situated in the County of _____ State of Texas: Lot _____ Block_____ Addition _____

Otherwise known as _____.
together with and including the following fixtures and articles of personal property attached to such real estate and owned by me(strike any that are not applicable): Air conditioning and heating equipment, venetian blinds, window shades, light fixtures, mail boxes, radio and television aerials and:

I hereby irrevocably appoint you my exclusive agent, with sole authority to sell said property at a price of $_____ or on such terms as I may approve:

    I understand that you as a member of the Multiple Listing Service of the Collin County Board of Realtors, and you have agreed to file this listing with said service. This agreement shall be considered a Multiple Listing as of the date of execution.

    You shall endeavor with all reasonable efforts to find a purchaser for said real estate on the terms set forth. You may take such actions to sell the property as you may deem advisable in your discretion, including the listing of the property with cooperating brokers, as well as the other members of the Multiple Listing Service.

    I agree to refer to you all inquiries which I may receive relating to such property, to conduct through you all negotiations relating to the sale of the property, and to cooperate with you fully in your efforts to sell the property.

    You shall have the exclusive right to place "For Sale" and Multiple Listing Service signs on or about the premises, and may enter the premises at any reasonable time for the purpose of showing the same to prospects. You shall not be responsible or liable in any way for vandalism, theft, or damage of any kind whatsoever sustained by said property during the period of this agreement, whether caused by prospects admitted to the property by you, or otherwise, unless caused by your failure to exercise reasonable precautions.

    The term of this agreement shall commence on _____ and shall continue for _____ days thereafter. If said property is sold prior to the termination of this agreement, whether by you, by me, or by any other person, or if the property is sold within 180 days after the termination of this agreement to anyone with whom you or any member of Multiple Listing Service negotiated during the period of this contract and of whose name you have notified me by written notice delivered to me personally or mailed to me at the address stated below within 10 days after the

termination of this agreement. In either such event, I agree to pay to you in _____ , Texas, a commission in cash equal to _____ per cent (_____%) of the selling price, except that no commission shall be payable to you if the property is sold after this agreement has terminated and while the property is under an exclusive listing with another member of the Multiple Listing Service of the _____ Board of Realtors. You may divide any commission payable hereunder with other licensed cooperating brokers or members of the Multiple Listing Service, but, it is agreed that, notwithstanding any such agreement to division of commissions, I shall be fully protected in paying all commissions payable hereunder solely to you.

    An exchange of said real estate shall be deemed a sale thereof for the purposes of this agreement. In the event of an exchange, you are authorized to represent and receive commissions from both parties.

    If this agreement is signed by more than one person, it shall constitute the joint and several obligations of each.

NOTICE: In accordance with the Law, this property is offered without respect to race, color, creed or national origin.

DATED_____

ACCEPTED:

Realtor, Member of the Collin County Board of Realtors

By _____   Address _____   Telephone _____

2-76

FIGURE 16–3

Multiple Listing Agreement for Income and Commercial Property

---

INCOME AND COMMERCIAL PROPERTY

NEBA Form   **EXCLUSIVE SALE AND LISTING AGREEMENT**   ....Washington

6-1-76   .... 19 ....

    In consideration of the services to be performed by the undersigned broker, herein after called Agent, the undersigned Seller does hereby grant to said Agent for a term of _____months (three months unless otherwise designated) from date hereof and effective immediately the sole and exclusive right to submit offers to purchase and to receipt for deposit in connection therewith, on the following described property situated

in the City of _____ County of

_____ ,Washington, to wit: All of that property, belonging to me, commonly known and designated as

_____ , legally described as follows or as on the reverse side hereof:

_____

_____

_____

The undersigned seller warrants that he has the legal right to sell the above described property at the terms and conditions set forth herein. The information given on the Listing Form on this agreement, and any provisions set forth on the reverse side hereof are hereby made a part of this Agreement.

SELLING PRICE $ _____ POSSESSION _____ TERMS _____

See PAGE 2 FOR PROPERTY DETAILS.

    The owner authorizes the Agent to install a key-box on the premises, which box may be opened by a master key held by all members of the North End Brokers Association, Inc., and their salesmen, and in said box one key to the premises will be kept; and allow Agent or North End Brokers Association, Inc., members to show said property at any reasonable time.

    Seller agrees to furnish purchaser's policy of title insurance from any title insurance company authorized to do business in the State of Washington evidencing ability to convey good and sufficient title and agrees to pay one-half of any escrow costs. Rents, insurance, taxes, interest and reserves on assumed encumbrances are to be prorated as of date of closing, which shall be within thirty days after title report, or after financing, whichever is later, with possession to be furnished not later than closing unless otherwise agreed. Sale shall be closed in office of agent or any escrow company or title insurance company or lending institution in the State of Washington unless otherwise agreed.

    When said Agent procures an offer to purchase on the terms set forth in this Agreement, or on other terms acceptable to the seller, or if seller removes said property from the market, or if seller directly or indirectly or through any other person or entity other than said Agent during the term hereof sells, contracts to sell, or exchanges or leases with option to purchase, or if seller within six months after the expiration of this Agreement, should sell, contract to sell, or exchange or lease with option to purchase said property to any person who has during the term of this Agreement been advised directly or indirectly through the offices of the Listing Broker or any member of the North End Brokers Association, Inc., that the property is for sale, then said Agent shall be conclusively presumed to be the procuring cause of such sale, contract of sale or exchange, or lease with option to

purchase and said seller agrees to pay said Agent a commission of .... % of selling price of said property.

    In the event that the Agent shall employ an attorney to enforce the foregoing or any other terms of this agreement, and shall be successful in enforcing the same, seller agrees to pay a reasonable attorney's fee and any court costs incurred in connection therewith.

    If the seller during the period of this agreement accepts any offer to purchase the premises and the sale pursuant to said acceptance fails to close for any reason whatsoever, the period of this agreement shall continue from effective date hereof until 30 days after expiration date, or,30 days after date upon which earnest money is forfeited or refunded, whichever is later.

    It is understood that said Agent is a member of the North End Brokers Association, Inc., and it is further agreed that said Agent shall refer this listing to said Association to be by it referred to all other participating members of said Association and said other members shall have the same rights and privileges under this Agreement as though each of them had executed a separate Agreement containing the terms and provisions hereof. The agents are not responsible for vandalism, theft, or damage of any nature whatsoever to the property.

    Seller agrees that he will not accept any offer unless submitted by the undersigned Agent or unless said offer recites that the submitting broker is a member, of the North End Brokers Association, Inc.

    Seller hereby acknowledges receipt of copy of this Agreement, and approves all information contained on this form and on reverse side hereof, however, seller hereby authorizes said agent to insert and amend legal description over all signatures but does not authorize said Agent to insert or change any of the financial details of the property over the signature.

    As a duly appointed Agent for seller and in consideration of the appointment thereof by the seller, the undersigned Agent does hereby agree during ther term hereof to make efforts to sell such property, and to process the listing through the North End Brokers Association, Inc., and to cause it to be delivered to all other participating members of said Organization. Said Agent further agrees to have a picture taken of the premises to be distributed to such members of the North End Brokers Association, Inc., who participate in the picture listing service.

    All rights extended to members of the NEBA, Inc. herein are likewise extended to members of cooperating Multiples. Any offer submitted to Seller by a broker who is not a member of NEBA, Inc. or a cooperating Multiple must be approved in writing by the undersigned agent.

    It is understood North End Brokers Association, Inc., is not a party to this agreement, and its sole responsibility is to, upon receipt of this agreement, and subject to its rules in respect thereto, refer it to its other members.

    There are no other agreements except as contained herein.

AGENT .... SELLER

BY   ....SELLER

                                                                   (Both husband and wife must sign if community property)

clusive right and authority to sell the property hereinafter described for the price and upon the terms hereinafter set forth." In addition, the seller grants exclusive "For Sale" sign privileges on the listed property and agrees to refer to the broker all inquiries received during the listing period.

Multiple Listings. The multiple listing combines features of the open listing and the exclusive right to sell agreement. Actually, the multiple listing is not a separate type of listing since it is based on an exclusive right to sell agreement. (See Figure 16–3 for a multiple listing form used by a multiple listing service in Seattle, Washington.)

> For example the seller agrees to grant to you, for the term of 120 days from the date hereof and to expire at midnight on January 15, 19—, the exclusive right and privilege to sell or exchange the above-described property for the sum of _____ or at such lesser price or terms to which I may consent.

In the multiple listing agreement, the seller acknowledges that the property will be submitted to a multiple listing service. With this agreement, members of the multiple listing group or service share commissions on an open listing basis. All listings of a member group are shared with other firms, effectively increasing the inventory of properties for sale among member brokers. As property is newly listed, details are immediately distributed to subscribing members. When a sale is made, the broker who originated the listing shares the commission with the selling broker. The success of the system depends on immediate distribution of the newly listed properties and on prompt reporting of sales to member brokers.

1. Multiple Listing Advantages. Provided that the multiple listing arrangement does not disturb the usual agency-principal relationship, the National Association of Realtors® recommends multiple listing service. It has defined multiple listing as "a means of making possible the orderly dissemination and correlation of listing information to Realtor® members who may better serve the buying and selling public" and has enumerated eight advantages of multiple listing:

1. Buyers and sellers receive the benefit of cooperation between Realtors® rather than being restricted to the offerings of a single agent or a series of agents.
2. Sellers of property, while retaining the professional services of a single agent, have access to the marketing facilities of all Realtors® who participate.
3. Buyers, by contacting only one Realtor®, may have access to the listings of all Realtors® who participate.
4. The needs of the buyer and seller are more readily matched, thus serving their interests, and saving time in more readily acquiring or disposing of property.
5. Negotiations are carried on under rules of procedure designed to assure effective practice, thus furthering the interest of clients and the public.

6. Communities can have a constant inventory of available residential property, useful in analyzing community needs and in attracting business and industry.
7. A centralized source of current market information is created, making available statistical data which is not otherwise accessible.
8. Current market information, which is readily available through Multiple Listing, means that Realtors®, their clients and the public are better served and informed.[8]

Multiple listing services often discourage the listing of properties that are overpriced or otherwise unmarketable. Through the multiple listing service the property owner benefits from exposure among member brokers who are assured of exclusive commission protection during the listing period. In this way the owner receives the benefits of the open listing as well as the promotional advantages of the exclusive right to sell agreement. Further, the owner retains the right to negotiate the commission since the multiple listing service is prohibited from controlling, establishing, or influencing commission rates.

2. Multiple Listing Administration. Though administrative practices vary, the experience of a multiple listing service of more than 200 members illustrates the administrative procedures followed by such services. The code of ethics in the bylaws of the North End Brokers Association, Inc., of Seattle, Washington, provides an additional advantage to listing sellers:

> The acceptance of an exclusive listing imposes the obligation of rendering skilled and conscientious service; when a Broker is unable to render such services either himself or with the aid of his member Broker, he should not accept the listing.
>
> Before offering a property listed with him by the owner, it is the Broker's duty to advise the owner honestly and intelligently regarding its fair market value.[9]

Membership in the association may be obtained by licensed real estate brokers who agree to abide by its rules, regulations, and bylaws and to carry the required insurance for membership. The initiation fees are equal to five times the book value of the association divided by the number of the broker members. The association's working capital is supplied by having members pay 2 percent of all real estate commissions to the listing service. For an exclusively listed property, the selling member is entitled to two thirds of the sale commission; one third of the commission is paid to the listing member broker. Rules provide for variations in these shares as agreed to in writing by cooperating brokers.

---

[8] *Handbook on Multiple Listing Policy* (Chicago: National Association of Realtors®, 1975), p. 9.

[9] Bylaws of North End Brokers Association, Inc., Seattle, Washington, 1976, p. 16.

Listing Termination

Listings are automatically terminated by a sale. An event that prevents performance—for example, death, physical incapacity of the principal, or destruction of the premises—also terminates the listing agreement. A listing may be ended before the date of termination by mutual consent of the agent and the principal. Suppose, however, that before the expiration date the seller cancels the listing agreement. In this event the broker is entitled to compensation for the time and money he has expended in exercising the agency.

On the other hand, if the broker has completed his agency assignment, finding a purchaser ready, willing, and able to buy on the seller's terms, the principal cannot intentionally cancel the agreement to avoid payment of a commission. To avoid misunderstanding, the listing agreement should require that both parties must give advance notice of termination. One good reason for a written listing is that it makes provision for a beginning and ending listing date. Agreement on the listing period minimizes controversies over payment of commissions.

Commission Liability

To enforce payment of a commission the real estate broker must satisfy special requirements: (1) the broker must prove employment; (2) the broker must hold a valid real estate license; (3) the broker must be the procuring cause of the sale; and (4) the broker must meet the purpose of the agency—to find a willing and qualified purchaser who agrees to the sale terms required by the seller. In many instances, each of these requirements is subject to interpretation.

Valid License Required. The state laws consistently hold that claims for payment of real estate commission are unenforceable unless the broker or salesperson held a valid license at the time the sale was made. Questions on the enforceability of commissions arise when brokers have not renewed their license, or when their license was revoked or suspended at the time the broker claimed a commission. On this point a typical statute reads:

> No person shall bring or maintain any action in the courts of this State for the collection of compensation for the performance of any of the acts mentioned in this Chapter without alleging and proving that he was a duly licensed real estate broker or salesman at the time the alleged cause of action arose.[10]

It therefore follows that brokers may not enforce payment of a commission unless their license is valid during the time the broker performs any act or service for which payment of a real estate commission is claimed.

---

[10] *Georgia Real Estate Manual, Chapter 84–14 and Rules and Regulations* (Atlanta: Secretary of State, 1974), p. 4.

Procuring Cause of the Sale. Most litigation over the payment of real estate commissions probably arises from disputes over who was the procuring cause of the sale. Assume that the broker shows a buyer a dwelling 30 days before an exclusive right to sell listing expires. Suppose that the asking price is $40,000, with a commission of 6 percent, or $2,400, and suppose that after the listing has terminated the same buyer buys directly from the seller for $38,000. If the seller accepts and it is later proven that the broker was the initial cause of the sale, the seller would be liable for payment of the commission of 6 percent on $38,000.

Brokers use several means to prove that they are the procuring cause of the sale. In sales of commercial and industrial properties, the experienced broker sends a letter to the principal which identifies the prospect. In sales of dwellings, the broker keeps the seller informed of prospects by submitting their names to the seller on printed forms. Because buyers may be shown the same house by more than one broker, the selling broker may have to prove that he was the procuring cause of sale. In disputes over commissions the facts of each case control. A mere letter stating that the broker has shown the property to a specific client may not in itself establish a valid claim.

The broker is on especially weak grounds if he abandons a prospect. Assume that a broker abandons a prospect for, say, 60 days, and that the same property is shown to the identical prospect by a second broker. Though the first broker was the first party to show the property to the prospect, he abandoned the prospect to a second broker who is the true cause of the sale and would therefore be entitled to the commission.

The rule is that the broker must perform within the time specified in the contract. If the broker abandons his efforts and the property is sold by a competing broker, a mere showing that the first broker was the party who initially introduced the purchaser to the property may be insufficient to establish the first broker as the procuring cause of sale. It should be added that the commission does not rest on the amount of work completed by a competing broker. Rather, it is a question of who has performed the agency —to find a buyer willing and able to purchase under terms acceptable to the seller.

Broker Employment. The listing agreement provides evidence of employment. To collect a commission the broker must prove that he was employed to sell the property. In most states permitting oral listing agreements, frequent disputes arise when the broker brings forth a buyer who later purchases the property directly from the seller. Though the sale is completed, in the absence of a finding that the broker was employed, the seller is not liable for a commission. Even though the broker may have been influential in executing the sale, he is not entitled to a commission unless he was employed.

Qualified Buyer. Buyers who offer to purchase a seller's property on terms unacceptable to the seller do not establish a claim for commission.

In the listing agreement the seller specifies the conditions under which the property will be sold. Unless the seller accepts the purchaser's offer to buy on terms other than the seller's original terms, the broker has not earned a commission. Similarly, if the buyer does not qualify for the required loan, the listing agreement will usually excuse the seller from paying a commission since the credit of the buyer was inadequate to meet the specified terms of sale.

REAL ESTATE MARKETING

Real estate salespersons and brokers must have the skills common to successful salesmanship. As these skills are developed, success in real estate depends heavily on technical real estate knowledge. On this score, new and compulsory educational programs, rising licensing requirements, and the growing number of real estate designations earned through real estate trade associations attest to the rising level of competence required of real estate brokers and their employees.

To show the emphasis on practical real estate knowledge, it is deemed worthwhile to highlight the leading informational sources developed by brokers to expedite sales; and since real estate brokers tend to specialize, the discussion centers on both residential and income-producing properties.

Single-Family Dwellings

The central problem in the sale of single-family dwellings is to classify prospects to save time and disappointment. Real estate offices are confronted with buyers who show only a casual interest in a purchase or are merely curious and without strong motives for purchase. Other buyers have the motive but not the down payment or the monthly income to finance a purchase. These buyers inspect model homes, attend home show exhibitions, and eagerly respond to advertisements, but they are not qualified prospects. Brokers qualify all real estate prospects according to their motives for purchase and their financial ability.

Qualifying the Prospect. In qualifying prospects, brokers conduct the initial interview to learn the minimum facts relevant to the purchase of a dwelling:

1. The full name of the prospect.
2. The address and phone numbers of the prospect's business and residence.
3. The type and class of property desired.
4. The motive for buying.
5. The location desired.
6. The prospect's occupational history.

7. Positions held by the prospect—past and present.
8. The family income bracket.
9. The marital status of the prospect.
10. The cash available for the down payment and closing.
11. The financial terms desired.
12. Property now owned by the prospect.
13. Current debts of the prospect.
14. The prospect's children, by sex and age.
15. School facilities desired.
16. Hobbies.
17. Club and other significant memberships.[11]

With this information at hand, the salesperson may match with current listings the desires of the prospect's family and the prospect's financial ability. Seldom will the buyer find the ideal house that meets his needs; seldom will the seller find a purchaser who is willing to pay his initial price and meet the terms of the first offer to sell. The salesperson's skill in helping the buyer and seller negotiate a sale may determine final sale results.

Contrast with Owner Sales.   It is estimated that less than 2 percent of owners who attempt to sell without the services of a real estate broker are successful.[12] To avoid payment of commission, a seller who advertises his or her property for a direct sale operates under certain handicaps. First, the seller must patronize prospects who are mere curiosity seekers, nuisances, speculators, dreamers, and/or high-risk buyers. Second, the seller is unaware of the preferences of the buyers—a large lot, garden space, a large master bedroom, a full basement, and the like. Third, the seller is usually unfamiliar with the financial arrangements that would expedite the sale. The seller has no way of determining whether the buyer would be financially able to arrange purchase and wastes much time in dealing with financially unqualified buyers. Fourth, without working through a third party, the seller is unable to overcome buyer resistance on minor points—buyers are reluctant to raise objections or questions about the seller's house. The seller may create added buyer suspicions by praising the property.

It is questionable whether the seller who burdens himself with these inconveniences saves the commission. The buyer, knowing that he is dealing directly with the seller, may submit an offer that is less the usual commission. Conversely, the buyer may find that the seller has increased his price to include the commission. More than likely, the seller has an inflated idea of the value of his property, overpricing it to such an extent that it remains

---

[11] Adapted from Harry Grant Atkinson and Percy E. Wagner, *Modern Real Estate Practice: An Introduction to a Career in Real Estate Brokerage* (Homewood, Ill.: Dow Jones-Irwin, Inc., 1974), pp. 191–92.

[12] William R. Beaton and Robert J. Bond, *Real Estate* (Pacific Palisades, Calif.: Goodyear Publishing Company, Inc., 1976), p. 52.

unsold for a long period, thus raising questions among prospects about possible undisclosed deficiencies.

Recall also that the seller has only one property. By working through a real estate broker, the buyer is able to select from an inventory that gives him the widest possible choice. Consequently, even though the buyer and the seller may negotiate a price that divides the commission, it is doubtful whether the saving is worth the inconveniences and risks.

The Listing Inventory. Listings of dwellings for sale may take the form of a simple card file or of printed forms with a photograph, the latter being more common for multiple listings and for offices with numerous branch offices. Brokers in some areas maintain computerized records accompanied by audio-video displays of offers to sell. In accepting the initial listing, certain information must be entered on the card to serve as a basis for sales persons' study of the property. A typical listing form for a single-family dwelling is shown in Figure 16–4.

Note that the form includes square footage; details of the building and its equipment; lot size; and more important the outstanding mortgage with its terms and the remaining balance at the date of listing. A photograph is helpful as a means of recalling other details of the property. It should be emphasized that these files are not for the prospect—they serve as a record for the sales staff and cooperating brokers.

Income-producing Property

As indicated in previous chapters, financing techniques and tax factors bear significantly on real estate decisions. It would be difficult to market income-producing real estate without a working knowledge of cash flow analysis and prevalent financing methods and their many variations. Some real estate brokers deal exclusively with income properties. They develop expertise in presenting conventional income properties for single ownership or multiple ownership in the form of a partnership, syndication, or purchase. The more sophisticated real estate brokers participate in real estate exchanges that appeal to investors who wish to postpone capital gains taxes.

The demands upon real estate brokers operating in this area have led to numerous specialized courses and forms that help brokers present investment advantages to the investor in income-producing property. While programmable calculators and computer facilities are available to analyze real estate investments, even the one person office may present complex income analysis by using standard forms. To illustrate, consider the cash flow form published by the Realtors® National Marketing Institute of the National Association of Realtors®.

A work sheet for calculating cash flow is shown in Figure 16–5. This sheet shows cash flow over 15 years, assuming a mortgage of $270,000, 25 years, 9 percent interest, with monthly payments of $2,265.83. Starting

FIGURE 16–4

A Listing Form for a Single-Family Dwelling Approved by the Texas Association of Realtors ®

LISTING CONTRACT

To_____, Agent, _____, Texas:

    For and in consideration of your listing for sale the property described on the reverse side hereof, said property being owned in fee simple by me or us, I or we hereby appoint you exclusive agent and grant you the exclusive right to sell said property for a period of

_____days from this date, at the price of $_____, and within the authority herein granted, you are hereby authorized to enter into a contract with any person, firm or corporation desiring to purchase said property, which contract shall be fully binding upon me or us.

    In the event a sale of said property is made within the time, at the price, and upon the terms as specified on the reverse side, or at such other time or price and upon such other terms as may be acceptable to me or us, I or we agree to execute and acknowledge and deliver to the purchaser or purchasers a good and sufficient general warranty deed to said property, to furnish sufficient title evidence, complete abstract of title or owner's title policy certified as to date of sale, to prorate taxes and rents as of the date of delivery of the deed, and to pay all other expenses customarily paid by the seller upon conveyance of real property, I or we further agree to pay you, at _____,

Texas, a commission of_____% of the price received from such sale, and you shall have the right to retain such commission out of any proceeds from such sale coming into your hands.

    Any person, firm or corporation you may interest in the purchase of said property either directly or indirectly shall be considered to be your customer for a period of_____months after the termination of this contract or any renewal thereof.

    I or we agree that attached list of furniture or other personal property, or a continuation of the description of the real property shall be considered a part of this contract.

    The agent holding this exclusive listing agrees to advertise the property mentioned herein and put forth every effort to sell the property at the amount stated above.

_____   _____
Realtor   Owner

_____   _____
By   Owner

Approved by the Texas Association of Realtors

FORM NO 18

Front

Date_____, 19 _____

Lot(s)_____Block_____Outlot(s)_____Div._____Addition_____

Locally known as_____, Texas_____Classification_____

Price $_____	Construction_____Stories_____Zoned_____
Loan_____Type_____	No. Rooms_____B. R._____Baths_____Porches_____
Int._____% Length loan_____yrs.	Roof_____Floors_____Age_____
Payments_____	Condition_____Heat_____Int. Walls_____
2nd Mtg._____	Tile in_____Gar._____Out Bldgs._____
Loan Comm._____	Lot Size_____Inside or Corner_____Facing_____
Contr. of sale_____	Paved_____Fences_____Trees_____Sewerage_____
Owner_____	Blks. to Bus_____School_____Comm. Cen._____
_____	Occupancy_____St. & Co. Tax $_____City Tax $_____
Res. Phone_____Bus. Ph._____	Will trade for_____
Other Phone_____	Abstr. or title policy_____Possession_____
Remarks_____	Remarks_____
How Shown_____	_____
Seller's Atty._____	_____
Title Co._____	Listing Agent_____Key_____

Back

FIGURE 16–5

Cash Flow Calculation for a Prospect

Cash Flow Analysis

Name _Potential Client_   Date_____   Purpose _15 Yr. Study_

Mortgage Data

	Encumbrances	Amount	Remaining Term	Payment Period	Interest Rate	Payment Period	Remarks
1	1st Mortgage	270 000	25 Yr.	Mo.	9%	2 265 83	
2	2nd Mortgage						
3	3rd Mortgage						

		(1) Year: 1	(2) Year: 2	(3) Year: 3	(4) Year: 4	(5) Year: 5	(6) Year: 6
4	Initial Investment	95 000					
5	1st Mortgage	270 000	266 988	263 693	260 089	256 147	251 836
6	2nd Mortgage						
7	3rd Mortgage						
8	Total Encumbrances						
9	Principal Reduction	3 012	3 295	3 942	4 311		4 717

Ownership Analysis of Property Income: Taxable Income

10	Total Gross Income	63 960					
11	– Vacancy & Credit Loss	3 840					
12	– Operating Expenses	23 650					
13	Net Operating Income	36 470	36 470	36 470	36 470	36 470	36 470
14	– Non-Operating Expense						
15	– Interest 9%	24 170	23 895	23 586	23 248	22 879	22 473
16	– Depreciation 25 Yr. 125% DB	14 636	13 935	13 270	12 637	12 036	11 466
17	Taxable Income	(2 344)	(1 360)	(386)	585	1 555	2 531

Cash Flows

18	Net Operating Income	36 470	36 470	36 470	36 470	36 470	36 470
19	Princp. & Int. Pymts.	27 190	27 190	27 190	27 190	27 190	27 190
20	– Funded Reserves						
21	– Capital Additions						
22	Cash Flow before Taxes	9 280	9 280	9 280	9 280	9 280	9 280
23	– Income Tax	(938)	(544)	(154)	234	622	1 012
24	Cash Flow after Taxes	10 218	9 824	9 434	9 046	8 658	8 268

Analysis of Sales Proceeds   Year:

	Adjusted Basis			Excess Depreciation			Tax on Gain %	
25	Original Basis			Total Depr.			Excess	
26	+ Capital Improvements			S L Depr.			Cap. Gain	
27	+ Costs of Sale			Excess Depr.			Cap. Gain	
28	Sub-Total						Total Tax Liab.	
29	– Depreciation			Gain			Sales Proceeds	
30	– Partial Sales			Sales Price			Sales Price	
31	AB at Sale			– AB			– Sales Costs	
32				Gain			– Mortgage	
33				– Excess			Proceeds before Taxes	
34				Cap. Gain			– Total Tax Liab.	
							Proceeds after Taxes	

FIGURE 16–5 (*continued*)

		(1) Year: 7	(2) Year: 8	(3) Year: 9	(4) Year: 10	(5) Year: 11	(6) Year: 12
4	Initial Investment						
5	1st Mortgage	247 119	241 961	236 318	230 147	223 396	216 012
6	2nd Mortgage						
7	3rd Mortgage						
8	Total Encumbrances						
9	Principal Reduction	5 158	5 643	6 171	6 751	7 384	8 077

Ownership Analysis of Property Income: **Taxable Income**

		(1)	(2)	(3)	(4)	(5)	(6)
10	Total Gross Income						
11	− Vacancy & Credit Loss						
12	− Operating Expenses						
13	Net Operating Income	36 470	36 470	36 470	36 470	36 470	36 470
14	− Non-Operating Expense						
15	− Interest 9%	22 032	21 547	21 019	20 439	19 806	19 113
16	− Depreciation 2.54n. 125%	10 923	10 408	9 919	9 454	8 392	7 972
17	Taxable Income	3 515	4 515	5 532	6 577	8 272	9 385

Cash Flows

		(1)	(2)	(3)	(4)	(5)	(6)
18	Net Operating Income	36 470	36 470	36 470	36 470	36 470	36 470
19	− Princp. & Int. Pymts.	27 190	27 190	27 190	27 190	27 190	27 190
20	− Funded Reserves						
21	− Capital Additions						
22	Cash Flow before Taxes	9 280	9 280	9 280	9 280	9 280	9 280
23	− Income Tax 40%	1 406	1 806	2 213	2 631	3 309	3 754
24	Cash Flow after Taxes	7 874	7 474	7 067	6 649	5 971	5 526

Analysis of Sales Proceeds   Year: 15

	Adjusted Basis		Excess Depreciation		Tax on Gain %		
25	Original Basis	365 000	Total Depr.	156 652	Excess		
26	+ Capital Improvements		S/L Depr.	174 395	Cap. Gain 50,000 25	12 500	
27	+ Costs of Sale 7%	25 550	Excess Depr.	0	Cap. Gain 81,102 30	24 331	
28	Sub-Total	390 550			Total Tax Liab.	36 831	
29	− Depreciation	156 652	**Gain**		**Sales Proceeds**		
30	− Partial Sales		Sales Price	365 000	Sales Price	365 000	
31	AB at Sale	233 898	− AB	233 898	− Sales Costs	25 550	
32			Gain	131 102	− Mortgage	178 868	
33			− Excess	0	Proceeds before Taxes	160 582	
34			Cap. Gain	131 102	− Total Tax Liab.	36 831	
					Proceeds after Taxes	123 751	

with an initial investment of $95,000 and a gross income of $63,960 in the first year, net operating income for the first year amounts to $36,470. Deducting mortgage interest and depreciation produces a tax shelter of $2,344. Considering income tax savings, depreciation allowances, and mortgage payment, in the first year the property shows a cash flow after taxes of $10,218. These calculations are projected over 15 years.

In addition, the form shows actual cash proceeds, assuming that the property is sold at $365,000. In short, presentation of an investment opportunity with such a form allows the trained real estate broker to present complex investments to the prospect, given the available financing, recommended depreciation schedule, estimated gross income, and operating expenses. Such a form may be completed for other sale terms and assumptions to show the potential cash flow and sale proceeds. It will be appreciated that this type of analysis, which is prepared for the prospect, calls for specialized training and instruction beyond the usual salesmanship skills.

THE FAIR HOUSING PLAN

In addition to observing state license laws, real estate brokers and salespersons must observe certain other state and federal legislation that affects real estate activities. The National Fair Housing Act of 1968 represents one of these statutes. Current policy of the United States is

> . . . to provide, within constitutional limitations, for fair housing throughout the United States.

With the August 22, 1974, amendment, Congress declared it unlawful

(a) To refuse to sell or rent after the making of a bona fide offer, or to refuse to negotiate for the sale or rental of, or otherwise make unavailable or deny, a dwelling to any person because of race, color, religion, sex, or national origin.

(b) To discriminate against any person in the terms, conditions, or privileges of sale or rental of a dwelling, or in the provision of services or facilities in connection therewith, because of race, color, religion, sex, or national origin.

(c) To make, print, or publish, or cause to be made, printed, or published any notice, statement, or advertisement, with respect to the sale or rental of a dwelling that indicates any preference, limitation, or discrimination based on race, color, religion, sex, or national origin, or an intention to make any such preference, limitation, or discrimination.

(d) To represent to any person because of race, color, religion, sex, or national origin that any dwelling is not available for inspection, sale, or rental when such dwelling is in fact so available.

(e) For profit, to induce or attempt to induce any person to sell or rent any dwelling by representations regarding the entry or prospective entry into the neighborhood of a person or persons of a particular race, color, religion, sex, or national origin.[13]

Financial institutions active in placing real estate mortgages are prohibited from discriminating in the fixing of the amount, interest rate, duration, or other terms and conditions of loans because of race, color, religion, sex, or national origin. Further, the same law prohibits denial of membership in real estate organizations because of race, color, religion, sex, or national origin.

The Department of Housing and Urban Development has listed certain other acts prohibited by the Fair Housing Law:

1. Refusing to sell or rent to, deal or negotiate with any person (Section 804[a]).
2. Discriminating in terms or conditions for buying or renting housing (Section 804[b]).
3. Denying that housing is available for inspection, sale, or rent when it really is available (Section 804[d]).
4. "Blockbusting"—for profit, persuading owners to sell or rent housing by telling them that minority groups are moving into the neighborhood (Section 804[e]).[14]

The same publication limits exemptions under the act to a fairly narrow group of activities:

The sale or rental of single-family houses owned by a private individual owner of three or fewer such single-family houses if:

A broker is not used.

Discriminatory advertising is not used.

No more than one house in which the owner was not the most recent resident is sold during any two-year period.

Rentals of rooms or units in owner-occupied multi-dwellings for two to four families, if discriminatory advertising is not used.

Limiting the sale, rental, or occupancy of dwellings which a religious organization owns or operates for other than a commercial purpose to persons of the same religion, if membership in that religion is not restricted on account of race, color or national origin.

Limiting to its own members the rental or occupancy of lodgings which a private club owns or operates for other than a commercial purpose.

---

[13] As amended, Public Law 93–383, Title VIII, Section 808(b) (1), August 22, 1974, 88 Stat. 729.

[14] *Fair Housing USA* (Washington, D.C.: Department of Housing and Urban Development, no date).

Persons seeking relief under the act may file a complaint with the Secretary of Housing and Urban Development, or file a complaint directly to federal, state, or local courts. If the courts find that a person has suffered discrimination as interpreted under this act, the complainant may be awarded actual damages, $1,000 punitive court costs, and reasonable attorney's fees. Because of the legal complexities in interpreting this act, parties should turn to state organizations and legal counsel for advice.

SUMMARY

Starting with a narrow definition of a real estate broker—a person who acts for another in buying or selling real property for a fee or in the expectation of a fee—some states define real estate brokers to include appraisers, managers, auctioneers, and related services. To regulate these activities in the public interest the 50 states, the Virgin Islands, Washington, D.C., and Puerto Rico enforce real estate license laws. License laws require applicants for a salesperson's or broker's license to successfully pass an examination on real estate laws, land use controls, appraising, finance, title closing, and similar subjects. By July 1, 1982, California proposes to license brokers as Certified Real Property Brokers, requiring new applicants to have a college degree and pass a high-level examination. Besides these increasing legal requirements, over the last few years a number of states have established compulsory educational prerequisites calling for a minimum number of hours of instruction or college credit as qualification for salesperson's and broker's licenses.

Real estate brokers who solicit buyers for the purchase of a listed property are agents serving the seller-principal. Acting as an agent, the broker must be *loyal,* and acting as a *fiduciary,* the broker must *account for money deposits.* Brokers must *obey instructions, act in person,* and have *no personal interest* in the property which is not fully disclosed. Brokers may act for both the buyer and the seller *only upon full disclosure* to both parties. In exercising the agency, the broker is barred from making false statements or misrepresentations to the buyer-prospect.

Brokers function through listing agreements, which are preferably in writing (if not legally required to be in writing) and must conform to the usual requirements of an enforceable contract. The types of listings vary from the *open listing,* in which the seller retains the right to list the same property with another broker, to the *exclusive right to sell,* which is an agreement to pay a real estate commission if the property is sold—even by the owner. The *exclusive agency,* in contrast, prohibits the listing of the property with other agencies, though the seller may sell his own property without commission liability. *Multiple listing* is based on an exclusive right to sell which is shared by members of the multiple listing service. *Net listings,* illegal in some states and discouraged by real estate brokers generally, provide for the payment of a specified net amount to the seller at closing.

The broker must recover his commission from the price above the net listing amount. Net listings are inconsistent with the objectives of the agent-principal relationship.

A broker may enforce the payment of a commission only if he is employed, holds a valid broker's license, is the procuring cause of the sale, and finds a purchaser willing to meet the terms of sale specified by the seller.

Real estate brokers and their employees and salespersons must demonstrate more than the usual qualities of good salesmanship. In dealing with single-family dwellings, they must take care in qualifying prospects. In this respect, they provide services, conveniences, and protection largely unavailable to buyers and sellers who deal directly. Through buyer qualification and an adequate listing inventory, the broker serves as the local marketplace for real estate.

In dealing with income property, brokers have developed simplified standard forms that help the prospect understand the complexities of cash flow analysis. Other forms developed by the Realtors® National Marketing Institute cover real estate exchanges, the net aftertax amount realized on the sale of property, and related topics. Real estate brokers generally learn to use these forms by attending special classes to study the calculations employed.

The Fair Housing Act of 1968, as amended, establishes an enforceable federal fair housing policy throughout the United States. As a result of this legislation it is unlawful to refuse to rent or sell a dwelling because of race, color, religion, sex, or national origin. The exemptions to this legislation are limited to the sale of dwellings by an owner who owns not more than three houses at one time, provided that the property is sold without the aid of brokers, agents, or salespersons; rentals in dwellings occupied by four families or less if the owner occupies one of the units; and under certain circumstances, the rental or occupancy of lodgings by religious organizations and private clubs.

REVIEW QUESTIONS

1. Define a real estate broker. What activities may be included in the legal definition of the term?
2. What topics are generally covered by real estate license laws?
3. From the subject content of real estate license examinations, would you say that these examinations properly qualify persons to act as salespersons and brokers? Give reasons for your answer.
4. Why is it in the public interest to require compulsory courses for real estate salespersons and brokers?
5. What is the relationship between a real estate broker and a listing seller who agrees to pay a commission on the sale of his property?

6. Explain the significance of agent duties to the principal. Give examples of each duty.

7. What are the chief elements of a listing agreement?

8. Discuss the advantages and disadvantages of the open listing compared to an exclusive right to sell.

9. Contrast a net listing with a multiple listing. Explain fully.

10. Give an example of each of the four requirements for enforcing the payment of a real estate commission.

11. What information helps qualify a prospect for a single-family dwelling? Explain.

12. What are the main difficulties faced by sellers in selling their own property?

13. Compare the listing information for a single-family dwelling with the presentation of an income-producing property.

14. What is the national policy with respect to fair housing?

15. What activities come under the National Fair Housing Act?

16. What are the exemptions under this legislation?

SELECTED REFERENCES

Beaton, William R., and Bond, Robert J. *Real Estate,* chap. 5. Pacific Palisades, Calif.: Goodyear Publishing Company, Inc., 1976.

Bowman, Arthur G. *California Real Estate Principles,* chap. 6. Pacific Palisades, Calif.: Goodyear Publishing Company, Inc., 1972.

Ficek, Edmund F.; Henderson, Thomas P.; and Johnson, Ross H. *Real Estate Principles and Practices,* chap. 15. Columbus: Charles E. Merrill Publishing Co., 1976.

Hines, Mary Alice. *Principles and Practices of Real Estate,* chap. 11. Homewood, Ill.: Richard D. Irwin, Inc., 1976.

Unger, Maurice A. *Real Estate,* chap. 17. 5th ed. Cincinnati: South-Western Publishing Co., 1974.

Weimer, Arthur M.; Hoyt, Homer; and Bloom, George F. *Real Estate,* chap. 16. 6th ed. New York: Ronald Press Co., 1972.

17

Real Estate Title Closing

After reading this chapter, you should be familiar with the following points:

1 The abstract of title, its limitations and advantages.

2 The types of title insurance available to parties transferring an interest in real estate.

3 The extent of title insurance coverage and common exclusions.

4 The characteristics of the Torrens land title registration system.

5 The objectives of the Real Estate Settlement Procedures Act.

6 The duties of the lender required by the Real Estate Settlement Procedures Act.

7 The requirements of the Truth in Lending Act.

8 The Equal Credit Opportunity Act.

9 The responsibilities of the escrow agent in title closing procedures.

10 The procedures followed in closing a real estate transfer.

TRANSFERRING real estate titles calls for cooperation between the buyer, the seller, their legal representatives, financial institutions, title insurance companies, and public officials. The conveyance of legal title depends heavily on the accuracy of legal documents and financial statements prepared under the supervision of many persons. Before detailing closing procedures, it is helpful to review the steps taken by the buyer to obtain a marketable title. Moreover, parties to a title closing must observe certain federal laws: the Real Estate Settlement Procedures Act (RESPA), the Truth in Lending Act, and the Equal Credit Opportunity Act. With this background, it is relevant to review the closing procedure—the concluding part of the chapter.

MARKETABLE TITLE

It is the duty of the seller to furnish a marketable title. Even though the seller proceeds in good faith, it is not always possible for the seller to perform on this point. It may be impossible to convey a marketable title because of acts that occurred before the seller acquired his ownership. If the seller conveys a real estate interest by a warranty deed or a comparable conveyance, the buyer may proceed against the seller for default on the warranties. Yet if the seller does not have a marketable title, the buyer may not secure a valid title for property which he has purchased. Further, there is no point in proceeding against a seller who defaults on his warranties if the seller has no assets. To guard against these eventualities, the buyer may require an abstract of title or title insurance.

Abstract of Title

The abstract includes a summary of the recorded documents affecting title. Each instrument appears in the order in which it was placed on record, starting with the first document and ending with the most recent. A person preparing the abstract executes a certificate citing the records examined and stating that no taxes, judgments, liens, or encumbrances appear on these records except as shown in the abstract. The seller holds the abstract until such time as the property is transferred. For the next transfer, the original abstract is updated by searching the title from the date of the last certificate to the present. From a summary copy of all documents appearing of record since the date of the last abstract of title, the abstractor prepares a new certificate for the period covered by the new abstract.

Abstractor Liability. Note that the abstractor makes no judgment concerning the condition of the title. Moreover, the abstract is subject to error: the original recorded documents may be in error; the abstractor may have copied incorrect information. Documents may have been executed by minors or other legally incompetent persons. The abstract will not reflect the claims of tenants or others in possession of the property. In some states, an abstractor must be bonded and subject to state supervision. Clients may hold the abstractor responsible for negligence in overlooking recorded documents or transcribing information incorrectly.

Certificate of Title Opinion.   The next step requires an opinion on the marketability of the title. This is executed by an attorney who studies the abstract. Frequently the attorney will recommend steps to make the title marketable. The certificate of opinion, rendered by an attorney, will state that the owner has a marketable title with exceptions as noted. The opinion will list outstanding liens or encumbrances, easements, and other exceptions of record.

As the abstractor system developed, the limitations of the abstract-opinion gradually became apparent. The abstract system is slow and costly, especially if the instruments establishing the title are numerous and cover extensive periods of time. More important, the system protects buyers only to the extent of the liability assumed by the abstractor and the attorney with respect to omissions and negligence. Even then, liability is limited to the financial resources of the abstractor and the attorney rendering an opinion.

The Beginnings of Title Insurance.   These limitations led abstractors to develop a title plant—a system of filing documents by legal description and not by the names of the grantor and grantee, as it is done in public records. With such a record of documents on file, abstract companies increased the speed and accuracy of title searching. Abstract companies were soon willing to guarantee title as disclosed by records. At first, these companies guaranteed against errors and assumed liability without regard to proof of negligence. Their next step was to add risks that were not ascertainable from public records. From these beginnings, title insurance policies gradually substituted for the guarantee of the abstractor.

Title Insurance

Virtually all states have title insurance available to protect the insured against losses arising from title defects as of the date of the policy. Title insurance is issued only to qualified risks. A title insurance company will not knowingly issue insurance on a defective title. In comparing title insurance to other forms of insurance, certain features stand out:

1. Title insurance protects against loss or damages arising from past events. Future events are not covered.
2. Title insurance protection begins from the time the loss or damage occurs, and not at the date of the policy. For example, an owner issued a title insurance policy ten years ago is protected against defects in title arising from events that occurred before the title policy was issued.
3. Title insurance premiums are fully paid on the date of issue. After the initial payment, no other fees or premiums are added, though the insurance continues in force.

4. An owner's title insurance policy remains effective as long as the insured or his heirs have an interest in the property. If the title insurance applies only to the lender's interest, the insurance terminates with the payment of the mortgage or foreclosure.

5. Title insurance may be purchased directly from a title insurance company or indirectly through title insurance company agents or an approved local attorney. General insurance agents do not handle title insurance.[1]

Title insurance applies to the interest of the owner (the owner's policy) or of the lender (the loan policy). Most title insurance companies use standard forms developed by the American Land Title Association in the interest of uniformity. Title insurance is also available for a leasehold owner's policy, a leasehold loan policy, and a construction loan policy.

The Owner's Policy. The owner's policy is issued for an amount equal to the value of the land and existing improvements at the date of the policy. The insurance covers loss and damage, including attorney's fees, which occur to the owner because of (1) loss of title to the estate or interest insured, (2) any defect in title or liens or encumbrances on title, (3) lack of the right of access to or egress from the land, or (4) unmarketability of title.

The title insurance company will pay damages for any defect in the title not excepted in the policy and will defend the title in court at no expense to the owner. Insurance against no access protects the owner from being landlocked with no means of access to his property, for example, land not located on a public road or land located on a nonaccess highway with no other means of access. In these circumstances, the land has no access over a private easement and the owner would be protected from the resulting loss.

Title Insurance Exclusions. Title insurance companies do not insure (1) against losses resulting from zoning ordinances. Suppose that a building does not conform to the local zoning ordinance and must be removed or demolished, for example, a mobile home permanently attached to the land in a residential district in which mobile homes are prohibited. The difficulty of determining compliance with local zoning ordinances has led to this exclusion.

(2) Actions under the right of eminent domain are excepted unless they appear in the public records. Some agencies file a notice of taking in the public record, which serves as a constructive notice of the eminent domain proceeding. Title insurance will protect against condemnation actions if such notice has been filed in the public records.

Other exclusions cover (3) defects created by the insured, (4) unrecorded defects known to the insured but not known to the title insurer, and (5) defects occurring after the date of the policy. In addition, title insur-

---

[1] See William R. Beaton and Robert J. Bond, *Real Estate* (Pacific Palisades, Calif.: Goodyear Publishing Company, Inc., 1976), p. 117.

ance will not insure against (6) losses or damage by reason of "the dower, curtesy, homestead, community property, or other statutory marital rights, if any, of the spouse of any individual insured."

Moreover, upon examining title, the insurance company may add other exclusions, such as a mortgage which on the record has not been satisfied or defects in the title arising from the failure to record necessary documents. An example of the standard owner's policy is shown in Figure 17–1.

Loan Policies.   These policies are issued for an amount equal to the outstanding principal balance of the loan. The insurance is effective against matters of survey and against loss or damage due to defects, liens or encumbrances, lack of the right of access, unmarketability of title, and unenforceability of the mortgage (usury and truth in lending laws excepted). The lender is protected against the priority of other liens, mechanics' liens, and the invalidity of any assignment of the mortgage.

Loan policy exclusions parallel the exclusions of the owner's policy— losses because of zoning issues, unrecorded eminent domain actions, defects created by the insured, unrecorded defects known to the insured but not known to the insurer, defects after the date of the policy—and, in addition, loan policies exclude losses arising from the unenforceability of a mortgage because the insured failed to comply with "doing business" laws.

The loan policy continues in force for property acquired at foreclosure or by deed in lieu of foreclosure. Statutory liens for labor or material are excepted if the liens gain priority over the lien of the insured mortgage. However, liens arising from construction started after the date of the policy are insured.

The premium rates for title insurance are graduated according to the value of the interest insured. The current schedule issued by the Lawyers Title Insurance Corporation provides for a loan policy premium of $125 on original title insurance on a $50,000 first mortgage ($2.50 × 50). Original title insurance for an owner's policy of $50,000 would be $175 ($3.50 × 50).

The Torrens Land Title Registration System

This system for registering land titles was initiated by Sir Robert Torrens, who in 1858 authored the "Torrens" law in South Australia. It is similar to the system followed in registering ships. The system spread to England, Canada, and the Philippines, and is now authorized in California, Colorado, Illinois, Massachusetts, Minnesota, New York, North Carolina, Ohio, Oregon, Virginia, and Washington.[2] In Cook County, Illinois, the owner has the option of registering title with the county or city while remaining under the system of transferring titles prescribed by Tor-

---

[2] Edna L. Hebard and Gerald S. Meisel, *Principles of Real Estate Law* (Cambridge, Mass.: Schenkman Publishing Company, Inc., 1967), pp. 342–44.

FIGURE 17–1

Standard Form: American Land Title Association Owner's Policy

Lawyers Title Insurance Corporation

A Stock Company
Home Office ~ Richmond, Virginia

POLICY OF TITLE INSURANCE

AMOUNT

SCHEDULE A

DATE OF POLICY

$_____

NAME OF INSURED

_____

1. The estate or interest in the land described herein and which is covered by this policy is:

2. The estate or interest referred to herein is at Date of Policy vested in:

3. The land referred to in this Policy is described as follows:

Countersigned: _____

Issued at :_____

SPECIMEN COPY

Authorized Officer or Agent

Page 1—Sched. A—Policy No.

ORIGINAL

Policy 85—Litho in U.S.A.

ALTA Owner's Policy—Form B—1970 (Rev. 10-17-70) Copyright 1969

FIGURE 17–1 *(continued)*

Policy 85—Litho in U.S.A.   ALTA Owner's Policy—Form B—1970 (Rev. 10-17-70) Copyright 1969

Lawyers Title Insurance Corporation
A Stock Company
Home Office ~ Richmond .Virginia

SUBJECT TO THE EXCLUSIONS FROM COVERAGE, THE EXCEPTIONS CONTAINED IN SCHEDULE B AND THE PROVISIONS OF THE CONDITIONS AND STIPULATIONS HEREOF, LAWYERS TITLE INSURANCE CORPORATION, a Virginia corporation, herein called the Company, insures, as of Date of Policy shown in Schedule A, against loss or damage, not exceeding the amount of insurance stated in Schedule A, and costs, attorneys' fees and expenses which the Company may become obligated to pay hereunder, sustained or incurred by the insured by reason of:

1. Title to the estate or interest described in Schedule A being vested otherwise than as stated therein;
2. Any defect in or lien or encumbrance on such title;
3. Lack of a right of access to and from the land; or
4. Unmarketability of such title.

IN WITNESS WHEREOF the Company has caused this Policy to be signed and sealed, to be valid when Schedule A is countersigned by an authorized officer or agent of the Company, all in accordance with its By-Laws.

Lawyers Title Insurance Corporation

George V. Scott
President

S E A L
1925

Attest:

Clifford B. Fleet
Secretary.

EXCLUSIONS FROM COVERAGE

The following matters are expressly excluded from the coverage of this policy:

1. Any law, ordinance or governmental regulation (including but not limited to building and zoning ordinances) restricting or regulating or prohibiting the occupancy, use or enjoyment of the land, or regulating the character, dimensions or location of any improvement now or hereafter erected on the land, or prohibiting a separation in ownership or a reduction in the dimensions or area of the land, or the effect of any violation of any such law, ordinance or governmental regulation.
2. Rights of eminent domain or governmental rights of police power unless notice of the exercise of such rights appears in the public records at Date of Policy.
3. Defects, liens, encumbrances, adverse claims, or other matters (a) created, suffered, assumed or agreed to by the insured claimant; (b) not known to the Company and not shown by the public records but known to the insured claimant either at Date of Policy or at the date such claimant acquired an estate or interest insured by this policy and not disclosed in writing by the insured claimant to the Company prior to the date such insured claimant became an insured hereunder; (c) resulting in no loss or damage to the insured claimant; (d) attaching or created subsequent to Date of Policy; or (e) resulting in loss or damage which would not have been sustained if the insured claimant had paid value for the estate or interest insured by this policy.

FIGURE 17–1 (continued)

Lawyers Title Insurance Corporation
A Stock Company
Home Office ~ Richmond ,Virginia

SCHEDULE B

This Policy does not insure against loss or damage by reason of the following:

1. The dower, curtesy, homestead, community property, or other statutory marital rights, if any, of the spouse of any individual Insured.

Page 1 of Sched. B—Policy No.

Policy 85—Litho in U.S.A.

ORIGINAL

ALTA Owner's Policy—Form B—1970 (Rev. 10-17-70) Copyright 1969

FIGURE 17–1 (*continued*)

Policy 85—Litho in U.S.A.   ALTA Owner's Policy—Form B—1970 (Rev. 10-17-70) Copyright 1969

Lawyers Title Insurance Corporation
A Stock Company
Home Office ~ Richmond ,Virginia

CONDITIONS AND STIPULATIONS

1. Definition of Terms

The following terms when used in this policy mean:

(a) "insured": the insured named in Schedule A, and, subject to any rights or defenses the Company may have had against the named insured, those who succeed to the interest of such insured by operation of law as distinguished from purchase including, but not limited to, heirs, distributees, devisees, survivors, personal representatives, next of kin, or corporate or fiduciary successors.

(b) "insured claimant": an insured claiming loss or damage hereunder.

(c) "knowledge": actual knowledge, not constructive knowledge or notice which may be imputed to an insured by reason of any public records.

(d) "land": the land described, specifically or by reference in Schedule A, and improvements affixed thereto which by law constitute real property; provided, however, the term "land" does not include any property beyond the lines of the area specifically described or referred to in Schedule A, nor any right, title, interest, estate or easement in abutting streets, roads, avenues, alleys, lanes, ways or waterways, but nothing herein shall modify or limit the extent to which a right of access to and from the land is insured by this policy.

(e) "mortgage": mortgage, deed of trust, trust deed, or other security instrument.

(f) "public records": those records which by law impart constructive notice of matters relating to said land.

2. Continuation of Insurance after Conveyance of Title

The coverage of this policy shall continue in force as of Date of Policy in favor of an insured so long as such insured retains an estate or interest in the land, or holds an indebtedness secured by a purchase money mortgage given by a purchaser from such insured, or so long as such insured shall have liability by reason of covenants of warranty made by such insured in any transfer or conveyance of such estate or interest; provided, however, this policy shall not continue in force in favor of any purchaser from such insured of either said estate or interest or the indebtedness secured by a purchase money mortgage given to such insured.

3. Defense and Prosecution of Actions—Notice of Claim to be given by an Insured Claimant

(a) The Company, at its own cost and without undue delay, shall provide for the defense of an insured in all litigation consisting of actions or proceedings commenced against such insured, or a defense interposed against an insured in an action to enforce a contract for a sale of the estate or interest in said land, to the extent that such litigation is founded upon an alleged defect, lien, encumbrance, or other matter insured against by this policy.

(b) The insured shall notify the Company promptly in writing (i) in case any action or proceeding is begun or defense is interposed as set forth in (a) above, (ii) in case knowledge shall come to an insured hereunder of any claim of title or interest which is adverse to the title to the estate or interest, as insured, and which might cause loss or damage for which the Company may be liable by virtue of this policy, or (iii) if title to the estate or interest, as insured, is rejected as unmarketable. If such prompt notice shall not be given to the Company, then as to such insured all liability of the Company shall cease and terminate in regard to the matter or matters for which such prompt notice is required; provided, however, that failure to notify shall in no case prejudice the rights of any such insured under this policy unless the Company shall be prejudiced by such failure and then only to the extent of such prejudice.

(c) The Company shall have the right at its own cost to institute and without undue delay prosecute any action or proceeding or to do any other act which in its opinion may be necessary or desirable to establish the title to the estate or interest as insured, and the Company may take any appropriate action under the terms of this policy, whether or not it shall be liable thereunder, and shall not thereby concede liability or waive any provision of this policy.

(d) Whenever the Company shall have brought any action or interposed a defense as required or permitted by the provision of this policy, the Company may pursue any such litigation to final determination by a court of competent jurisdiction and expressly reserves the right, in its sole discretion, to appeal from any adverse judgment or order.

(e) In all cases where this policy permits or requires the Company to prosecute or provide for the defense of any action or proceeding, the insured hereunder shall secure to the Company the right to so prosecute or provide defense in such action or proceeding, and all appeals therein, and permit the Company to use, at its option, the name of such insured for such purpose. Whenever requested by the Company, such insured shall give the Company all reasonable aid in any such action or proceeding, in effecting settlement, securing evidence, obtaining witnesses, or prosecuting or defending such action or proceeding, and the Company shall reimburse such insured for any expense so incurred.

4. Notice of Loss—Limitation of Action

In addition to the notices required under paragraph 3(b) of these Conditions and Stipulations, a statement in writing of any loss or damage for which it is claimed the Company is liable under this policy shall be furnished to the Company within 90 days after such loss or damage shall have been determined and no right of action shall accrue to an insured claimant until 30 days after such statement shall have been furnished. Failure to furnish such statement of loss or damage shall terminate any liability of the Company under this policy as to such loss or damage.

5. Options to Pay or Otherwise Settle Claims

The Company shall have the option to pay or otherwise settle for or in the name of an insured claimant any claim insured against or to terminate all liability and obligations of the Company hereunder by paying or tendering payment of the amount of insurance under this policy together with any costs, attorneys' fees and expenses incurred up to the time of such payment or tender of payment, by the insured claimant and authorized by the Company.

6. Determination and Payment of Loss

(a) The liability of the Company under this policy shall in no case exceed the least of:

(i) the actual loss of the insured claimant; or

(ii) the amount of insurance stated in Schedule A.

(b) The Company will pay, in addition to any loss insured against by this policy, all costs imposed upon an insured in litigation carried on by the Company for such insured, and all costs, attorneys' fees and expenses in litigation carried on by such insured with the written authorization of the Company.

(c) When liability has been definitely fixed in accordance with the conditions of this policy, the loss or damage shall be payable within 30 days thereafter.

Continued on cover sheet

FIGURE 17–1 (continued)

CONDITIONS AND STIPULATIONS—CONTINUED

7. Limitation of Liability

No claim shall arise or be maintainable under this policy (a) if the Company, after having received notice of an alleged defect, lien or encumbrance insured against hereunder, by litigation or otherwise, removes such defect, lien or encumbrance or establishes the title, as insured, within a reasonable time after receipt of such notice; (b) in the event of litigation until there has been a final determination by a court of competent jurisdiction, and disposition of all appeals therefrom, adverse to the title, as insured, as provided in paragraph 3 hereof; or (c) for liability voluntarily assumed by an insured in settling any claim or suit without prior written consent of the Company.

8. Reduction of Liability

All payments under this policy, except payments made for costs, attorneys' fees and expenses, shall reduce the amount of the insurance pro tanto. No payment shall be made without producing this policy for endorsement of such payment unless the policy be lost or destroyed, in which case proof of such loss or destruction shall be furnished to the satisfaction of the Company.

9. Liability Noncumulative

It is expressly understood that the amount of insurance under this policy shall be reduced by any amount the Company may pay under any policy insuring either (a) a mortgage shown or referred to in Schedule B hereof which is a lien on the estate or interest covered by this policy, or (b) a mortgage hereafter executed by an insured which is a charge or lien on the estate or interest described or referred to in Schedule A, and the amount so paid shall be deemed a payment under this policy. The Company shall have the option to apply to the payment of any such mortgages any amount that otherwise would be payable hereunder to the insured owner of the estate or interest covered by this policy and the amount so paid shall be deemed a payment under this policy to said insured owner.

10. Apportionment

If the land described in Schedule A consists of two or more parcels which are not used as a single site, and a loss is established affecting one or more of said parcels but not all, the loss shall be computed and settled on a pro rata basis as if the amount of insurance under this policy was divided pro rata as to the value on Date of Policy of each separate parcel to the whole, exclusive of any improvements made subsequent to Date of Policy, unless a liability or value has otherwise been agreed upon as to each such parcel by the Company and the insured at the time of the issuance of this policy and shown by an express statement herein or by an endorsement attached hereto.

11. Subrogation Upon Payment or Settlement

Whenever the Company shall have settled a claim under this policy, all right of subrogation shall vest in the Company unaffected by any act of the insured claimant. The Company shall be subrogated to and be entitled to all rights and remedies which such insured claimant would have had against any person or property in respect to such claim had this policy not been issued, and if requested by the Company, such insured claimant shall transfer to the Company all rights and remedies against any person or property necessary in order to perfect such right of subrogation and shall permit the Company to use the name of such insured claimant in any transaction or litigation involving such rights or remedies. If the payment does not cover the loss of such insured claimant, the Company shall be subrogated to such rights and remedies in the proportion which said payment bears to the amount of said loss. If loss should result from any act of such insured claimant, such act shall not void this policy, but the Company, in that event, shall be required to pay only that part of any losses insured against hereunder which shall exceed the amount, if any, lost to the Company by reason of the impairment of the right of subrogation.

12. Liability Limited to this Policy

This instrument together with all endorsements and other instruments, if any, attached hereto by the Company is the entire policy and contract between the insured and the Company.

Any claim of loss or damage, whether or not based on negligence, and which arises out of the status of the title to the estate or interest covered hereby or any action asserting such claim, shall be restricted to the provisions and conditions and stipulations of this policy.

No amendment of or endorsement to this policy can be made except by writing endorsed hereon or attached hereto signed by either the President, a Vice President, the Secretary, an Assistant Secretary, or validating officer or authorized signatory of the Company.

13. Notices, Where Sent

All notices required to be given the Company and any statement in writing required to be furnished the Company shall be addressed to its Home Office, 3800 Cutshaw Avenue, Richmond, Virginia 23230.

Lawyers Title Insurance Corporation

A Stock Company
Home Office ~ Richmond, Virginia

SPECIMEN COPY

FIGURE 17–1 *(concluded)*

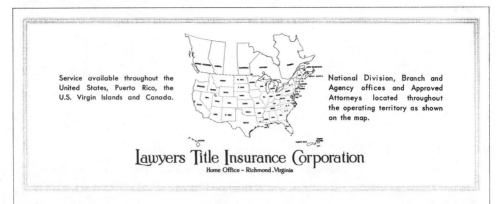

Service available throughout the United States, Puerto Rico, the U.S. Virgin Islands and Canada.

National Division, Branch and Agency offices and Approved Attorneys located throughout the operating territory as shown on the map.

Lawyers Title Insurance Corporation
Home Office ~ Richmond , Virginia

Lawyers Title
Insurance Corporation
A Stock Company
Home Office
Richmond , Virginia

Policy
of
Title Insurance

A word of thanks to our insured .....

As we make your policy a part of our permanent records, we want to express our appreciation of this evidence of your faith in Lawyers Title Insurance Corporation.

There is no recurring premium.

This policy provides valuable title protection and we suggest 'you keep it in a safe place where it will be readily available for future reference.

If you have any questions about the protection provided by this policy or wish to contact us for any other reason, write to:

Consumer Affairs Department
Lawyers Title Insurance Corporation
P.O. Box 27567
Richmond, Virginia 23261

TABLE 17–1

Title Insurance Premium Rates: First-Mortgage Title Insurance Rates and Original Title Owners' Policies*

	Per Thousand
Original title insurance rates for first mortgages	
Up to $50,000 of liability written...............................	$2.50
Over $50,000 and up to $100,000, add..........................	2.00
Over $100,000 and up to $500,000, add........................	1.75
Over $500,000 and up to $10,000,000, add.....................	1.50
Over $10,000,000 and up to $15,000,000, add..................	1.25
Over $15,000,000, add...	1.00
Minimum premium..	$7.50

	Per Thousand
Original title insurance rates for owners' policies	
Up to $50,000 of liability written...............................	$ 3.50
Over $50,000 and up to $100,000, add..........................	3.00
Over $100,000 and up to $5,000,000, add.......................	2.00
Over $5,000,000 and up to $10,000,000, add....................	1.75
Over $10,000,000 and up to $15,000,000, add..................	1.50
Over $15,000,000, add...	1.25
Minimum premium..	$10.00

* A first-mortgage policy cannot be issued for an amount less than the full principal debt; an owner's policy insuring a fee simple estate will not be issued for less than the full value of the premises.
Source: Lawyers Title Insurance Corporation, October 1976.

rens recording statutes. Once the property has been registered, the property cannot be removed from the Torrens system except by court order.

The Torrens system requires that county courts and recorders act as registrars of title in each county. An owner who wishes to register title must file a petition requesting registration with the recorder of the county in which the land is located. The Torrens official publishes a notice in the official county newspaper of the hearing on the petition to be held before a court of law. Copies of the notice of the hearing are sent to all parties having an interest in the real estate. After the hearing the court renders a final order and the title is marketable. The court issues a final judgment decreeing that title is vested in the petitioner and orders the registrar to register title subject to known encumbrances.

On the strength of the final order of registration, the registrar issues a certificate of title showing the title owner, the date of registration, the number of the certificate, and all encumbrances on the title. Upon transfer of title, the owner conveys title by deed and transfers the title registration certificate, both of which are filed with the registrar, who issues a new certificate to the buyer.

Though the Torrens registration eliminates the continual search required by the abstract and title insurance, critics of the Torrens system point to the high cost of undertaking the initial registration. The loss to parties who may sustain damage because of title registration through error, omission, or fraud is restricted to the amount of funds in the assurance fund built up from registration fees. Unlike title insurance, the registrar is not required to defend registered titles in court. Claims against the title must be defended at the owner's expense. Because of these and other limitations, the Torrens system has not been widely used in the United States.

THE REAL ESTATE SETTLEMENT PROCEDURES ACT

First enacted by Congress in 1974 and amended in 1975, the Real Estate Settlement Procedures Act initiated certain changes in the procedure for closing loans on one- to four-family residential properties to "insure that consumers throughout the nation are provided with greater and more timely information on the nature and costs of the settlement process and are protected from unnecessarily high settlement charges caused by certain abusive practices that have developed in some areas of the country." The purposes of the act were:

1. To provide more effective advance disclosure of settlement costs to home buyers and sellers.
2. To eliminate kickbacks or referral fees that tend to increase unnecessarily the costs of certain settlement services.
3. To reduce the amounts home buyers are required to place in escrow accounts established to insure the payment of real estate taxes and insurance.
4. To significantly reform and modernize local record keeping of land title information.[3]

The act applies to all federally regulated lenders. These are defined to include institutions supervised by the Federal Reserve Board, the Federal Home Loan Bank Board, the Federal Deposit Insurance Corporation, the Veterans Administration, and other government agencies. The act covers federally related mortgage loans secured by single-family dwellings, condominiums, and cooperatives occupied by one–four families. Thus the act encompasses virtually all loans on one- to four-family dwellings insured by financial institutions.

Exemptions under the Act

The exclusions under the act are rather limited. Mortgaged property in excess of 25 acres and home improvement loans are exempted from the

---

[3] *Real Estate Settlement Procedures Act of 1974* (Public Law 93–533), as amended by *Real Estate Settlement Procedures Act of 1975* (Public Law 94–205).

provisions of RESPA. Loans to finance the purchase of a vacant lot and to construct a home are exempt. The assumption of an existing loan is generally exempt. A mortgage loan on a lot, where the proceeds of the loan are used to finance construction, is exempt. Land sales, contracts, and loans to finance the purchase of a property for resale do not come under the act.

Lender Duties

To be sure, the act places the burden of compliance on federally regulated mortgage lenders. Yet, since compliance with RESPA requires the cooperation of real estate brokers and others, and since title may not be transferred unless the provisions of RESPA are fulfilled, real estate agents have an interest in the operations required by the act. RESPA expedites title transfer at final settlement to the extent that all interested parties understand its main provisions. Before the Settlement Statement is presented, the duties of the lender warrant mention.

The Settlement Booklet. At the time the borrower makes application for a mortgage or within the following three days, the lender is required to give the borrower a copy of the new *Settlement Procedures Special Information Booklet*. Prepared by the Department of Housing and Urban Development, the booklet describes the main procedures specified by RESPA and lists unfair practices prohibited by the act. The table of contents shows how the booklet serves the interest of consumers.

TABLE OF CONTENTS

INTRODUCTION

PART I

WHAT HAPPENS AND WHEN

SHOPPING FOR SERVICES

Role of the Broker
Negotiating a Sales Contract
Selecting an Attorney
Selecting a Lender
Selecting a Settlement Agent
Securing Title Services

HOMEBUYER'S RIGHTS

Information Booklet
Good Faith Estimates
Lender Designation of Settlement Service Providers
Disclosure of Settlement Costs One Day before Closing and Delivery
Escrow Closings
Truth-in-Lending
Protection against Unfair Practices
The Right to File Complaints

HOMEBUYER'S OBLIGATION
Repayment of Loan
Maintenance of Home
PART II
UNIFORM SETTLEMENT STATEMENT
Settlement Costs Worksheet
SPECIFIC SETTLEMENT SERVICES
COMPARING LENDER COSTS
CALCULATING THE BORROWER'S TRANSACTIONS
RESERVE ACCOUNTS
ADJUSTMENTS BETWEEN BUYER AND SELLER
APPENDIX A—Bibliography

The booklet describes how settlement costs are calculated. The booklet explains that advance disclosure serves two purposes: such disclosure gives the borrower an estimate of the cash required at the date of settlement, and it allows the borrower to compare the settlement charges of the lender with those of other lenders, thus helping the borrower to obtain the most reasonable closing terms. The rights of the borrower when dealing with the lender, closing agents, and others are outlined in the booklet.

Advance Disclosure of Settlement Costs. The lender must give a written statement of "good faith estimates" of the closing costs likely to be incurred at the date of closing. The form must include the name of the lender and must be easily read. Exceptions are allowed for costs which the borrower pays directly. For example, a borrower may negotiate directly with a private company for a termite inspection. Such direct expenditures of the borrower need not appear on the advance disclosure form.

Inspection of the Settlement Statement. The prospective home buyer must be allowed to inspect the final settlement statement on the business day before the settlement.

Uniform Settlement Statement Form. Although the lender may use his own settlement statement form for the advance disclosure, at the time of closing the buyer must be given the Uniform Settlement Statement prepared by HUD. Information relating to the borrower and the seller must be given to each of the parties. This form must not be provided later than settlement except (1) where the borrower or the borrower's agent does not attend the settlement, or (2) where the person conducting the settlement does not require a meeting of the parties for that purpose. In these instances, the settlement statement must be supplied "as soon as practicable after settlement." This latter provision allows settlements undertaken by third-party escrow agents acting under strict instructions of the buyer and the seller.

Unearned Fees. Section 8 of RESPA provides that

No person shall give and no person shall accept any fee, kickback, or thing of value pursuant to any agreement or understanding, oral or otherwise, that business incident to or a part of a real estate settlement service involving a federally related mortgage loan shall be referred to any person.

This means that persons may not accept a thing of value representing compensation for referral of business incident to a real estate settlement service. The act is directed, for example, to payments made by a title insurance company to persons who perform no service for the title company other than placing an application for insurance with the company. Similarly, the act prohibits payments by an attorney who gives a portion of his or her fee to another attorney, a lender, or a real estate agent for referral of clients. Title insurance companies may not pay commissions to others for referral of business.

No seller of property who comes under RESPA may require that title insurance be purchased by the buyer from a particular title company. Apparently this section of the law is aimed at contractors who divert all business to a particular title company. Violation of this section subjects the seller to damages equal to three times all charges made for such title insurance. In effect, this provision allows buyers to shop for the most advantageous title insurance policy.

Escrow Deposits.   Escrow deposits are advance payments collected with monthly mortgage payments into an account maintained by the lender for the payment of annual property taxes and insurance. Basically, the law prohibits lenders from establishing escrow accounts for property taxes, insurance, and other charges for more than the amount needed to make payment plus two months' deposits.

While compliance with RESPA turns mostly on the lender, interrelationships among real estate brokers and the lender and others are such that the lender is dependent on the broker to secure information on such matters as real estate commission costs and other title transfer costs. Note also that the broker may not participate in any referral or kickback fees for which no service was rendered.

The Settlement Statement

To illustrate the settlement statement form, the entries required by RESPA are shown in Figure 17–2. Note that the settlement statement covers a conventional uninsured loan, for a closing date as of September 18, 19—. The statement is divided into two parts that summarize the borrower's transaction and the seller's transaction.

Summary of Borrower's Transaction.   The entries for the borrower are shown in the three sections ending with the final cash due from the borrower. Paragraph numbers correspond to line numbers on Figure 17–2.

100. Gross Amount Due from Borrower.   The borrower is committed to paying the sales price, $29,000, and certain settlement charges at the time of settlement. Figure 17–2 details the settlement charges, including the expenses of closing and the borrower's share of prepaid expenses. In

FIGURE 17–2

Settlement Statement (page 1)

HUD-1 REV. 5/76		FORM APPROVED OMB NO. 63-R-1501

A.	B.	TYPE OF LOAN

U. S. DEPARTMENT OF HOUSING AND URBAN DEVELOPMENT

SETTLEMENT STATEMENT

TYPE OF LOAN
1. ☐ FHA   2. ☐ FmHA   3. ☒ CONV. UNINS.
4. ☐ VA   5. ☐ CONV. INS.
6. FILE NUMBER: 7. LOAN NUMBER: 14912
8. MORTGAGE INSURANCE CASE NUMBER:

C. NOTE: *This form is furnished to give you a statement of actual settlement costs. Amounts paid to and by the settlement agent are shown. Items marked "(p.o.c.)" were paid outside the closing; they are shown here for informational purposes and are not included in the totals.*

D. NAME OF BORROWER:	E. NAME OF SELLER:	F. NAME OF LENDER:
William R. Davis	John G. Jones	Federal Savings & Loan Association

G. PROPERTY LOCATION:	H. SETTLEMENT AGENT:	I. SETTLEMENT DATE:
150 Parkway Drive Atlanta, Georgia	Federal Savings and Loan Association	9-18-75
	PLACE OF SETTLEMENT: Federal Savings and Loan Association	

J. SUMMARY OF BORROWER'S TRANSACTION		K. SUMMARY OF SELLER'S TRANSACTION	
100. GROSS AMOUNT DUE FROM BORROWER:		400. GROSS AMOUNT DUE TO SELLER:	
101. Contract sales price	29,000.00	401. Contract sales price	29,000.00
102. Personal property		402. Personal property	
103. Settlement charges to borrower (line 1400)	1,253.10	403.	
104.		404.	
105.		405.	
Adjustments for items paid by seller in advance		*Adjustments for items paid by seller in advance*	
106. City/town taxes 9-18-75 to 12-31-75	28.19	406. City/town taxes 9-18-75 to 12-31-75	28.19
107. County taxes to		407. County taxes to	
108. Assessments to		408. Assessments to	
109.		409.	
110.		410.	
111.		411.	
112.		412.	
120. GROSS AMOUNT DUE FROM BORROWER	30,281.29	420. GROSS AMOUNT DUE TO SELLER	29,028.19
200. AMOUNTS PAID BY OR IN BEHALF OF BORROWER:		500. REDUCTIONS IN AMOUNT DUE TO SELLER:	
201. Deposit or earnest money	500.00	501. Excess deposit (see instructions)	
202. Principal amount of new loan(s)	23,200.00	502. Settlement charges to seller (line 1400)	1,794.50
203. Existing loan(s) taken subject to		503. Existing loan(s) taken subject to	
204. Application fee	45.00	504. Payoff of first mortgage loan	20,193.99
205. Commitment fee	232.00	505. Payoff of second mortgage loan	
206. Second loan to Seller	2,900.00	506. The Citizens & Southern	
207.		507. National Bank (373-71)	
208.		508. Second loan from buyer	2,900.00
209.		509.	
Adjustments for items unpaid by seller		*Adjustments for items unpaid by seller*	
210. City/town taxes to		510. City/town taxes to	
211. County taxes 1-1-75 to 9-18-75	143.42	511. County taxes 1-1-75 to 9-18-75	143.42
212. Assessments to		512. Assessments to	
213.		513.	
214.		514.	
215.		515.	
216.		516.	
217.		517.	
218.		518.	
219.		519.	
220. TOTAL PAID BY/FOR BORROWER	27,020.42	520. TOTAL REDUCTION AMOUNT DUE SELLER	25,031.91
300. CASH AT SETTLEMENT FROM/TO BORROWER		600. CASH AT SETTLEMENT TO/FROM SELLER	
301. Gross amount due from borrower (line 120)	30,281.29	601. Gross amount due to seller (line 420)	29,028.19
302. Less amounts paid by/for borrower (line 220)	27,020.42	602. Less reductions in amount due seller (line 520)	25,031.91
303. CASH (☒ FROM) (☐ TO) BORROWER	3,260.87	603. CASH (☒ TO) (☐ FROM) SELLER	3,996.28

THIS IS A FIVE PART FORM; WHITE, GOLDENROD, BLUE, PINK AND CANARY

this case they total to $1,253.10. Shown separately in this section is the borrower's share of city property taxes prepaid by the seller from the date of closing to the end of the year. With these adjustments, the gross amount due from the borrower totals $30,281.29.

200. Amounts Paid by or in Behalf of Borrower. In this section the borrower is credited for (*a*) the $500 earnest money which was paid directly to the real estate agent, (*b*) the amount of the new loan, (*c*) fees previously paid to the lender, $45 and $232, and (*d*) the second loan of $2,900, accepted by the seller in lieu of cash. In addition, the buyer is given credit for county property taxes unpaid to the date of closing. With these adjustments, the borrower is credited for $27,020.42.

300. Cash at Settlement from/to Borrower. The difference between the gross amount due from the borrower and the total paid by or for the borrower gives the final amount, in this case due *from* the borrower, of $3,260.87.

Summary of Seller's Transaction. The second half of the settlement statement divides the seller's transaction into three parts, ending with the total amount of cash due the seller at the date of closing.

400. Gross Amount Due to Seller. In this instance, the seller is due the sales price and property taxes prepaid from the date of closing to the end of the year, totaling $29,028.19. Personal property included in the sale would be added to this sum.

500. Reductions in Amount Due to Seller. The seller is responsible for the real estate commission and recording and document preparation for the deed, which total $1,794.50. Deducting (*a*) the amount of the outstanding first mortgage that would be paid by the lender, (*b*) the amount of the second loan the seller accepts in lieu of cash, and (*c*) the unpaid taxes to the date of closing ($143.42) gives the total reduction from the amount due to the seller, $25,031.91.

600. Cash at Settlement to/from Seller. The difference between item 601 and item 602 shows that the seller is entitled to $3,996.28.

A Summary of Settlement Charges. Figure 17–3, a reproduction of page 2 of the settlement statement, shows how the settlement charges were calculated for the borrower and the seller. These charges are divided into seven groups.

700. Total Sales/Broker's Commission. In this section the sales price and the stated real estate commission must be shown, and if the real estate commission is divided between two agents, this information is shown in subsections. In the present case the earnest money deposit of $500 was retained by the broker and paid into the broker's escrow account in trust for the buyer. On the final closing, the seller will be charged an additional $1,240 for the real estate commission and the broker will be authorized to transfer $500 from his escrow account to his personal account.

800. Items Payable in Connection with Loan. In this section are normal costs for originating a new loan. In the present case, the loan origina-

FIGURE 17–3

Settlement Charges

			Page 2
L.	**SETTLEMENT CHARGES**	**PAID FROM BORROWER'S FUNDS AT SETTLEMENT**	**PAID FROM SELLER'S FUNDS AT SETTLEMENT**
700. TOTAL SALES/BROKER'S COMMISSION based on price $ 29,000.00 @ 6 % =			
Division of Commission (line 700) as follows:			
701. $ 1,240.00 to Shields Realty			
702. $ 500.00 **xx** earnest money retained by Broker			
703. Commission paid at Settlement			1,740.00
704.			
800. ITEMS PAYABLE IN CONNECTION WITH LOAN			
801. Loan Origination Fee 2 % + $100.00 (204 & 205) Lender		564.00	
802. Loan Discount %			
803. Appraisal Fee to			
804. Credit Report to			
805. Lender's Inspection Fee			
806. Mortgage Insurance Application Fee to			
807. Assumption Fee			
808.			
809.			
810.			
811.			
900. ITEMS REQUIRED BY LENDER TO BE PAID IN ADVANCE			
901. Interest from 9-18-75 to 10-5-75 @$5.48 /day 17days		93.16	
902. Mortgage Insurance Premium for · months to			
903. Hazard Insurance Premium for years to p.o.c.			
904. years to			
905.			
1000. RESERVES DEPOSITED WITH LENDER			
1001. Hazard insurance 1 months @ $ 8.34 per month Lender		8.34	
1002. Mortgage insurance months @ $ per month			
1003. City property taxes 5 months @ $ 8.57 per month Lender		42.58	
1004. County property taxes 11 months @ $ 16.75 per month Lender		184.25	
1005. Annual assessments months @ $ per month			
1006. months @ $ per month			
1007. months @ $ per month			
1008. Total Escrow $235.44 months @ $ per month			
1100. TITLE CHARGES			
1101. Settlement or closing fee to			
1102. Abstract or title search to			
1103. Title examination to			
1104. Title insurance binder to			
1105. Document preparation $25.00 to Frank Spitzer			25.00
1106. Notary fees to			
1107. Attorney's fees 282.00 to Frank Spitzer		282.00	
(includes above items numbers;)			
1108. Title insurance to			
(includes above items numbers;)			
1109. Lender's coverage $			
1110. Owner's coverage $			
1111.			
1112.			
1113.			
1200. GOVERNMENT RECORDING AND TRANSFER CHARGES			
1201. Recording fees: Deed $ 2.00* ; Mortgage $ 6.00* ; Releases $ .50*		8.00	.50
1202. City/county tax/stamps: Deed $; Mortgage $			
1203. State tax/stamps: Deed $ 29.00± ; Mortgage $70.50±±		70.50	29.00
1204. *King Crawford, Clerk **Homer G. Hale, T. C.			
1205.			
1300. ADDITIONAL SETTLEMENT CHARGES			
1301. Survey to			
1302. Pest inspection to			
1303.			
1304.			
1305.			
1400. TOTAL SETTLEMENT CHARGES *(enter on lines 103, Section J and 502, Section K)*		1,253.10	1,794.50

HUD-1 REV. 5/76

THIS IS A FIVE PART FORM; WHITE, GOLDENROD, BLUE, PINK AND CANARY

tion fee of 2 percent plus $100, representing appraisal and credit report fees, add to $564 allocated to the borrower. Note that the form includes space for entering the assumption fee, a charge usually paid by the buyer. The loan discount is usually assumed by the seller.

900. Items Required by Lender to Be Paid in Advance. Here the lender details advance payments held in escrow for insurance and property taxes. Since the seller will be charged for mortgage interest for the month of September through October 5—the due date of the monthly mortgage payment—the interest cost for 17 days is charged back to the borrower. Note also that the form shows the entry "p.o.c.," meaning *paid out of closing,* since the borrower paid the first year's hazard insurance directly to the insurance company.

1000. Reserves Deposited with Lender. The reserves deposited with the lender may not be more than two months in excess of the monthly cost of insurance and property taxes. In this case the total reserves deposited with the lender amounted to $235.44, charged to the borrower at the time of settlement.

1100. Title Charges. In the present case the lender required an abstract and a legal opinion of the title, which cost the buyer $282. The seller paid a $25 legal fee for preparing the warranty deed.

1200. Government Recording and Transfer Charges. Note that recording fees for the deed and mortgage are charged to the borrower; the seller agreed to pay the recording fee for filing a mortgage release on the paid-out mortgage. The cost of state document stamps on the deed was charged to the seller. The buyer paid the intangible tax on the mortgage.

Totaling all charges assumed by the buyer and seller gives the total settlement charges entered in Figure 17–3.

TRUTH IN LENDING

Though not directly concerned with mortgage credit, new legislation enacted by Congress affects the procedures used in establishing mortgage credit. Two laws of interest here are the Truth in Lending Act and the Equal Credit Opportunity Act.

The Truth in Lending Act

The purpose of the Truth in Lending Act was to encourage competition among financial institutions by informing consumers of the cost of credit and permitting consumers to compare the various credit terms available. Creditors must report the amount of the finance charge, including (1) interest and any amount payable under a point discount or other system of additional charges; (2) service or carrying charges; (3) loan fees, finder's fees, or similar charges; (4) fees for credit reports and other investigations; and (5) premiums or other charges or guarantees for insurance protecting the creditor against default. This information must be supplied by the lender when the loan is approved. Creditors must observe Regulation Z issued by the Board of Governors of the Federal Reserve System.[4] Regulation Z requires lenders to disclose the annual percentage rate (APR), or the effective interest rate paid on the mortgage loan. This rate is usually higher than the contract rate because the APR includes discount points, fees, and financing charges as well as the contract interest rate. The truth in lending statement reveals additional charges for prepayment, assuming that the remaining balance of the mortgage is paid before it is due. This statement must be given to the borrower at the time the loan is granted.

Equal Credit Opportunity Notice

In dealing with buyer prospects, real estate agents should understand that mortgage lenders must observe Regulation B of the Federal Reserve Board, which outlines procedures to follow in judging mortgage loan applicants with respect to marital status and sex. Under the present law, a creditor cannot make any statements to applicants on the basis of sex or marital status that would discourage a reasonable person from applying for credit.[5]

Regulation B confines inquiries about the loan applicant's marital status to the terms *married, unmarried,* and *separated.* A creditor may inquire whether income stated in an application is derived from alimony, child support, or maintenance. When making a mortgage application, each applicant must be given the following notice:

> The Federal Equal Credit Opportunity Act prohibits creditors from discriminating against credit applicants on the basis of sex and marital status.

Beginning March 23, 1977, the act prohibits discrimination against credit applicants because of race, color, religion, national origin, or age, because all or part of the applicant's income is derived from any public assistance program, or because the applicant has in good faith exercised any right under the Consumer Credit Protection Act.

However, the Act states:

> A request for the signature of both parties to a marriage for the purpose of creating a valid lien, passing clear title, waiving inchoate rights to property, or assigning earnings, shall not constitute discrimination under this subchapter: Provided, however, That this provision shall not be construed to permit a creditor to take sex or marital status into account in connection with the evaluation of creditworthiness of any applicant.[6]

---

[4] Title 12, *CFR,* part 226, as amended.

[5] See Federal Reserve Board Regulation B, 12 CFR 202.4(*d*), and the Equal Credit Opportunity Act, 15 U.S.C. 1691, et seq.

[6] Ibid.

ESCROW AGENT

In some states it is common practice for the buyer and the seller, acting through the real estate broker, to close the transaction through an escrow agent. The escrow agent may be a lender, a real estate agent, a title company, an attorney, or an escrow company. The escrow agent operates under a written agreement stating the terms and conditions under which title is to be transferred. The escrow agent must obey the instructions of the escrow agreement; the escrow agent favors neither buyer nor seller, and in fact represents both parties.

Functions of an Escrow Agent

The escrow agent performs a useful function in arranging for title transfers. Frequently title is not conveyed until certain events have taken place: primarily, completion of the appraisal, termite inspection, credit report, financing, surveys, title searches, repairs to the property, and like tasks. Since these events take time, the buyer and the seller in effect instruct the escrow agent to convey title under certain conditions and provided that certain required events have taken place. Consequently, though the seller delivers a deed to the escrow agent, title is not conveyed to the buyer until the stated conditions have been met. Further, the escrow agent is prohibited from transferring funds of the buyer to the seller unless a marketable title has been delivered.

In short, the escrow agent performs everything that the buyer and seller would normally undertake in completing the transaction. An escrow is complete when all terms of the instruction have been met, and title documents have been delivered.

Transfer of title by escrow protects both the buyer and the seller. For example, assume that John Jones sells Bill Smith a dwelling for $40,000 on January 15. A title search on January 20 shows no liens of any kind. Suppose that on January 25 John Jones delivers the deed to Bill Smith, who pays the agreed price of $40,000 plus closing costs. However, on August 22 a lien was recorded against the property for $20,000. Though Bill Smith has a rightful claim against John Jones for the amount of the lien, he does not own the property free and clear. An escrow agent would avoid this since title would not be conveyed unless title were clear as of the date of conveyance.

Escrow Procedures

The procedures followed under an escrow where the property is financed may be briefly summarized as follows:

1. The seller deposits his deed and other documents into escrow with the provision that the deed will be transferred to the buyer in return for cash.

2. The buyer makes a down payment to the escrow with the understanding that additional funds will be supplied by the lender in full satisfaction of the purchase price and closing costs.

3. The lender deposits the balance of the payment, representing the mortgage loan, with instructions to the escrow agent that funds will be disbursed only if a lender's title insurance policy insuring the mortgage as a first lien with necessary mortgage and promissory note or deed of trust is obtained.

4. Assuming that all parties have fulfilled the requirements of the escrow, the escrow agent conveys the deed to the purchaser, the lender receives a deed of trust or a mortgage and promissory note, and the funds are transferred to the seller.

In a sense, the escrow is a binding contract ensuring performance, but only if the seller, the buyer, and the lender have met the conditions of the escrow. The seller is protected in that title will not be conveyed until the terms of the sale have been completed; the buyer retains control of the down payment until the conditions of transfer have been met; and the lender does not disburse funds unless all documents for the loan have been completed.

The importance of the escrow arrangement has led some states, such as California, to license escrow agents. Each applicant must submit a bond of $5,000 and have a tangible net worth of $10,000 and must maintain bonds, accounts, and records in accordance with legal requirements. The applicant must be a corporation organized for escrow business. Exemptions are granted to banks, trust companies, savings and loan associations, insurance companies, title companies, and under certain circumstances, licensed attorneys and real estate brokers.[7]

Indeed, the special skills required for the escrow agent have led at least one college to sponsor an escrow certificate and degree program. The College of San Mateo, in California, offers a certificate approved by the California Escrow Association. For advanced work, which requires 60 college course units with a grade of C or better, the college offers an Associate in Arts degree with escrow specialization. Graduates of this program qualify for work with title insurance companies, escrow companies, banks, savings and loan associations, and other financial institutions.

CLOSING PROCEDURES

A real estate transfer begins with the listing agreement. Here the seller outlines the conditions under which he will transfer title. Frequently the prospect rejects the seller's original offer and submits his own offer, which must be accepted by the seller. When the buyer and seller are in agreement,

---

[7] See Arthur G. Bowman, *California Real Estate Principles* (Pacific Palisades, Calif.: Goodyear Publishing Company, Inc., 1972), pp. 118–19.

the broker must execute a document evidencing the buyer's offer and the seller's acceptance. Generally states follow one of three methods in initiating title transfer. Each of these initial documents states the terms under which title will be transferred and to a large degree governs the final closing.

Methods of Closing

Some states require the broker to prepare a *binder* which serves as a receipt of the buyer's deposit pending final closing or disposition of the offer. The binder submitted to the seller describes the terms of sale and includes the legal description. If the binder is accepted and signed by the seller, it serves as the basis for the preparation of a contract for sale which is prepared by an escrow agent or attorney.

In states such as California, the broker prepares a receipt for deposit and real estate purchase contract, using standard forms approved by the California Real Estate Association and the State Bar of California. In some instances, the attorney must prepare the form if the standard form does not serve the interests of buyer and seller.

In other states, a detailed *contract for sale* serves as the deposit receipt and describes details of the sale that control final title transfer. In this respect, the initial document must observe elements of an enforceable contract: (1) an offer and acceptance, (2) a valid consideration, (3) parties capable of contracting, and (4) a lawful object.

The Earnest Money Contract

For an example of this procedure, refer to Figure 17–4, which illustrates the deposit form required by the Texas Real Estate Commission. This form constitutes a *residential earnest money contract* that covers normal situations in a typical assumption of loan transfer. In unusual situations, the broker must refer preparation of the form to an attorney to avoid the unauthorized practice of law. The more important elements of the earnest money contract warrant further comment.

Elements of the Earnest Money Contract. Note that the parties are identified especially with respect to their marital status. Both the address and the legal description identify the property and describe the fixtures to be included in the sale. The form provides for listing of the sales price, the down payment, and assumption of an existing loan. It also provides for the addition of a second lien.

The earnest money deposit and the appointment of the escrow agent are covered in paragraph 4. Special provisions, the existing lien, and provision for the owner's policy and title insurance are stated. The parties have agreed in this case to certain repairs as a condition for the final sale. Responsibility for the payment of prorates on taxes, insurance, rents,

FIGURE 17-4

Residential Earnest Money Contract

ASSUMPTION OF LOAN   -   RESIDENTIAL EARNEST MONEY CONTRACT
PROMULGATED BY TEXAS REAL ESTATE COMMISSION

1. PARTIES: __ISA SELLER and Wife WEDA R. SELLER_____ (Seller) agrees
to sell and convey to __IMA BUYER (femme sole)_____ (Buyer)
and Buyer agrees to buy from Seller the following property situated in ___Bexar_____ County, Texas,
known as __8127 Dry Gulch Trail_____ (Address).

2. PROPERTY: Lot __East 25 ft. of Lot 5, All of Lot 6_____ Block ___2___ NCB 10001
Harmony Valley_____ Addition, City of ___San Antonio_____, or as described on
attached exhibit, together with the following fixtures, if any: curtain and drapery rods, venetian blinds, window shades,
screens and shutters, awnings, wall-to-wall carpeting, mirrors fixed in place, attic fans, permanently installed heating
and air conditioning units and equipment, lighting and plumbing fixtures, TV antennas, mail boxes, water softeners,
shrubbery and other property attached to the Property and owned by Seller. All property sold by this contract is called
"Property."

3. CONTRACT SALES PRICE:
   A. The   Exact [X]   Approximate ☐   Cash down payment .... $ ˙3,050.00
   B. Buyer's assumption of the unpaid balance of a promissory note, payable to Noteholder, with
   present monthly installments of $ __231.00__, including principal, interest and escrow
   deposit, with Buyer's first payment due __Dec. 1, 1975_____, the unpaid
   principal balance of which (allowing for an agreed $100 variance) is .... $ __25,452.13__
   C. Any balance of Sales Price to be evidenced by a second lien note payable to [check (1) or (2)
   below]:
      ☐ (1) Seller, bearing interest at the rate of _____ % per annum, either in
         ☐ lump sum on or before _____ or
         ☐ principal and interest installments of $_____, or more per _____,
         with first installment payment on _____.
      ☐ (2) Third Party in principal and interest installments not in excess of $_____
      per month;
   and in the   Exact ☐   Approximate ☐   (check "Approximate" only if A. above
   and D. below are "Exact") amount of .... $ __-0-__
   D. The   Exact ☐   Approximate [X]   total Sales Price of (Sum of A., B. and C. above) $ __28,492.13__

4. EARNEST MONEY: $ __500.00__ of the cash down payment is herewith tendered and is to be deposited as
Earnest Money with __First Fidelity Title Co._____ as Escrow Agent, upon execution of
the contract by both parties. Additional Earnest Money, if any, shall be deposited with the Escrow Agent on or before
the __15th__ day of __November_____, 1975, in the amount of $ __1,500.00__.

5. SPECIAL PROVISIONS: This contract subject to successful closing of sale of buyer's
home at 223 Breese Ave., San Antonio, to Mr. and Mrs. John Doe, now in escrow at
First Fideltiy Title Co. concurrently with purchase of subject property. Buyer
agrees to cooperate with sellers' securing release of liability and to furnish all
necessary information and sign applicable papers.

(Set forth above terms and conditions of a factual nature applicable to this sale, e.g., personal property included in sale,
prior purchase or sale of other property, lessee's surrender of possession, and the like.)

6. REPRESENTATIONS: Seller represents that at the time of closing there will be no Title I liens, unrecorded liens or
Uniform Commercial Code liens against any of the Property, that loan(s) will be without default, and escrow account
will not be deficient. If above representations are untrue or if Noteholder raises the existing interest rate above __7-3/4%__
or requires Buyer to pay an assumption fee in excess of $ __35.00__, then this contract may, at Buyer's op-
tion, be declared null and void and Earnest Money shall be returned without delay. Representations shall survive closing.

7. TITLE: Seller at Seller's expense shall furnish either:
   [X] A. Owner's Policy of Title Insurance (the Title Policy) issued by __First Fidelity Title Co.__
   _____ in the amount of the Sales Price dated at or after closing, OR,
   ☐ B. Complete Abstract of Title certified by _____ to current date.
   NOTICE TO BUYER: If neither an Abstract of Title nor a Policy of Title Insurance is provided for herein, then AS
   REQUIRED BY LAW, Broker hereby advises YOU that YOU should have an abstract covering the real estate which
   YOU are hereby buying examined by an attorney of YOUR own selection, or that YOU should be furnished with or ob-
   tain a Policy of Title Insurance.

8. PROPERTY CONDITION (Check "A" or "B"):
   [X] A. Buyer accepts the Property in its present condition, subject only to the following exceptions: __Seller to__
   __repair back fence, air conditioning to be in good operating condition__
   ☐ B. Buyer requires inspections and repairs as provided by the attached addendum.
   Buyer acknowledges that Broker and sales associates have no responsibility or liability for the repair or replacement
   of the Property or related equipment or fixtures.

9. PRORATION: Taxes, insurance, rents, interest and maintenance fees, if any, SHALL ☐   SHALL NOT [X]   be prorated to the date of closing. If these are not prorated, all funds held in escrow for payment of taxes, maintenance fees
and insurance shall be transferred to the account of Buyer by Seller without cost to Buyer.

10. BROKER'S FEE: __Guy Chipman Co._____, as Real Estate Broker ("Broker") has
negotiated this sale and Seller agrees to pay Broker in __Bexar_____ County, Texas, a fee in
cash in the amount of __6%__ of the total Sales Price at closing or upon Seller's default when completion of sale is prevented through fault of Seller.

11. CLOSING: The closing of the sale shall be on or before __November 27, 1975__ or within 7 days after
objections to title have been cured, whichever date is later.

12. POSSESSION: The Property shall be delivered to Buyer on __December 1, 1975__
in its present condition, ordinary wear and tear excepted, unless otherwise specified herein.

FIGURE 17-4 (continued)

13. ASSUMPTION APPROVAL: If Noteholder requires approval of Buyer, or can accelerate note upon assumption, or both, then approval of Buyer and waiver of right of acceleration in writing by Noteholder prior to closing shall be required, otherwise this contract may, at Buyer's option, be declared null and void and Earnest Money shall be returned without delay. Buyer will use every reasonable effort to obtain such approval and waiver.

14. TITLE APPROVAL: If Abstract of Title is furnished, Seller shall deliver same to Buyer within 20 days from the date of application therefor. Buyer or Buyer's attorney shall have 20 days from date of Buyer's receipt of Abstract to examine and deliver a copy of the written report thereon to Seller, stating any objections to title made by Buyer, and only objections thereto so stated shall be considered. If Owner's Policy of Title Insurance is furnished, Seller shall have 20 days from the date of application therefor to secure assurance that Title Insurance may be issued. In either instance, if title objections are disclosed, Seller shall have 30 days to cure the same. Exceptions permitted to the Deed and zoning ordinances shall not be valid objections to title.

   The Title Policy (form prescribed by State Board of Insurance of the State of Texas) shall guarantee Buyer's title to be good and indefeasible subject only to the following:

   A. Restrictive covenants affecting the Property.

   B. Any discrepancies, conflicts, or shortages in area or boundary lines, or any encroachments, or any overlapping of improvements.

   C. All taxes for the current and subsequent years.

   D. Any existing building and zoning ordinances.

   E. Rights of parties in possession.

   F. Any liens which are recited as part of the consideration for the Property being purchased.

   Seller agrees to furnish at Seller's expense tax certificates showing no delinquent taxes, and a general Warranty Deed conveying title subject only to liens created or assumed as a part of the consideration, taxes for the current year, usual restrictive covenants and utility easements common to any regularly platted subdivision where Property is located and any other reservations or exceptions acceptable to Buyer. Each note herein provided shall be secured by a Vendor's and Deed of Trust lien. A Vendor's lien shall be retained and a Deed of Trust to Secure Assumption required, which liens shall be automatically released on execution and delivery of a release by Noteholder. Unless otherwise mutually agreed, the Deed, Notes and Deeds of Trust shall be upon forms currently published by the State Bar of Texas, or those required by any lending institution or governmental agency providing funds, guaranties or insurance for financing.

15. LOSS: If any part of Property is damaged or destroyed by fire or other casualty loss, Seller shall restore the same to its previous condition as soon as reasonably possible, but in any event within 30 days after the herein recited period of time for closing (and the closing date shall be extended accordingly); and if Seller is unable to do so, Buyer may cancel and terminate this Contract, whereupon all Earnest Money shall be returned to Buyer, and Broker shall not be entitled to any fee.

16. DEFAULT: If Buyer fails to comply herewith, Seller may either enforce specific performance or receive the Earnest Money as liquidated damages, one-half of which (but not exceeding the amount of the Broker's fee recited herein) shall be paid by Seller to Broker in full payment for Broker's services. If Seller is unable, through no fault of his own, to obtain abstract or title information from the Title Company or to make any repairs required herein, within the time herein specified, Buyer may, at his option, extend the time or terminate the contract, and receive the Earnest Money back as the sole remedy. If Seller fails to comply herewith for any other reason, Buyer may demand the Earnest Money, thereby releasing Seller from this contract, or Buyer may either enforce specific performance hereof or seek such other relief as may be provided by law. If completion of sale is prevented by Buyer's default, and Seller elects to enforce specific performance, the Broker's Fee is payable only if and when Seller collects judgment for such default by suit, compromise, settlement or otherwise, and after first deducting the expenses of collection, and then only in an amount equal to one-half of that portion collected, but not exceeding the amount of Broker's fee.

17. ESCROW: Funds are deposited with Escrow Agent with the understanding that Escrow Agent (i) does not assume or have any liability for performance or nonperformance of any party (ii) has the right to require the receipt, release and authorization in writing of all parties before paying the deposit to any party and (iii) is not liable for interest or other charge on the funds held. Any excess of Earnest Money over the amount required for down payment shall be applied against Buyer's closing costs.

18. EXPENSES OF SALE: Preparing and recording Deed of Trust to Secure Assumption and one-half of Escrow Fees shall be Seller's expense. All other costs and expenses incurred in connection with this contract which are not recited herein to be the obligation of Seller, shall be the obligation of Buyer. Unless otherwise paid, before Buyer shall be entitled to return of Earnest Money, any such costs and expenses shall be deducted therefrom and paid to the creditors entitled thereto.

19. THIRD PARTY FINANCING: If financing by third party is provided herein, Buyer shall have 15 days to obtain the same, and failure to secure the same after reasonable effort shall render this contract null and void, and the Earnest Money returned without delay.

20. EXTENDED CLOSING: If necessary to comply with REAL ESTATE SETTLEMENT PROCEDURES ACT of 1974, closing shall be extended daily up to 30 days.

21. AGREEMENT OF PARTIES: This contract contains the entire agreement of the parties and cannot be changed except by their written consent.

22. CONSULT YOUR ATTORNEY: This is a legally binding contract. READ IT CAREFULLY. If you do not understand the effect of any part, consult your attorney BEFORE signing. The Broker cannot give you legal advice - only factual and business details concerning this land and its improvements. If desired, attorneys to represent parties may be designated below, and, so employment may be accepted, Broker shall promptly deliver a copy of this contract to such attorneys.

Seller's Atty: _____ Buyer's Atty: _____

EXECUTED in multiple copies effective the _____ day of _____ 197__ (Broker fill in date after last party signs).

Receipt of $ _____ Earnest Money is acknowledged in the form of _____

Escrow Agent	Date	Seller	
By_____		Seller	
Broker	License No.	Seller's Address	Tel.
By_____		Buyer	
Broker	License No.	Buyer	
By_____		Buyer's Address	Tel.

The form of this contract has been approved by the Texas Real Estate Commission and the State Bar of Texas. No representation is made as to the legal validity or adequacy of any provision in any specific transaction. It is not suitable for complex transactions and extensive riders or additions are not to be used. (9-75) TREC No. 1-0.

FIGURE 17–4 (concluded)

ADDENDUM TO EARNEST MONEY CONTRACT
BETWEEN THE UNDERSIGNED PARTIES

DATED _____ _____

CHECK APPLICABLE BOXES:

☐ A. TERMITES: Seller agrees at his expense to furnish Buyer with a letter of current date from a licensed exterminator stating there is no visible evidence of active termites or other wood destroying insects or damage from same in need of repair to the improvements on the Property. Said letter shall guarantee the improvements free of infestation for a period of 90 days.

☐ B. INSPECTIONS BY BUYER. REPAIRS BY SELLER: Buyer, at Buyer's option and expense, shall have 10 days from the effective date of the contract to have the structure, foundation, roof, dishwasher, disposal, trash compactor, range, oven exhaust fan, heating and air conditioning system, plumbing (including well and septic tank) system, electrical system, swimming pool and _____

_____ inspected by specialists of Buyer's choice and shall give Seller written notice of required repairs to any of the above items which are not performing the function for which intended or which are in need of immediate repair. Failure to do so shall be deemed a waiver of Buyer's inspection and repair rights and Buyer agrees to accept Property in its present condition. Seller shall cause the repairs to be made without delay and prior to closing. Any inspections or repairs shall be by trained and qualified parties who are licensed or bonded whenever such license or bond is required by law or by a manufacturer-approved service person in the event of equipment items.

REPAIR EXPENSES: Seller's repair expenses from A and B shall not exceed $_____. If such repairs exceed such amount and Seller refuses to pay the balance of the cost, Buyer may pay the additional cost or accept the Property with the above limited repairs, and this sale shall be closed as scheduled, or Buyer may declare this contract null and void and the Earnest Money returned, less any inspection expenses to be paid to third parties. If Seller fails to commence immediately and complete the agreed repairs, Buyer may make the repairs and Seller shall be liable up to the amount specified, and the same paid from the proceeds of the sale.

If Broker and sales associates are requested to recommend inspectors or repairmen, Broker and sales associates are not liable for the results and have no responsibility for the performance of any firms making inspections or repairs pursuant to this contract.

_____   _____
SELLER   BUYER

_____   _____
SELLER   BUYER

PROMULGATED BY TEXAS REAL ESTATE COMMISSION

interest, and maintenance fees is stipulated. The earnest money contract identifies the closing and possession dates.

Broker Restrictions. Using this form, brokers are prohibited from altering or amending the contract; it is not to be used for any purpose other than a transfer of residential property where there is assumption of an existing loan. Though the broker is permitted to fill in blanks, he or she may not add matter to or strike matter from the form. Only factual statements may be added as directed by the buyer and the seller. If it is necessary to attach long additions to the contract, the advice of an attorney is required.

Closing Steps

Strictly interpreted, the broker's role is completed when he has fulfilled the purposes of the agency: to find a purchaser willing and able to meet terms acceptable to the seller. Yet it is helpful for the real estate agent to understand the steps that must be taken before the sale is completed. The real estate agent has an interest in these procedures since final commissions are usually not paid until the time of closing. Though the details vary according to the agreement and local custom, normally the buyer, the seller, and the closing agent have mutually dependent duties.

Seller Responsibilities before Closing. The seller through his attorney must be prepared to transfer title by the conveyance instrument required. If a warranty deed is specified in the agreement, the seller must be prepared to execute the deed before the closing date. If hazard insurance is to be transferred, steps must be taken to transfer insurance in the name of the buyer with appropriate pro rata allocations of insurance costs. Outstanding liens that are not assumed by the buyer must be paid, termite inspections must be arranged, and the seller must repair items specified by contract. Real estate appraisals and surveys required must be completed, and the seller must remove outstanding encumbrances that interfere with title closing.

The closing costs assumed by the seller are subject to agreement. They are determined by a binder, a contract for sale, or an earnest money and deposit receipt. Ordinarily, closing costs are assumed by both the borrower and the seller and are noted in the listing agreement. Though subject to much variation, the seller usually would be expected to assume:

1. Legal fees in preparing the deed and other instruments for the buyer.
2. The cost of recording the mortgage release if an existing loan is paid out.
3. The payment of outstanding encumbrances agreed to as part of the terms of sale. In this category are included outstanding special assessments or similar liens.
4. Document stamps required for the warranty deed or expenses in preparing conveyance instruments given to the buyer.

5. Loan discount fees, especially FHA and VA discount points.
6. The cost of title abstract or title insurance, though local practices on this point may shift these costs to the buyer.

Buyer Responsibilities before Closing. Depending on the details of the sale, the buyer must arrange for a new loan which must be approved before closing. The buyer must be prepared to transfer the final down payment and closing costs. The buyer must specify his wishes on title insurance or abstract and opinion of title. The buyer must cooperate in furnishing credit references, employment verification, and current income. If the purchase covers property leased to tenants, the buyer should have a letter of introduction prepared for tenants.

The costs of closing assumed by the buyer vary widely, but usually would include:

1. Appraisal fees for a new mortgage.
2. Assumption fees required by the lender as a condition to assuming an existing loan.
3. In the case of a new mortgage, loan origination fees.
4. The cost of a survey if required by a lender issuing a new mortgage.
5. Title insurance, especially if the lender requires a mortgagee's title insurance policy.
6. Legal fees for the preparation of mortgages, notes and recording fees, conveyance or document stamps applying to mortgages, deeds of trust, and notes.
7. Legal fees for examining title and rendering an opinion on an abstract.
8. Termite inspection, usually required by the lender.

Duties of the Closing Agent. The escrow agent or the attorney responsible for the final closing must review the accuracy of documents for

1. The date of closing.
2. The name and address of the seller or sellers.
3. The seller's marital status, age, and legal competence, especially for corporations and partnerships.
4. The name and address of the purchaser.
5. An accurate, full legal description.
6. The selling price and the final amount to be paid at closing.

The attorney should determine whether the property is purchased by *assuming* an existing mortgage or *subject to* an existing mortgage. Special agreements on personal property to be conveyed with the property and other conditions, such as repairs or special occupancy arrangements, should be stated in the contract for sale. All leases, rents, or rights of other parties in possession must be identified. The attorney or the closing agent is responsible for seeing that the survey, the appraisal, and the mortgage payoff of old loans are completed on time. The release of an existing mortgage should be recorded. Disbursement from the new lender and funds from the seller should be determined. Documents to clear title, such as quitclaim deeds, affidavits, or other necessary instruments, must be available before closing.

The Final Closing.   If documents are signed beforehand, the seller need not be present at closing. The closing statement for both the buyer and the seller, prepared in advance, must be signed by the buyer and the seller. All notes, deeds, and other documents must be signed, acknowledged, and delivered. Funds must be issued to the seller and the buyer, and disbursed for state taxes, intangible taxes, document stamps, and recording fees. The closing officer retains all documents for recording. After closing the closing agent records the documents, and on return of the recorded documents he or she sends deeds, tax receipts, and title policies to the purchaser or the purchaser's attorney.

SUMMARY

Steps taken to insure—but not guarantee—a marketable title include the abstract of title and title insurance. The abstract includes a summary of recorded documents affecting title. The document serves as the basis for an opinion of title by an attorney. Gradually, as abstractor records developed, abstract companies first guaranteed against errors and later assumed liability without regard to proof of negligence.

Title insurance insures against losses from certain title defects occurring on or before the date of the policy. Future events are not covered. Title insurance premiums are paid in a lump sum on the date of issue. No other fees or premiums are added, though the insurance continues in force. It remains effective as long as the insured continues to have an interest in the title insured. Title insurance is available only through title insurance companies or approved attorney agents. Such insurance may apply to various interests in the property, primarily the owner's or the lender's interest.

Title insurance usually exempts losses occurring from the exercise of zoning ordinances, actions under the right of eminent domain not appearing in the public record, defects created by the insured, and certain other losses accepted by the title insurance company. The Torrens system, used only in selected areas, is based on a registration certificate issued by the Torrens official. Registered titles under the Torrens system must be defended at the owner's expense.

The Real Estate Settlement Procedures Act covers one- to four-family residences financed by federally regulated lenders. Under the act, lenders must issue a settlement booklet to the mortgage applicant, provide an advance disclosure of the settlement cost, and at the time of settlement, issue a uniform settlement statement form which the home buyer is allowed to inspect on the business day before settlement. Unearned fees are prohibited. Escrow accounts for prepaid property taxes, insurance, and other charges are limited by the act. The Truth in Lending Act requires mortgage lenders to issue a statement on the effective interest rate paid on a mortgage loan. Similarly, the Equal Credit Opportunity Act prohibits discrimination on the basis of sex or marital status.

The escrow agent operates under a written agreement which states the terms and conditions under which title is to be transferred. The escrow agent performs everything the buyer and seller would normally undertake in completing a transaction. When all the terms of the escrow instruction have been met and title documents have been delivered, the escrow is terminated.

Closing a sale may require the execution of a binder in some states, in others a receipt for deposit and a real estate purchase contract, and in still others a contract for sale. In Texas, an earnest money contract specified by the Texas Real Estate Commission must be used for residential property for a typical assumption of loan sale. Brokers fill in blank spaces on the form but must not amend the form or make substantial additions.

Final closing of a sale will not be effective unless the seller observes his or her responsibilities and assumes certain costs of closing. The buyer has the responsibility for meeting closing costs and arranging for other necessary steps, primarily in the interest of the lender, before title is transferred.

REVIEW QUESTIONS

1. To what extent does an abstract of title insure marketable title? Explain fully.
2. What protection does title insurance give a buyer under an owner's policy?
3. What are common exclusions to an owner's policy?
4. Explain the Torrens land title registration system.
5. What duties does the lender have under the Real Estate Settlement Procedures Act?
6. What function does the settlement booklet serve?
7. What is the purpose of the Uniform Settlement Statement? Explain how the form accomplishes its function.
8. What duties must the lender perform under the Truth in Lending Act?
9. What is the impact of the Equal Credit Opportunity Act on mortgage lending?
10. What are the functions of an escrow agent in closing a real estate sale?
11. What is the significance of the earnest money contract to a real estate title transfer? Explain fully.
12. Explain the seller's responsibilities before closing.
13. What are the buyer's responsibilities in acquiring title?

14.   What functions does the closing agent perform in planning and completing a title closing?

SELECTED REFERENCES

Beaton, William R., and Bond, Robert J.   *Real Estate,* chap. 8. Pacific Palisades, Calif.: Goodyear Publishing Company, Inc., 1976.

Bowman, Arthur G.   *California Real Estate Principles,* chap. 7. Pacific Palisades, Calif.: Goodyear Publishing Company, Inc., 1972.

Ficek, Edmund F.; Henderson, Thomas P.; and Johnson, Ross H.   *Real Estate Principles and Practices,* chap. 17. Columbus: Charles E. Merrill Publishing Co., 1976.

Hines, Mary Alice.   *Principles and Practices of Real Estate,* chap. 10. Homewood, Ill.: Richard D. Irwin, Inc., 1976.

Levine, Mark Lee.   *Real Estate Fundamentals,* chap. 41. St. Paul: West Publishing Co., 1976.

Shenkel, William M.   *The Real Estate Professional,* chap. 9. Homewood, Ill.: Dow Jones-Irwin, Inc., 1976.

Unger, Maurice A.   *Real Estate,* chap. 23. 5th ed. Cincinnati: South-Western Publishing Co., 1974.

18

Property Management

After reading this chapter, you should be familiar with the following points:

1 The functions of a real property manager.
2 The main elements of a management agreement.
3 Tenant selection procedures.
4 The content of a residential lease.
5 The duties of a resident manager.
6 Management consulting practices.
7 The contents of the management survey.
8 The manager's role in converting apartments to condominiums.
9 Critical issues in managing low-income properties.

A PROPERTY MANAGER is one who directs, controls, or operates real property for a fee. The Institute of Real Estate Management defines real estate management as

> . . . the art or science of operating, dealing with, or otherwise handling real estate or the improvements thereon which is held for rent or for the production of income, herein referred to as "rental properties," in a manner or fashion as to produce for the owners thereof, within the limitations of applicable law and responsibility to the community, a maximum of economic return over the period of management.[1]

The same organization defines a property manager as "any person who, as an owner, employee or independent contractor, directs, controls or advises in respect to rental properties in such manner and with such degree of skill, executive ability, judgment and integrity as to demonstrate . . . knowledge of and proficiency in real estate management."

Managers deal primarily with real estate which is leased or rented, and in this sense their main function is to secure the highest net income over the useful life of the property. While maximizing net income, the manager works to maintain and preserve the utility of the property under management. This latter qualification means that the professional manager recommends necessary repairs and maintenance so that net income is not earned at the sacrifice of long-term losses.

THE MANAGEMENT FUNCTION

To the layman, property management may be viewed as a person who collects rents. But the duties of the property manager cover a wide range of operations. Some property managers serve as consultants, guiding the property to some new use that maximizes income. Others specialize in the management survey—a report that outlines alternative plans to operate a property. Property managers may supervise resident managers who are responsible for the day-to-day management of an apartment complex, a shopping center, or similar properties.

More specifically, the main activities of the property manager may be classified into four categories:

1. The renting or merchandising of space in the buildings under his management.
2. The operation and maintenance of the property.
3. The remodeling, rehabilitation, or modernization of the building.
4. Record keeping and rent collecting.

The specialization required to operate as a real property manager has led to the formal recognition of three designations: the Certified Property

---

[1] James C. Downs, Jr., *Principles of Real Estate Management,* 11th ed. (Chicago: Institute of Real Estate Management, 1975), p. 25.

Manager (CPM), the Accredited Resident Manager (ARM), and the Accredited Management Organization (AMO).

Professional Management Designations

The Institute of Real Estate Management, one of the affiliates of the National Association of Realtors®, which awards professional designations, was formed in 1934 from an informal group which met to enforce certain ethical standards of real estate managers. Beginning in 1938, the bylaws were changed to provide for the Certified Property Manager.

The Certified Property Manager (CPM). To qualify for the designation, a CPM applicant must (1) be a candidate for membership in the Institute of Real Estate Management, which requires a high school education, legal age, and one full year of management experience; (2) be recommended for membership by the admissions committee; (3) have not less than three years' experience as a real estate manager and a college degree in business administration (without a college degree, five years of management experience are required); (4) hold some form of membership in a member board of the National Association of Realtors® or an individual membership in the Association; and (5) pass at least three examinations given by the Institute as prescribed by regulations.

It was recently reported that property managers were managing in excess of $68 billion of real estate. CPMs spend some 61 percent of their time in property management and the balance in related activities, such as real estate brokerage, syndication, and counseling and appraisal.[2]

The Accredited Resident Manager (ARM). The resident manager is the on-site manager who serves as the communication link between the executive manager (for example, a Certified Property Manager) and tenants. The resident manager is expected to report on neighborhood changes, trends in tenancy preferences, and the condition of the rental property. The resident manager is responsible for implementing management policies. Persons who have taken the resident manager's course and successfully passed the final examination are awarded the ARM designation.

The Accredited Management Organization (AMO). After 1945, real estate firms could be designated as Accredited Management Organizations by the Institute of Real Estate Management. To qualify, a firm must have an officer or a management executive who holds the CPM designation. The firm must be actively engaged in the business of real estate management, and must conform to the standards of ethics established for an accredited management organization. The AMO designation may be used on company stationery and advertising.[3]

---

[2] Educational Courses, Books, and Publications and Professional Certification (Chicago: Institute of Real Estate Management, 1976), pp. 2–3.

[3] Downs *Real Estate Management,* p. 28.

The Management Agreement

Like the real estate broker who operates under a listing agreement, the manager works under a management agreement signed by the property owner and the management agency. Although the management agreement may be arranged for virtually any time period, most managers prefer a three-year contract. Three years provides time to revise management policy and secure tenants ideally adapted to the property. If repairs, modernization, or rehabilitation programs are necessary, a three-year period allows the manager to complete a logical plan of development. The main duties of the manager are described by paragraph 2 of the model management agreement prepared by the Institute of Real Estate Management. Under this agreement the management agent agrees:

> (*a*) To accept the management of the Premises, to the extent, for the period, and upon the terms herein provided and agrees to furnish the service of its organization for the rental operation and management of the Premises.
>
> (*b*) To render a monthly statement of receipts, disbursements and charges to the following person at the address shown . . .
>
> *   *   *   *   *
>
> and to remit each month the net proceeds (provided Agent is not required to make any mortgage, escrow or tax payment on the first day of the following month). Agent will remit the net proceeds or the balance thereof after making allowance for such payments to the following persons, in the percentages specified and at the addresses shown. . . .

The management agreement requires the bonding of the agent and his or her employees. So that the manager may exercise his best efforts, the owner gives the agent limited authority and allows the manager to make certain necessary outlays in the name of the owners. The management agreement gives the manager authority to:

1. Advertise the property for rent.
2. Hire, discharge, and pay employees to operate the property.
3. Collect rents.
4. File all necessary reports to federal, state, and local agencies.

The owner authorizes the management agent to rent and grant leases to tenants for a stated number of years. The management agent has the authority to renew and cancel leases and to execute new leases. The manager may sue tenants for the recovery of rent in the name of the owner. The management agent may negotiate maintenance and service contracts, such as elevator maintenance, window washing, and landscaping contracts, up to a stated amount, which is entered on the contract.

The management agreement provides for a management fee, which is usually based on a percent of the gross income. Ordinarily, the percentage is lower for larger projects, for example, a 500-unit luxury apartment, and higher for smaller, low-income units. The range probably extends from 4 percent for larger projects to as high as 10 percent for smaller units. The economies of scale are such that a 4 percent fee would be reasonable for operating a large luxury apartment house complex with few tenant problems, while a 10 percent fee for managing a 100-unit, low-income apartment house project would cover the additional costs of dealing with high tenant turnover, vandalism, delinquent rents, and other problems associated with low-income projects.

A management firm will have both fixed and variable costs of operation. Suppose that a management firm experienced an annual cost of operation of $1,000,000, including a 20 percent profit. If the firm was staffed to manage 10,000 apartment units, its management fee would average $100 per unit. In calculating its cost of operation, one firm prices apartment management fees according to the following schedule:

Number of Units	Price per Unit
25 or less	$120 per unit per year, plus $50 for rental.
26–50	$115 per unit per year, plus $50 for rental.
51–100	$110 per unit per year, plus $50 for rental.
101–150	$105 per unit per year, plus $50 for rental if there is no on-site manager or janitor who can handle rentals.
151–200	$100 per unit per year. Property requires on-site manager. No rental fee except on new construction (first-time rent-up).
201–300	$95 per unit per year. Property must have on-site manager and secretary-receptionist. No rental fee except on new construction.
Over 300	$90 per unit per year. Property must have on-site manager, secretary-receptionist, part-time rental consultant. No rental fee except on new construction.

Source: William D. Sally, "Pricing Residential Management Fees . . . Fairly and Accurately," *Journal of Property Management,* September/October 1976, p. 235. Reprinted with permission.

Note that a $50 fee is charged for rental of an apartment that has no resident manager. The rental fee compensates the manager for extra costs incurred with buildings that have a high tenant turnover, including frequent visitations to the project site.

Under the management agreement, the manager must obtain permission before making any structural changes, and then only with a specific grant of authority from the owner. For example, the management agreement typically reads:

> The owner expressly withholds from the agent any power or authority to make any structural changes in any building or to make any other major alterations or additions in, or to any such building or equipment

therein, or to incur any expense chargeable to the owner other than expenses relating to exercising the express powers above invested in the agent without prior written direction of the following persons.

In sum, the authority of the agent is limited to the normal operating tasks of managing real estate. Rehabilitation, modernization, and conversion are covered by other express grants of authority by the owner.

Tenant Selection

The real estate broker markets titles in real estate—the right to possession and exclusive use in perpetuity; the real estate manager markets the right to possession and exclusive use over a specific time. To this extent, the real estate manager has a continuing interest in tenant activities. The interaction of tenants in part determines the continued success of the investment and even the neighborhood. A tenant unsuited to a location in a shopping center, for example, an accounting office, is not likely to generate customers for an adjoining women's dress shop; if the property manager leases the same space to a family shoe store, the shoe store generates customers for the women's dress shop. Ideally the property manager tries to select a compatible group of tenants in the interest of maximizing tenant satisfaction and net income.

The same rules apply to office buildings, industrial parks, and apartment complexes. For instance, it is not unusual to commit an apartment unit to a three-year lease. The property manager may agree to undertake decorating and to supply other services to the tenant provided that the credit and employment of the tenant prove satisfactory. As a condition to renting the property, the property manager requires tenants to complete an application form granting the manager the right to investigate credit, employment, and former rental references.

Such a form is shown in Figure 18–1. Note that in this form the applicant agrees to pay for the credit report, and that he provides a rental history, an employment record, his present salary, and personal references. With this information, the manager determines the applicant's past record on promptness of rent payments and rental delinquencies. Selecting tenants on this basis lowers vacancies, leads to a compatible group of tenants, reduces tenant turnover, and lowers rental collection expenses.

Residential Leases

Most property owners approving a lease for more than 30 days require a written lease between the tenant and the owner or the management agent. Leases grant the exclusive right to use premises for a stated period, over a specified rental term. Most of the lease agreement is devoted to qualifying a tenant's right to the exclusive use of the property. A lease that conforms to Virginia law is shown in Figure 18–2.

FIGURE 18–1

A Tenant Application for a Rental Apartment

APPLICATION TO RENT FROM
W.F. BALDWIN AND SON REALTORS

Application to rent_____

Rent per week or month_____

_____
date

CREDIT REPORT

    I herewith deposit $1.00 with W.F. Baldwin & Son, Realtors for the purpose of processing a credit report that a determination may be made by W.F. Baldwin & Son, Realtors if they can, or can not rent to me; it being understood and agreed herewith that no information from this credit report can be given to me and it is also understood and agreed that the $1.00 deposited herewith is not refundable to me if I rent or do not rent this property. The $1.00 is for servicing a local credit report only.

_____(SEAL)   _____(SEAL)
FOR W.F. BALDWIN & SON, REALTORS   APPLICANT AGREES

- -

APPLICATION

NAME_____
    LAST   FIRST   MIDDLE   SPOUSE   NO. OF CHILDREN

I NOW LIVE AT_____
    ADDRESS

I HAVE BEEN PAYING $_____RENT EACH WEEK OR MONTH AT THE ABOVE ADDRESS.
AND I HAVE BEEN RENTING FROM_____FOR_____YEARS
    REAL ESTATE CO. (ETC.)

I WORK (MY EMPLOYMENT IS)_____

AND I HAVE WORKED THERE FOR _____YEARS AND MY SALARY IS $_____,

MY DATE OF BIRTH IS _____AND I AM _____YEARS OLD.

    BELOW I GIVE TWO (2) PERSONAL REFERENCES OR PEOPLE THAT KNOW ME AND THAT W.F. BALDWIN & SON MAY CALL

(1)_____
    NAME   ADDRESS   TELEPHONE

(2)_____
    NAME   ADDRESS   TELEPHONE

    I HAVE LIVED FOR THE LAST THREE (3) YEARS AT _____
_____   _____
_____   _____

*   If the above property is rented to me this application is to be attached to and made a part of that agreement.

Source: *The Property Manager's Guide to Forms and Letters,* book 1, "Renting the Residential Unit" (Chicago: Institute of Real Estate Management, 1971), p. 5.

FIGURE 18–2

An Apartment Lease

(Page 1 of 3-page form)

DRUCKER & FALK

APARTMENT LEASE

This Agreement of Lease. Made this   day of   19

between   , hereinafter styled lessor,

and

(All words herein referring to Lessee to be taken to be of such gender and number as the circumstances may require), hereinafter called tenant. WITNESSETH, That the lessor lets unto the lessee or tenant, all that certain property, to-wit:

to be used as a private residence and for no other purpose,

for the term of

beginning on the   day of   , 19   , and ending on

the   day of   , 19   , at noon of each of the said

days, paying therefor unto the said parties of the first part, or their agents, in lawful money of the United States, the

term rental, or sum of

payable in advance, as follows:

without formal demand, during business hours, at the office of Drucker & Falk,

The above letting is on the following terms and conditions:

FIRST: Tenant has deposited with Lessor the sum of $.. Dollars, as security for the full and faithful performance by Tenant of all the terms, covenants and conditions of this lease to be performed by Tenant against which sum Lessor is authorized to charge any damages occasioned by Tenant's not fully and faithfully performing any of said terms, covenants or conditions. At the expiration of the term of this lease (or renewal thereof) any unused portion of said sum shall be returned to Tenant, but only after an inspection of the premises (to be made as soon as convenient to management) has been made after vacation thereof by tenant and before occupancy by another tenant. NO SECURITY DEPOSIT SHALL BE RETURNED TO ANY TENANT OCCUPYING THE APARTMENT FOR LESS THAN THE ORIGINAL TERM OF THIS LEASE OTHER THAN MILITARY AND GOVERNMENT PERSONNEL TRANSFERRED ON MILITARY ORDERS.

MANNER OF PAYMENT AND REMEDIES OF LESSOR.

SECOND: The tenant will without previous demand therefor pay the rent at the time and in the manner above provided, and in case of non-payment of said rent; or in case the leased premises shall be deserted or vacated, lessor shall have the right to enter the same at once either by force or otherwise, without being liable to any prosecution therefor, and to distrain for rent, and also re-let the said premises as agents of lessee for any unexpired balance of the term and receive the rent therefor. The tenant also agrees that all property on the said premises and for thirty days after removal shall be liable to distress for rent, and waives the benefit of all laws exempting any of his property from levy and sale either on distress for said rent, or on judgment obtained in a suit therefor.

RENT IN ARREARS AND REMEDIES.

THIRD: It is further agreed, that if said rent in whole or in part shall at any time be in arrears and unpaid, said lessor may distrain or sue therefor; and if the tenant shall fail to comply with any of the conditions of this lease, or notice given under the terms hereof, then lessor may at his option re-enter upon the premises hereby rented without further form of process of law, and such re-entry shall, at the option of the lessor, constitute a termination of this lease. No such termination of this lease, however, nor re-covering possession of the premises, shall deprive the lessor of any other action or remedy against the tenant for possession, for rent or for damages.

NOTICE TO QUIT OR SURRENDER.

FOURTH: Either party hereto may terminate this lease at the end of said term by giving the other WRITTEN NOTICE OF AT LEAST TWO MONTHS PRIOR THERETO. The lessor reserves the right to mail by ordinary mail said notice to terminate lease, or to deliver said notice to the lessee, or any member of his family, or employees. The lessee accepts these conditions as the legal means to cancel lease. BUT IN DEFAULT OF SUCH NOTICE THIS LEASE SHALL CONTINUE UPON SAID TERMS AND CONDITIONS AS ARE HEREIN CONTAINED FOR A PERIOD OF ONE YEAR AND SO ON FROM YEAR TO YEAR until terminated by either party hereto, giving to the other at least two months notice for removal prior to expiration of current term, provided, however, that if the lessor shall have given at least two months notice in writing previous to the expiration of said term (or any extension of renewal thereof as above), of his intention to change the terms or conditions of this lease, and if tenant shall hold over into another term, he shall be considered a tenant under the terms and conditions mentioned in such notice for another similar term, and until the lease is again terminated by notice as hereinabove provided.

If the lessee is in the military service of the United States and is transferred out of the Hampton Roads Area or if he is discharged from the service, after signing this lease, he may cancel it by giving 30-days written notice. However, liability under the lease will not terminate until orders of such transfer or discharge are displayed.

If the lessee should be transferred by his employer or changes employment and is required to live outside the Hampton Roads Area, he may cancel this lease by giving one calendar months notice effective the last day of the first month following such notice. However, liability under this lease will not terminate until evidence satisfactory to lessor has been submitted of such transfer or change of employment.

FIGURE 18–2 (continued)

(Page 2)

NO ASSIGNMENT OR SUB-LETTING.

FIFTH: Tenant shall not without written consent of the lessor first endorsed on this lease use or allow to be used the said premises for any purpose other than above mentioned, nor assign this lease for the whole or any part of the term, nor underlet the whole or any part of the said premises, nor allow said premises or any part thereof to be occupied by any other person than tenant, or other persons authorized by owner or agent. Any lawful levy or sale or execution or other legal process, and also any assignment, or sale, in bankruptcy, or insolvency, or under any compulsory procedure, shall be deemed an assignr within the meaning of this lease.

EXPIRATION OF LEASE AND TERM HEREOF. IMPROVEMENTS AND FIXTURES.

SIXTH: Tenant will during the term keep and at the expiration thereof deliver up said premises in as good order and condition as the same now are, reasonable wear and tear and damage by accident or fire alone excepted. Tenant shall not make any alterations or additions without lessor's consent, endorsed on this lease, and all alterations, additions or improvements made by either of the parties thereto upon the premises except movable furniture and fixtures put in at the expense of the tenant, shall be the property of the lessor, and shall remain upon and be surrendered with the premises at the termination of this lease.

SEVENTH: It is further understood that should the tenant, who now occupies the property above leased, refuse to move prior to the inception date of this lease, that the lessor shall use every legal effort to compel him to vacate so that the lessee may have possession of same, but that the lessor shall not be liable for any damages other than rebate of rent and deposit paid, and if possession cannot be given within 30 days, then either party may terminate this lease upon giving written notice before possession of the property can be secured.

EXAMINATION OF SHOWING PREMISES,

EIGHTH: The tenant agrees to allow the lessor or his representatives, at any reasonable hour to enter the said premises for the purpose of inspecting the same, for making repairs that they may deem necessary or desirable; or for showing the premises to any parties after a vacating notice has been given.

NINTH: The tenant will not hold the lessor liable for any damage to his property. He agrees to assume all risks of every kind, whether relating to property or person in connection with his occupancy of the leased premises, whether the same arise from defects latent or patent in connection with the building or other parts of the leased premises and whether or not the same were known by the lessor at the time of making this lease and were not disclosed by the lessor at that time, or at any subsequent time.

It is understood as a part of this lease that any repairs or alterations which may be made by the Lessor at the request or by permission of the tenant, during this lease or any renewals or continuance of the same, are to be construed as done by them only for the preservation or improvement of the property. No matter how often, nor for what purpose they may be done, they are not to be taken as indicating the existence of any agreement implied or otherwise, that it shall be the duty of the Lessor to do such things, nor any similar nor other things in connection with the leased property, no matter how long this lease may be continued, nor how often such things may arise.

DAMAGES FROM WATER, ICE, GAS, SNOW, STEAM, ETC.

TENTH: That the said lessor shall not be liable for any damage or injury occasioned by or from electric wiring, plumbing, water, ice, snow, gas, steam or sewerage or any other damages or injury howsoever caused nor shall the lessor be responsible for any accident to the tenant or any occupant of premises, resulting form any cause whatsoever, and the tenant agrees that he will not hold the lessor liable in any way, whether such accident occur in the said premises, or in any part of the said building.

DAMAGES BY FIRE TO PREMISES.

ELEVENTH: If during the term the demised premises be damaged by fire or the elements, they shall be repaired by the lessor with all reasonable diligence; and in case they shall be so badly injured that they cannot be repaired with such diligence so as to be fit for occupancy the rent shall cease from the date of the injury until they shall be repaired, and the tenancy shall not be terminated unless such repairs shall require more than sixty days, in which case tenant shall have the option of vacating the premises, provided always, that there shall be no cessation of rent if the damages shall have been the result of negligence, default, or wilful act of the tenant or his agent or employees.

DAMAGES TO PREMISES.

TWELFTH: The tenant agrees that he will not use, or permit to be used, the roof of the said premises, nor will he injure or disfigure the said premises nor any part thereof in any way, nor allow the same to be done, and that he will be responsible for the breakage of all glass in the said premises, and agrees to replace the same without delay, regardless of how same was broken.

THIRTEENTH: That to secure this lease, lessee represents that he is of good moral character and not engaged in any illegal or immoral business on or off the premises. The untruth of which now or during the term of the lease shall be grounds for terminating this lease.

HEIRS, EXECUTORS, ETC., BOUND.

FOURTEENTH: All rights and liabilities herein given to or imposed upon either of the parties hereto shall extend to the heirs, executors, administrators, successors, and so far as same is assignable by the terms hereof, to the assigns of such parties.

FIFTEENTH: The tenant further agrees to do at his own expense, such improvements, repairs, decorations, and upkeep to the premises during the term of this lease as he desires for his convenience and comfort, and to keep the plumbing, sewerage, heating and lighting fixtures in good order, and to keep the premises in sanitary condition.

STOREROOMS, LOSS, DAMAGE, ETC. STEAM HEATING AND WATER.

SIXTEENTH: Where storerooms are provided by the lessor to accommodate the tenants in the storage of trunks or other articles, it is with the express understanding that space is furnished gratuitously by the lessor and that tenants using the same for any purpose do so at their own risk and upon express stipulation and agreement that the lessor shall not be liable for any loss, damage, or injury whatsoever. Lessor will keep in the premises a central heating plant for the use of the tenants during such periods as the same may be necessary between the first of October and the fifteenth day of May in each year. In consideration of the fact that no extra charge is made for heat and water, lessor shall not be liable for any failure to supply the same.

RULES AND REGULATIONS PART OF THIS AGREEMENT

SEVENTEENTH: The rules and regulations in regard to said building, annexed to this lease, and such amendments and modifications thereof as may from time to time be made by the lessor, shall be considered a part of this agreement, and tenant covenants that said rules and regulations shall be faithfully observed by tenant and his employees, and all persons invited by tenant into said building.

FIGURE 18–2 (concluded)

(Page 3)
RULES AND REGULATIONS

NO OBSTRUC-
TIONS.

    A.—The sidewalks, entry, passages, and stairways shall not be obstructed by the tenants, nor used by them for any other pur-pose than for ingress and egress to and from their respective apartments.

'GHTS, WATER
CLOSETS, ETC.

    B.—The doors, floors, skylights and windows that reflect or admit light into passageways or into any place in said building shall not be covered or obstructed by any of the tenants. The water closets and other water apparatus shall not be used for any other purpose than those for which they were constructed and no sweepings, rubbish, rags or other substance shall be thrown therein. Any damage resulting to them from misuse shall be borne by tenant who shall cause it.

PROPERTY AFFECT-
ING INSURANCE
RATES, ETC.

    C.—No tenant shall do or permit anything to be done in said premises, or bring or keep anything therein, which will in any way increase the rate of fire insurance on said building, or on property kept therein, or obstruct or interfere with the rights of other tenants, or in any other way injure or annoy them, or conflict with the laws relating to fires, or with the regulations of the Fire Department, or with any insurance policy upon the said building or any part thereof, or conflict with any of the rules of the Board of Health.

HEATING

    D.—No tenant shall use any method for heating other than that provided for in the within lease.

NUISANCES

    E. No domestic or wild animals shall be kept in or about the premises.

RENT INCLUDES

    F.—The rent of an apartment will include heat and water.

PERSONAL
PROPERTY RISK.

    G.—All personal property placed in the leased premises or in any other portion of said building or any place appurtenant thereto, shall be at the sole risk of the Lessee or the parties owning the same, and the Lessor shall in no event be liable for the loss, destruction, theft of or damage to such property.

TELEGRAPH AND
TELEPHONE

    H.—If tenants desire telephone connection, the lessor will direct the electricians as to where and how the wires are to be introduced, and without such direction no boring or cutting for wires will be permitted.

    I.—It is understood and agreed that reasonable observance by the lessee of the rights, privileges and welfare of the other tenants in the building is to be maintained at all times and in the event the conduct of the lessee is, in the opinion of the lessor or its agent, prejudicial to the interest of the lessor and the rights, privileges and welfare of the other tenants in the building, then the lessor may terminate this lease at any time by serving upon the lessee five (5) days notice of his desire and intention to so ter-minate this lease. A letter sent by registered or certified mail shall be sufficient notice under the provision set forth above. Any unearned portion of the rent is to be refunded the lessee following vacation of the premises.

POSSESSION

    J.—The Lessor shall not be liable for failure to deliver possession of the leased premises at the time stipulated herein as the date of the commencement of the tenancy nor shall such failure excuse the Lessee's obligation hereunder, except that in the event of delay, the rent herein stipulated to be paid shall be abated for the period from the date of the commencement specified in this lease to the day possession is tendered to the Lessee.

WITNESS the following signatures and seals.

DRUCKER & FALK, Agents

APARTMENT INCLUDES THE FOLLOWING
ITEMS IF SO DESIGNATED:

By: _____

_____(SEAL)

ITEM	YES	NO
Range		
Refrig.		
Furn.		

_____(SEAL)

I have read the "FOURTH" paragraph of this Lease.

_____(SEAL)

It is understood that in the event Agent saves Lessee from any rent liability under this lease by entering into another lease for these premises, a $5.00 fee will be charged for Agent's services.

The first part of the lease commits the property to the tenant for a stated period of time. ". . . The lessor lets unto the lessee or tenant, all that certain property, to wit: . . . to be used as a private residence and for no other purpose . . ." The succeeding part of the lease defines the lease term and states the rental and the conditions of its payment. Other portions of the lease qualify the tenant's rights.

For example, paragraph 3 outlines the rights of the owner if the tenant defaults in any terms of the lease. Further, the tenant is required to surrender the premises by written notice at least two months prior to lease termination. The tenant is prohibited from assigning or subleasing the premises without permission of the owner (paragraph 5), and is directed to keep the premises "in as good order and condition as the same now are, reasonable wear and tear and damage by accident or fire alone excepted."

The tenant must allow the owner or his representatives to inspect the premises at reasonable times; the tenant is prohibited from injuring or disfiguring the premises in any way (paragraph 12). Other paragraphs of the lease concern tenant obligations to make interior repairs, qualify the use of storage space, and direct the tenant to observe building rules and regulations which are made part of the lease (paragraphs A to J).

Note further that the rules and regulations further qualify tenant rights of use. These rights are mutually enforceable against all tenants and tend to preserve the utility of the property. For instance, entry passageways must be kept clear; tenants must not obstruct windows or skylights in common areas; tenants must not use the property so as to increase the rate of fire insurance; and tenants must not interfere with the rights of other tenants—for example, "No domestic or wild animals shall be kept in or about the premises."

Other responsibilities of the management relate to negotiating lease extension or renewal, the issuance of delinquency and eviction notices, and enforcing the rules and regulations. Some of these operations may be delegated to the resident manager.

The Resident Manager

The resident manager—the on-site manager representative—has the overall responsibility for daily operations. These responsibilities may be divided into three categories:

1. Marketing and public relations.
2. Rental collection and record keeping.
3. Operational supervision.

In the public relations role, the on-site representative helps create an image for the project. In the marketing function, the resident manager helps sell space to the public that needs a particular type of accommodation. In this task, the resident manager implements the marketing program. The on-site representative makes the first point of contact and must carefully qualify the prospect. Proper greeting and qualifying of rental prospects are among the main marketing responsibilities of the resident manager. To help in the marketing program, the prospect must be informed about the neighborhood and its churches, schools, and recreational, shopping, and transportation facilities. And above all, he must be informed about the building and its features in comparison to competing space.

In exercising the rent collection and records system, a checklist is used for inspections of apartments in preparation for new occupancy, and the checklist also helps to maintain proper records for each tenant. In organizing and supervising operations, the resident manager must observe a monthly maintenance calendar, initiate purchase order requests, and maintain employee work records.

MANAGEMENT CONSULTING

Real estate managers wear many hats. Probably most of their consulting work relates to recommendations on rehabilitation, modernization, and the conversion of existing properties to alternative uses. Property managers are consulted by developers to establish a rental schedule and make other management proposals for new apartment house projects. In addition, real estate managers specialize in undertaking management surveys. Management surveys are usually made for problem properties.

Rehabilitation, Modernization, and Conversion

Property managers consult owners on methods of managing property for maximum income. If the property is an existing structure, the property manager studies the feasibility of rehabilitating or modernizing the property or of converting it to some other use.

To the manager, these terms have a special meaning. *Rehabilitation* refers to a structure which is restored to a like-new condition but whose present use and design are unchanged.

Modernization refers to the replacement of equipment that is wearing out or is functionally obsolete. Again, no change in use is recommended, if all that needs to be done is to replace, say, the heating system, the lighting fixtures, or the plumbing with more modern facilities. Modernization extends the useful life of the building and maintains or increases net income or, conversely, prevents net income from decreasing, which may result with continued deterioration.

Property *conversions* are more complex. Conversion to a new use is advised if the current use is no longer profitable and a change in design or use must be made for continued operation. Cases in point are the conversion of an apartment building to a condominium or the development of an abandoned downtown industrial property to a new use, such as a discount store or a warehouse. Property managers recommending a conversion first estimate the highest and best use and then show the cost of conversion.

Proposed Construction

Developers contract with real estate managers to recommend rental schedules for proposed buildings. Such a consulting contract is demonstrated by a real estate manager operating in the Chicago rental market. The contract reads:

1. [The property manager] will define the upper and lower limitations of the rental structure, i.e., what is the maximum rental to be achieved without inviting fast turnover from initial occupancy or slow initial rent-up. This analysis will include recommendations for both the initial marketing phase and the operational phase of the rental program, together with the effect of specific amenities on said marketing program.
2. [The property manager] will furnish the necessary qualified personnel to work directly with your organization in scanning all architectural and engineering details on a consulting basis as these relate to the physical management of the properties to insure that major architectural designs will not hinder or increase the cost of future operation.
3. [The property management firm] will utilize its background and knowledge concerning the initial marketing of apartments and the sale of condominiums and/or townhouses to advise you as to which stage should be constructed first as a part of your critical path planning.

A second management consulting responsibility relates to questions on the management of the proposed project: recommendations on the initial staff, office procedures, bookkeeping and record systems, leasing policies, forms and reports. Such an analysis will project a program and staff for interior and exterior maintenance, miscellaneous repairs, supplies and utility expenses, scavenger pickup, and preventive maintenance, security, and recreational programs.

The blueprints will be analyzed to project an operational and maintenance budget for the first two years of operation. Recreational facilities will be judged according to their competitive impact on the local rental and sales market. The recreational program staff will be recommended. If the project covers a condominium conversion, the manager makes recommendations to an attorney on points to incorporate in the declaration which will reduce problems in common area management and in developer-owner relations. The manager may even consult on or supervise the preparation of signs, graphics, advertising, and model apartments.

The Management Survey

As defined by the Institute of Real Estate Management (IREM), The management survey is a comprehensive economic analysis of an income property. The survey may be requested by the owner, who may want to buy, sell, refinance, redevelop, or change the property use. In the final analysis, the management survey includes a plan under which the owner will realize the highest net income.

The recommended plan of action, however, may not always produce higher rents. If the same use is continued, tenants may already be paying market rent. But modernization or rehabilitation may result in lower vacancy rates, lower tenant turnover, or lower operating expenses. To accomplish these objectives, the management survey covers six topics:

1. Physical real property inventory.
2. Neighborhood analysis.
3. Market analysis.
4. Gross income analysis.
5. Operating expense analysis.
6. Economic analysis of alternative plans.

The Physical Real Property Inventory. In this part of the report, the property manager describes the condition of the interior and exterior of the building from the standpoint of tenant needs. He also considers the advisability of replacing worn and outmoded materials according to the contribution that replacements make to net income.

An example of an inspection report form for an office building exterior is shown in Figure 18–3. A similar inspection report form for an office building interior is available from the Institute of Real Estate Management. Note that the form provides space for listing suggested repairs and their estimated cost. Both deferred maintenance and obsolescence are shown on this checklist. It would be uneconomic to correct some obsolete building features—in an office building, for example, wide corridors, outdated floor plans, and old style architecture. The physical inventory serves as the basis for final recommendations of the management survey report.

Neighborhood Analysis. The property manager advises owners on the long range desirability of a specific location. The manager indicates whether the neighborhood is improving or declining and analyzes the forces that determine neighborhood trends. The neighborhood analysis helps structure the rent schedule competitively with that of other rental buildings.

Moreover, the manager advises on rental prospects. In doing so, he

FIGURE 18–3

Office Building Inspection Report of the Exterior

_____ 19___

OFFICE BUILDING INSPECTION REPORT

Name of Property..Address..

Type of Property..Office Area Rental Rate..

No. of Stores..Store Area Rental Rate..

Report Submitted By..Basement Area Rental Rate..

Owner..

EXTERIOR

Items	Character & Condition	Needs	Est. Expenses
Roofs			
1. Type			
2. Flashing			
3. Valleys			
4. Drains			
Walls - North			
5. Type			
6. Base			
7. Top			
8. Tuck pointing			
9. Stone sills			
10. Coping			
11. Parapet walls			
12. Terra cotta			
13. Metal trim			
Walls - East			
14. Type			
15. Base			
16. Top			
17. Tuck pointing			
18. Stone sills			
19. Coping			
20. Parapet walls			
21. Terra cotta			
22. Metal trim			
Walls - West			
23. Type			
24. Base			
25. Top			
26. Tuck pointing			
27. Stone sills			
28. Coping			
29. Parapet walls			
30. Terra cotta			
31. Metal trim			
Walls - South			
32. Type			
33. Base			
34. Top			
35. Tuck pointing			
36. Stone sills			
37. Coping			

Source: Institute of Real Estate Management, Chicago, Illinois.

FIGURE 18–3 (continued)

GENERAL EXTERIOR			
Items	Character & Condition	Needs	Est. Expenses
Walls - South (Cont'd)			
38. Parapet walls			
39. Terra cotta			
40. Metal trim			
Walls - Court			
41. Type			
42. Base			
43. Top			
44. Tuck pointing			
45. Stone sills			
46. Coping			
47. Parapet walls			
48. Terra cotta			
49. Metal trim			
Chimney			
50. Type			
51. Comment			
Sidewalk Elevators			
52. Permits - expiration date			
53. Make			
54. Type			
55. Capacity			
56. Parts, oil, grease contr.			
57. Sidewalk doors			
58. Shaft			
59. Platform size			
60. Shaft gates			
61. Motors			
62. Pumps			
63. Tanks			
64. Generator			
65. Signal			
66. Safety locks			
67. Controls			
68. Pits			
69. Signs			
70. Comments			
Bldg. Entrance			
71. Doors			
72. Hinges			
73. Locks			
74. Checks			
75. Side lights			
76. Transoms			
77. Canopy			
78. Signal button			
79. Lighting			
80. Building name			
81. Street numbers			
82. Entry steps			
Exterior Fire Escapes			
83. Signs			
84. Access windows			
85. Access ladders			
86. Maintenance			
87. Ladder treads			
88. Hand rails			
Sidewalks			
89. Comments			

FIGURE 18–3 (*concluded*)

GENERAL EXTERIOR

Items	Character & Condition	Needs	Ext. Expenses
Light Wells			
90. Skylights			
91. Roof			
92. Comments			
Fire Hazards			
93. Defective wiring			
94. Trash and rubbish			
95. Oil, gasoline or paint storage			
96. Gas leaks			
97. Self-closing doors			
98. Breeching and flues			
99. Dumbwaiter enclosures			
100. Hot ash disposal			
101. Defective fire hose			
102. Fire extinguishers			
Windows - Office			
103. Type			
104. Frames			
105. Stops			
106. Sash			
107. Sills			
108. Lintels			
109. Anchor bolts			
110. Glass			
111. Glazing			
112. Caulking			
113. Weather strip			
114. Screens			
115. Locks			
Windows - Store			
116. Frames			
117. Transoms			
118. Sash			
119. Glass			
120. Caulking			
121. Glazing			
122. Screens			
123. Hinges			
124. Sash			
125. Locks			
Penthouse - Elevator			
126. Roof			
127. Walls			
128. Steps			
129. Doors			
130. Windows			
131. Flooring			
132. Fire protection devices			
Other Roof Structures			
Miscellaneous Extras			

outlines the main features of the neighborhood. For instance, if the property under survey is an apartment dwelling, the rental structure, property use, and marketing program depend on the character of the neighborhood. The more important factors to consider would be.

1. Transportation facilities to urban centers.
2. Highway access from the neighborhood to industrial and business areas.
3. Access to shopping centers and local convenience stores.
4. The distance to educational facilities.
5. The location of churches of different denominations.
6. Population characteristics—observed shifts in population.
7. The relative desirability of the building in comparison to competing buildings.
8. The desirability of the neighborhood from the standpoint of tenants.

Given these data, the property manager recommends a rental schedule compatible with the advantages and disadvantages of the neighborhood.

Market Analysis.   The property manager examines each lease: its date of termination, renewal options, and the annual rent per square foot or per room. The vacancy rate and credit loss may suggest management deficiencies and poor tenant selection. An unusual rate of tenant turnover may suggest dissatisfaction with existing management policies.

Part of this analysis deals with the main source of tenant income. Recommendations on the level of tenant services and the rental structure depend on the source of tenants and their income. The rents and tenant services recommended for an apartment complex serving primarily employees of an aircraft manufacturing facility would be considerably different from those recommended for an apartment project oriented to retirees in St. Petersburg, Florida.

Gross Income Analysis.   Gross income for the project will be shown per square foot of rentable area, per apartment, and per room, so that the rents may be compared with rents for similar properties. Some allowance must be made for variations in the services provided by different buildings. The availability of parking, extra storage, and such tenant services as swimming pools, sauna baths, air conditioning, and furnished utilities affects the reported gross income level. In some circumstances, the manager may suggest the withdrawal of free utilities or recommend that additional services be provided tenants without charge, for example, parking garages and extra storage. These recommendations depend on the current rental market and the competition for tenants.

Operating Expense Analysis, Short and Long Term.   Starting from an operating statement prepared for income tax purposes, the manager develops a statement of operating expenses for decision-making purposes. The profit and loss statement must be classified to permit a separate study of *current* expenses and *stabilized* expenses.

Current expenses are actual out-of-pocket expenses paid over an operating year. A statement of current expenses does not show the true cost of earning gross income since some expenses may be deferred and others are incurred only as repairs are made or items are replaced.

In contrast, a stabilized expense statement will include an annual sum to cover the replacement of short-lived items. In an apartment project, for example, allowance must be made to replace kitchen appliances, ranges, ovens, refrigerators, furniture, and lobby fixtures. The cost of these items will be prorated over their expected life, say, three to five years. A stabilized expense statement shows the projected expenses, indicating the true annual cost of earning annual gross income. The resulting answer is the stabilized net operating income.

The Economics of Alternative Plans. At this point the manager may recommend a program of modernization, rehabilitation, or conversion to some other property use. In each case the manager will present a capital improvement budget—the budget will show the costs of repairing, replacing, or converting the project to another use.

The management survey will report the cost of correcting physical deficiencies or the cost of correcting functional obsolescence. In more advanced reports, the income tax aspects of capital improvements will also be explained (higher depreciation allowances, interest deductions on improvements financed by additional mortgage money). The property manager separately reports the expenses and the expected gross income to be earned under alternative plans. The final recommendation will relate the rate of return to the risks undertaken in following suggested management recommendations. In short, the management survey starts with a study of the local market, and concludes with a plan for adapting the property to meet current needs to the end of maximizing investment objectives.

CONVERTING AN APARTMENT RENTAL UNIT TO CONDOMINIUM OWNERSHIP

The conversion of apartment units to condominiums appeals to developers because of the potential profit which may be earned over a relatively short time. The conversion of an existing building to a condominium takes less planning and is subject to fewer delays than planning and constructing a new condominium. Yet not all rental projects are suitable for such conversion, and because the success or failure of a conversion depends partly on factors not under the control of the developer, the property manager reduces investment risks by selecting a building ideally adapted to condominium conversion. Even then, the profitability of conversion depends on general economic conditions, the availability of financing, favorable interest rates, and local government cooperation. Because it may take several months to complete a condominium conversion, the market conditions may not be predicted accurately.

Conversion Problems

The conversions of rental apartments to condominium units have been criticized on the ground that tenants and condominium purchasers are frequently abused by incompetent or unethical developers. The main objections to conversions center on three main problems: tenant displacement, tenant treatment, and construction deficiencies. Certain other minor problems have been disclosed by investigations conducted by the Department of Housing and Urban Development.[4]

Tenant Displacement. The current record shows that nationally approximately 75–80 percent of tenants affected by conversions are displaced. In some instances the tenant must either purchase or secure other rental housing after a 30-day eviction notice. Tenants with relatively low income are especially vulnerable to displacement. Such tenants must relocate because they cannot meet the financing terms of the purchase. In these circumstances a one-month notice to relocate is inadequate, especially if the local apartment vacancy rate is less than 5 percent.

As a result, some communities (for example, Washington, D.C.) have issued temporary moratoriums on conversions, while in other areas, such as the state of Maryland, a tenant is given six months to relocate. Further restrictions are illustrated by the city of San Francisco, which prohibits an apartment conversion if the plan is opposed by 35 percent of the tenants.

Tenant Treatment. A developer depends on tenants to acquire a certain percentage of converted units. The developer realizes rental income from tenants during the conversion process. On sale of a converted unit, the developer hopes that the tenant will vacate quickly to allow immediate renovation or redecoration of the unit for owner occupancy. Uncooperative tenants and impatient developers lead to expensive controversies. In this environment, authorities have found instances of tenant harassment and maltreatment and unlawful issuance of eviction notices.

Construction Quality. Questionnaire surveys by the Department of Housing and Urban Development revealed that approximately one third of the purchasers reported misrepresentation by the developer as to the nature of the apartment or project after conversion. Problems have also been created by the malfunctioning of mechanical, electrical, plumbing, or structural systems soon after the purchase.

Other Problems. Because condominium units usually sell for 30 percent above the rental value, unit owners have occasionally faced unexpected property tax assessments. In addition, if all converted units are not sold, conflicts arise between renters and unit owners. For instance, it is claimed that renters are less likely to obey rules and respect the rights of

---

[4] This discussion is based on the HUD report entitled *HUD Condominium/Cooperative Study,* vol. 1 (Washington, D.C.: U.S. Government Printing Office, 1975), pp. V–34 to V–40.

other occupants. Some of these issues may be resolved by a study of conversion feasibility.

Conversion Feasibility

The more successful conversions have dealt with middle-income and luxury apartments in the central locations of large urban centers. Moreover, buildings constructed in the shape of letters, that is, E, H, and U, have restricted views, which do not have the appeal of open-view apartments, and which do not make good subjects for conversion.

Feasibility will be determined in part by the costs of conversion: (1) the costs of restoration and (2) the costs of improvements that enhance marketability. Restoration returns the building to a like-new condition. Correcting for deferred maintenance and replacing worn-out equipment—the heating system, air conditioning, elevators—enhances marketability. Features that enhance marketability include adequate clubhouse space, swimming pools, recreational facilities, and structural changes to individual apartments, such as kitchen and bathroom remodernization.[5]

Apartment Conversion Demonstrated

To emphasize the main issues in estimating the feasibility of converting an apartment to a condominium, consider the conversion of a multiple-family housing development, referred to here as the Hill View Apartments.[6]

Building Description. The 120-apartment unit was constructed in 1968. It was located on a five-acre site and consisted of four two-story buildings and two three-story buildings. It was a garden apartment with outside entries from ground level or exterior walkways. It had no interior hallways. The buildings were concrete, had a slab foundation and intermediate floors of lightweight concrete, stucco exterior walls and wood shingles, interior dry wall construction, vinyl tile bathroom and kitchen floors, and ceramic tile baths and showers.

Construction quality was above average. Each apartment unit was supplied with an air conditioning system, a range, a refrigerator, a dishwasher, a garbage disposal, and a television antenna hookup. Washers and dryers were available for common use in two locations. Some units had fireplaces. All units had a carport and a large storage locker. The common areas included heavily landscaped grounds, a swimming pool, a small clubhouse, and parking space. The building was in a good, well-maintained condition.

The location, a medium-sized suburban community of 100,000 was an upper middle-class and above-average neighborhood. The area was sur-

---

[5] See William M. Shenkel, *The Real Estate Professional* (Homewood, Ill.: Dow Jones-Irwin, Inc., 1976), pp. 234–36.

[6] This material is adapted from *HUD Condominium/Cooperative Study*, vol. 2, appendix B.

rounded by relatively high-priced, single-family dwellings, modern rental apartments, and other condominiums developed over the past 15 years. The site was well located with respect to employment, schools, and shopping, and access to all of these facilities was readily available from a limited-access freeway which was one mile distant. It is fairly clear that the amenities favored condominium ownership.

Rental Data. The economics of conversion depend partly on the rental structure. Electricity, water, and natural gas were included in the monthly rent. The annual gross income totaled $428,000, giving a spendable income after debt service of $56,600. These figures are shown in Table 18–1.

TABLE 18–1

Preconversion Operating Statement: Hill View Apartments

Gross rent.............................		$ 441,000
Less vacancy...........................		−13,000
Actual gross income.....................		$ 428,000
Expenses:		
Real estate taxes......................	$76,900	
Insurance.............................	3,800	
Utilities..............................	10,500	
Management fee.......................	20,000	
On-site management...................	31,000	
Improvements.........................	2,500	
Building maintenance..................	7,000	
Grounds maintenance..................	7,300	
Supplies..............................	1,600	
Advertising...........................	2,400	
Other.................................	3,800	−166,800
Net income before debt service..........		$ 261,200
Debt service...........................		−204,600
Net spendable income...................		$ 56,600

Source: *HUD Condominium Cooperative Study,* vol. 2 (Washington, D.C.: U.S. Government Printing Office, 1975).

The apartments, which showed a net operating expense ratio of 38 percent ($166,800/$428,000) and a vacancy rate of 2.94 percent, would be regarded as a profitable operation. A condominium conversion study indicated very favorable prospects for converting rental income to substantial capital gains. Part of the success of the project depended on the expected number of tenants who would purchase condominium units.

Tenant Characteristics. The tenants were professional people with above-average incomes. Most of the tenants were middle-aged, and some lived with older children (children under 16 were not permitted). Since nationally, approximately 50 percent of tenants had purchased condominium units on conversion, the present tenant mix favored an even higher higher level of purchases by existing tenants.

The Condominium Plan.   The apartment owners favored conversion. The rental unit was owned by 70 limited partners who purchased Hill View shortly after construction. Accelerated depreciation of 1.25 times straight-line rates sheltered all project cash flow. By the time of conversion, the partners were experiencing diminishing benefits of tax shelter and the property had *appreciated* approximately $3 million since purchase. The developer-converter offered to purchase the property outright from the partners for $3.93 million.

The next step was to secure local government approval of the condominium plan. The tenants originally opposed the conversion on these grounds: (1) they could not afford to purchase an apartment unit; (2) condominium conversions would decrease the supply of available rental housing; (3) relocation would cost each tenant an average of $500; and (4) the building was not structurally suited for condominium ownership. The city approved a condominium conversion provided that the tenants were given six months to relocate, that each tenant was given the right of first refusal to purchase units in the project, and that the developer would bring the property up to "as built" condition.

The Financing Plan.   To finance the project, the developer requested an 80 percent loan of $4,050,000, based on an estimated combined condominium value of $5,070,000. Such a loan was approved at a 10 percent interest rate for 18 months. The developer invested an equity of $50,000 to finance the project. The estimated cash flow was based on an expected sales rate of ten units per month. The purchasers of condominium units were able to finance their purchase with an 80 percent loan with 30-year repayments at current market interest rates. Some loans were available at 90 percent of the sales price with slightly higher interest rates.

The Condominium Budget.   The conversion expenses totaled $617,300. (See Table 18–2.) Interest on the 18-month loan, commissions, personnel costs, and renovation expenses accounted for the major share of the conversion expenses. Rental income of $110,000 received from tenants during conversion reduced the total cost of conversion.

The Marketing Plan.   The marketing plan offered tenants the right to purchase a condominium unit prior to public sale with $1,500–$2,700 discount from the public sales price, depending on the size of the unit purchased. Forty of the 120 units were purchased by tenants, and in four months 50 percent of the units were sold. About 15 of the original tenants rented units purchased by individual investors at a rental approximately 30 percent above the previous rental. Final sales of all units were completed in about 15 months.

The conversion required the developer to repair driveways, exterior building cracks, sidewalks, balconies, and walkways; to install drainage tile; to replace some defective plumbing; and to paint building exteriors. The developer undertook no decorating or repainting of individual interiors, but instead offered individual purchasers a $600 to $1,200 deco-

TABLE 18–2

Conversion Expense Budget: Hill View Apartments

Marketing		
Advertising.............................	$ 35,000	
Models.................................	7,500	
Printing brochures, etc..................	3,000	
Other..................................	10,500	
Total...............................		$ 56,000
Personnel		
Project manager........................	12,500	
Receptionist...........................	7,500	
Commissions to sales representatives...	160,000	
Total...............................		$180,000
Legal and professional services		
Legal fees.............................	8,000	
Documentation.........................	3,500	
Title insurance and recording...........	25,000	
Legal survey...........................	7,500	
Accounting............................	4,800	
Other..................................	3,500	
Total...............................		$ 52,300
Finance—interest........................		$269,000
Renovation		
Interior (credits)........................	120,000	
Exterior...............................	25,000	
Total...............................		$145,000
Operations		
Rental income.........................	(235,000)	
Rental expense........................	125,000	
Total...............................		($110,000)
Contingency.............................		25,000
Grand Total....................		$617,300

Source: *HUD Condominium/Cooperative Study,* vol. 2 (Washington, D.C.: U.S. Government Printing Office, 1975).

rating credit. The prices of units ranged from $33,500 to $61,000, with monthly condominium maintenance fees ranging from $33.50 to $62.20.

Project Profitability. Table 18–3 indicates a profit of $350,000 for the developer converter. Profitability was lower than expected because (1) sales took 15 months instead of the projected 12 months; (2) the cost of an engineering report required by the city was not anticipated; (3) legal and interest costs on the loan exceeded the original estimates; (4) the rental income was reduced because some tenants moved out, causing a temporary 20 percent vacancy; and (5) there were unanticipated repair and renovation expenses.

TABLE 18–3

Comparison of Estimated Original Budget and Outcome: Hill View Apartments

	Original Budget	*Estimated Outcome*
Profit summary		
Sales price	$5,066,000	$5,070,000
Purchase price	3,780,000	3,930,000
Gross profit	$1,286,000	$1,140,000
Conversion expenses	617,000	790,000
Net profit	$ 669,000	$ 350,000

Source: *HUD Condominium/Cooperative Study,* vol. 2 (Washington, D.C.: U.S. Government Printing Office, 1975).

Nevertheless, the conversion was successful, and its success probably turned on a number of favorable points:

1. The developers of the rental unit experienced a capital gain after some four years of ownership.
2. The developer was able to sell the condominium for a total value of $5,070,000, which was $1.14 million above the original purchase price.
3. Tenants were in the middle-income class with sufficient assets to make down payments.
4. The structure had amenities associated with condominium ownership —a swimming pool, landscaped grounds, and a clubhouse.
5. Tenants were able to purchase property and finance an 80 percent loan with monthly payments comparable to rental expense.
6. Tenants realized that condominium ownership would give them the benefit of a constant mortgage payment compared to annually increasing rent.
7. Tenants anticipated gains from appreciation. In fact, during the 14-month sales period a tenant who purchased a $42,000 unit resold for $49,500.

Apparently these benefits were sufficient to overcome the limitations of condominium ownership. In this case purchasers assumed responsibility for maintaining unit interiors, sacrificed freedom to move, subjected themselves to the governing rules of the project, and assumed financial obligations for the operating budget.

THE MANAGEMENT OF LOW-INCOME APARTMENT UNITS

Owners of public and private projects have an incentive to use professional real estate managers for low-income housing projects. The importance of this area is indicated by Department of Housing and Urban

Development estimates that 20 percent of FHA rent supplement projects and 30 percent of below-market interest rate projects would be foreclosed during the first ten years of project life.[7]

In a survey of 20 federally subsidized multiple-family projects in Pittsburgh, it was discovered that management was the most significant factor in explaining tenant satisfaction. Tenants judged management according to (1) the quality of maintenance, (2) the trustworthiness of management, (3) the degree of response management gave tenant complaints, and (4) management strictness in enforcing rules. The study concluded, "Management is the most important determinant of tenant satisfaction, more important than neighborhood services, neighboring project cleanliness, security, or the physical unit."[8]

Improving Resident Relations

Professional managers have recommended elimination of the term *tenant*. Accordingly tenant unions are changing into resident councils, advisory committees, and open town hall meetings. Apparently these changes help residents and management to work toward common goals. In the face of rising utility costs, improved relations with project residents may lead to measures to compensate for added costs of operation.[9]

In subsidized housing, for example, managers solicit volunteers through the resident council to help supplement the operating staff in cleaning interior hallways, eliminating trash, and keeping the laundry room and the grounds clean. Members of the tenant council form rent collection committees, and they may give emergency assistance, but more important, they explain that rent must be paid on the due date.

Improving Resident Satisfaction

One study has recommended that resident satisfaction must incorporate every aspect of the living environment—that management should take a broad perspective in coping with the forces that infringe upon residents. This means that management must respond quickly to resident complaints and ensure that repair work meets minimum standards. The following points are also helpful in dealing with low-income management problems:

1. It is important to improve the management qualities of trust and fairness.
2. It is important that management be responsive not only to maintenance problems but also to other tenant problems.

---

[7] Roger S. Ahlbrandt, Jr., et al., "The Key to Satisfied Tenants: Good Management," *Journal of Property Management*, September/October 1974, p. 213.

[8] Ibid., p. 215.

[9] See *Tenant Councils: Preparing the Climate* (Champaign: Housing Research and Development, University of Illinois at Urbana-Champaign, no date), p. 47.

3. Strictness or firmness in the enforcement of rules is positively associ-
    ated with tenant satisfaction. Management must not only set rules of
    behavior but must communicate those rules to the residents and must
    enforce the rules in a reasonable manner. Enforcement of the rules
    also requires an element of consistency over time and among tenants.
4. Increasing maintenance expenditures may not be the correct approach
    for raising the level of tenant satisfaction; improving quality and re-
    sponse time may be more important.

It is fairly clear that management competence reduces operating costs and
improves rent collections and the physical condition of the unit and its
surroundings.

Resident Councils

Increasingly, management has turned to resident councils to improve
resident relations. Management councils encourage tenants to accept management policy. For example, before a complaint becomes an emotionally
charged issue, residents turn to the council to make recommendations to
management.

Managements that participate in resident councils help establish a
formalized structure with elected officers and a written constitution or bylaws. If the project is a nonprofit or public housing unit, a formalized
written agreement may be drawn between management and the resident
council.

Management may even introduce members to resident council training
programs directed to understanding housing operations. The training of
resident representatives covers tenant selection and move-in policies, the
computation of rent, management, modernization and maintenance programs, and procedures for requesting management maintenance services.
Residents working through a council are less prone to make excessive and
unreasonable demands.[10]

SUMMARY

A property manager directs, controls, or operates real property for a
fee. The property manager's main task is to secure the highest net income
over the useful property life. Management activity concentrates on four
areas: (1) merchandizing space; (2) operation and maintenance; (3)
remodeling, rehabilitation, or modernization; and (4) record keeping and
rent collecting.

Professional managers are designated as Certified Property Managers
by the Institute of Real Estate Management. To gain the CPM designation,
a candidate must pass examinations and have not less than three years'

---

[10] Ibid.

experience as a real estate manager. Accredited Resident Manager (ARM) and Accredited Management Organization (AMO) are designations attesting to the competence of managers and management firms, respectively.

Property managers operate under a management agreement that defines the duties and authority of the managing agent. The agent must secure the owner's permission before exceeding the authority delegated by the management agreement. To function effectively, management qualifies tenants with respect to their credit rating and their past rental history. Managers typically rent apartment space under a lease that grants the tenant exclusive rights of use and possession over the lease, and stipulates the conditions under which the tenant may use the property. Particular attention is placed on the enforcement of rules and regulations that help maintain the utility of the property for the mutual benefit of tenants and owner.

The resident manager serves as the on-site management representative. In this capacity the resident manager assists in (1) marketing and public relations, (2) rent collection and record keeping, and (3) operational supervision.

Property managers advise clients on rehabilitation, which restores a building to a like-new condition; on modernization, which replaces worn-out or functionally obsolete equipment; or on conversion, which changes an existing property use to a more profitable use. In their capacity as real estate managers, they advise on rental schedules for proposed buildings. They recommend a management organizational structure and a marketing and record-keeping program.

The management survey parallels the appraisal report prepared by a qualified real estate appraiser. The survey is a comprehensive economic analysis of an income property. Among the subjects analyzed in the report are the physical real property inventory, the neighborhood, the market, gross income, operating expenses, and alternative plans.

The problems encountered in management consulting are demonstrated by the analysis of an apartment rental unit considered for conversion to condominium ownership. Conversion feasibility rests largely on features that enhance marketability, for example, adequate clubhouse space, a swimming pool, recreational facilities, and minimum restoration costs.

Conversion may be advised if tenant characteristics favor a condominium plan, namely, if tenants have above-average incomes and assets to make down payments. Moreover, condominiums are likely to be feasible if the combined condominium value is considerably above the value of the project operated as a rental property. Favorable financing may reduce equity requirements to fairly nominal amounts. Assuming favorable financing, a condominium budget and marketing plan are prepared to estimate conversion profitability.

The management of low-income apartment units emphasizes the significance of the management function. Surveys have shown that management is the most significant factor in explaining tenant satisfaction. Professional managers working with low-income groups in subsidized housing operate through tenant councils to improve resident satisfaction. Such councils assist in recruiting volunteers who perform custodial operations and help communicate management policy to residents.

REVIEW QUESTIONS

1. Define a real estate manager.
2. What are the main functions of a real estate manager?
3. What qualifications are associated with professional management designations?
4. What is the purpose of the management agreement?
5. Explain how a manager arrives at an equitable management fee.
6. Why is the problem of tenant selection so critical to income property management?
7. Why are managers advised to rent space under a certain lease? Explain fully.
8. Explain the main duties of a resident manager.
9. Give examples showing the difference between rehabilitation, modernization, and conversion.
10. What contributions do managers make in consulting owners on new construction?
11. What are the main elements of a management survey?
12. What is meant by the "economics of alternative plans"?
13. What are the factors that seem significant to successful apartment rental conversion to condominium ownership?
14. Explain how a real property manager contributes to the efficient management of low-income rental housing.

SELECTED REFERENCES

Beaton, William R., and Bond, Robert J. *Real Estate,* chap. 9. Pacific Palisades, Calif.: Goodyear Publishing Company, Inc., 1976.

Brauer, William; Sachar, Roger; Shepard, Reba; and Walters, William. *The Resident Manager.* Chicago: Institute of Real Estate Management, 1973.

Downs, James C., Jr. *Principles of Real Estate Management.* 11th ed. Chicago: Institute of Real Estate Management, 1975.

Ring, Alfred A., and Dasso, Jerome. *Real Estate Principles and Practices,* chap. 23. 8th ed. Englewood Cliffs, N.J.: Prentice-Hall, Inc., 1977.

Unger, Maurice A. *Real Estate,* chap 21. 5th ed. Cincinnati: South-Western Publishing Co., 1974.

Weimer, Arthur M.; Hoyt, Homer; and Bloom, George F. *Real Estate,* chap. 17. 6th ed. New York: Ronald Press Co., 1972.

19

Land Development: Residential, Commercial, Industrial Parks

After reading this chapter, you should be familiar with the following points:

1 The advantages and limitations of land investment.
2 Techniques of developing residential land.
3 Methods of evaluating subdivision feasibility.
4 Judging prospects for commercial development.
5 Development under net ground leases.
6 Commercial development under syndication financing.
7 Procedures followed in developing organized industrial parks.

IT IS POPULARLY BELIEVED that land provides a universal and relatively safe hedge against inflation. The record does not always support this conclusion. Land values are subject to economic, physical, and political forces that are difficult to predict. Moreover, vacant land merely held for investment provides no cash flow. The profitability of holding vacant land rests on (1) the potential use of the land and (2) the present worth of expected sales proceeds.

To explore these concepts, land is treated first as an investment, then as an asset for urban development: mainly residential, commercial, and industrial. The first part of the chapter explains the unique characteristics of land investment. The remainder of the chapter treats specific land use investments.

LAND INVESTMENTS

Land investment presents opportunities for capital gains. Under our system of ownership, land must be held by an owner—public or private. In one sense capital gains represent the reward for holding land until the land succeeds to a higher use. Before evaluating land investments, certain qualifications seem advised.

Qualifying Land Investments

Homer Hoyt, a well-known land economist, advises investors to observe several generalizations before committing funds to vacant land. Starting with the proposition that land must have a potential use to earn a reasonable return, Homer Hoyt advises:

1. Vacant land that will never yield an income in the foreseeable future may have no justified value—even in times of inflation. Though speculation may increase sales prices, this possibility cannot be safely relied on for investment purposes.
2. Even in metropolitan areas there is more vacant land than can be absorbed for urban use.
3. Zero population growth lessens the total demand for land.
4. The no-growth policies of some communities prevent future building.
5. Redevelopment by building high-rise apartments, town houses, and suburban apartments lowers the total demand for subdivision acreage.
6. The movement from metropolitan centers increases the demand for land in fringe areas.
7. Overbuilding of urban properties, offices, apartments, shopping centers, or factories decreases the short-run demand for urban land.
8. Environmental controls increase the cost of developing land, lowering vacant land values.
9. The demand for vacant land is contingent upon the availability of

credit for new construction. Credit sources are scarce under inflationary conditions.[1]

With these points in mind, more specific comments on land investments may be cited.

Land Investment Advantages

Investors typically look to the proceeds of sale in buying land for investment. In contrast to investors who pay cash and hold land for long-run appreciation, most investors finance land purchases. The most popular approach is to buy land with a low down payment and with low carrying costs and to sell within three–five years.[2] To illustrate, assume a 100-acre purchase of $200,000 which is held for four years and then sold for a net price of $300,000. Assume further a $20,000 down payment, four annual payments on a purchase money mortgage, and annual property taxes of $3,500. With an annual interest cost of $14,400 and annual property taxes of $3,500, the carrying costs would total $17,900 per year or $71,600 over four years. For an investor in the 50 percent income tax bracket, the $71,600 carrying cost would have a *net* carrying cost after taxes of $35,800 (50 percent of $71,600). Hence, the total investment after taxes would total $55,800:

Down payment	$20,000
Aftertax carrying cost	35,800
Total aftertax investment	$55,800

Under these assumptions, which are based on an expected increase in land values of 50 percent over four years, or 12.5 percent average appreciation per year, the investor doubles his money in four years.

These results appeal to investors who look to proceeds of the sale for a return on their investment. Land investments financed in this way provide

Net sales price	$300,000	
Less mortgage	−180,000	
Pretax proceeds	$120,000	
Less capital gains tax	−25,000	
Aftertax proceeds		$95,000
Total *aftertax* investment		
Down payment	$ 20,000	
Aftertax carrying cost	35,800	−55,800
Aftertax profit		$39,200

For a more detailed explanation, see Maury Seldin, *Land Investment* (Homewood, Ill.: Dow Jones-Irwin, Inc., 1975), pp. 23–25.

---

[1] See Homer Hoyt, "Investment in Vacant Urban Land as a Hedge against Inflation," *MGIC Newsletter,* November–December 1974.

[2] Maury Seldin, *Land Investment* (Homewood, Ill.: Dow Jones-Irwin, Inc., 1975), p. 23.

some tax shelter (but not as much as a building which may be depreciated under accelerated depreciation methods). Land investments are suitable for high-leverage short-term investments. They require that investors have sufficient cash to pay carrying costs, for example, interest and property taxes. Even so, however, investors must assume the risk that land values may depreciate.

Land Investment Limitations

The first limitation of land investment is that, unlike commercial property, which earns income and provides cash flow, land investment requires the payment of an annual carrying cost—the investor must have sufficient income from other sources to meet real estate taxes, interest payments, and other outlays during the time that the land produces no income. Agricultural or other temporary uses seldom yield enough to pay carrying costs.

Second, the rate of land appreciation is uncertain. It is unrealistic to anticipate that land will increase in value at some constant rate. In fact, it is more likely that land values will remain stable for several years and then suddenly increase in value as the result of new zoning, highways or utilities, or changes in surrounding land use. Conversely, local land values may decrease as the result of adverse economic, political, or physical changes.

Third, buying vacant land subjects investors to title risks not encountered in the purchase of government bonds, stocks, or other intangible investments. Ownership of land follows from the title acquired by the buyer —which may be subject to judgment liens, easements, zoning controls, land use restrictions, and other ownership risks. While title insurance, title abstracts, and warranty deeds minimize these risks, they do not eliminate all risks of ownership.

Fourth, landowners may not have the inside information held by local real estate dealers or public officials. As a result, they may sell below market to others who have knowledge of impending public or private activities that affect local real estate values.

Fifth, the highest returns on land are found in the acquisition of large tracts. Ordinarily, the purchasers of small lots do not have the same opportunities for leverage and capital gains as the buyer of large tracts.

Consider further certain *financial risks* associated with land investment. An investor in land assumes numerous financial risks, not shared by depositors in a savings institution who earn interest with relatively little risk of capital. The land investor receives no assurance that the investment capital will be recovered. Vacant land earns no annual income. Compared to an income-producing property subject to depreciation allowances, the land investment earns no cash flow.

Consider also the *risks of the market*. Unpredictable changes in the economy or local factors that change land use subject the investor to a market risk. There is no way to predict future property value. The buyer purchases the present worth of future benefits, and though the expectations may be favorable, expectations are not always realized in a market where land values are subject to change.

Next, consider that the investor in land gives up *liquidity*. Again, in contrast to a deposit which may be withdrawn on demand, typically an investment in land cannot be converted to cash without allowing sufficient time to find a buyer. In the short run, the market value may not have changed, so that the land may be converted to cash only by paying selling costs and assuming a capital loss.

Last, consider the point that landowners must *risk losses from natural hazards:* flooding, fire, problems arising from drainage, water, air, and noise pollution. Tornadoes and hurricanes are other hazards that may materially affect land values.

RESIDENTIAL DEVELOPMENT

At one time, developing land for residential purposes, primarily subdivisions for single-family dwellings, was a matter of judging the suitability of the site, estimating the costs of development, projecting sales proceeds, and calculating cash flow requirements. A project was deemed feasible if the present worth of expected sales exceeded costs. And provided that cash flow was positive and favorable, the project would be recommended.

Entitlement to Use Strategy

This reasoning is still valid. But new land use controls add a further dimension. Land developers must proceed under an entitlement to use strategy program—a program that describes an internal policy to process land development, required because so many agencies must approve a new project. The Irvine Company, a large-scale land developer near Newport Beach, California, states that "a complete understanding of the law and the administrative process is a necessity in the course of land development." According to this source, a potential challenge to land development may occur at any point before a final development permit is reached. "Continual monitoring is no longer a luxury—it is now a required necessity."[3]

The issue is particularly pressing for land developments that fall within coastal zone areas. A developer in the California coastal zone area proposing to develop subdivision land must consider regulations that cover at least 11 issues:

---

[3] Statement by Hardy M. Strozier, Manager and Entitlement to Use Task Force Coordinator, The Irvine Company, Newport Beach, California, in letter dated November 17, 1975.

1. Environmental impact reports (EIR).
2. Zoning codes.
3. Compliance with the general plan of local agencies.
4. Tentative map (subdivision map act).
5. Air pollution, including indirect sources and parking.
6. Water pollution.
7. Land use legislation, open space and agricultural use legislation.
8. Environmental management regulations promulgated by local governments, including phased development permits.
9. Noise controls.
10. Housing codes, density controls.
11. Antiquity laws: archaeological and historical preservation.

It will be appreciated that these problems must be resolved in addition to the usual feasibility studies and financial analysis reports. The environmental impact report calls for a detailed checklist supervised by the project planner.

Step   1—Test for Ministerial Project

Step   2—Test for Categorical Exemption

Step   3—Test for Emergency Projects

Step   4—Initial Studies Preparation
            (Environ Evaluation)

Step   5—Negative Declaration Preparation

Step   6—EIR Preparation

Step   7—Draft EIR Review and Comment

Step   8—Public Circulation and Comment

Step   9—Planning Commission Hearing

Step 10—City Council Hearing

Step 11—Final EIR Completion[4]

The negative declaration called for in Step 5 is prepared if it is indicated that the project will not have a significant effect on the environment. Even here, the project developer must determine whether more than one agency requires project approval. In this instance, the negative declaration must be made available for public comment some 30 days before the agency conducts a hearing to approve the project.

Evaluating Potential Residential Land

Subdivisions create deferred income. The initial outlay for land, capital, planning, and project processing through the required agencies must be advanced under the expectation of future land sales. If sales are not realized, capital losses result which are difficult to recoup. A subdivision that

---

[4] *Entitlement to Use Strategy Program* (Newport Beach, Calif.: Irvine Co., no date), pp. 3–1 and 3–5.

suffers deficiencies in some major respect commits fixed capital to an investment which has few alternative uses. Both investors and the community lose from poorly designed, poorly located, and ill-conceived subdivisions.

Land developers recommend checklists so that issues relevant to subdivision feasibility are not overlooked. Such a checklist is shown in Figure 19-1. The checklist does not indicate the relative importance of the items

FIGURE 19-1

A Checklist for Evaluating Potential Residential Land

A. *Protection against inharmonious land uses*
   1. Zoning
   2. Protective covenants
   3. Geographic position of neighborhood in relation to other functional areas of the city
   4. Character of neighboring structures
B. *Physical and social attractiveness*
   1. Special hazards and nuisances
   2. Natural physical features and landscaping
   3. Neighborhood design
   4. Architectural appearance of neighboring buildings
   5. Compatibility among neighborhood occupants
   6. Prestige
   7. Friendship location pattern
C. *Adequacy of civic, social, and commercial centers*
   1. Quality and access of schools
   2. Quality and access of shopping centers
   3. Churches, recreational centers, and theaters
   4. Local government
D. *Adequacy of transportation*
   1. Diversity and cost
   2. Quality and frequency
   3. Distance from site to boarding point
   4. Time required to destination
   5. Convenience
   6. Private transportation
   7. Roads
E. *Sufficiency of utilities and services*
   1. Quantity
   2. Quality
   3. Cost
F. *Level of taxes and special assessments*
   1. Taxes
   2. Special assessments
G. *Relative marketability*
   1. Location of competing sites
   2. Finished home costs

      3.   Financing

      4.   Market situation for site and ripeness

      5.   Housing and location to suit market demand

H. *Land acquisition and development costs*

      1.   Land availability

      2.   Land cost per area or lot

      3.   Physical suitability

      4.   Extent of clearing

      5.   Financing

      6.   Sites for community facilities

      7.   Total estimated development costs

 I. *Local regulations*

      1.   Zoning.

      2.   Rehabilitation of previously platted land

      3.   Building regulations

 J. *Utilities*

      1.   Extent of installations existing and required

      2.   Water and sewerage

      3.   Electricity, gas, and telephone

Source: William J. Casey, *How to Buy and Sell Land* (New York: Institute for Business Planning, 1962), pp. 15–16.

listed under each heading. For instance, a subdivision may be rendered relatively unmarketable by protective covenants that insure compatible land use or by buildings, if absent or inappropriate.

For example, if property owners are allowed to construct unsightly accessory buildings, garden sheds, garages, or other structures not in harmony with other subdivision buildings, the neighborhood depreciates. And while the physical and environmental attractions may meet the highest standards, the land may be unmarketable. Subdividers should know the rate of land absorption among competing sites. Their projection of sales must be related to estimates of the local market for housing at a specific location for the type of project under development. Given realistic projections, the land acquisition and development costs and the financing terms largely determine the subdivision's potential.

Subdivision Development Costs

Besides the environmental and land use studies required by local, state, and federal agencies, an engineering cost survey must be made for the proposed acreage and reduced to an estimated cost per lot. For example, assuming no land leveling costs or expensive street grading, the costs would be broken down into the following categories:

Estimated Costs of Subdividing 40 Acres

Streets
    Excavation
    Base course

Curb and gutter
Sidewalk
Pavement
Sewers
Eight-inch sewer mains
Four-inch house laterals
Manholes
Water
Eight-inch water main
Six-inch water main
Fire hydrants
Service connections
Underground power
Underground telephone
Gas mains
Engineering fees
Preparation of tentative map
Final map, street and sewer
Improvement plans
Tract map
Tentative map check
Flood control check
Final map check
Improvement plan check
Recording fee
Property taxes
Financing charges

Assuming a land cost of $3,000 an acre, the proposed 80-acre sub-division would require a $240,000 land investment. Allowing three lots per acre, the land cost per lot would be $1,000. If the property is fully developed as planned, assume also a development cost of $5,000 per lot, or a total of $1,200,000. Land and subdivision improvements would result in a per lot investment of $6,000.

$1,200,000	Subdivision improvements
240,000	Land cost
$1,440,000	Total cost
($6,000 per lot)	

Even assuming that lots could be developed according to this schedule and sold for $12,000 per lot—a profit of $6,000 per lot—it does not follow that the project would be feasible. The central problem is to compare the costs incurred by stages in comparison to the expected sales.

Table 19–1 shows how development costs are incurred in relation to expected gross income. Note that the subdivision requires a land purchase of $300,000 and a $35,000 closing cost. In the first and second years, the direct costs of development total $256,500. It is not until the third year that sales of $120,000 less sales expenses produce a net income of $7,500.

TABLE 19–1

A Schedule of Projected Cash Flow for a Proposed Subdivision, Landco Development Company

							Year						
	Close	1	2	3	4	5	6	7	8	9	10	11	12
Inflow:													
Sales..............				$120,000	$120,000	$150,000	$150,000	$150,000	$150,000	$90,000	$90,000	$90,000	$90,000
Loan draws.......	$335,000	$150,000	$106,500	100,000	56,500								
Total inflow........	335,000	150,000	106,500	220,000	176,500	150,000	150,000	150,000	150,000	90,000	90,000	90,000	90,000
Outflow:													
Land purchase....	300,000												
Closing fees.......	35,000												
Loan repayment.......				106,500	106,500	133,125	133,125	133,125	133,125	79,875	36,648		
Direct costs.......		150,000	106,500	100,000	56,500								
Other expenses:													
General and administrative					3,000	3,000	3,000	3,000	3,000	3,000	2,000	2,000	2,000
Property tax......					3,000		2,500		2,500		2,000		1,500
Sales expense......				6,000	6,000	7,500	7,500	7,500	7,500	4,500	4,500	4,500	4,500
Total outflow........	335,000	150,000	106,500	212,500	175,000	143,625	146,125	143,625	146,125	87,375	45,148	6,500	8,000
Net cash in (out)..	0	0	0	$ 7,500	$ 1,500	$ 6,375	$ 3,875	$ 6,375	$ 3,875	$ 2,625	$44,852	$83,500	$82,000

Source: Henry E. Hoagland, Leo D. Stone, and William B. Brueggeman, *Real Estate Finance*, 6th ed. (Homewood, Ill.: Richard D. Irwin, Inc., 1977).

Development costs are not completed until the end of the fourth year, and even with sales of $150,000 per year from the fifth year to the eighth year, the loan repayment and sales expenses absorb most of the gross receipts. Not until the tenth year does the developer realize a net income of more than $6,375 (the fifth and seventh years).

While subdivisions may not follow this precise pattern, the example illustrates the problem of deferred income. If the expected sales do not meet the planned schedule, the subdivision stands in danger of foreclosure. Further, the net income for each year must be discounted to present worth to show the value of the proposed project.

COMMERCIAL DEVELOPMENT

The procedures outlined for residential land development are germane to commercial land development. According to one authority, the first step in developing an apartment house project is to select a city which shows prospects for a growing rental market. For example, a favorable multiple-family market occurs if the following conditions are present:

1. *Population Growth*—A growth rate of 5 percent a year or more is a good rate.
2. *Net In-Migration*—This figure is the number of newcomers, offset by the number of out-migrants. If migration accounts for more than half the population gain, the situation is most promising.
3. *Low Multifamily Ratio*—If the multifamily percentage is less than 15 percent, an unfilled demand may exist.
4. *High Absorption Rate*—Check the number of new rental units the city has absorbed during 10-year periods. This figure provides a basis for future probable absorption.
5. *Low Vacancy Rate*—Although broad overall measures of vacancy can sometimes be misleading, at least they are an initial measuring stick. If a city shows an overall vacancy rate below 5 percent, or even below the prevailing national average, it could be a good market for new rental housing in the right price ranges.
6. *Growth of the Economic Base*—Apart from temporary ups and downs, the long-term growth or shrinkage of the local housing market is related to the economy of the local area. Planning groups, universities, and industrial development organizations have already made long-range studies and projections. These studies may be readily obtained and evaluated.
7. *Shift in Population Mix*—Because of varying birth and death rates, migration, immigration, employment opportunities, and other factors in the population mix of a city tend to vary over a period of years, and these variations cause fundamental changes in housing demand.[5]

---

[5] William R. Smolkin, "Marketing for the Apartment Builder," in *Land Development Manual* (Washington, D.C.: National Association of Home Builders, 1974), pp. 285–86.

Assuming that a city qualifies for further investigation, the apartment developer selects a site that shows a strong demand for multiple-family units. Before the site is selected, the developer reviews the competition. This means that the developer should make a field inspection of competitive units, survey occupants of existing competitive buildings, and even employ comparative shoppers to elicit rental data. The review may include interviews with property managers and owners and the usual sources of local data, including the tax assessor, local planning and zoning offices, and the like.

Before proceeding further, the project must show a favorable ratio of income to operating costs, and in particular, the project must show favorable ratios with respect to the following items:

1. Net operating income should be 125 percent of mortgage payments.

    a. Debt service ratio $= \dfrac{\text{Net operating income}}{\text{Annual mortgage payments}}$
    $= \$125,000/\$100,000$
    $= 125$ percent

    b. With these relationships, net operating income may decrease some 20 percent before net income is inadequate to make mortgage payments.

2. The sum of operating expenses and mortgage payments should not exceed 85 percent of gross potential income.

    a. The total of operating expenses plus debt service divided by the gross potential income shows the break-even ratio. For example:

    $$\text{Break-even ratio} = \text{Operating expenses} + \text{debt service}/\text{Gross potential income}$$
    $$\dfrac{\$30,000 + \$55,000}{\$100,000}$$
    $$= 85 \text{ percent}$$

    b. This is another way of saying that actual gross income must be equal to 85 percent of the *potential* gross income to meet operating expenses and mortgage payments. Even at this point, the developer is only breaking even. Under these assumptions, net income will not be realized until the project earns more than 85 percent of gross possible income.[6]

Commercial Property Promotion

Even with favorable financial ratios and feasibility studies, financial success turns on marketing strategy. In the case of multiple-family units,

---

[6] For a more complete discussion of financial ratios consult Henry E. Hoagland, Leo D. Stone, and William B. Brueggeman, *Real Estate Finance,* 6th ed. (Homewood, Ill.: Richard D. Irwin, Inc., 1977).

some developers allocate $100 per apartment unit or 5 percent of projected, effective gross income for promotion. A promotional program includes:

Publicity releases.

Advertising brochures.

A sales promotion manual, including prospect forms.

Off-site displays.

Rental office and displays.

Furnished model apartments.

Landscaping.

On-site signs.

Special events and promotions.

A paid advertising program.

Training a sales management staff.

Developing a promotion plan and schedule.[7]

While these steps agree with conventional commercial development, two other devices warrant further explanation: net ground leases and syndications.

Net Ground Lease Development

Long-term net ground leases represent a means of financing land. In most respects, land leased for improvement conveys the right of possession and exclusive use over the lease term. If the lease term extends from, say, 55 years to 99 years, the economic rights acquired by the tenant are comparable to a leased fee interest. In contrast to the fee simple estate, which is acquired in return for a lump-sum payment (the sales price), the lease allows the occupant to pay for use rights over the lease term and as the property earns income. In this respect, long-term net ground leases may benefit both the owner-lessor and the tenant-lessee.

Advantages to the Lessor.   Net ground leases appeal to the lessor because of four main advantages.

1. The main attraction to an owner committing land for a long-term net ground lease may rest on the *income tax effects of leasing* versus a sale. Under a lease the lessor avoids capital gains taxes. In place of a capital gains tax on a sale, the owner pays income taxes on the net ground rent at ordinary income tax rates. Depending on the tax status of the owner, this leasing may be the preferred way to minimize aftertax income.

2. Under a net ground lease, an owner may create an *income comparable to an annuity.* The income is secured by a tenant of the owner's selection. A net ground lease to a national corporation with a high credit standing is a case in point.

---

[7] Smolkin, "Marketing for Apartment Builder."

3. At the same time, if the owner requires the tenant to construct buildings adapted to the site, *tenant buildings improve the capital values* of the site and surrounding property. This assumes that the property development is operated by a competent, successful tenant who, by skilled development and management techniques, increases the capital value of the leased land.

4. Add to these advantages the fact that a net ground *lease shifts management responsibility* from the owner to the tenant. Indeed, the owner benefits from tenant investment, financing ability, and management. If a later sale is desired, a successfully leased property is readily marketable.

Advantages to the Lessee. A net ground lease may be mutually advantageous to owner and tenant. (1) The tenant secures the *equivalent of a 100 percent loan* equal to the value of the leased land. Most lenders are reluctant to lend on vacant land—at least not up to 100 percent of its appraised value. Yet the tenant may regard the rent as equivalent to interest paid for the use of capital, which in this case is invested in land. (2) Moreover, the tenant, like the owner, benefits from certain tax advantages —*land rent is deductible from taxable income.* The land cost of the fee simple estate is not deductible as an expense item since it is presumed that land is not a depreciable asset. (3) Furthermore, leasing allows the tenant to *convert available capital to buildings and other improvements*—the tenant reduces the required equity by leasing compared to landownership.

Net Ground Lease Terms. Because a net ground lease typically conveys use rights over relatively long terms—up to 99 years—it will be appreciated that such lease agreements must be lengthy and complex. Ordinarily, long-term leases will cover six main topics, though they may not follow the order of presentation given here. No standard form is followed.

1. Introductory material.
   a. Definitions (gross receipts, refunds, tax receipts).
   b. Land description.
2. Financial covenants.
   a. Term.
   b. Rental.
   c. Annual accounting.
   d. Rental bond.
   e. Performance bonds.
   f. Bonding companies.
   g. Nonresponsibility notices.
   h. Holding over.
3. Improvement clauses.
   a. Improvements.
   b. Plans and design.
   c. Construction, maintenance, repairs, and alterations.
   d. Completion of development.
4. Other rights.
   a. Sublease, assignments, and transfers.
   b. Agreements for utility lines and streets.

       c.   Encumbrances.
       d.   Liens, taxes, assessments, and utility charges.
       e.   Lessor's paying claims.
   5. Insurance.
       a.   Public liability.
       b.   Fire and damage insurance.
       c.   Unlawful use.
   6. Miscellaneous.
       a.   Eminent domain.
       b.   Arbitration.
       c.   Default.
       d.   Attorney's fees.
       e.   No partnership.
       f.   Term of trust.
       g.   Obligations of lessee.
       h.   Status of subleases.
       i.   Payments and notices.

In some respects the lease resembles other instruments conveying an interest in land. For example, the introductory material defines the terms used in the lease and identifies the property by a proper legal description. The section covering financial covenants includes items dealing with the lease term, the rent, the duties of the tenant with regard to constructing buildings, and the rights of the parties with respect to subleases, easements, mortgages, assessments, and other potential liabilities.

Since the landowner benefits from buildings constructed by the tenant, tenant buildings may even be the main reason for leasing—the lease usually allows the owner to control the quality of construction. Typical net ground leases read:

> No structure or material or addition to or alteration of the exterior of any building constructed on the leased land shall be commenced unless and until plans and specifications covering the proposed structure, addition, or alteration shall have been first submitted to and approved by the lessor.

Lease provisions concerning commercial buildings to be constructed on leased land require tenants to complete buildings of a minimum cost by a stated date. Such controls insure that the tenants improve the land partly for the benefit of the owner, who hopes to realize increasing rents from proper improvement of a vacant site. If a lease provides for rents based partly on gross receipts, this clause is particularly important.

Net Ground Lease Percentage Rents. Percentage rents are commonly associated with commercial stores and shopping centers. As a rule, owners resist long-term leases at fixed rents. Some long-term leases provide for higher rents as the consumer price index or some other index moves upward. However, changes in price indexes correlate poorly with commercial real estate values or ground rent. As a result, net ground lease rents may be adapted to developers who propose to construct buildings and sublease portions of the property under shorter terms to multiple tenants for 3, 5, 10, or 15 years. In these circumstances, rents will be partly based on a share of the business earned by the developer on subleases.

To illustrate, consider the ten leases shown in Table 19–2. Each lease commits vacant land for commercial, resort, or residential use. The acreages vary from half an acre to a 680-acre, multimillion dollar development. Note that in the first lease the 40 acres require single and multiple residences, apartments, and hotel and tennis facilities as part of a proposed resort golf course development. The tenant agrees to pay a percentage, for example, of hotel sublease rents, subdivided residential lots under sub-

TABLE 19–2

Percentage Rents on Selected Net Ground Leases, Palm Springs, California

Lease Number	Property Use	Number of Acres	Percentage Lease Rent on Subleases
1.	Single and multiple residences, apartments, hotel, golf course, tennis club, miscellaneous...............	40.0	
	Hotel...		5.0
	Residential lots....................................		35.0
	Golf course..		10.0
	Bar..		2.5
	Food restaurant....................................		2.0
	Other..		10.0
2.	Campground and residential mobile home park.......	12.0	
	Trailer space......................................		11.0
	Food restaurant....................................		4.0
	Drugstore..		4.0
	Auto sales...		4.0
	Utility..		4.0
	Other..		4.0
3.	Mobile home park..................................	20.0	
	Trailer space......................................		20.0
	Other..		10.0
4.	Hotel, apartments, condominiums, residences, bar, golf course and club, community office..........	20.0	
	General subleases.................................		25.0
	Hotel...		5.0
	Apartments..		5.0
	Residential lots....................................		35.0
	Golf club...		10.0
	Golf course..		10.0
	Bar..		2.5
	Food restaurant....................................		2.0
5.	Mobile home park..................................	22.325	
	Trailer space......................................		20.0
	Utility..		10.0
	Other..		10.0
	Utility net..		1.0

TABLE 19–2 (continued)

Lease Number	Property Use	Number of Acres	Percentage Lease Rent on Subleases
6.	Residences, cooperatives, condominiums, apartments, golf club, bar, restaurant	680.0	
	Apartments		5.0
	Residential lots		30.0
	Golf course		10.0
	Bar		2.5
	Food restaurant		2.0
	Pro shop		4.0
	Other		5.0
7.	Restaurant	0.5	
	Bar		2.0
	Food restaurant		2.5
8.	Hotel, restaurant, bar	7.9	
	General subleases		25.0
	Hotel		2.5
	Motel		2.5
	Bar		1.3
	Food restaurant		1.0
9.	Hotel, apartment houses, restaurant, coffee shop, bar, residential lot rentals	20.0	
	Hotel		5.0
	Apartments		5.0
	Residential lots		30.0
	Golf course		10.0
	Bar		2.5
	Food restaurant		2.0
	Grocery		5.0
10.	Residences, apartments, hotel, restaurant, bar, golf driving and practice range	15.9	
	Hotel		5.0
	Apartments		5.0
	Residential lots		30.0
	Driving range		10.0
	Bar		2.5
	Food restaurant		2.0

Source: Bureau of Indian Affairs, Palm Springs, California.

leases, receipts from the golf course, and receipts earned from other planned land uses.

Even for a 20-acre mobile home park, the lessor earns a minimum ground rent and in addition 20 percent of gross trailer space rents. In sum, each net ground lease provides for a minimum rent in addition to a percentage share of the developer's income from subleases or business operations.

Land Development under Syndication

An increasingly popular method of financing income property lies in syndication developments. Syndicates take many business forms, including the limited partnership arrangement. Here the syndicator serves as a general partner, originating and managing the syndicate, while the limited partners provide equity funds. To the limited partner, the syndicate has the advantages of (1) limiting liability to the amount of his investment and (2) avoiding corporate taxes. Syndicates range from complex offerings requiring Security Exchange Commission registration to local syndicates formed to develop and market relatively small commercial properties.

The Syndicate Offering. To illustrate the syndication of a relatively small project, reference is made to a syndicate formed for the purchase of an apartment earning a gross income of some $80,000. Under this plan, an equity of $80,000 was required which would be contributed by eight investors who would have a limited partner interest of $10,000 each or a one-ninth interest. The syndicator would be given a one-ninth interest as compensation for forming the syndicate.

While the nine limited partners have a joint interest, they are not acting as tenants-in-common and they are not liable for the actions of other syndicate owners. A judgment or lien against one of the limited partners attaches only to his interest in the property. The death of a syndicate owner does not affect the interests of the surviving partners.

In this case, the syndicator subordinates his one-ninth interest to the interests of the other eight limited partners. The syndication agreement provides that the syndicator receives a proportionate cash distribution of current income only after each syndicator receives a yield of 11 percent on his equity interest. Similarly, if the property is sold, the investors are entitled to recover their original investments from the proceeds of the sale before the syndicator receives a similar amount. After each of the nine partners receives his original investment ($10,000), the proceeds of the sale are divided equally among the nine parties.

Financial Projections. The syndicate was formed to purchase an existing building showing 100 percent occupancy. With depreciation based on 150 percent declining balance, the net taxable loss for the first year was projected at $927.

Gross income		$80,220
Interest, first mortgage	$20,480	
Interest, second mortgage	2,520	
Depreciation:		
Building ($380,600—40 years)	14,273	
Appliances ($15,539—7 years)	3,330	
Furniture and carpeting ($19,361—4 years)	7,260	
Operating expenses	33,284	−81,147
Net taxable loss, first year		$ 927

With first- and second-mortgage financing, net spendable income was projected at $14,747:

```
Net operating income............................................. $46,936
     Financing:
         First-mortgage payments................................  −28,008
         Cash flow before second-mortgage payments............   $18,928
         Second-mortgage payments..............................   −4,181
             Net spendable income..............................   $14,747
```

Under these terms, the investors would acquire property valued at
$433,000:

```
Cash equity supplied by eight limited partners............ $  80,000
First mortgage...............................................   313,000
Second mortgage.............................................    40,000
     Total purchase price.................................. $433,000
```

Under the syndication offering, these figures would allow an initial
distribution of approximately 16 percent on the equity invested by each
syndicate owner. The syndicate plan provided for the distribution of only
11.0 percent annually by the syndicator, with the balance to be deposited
in a special reserve account until the reserve reached $10,000.

In addition, the syndicate owners would make payments against the
mortgage principal of approximately $9,500 the first year, which is equal
to 10.5 percent of the equity capital. If this amount were added to the
projected yield, limited partners would recover 21.5 percent on the equity
investment (11.0 percent cash, 10.5 percent mortgage principal reduction). This latter conclusion assumes that the property will be sold for
its original cost plus mortgage principal reduction. In this syndication offering, syndicate partners receive tax shelter, cash flow, an effective yield
projected at 11 percent, and opportunities for capital gains on the sale of
the property.

Syndicate Problems.   Not all syndicates operate in this way. Real estate
syndicates are subject to certain problems:

1. Excessive compensation to the general partner, the syndicator-origina-
    tor.
2. Conflicts of interest when the syndicator places his own interest above
    the interests of limited partners.
3. Overly optimistic net income projections.
4. Inadequate control over the syndicator's use of partnership funds.

Regulatory bodies seek to minimize these problems by enforcing full
disclosure laws and controlling the compensation paid the syndicators.
National and state regulators controlling syndication securities have led to
recommendations by the National Association of Realtors® on syndicate
regulations.[8]

---

[8] See appendix A–1 in Stephen Roulac (ed.), *Real Estate Securities and Syndication* (Chicago, Ill.: National Association of Real Estate Boards, 1973).

INDUSTRIAL PARKS

Industrial development today encompasses all aspects of the environment: the physical, social, regulatory, and technological aspects of industrial land use. For the present purpose, an industrial park or organized industrial district has been defined in the following terms by the National Association of Industrial Parks:

> An industrial park is the assembly of land, under one continuing control, to provide facilities for business and industry consistent with a master plan and restrictions, resulting in the creation of a physical environment achieving the following objectives:
>
> consistency with community goals,
>
> efficient business and industrial operations,
>
> human scale and values,
>
> compatibility with natural environments,
>
> achieving and sustaining highest land values.[9]

In essence, industrial parks provide for exclusive industrial use by a selected group of industries. The industrial park, with its superior facilities, special planning for industries, and an enforced set of land use controls, substitutes for the mixed land uses permitted in the older industrially zoned corridors of central cities.

Some industrial sponsors provide buildings for sale or lease and offer special services in the form of financing, engineering aids, and technical counsel to district occupants. The more specialized industrial parks stress the highest standards of openness and attractiveness, making such industrial parks popular among corporations that cite these locations to enhance their public image.

The more successful industrial parks are characterized by the following qualities:

> Comprehensive planning both beyond the periphery as well as within.
>
> Joint action and investment both by public agencies and the private sector.
>
> Resource oriented toward market, transportation, or materials.
>
> Developed at a prime location.
>
> A major land use element in the community and in regional land use plans.
>
> A focal point for multi-modal transportation facilities for goods and people.
>
> Provides for industries linked by process, product, or service.
>
> Designed for optimum efficiency for occupant industries.
>
> On-site essential services both public and private for industries, employees, and clients to minimize vehicular movements.

---

[9] *Industrial Development Handbook* (Washington, D.C.: Urban Land Institute, 1975), p. 7.

Pleasant, convenient, and satisfying work conditions for employees, including the opportunity for a short journey to work.

Walk-to-work residential areas.

Protection and enhancement of the physical environment.

An industrial center, sharing facilities, minimizing redundancy.

A durable as well as attractive appearance.

A profitable return to the community in taxes, wages, and local sales.

A reasonable return to the entrepreneur and investors.[10]

Industrial districts that meet these standards benefit the public through efficient land management and the compatible operation of productive activities. Such industrial districts serve the locational requirements of compatible industrial firms while providing new employment opportunities, expanding the local property tax base, and contributing to community appearance without overly disturbing the natural environment.

The Industrial Development Process

Developing industrial property requires special attention to planning and engineering studies. Even with competent planning and engineering, marketing and financing become highly critical to project feasibility. As development takes place, land use controls continue to be enforced against industrial occupants to preserve the amenities of the organized industrial park. Figure 19–2 outlines a formal, five-part process for developing an industrial park.

FIGURE 19–2

Industrial Park Development Steps

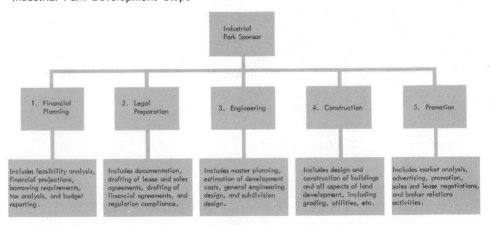

Source: Adapted from *Industrial Development Handbook* (Washington, D.C.: Urban Land Institute, 1975), p. 174.

---

[10] Ibid.

Financial Planning. As the term is used here, financing incorporates the feasibility study, the cash flow projection, sources of funds, tax analysis of the proposed project, and the pro forma budget. To this end, some industrial districts stress rail access; others, a location convenient to limited-access highways near metropolitan areas. Government-sponsored districts in smaller communities may emphasize employment. Such districts are typically found in rural small-town areas serving the needs of agricultural processing centers and showing an orientation toward transportation and distribution facilities. Ideally, organized industrial districts are generally located in the direction of industrial growth near highways, airports, rail centers, or water transportation.

Industrial park sponsors study the land absorption rate for industry—by type of industry—attempting to identify industrial land use trends. The land must be suitable for industrial development, for example, level, well drained, with the soil suitable for heavy construction. Utilities must be available at reasonable cost.

Legal Preparation. Since industrial parks represent a specialized land use, a special set of leases, sale agreements, and land use controls must be prepared. Compliance with government environmental regulations and arrangements for on-site utilities may call for easements and other documents.

Engineering. Land preparation starts with engineering studies of the site. Land grading and the platting of sites to maximize industrial utility must be presented to local agencies for approval. The detail required is shown by the site plan prepared for the Andover Industrial Park in Seattle, Washington. (See Figure 19–3.)

Note that the industrial park adjoins an access road to the interstate highway between Tacoma and Seattle. Note in addition that rail spurs are located so that industrial buildings front on both rail and streets—giving occupants relatively unrestricted access to both rail and truck services. The sponsor has also left the undeveloped portion in large tracts—a technique that gives maximum flexibility in meeting space demands for future occupants.

As illustrated in Figure 19–3, sponsors generally select locations near freeway interchanges. The interstate highway system allows occupants to move from the congested, blighted industrial areas of central cities to outlying freeway locations with little loss in access to their employees, customers, or suppliers.

The advantages of a freeway location turn on (1) transportation savings that improve access in time rather than miles. A customer may be able to reach a location 20 miles away in less time than a location 5 miles away if the latter location is handicapped by traffic congestion. (2) Skilled and professional employees in the suburbs live closer to industrial developments centered on freeways. The industrial freeway location is more convenient to employees. (3) By locating near a freeway, industrial firms may

FIGURE 19–3

Industrial Layout for the Andover Industrial Park, Seattle, Washington

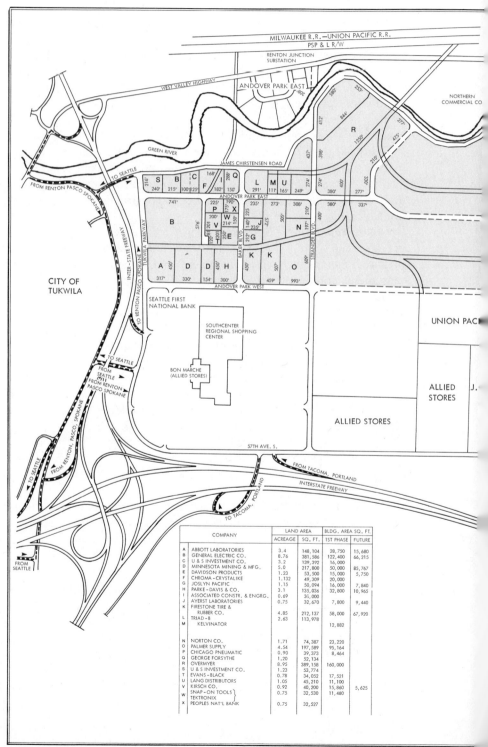

	COMPANY	LAND AREA		BLDG. AREA SQ. FT.	
		ACREAGE	SQ. FT.	1ST PHASE	FUTURE
A	ABBOTT LABORATORIES	3.4	148,104	28,750	15,680
B	GENERAL ELECTRIC CO.	8.76	381,586	122,400	66,215
C	U & S INVESTMENT CO.	3.2	139,392	16,000	
D	MINNESOTA MINING & MFG.	5.0	217,800	50,000	85,767
E	DAVIDSON PRODUCTS	1.23	53,500	15,000	5,750
F	CHROMA – CRYSTALIKE	1.132	49,309	20,000	
G	JOSLYN PACIFIC	1.15	50,094	16,000	7,840
H	PARKE – DAVIS & CO.	3.1	135,036	32,800	10,965
I	ASSOCIATED CONSTR. & ENGRG.	0.69	30,000		
J	AYERST LABORATORIES	0.75	32,670	7,800	9,440
K	FIRESTONE TIRE & RUBBER CO.	4.85	212,137	58,000	67,920
L	TRIAD – B	2.63	113,978		
M	KELVINATOR			12,882	
N	NORTON CO.	1.71	74,387	23,220	
O	PALMER SUPPLY	4.54	197,589	95,164	
P	CHICAGO PNEUMATIC	0.90	39,373	8,464	
Q	GEORGE FORSYTHE	1.20	52,134		
R	OVERMYER	8.95	389,158	160,000	
S	U & S INVESTMENT CO.	1.23	53,774		
T	EVANS–BLACK	0.78	34,052	17,521	
U	LANG DISTRIBUTORS	1.05	45,210	11,100	
V	KIRSCH CO.	0.92	40,200	15,860	5,625
W	SNAP–ON TOOLS TEKTRONIX	0.75	32,530	11,480	
X	PEOPLES NAT'L BANK	0.75	32,527		

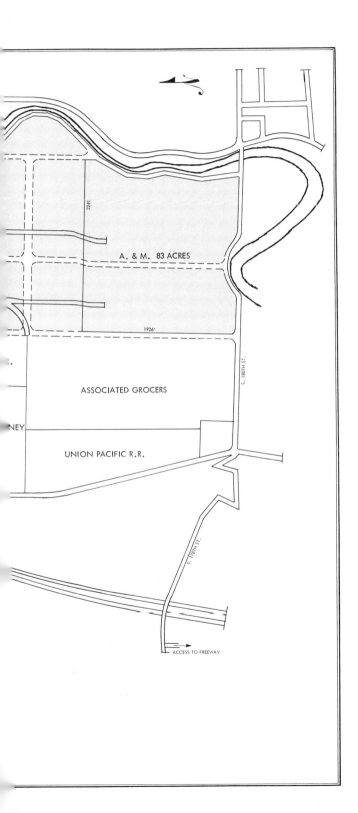

serve the central city and still compete for business in the expanding suburbs.

Construction Costs. Construction costs are especially critical for industrial parks because the land absorption rate is relatively low. While a residential subdivision may be sold out over 3, 5, or 10 years, industrial parks may take 10, or more years for full development. Industrial park sponsors reduce risks by developing large acreages in phases. Development costs fall into these categories:

> Clearing, grading, and fill compaction.
> Storm sewers and drainage.
> Rail.
> Utilities.
>> Water lines.
>> Sanitary sewers.
>> Electrical lines.
>> Gas lines.
>> Lighting, striping, and signing.
> Paving and surfacing.
> Curb, gutters, and sidewalk.
> Landscaping, trees, and shrubbery.
> Off-site improvements and miscellaneous.
> Planning, engineering, and professional fees
>> Site concept engineers.
>> Soil engineer.
>> Topographical mapping and survey.
>> Landscape architect.
> Professional fees.
>> Traffic consultant.
>> Environmental expert.

These costs may range from a minimum of $3,000 an acre to $20,000 per net acre.[11]

Promotion. Industrial sponsors recommend that project directors should be sales oriented, with broad contacts in industrial real estate. Successful promotion turns on personal contacts with banks, investment bankers, utilities, railroads, state development officials, and local agencies, among others. The marketing agent must be familiar with the locational requirements of industry, the special problems and vocabulary of particular industries, and even industrial construction.

The industrial park management must have data on competing industrial areas. In discussing industrial property with prospects, the sponsor must be able to recite the advantages and disadvantages of competitive properties

---

[11] Ibid., p. 185.

and must undertake on request cost studies comparing the features of competitive sites with those of the industrial park.[12]

Land Use Controls

Land use controls govern all occupants of an industrial park. They guard against the sale of land to occupants incompatible with other occupants. In this respect, the land use controls of private park developers are more rigidly enforced and more restrictive than public land use controls.

Land use regulations further the long-run objectives of the sponsor. Usually private sponsors tend to maintain the highest degree of utility for industrial land use. For instance, in an industrial park adapted to the distribution centers of national corporations, developers would normally prohibit the sale of land to retailers, to industries that store building materials on the premises for sale to customers, or to occupants who market secondhand machinery.

Privately enforced land use controls protect the occupants of the industrial park. Landowners selling acreage for industrial purposes in uncontrolled areas have no continuing interest in enforcing land use regulations. In contrast, land use controls conserve site utility and retard industrial blight by requiring architectural approval of building construction, by providing off-street truck loading, and by planning for employee and customer parking. Professionally developed land administered in this way helps create a continuing demand for industrial sites.

As a consequence, the industrial land use controls of the organized industrial property concentrate on (1) covenants that guide industry selection, prohibiting, for instance, industries "which shall cause a nuisance or which shall be injurious to products manufactured upon other lots, or which shall injure the reputation of the park or of neighboring property"; (2) covenants that regulate the maximum land area covered with buildings (such controls often require that high buildings be set back from the street or prohibit buildings that occupy more than a specified maximum percent of the land area); (3) covenants covering architectural and aesthetic design. Some industrial sponsors require occupants to submit building plans for approval. The more restrictive industrial parks prohibit metal face buildings and require more permanent construction, such as brick or masonry exterior walls.

SUMMARY

To anticipate profitable land investments, certain qualifications are necessary: land values do not always appreciate; land values relate closely

---

[12] Robert E. Boley, *Industrial Districts: Principles in Practice,* Technical Bulletin 44 (Washington, D.C.: Urban Land Institute), 1962.

to the prospects for potential use—a local market phenomenon. Given these qualifications, land investments provide after-sale proceeds. However, even with projected profit opportunities, vacant land earns no cash flow pending development. The land appreciation rate is uncertain. Land investment subjects the owner to title risks, financial risks, market risks, illiquidity risks, and risks associated with natural hazards.

Residential development typically involves complicated procedures relating to environmental land use controls. Determining the prospects for residential development begins with feasibility studies and a careful projection of costs, the rate of land absorption, and cash flow studies. Commercial developments call for careful analysis of the market, financial ratios, and competitive properties.

Net ground lease developments tend to be highly specialized and provide the lessor with certain income tax and financial advantages not found in alternative investments: namely, avoidance of capital gains taxes, income comparable to an annuity, tenant buildings that improve capital values, and a shift of management responsibility to the tenant.

There are also financial advantages for the lessee: the lease is equivalent to a 100 percent loan equal to the value of the leased land; land rent is deductible from federal net income taxes; and leasing allows the tenant to convert available capital to buildings and other improvements. Net ground leases call for a detailed list of lease terms, with particular attention drawn to the rental clause, which may include percentage rents on subleases and on the income of the tenant-developer.

Land development under syndication creates certain financial advantages to small investors which are qualified by syndicate problems. Among these problems are excessive compensation to general partners, conflicts of interest, overly optimistic projections, and inadequate control over the general partners' use of funds.

The industrial park is a specialized type of development not found in land subject only to industrial zoning ordinances. The industrial park follows a fairly formal development process turning on five points: (1) financial planning, (2) legal preparation, (3) engineering, (4) construction, and (5) promotional activities. Land use controls, while comparatively restrictive, preserve the amenities of the industrial park.

REVIEW QUESTIONS

1. Discuss the qualifications that you would make in considering a land investment.
2. Cite three advantages of investing in vacant land and give an example showing the financial results of a land purchase and sale.
3. Explain the leading limitations to a land investment.
4. What is meant by "entitlement to use strategy"?
5. What factors would you consider in evaluating potential residential land?

6. Why is it desirable to prepare a schedule of projected cash flow for a proposed subdivision? Explain thoroughly.

7. What factors associated with a city indicate favorable prospects for multiple-family development?

8. Give an example of two operating ratios essential to the success of a multiple-family development.

9. Explain the advantages of a long-term net ground lease to an owner-lessor.

10. What advantages does a net ground lease create for the tenant-lessee?

11. What are several terms that are included in a long-term net ground lease?

12. Indicate how a syndication operates under a limited partnership arrangement.

13. Contrast an industrial park to industrial acreage.

14. What steps would you follow in developing an industrial park?

15. Compare the industrial land use controls of an industrial park with the industrial land use controls of a local zoning ordinance.

SELECTED REFERENCES

Beaton, William R., and Robertson, Terry. *Real Estate Investment,* rev. ed. Chap. 6. Englewood Cliffs, N.J.: Prentice-Hall, Inc., 1977.

Messner, Stephen D.; Schreiber, Irving; and Lyon, Victor L. *Marketing Investment Real Estate: Finance Taxation Techniques,* chap. 2. Chicago: Realtors® National Marketing Institute of the National Association of Realtors®, 1975.

Pearson, Karl G. *Real Estate: Principles and Practices,* chap. 22. Columbus: Grid, Inc., 1973.

Ring, Alfred A., and Dasso, Jerome. *Real Estate Principles and Practices,* chap. 24. 8th ed. Englewood Cliffs, N.J.: Prentice-Hall, Inc., 1977.

Roulac, Stephen E., ed. *Real Estate Securities and Syndication.* Chicago: National Association of Real Estate Boards, 1973.

Seldin, Maury. *Land Investment,* chaps. 2 and 3. Homewood, Ill.: Dow Jones-Irwin, Inc., 1975.

Unger, Maurice A. *Real Estate,* chap. 7. 5th ed. Cincinnati: South-Western Publishing Co., 1974.

20

Condominiums, Cooperatives, and PUDs

After reading this chapter, you should be familiar with the following points:

1   The legal status of condominium ownership.
2   Points important to an evaluation of condominiums.
3   The general purpose and content of a condominium declaration.
4   The subject matter of condominium bylaws.
5   Elements of the management agreement.
6   The investment analysis of condominium units.
7   Points important to cooperative housing evaluation.
8   The main provisions of a cooperative proprietary lease.
9   The purpose of planned unit developments.
10 The main problems encountered in organizing a planned unit development.

RISING LAND COSTS and the growing number of households have popularized new dwelling arrangements. Households are no longer faced with renting an apartment as the only alternative to housing ownership. The condominium and the cooperative provide some of the advantages of ownership together with the economies associated with multiple-family occupancy. The planned unit development (PUD)—the new town concept—is a reaction against the high-density, mixed, and unplanned land uses of the older urban centers. The characteristics of each of these housing options vary considerably. Their analysis helps identify the best investment opportunities and the optimum housing choice.

CONDOMINIUM OWNERSHIP

Condominiums provide for a unique type of ownership which has certain advantages over both single-family ownership and rental occupancy. In this sense the condominium may be viewed as (1) a special form of housing and (2) as an income property. In the latter case condominium units are purchased as income units operated as part of a resort hotel.

Simply stated, a condominium provides for fee title ownership of a designated portion of a building and an undivided interest in the common elements. The common elements of an apartment condominium refer to the land and such facilities as the swimming pool, parking space, the halls, elevators, and building equipment. The common elements are enjoyed jointly by all owners. The term *common elements* has been defined by statute as

> That form of ownership of condominium property under which units are subject to ownership by one or more owners, and there is appurtenant to each unit as part thereof an undivided share in the common elements.[1]

The condominium project may include separate ownership of town houses, detached housing units, or more commonly, a separate unit in a multiple-unit project. These various forms are illustrated in Figure 20–1, which shows that individual owners A to Z each owns an individual unit and has an undivided interest in the common elements (including roofs and other structural elements). In the example, the individual owners (identified as owners A–Z) have an undivided interest in the land, the clubhouse, and the pool.

Condominium Origin

While fairly new in the United States, ownership in the condominium form has been traced to the Roman Empire. Indeed, the term is taken from the Latin words *con,* meaning jointly or together, and *dominium,* meaning control or ownership. A Babylonian document dating back to 2,000 B.C.

---

[1] *Florida Statutes Annotated,* chap. 711.

509

FIGURE 20–1

Various Arrangements of Condominiums Indicating that Owners A to Z Own an Individual Unit and an Undivided Interest in the Common Elements

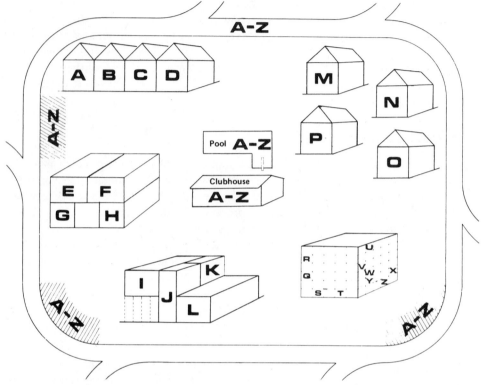

Source: *HUD Condominium/Cooperative Study,* vol. 3 (Washington, D.C.: U.S. Government Printing Office, 1975), p. G–10.

mentions the sale of the first floor of a house with the owner retaining title to the second floor. The Brooklyn Museum has papyrus No. 4721891, dating from 434 B.C., which describes an apartment and its boundaries and is purported to be the oldest condominium deed in existence. The condominium form of ownership appeared in France in the 12th and 13th centuries and was included in the Napoleonic Code of 1804. Today it is reported that the condominium is the most prevalent form of apartment living in Paris. The word *condominium* was included in the Italian Code of 1930, and in South America condominium laws were common in the 1940s and 1950s.[2]

---

[2] For further information consult Arthur E. Warner, *Condominium: Concept, Control, Consumer Acceptance,* Research Report No. 11 (Columbia: Center for Real Estate and Urban Economics, College of Business Administration, University of South Carolina, July 1976); *HUD Condominium/Cooperative Study,* vol. 2 (Washington, D.C.: U.S. Government Printing Office, 1975); and *Condominium Housing for Tomorrow* (Boston: Management Reports, 1964).

In the United States, condominiums originated with the Puerto Rican Horizontal Property Regime Act of 1958, which led to Section 234 of the National Housing Act of 1961, extending FHA mortgage insurance to individual condominium units. By now, all 50 states have enacted legislation that permits the condominium form of ownership. Statutory changes were necessary to allow for (1) three-dimensional legal descriptions referring to cubic areas and not merely flat planes and (2) property taxes levied against a condominium and its undivided interest in the common elements. Legislation was also required to prohibit "tenants in common" from partitioning the undivided common interest.

Condominium Evaluation

Some authorities expect condominium ownership to increase because rising land costs and the rising costs of constructing single-family dwellings have priced such dwellings out of the reach of middle-income households. The advantages of a condominium further encourage their popularity.

Advantages. In comparison to the conventional apartment living of renters, condominiums change life-styles. Condominium owners usually expect a higher level of services in the form of swimming pools, recreational facilities, and other amenities. There also seems to be some appeal in living in an apartment unit under occupant control. Added to these features are certain economic advantages:

1. A condominium tends to protect occupants from the rising rents experienced by apartment renters.
2. The condominium provides for multiple-family living with certain amenities which are not always supplied by comparable rental housing.
3. Condominium owners benefit from the income tax deductibility of mortgage interest and property taxes. In some states, property tax exemptions extended to homeowners are also allowed to condominium owners.
4. The lower vacancies and turnover of condominium housing compared to rental housing make condominiums more economical.
5. The condominium owner does not pay rent toward the apartment owner's profit.
6. The condominium provides ownership rights in fee without the daily problems of maintenance and the operating chores of a dwelling owner. These tasks are assumed by the condominium management.

Limitations. To be sure, not all occupants weigh these advantages favorably. There still remain households that are unwilling to make the long-term commitment of a condominium. There is also the risk of experiencing a capital loss if the local market is oversupplied with condominium units. Consequently, the condominium tends to appeal to households that view it as a fairly long-term investment or that purchase it in a resort area partly for rental purposes.

In addition, condominium units may be more expensive in that they rely on union or contract maintenance. In central cities, condominium maintenance costs substitute for the owner's contribution in the form of landscaping, labor, minor house repairs, interior and exterior painting, and the like. Moreover, the condominium unit is dependent on group approval for changes in operation, remodeling, and the level of services provided. These are freedoms enjoyed by the owner of a single-family dwelling that give way to group control under condominiums. And as with apartment occupancy, the condominium owner gives up the privacy of a single-family dwelling—though for some individuals this could be a minor point.

Condominium Characteristics

The rights of the condominium owner are controlled by three documents: the declaration, the corporation bylaws, and the management agreement. In some instances, state law requires that these and other documents be supplied to the prospective purchaser. The descriptive detail associated with each condominium purchase frequently results in a lengthy legal-sized document which most households are poorly prepared to analyze. The main points covered by the three condominium documents show the difference between condominium ownership and fee simple ownership.

The Declaration.   Known also as the master deed, or the covenants, conditions, and restrictions, the declaration creates the condominium entity. The declaration is prepared with all the legal formality of a contract, and it is recorded as a deed or other conveyance instrument. Its importance lies in the identification of each condominium unit, the pro rata interest held in the common elements, the governing rules of the condominium, and the rights of the condominium owners. The inclusive nature of the document is illustrated by a condominium organized in Florida whose declaration covers some 28 main subjects in 22 closely typed pages. The list of topics is shown in Figure 20–2. Because of the directive nature of

FIGURE 20–2

Table of Contents for a Condominium Declaration

1.   Submission Statement
2.   Name
3.   Leasehold Estate
4.   Explanation of Terminology: Description of Improvements
5.   Survey, Plot Plan, and Graphic Description
6.   Undivided Shares in Common Elements and Use of Common Elements
7.   Shares in Common Expenses and Owning Common Surplus
8.   Association Membership and Voting Rights of Apartment Owners Therein
9.   Bylaws
10.   Easements
11.   Management Agreement and Facilities

FIGURE 20-2 (continued)

12. Apportionment of Tax or Special Assessment if Levied and Assessed against the Condominium as a Whole
13. Occupancy and Use Restrictions
14. Transfer of Parking Spaces
15. Transfers
16. Maintenance and Repairs
17. Common Expenses and Assessments
18. Insurance
19. Destruction of Improvements and Casualty Insurance
20. Prohibition of Further Subdivision
21. Severability
22. Interpretation
23. Remedies for Violation
24. Provisions for Alteration of Apartments by Sponsor and Provisions for Amendments by Sponsor's and Members' Vote
25. Rights of Sponsor, Including Sale or Lease of Apartments Owned by It Free of Restrictions Set Forth in Article
26. Additional Rights of Approved Mortgagees
27. Renewal or Assumption of Ground Lease
28. Termination

this document, more important points included in the declaration deserve added comment.

1. *Definition of Terms.* The condominium uses new terms foreign to other types of ownership. Because these terms are used in the declaration, the articles of incorporation, the bylaws, the management agreement, and other documents, they are carefully defined by state statute. The more commonly defined terms include the following:

Unit
   A part of the condominium property which is subject to private ownership, such as an apartment unit.
Common elements
   That portion of the condominium property not included in a unit.
Limited common elements
   Common elements which are reserved for the use of certain units to the exclusion of other units.
Common expenses
   Expenses for which the unit owners are liable to the association.
Association
   The entity responsible for the operation of a condominium.

Purchase of a condominium unit gives the owner (1) an undivided share in the common elements and (2) the exclusive right to use common elements as provided by the declaration. The use of common elements must not encroach upon the rights of other unit owners. In short, the owner of a unit is entitled to the *exclusive possession of his unit* and *the right to use the common elements* as provided by the declaration.

2. *The Legal Description.* Not only must the declaration legally describe the land committed to the condominium, but each unit must be designated by letter, name, or number in sufficient detail to identify each unit and the common elements. State legislation may require an exhibit given each owner that legally describes the land and graphically indicates the location of each unit on a plot plan. The survey, plot plan, and description are usually in the form of an exhibit given to each unit owner. An example of a recorded survey is shown in Figure 20–3.

The description includes a conventional survey and further defines the unit, including balconies, stating that each unit has an undivided share of the common elements. The three-dimensional part of the survey is included in exhibits of each floor that give the elevation and ceiling heights of each apartment unit. Bearing walls to the unfinished surface of each apartment unit are identified as parts of the common elements. In short, the legal description describes the cubic foot area of each unit which is subject to fee ownership.

3. *Undivided Shares in Common Elements.* The undivided share in the common elements determines the pro rata share of operating expenses borne by unit owners. Moreover, the liability of unit owners for claims against the association is limited to this share. Usually based on square foot area, the share is stated in the declaration for each unit. For example, a condominium of one-, two-, and three-bedroom apartments allocates shares according to the following schedule.

Type of Unit	Percent of Share
One-bedroom apartment............................	0.9427212
Two-bedroom apartment............................	1.4048
Three-bedroom apartment..........................	1.88539

If annual expenses of operation, including property taxes on common elements, amount to $100,000, the owner of a one-bedroom apartment would pay $942.72, the pro rata share of expenses. By assigning these shares to each unit owner, all expenses of operating a 70-unit project will be paid.

Number of Units		Share per Unit	Percent of Total Shares
12	One-bedroom units...............................	0.9427212	11.3126544
43	Two-bedroom units...............................	1.4048	60.4064000
15	Three-bedroom units.............................	1.88539	28.2808500
70	Total shares all units......................		99.9999044
		(rounded)	100.0

The declaration gives the association board of directors the duty of preparing a budget, which is assessed against unit owners. For example:

FIGURE 20-3

Legal Description of a Condominium Project

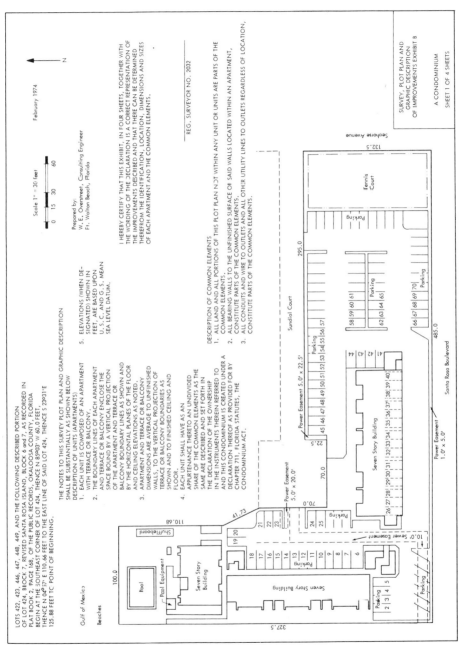

> It is hereby stated to be the express duty of each apartment owner to promptly pay his share of the common expenses and all assessments levied by the board.

The individual share of each owner determines his pro rata share of the budget:

> After the adoption of a budget and determination of the annual assessments against the apartment owners in accordance with the shares of common expenses, . . . the board shall assess such sums promptly, notifying all apartment owners by delivering or mailing notice thereof. . . ."

4. *Condominium Management.* The condominium association is responsible for the affairs of the condominium: the daily management, repair, and operation. Each unit owner ordinarily has one vote. State statute controls the ability of the developer-owner to cast votes during the period of development and the sale of condominium units. According to the declaration, the members of the board of directors are elected by unit owners, and the board in turn usually signs a management agreement. The management agreement provides for a delegation of authority to a real estate manager who pays bills, employs help, and maintains the building in good condition. Alternatively a few condominiums are directly managed by a board of directors which hires an on-site resident manager.

Other features of the declaration define the legal liabilities, and the rights and duties of unit owners with respect to easements for public access, use restrictions, provisions for bylaws, and the sale and lease of individual units. The rights of unit owners in the operation of the condominium are defined in the bylaws.

Condominium Bylaws. Rules governing the organization and authority of the condominium association are specified in the bylaws. Provisions for voting rights, a board of directors, and the powers and duties of the board are normal to corporate organization. The bylaws usually cover these points:

1. Identification of the condominium association.
2. Membership, meetings, voting, and proxies.
3. Board of directors.
4. Powers and duties of the board of directors.
5. Election of officers.
6. Fiscal management.
7. Parliamentary rules.
8. Provision for amendment of the bylaws.

A critical issue covered by the bylaws is the appointment of the first board. For the sponsor or developer must manage the project while units are conveyed to unit owners. For instance, a condominium near Fort Lauderdale, Florida, provides that

The first board shall consist of three persons, none of whom need be members of the association. The first board shall consist of persons designated by the sponsor and they shall serve so long as the sponsor is the owner of any unit, or until December 31, 1982, or until the sponsor elects to terminate its control of the condominium, whichever occurs first, and the successors are elected.

After the tenure of the first board ends, the directors are elected during annual membership meetings, at which time a nominating committee proposes members for election to the board. The board is given all the powers and duties of the association, including the collection and levying of assessments for maintenance, repair, and other expenses. In practice, operating functions are delegated to a professional manager under the management agreement.

The Management Agreement. The management agreement for a new condominium usually provides that the sponsor execute the management agreement with the association temporarily or until control of the board of directors is turned over to unit owners. The interim agreement may extend over a one-year term and provide that the manager will assist the board of directors to implement management policy. Under the initial agreement, the manager collects expense assessments and uses a unit as an office and storage area during the transition period. The management agreement will provide for a management fee, say, $8 per month per apartment. At some point the association assumes responsibility for executing a management agreement with a condominium management firm.

1. *Management Duties.* The duties of the management firm are, *first,* to perform normal management services, namely, to hire, supervise, and employ maintenance personnel and without board approval to make outlays of up to some maximum amount for the maintenance and repair of condominium property and the common elements. *Second,* the management firm is responsible for enforcing bylaws, house rules, and provisions of the declaration. *Third,* the management firm makes payments on insurance contracts and taxes and maintains records for review by the board. Typical fees earned for management service vary from a minimum fee per apartment unit to a fee based on a percentage of assessments. For example,

as compensation for its services hereunder, the management firm shall receive from the association, in addition to all costs and expenses, a net fee, free of all charge and expenses, of three (3) percent of assessments of every kind of such association. . . .

2. *Enforcement of House Rules.* Since condominium occupancy is a form of multiple-family housing, the management must introduce house rules governing the conduct of the occupants. Since the occupants share common elements, the house rules tend to be more critical in condominiums than in rental apartments. It has been observed by competent managers that the attractiveness of condominiums depends largely on suitable

house rules that are uniformly enforced against all occupants. The house rules govern the occupants' use of the property. Thus, occupants must not unreasonably disturb other unit owners and equipment must not be abused. Other rules maintain attractively appearing buildings. For example:

> The public halls, sidewalks and stairways shall not be obstructed or used for any other purposes than for ingress to and egress from the apartments.

And further:

> No shades, awnings, or window guards shall be used except such as shall be put up or approved by the association. No sign, signal, advertisement or illumination shall be inscribed or exposed on or at any window or other part of the building except such as shall be approved in writing by the association.

Control over unit owners which may disturb tenants is usually accomplished by a house rule that provides:

> No unit owner shall make or permit any disturbing noises in the building by himself, his family, friends or servants; nor permit anything to be done by such persons that will interfere with the rights, comforts or convenience of other unit owners. No occupants shall play upon or suffer to be played upon any musical instrument in the premises between the hours of 11:00 P.M. and the following A.M. if the same shall disturb or annoy other occupants of the building.

In other words, fairly restrictive rules apply to the condominium owners in contrast to single-family occupancy. In return for observing these restrictions, however, each unit owner benefits from observance of these rules by neighbors. In this way, each owner knows that the project will be operated for the convenience of its occupants, preserving the advantages of ownership with the best features of multiple-family occupancy.

Condominium Income Units

While residential condominiums accounted for almost 50 percent of the dwelling units built during 1973, industrial, commercial, office, and vacation resort condominiums have also been developed. Condominiums operated as resorts are often structured as offerings of securities coming under federal and state security laws. The first such offering was registered with the Securities and Exchange Commission in 1967, and by 1974 there were 75 such registrations with a total value of $713.3 million.[3] Most condominiums of this type are sold to absentee owners as a source of income. The return to the condominium investor depends heavily on the compe-

---

[3] *Condominiums Registered under the Securities Act of 1933: 1967–1974*, Economic Staff Paper 74–No. 1, Office of Economic Research, Securities and Exchange Commission, July 1974, p. 3.

tence of the manager and the method of calculating management compensation.

Monthly Costs. The incentive for investing in a resort condominium as a part-time occupant and absentee owner is indicated by a condominium offered for $46,900. Financing was available at approximately 5 percent down, 8¾ percent interest, and a 30-year mortgage. The monthly tax benefit would amount to $146.51 for a person in the 40 percent net income tax bracket.

Selling price...		$46,900.00
Less down payment.................................		−2,400.00
First mortgage......................................		$44,500.00
Monthly expense		
Mortgage payment................................		$ 350.09
Monthly maintenance.............................		50.04
Property taxes.....................................		39.32
		$ 439.45
Less tax savings		
Mortgage interest................................	$3,923.75	
(First year)		
Property taxes.....................................	471.84	
Income tax deduction.............................	$4,395.59	
Annual tax benefit (40% bracket)..................	1,758.23	
Monthly benefit ($1,758.23/12)....................		−146.51
Net monthly expense...........................		$ 292.94

By considering income tax deductions, the monthly expense of $439.45 is reduced to a net expense of $292.94. With weekly rental rates ranging from $300 to $335 for this apartment (depending on the floor), the owner would have a potential maximum gross income of $1,200 to $1,340 per month from the end of May to the first of September. The same apartment would rent for approximately $300 per month during the off-season. The management fee would be 20 percent of the gross rent collected during the summer and 10 percent of the gross rent collected during the off-season.

To qualify for rental income, the owner must furnish the apartment, supply cooking utensils, and bear a weekly maid and linen expense of approximately $10 per week. From this fairly simple arrangement, sponsors of condominiums developed for resort purposes can provide a project in which the owner may participate in the rental arrangement as a limited partner.

Figure 20–4 diagrams such an arrangement in which unit owners of a 620-unit project have the option of committing their unit to the income project. In effect, unit owners become limited partners with the sponsor, who becomes the manager and general partner. Under this plan, recreational facilities are available only to unit owners who join the recreation

FIGURE 20–4

Ownership Flowchart of Sundial Associates, Sanibel Island, Florida

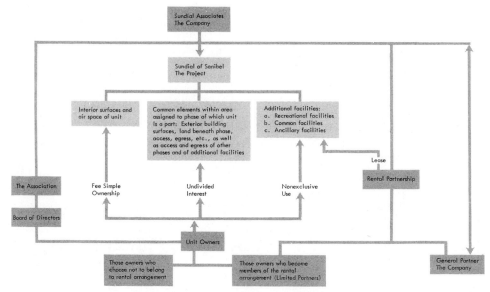

Source: *Condominiums Registered under the Securities Act of 1933: 1967–1974*, Economic Staff Paper 74–No. 1, Office of Economic Research, Securities and Exchange Commission, July 1974, p. 34.

club and pay monthly dues. A representative summary of management fees is listed in Table 20–1.

Income Allocation. As Table 20–1 indicates, the fee schedule varies greatly among projects. The net income allocated to each unit owner closely follows a well-accepted formula used in computing income attributable to each unit owner. In this formula each owner's interest is calculated according to (1) the proportionate time his unit was available and (2) the proportionate value of the unit relative to the value of other units.

$$\frac{\text{Base value of rental unit}}{\text{Aggregate base value of all rental units in rental pool}} \times \frac{\text{Number of days unit was available to rental pool}}{\text{Total number of days in applicable period}} = \text{Availability percentage of rental unit}$$

$$\frac{\text{Availability percentage of rental unit}}{\text{Availability percentage of all rental units in rental pool}} \times \begin{array}{l}\text{Allocable net profits (or losses) during applicable period}\end{array} = \begin{array}{l}\text{Allocable net profits (or losses) for rental unit owners for single rental unit}\end{array}$$

Suppose that $200,000 was earned by the rental pool. With a unit value of $55,000, and assuming that the available percentage of all units in the pool is 95 percent, and that the unit in question was available for 80 days of 90 days, the income allocated to the unit owner would be \$2,273.68.[4]

$$\frac{\$55,000}{\$4,500,000} \times \frac{80}{90} = 0.0108$$

$$\frac{0.0108}{0.95} \times \$200,000 = \$2,273.68$$

From the investor's point of view, the unit is available at his or her option at a cost partly offset by potential rental income. To the extent that units are sold, the sponsor, general partner, or developer shifts the financing of rentable units to the purchaser.

COOPERATIVE APARTMENTS

Occupancy in multiple-unit apartments under the cooperative plan has proven especially popular in Chicago and New York City. The Amalgamated Clothing Workers originally sponsored cooperative housing in New York City under a 1926 state law that partially exempted nonprofit housing corporations from taxation. The Foundation for Cooperative Housing, formed in the 1950s, has spearheaded low-cost cooperative housing in some 24 states.[5] The legal relationships among the shareholders of a cooperative and the owners of a condominium differ materially.

Cooperative Housing Evaluated

Some advantages claimed for the condominium owner are also enjoyed by the cooperative shareholder. Their main advantages turn on seven points.

Advantages. (1) A cooperative shareholder, as a member of a nonprofit corporation, benefits from the elimination of the owner's profit of a conventional rental. (2) Like the condominium owner, the cooperative shareholder benefits from lower vacancies. (3) Both the condominium owner and the cooperative shareholder benefit from the income tax deductibility of mortgage interest and property taxes. (4) Cooperatives tend to be more restrictive in the selection of shareholders joining the cooperative. (5) The transfer costs of cooperatives are relatively low. Single-mortgage financing and the transfer of an interest by exchanging shares eliminate title reports, loan origination fees, and financing costs. (6) Cooperative shareholders, like condominium owners, have a voice in the operation of the cooperative. (7) Cooperative shareholders are not personally responsible for the mortgage debt. The cooperative is financed

---

[4] Consult ibid., p. 13.

[5] National Commission on Urban Problems, *Building the American City*, Report of the National Commission on Urban Problems (New York: Frederick A. Praeger, Publishers, 1971), p. 136.

TABLE 20–1

Management Fees and Method of Sharing Revenues of Sampled Condominium Registrations: 1967–May 31, 1974

Developer	Manager's Base Fee	Incentive Arrangement	Method of Sharing Revenues
1. Carefree Resorts	40% of gross revenues		Net—based on availability of owner's unit
2. Carlton House Resort Inns	10% of gross revenues	50% of net profit over $4.0 million	Net to owners (after payment of rental expenses)
3. Condominiums Northwest (Inn at Otter Crest)	40% of rentals		10% to owners of rental units and 50% to owners based on availability
4. Condominiums Northwest Inc. (Inn of the Seventh Mountain)	40% of gross rentals		10% based on use and 50% pooled by availability
5. Dorado Beach	15% of gross rents		Net to owners: based on availability
6. Elkhorn at Sun Valley	15% of gross rentals plus $15/month/owner		Rental pool: based on availability; rental agency: based on actual use
7. Hawaiian Enterprises Ltd.	10% or $700 of gross receipts (higher) plus $427 per month	5% of net profit	Net to partners (except for 5%) after payment of rental expenses
8. John Colter Development Co., Ltd.	15% of the gross rentals plus average basic monthly fee per unit—annualized at $380		Not clear
9. Marriott Condominium Development Corp.	20% of gross revenues		Net to limited partners
10. Montaneros (Shareholders Recreation Programs Inc.)	$10/unit/month and reimbursement for any direct expenses		Based on rental points (owners' interest and availability
11. Ocean Pines Condominiums	20% of gross rents (15% of rents of more than 90 days)		Net to owners after deductions of rental expenses
12. Plan-Com Ltd.	15% of gross rental income to general partner and 18% to rental agency to promote project		Net to partners after payment of rental expenses based on availability and interest
13. Plantation Hale	10% of gross income on rents		10% to owners of rental units, net to owners from which all rental expenses are paid
14. Palmetto Dunes Resort	15% of gross rents		1% of net to general partners; remainder based on availability and owner interest

15. Pope and Talbot Properties Inc.	55% of gross plus 5% for maintenance	30% of gross revenues based on owner interest and availability and 10% on actual use
16. Port industries	30% of gross rentals	Net to owners
17. Ranch at Roaring Fork	2% of gross revenues to general partner, 8% of gross revenues to manager	Net to partners after payment of rental expenses
18. Residential Resort Developments	10% service charge	Balance to participants based on square footage interests
19. Resort One	$900/month to each of two managers	Based on rentals
20. San Diego–Maui Group	$9,240 per annum or 20% of operating profit (whichever is greater)	At the direction of the association
21. Sapphire Hill Village	15% of gross rents	Based on interest in project
22. Sundial of Sanibel	5% of gross revenues of partnership for service fee (plus 15% of gross revenues as facilities rental)	Room rentals (less resort hotel operational expenses)
23. Tamarron–Golf Host West	51% of all gross rental income (from which rental pool expenses are paid)	34% pooled, by availability; 15% to participants based on actual unit rental
24. Treasure Mt. Corp.	1/3 of annual excess (net rental income)	Net to owners: based on availability
25. Wailea Development Company	10% of maintenance assessments 5% of gross proceeds (operating profits) less partnership expenses plus occupancy incentives	Net to owners after payments of rental expenses

10% of net profit

Source: See Figure 20-4.

through a single mortgage that commits the nonprofit cooperative corporation, and not the individual shareholders. Shareholders assume their pro rata share of the mortgage according to the value of their apartment unit.

Disadvantages. It is true that shareholders are individually responsible for the debts of the cooperative. Hence the first disadvantage is that surviving shareholders assume liability for the defaulted payments of other occupants. Unlike condominium owners, individual shareholders do not pay property taxes; likewise, the mortgage payments are the responsibility of the cooperative, which allocates a pro rata share of the monthly payments to tenant shareholders.

Typically, the release clause allows shareholders to relinquish shares to the cooperative and escape further legal liability for the cooperative's obligations. In so doing, the shareholder gives up his equity interest—a second disadvantage. In the condominium, since the individual negotiates a mortgage and promissory note, he or she remains personally liable for the mortgage.

The Proprietary Lease

Strictly speaking, the purchaser of a cooperative apartment is not an apartment owner—the purchaser buys a share in the cooperative which is priced according to the value of the unit occupied. Initially the number of shares is allocated to each apartment according to the proportion that the apartment rental value bears to the total rental value of the project. The number of shares usually establishes the purchase price and the ratio of monthly maintenance charges allocated to each tenant-shareholder.

Ownership of a share entitles the tenant-shareholder to a long-term lease on an apartment in which the rental is equal to the cost of operation, including a pro rata share of the principal and interest payments on the mortgage. Since ownership rests in the hands of tenant-shareholders, rents cover only the "economic" rent which is sufficient to operate the property and pay the mortgage. Hence, tenant-shareholders own stock in a nonprofit corporation that holds title to the property.

Rental Terms. The basis of this arrangement is the proprietary lease, which conforms to the same pattern for all tenant-shareholders. Leases of a cooperative begin and end on the same date and usually extend over 99 years. The cooperative assigns an apartment lease to succeeding shareholders. There is no fixed rent; each tenant agrees to pay his pro rata share of the budget for repairs, upkeep, wages, supplies, heat, taxes, reserves, and amortization of the mortgage. Typical language states:

> The rent under the lease shall be the lessee's proportionate share of the cash requirements of the lessor (the tenant-owning corporation) for each year as determined by the board of directors at the same ratio as that which the number of shares of stock of the lessor owned by the lessee bears to the aggregate of all the shares outstanding at the time such rent shall be payable.

The usual proprietary lease requires the tenant to make interior repairs and decorating, while the corporation is responsible for landscaping, exterior maintenance, and building equipment. In agreement with the condominium document, the proprietary lease identifies the space assigned to the tenant-shareholder by virtue of stock ownership. A board of directors elected by tenant-shareholders has the right to levy special assessments and rents (for mortgage payments and operating expenses) against tenant-shareholders.

Release Clauses. Leases may provide for termination on six months' written notice after the first year. In these circumstances, the tenant-shareholder returns the stock and the lease and thereby avoids further obligations to the cooperative, though he loses the amount of his equity and his accumulated payments on the mortgage principal. The mortgage of the corporation is secured by land and building with no personal liability on the part of tenant-shareholders. The proprietary lease carries the right of the tenant-shareholder to sell his interest back to the corporation or to sublease his interest if the board of directors approves the new occupant.

Low- and Middle-Income Cooperative Housing

Housing cooperatives were organized under the Rochdale Plan,[6] and Section 213 of the National Housing Act of 1950 extended mortgage insurance to apartment buildings dedicated to cooperative ownership. The mortgage term was 40 years, with loan-to-value ratios of not more than 97 percent of replacement value. By the end of 1968, FHA insurance had been extended to over 2,000 cooperative apartment projects.[7] Further incentives were given under Section 221(d)(3) of the 1961 Housing Act, which allowed below-market interest rates to be used to finance cooperative housing.

Resale of Cooperative Apartments. Under cooperative plans financed by the FHA and sponsored by nonprofit organizations, upon resale co-op members receive only the initial down payment on their apartments. The cooperative apartment is then offered to new occupants at the original price. Under this plan the capital gain (if any) is distributed in the form of low initial payments and monthly carrying charges for future members.

A second method allows a selling member to seek the highest price in the open market. The original member benefits from capital gains at the expense of the new member. This is generally the procedure followed in commercially sponsored nonsubsidized cooperatives.

The third method followed by FHA-insured cooperatives allows the

---

[6] This plan refers to the principles under which the early cooperatives of Great Britain were organized: (1) membership is open to all persons; (2) members make initial payment for shares of stock; (3) voting is on the basis of one member one vote; (4) the net income of the cooperative is distributed to members in proportion to their purchases; and (5) the cooperative is run for the benefit of consumers.

[7] National Commission on Urban Problems, *Building the American City,* p. 135.

departing member to recover his down payment and his share of equity buildup from principal repayments and cost-of-living payments. For example, if the consumer price index has increased by 20 percent over the ownership period, the selling price would be the original cost plus 20 percent in addition to total mortgage principal repayments.

Social Aspects. Proponents of cooperatives emphasize their social benefits. These benefits arise from the fact that cooperators elect their own boards under full democratic control. Cooperative members participate in other cooperative enterprises, such as nurseries, day-care centers, summer camps, and recreation centers. Vandalism, crime, and delinquency have been held to a very low level in the more prominent cooperatives of New York and Baltimore, for example. To some observers the cooperative provides a mechanism for dealing with housing problems in a constructive way. If the cooperative fails to control behavior which disrupts or disturbs the community, the cooperative enforces democratic methods for applying sanctions.

PLANNED UNIT DEVELOPMENTS

Local ordinances that authorize planned unit development refer to *a proposed development with a minimum contiguous acreage of ten acres or more developed as a single entity according to a plan for planned unit residential development and providing for public, commercial, or industrial areas.*[8] Zoning for planned unit developments gives exclusive protection to residential, commercial, and industrial zones. That is, an area zoned for commercial use must be used only for this purpose. The same principle applies to other land use categories. Parking, traffic, and population density are controlled by provisions specifying the percent of land used for dwellings, apartments, and commercial stores. Typically parking for shopping purposes requires three square feet of parking space for one square foot of net retail area. Similar provisions specify the proportion of land devoted to industrial use, open spaces for parks, recreation areas, golf courses, playgrounds, and school sites. Ordinarily the number of dwelling units per acre will be controlled according to the type of residential zoning.

Planned Land Uses

Traditionally the planned unit development substitutes for zoning that divides districts into segregated land uses. Under conventional practices, residential districts offer poor access for convenience goods and other

---

[8] In practice, planned unit developments may cover several hundred or even several thousand acres. See Robert W. Burchell, *Planned Unit Development* (New Brunswick, N.J.: Center for Urban Policy Research, Rutgers—The State University, 1972), p. 224.

community facilities of a nonresidential nature. A PUD ordinance describes the purpose of the planned unit development:

> . . . to provide for necessary commercial and educational facilities conveniently located to such housing; to provide for well located, clean, safe, pleasant industrial sites involving a minimum of strain on transportation facilities, to encourage the planning of new towns; to encourage innovations in residential, commercial and industrial development and renewal so that the growing demands of the population may be met by greater variety in type, design and layout of buildings and by the conservation and more efficient use of open space ancillary to said buildings; so that greater opportunities for better housing and recreation, shops and industrial plants conveniently located to each other may extend to all citizens and residents of this municipality. . . .[9]

Similarly, the purpose of a planned unit development is indicated by the Fairfax County, Virginia, Zoning Ordinance, which states

> Within such planned communities the location of all residential, commercial, and industrial and government uses, school sites, parks, playgrounds, recreation areas, parking areas and other open spaces shall be controlled in such manner as to permit a variety of housing accommodations and land uses in orderly relationship to one another.[10]

Densities in the planned community of Columbia, Maryland, were limited to 3.8 persons per acre in residential areas—high-density areas could not exceed 60 persons per acre.[11] In short, the integration of superior site planning with community facilities, shopping, and employment centers characterizes the concept of the Planned Unit Development.

This idea is illustrated in the Twin Rivers Community, started in 1964 in New Jersey. The land use plan shown in Figure 20–5 is based on principles common to planned unit development: (1) a neighborhood is recognized as a sociophysical concept; (2) the plan creates a civic entity rather than a residential suburb; (3) the neighborhood superblock serves as a design element, providing internal safety from traffic; and (4) the plan minimizes commuting through nearby or self-contained housing, employment, recreation, and shopping areas.[12]

Organizing a Planned Unit Development

James W. Rouse, the sponsor of the Columbia, Maryland, PUD assembled some 15,000 acres specifically for a PUD. The initial problem was to convert conventional, segregated land use districts to a planned

---

[9] Ibid., pp. 227–28.

[10] Philip David, *Urban Land Development* (Homewood, Ill.: Richard D. Irwin, Inc., 1970), p. 495.

[11] Ibid., p. 496.

[12] Burchell, *Planned Unit Development,* p. 88.

FIGURE 20–5

Twin Rivers, New Jersey, Land Use Plan

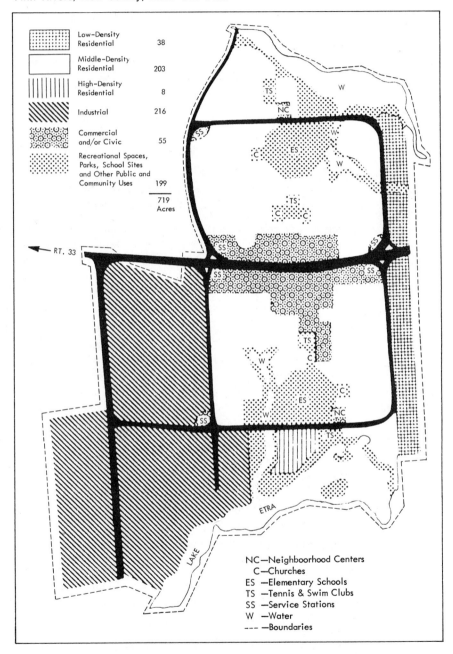

Low–Density Residential	38	
Middle–Density Residential	203	
High–Density Residential	8	
Industrial	216	
Commercial and/or Civic	55	
Recreational Spaces, Parks, School Sites and Other Public and Community Uses	199	
	719 Acres	

RT. 33

NC—Neighboorhood Centers
C—Churches
ES —Elementary Schools
TS —Tennis & Swim Clubs
SS —Service Stations
W —Water
- - - —Boundaries

Source: Robert W. Burchell, *Planned Unit Development* (New Brunswick, N.J.: Center for Urban Development, Rutgers—The State University, 1972), p. 89.

unit development scheme. At the beginning it was necessary to request five assurances from the local county government:

1. Zoning permitting higher residential densities and industrial and commercial uses.
2. The authority to create a special entity that could issue tax-exempt bonds for major roads and utilities on the site.
3. The assurance that at public expense peripheral roads and utilities adequate to handle a development of this size would be brought to the site.
4. A legal basis that would guarantee to the developer that he would not, over the long-term development period, be forced to change zoning and other controls as the result of pressure from either the county or his own residents.
5. A commitment to improve the level of municipal services so that the project could attract residents.[13]

FIGURE 20–6

Cash Flow Diagram of a Planned Unit Development

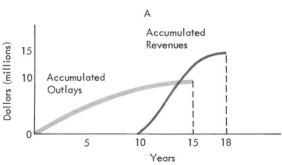

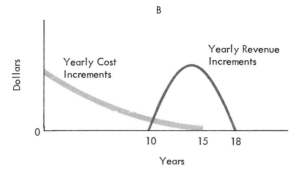

Source: Wallace F. Smith, *Urban Development*. Copyright © 1975 by The Regents of the University of California; reprinted by permission of the University of California Press.

---

[13] David, *Urban Land Development,* p. 483.

Rejecting conventional zoning controls, Columbia, Maryland, was projected as a community of 100,000 population, with an overall cost of $1 billion. Although the market projection anticipated an eventual profit, the project required an initial investment of $144 million for land and some $90 million in planning, land improvement, financing, and sales administration.

Initiating a planned unit development calls for heavy investments over the initial years in anticipation of revenues postponed for a considerable period of time. Figure 20–6 assumes that accumulated revenues will not begin until the 10th year, reaching a peak at the 18th year, the end of development (Part A). Part B of Figure 20–6 plots annual expenses with revenue expectations over 18 years. If costs and revenues follow the projection of Figure 20–6, some means of financing the land purchase, utility costs, and planning must be assured until the development is in salable condition. For this reason, a planned unit development, though improving the community environment, tends to be very risky for large-scale developers.

SUMMARY

Condominium ownership provides for fee title ownership of a designated unit and an undivided interest in the common elements. The common elements refer to facilities used jointly with other unit owners. In the United States, condominiums originated from a Puerto Rican law of 1958 and the National Housing Act of 1961. The Housing Act extended FHA mortgage insurance to individual condominium units. Today all states provide for condominium ownership, allowing the description of a fee interest in a three-dimensional legal form and the levying of property taxes against unit owners and their share of the undivided interest in the common elements.

The rising costs of single-family dwelling ownership have encouraged condominium housing. Condominiums protect unit owners from the periodic rental increases of conventional apartments. Condominiums provide a high level of amenities not always supplied by comparable rental housing and usually with covenants. Condominium owners enjoy the same income tax deductions extended to the owners of single-family dwellings. Moreover, condominium purchasers benefit from lower vacancies relative to conventional apartment rentals. To the extent that the condominium eliminates the apartment owner's profit, condominiums are more economical than rental units. In addition, the condominium owner acquires a fee interest in his unit without the yard and maintenance chores associated with single-family dwelling ownership.

Against these advantages are relatively high monthly maintenance charges. Compared to the owners of single-family dwellings, condominium unit owners sacrifice privacy. There is the added risk of poor marketability if the condominium is resold and refinanced. To estimate the value of a single condominium unit for mortgage purposes, the lender must appraise the entire condominium project. If the lender has not previously financed other units in the project, reappraisal costs for a resale and refinancing could be prohibitively expensive.

Condominium rights are controlled by the declaration, the corporate bylaws, and the management agreement. The declaration commits the property to condominium status. It identifies each condominium unit and the pro rata interest held in the common elements by each unit owner, and it provides the operating rules of the condominium and describes the rights of individual owners. The undivided shares of the common elements are usually determined by square foot area. The pro rata area of each unit owner determines his liability for property taxes and the expenses of the condominium association.

Condominium bylaws control the government of condominiums, that is, the election of the board of directors, and describe the powers and duties of the board. The management agreement is a contract delegating powers of the board of directors to a management agent—mainly the authority to hire, supervise, and employ maintenance workers and to maintain and repair the common elements. Management is responsible for enforcing the bylaws, house rules, and the declaration. Management has the authority to collect and pay contracts of the condominium.

The house rules of condominiums tend to be fairly restrictive, controlling tenant use of the premises and preserving the structure from damage. However, each unit owner benefits from the observance of the house rules by his neighbors.

Condominium units are purchased as an investment in resort areas. Under these arrangements, the unit owner dedicates his unit to rental purposes during specified times of the year. At the end of the year, each unit owner receives a portion of the net condominium income, according to the relative time his unit was available and the proportionate value of his unit relative to the value of other units.

Cooperative apartments provide for the purchase of cooperative shares in return for a proprietary lease. Title is held by the cooperative. Accordingly, transfer costs are relatively low—the cooperative avoids title reports, loan origination fees, and financing costs. Only shares are exchanged.

In comparing cooperatives with condominiums, it should be realized that cooperative shareholders are not personally liable for the mortgage debt of the cooperative; yet cooperative shareholders are liable for the defaults of other shareholders. The rights of the cooperative owner are stated in the proprietary lease, a lease that is uniform for all tenant-shareholders. The rent or assessment provided by the lease is determined by the value of the shares held by each tenant-shareholder.

Upon resale, cooperatives vary in the manner in which the selling owner benefits from capital gains. Arrangements vary from co-ops that offer a selling shareholder only the initial down payment to co-ops that allow the selling member to seek the highest price on the open market. Under FHA-insured cooperatives, the departing member is allowed to recover his down payment, his share of equity buildup from mortgage principal repayments, and a cost-of-living increase allowance.

For zoning purposes, the Planned Unit Development may legally refer to an area of ten acres or more developed as a single entity according to a plan for residential, public, commercial, or industrial use. Land use areas are reserved exclusively for the designated use. The Planned Unit Development replaces the segregated land use scheme under conventional zoning ordinances.

Because PUDs require a high initial outlay and considerable advance planning, local government must grant concessions that give sponsors sufficient time to complete a suitable land use plan. A high initial capital cost undertaken in the face of deferred revenues realized over several years makes these projects highly risky.

REVIEW QUESTIONS

1. Describe the condominium as a legal entity.
2. Critically evaluate the following statement: Condominium ownership is preferred over conventional apartment rentals.
3. What is the purpose of the condominium declaration? Explain fully.
4. Define terms associated with condominium ownership.
5. In what manner does the legal description of a condominium unit vary from a legal description of a single-family dwelling?
6. What is the significance of the undivided share in common elements?
7. What is the function of condominium bylaws?
8. What are the main topics covered by the management agreement?
9. In a condominium unit purchased partly as a source of income, how is net income allocated to unit owners? Give an example in illustration of your answer.
10. Critically evaluate the following statement: Cooperative housing is preferred over condominium ownership. Do you agree or disagree? Why or why not?
11. What is the function of a proprietary lease in a cooperative apartment?
12. How do cooperatives arrange for the resale of cooperative apartments?
13. Define a planned unit development.
14. How do planned unit developments vary from the land use districts established under zoning codes?
15. What is the purpose of a planned unit development?
16. What are the main problems in organizing a planned unit development?

SELECTED REFERENCES

Burchell, Robert W., and Hughes, James W. *Planned Unit Development.* New Brunswick, N.J.: Center for Urban Policy Research, Rutgers—The State University, 1972.

David, Philip. *Urban Land Development,* part 6. Homewood, Ill.: Richard D. Irwin, Inc., 1970.

National Commission on Urban Problems. *Building the American City,* chap. 4. New York: Frederick A. Praeger, 1971.

Roulac, Stephen E. *Case Studies in Property Development.* Menlo Park, Calif.: Property Press, 1973.

Shenkel, William M. *The Real Estate Professional,* chap. 11. Homewood, Ill.: Dow Jones-Irwin, Inc., 1976.

Smith, Wallace F. *Urban Development,* chap. 10. Berkeley: University of California Press, 1975.

21

Home Ownership
Analysis

After reading this chapter, you should be familiar with the following points:

1 The components of acquisition costs in purchasing a dwelling.
2 The calculation of monthly housing expenses.
3 The manner in which income tax deductions favor home ownership.
4 The calculation of the net sales proceeds of ownership.
5 The relative advantages of renting versus owning.
6 Methods of judging housing as an investment.
7 Guides to follow in making a housing purchase.

AMERICANS prefer home ownership to rental housing—64.4 percent of all occupied housing is owner-occupied. The main alternatives facing households include single-family ownership, condominium and cooperative housing, mobile home occupancy, and rental units. To a large degree, the final choice depends on personal preferences. For this reason, it is impossible to hold that ownership is "better" than renting an apartment.

For most people, it is helpful to compare the economic cost of ownership relative to renting. There is also the question of treating housing not only as a consumer good but as a long-term investment. For this reason, suggestions are offered to analyze the costs of home ownership relative to renting similar space. This material is supplemented by an explanation of how housing may be analyzed as an investment. Certain guides to follow in the purchase of a house conclude the chapter.

It will be appreciated that the decision to rent or buy is not solely an economic or business decision. Young persons faced with frequent job changes and workers who require mobility are automatically in the rental market. Add to these groups the confirmed apartment dweller, who prefers the amenities of apartment living, and others who, because of limited income, must continue to rent.

Moreover, prospective homeowners may be motivated by noneconomic factors associated with the amenities of owner-occupancy. Amenities refer to qualities that add to the satisfaction of ownership. For many Americans the choice of home ownership is based on amenities associated with the pride of ownership and with the personal freedom accompanying ownership status. The added privacy and independence that come with home ownership may override the economic advantages of rental over ownership. In part, the final decision is an emotional decision based on consumer preferences.

Generally speaking, the costs of sale make short-term home ownership uneconomic. The Department of Housing and Urban Development has reported that sellers typically pay costs approximating 8 percent of the sales price. The burden may be inescapable since the homeowner is subject to involuntary changes in job and family status. In contrast, renters may change residences without incurring large capital costs. Because of transfer costs, one study shows that renting is less expensive for up to a three-year occupancy while ownership is less expensive over an occupancy of four years or more.[1]

COSTS OF OWNER-OCCUPANCY

Some authorities contend that an owner avoids two costs encountered in rental housing: charges arising from vacancies in rental housing and

---

[1] The relatively higher rates of inflation experienced from 1972 to 1976 may shorten the period in which rental occupancy is more economical. See John P. Shelton, "The Cost of Renting versus Owning a Home," *Land Economics,* February 1968, p. 72.

property management fees. To some extent, these savings offset the costs of selling a home. The impact of these differences will be shown by considering specific costs of owner and rental occupancy.

It is convenient to consider ownership costs in terms of acquisition costs, housing expenses, and the income tax deductions available to home-owners. The deductibility of property taxes and mortgage interest generally favors ownership. In addition, on resale, homeowners may be exempt from capital gains taxes.

Acquisition Costs

A buyer who finances a dwelling must pay settlement costs in addition to the down payment. The required down payment varies according to the source of credit. An FHA-financed dwelling requires at least a 3 percent down payment, while a loan guaranteed by the Veterans Administration legally requires no down payment unless the price exceeds the Veterans Administration estimate of reasonable value. Conventional loans with mortgage insurance may be arranged for up to 95 percent of the property value, but typically conventional loans require a 20 percent down payment. In comparing ownership with rental costs, an allowance must be made for the loss of income from the down payment or equity investment. For the renter has the alternative of investing a sum equal to the down payment in a deposit that would earn annual interest.

There is no legal requirement for the division of settlement costs between buyer and seller. Closing costs assumed by each party are determined by the contract of sale. Usually closing costs follow local custom. A list of closing expenses usually includes the following items:

Title abstract	Loan origination fee
Title insurance	Mortgage discount points
Legal fees	Appraisal fee
Land survey	Recording fees
Preparation of legal documents	Transfer taxes
Closing fees	Mortgage insurance premium
Credit report	Escrow fees
Termite inspection	Adjustments of prepaid items

While these closing charges are largely self-explanatory, some deserve explanation. Usually an abstract and title insurance are not both required. Lenders charging origination fees are restricted to a fee of 1 percent of the mortgage for FHA and VA loans. Though the seller pays mortgage discount points, the cost may be shifted to the buyer in a higher selling price. Mortgage insurance premiums may be paid in a lump sum for private mortgage insurance; FHA loan premiums are equal to one half of 1 percent of the loan. The buyer and seller ordinarily allocate prepaid items, such as property taxes, insurance, and mortgage payments on existing mortgages as their interests may appear. Again, the seller and buyer are free to negotiate settlement costs. In the final analysis, settlement costs borne by the seller and buyer must be allocated over their period of home ownership.

Monthly mortgage payments dominate the expense of owning a house. Mortgage terms affect the interest deduction for income taxes and the capital gain (or loss) upon sale. In a sense, that share of the mortgage payment allocated to the principal is a form of "forced saving" which reverts to the seller upon sale. Other monthly costs include property taxes, insurance, maintenance, and utility expenses. Finally, the impact of federal income taxes and transfer costs reveals the economic costs of ownership relative to rental occupancy.

Mortgage Payments

Most dwelling mortgages provide for a 20-, 25-, or 30-year amortization. Monthly costs of mortgage services (including interest and principal) are shown in Table 21–1 for a $1,000 loan. The table shows monthly costs for three amortization terms with interest rates ranging from 5½ percent to 10 percent. For example, a $30,000 mortgage financed for 30 years at 9.0 percent has a monthly cost of

$$\$8.05 \times 30 = \$241.50$$

If the above mortgage were held to maturity, the payments would total $86,940 ($2,898 × 30).

TABLE 21–1

Monthly and Total Costs to Finance $1,000 for Selected Interest Rates and Years

| Rate of Interest | Years Financed | | | | | |
| | 20 Years | | 25 Years | | 30 Years | |
	Monthly Cost	Total Cost	Monthly Cost	Total Cost	Monthly Cost	Total Cost
5½%..........	$6.88	$1,651	$6.15	$1,845	$5.68	$2,045
6..............	7.17	1,721	6.45	1,935	6.00	2,160
6½............	7.46	1,790	6.76	2,028	6.33	2,279
7..............	7.76	1,862	7.07	2,121	6.66	2,398
7½............	8.06	1,934	7.39	2,217	7.00	2,520
8..............	8.37	2,009	7.72	2,316	7.34	2,642
8½............	8.68	2,083	8.06	2,418	7.69	2,768
9..............	9.00	2,160	8.40	2,520	8.05	2,898
9½............	9.32	2,237	8.74	2,611	8.41	3,027
10.............	9.66	2,318	9.09	2,727	8.78	3,161

Source: U.S. Department of Labor, Bureau of Labor Statistics, *Rent or Buy*, Bulletin 1823, U.S. Government Printing Office, (Washington, D.C.: 1974), p. 26. See also the rates published in such sources as *Payment Table for Monthly Mortgage Loans* and *Comprehensive Mortgage Payment Tables*, publication Nos. 292 and 392, respectively (Boston: Financial Publishing Co.).

Mortgage Interest. At the end of the first year, interest payments would amount to 93 percent of annual mortgage payments. In the preceding example, monthly payments of $241.50 total $2,898 annually, which would include an interest expense of $2,695.14 (93 percent). At the end of the tenth year, the proportion going to interest would be 84 percent. Consequently, for a 30-year, 9 percent mortgage a relatively large proportion of each mortgage payment is income tax deductible over the first 10 years. Table 21–2 shows the interest share for selected years under different mortgages and interest rates.

It should be added that monthly principal payments are not always comparable to "forced savings." Forced savings are realized only if the

TABLE 21–2

Mortgage Interest as a Percent of Annual Mortgage Payments in Selected Years under Different Mortgages and Interest Rates

Interest Rate	1st Year	5th Year	10th Year	15th Year	20th Year	25th Year	30th Year
Life of Mortgage—30 years							
5%	77	72	64	54	40	24	3
5½	81	75	68	57	43	26	3
6	83	78	71	60	47	28	3
6½	85	80	73	63	49	30	3
7	87	83	76	66	52	32	4
7½	89	86	79	68	55	34	4
8	91	88	81	71	57	36	4
9	93	90	84	75	61	39	5
10	95	92	87	79	65	42	5
Life of mortgage—25 years							
5%	71	64	54	40	24	3	
5½	74	68	57	43	26	3	
6	77	71	60	47	28	3	
6½	79	73	63	49	30	3	
7	82	76	66	52	32	4	
7½	84	79	68	55	34	4	
8	86	81	71	57	36	4	
9	89	84	75	61	39	5	
10	92	87	79	65	42	5	
Life of mortgage—20 years							
5%	62	54	40	24	3		
5½	66	57	43	26	3		
6	69	60	47	28	3		
6½	72	63	49	30	3		
7	74	66	52	32	4		
7½	77	68	55	34	4		
8	79	71	57	36	4		
9	82	75	61	39	5		
10	85	79	65	42	5		

* Only the first-year percentages shown here are used to compare the investment advantages of owning and renting.

Source: U.S. Department of Labor, Bureau of Labor Statistics, *Rent or Buy*, Bulletin 1823 (Washington, D.C.: U.S. Government Printing Office, 1974), p. 26. See also the rates published in *Payment Table for Monthly Mortgage Loans* and *Comprehensive Mortgage Payment Table*, publication Nos. 292 and 392 (Boston: Financial Publishing Co.).

dwelling sells for its original cost or more. This is not always a safe assumption. The rate of obsolescence may exceed the amount of mortgage principal payments. If a house is sold at the original purchase price or more, the owner recovers the down payment less selling costs plus that portion of the mortgage payment applied to the principal. If the sales price is less than the sum of (1) the remaining balance of the mortgage, (2) the original down payment, and (3) mortgage principal payments, the seller has a capital loss.

Financing Charges. Although the interest rate, loan-to-value ratio, and term of the mortgage control monthly payments certain steps may be taken to reduce financing charges. By searching for the most favorable financing charges among institutional lenders, total financing costs may be reduced. For example, *lenders vary in charges* for appraisals, credit reports, origination fees, and other tasks associated with qualifying a borrower. Determine also whether the lender levies a *late payment charge*. It is sometimes significant to determine how late monthly payments may be before late payment charges are assessed. *Prepayment penalties* apply if the mortgage is prepaid because the owner sells or refinances the house. Prepayment penalties increase financing costs.

Frequently, it is to the borrower's advantage to sell to a buyer who assumes the existing loan. The most favorable sales price may be realized if the *lender allows loans to be assumed* by third parties. Check also to determine whether the lender has the right to charge an *assumption fee*. In addition, in financial emergencies an *open-end mortgage* permits the borrower to secure additional money on the mortgage after part of the original loan has been repaid.

Monthly Housing Expenses

Besides debt service, monthly charges include an allowance for annual property taxes, insurance, maintenance, and utilities. Although communities vary in property tax policy, it would be reasonable to assume that annual property taxes would normally approximate 1.5 percent of the cost of housing. Typically property taxes would be higher in the northeastern states and lower in the southern states. Compared to other expenses, insurance costs are fairly nominal, but for a $40,000 house, insurance could amount to $150 a year, depending on location, construction, and policy terms.

Maintenance expenses, while not a monthly cash outlay, would approximate an annual expense of 1.5 percent of the dwelling value. This is an average figure that would be higher for older houses, for example, 20 years old or more. Fuel and utilities, which according to the Bureau of Labor Statistics increased in price some 37.3 percent from 1965 to 1973, are the final element in calculating monthly housing costs.[2]

---

[2] U.S. Department of Labor, Bureau of Labor Statistics, *Rent or Buy*, Bulletin 1823 (Washington, D.C.: U.S. Government Printing Office, 1974), p. 9.

Total Monthly Expenses. The monthly costs of ownership would include the mortgage payment plus monthly housing expenses. For the $30,000 mortgage outlined above, these costs would be calculated as follows:

Monthly Expenses of Ownership

Monthly mortgage payment...............		$241.50
Other monthly expenses		
Real estate taxes.....................	$50.00	
Property insurance...................	15.16	
Maintenance.........................	30.00	
Utilities..............................	65.00	160.16
Total monthly expense...........		$401.66

Starting with a $30,000, 9 percent, 30-year mortgage, real estate taxes are based on 1.5 percent of a $40,000 dwelling, while the amounts allowed for property insurance and utilities are believed to be fairly typical for a $40,000 ownership, though these figures vary locally. On maintenance, the usual assumption is that over the economic life of a house annual maintenance costs approximate 1 percent of cost, or in this instance $400 a year. If relatively short-term ownership of a *new house* is anticipated, say, between five and ten years, this allowance is reduced to $30 per month. The point is that the total monthly expense of $401.66 covers the four monthly expenses and the mortgage payment. Income tax deductions reduce this value to a lower *effective* monthly expense.

Energy Conservation. Preliminary studies have shown that energy conservation can reduce heating and air conditioning costs. Economic benefits are realized in existing houses by adjusting furnaces to increase efficiency; adding extra insulation in ceiling, walls, and floors; caulking around windows and door frames; and sealing cracks and openings. Preliminary studies have shown that existing houses can be *retrofitted* to reduce energy costs by borrowing money under FHA Home Improvement loans (which provide for 10 percent interest or more) to pay for (1) adding ceiling insulation, (2) wall insulation, (3) floor insulation, (4) insulation of ducts in unheated spaces, (5) storm windows, and (6) storm doors and weather stripping.[3] Studies have shown that the savings in fuel may more than pay for interest on a loan and the cost of retrofitting.

For instance, a single-family dwelling may be modified to conserve energy to result in a net savings per year after increasing the mortgage to finance the cost. See, for example, Table 21–3, which shows modification costs totaling $844, resulting in an annual heating and air conditioning

------

[3] Stephen R. Petersen, *Retrofitting Existing Housing for Energy Conservation and Economic Analysis* (Washington, D.C.: Center for Building Technology, Institute for Applied Technology, National Bureau of Standards, December 1974), p. 41.

TABLE 21–3

Annual Savings Realized by Retrofitting a Single-Family Dwelling*

House Modification	Cost	Annual Savings	Annual Additional Mortgage Payments	Net Savings per Year
High-efficiency air conditioner...........	$250	$ 12.77	$24.33	−$11.56
Wall insulation..........................	54	12.73	5.26	7.47
Storm windows..........................	180	45.83	17.52	28.31
Storm doors............................	75	18.90	7.30	11.60
Double-pane glass door.................	50	9.02	4.87	4.15
Ceiling insulation.......................	180	23.15	17.52	5.63
Partition insulation.....................	25	5.10	2.43	2.67
Slab insulation.........................	30	15.81	2.92	12.89
All modifications..................	$844	$143.31	$82.15	$61.16

* The example applies to a one-story, 1,532-square-foot dwelling financed with a 30-year, 9 percent mortgage (Chicago, Illinois).
Source: Society of Real Estate Appraisers, *Appraisal Briefs,* January 28, 1976, p. 1.

cost savings of $143.31. If the mortgage is increased to finance these charges, a net annual savings of $61.16 is realized.

In a like development, considerable interest has been expressed in the development of *solar energy homes.* In some areas, the single-family home may be fitted with solar equipment costing $4,000–$5,000. A solar energy project would be economic if the added debt service and operating expenses of solar equipment were less than the cost of the heating fuel saved. The Department of Commerce reports that the feasibility of converting to solar energy depends on (1) the local climate, (2) personal comfort requirements, (3) building characteristics, (4) present and future fuel costs, (5) the cost of solar and conventional heating components, and (6) the cost of installation and other energy conservation techniques.[4]

Income Tax Deductions

The benefits homeowners realize from income tax deductions vary with the individual's tax bracket. For instance, the benefits realized from a given home will be greater for an owner in the 50 percent net income tax bracket than for an owner in the 20 percent income tax bracket. Moreover, the income tax deduction rises in proportion to the value of the dwelling. Deductions are greater for a $40,000 house than for a $10,000 house, given the same financing terms and proportionate property taxes.

The economic advantage realized by homeowners is shown in Table 21–4. The example covers a $40,000 house purchased with a $10,000

[4] Rosalie P. Ruegg, *Solar Heating and Cooling in Buildings: Methods of Economic Evaluation* (Washington, D.C.: National Bureau of Standards, Department of Commerce, July 1975), p. 39.

TABLE 21–4

Effective Monthly Payment after Income Tax Deductions

1.	Sales price of home...	$40,000.00
2.	Cash required: $10,000	
3.	Loan: $30,000, 30 years at 9% interest	
4.	Monthly payments, principal and interest....................	241.50
5.	Monthly deposit for property taxes, approximately...........	58.00
6.	Monthly deposit for insurance, approximately................	11.52
7.	Total monthly cost...	311.02
8.	Expense items for income tax purposes:	
9.	First month's interest....................................... $225	
10.	Monthly tax deposit... $ 58	
11.	Total deductions... $283	
*12.	In 50% tax bracket, deduct cash savings per month.........	141.50
13.	In 40% tax bracket, deduct cash savings per month.........	113.20
14.	In 30% tax bracket, deduct cash savings per month.........	84.90
15.	In 20% tax bracket, deduct cash savings per month.........	56.60
16.	Total monthly cost (line 7)..................................	311.02
17.	Subtract applicable deduction (assumed line 15)..............	56.60
18.	Effective monthly cost.......................................	254.42

* To calculate, multiply tax bracket by "Total deductions," line 11.
Source: Adapted from Donald N. McIntosh, "Making the Most of Financing," *Real Estate Today*, May/June 1976, p. 49.

down payment and a $30,000, 30-year loan at 9 percent. The table shows the income tax deduction for the first month only. In this case, the first month's interest and property tax total $283. After income tax deductions and assuming a 20 percent income tax bracket, the effective monthly payment is $254.42, ranging downward to $169.52 for the 50 percent income tax bracket. The effective monthly cost for the four income tax brackets of Table 21–4 is shown below.

	Income Tax Brackets			
	20%	30%	40%	50%
Total monthly cost.....................	$311.02	$311.02	$311.02	$311.02
Less deductions.......................	− 56.60	− 84.90	−113.20	−141.50
Effective monthly cost..........	$254.42	$226.12	$197.82	$169.52

Since the first monthly payment to principal is $16.50, assuming that the down payment and principal payments will be recovered at sale, the principal payment of $16.50 would be considered an added benefit of ownership. Note that the effective monthly cost includes mortgage interest, principal payments, property taxes, and prorated monthly insurance costs (less income tax savings).

A more realistic method of comparing ownership with rental is to include total personal income tax deductions and exemptions to show the actual tax savings arising from mortgage interest and property tax deductions. For this purpose, assume a $25,000 income and a tax bracket of 20 percent.

TABLE 21–5

Tax Liability with Deductions for Mortgage Interest and Real Estate Taxes

	Ownership		Rental	
Income before taxes.......................	$25,000			$25,000
Less deductions:				
Real estate taxes ($58/month).............	696		—	
Mortgage interest........................	2,695		—	
Other....................................	2,000		2,000	
Less personal exemptions...................	3,000	8,391	3,000	5,000
Equals taxable income................		$16,609		$20,000
Tax liability (20%)				
Annual....................................		3,322		4,000
Monthly...................................		276.83		333.33
Monthly tax saving by itemizing mortgage interest and taxes*				
($333.33 – $276.83)...................				56.50

* The tax savings equal the difference between monthly tax liability without home ownership deductions and monthly liability with deductions.

Without the deduction of mortgage interest and real estate taxes, taxable income totals $20,000, with an annual tax liability of $4,000 or a monthly tax liability of $333.33. With mortgage interest and property tax deductions, the monthly tax liability is $276.83—a monthly tax savings of $56.50, or a $678 annual tax savings. These data are summarized in Table 21–5.

Net Sale Proceeds

The decision to own or rent is based partly on expected proceeds from the eventual sale. It is based on highly personal judgments: first, the period of ownership must be estimated, and second, the anticipated sales price must be assumed for this calculation. Anticipated costs of sale and the remaining mortgage balance indicate a relative gain or loss from ownership.

Anticipated Sales Price. Assumptions on this point are highly critical to the final decision. For example, a $40,000 dwelling that appreciates at the rate of 2 percent per year will have a value of $44,160 at the end of five years; of $58,756 after ten years. Other annual rates of appreciation are shown in Table 21–6. If a $40,000 house appreciates at the annual compound rate of 6 percent, at the end of five and ten years the property would have a value of $53,528 and $71,632, respectively. In Table 21–6, the rate of appreciation is compounded since each succeeding increase is based on the added increment of the preceding year.

Note also that if the property is purchased with a $10,000 down payment and assuming a 6 percent compound rate of appreciation, in five years the property would sell for $13,528 above the original equity pay-

TABLE 21–6

The Increase in the Value of a $40,000 Dwelling
for Selected Annual Rates of Appreciation

Annual Percent of Appreciation	End of Five Years	End of Ten Years
2.....................	$44,160	$ 48,756
4.....................	48,668	59,208
6.....................	53,528	71,632
8.....................	58,772	86,356
10.....................	64,420	103,748

ment and mortgage. In other words, with a down payment of $10,000 the sale would net a capital gain of $13,528, 135.28 percent of the initial equity investment. In addition, the property owner would recover principal payments made over a five-year ownership period.

Deductions from the Sales Price. It would not be unrealistic to assume average selling costs of 8 percent. The next problem is to deduct the mortgage balance owed, which is given in standard mortgage tables. For instance, a 9½ percent, 30-year mortgage would have an unpaid remaining principal of 96 percent of the loan after 5 years and 89 percent after 10 years.[5] To illustrate, assume that a $40,000 house with a $30,000, 9½ percent, 30-year loan sells for $53,528—an annual rate of appreciation of 6 percent. With selling costs of 8 percent, net sales proceeds after five and ten years would be $20,450 and $39,052, respectively.

	End of 5 Years	End of 10 Years
Market value.....................................	$53,500	$71,600
Less selling costs, 8 percent....................	− 4,280	− 5,728
	$49,220	$65,872
Less remaining mortgage balance..............	−28,770	−26,820
Net sales proceeds.......................	$20,450	$39,052

---

[5] The percent of the remaining mortgage balance may be calculated from the following formula:

$$\text{Remaining mortgage balance} = \frac{\text{Present worth of the remaining debt service}}{\text{Present worth of the debt service over the mortgage term}}$$

Hence, to calculate the percent of the remaining balance of a 30-year mortgage for $30,000, 9½ percent interest, at the end of the fifth year:

1. Multiply the installment of one, 30 years, monthly payments (360 periods), 9½ percent (0.0084085421) times $30,000. The product gives the monthly payment of $252.26.
2. The present worth of one per period, 9½ percent, 300 periods (25 years) of 114.456200 times $252.26 gives the present worth of the remaining mortgage payments of $28,872.72. Since the present worth of mortgage payments is equal to $30,000, the remaining mortgage balance is equal to 96 percent of the original principal:

$$\frac{\$28,872.72}{30,000} = 96\%$$

To repeat, these data are based on presumed rates of appreciation—which may or may not be realized. It is not implied that dwelling purchases always result in property appreciation. The final sales price depends on local market conditions—conditions which are affected by local employment, government policies, interest rate changes, credit availability, household formation, and the like. The main purpose here is not to establish a given rate of appreciation on home ownership; the data are presented to illustrate the analytic procedure in measuring anticipated home ownership costs.[6]

Income from Invested Savings

Renting presents the option of investing down payment and settlement costs. Considering only the down payment of the previous example, sup-

TABLE 21–7

The Net Savings Realized by Renting and Investing Forgone Down Payment and Settlement Costs of $11,200

End of Year	Compound Amount of One, 6%	Accumulated Income on Forgone Down Payment and Buyer Settlement Costs	Annual Interest Income	Less 20% Income Tax	Net Savings Realized
Beginning of—year 1.........		$11,200.00	—	—	—
1...................	1.0600	11,872.00	$672.00	$134.40	$537.60
2...................	1.1236	12,584.32	712.32	142.46	569.86
3...................	1.1910	13,339.20	754.88	150.98	603.90
4...................	1.2625	14,140.00	800.80	160.16	640.64
5...................	1.3382	14,987.84	847.84	169.57	678.27

pose that the occupant opts to rent, investing the $10,000 in a 6 percent certificate of deposit. At the end of five and ten years at 6 percent interest, the deposit would have a value of $13,382 and $17,908, respectively—a net gain of $3,382 and $7,908. In addition, costs of purchase or settlement costs should be added to the deposit. Since interest income is taxable, the net amount realized is decreased by an assumed 20 percent income tax rate. At the end of five years, this calculation shows that a $10,000 down payment and $1,200—the buyer's settlement costs—accumulate to $14,987.84.

---

[6] In this discussion it is assumed that the dwelling is exempt from capital gains taxation. Under the present law, if a house used by the taxpayer as his principal residence is sold and another dwelling is purchased within 18 months, capital gains are recognized only to the extent that the adjusted sales price of the old residence exceeds the taxpayer's cost of purchasing a new residence. See Section 1034, Internal Revenue Code, 1975, as amended.

This figure is used to make the final calculation. The value of money not invested in a house—the down payment and settlement costs plus the interest earned thereon, less annual income taxes—must be deducted from the net proceeds from owning. Using the assumptions presented so far, the net advantage of owning over renting at the end of five years is $5,462.16, or a $91.04 savings per month.

```
Net sales proceeds.............................. $20,450.00
Less alternative investment returns at 6 percent.. −14,987.84
Net advantage of owning........................ $ 5,462.16
Monthly savings ($5,462.16/60).................... $   91.04
```

The final step is to equate the monthly expense of ownership with the amount of rent that will place the renter in an equal economic position with the homeowner. It was previously shown that the total monthly expenses of the $40,000 house purchased with a $30,000 mortgage was $401.66. If the renter enjoys a monthly savings of $91.04, then the difference between these figures gives the remainder available for rent, $310.62.

```
Total monthly expense
  (mortgage payments, property taxes,
  insurance, and utilities)........................ $401.66
Less monthly savings by renting.................. −91.04
Remainder available for rent..................... $310.62
```

In this example, the renter may spend $310.62 per month to equate the advantages of renting with the advantages of owning. Economically, the renter would be worse off than the owner if rental costs per month were above this amount. Or conversely, a monthly rental housing cost of less than $310.62 would give the renter an economic advantage over the owner.

The steps outlined in judging homeowner costs may be summarized in six points:

1. Determine the mortgage payments, interest, and principal payments for a proposed housing purchase.
2. Estimate the down payment requirements plus the settlement costs to the buyer.
3. Calculate the monthly expenses for real estate taxes, property insurance, maintenance, and utilities.
4. Estimate the net sales proceeds after deducting the costs of sale and the remaining mortgage balance.
5. Calculate the forgone earned income after taxes on settlement costs that would be realized under the rental option.
6. From the total monthly expenses of owning, deduct the savings realized by renting. The difference is the maximum monthly rental cost that gives the renter an advantage equal to that of the owner.

To be sure, these calculations are highly subjective. Yet if the prospective homeowner may base estimates on the most probable outcome, even though each calculation may not be realized, the procedure provides a logical means of comparing the economic advantages of renting versus owning. To this calculation would be added the respective amenities associated with home ownership and rental occupancy. Indeed, a renter may not realize the unique services of an owner-occupied single-family dwelling, namely, a unique location, privacy, and the personal freedom of an owner relative to that of a renter. The weight attached to amenities depends on personal preferences.

HOUSING INVESTMENTS

Rising land values, construction costs, and interest rates have induced households to rent rather than purchase dwellings. Households seeking a temporary residence prefer rentable single-family dwellings to undertaking home ownership over a few months. Similarly, single-family dwellings purchased for investment appeal to small investors and the investor who profits from tax deductions from a dwelling held for income purposes.

To the relatively small investor, with $5,000 to $10,000, rental houses are ideal. They require relatively small equity investments. Add to this the advantage of long-term financing available to investors with good credit secured by an asset that has prospects for continued rental income. It is claimed that middle-income housing meeting standard construction requirements leads to low maintenance costs. On resale, such houses appeal to two markets: the investor in income property and potential owner-occupants. They also have the advantage of the relatively low vacancy rates experienced by well-located dwellings in stable communities.

Tax Shelter

A single-family dwelling purchased for investment is usually a poor source for net income or cash flow. The rent is usually insufficient to pay operating expenses and mortgage payments. The main objective in operating single-family dwellings as a source of investment lies in tax shelter. Provided that losses on real estate may be carried over to other income, such an investment appeals to investors in relatively high income tax brackets. Table 21–8 shows the projections for a $47,500 dwelling financed with a $42,500, 9 percent, 25-year mortgage.

Beginning with an initial monthly rent of $350, both annual gross income and operating expenses are increased at a 6 percent rate for each year. Note that with operating expenses approximating 25 percent of gross income and mortgage payments of $4,284, net spendable income is a *negative sum:* $1,399 for the first year. In this instance, the investor must

TABLE 21–8

Tax Shelter from a Rental Dwelling

	Year				
	1	*2*	*3*	*4*	*5*
Net spendable income					
Gross possible income..........	$4,200	$4,452	$4,719	$5,195	$5,506
Less vacancy, one month.......	− 350	− 371	− 393	− 433	− 458
	$3,850	$4,081	$4,326	$4,762	$5,048
Less operating expenses........	− 965	−1,022	−1,084	−1,149	−1,218
Net operating income..........	$2,885	$3,059	$3,242	$3,613	$3,830
Less mortgage payments.......	−4,284	−4,284	−4,284	−4,284	−4,284
Net spendable income......	($1,399)	($1,225)	($1,042)	($ 671)	($ 454)
Taxable income					
Net operating income..........	$2,885	$3,059	$3,242	$3,613	$3,830
Less interest payments.........	−3,816	−3,774	−3,689	−3,689	−3,604
	($ 931)	($ 715)	($ 477)	($ 76)	($ 226)
Less depreciation...............	−1,173	−1,137	−1,101	−1,067	−1,034
Tax shelter.................	($2,104)	($1,852)	($1,548)	($1,143)	($ 808)

The table assumes a $47,500 purchase, $42,500 9 percent, twenty-five year mortgage, a depreciable base of $37,500, and 125 percent declining balance depreciation, 40-year life.

meet mortgage payments partly out of personal funds, though negative net spendable income decreases to $454 at the fifth year.

The advantage lies in tax shelter since interest payments and depreciation provide a paper loss of $2,104 for the first year, decreasing to $808 at the end of the fifth year. Note further that with an annual net operating income of $2,885 in year 1, the investor earns some 57 percent on his equity investment ($2,885/$5,000). If the property were purchased for cash, the annual return for the first year would be some 6 percent of invested capital ($2,885/$47,500). Note that these projections assume that the property will be vacant at least one month per year.

Net Sales Proceeds

Assuming that the property is purchased with a relatively small equity ($5,000), and assuming further the annual 6 percent price increases of the previous example, considerable capital gains will be realized over a five-year term. For example, at the end of the first year, a 6 percent price increase would mean a sales price of $50,350, or a capital gain, including mortgage principal payments, of $3,318. Projecting these same figures to the fifth year, a capital gain of $18,913 would be realized. From this figure the net sales proceeds would be reduced by approximately 8 percent, accounting for the costs of sale. These data are summarized in Table 21–9 for an assumed sales price increase of 6 percent over one–five years.

Because of declining depreciation and mortgage interest deductions,

TABLE 21–9

Capital Gain on $5,000 Equity, $47,500 Purchase, 6 Percent Annual Price Increase over One–Five Years

Year	Sales Price	Capital Gain	Add Mortgage Principal	Total Gain	Total Gain as a Percent of Equity $5,000
1...............	$50,350	$ 2,850	$ 468	$ 3,318	66
2...............	53,371	5,871	978	6,849	136
3...............	56,573	9,073	1,573	10,646	212
4...............	59,967	12,467	2,168	14,635	292
5...............	63,565	16,065	2,848	18,913	378

some authorities recommend sales of dwellings by the fifth year. An earlier sale does not provide much gain after payment of selling costs. Note that under the assumptions of Table 21–9, the gain before selling costs totals some 378 percent on a $5,000 equity.

These figures are subject to considerable qualification. The expected sales price may not be realized—it may even go down. Further, the used house may have extraordinary remodeling expenses, such as a new roof or repairs to the plumbing and heating system. Provided that a capital gain is realized, consider also the fact that capital gains are taxed at a maximum of 30 percent. For investors in higher income tax brackets, the conversion of income to capital gains provides a further investment incentive.

It should be noted that if the property is held for income purposes and if accelerated depreciation methods are used, the sale is subject to the recapture of accelerated depreciation. Using the example shown in Table 21–8 and assuming further (1) that at the end of five years the property is sold for $60,000, (2) that the taxpayer is subject to a 40 percent personal income tax rate, and (3) that the capital gain is taxed at one half of ordinary personal income tax rates, the net proceeds would be reduced as follows:

Sales price................................		$60,000.00
Cost....................................	$47,500	
Less accumulated depreciation...........	−5,512	−41,988.00
Total gain...........................		$18,012.00
Depreciation recapture		
Accumulated depreciation..	$ 5,512.00	
Less straight line........................	−4,687.50	
Ordinary income...........................		$ −824.50
Capital gain.........................		$17,187.50
Taxes		
Ordinary income, $824.50 × 0.40..........		329.80
Capital gain, 20% × $17,187.50		
(½ of ordinary income tax rate)........		3,437.50
Total tax due.......................		$ 3,767.30

The accumulated depreciation of 125 percent, declining balance, totals $5,512, producing a total gain of $18,012. Recapturing accelerated depreciation indicates an ordinary income of $824.50 and a capital gain of $17,187.50. The additional tax due represents a 40 percent tax on the ordinary income and an effective capital gains tax of 20 percent of the gain ($3,437.50). The net sales proceeds shown in Table 21–8 would be reduced by $3,767.30.[7]

THE HOME PURCHASE DECISION

The decision to buy a dwelling is the largest single investment most families will face. In making this decision, the first step requires a projection of the family's housing preferences over five or ten years. Given these preferences, they must be adapted to the family's budget restraints. The family's preferences and its ability to finance or purchase housing must be known to the broker or seller. The real estate broker will qualify the buyer before showing houses. If the prospective buyer elects to purchase directly from the seller, special precautions must be taken to ensure a favorable purchase, suitable financing, and a secure title. Given alternative housing choices, each dwelling must be evaluated with respect to its general suitability, construction standards, and personal preferences. Even after the decision to purchase is made, the steps taken in initiating the closing are critical to buyer welfare.

Determining Family Housing Needs

Personal preferences concentrate on the neighborhood, the site, and the dwelling itself. The neighborhood is judged with respect to schools, churches, shopping facilities, transportation, and distance to work. The neighborhood will be evaluated according to the level of maintenance of other houses and the conformity of houses to the type and price range required. Factors that encourage neighborhood stability include the enforcement of local zoning laws, subdivision covenants, and deed restrictions. Other relevant items that should be considered include the degree of protection from noise, dirt, and heavy traffic, and off-site improvements, such as sidewalks, streets, curbs and pavements, and sewers. Personal preferences will govern the final judgments over the suitability of the site. At a minimum, the lot should slope away from the house for proper drainage. A checklist will help evaluate the condition of the house.

Housing authorities recommend the preparation of a monthly family budget prior to committing the family to a house purchase. A form for that purpose, listing common monthly family expenses, is shown in Figure

---

[7] For further examples see Henry E. Hoagland, Leo D. Stone, and William B. Brueggeman, *Real Estate Finance,* 6th ed. (Homewood, Ill., Richard D. Irwin, Inc., 1977).

21–1. The net amount for mortgage amortization will be indicated by reducing gross income by average monthly expenses. While many lenders follow the general rule that a housing purchase should not be more than 2½ times gross income, and that monthly mortgage payments should not be more than 25 percent of income, these figures are subject to much variation. Lower income families tend to exceed these limits; higher income families spend a much smaller proportion of income for housing than these

FIGURE 21–1

Family Budget Showing Income Available for Mortgage Payments

Subtract from your family's estimated monthly
   expenses:
Food... $_____
Clothing (including upkeep)........................ $_____
Commuting... $_____
Children's education (including tuition, board,
   travel)... $_____
Installment debt (household furniture, appliances,
   revolving charge accounts, extended payments
   on credit cards)................................ $_____
Automobile payments (financing of purchase,
   insurance, repairs)............................. $_____
Taxes (federal, state, and/or city withholding or
   estimate of liability if not withheld, social
   security, pension payments, union dues)........ $_____
Life insurance..................................... $_____
Medical expenses (including health insurance
   payments)...................................... $_____
Recreation and entertainment (movies, plays,
   family outings, sports, hobbies, books, records,
   reserve for vacation).......................... $_____
Charity, personal gifts............................ $_____
Other fixed expenses (alimony, support payments
   to children or elderly relatives)................ $_____
Regular savings................................... $_____ $_____
Leaves sum available monthly for housing   Total
   (amortization and interest on mortgage, property
   taxes, heating and air conditioning, reserve for
   repairs to house)................................... $_____

Less
   $\frac{1}{12}$ annual estimated taxes........................ $_____
   $\frac{1}{12}$ annual insurance premiums.................... $_____
   Average monthly heating and airconditioning
     cost.. $_____
   Prorated outlay for repairs (if large amount of
     work to be done at outset, spread cost over a
     five-year period, add 15 percent for total interest
     charges)...................................... $_____ $_____
                                           Total

Leaves net amount available for mortgage
   amortization and interest (your payments
   to the lending institution)......................... $_____

Source: From *How to Buy a Home/How to Sell a Home,* by Glenn Fowler, pp. 15–16. Copyright © 1969 by Rutledge Books, Inc., and The Benjamin Company, Inc. Used by permission of the publisher.

figures suggest. Advance preparation of the form in Figure 21–1 will be helpful to the broker and the lender.

Most buyers elect to work through real estate brokers. In this respect, there is an advantage in dealing with a Realtor®, who holds not only a real estate license but also membership in the National Association of Realtors® through the local Realtor's® organization. Membership requires observance of the Code of Ethics. Membership usually requires participation in educational programs sponsored by state, local, and national member organizations.

To a large extent, the real estate broker provides a central marketplace, however imperfect, which allows sellers and buyers a place to submit offers

FIGURE 21–2

A Form to Qualify Prospective Home Buyers

1.	Type of home:	Existing _____	New _____
		Ranch _____	Split-level _____
		Two-story _____	Other _____
		Traditional _____	Contemporary_____
2.	Construction:	Brick _____	Wood siding _____
		Cement _____	Asbestos shingles _____
		Cedar shingles_____	Other _____
3.	Lot:	Size: _____	Type _____
4.	Rooms—		
	Number and		
	type:	Bedrooms _____	Bath _____
		Dining _____	Family _____
		Basement _____	Other _____
5.	Extras:	Fireplace _____	Garage _____
		Porch _____	Air conditioning _____
6.	Heat:	Hot air: _____ Hot water _____ Other _____
7.	Fuel:	Gas _____ Oil _____ Other _____
8.	Neighborhood:	_____
9.	Transportation requirements:	_____
10.	School requirements:	_____
11.	Church:	_____
12.	Price range:	$_____ to _____
13.	Cash down payment:	$_____
14.	Special requirements or preferences: _____

_____

_____

_____

15.	Family members:	Adults_____
		Children_____
	Name:	_____
	Address:	_____
	Telephone:	_____Date_____

Source: Glenn C. Fowler, "Tips on House Hunting: How Best to Use the Real Estate Man and Find Other Assistance," in Melvin Mencher (ed.), *The Fannie Mae Guide to Buying, Financing, and Selling Your Home.* Copyright © 1973 by The Federal National Mortgage Association. Reprinted by permission of Doubleday & Company, Inc.

to buy and sell. The broker shows houses only to buyers who he believes are in the market for a specific house and are qualified to finance the purchase. By matching preferences and ability with available houses for sale, the broker serves the interest of buyer and seller alike. Figure 21–2 is a reproduction of a questionnaire recommended by Realtors® to help qualify the personal preferences and financial ability of the buyer. With this initial information, the real estate broker may match offers to sell with the needs of specific buyers.

Evaluating a Proposed Purchase

Few families find houses ideally suited to their needs. Usually a compromise must be reached; the buyer must focus on the elements of the purchase that seems more significant. And because of the details affecting neighborhoods, the site, and the house—its exterior, interior, and equipment—it is helpful to be guided by a checklist. A checklist recommended by the Veterans Administration is shown in Figure 21–3.

FIGURE 21–3

A Checklist to Evaluate a Proposed Housing Purchase

Neighborhood

Consider each of the following to determine whether the location of the property will satisfy your personal needs and preferences:

Remarks

Convenience of public transportation . . . . ☐
Stores conveniently located . . . . ☐
Elementary school conveniently located . . . . ☐
Absence of excessive traffic noise . . . . ☐
Absence of smoke and unpleasant odors . . . . ☐
Play area available for children . . . . ☐
Fire and police protection provided . . . . ☐
Residential usage safeguarded by adequate zoning . . . . ☐

Lot

Consider each of the following to determine whether the lot is sufficiently large and properly improved:

Size of front yard satisfactory . . . . ☐
Size of rear and side yards satisfactory . . . . ☐
Walks provide access to front and service entrances . . . . ☐
Drive provides easy access to garage . . . . ☐
Lot appears to drain satisfactorily . . . . ☐
Lawn and planting satisfactory . . . . ☐
Septic tank (if any) in good operating condition . . . . ☐
Well (if any) affording an adequate supply of safe and
  palatable water . . . . ☐

FIGURE 21–3 (continued)

Exterior Detail

Observe the exterior detail of neighboring houses and determine whether the house being considered is as good or better in respect to each of the following features:

Porches .... ☐
Terraces .... ☐
Garage .... ☐
Gutters .... ☐
Storm sash .... ☐
Weather stripping .... ☐
Screens .... ☐

Interior Detail

Consider each of the following to determine whether the house will afford living accommodations which are sufficient to the needs and comfort of your family:

Remarks

Rooms will accommodate desired furniture .... ☐
Dining space sufficiently large .... ☐
At least one closet in each bedroom .... ☐
At least one coat closet and one linen closet .... ☐
Convenient access to bathroom .... ☐
Sufficient and convenient storage space (screens, trunks, boxes, off-season clothes, luggage, baby carriage, bicycle, wheel toys, etc.) .... ☐
Kitchen well arranged and equipped .... ☐
Laundry space ample and well located .... ☐
Windows provide sufficient light and air .... ☐
Sufficient number of electrical outlets .... ☐

Exterior Construction

The following appear to be in acceptable condition:

Wood porch floors and steps .... ☐
Windows, doors, and screens .... ☐
Gutters and wood cornice .... ☐
Wood siding .... ☐
Mortar joints .... ☐
Roofing .... ☐
Chimneys .... ☐
Paint on exterior woodwork .... ☐

CAUTION: Cracking, peeling, scaling, and loose paint on stairs, decks, porches, railings, windows, and doors may contain amounts of lead which are harmful if eaten by children under seven years of age. Examine these areas carefully.

FIGURE 21–3 (concluded)

Interior Construction

Plaster is free of excessive cracks .... ☐
Plaster is free of stains caused by leaking roof or sidewalls .. ☐
Door locks in operating condition .... ☐
Windows move freely .... ☐
Fireplace works properly .... ☐
Basement is dry and will resist moisture penetration .... ☐
Mechanical equipment and electrical wiring and switches
    adequate and in operating condition .... ☐
Type of heating equipment suitable .... ☐
Adequate insulation in walls, floor, ceiling, or roof .... ☐

The following appear to be in acceptable condition:

                                                                                         Remarks

Wood floor finish .... ☐
Linoleum floors .... ☐
Tile floors—vinyl asbestos, asphalt .... ☐
Sink top .... ☐
Kitchen range .... ☐
Bathroom fixtures .... ☐
Painting and papering .... ☐
Exposed joists and beams .... ☐

Source: *To the Home Buying Veteran,* VA Pamphlet 26—6, rev. (Washington, D.C.: Veterans Administration, June 1973), pp. 16–18.

In Figure 21–3, the buyer is encouraged to judge the neighborhood, the lot, and the exterior detail of the house. Probably not all houses will conform to personal preferences. For example, the interior detail may not accommodate all of the desired furnishings. Storage space may be lacking, or the kitchen may be poorly arranged and equipped. Yet the checklist provides a means of comparing houses considered for purchase. Incidentally, the neighborhood, the lot, and exterior and interior detail control decisions before construction details are evaluated. Deficiencies in these first three items may render a dwelling unsuitable even if the construction details are more than acceptable.

Judgment of the exterior and interior, as listed in Figure 21–3, provides a means of estimating rehabilitation costs. The house may represent an acceptable purchase if the price is lowered to account for replacement of the gutters and downspouts, replacement of the roof, or other details. Again, by completing such a checklist for selected houses, the buyer may more easily identify the "best buy."

Even with such a checklist, other precautions must be observed. The basement should be free from flooding, and the lot should be adequately drained. There should be a suitable sewer and water supply system, a sound foundation with no cracks or evidence of settlement, and no termite or dry rot damage.

Title Closing

The numerous documents assembled for a title transfer call for a lawyer representing the buyer. The lawyer will usually insure that:

1. The sales price and purchase terms are stated in the contract.
2. A date of closing is given with the type of conveyance document identified, for example, a warranty deed.
3. Agreement is reached on responsibility for the property before the date of closing.
4. Buyer and seller agree on the transfer and purchase of built-in equipment and appliances.

Above all, the attorney will insure that the property is transferred with an adequate legal description, survey and title documents, and either title insurance or an abstract and opinion of title. Prudent selection of a lender to gain the maximum financing terms at the least cost helps lower monthly housing costs.

SUMMARY

Home ownership is usually more expensive than renting if occupancy is anticipated for less than three years. In estimating home ownership costs, a buyer must consider the costs of acquisition, namely, the down payment and the buyer's share of the settlement costs, which may be as high as 3 percent of the selling price. Mortgage interest and property tax deductions favor home ownership, especially for higher priced housing and for buyers in the middle and upper income tax brackets.

A buyer may reduce his overall financing costs by selecting a lender that processes loans at the least cost, that levies reasonable late payment charges, and that grants prepayment privileges at the least cost. Loan assumption fees and open-end mortgage privileges are other factors affecting mortgage expenses.

In judging the monthly expenses of ownership, allowance must be made for real estate taxes, insurance, maintenance, and utilities. Some of these costs may be reduced by energy conservation measures that lower fuel and air conditioning costs. Some authorities recommend solar energy houses where the fuel savings justify the added expense.

Financial advantages accrue to the homeowner not only because of mortgage interest and property tax deductions for income taxes, but because of net sales proceeds. To measure the impact of an anticipated sales price, a prospective buyer must assume an expected occupancy period. From the anticipated sales price, deduct the remaining balance of the mortgage and the selling costs, which in this work are assumed to approximate 8 percent of the price.

The final answer is obtained by comparing the monthly expense of owning a house with the monthly savings of renting. The last item represents earnings on forgone deposits and settlement costs. The resulting answer provides the maximum money available for rent before a renter is economically worse off than an owner.

Housing purchased for rental seldom provides much cash flow and net income. The advantage lies in tax shelter because of the deductibility of mortgage interest and depreciation allowances permitted for income-producing property. The tax shelter is attractive to investors with outside income that may be sheltered from the housing investment. Provided that housing tends to appreciate over a relatively short period of ownership, net sales proceeds may be fairly substantial as measured against the actual equity investment.

The home purchase decision starts with the qualification of the family's housing needs and of its ability to finance a house. Decisions on the purchase are refined by using checklists that evaluate the neighborhood, the lot, and the exterior and interior features of the house. An evaluation of construction allows the buyer to measure the condition of the house and the sales price among alternative purchases. The closing requires specialists who act on behalf of the buyer: the attorney, the lender or escrow agent, and the real estate broker.

REVIEW QUESTIONS

1. What is meant by acquisition costs incurred in a housing purchase? Explain thoroughly.
2. What is the effect on the monthly payment of extending a 9 percent mortgage from 20 years to 30 years?
3. With respect to the total cost, what is the economic effect of extending a 9 percent mortgage from 20 years to 30 years?
4. From Table 21–1, demonstrate how higher interest rates have been offset by longer term mortgages (compare a 20-year, 7.5 percent mortgage with a 30-year, 9 percent mortgage).
5. Explain financing charges that bear on the final financing cost of a home purchase.
6. Explain how you would calculate the monthly expenses of ownership.
7. Illustrate the economic advantage realized by homeowners with respect to net income taxes.
8. What elements are considered in calculating net sales proceeds?
9. Explain the steps you would follow in judging homeowner costs relative to the cost of renting.
10. What are the financial advantages of purchasing a single-family dwelling for rental purposes? Explain thoroughly.

11. In determining family housing needs, what is the purpose of preparing a family monthly budget?

12. What are the main elements of a checklist for evaluating a proposed dwelling?

SELECTED REFERENCES

Beaton, William R., and Bond, Robert J. *Real Estate,* chap. 20. Pacific Palisades, Calif.: Goodyear Publishing Company, Inc., 1976.

Ficek, Edmund F.; Henderson, Thomas P.; and Johnson, Ross H. *Real Estate Principles and Practices,* chap. 9. Columbus: Charles E. Merrill Publishing Co., 1976.

Hines, Mary Alice. *Principles and Practices of Real Estate,* chap. 16. Homewood, Ill.: Richard D. Irwin, Inc., 1976.

Levine, Mark Lee. *Real Estate Fundamentals,* chap. 15. St. Paul: West Publishing Co., 1976.

Weimer, Arthur M.; Hoyt, Homer; and Bloom, George F. *Real Estate,* chap. 21. 6th ed. New York: Ronald Press Co., 1972.

22

The International Real Estate Market

After reading this chapter, you should be familiar with the following points:

1 The trend in international real estate markets.
2 Reasons for the foreign demand for U.S. real estate.
3 Characteristics of foreign demand as indicated by selected countries.
4 The factors creating a demand for foreign real estate among U.S. investors.
5 Brokerage procedures unique to foreign real estate operations.
6 Methods that foreigners use to acquire ownership interests in U.S. real estate.
7 Methods of acquiring foreign clients.
8 The evaluation of foreign real estate investments.

TECHNOLOGICAL CHANGES in international monetary conditions have created an unusually favorable market for international real estate. Buyers in the United States continue to make purchases of foreign residential, resort, and industrial property; foreigners, in turn, invest heavily in U.S. real estate: real estate for immediate use in industry and business and real estate for long-term investment. The Kuwait Investment Company, 50 percent of which is owned by the Kuwait government and Kuwait investors, purchased Kiawah Island, 15 miles south of Charleston, South Carolina, for $17.4 million cash. The island of 3,500 acres, 3 miles by 11 miles, will be developed as a resort which will require a multimillion dollar investment. The same company purchased a 50 percent interest in the new Atlanta, Georgia, Hilton Hotel for a reported $10 million as well as a 27 percent interest in an Idaho cattle feedlot.

Shah Mohammed Reza Pahlevi of Iran purchased the DePinna Building in New York for $3.6 million. Since 1971 the English Property Corporation has acquired over $150 million of urban real estate, including the Fisher and First National buildings in Detroit. The British Land Corporation has spent $30 million on office buildings in Baltimore and Los Angeles. Some of the leading examples of foreign investment in the United States are illustrated by the following list:

Foreign Investors	U.S. Investment
Hammerson Property, London	$75 million, office buildings in Houston*
Town and City Properties, London	$55 million, Boston†
Hitachi Company, Japan	75 thousand square feet, office building, Long Island City, New York
Trizec Corporation, Ltd., Canada	$200 million, commercial property, southeastern United States‡
Mitsui and Company, Japan	$125 million, aluminum smelter plant, western United States§
Tsukamoto, Sogyo Company, Ltd., Japan	$3 million, Montecito Country Club, Santa Barbara, California
Mazda Motors of America, Japan	$16 million, Irvine, California‖

* *Dun's Review*, 1974.
† Ibid.
‡ *National Real Estate Investor*, October 1974.
§ Art Detman, Jr., "Japan Investments: The Boom Is Dead," *California Real Estate Magazine*, March 1974, p. 30.
‖ Ibid.

Japanese industrialists have purchased luxury housing in California, and Japanese companies have actively pursued investments in U.S. timberland and new factory sites. These developments have led some observers to predict foreign real estate holdings in the United States of some $35 billion in the next ten years.[1]

[1] *Dun's Review*, May 1974, p. 58.

Americans and foreigners alike have purchased residential lots from foreign nationals. Lots from the ITT Community Development Corporation's 92,000-acre development on Florida's Palm Coast are marketed in Switzerland and West Germany. Similarly, the Deltona Corporation of Miami has sold lots on Florida's Marco Island to European investors. Some 8,500 Americans served by two U.S. airlines live along the Pacific coast of Costa Rica, ten days' driving time from Texas. Americans are purchasing lots in a 600-acre mountainside near Taxco, Mexico.[2] Numerous other examples of the growing interest in the international market for real estate may be cited.

THE DEMAND FOR U.S. REAL ESTATE

Some of the reasons for foreign purchases are technological, some are institutional, and others turn on a valid economic basis. These factors virtually guarantee a continuing demand for American real estate among foreign individuals and companies.

Improved Communication

Transoceanic flight by jet airplane has broadened the potential market for real estate. Potential buyers from Europe, South America, Japan, and the Middle East may inspect property and return home over a weekend. Improved air travel has expanded the development of luxury condominiums, hotels, and other properties for foreign buyers. The American executive taking advantage of three-day holidays seems attracted to foreign second homes and resorts. Real estate brokers dealing in the international market may communicate with foreign customers by long-distance telephone, teletype, and airmail with virtually the same ease and efficiency experienced in dealing with out-of-town buyers.

These and other technological developments reduce the risk of complex foreign real estate investments. In the past, international operations have been considerably more complex, time-consuming, and risky. Computer records and analysis enable managers to make investment decisions more quickly and with more significant information. Today the combination of computer analysis, rapid duplicating facilities, new telecommunication systems, and jet travel permits real estate specialists to operate efficiently in the expanding international real estate market.

Stability of Government

Capital investment in some countries is subject to the risks of changing governments and tax policies and of land expropriation. The political en-

---

[2] H. Bob Fawcett, "International Opportunities: How to Capture Them," *Farm and Land Realtor,* vol. 25, no. 6, June 1973, p. 1.

vironment in the United States appeals to investors in South America, the Middle East, and Europe. Foreign investors who pursue long-run objectives prefer the relative stability of government institutions in the United States to the institutional environment in their own country. Some investors fear that private landownership in some countries faces the possibility of stringent land use controls, prohibitive land taxes, or even government expropriation.

Higher Net Return

Foreign investors measure the net return on real estate investments very differently than American investors. In the United States the net income before depreciation is compared to the total property value to produce the overall return or capitalization rate. Alternatively, investors compare the rate of return on their equity investment after payment of mortgage principal and interest. The third procedure calculates cash flow: the return on the investment after payment of mortgages and income taxes.

The Rate of Return, United States. Considering the first calculation (the overall rate of return), an apartment dwelling available at $1,700,000 and earning a net income of $178,000 before depreciation would indicate an overall rate of return of 10.5 percent.

Overall Rate of Return (United States)

Annual net income (before depreciation)...................	$ 178,000
Property value.....................	1,700,000
Overall rate ($178,000/$1,700,000)..............	10.5%

The same property would be viewed by the foreign investor as earning a higher rate of return because the return would be increased by the amount

TABLE 22-1

The Annual Inflation Rate Indicated by the Consumer Price Index: 1966–1975

Year	Consumer Price Index	Annual Percentage Change
1966..................	97.2	—
1967..................	100.0	2.9
1968..............	104.2	4.2
1969..................	109.8	5.4
1970..................	116.3	5.9
1971..................	121.3	4.3
1972..................	125.3	3.3
1973..................	133.1	6.2
1974..................	147.7	11.0
1975..................	161.2	9.1

Source: *Monthly Labor Review*, vol. 99, no. 3, March 1976, p. 85.

FIGURE 22–1

The Rate of Inflation as Indicated by the Consumer Price Index: 1965–1975

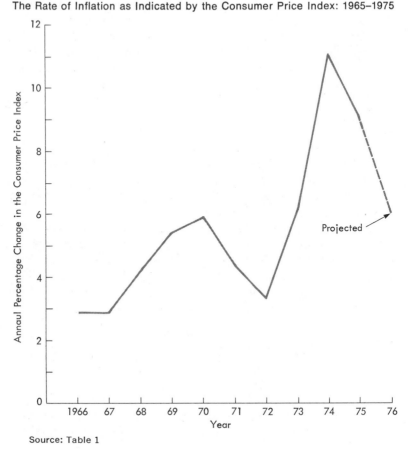

Source: Table 1

of equity buildup resulting from mortgage principal payments. Moreover, foreign investors include an assumed capital appreciation resulting from a projected inflation rate. The same property which under the American practice would show a return of 10.5 percent would be viewed as earning a 16.5 rate of return, assuming an annual inflation rate of 6 percent. Table 22–1 partly indicates the attraction of U.S. real estate investments. These data are also shown in Figure 22–1 with a projection for 1976. If foreign investors believe real estate values increase in proportion to changes in the consumer price index, you would interpret Table 22–1 as indicating a return of 26.3 percent from the end of 1972 to the beginning of 1976. The presumed increase in capital value is viewed as a capital return.

The Rate of Return, Foreign. By adding the mortgage principal payments to annual net income and an assumed inflation factor, say, 6 percent annually, an investment yields a considerably higher annual return. In this light, the same apartment earning an annual net income of $178,000 would earn an annual return of 22.5 percent.

The foreign interpretation of investment return on real estate is unacceptable to American investors. The foreign interpretation is based on the assumptions that the property will be resold for an amount equal to the original investment cost plus (1) the amount of the cumulative mortgage principal payments and (2) an amount that increases in proportion to an assumed future rate of inflation. These assumptions are too speculative for general American acceptance. Nevertheless, the foreign method of inter-

Rate of Return Calculation (foreign)

Annual net income (before depreciation).................	$ 178,000
Add mortgage principal payments (first year)..............	101,909
	$ 279,909
Property value...	$1,700,000
Rate of return ($279,909/$1,700,000).......................	16.5%
Add annual inflationary rate (assumed)..................	6.0%
Rate of return (first year)..................................	22.5%

preting real estate yields makes U.S. investments look considerably more profitable to foreigners than to Americans.

Compounding this factor are the relatively high interest rates that reduce the profitability of real estate investments in countries with a shortage of capital.

Dollar Devaluation

The rate of return for foreign investors has been increased indirectly by the devaluation of the U.S. dollar in terms of gold. Starting in December 1971, the United States devalued the dollar by some 8.6 percent by increasing the price of gold from $35 to $38. This increased the purchasing power of foreign currency in terms of U.S. dollars. Again, on February 12, 1973, the dollar was devalued with respect to gold by another 10 percent, which had the effect of decreasing the price of real estate to foreigners by a proportionate amount. To illustrate, the German mark was equal to 25.04 cents in 1965. In January 1976, one mark could buy 38.42 cents of U.S. goods—an increase of 53.4 percent.[3]

Favorable Tax Treatment

Foreign investors have the option of classifying income as *investment* or *business* income. Under U.S. tax law, the investment income of a non-

---

[3] *Federal Reserve Bulletin*, vol. 62, no. 2, February 1976, p. A75.

resident alien is exempt from federal income and capital gains taxes. The exemption was introduced by the Foreign Investors Tax Act of 1966 as an incentive for foreign investment in the United States. As a substitute for the federal income tax, foreign investors are subject to a flat rate tax of 30 percent on their gross income from U.S. sources, with no allowable deductions. According to a tax treaty, investors from Canada, Great Britain, and Ireland are subject to a 15 percent flat rate tax on their U.S. investment income.

Business income is defined as income connected with a U.S. business and is subject to the same federal income tax laws that apply to U.S. taxpayers. Depending on deductions for depreciation, interest, real estate taxes, and operating expenses, foreign investors may pay less tax on business income than on income treated as investment income and subject to the 30 percent flat rate tax. Further, capital gains realized by a nonresident alien individual on U.S. real estate are tax free unless one or both of the following conditions apply:

1. The nonresident alien is present in the United States for at least 183 days during the taxable year.
2. The capital gains are effectively connected to the conduct of a trade or business within the United States.

A capital gain is taxed at a flat 30 percent rate if the nonresident alien is present in the United States for 183 days or more during the taxable year. If the capital gain is related to the conduct of the business in the United States, the gain is taxed at the regular tax rates that apply to U.S. citizens. (See Figure 22–2.)

FIGURE 22–2

Tax Options on U.S. Real Estate Investment by Nonresident Aliens

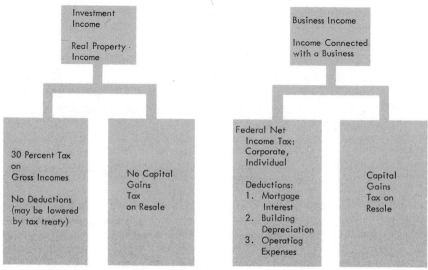

These provisions enable the foreign investor to undertake a real estate purchase as investment income that has a strong possibility of a capital gain. The payment of a flat rate tax on gross income of 30 percent and the exemption of capital gains taxes on U.S. income properties may be much more profitable than investments in the foreigner's own country.

Alternatively, U.S. tax laws that allow interest and depreciation tax deductions in combination with favorable financing may give a much higher rate of return than would be available in capital shortage countries of the Far East, Europe, and South America. The U.S. treatment of long-term capital gains favors investment considerably more than does the treatment of investors in Great Britain and other countries.[4]

Favorable Financing

Mortgage lenders in the United States are more liberal in financing than their foreign counterparts. Real estate investments in South America, the Far East, and Europe are subject to a 50 percent maximum loan-to-value ratio and a term of two to five years with interest rates above 10 percent.[5] More leverage is gained and the return on equity is increased by taking advantage of the terms available in the United States on well-secured real estate. Refer to Table 22–2 for an illustration of leverage under two assumed mortgages.

The example of Table 22–2 indicates a return on equity of 52.4 percent under a first mortgage of 25 years, 9 percent interest, and a loan-to-value ratio of 80 percent. If the foreign investor has similar opportunities in his own community, but with only a 50 percent loan-to-value ratio, a 15 percent interest rate, and a ten-year mortgage, the return on equity decreases substantially to 20.9 percent. Note also that net income after mortgage payments varies from $41,045 for the 80 percent mortgage to $13,440 for the 50 percent mortgage. Consequently, the foreign investor, who may be faced with even less favorable financing, has a strong inducement to invest in U.S. real estate.

Foreign Trade Developments

The lowering productivity of labor and the relatively high wages of foreign countries have encouraged foreign industrial investments in the United States. Japan, for example, facing higher wages and lower productivity relative to the United States, has established plants in the United States for manufacturing textiles and assembling motorcycles, electronic equipment, and automobiles. Countries that export heavily to the United States have

---

[4] Robert Feinschreiber and Lana Feinschreiber, "Foreign Investment in U.S. Real Estate: The Federal Tax Considerations," *Real Estate Law Journal*, Fall 1974, pp. 145–46.

[5] Williston H. Clover, "Outlining the Possibilities," *Real Estate Today*, July 1974, p. 38.

TABLE 22-2

An Illustration of Leverage under Two Assumed Mortgages

First-mortgage terms	*First-mortgage terms*
1. 80% loan-to-value ratio	2. 50% loan-to-value ratio
25-year term, monthly pay-ments	10-year term, monthly pay-ments
9% interest rate	15% interest rate

$1,700,000	market value	$1,700,000	market value
−1,360,000	first mortgage	− 850,000	first mortgage
$ 340,000	equity	$ 850,000	equity

Return on equity   *Return on equity*

$178,000/\$340,000 = \underline{52.4\%}$ $178,000/\$850,000 = \underline{20.9\%}$

    (before deprecia-   (before deprecia-
    tion and income   tion and income
    tax and mortgage   tax and mortgage
    payments)   payments)

Spendable income   *Spendable income*

    (Net income before deprecia-   (Net income before deprecia-
    tion, after annual mortgage   tion, after annual mortgage
    payments)   payments)

$178,000	annual net income	$178,000	annual net income
−136,955	less annual mort-gage payments	−164,560	less annual mort-gage payments
$ 41,045	spendable income	$ 13,440	spendable income

an economic advantage in locating factories near Canadian and U.S. markets.[6]

Land Relatively Inexpensive

In comparing land values, foreign investors frequently find U.S. land a relatively good buy. Land that sells for $1,000 to $1,500 a square foot in downtown Tokyo would cost $20 million to $30 million for a site of 100 feet by 200 feet. In comparison, the most desirable land in downtown Los Angeles has been purchased by Japanese interests for $150 to $175 per square foot; at this price a site of 100 feet by 200 feet would cost between $3 million and $3.5 million. Similar experiences have been reported for investors in South America, England, and Western Europe.[7]

CHARACTERISTICS OF FOREIGN DEMAND

Not all foreign investors are in the market for the same type of real estate. Foreign demand changes with changes in the economic conditions of each country.

---

[6] Art Detman, Jr., "Japan Investments: The Boom Is Dead," *California Real Estate Magazine,* March 1974, p. 30.

[7] Ibid., p. 32.

Japanese Investors

Investments in U.S. real estate by the Japanese have shown a marked change. Before December 1973, the Japanese paid $3.50 per barrel of crude oil from Arab sources. Early in 1974, the price increased to $10 per barrel, with the result that the Japanese had to spend an additional $10 billion per year for oil imports. Hence, the Japanese are now more selective in the purchase of real estate in the United States. Formerly, Japanese companies purchased land and built factories for the assembly of motorcycles, automobiles, pianos, and kitchenware; Japanese businesses were also heavily concentrated in hotels, golf courses, and banks; other Japanese investments included office buildings, industrial parks, and apartment complexes—strictly income-producing investments. Now the Japanese are concentrating in raw material–oriented investments.

To some extent the concentration in raw material–oriented investments is a continuation of policies established before the Arab oil crisis. It is reported that the Kyokuyo Company owns 37 percent of Whitney-Fidalgo Seafoods, Inc., a major salmon processor, and some 3,400 acres of Washington State timberland. In Oregon, Mitsui and Company has committed $125 million in a joint venture with the American Metal Climax Company to build an aluminum smelting plant.[8] These and other Japanese investments, according to some estimates, total over $1.5 billion.

Observers now report that the government of Japan favors investments that are urgent and necessary for the Japanese economy. Japan's less favorable balance of payments, because of the rise in oil prices, makes the Japanese favor investments in mines, oil wells, timberlands, farms, and factories. These investments increase the supply of raw materials and foodstuffs and lower the price of consumer goods for the Japanese people. New investments in land, hotels, or office buildings, which tend to be speculative or only income producing, are now less likely to be favored.

European Investors

Authorities point out that the British have traditionally been heavy investors in American real estate. One English company has acquired over $150 million worth of U.S. urban real estate, including the Fisher and First National buildings in Detroit and the $21 million Park Regent Apartments in New York City. The British Land Corporation has discontinued investments in Britain, concentrating instead on office buildings in Baltimore, Los Angeles, and other U.S. cities.

A British spokesman has said that because U.S. construction costs are rising so rapidly, it is unlikely that new buildings will be replaced at current costs. To illustrate further, London's Town and City Properties has acquired over $55 million worth of real estate in Boston. Travelodge Inter-

---

[8] Ibid., p. 32.

national, with 460 motels and the elegant Hotel Pierre in New York City, is British owned. These illustrations indicate that the British seek urban properties with proven income-producing ability. They apparently prefer capital gains opportunities and favorable prospects for long-term rentals.[9]

A recent survey of 1,000 foreign manufacturing companies revealed that 36 companies plan to build new plants or to expand their present facilities in the United States. The main reason foreign companies gave for U.S. investment was to build plants to expand their share of U.S. and Canadian markets. Other reasons offered included the availability of a skilled labor force and the opportunity to apply U.S. research.[10]

Middle East Investors

Observers have noted that Arab investors tend to be very conservative and highly concerned over the preservation of capital. Hence, they have preferred short-term investments. Arab investors have acquired a diversified portfolio of office buildings, shopping centers, and apartment houses. Well-secured land and buildings are considered relatively safe assets that will appreciate and preserve capital. For example, the Chase Manhattan Bank has reported the placement of Arab investments in over 50 projects. Arab-controlled investors have purchased industrial buildings, shopping centers, downtown office buildings, and industrial parks.[11]

In sum, real estate experts indicate that the foreign investor must be assured of a growing community where investment may be expected to appreciate. Foreign investment seems to be primarily moved by safety of principal and not primarily by the rate of return. A real estate investment in the United States diversifies a foreigner's holdings and may avoid heavy inheritance taxes levied in his own country. A major category of Arabian investment relates to joint venture projects. Among the firms active in joint venture projects with Arabs are Enck, Hollingsworth and Reveaux firm in Louisville, Kentucky, which has reportedly a $200 million line of credit; Wooten and Associates in Dallas, Texas; and the Eastdil Realty Company, which is affiliated with Blyth Eastman Dillon Company. These firms plan a mixed pool of Arab and other investor funds.[12]

U.S. DEMAND FOR FOREIGN REAL ESTATE

Richard A. Keefe, president of Blair International, Inc., of Chicago, cites several reasons for the burgeoning demand for overseas property. Aircraft which transport 490 travelers on one trip, such as the Boeing 747,

---

[9] A. Patrick Giles, "International Investors in United States Real Estate," *Real Estate Appraiser,* July/August 1973, p. 19.

[10] *Plants, Sites, and Parks,* March/April, 1975, p. 1.

[11] *Site Selection Handbook,* 1975, p. 16.

[12] Ibid.

have expanded the need for tourist and other travel facilities, such as motels and hotels, in all parts of the world. In addition, industry requirements for offices and manufacturing plants have increased the search for available land and buildings in major cities of the free world. Large corporations have diversified their holdings by developing hotel-motel property, while airlines and related transportation services have expanded their hotel-motel business.[13]

Another authority describes the growing demand for vacation and resort sites on the Pacific coast of Costa Rica, which currently serves 8,500 Americans with second or retirement homes. Costa Rica, available by flight from Miami or San Jose or via Pan American Airlines, is also only some ten days' driving time from Texas by the Inter-American Highway. Homesites in Costa Rica were sold for from $4,500 for a quarter acre to $24,000 for 2 acres.[14]

Brokers active in serving Americans who invest in overseas real estate insist on the free convertibility of foreign money to U.S. dollars. If the United States experiences continuing inflation, the investment return is calculated to include the projected rate of inflation. In other countries, investment procedures follow local custom. In England, for example, because the tenant pays property taxes, the owner of an office building may hold the property off the market for several months until rental rates increase.[15]

Americans purchasing foreign real estate are confronted with laws and regulations that require competent, legal interpretation. For instance, the Costa Sur condominium development owned by Gulf and Western Foods, Inc., is unable to transfer title to non-Dominican citizens. As an alternative, the resort is developed under a combination long-term lease and condominium ownership plan. The lease establishes title and the right of possession under the following clause:

> THE LESSOR justifies its right of ownership over the mentioned real estate, with Certificate of Title No. 72–75, which was issued to him by the Register of Titles of the Department of San Pedro de Macorís, on the 9th day of October, 1973, the duplicate of the corresponding Owner.

The rights of the tenant–condominium purchaser are governed by a separate law. As quoted in the 99-year lease:

> THE LESSOR has organized or will organize the real property subject of the present leasing contract, according to condominium rule established by Law No. 5038, dated November 21, 1958, which is known by THE LESSEE and who compels himself to accept such rule, and

---

[13] "Air Travel Revolution Creates Big Market for Foreign Property," *National Real Estate Investor,* February 1970, p. 26.

[14] *The Mortgage and Real Estate Executives Report,* Boston, Massachusetts, August 15, 1974, p. 6.

[15] "International Real Estate: A Two-Way Street," *Real Estate Forum,* April 1969, p. 34.

who also states that he formally accepts each of the dispositions contained in such Law No. 5038 earlier mentioned, and which has been or will be filed at the Register of Titles Department in San Pedro de Macorís. . . .

The U.S. investor must accept a different set of customs, laws, and regulations that govern titles, land use, and the financing of foreign real estate. The broker who specializes in such properties must also be knowledgeable about real estate practices in both the United States and the foreign country in which he markets real estate.

FOREIGN REAL ESTATE OPERATIONS

Specialists in foreign real estate must adapt brokerage procedures to policies common to the international real estate market. The marketing plan and the tax aspects of foreign real estate deserve special attention. The complexity of these issues requires a special plan of presentation not found in the marketing of real estate in the United States.

The Brokerage Agreement

At the outset a U.S. broker operating in the international market must adapt himself to the cultural and social attitudes of his foreign client. Problems develop if the U.S. broker follows American business practices while the foreign client expects him to observe foreign practices. Both parties must recognize national differences in business customs and practices. Foreign brokers report that it is often necessary to establish a personal, friendly relationship to achieve favorable business results. Jack H. Lee of Milwaukee, Wisconsin, advises the U.S. broker to:

1. Define the needs and capabilities of the foreign client.
2. Define the U.S. broker's role.
3. Establish a viable financial relationship with the client.[16]

On the first point it has been observed that a foreigner may hire a consultant or a broker to acquire an investment property. Others may prefer to buy a business, merge with a U.S. business, or participate in a joint venture with a U.S. partner. In some instances it has been reported that a client thinks he knows his needs but needs careful counseling because he is not familiar with the U.S. economy or with state and local laws. To guard against misunderstanding, brokers qualify the client by resolving the following questions:

1. Is the client able to transfer funds to the United States?
2. About how much money can the client transfer to the United States?

---

[16] Jack H. Lee, "Working with Foreign Buyers," *Real Estate Today,* July 1975, p. 24.

3. What funds does the client have on hand for a U.S. acquisition?
4. Does the client require U.S. financing?
5. Are legal and accounting services available to the client?
6. Does the client own other U.S. real estate, or is this his first acquisition?
7. Is the client capable of operating or managing the proposed purchase?
8. Has the client worked with other U.S. real estate brokers?
9. Will the client make his own decisions on value and price (the client may require an independent appraisal opinion)?
10. Is the client the sole purchaser or a partner in a joint venture?
11. Does the client have a U.S. office or a legally recognized real estate corporation?
12. What are the client's U.S. banking connections?
13. Does the client understand English technical and legal terms?[17]

Experienced brokers in the foreign real estate market identify money as black, gray, or white, which gives another reason for seeking competent legal council. Black money is money which investors have transferred outside the country in violation of the exchange or tax laws. Investment funds from Hong Kong, Singapore, the Far East (except Japan), and Latin America (except Panama and Uruguay) fall into this category. With certain exceptions, nationals in Norway, Sweden, Denmark, Finland, and Spain must observe stringent restrictions on foreign investment. Money from Belgium and Italy is termed gray money because nationals in these countries commonly violate exchange control laws to the point that violation is almost an accepted business practice. White money refers to funds from countries in which there are no exchange control regulations prohibiting their investment abroad. Typically money from Germany, Switzerland, and the Netherlands falls into this category.[18]

The answers to the questions raised above dictate the extent of the broker's services and responsibilities. The listing agreement is the determination of the broker's consulting fee.

Marketing property internationally is considerably more expensive than marketing it domestically. If property is advertised in foreign media, a lead time of at least 60 days is required to place an advertisement. Extra time and care must be taken to prepare brochures in different languages. It takes more time to clear a deposit with an offer to buy, and delays are encountered in conducting on-site inspections by foreign prospects. Experienced brokers therefore recommend a listing term of one year, granted on an exclusive right to sell agreement.[19]

---

[17] Ibid.

[18] Giles, "International Investments," p. 19.

[19] Williston H. Clover, "Merchandising the Property," *Real Estate Today,* July 1974, p. 40.

Exclusive listing agreements typically will call for a 6–8 percent commission on income and industrial property and 10–12 percent on vacant land. Commissions may vary from these figures because of local customs and the tendency to accept lower commissions for higher priced property. Advertising and promotion fees and inspection costs are budgeted in advance and paid for by the listing client. Promotional expenses of from $2,500 to $7,500 to advertise and promote foreign sales are not unusual.

A company specializing in international real estate markets accepts listings from a network of affiliated U.S. real estate brokers for the sale of property to foreign buyers. Listings by affiliated U.S. brokers are given to Panorama Properties, Inc., which then exposes the listing to some 900 major U.S. and foreign buyers. Panorama Properties' marketing network includes 60 affiliated U.S. brokers and some 45 affiliated overseas brokers.[20]

The Property Brief

A written description of the property, with photographs, maps, detailed floor plans, and the financial data normally included in a professional narrative appraisal report, constitutes the property brief. It is difficult to market real estate in foreign countries without special and professional attention to the preparation of a comprehensive property brief. The extra effort arises from the inherent disadvantages a foreign prospect has in considering the purchase of U.S. real estate: generally, foreign investors are not well informed on prospects for local community growth and on the rates of return typical of various types of real estate; they are usually unfamiliar with our real estate terms, such as amortized mortgages, cash flow, and accelerated depreciation, and with our corporate and personal income tax laws.

In addition to photographs, maps, and a written property description, the property brief includes certain *background information* found in the narrative appraisal report: (1) descriptive information on the city in which the property is located, including an analysis of the economic base and information revealing historical growth patterns, and (2) site location analysis.

The *financial information* of the property brief begins with a list of tenants, the rent roll, the date leases expire, and an identification of the space leased by tenants. The operating expense statement would be taken from an annual audit, which would include a projection of annual real estate taxes, the recommended insurance coverage, and its cost. The terms of the mortgage would be noted, with due dates and provisions for prepayment.

While these data are taken from past operating experience, the property brief preferably includes a projection of net operating income over the first

---

[20] *Real Estate "Insider" Newsletter,* vol. 5, no. 10, December 17, 1973.

ten years of ownership. The statement allows for a reasonable estimate of future vacancies and an estimate of the annual costs incurred in replacing personal property: furniture and equipment which must be periodically replaced. The broker would comment on the probability of increasing the rent roll and on the possibility of decreasing expenses over the early years of ownership.

The experienced commercial and industrial broker would recognize that most of these requirements of the property brief are common to offers extended to U.S. prospects. However, these requirements would be supplemented by certain other information deemed significant to the foreign prospect. The additional points include:

1. Recommendations on the type of ownership interest acquired: an individual purchase, a corporate purchase, a joint venture.
2. Recommendations on conversion to *investment* income or *business* income.
3. A projection of income and expenses over ten years, showing interest and principal payments on mortgages and projected income taxes.
4. A statement of the fees charged for leasing, managing, and preparing accounting statements for the client.
5. A summary of the U.S. taxes the foreign investor may expect, and of the anticipated net cash income after taxes. The analysis will also contain an estimate of the rate of return, which includes the repayment of mortgage principal.
6. A conservative estimate of the capital gains which the foreign prospect may anticipate after ten years of ownership.

Clearly the broker operating in the international real estate market must know technical details not usually encountered in domestic selling. Considerable emphasis is placed on the written property brief. The written statement allows the prospect to counsel through a so-called hidden adviser—the banker or attorney who is frequently requested to review the brief. Prospects tend to be impressed by the detail of a well-written brief, a brief that creates confidence and allows the prospect to repeatedly review reasons for acting on the recommended investment.

FOREIGN OWNERSHIP INTERESTS

Foreign investors may acquire ownership interests in numerous forms: a U.S. partnership interest, a foreign partnership, a U.S. trust, a foreign trust, an offshore real estate fund, individual ownership, a foreign corporation, or a U.S. corporation. The final decision *rests* on legal and tax counsel recommendations. Here it is considered relevant to cover the main foreign investment practices. The final ownership form turns on the party making the investment, on investment objectives, and on the tax status of the investor, both in the United States and in the investor's own country.

Foreign Investors

Most international investors fall into one of three categories: professional developers, institutional investors, and individuals. Professional developers usually prefer the corporate form, illustrated by the Trizec Corporation. Though a Canadian real estate company owned by the English Property Corporation of London, the corporation actively invests in the United States. Because Canada places prohibitive taxes on foreign investments, Trizec has joined with German financial institutions to invest some $200 million in U.S. property.[21]

International institutional investors include commercial and private banks, insurance companies, pension funds, and professional associations. These institutions frequently prefer to invest in acreage with capital gains opportunity. The third type of foreign investor, the individual, has the largest degree of investment flexibility. The individual can more easily adapt investment objectives to minimize taxes and maximize long-term objectives.

The Ownership Interest

Suppose that the foreign investor elects to develop land. In this case the investor would usually choose among three options: (1) the purchase of shares in a land company, (2) the purchase of shares in financial institutions which invest in land development projects, or (3) the direct purchase of land as a joint venture with U.S. firms active in land development projects.

If the foreign investor's ownership interest is acquired through a foreign corporation, such as the Canadian-owned Tristar Corporation, the development, subdivision, and sale of real estate would constitute conduct of trade or business subject to the tax laws that apply to U.S. nationals. Brokers confronting these problems seek professional legal counsel experienced in the taxation of income on real estate owned by foreigners. The taxation of foreign-owned real estate in the United States is complicated by treaties, protocols, and tax conventions between the United States and other countries that have the effect of revising provisions of the Internal Revenue Code. For this reason it is necessary for the broker handling international real estate to work closely with tax attorneys experienced in international tax law.

For income properties involving more than one buyer, a joint venture is usually preferred. The acquisition may be as tenants in common with either individuals or a corporation or by a corporation and an individual. For U.S. tax purposes, the joint venture may involve a business undertaken for profit which may be treated as a partnership.

The joint venture appeals to foreign investors operating on a large scale.

---

[21] "National Real Estate Newsletter," *National Real Estate Investor,* October 1974.

The Kuwait Real Estate Bank and the Bank of America International Realty Company formed a third company, the Kuwait Properties International (52 percent and 48 percent interests, respectively), to invest more than $20 million in U.S. office buildings, industrial and retail properties, and established apartment buildings. The Bank of America organization was formed to provide foreign nations with real estate advisory services. In these examples the broker refers clients to tax counsel who analyze the tax consequences of annual income earned from the investment and the tax treatment of capital gains. The nonresident alien may obtain the maximum return only by selecting the tax option that meets his investment objectives.[22]

Acquiring Foreign Clients

Developing a business with potential foreign investors in real estate involves special procedures adapted to such investors. One source explains that affluent residents of Chile, Peru, Columbia, and El Salvador, and to a lesser extent citizens of Venezuela, Ecuador, Nicaragua, and Panama, deal with U.S. lawyers in order to keep land purchases confidential. The U.S. lawyer organizes a company to take title to the real estate purchased by the foreign client. Such companies are commonly headquartered in a Caribbean country which exempts resale profits. The attorney deals directly with a U.S. broker who is commissioned to find a suitable investment.

To develop a business from this source, brokers are advised (1) to make inquiries to local bankers for names of local attorneys and tax lawyers known to represent foreign clients or (2) to place ads in magazines published by airlines that service Latin American countries. These ads would describe real estate services to foreign investors.

The second main method of developing a foreign real estate business requires a working relationship with the trust departments of certain U.S. banks. Usually these are banks centered in New York City, California, and Chicago which deal frequently in foreign trade; many of these banks have foreign branch offices. Typically the foreign investor is referred to the trust office of banks in New York City, California, and Chicago. The banks, in turn, work with real estate brokers known to deal in income properties and to have the capability of servicing foreign investors.

FOREIGN INVESTMENTS EVALUATED

Concern over foreign investments, both portfolio investments and direct investments in real estate, led the president of the United States under Executive Order 11858, May 7, 1975, to establish the Committee on Foreign

---

[22] Dwaine E. Carr, "Taxes and the International Transaction," *Real Estate Today*, July 1974, p. 51.

Investment. The committee is made up of representatives of the Secretaries of State, the Treasury, Defense, and Commerce as well as the Assistant to the President for Economic Affairs and the Executive Director of the Council on International Economic Policy. The committee has primary responsibility for monitoring the impact of foreign investment in the United States. In this respect the committee is directed to:

1. Arrange for the preparation of analyses of trends and significant developments in foreign investments in the United States.
2. Provide guidance on arrangements with foreign governments for advance consultations on prospective major foreign governmental investments in the United States.
3. Review investments in the United States which, in the judgment of the committee, might have major implications for U.S. national interests.
4. Consider proposals for such new legislation or regulations relating to foreign investment as may appear necessary.

While much concern has been directed to purchases by corporations, others have voiced fears over the ownership of real estate by nonresident aliens. On this point Dean R. Hinton, Deputy Executive Director of the President's Council on International Economic Policy, stated, ". . . the Administration has concluded that an open door policy or a policy of 'National Treatment' whereby foreigners should be treated like Americans is in our best interest." He added that foreigners are expected to adhere to U.S. laws, and that if this is done, there are no problems. He stated further that the fear of foreign investment in U.S. real estate is an emotional one. On this issue, "we must remember that there is more American investment abroad than foreign investment here." Apparently the national policy has produced a more open economic system; in the past administration's view, restrictions on foreign investment tended to divide countries when we were striving for unity.[23]

Another authority has stated that foreign investment in the United States narrows the dollar gap in our balance of payments. Foreign investment in real estate projects, moreover, creates jobs in the United States and increases federal and local tax revenues. In addition, investment in the United States stimulates the inflow of foreign equity capital. Consequently, provided that foreign investors conform to U.S. laws and procedures, they are apparently viewed favorably by the majority as a means of increasing jobs, tax revenues, and U.S. economic development.

SUMMARY

International conditions favor expansion of the international real estate market. In the United States, individuals have turned to resort, condominium, and retirement property overseas, largely as a consequence of the

---

[23] "Foreign Investment in U.S. on Upswing," *Farm and Land Realtor,* June 1974, p. 11.

availability of jet travel, car rental, and improved communications. Foreign companies in the United States continue their investment in real estate as part of their industrial and marketing functions. Foreigners have favored the purchase of U.S. real estate for business purposes, as illustrated mainly by the Japanese, and for long-term investment, as demonstrated by the British, Canadians, South Americans, and Western Europeans.

Foreign investment is attracted by the stability of the U.S. government and the relatively high net return earned on U.S. income property. Devaluation of the U.S. dollar, favorable tax treatment of foreign investments, attractive financing of real estate projects, expansion of foreign trade, and the relatively inexpensive land in the United States have contributed to an increase in foreign investment in U.S. real estate.

More recently the Japanese have been heavy investors in raw material– and manufacturing-oriented investments. This new emphasis is largely the result of a decline in the capital available to the Japanese because of the increased cost of Japan's imported oil. British corporations and West German investors have favored long-term returns with opportunities for capital gains. Similarly, investors in the Middle East have favored investments that preserve capital; they have shown a preference for a lower rate of return on properties that have a proven prospect of long-term income. U.S. investors in foreign real estate are dominated by corporations that have expanded overseas hotel and resort developments and by individuals who have purchased foreign resort, vacation, and retirement properties.

Foreign real estate operations start with the definition of the needs and capabilities of the client, an understanding of the U.S. broker's role, and an agreement on the financial arrangement between the foreign client and the U.S. broker. The listing agreement extends for a longer term than do listing agreements with U.S. clients, typically 12 months. The commissions include an allowance for the extra expense of international advertising, travel, and inspection.

In selling U.S. real estate to foreigners, the broker depends heavily on the property brief. The brief includes not only photographs, maps, and a written property description and other background information common to a narrative appraisal report, but also detailed financial information: a tenant list, an operating expense analysis, and a review of gross income and mortgage terms. The broker adds his ten-year projection of net operating income. In addition, a property brief for foreign investors includes recommendations on the type of ownership interest to be acquired and the tax consequences of the purchase.

The foreign investor may be a professional developer, an institutional investor, or an individual. Foreign investors may take title to U.S. real estate in the form of shares in a land company, shares in a financial institution, or by direct purchase of land as a joint venture with a U.S. company. Brokers seeking to attract foreign clients work through lawyers specializing in foreign clients and with the trust departments of leading metropolitan banks.

REVIEW QUESTIONS

1. Explain how improved communications have created a demand for U.S. real estate.

2. Why has the stability of the U.S. government increased the demand of nonresident aliens for the ownership of U.S. real estate?

3. Illustrate how income from an office building would show a considerably higher overall rate of return to the foreign investor compared to the U.S. investor.

4. In your view, should the mortgage principal be regarded as part of the rate of return earned on real estate assets? Why or why not?

5. Why is it inappropriate to consider the rate of inflation as part of the return earned on real estate? Explain thoroughly.

6. Illustrate how dollar devaluation increases the demand for real estate in the devaluing country.

7. Would you advise the foreign investor to classify his real estate investment as *business* income or as *investment* income? Give an example to illustrate your answer.

8. What is the effect of more favorable financing on the return on equity? On spendable income?

9. How can international foreign trade conditions affect the demand for ownership of U.S. real estate by foreign nationals?

10. What is the policy of Japanese investors on U.S. investment real estate?

11. What are the investment preferences of British investors in U.S. real estate?

12. What developments help explain the demand for foreign investments by U.S. nationals?

13. Discuss why a broker must qualify a prospective foreign purchaser of U.S. real estate.

14. What is a property brief?

15. How is the property brief adapted to the needs of the foreign prospect?

16. What are the characteristics of foreign investors?

17. In developing land, what forms of ownership interests are open to the foreign investor? Explain fully.

18. How would a real estate broker acquire foreign clients?

19. What objection may be raised against the further increase in the acquisition of U.S. real estate by foreign investors?

20. What arguments are offered in defense of continued foreign investment in U.S. real estate? Critically evaluate.

SELECTED REFERENCES

Conser, Eugene P. *Real Estate—European Style,* p. 634. New York: Exposition Press, 1976.

Feinschreiber, Robert, and Feinschreiber, Lana. "Foreign Investment in U.S.

Real Estate: The Federal Tax Considerations," *Real Estate Law Journal,* vol. 3, no. 2 (Fall 1974), pp. 144–54.

Giles, A. Patrick. "International Investors in United States Real Estate." *Real Estate Appraiser,* vol. 39, no. 4 (July/August 1973), pp. 18–22.

Hines, Mary Alice. *Principles and Practice of Real Estate,* chap. 24. Homewood, Ill.: Richard D. Irwin, Inc., 1976.

Klein, Susan Fayth. "Investments by Foreign Persons in United States Real Estate," *Journal of Real Estate Taxation,* vol. 2, no. 3 (Spring 1975), pp. 265–91.

Weimer, Arthur M.; Hoyt, Homer; and Bloom, George F. *Real Estate,* chap. 24. 6th ed. New York: Ronald Press Co., 1972.

appendix

Capitalization Tables and Their Explanation

CAPITALIZATION tables are shown for interest rates of 8, 9, 10, 11, and 12 percent. Each table is limited to 50 periods. For other interest rates and periods, consult readily available published capitalization tables. These tables are included to allow students to experiment with problems and cases solved with a range of interest rates and discount factors. An explanation of capitalization tables follows the last table.[1]

---

[1] The capitalization tables are adapted from William M. Shenkel, *Capitalization Tables for Investment Purposes* (Athens, Ga.: Department of Real Estate and Urban Development, College of Business Administration, University of Georgia, 1972), 161 pp.

Capitalization Tables: Compounded Annually, Nominal Rate 8.0 Percent

Periods	Amount of One	Amount of One per Period	Sinking Fund	Present Worth of One	Present Worth of One per Period	Partial Payment
1............	1.0800	1.0000	1.0000	.9259	.9259	1.0800
2............	1.1664	2.0800	.4808	.8573	1.7833	.5608
3............	1.2597	3.2464	.3080	.7938	2.5771	.3880
4............	1.3605	4.5061	.2219	.7350	3.3121	.3019
5............	1.4693	5.8666	.1705	.6806	3.9927	.2505
6............	1.5869	7.3359	.1363	.6302	4.6229	.2163
7............	1.7138	8.9228	.1121	.5835	5.2064	.1921
8............	1.8509	10.6366	.0940	.5403	5.7466	.1740
9............	1.9990	12.4876	.0801	.5002	6.2469	.1601
10............	2.1589	14.4866	.0690	.4632	6.7101	.1490
11............	2.3316	16.6455	.0601	.4289	7.1390	.1401
12............	2.5182	18.9771	.0527	.3971	7.5361	.1325
13............	2.7196	21.4953	.0465	.3677	7.9038	.1265
14............	2.9372	24.2149	.0413	.3405	8.2442	.1213
15............	3.1722	27.1521	.0368	.3152	8.5595	.1168
16............	3.4259	30.3243	.0330	.2919	8.8514	.1130
17............	3.7000	33.7502	.0296	.2703	9.1216	.1096
18............	3.9960	37.4502	.0267	.2502	9.3719	.1067
19............	4.3157	41.4463	.0241	.2317	9.6036	.1041
20............	4.6610	45.7620	.0219	.2145	9.8181	.1019
21............	5.0338	50.4229	.0198	.1987	10.0168	.0998
22............	5.4365	55.4568	.0180	.1839	10.2007	.0980
23............	5.8715	60.8933	.0164	.1703	10.3711	.0964
24............	6.3412	66.7648	.0150	.1577	10.5288	.0950
25............	6.8485	73.1059	.0137	.1460	10.6748	.0937
26............	7.3964	79.9544	.0125	.1352	10.8100	.0925
27............	7.9881	87.3508	.0114	.1252	10.9352	.0914
28............	8.6271	95.3388	.0105	.1159	11.0511	.0905
29............	9.3173	103.9659	.0096	.1073	11.1584	.0896
30............	10.0627	113.2832	.0088	.0994	11.2578	.0888
31............	10.8677	123.3459	.0081	.0920	11.3498	.0881
32............	11.7371	134.2135	.0075	.0852	11.4350	.0875
33............	12.6760	145.9506	.0069	.0789	11.5139	.0869
34............	13.6901	158.6267	.0063	.0730	11.5869	.0863
35............	14.7853	172.3168	.0058	.0676	11.6546	.0858
36............	15.9682	187.1021	.0053	.0626	11.7172	.0853
37............	17.2456	203.0703	.0049	.0580	11.7752	.0849
38............	18.6253	220.3159	.0045	.0537	11.8289	.0845
39............	20.1153	238.9412	.0042	.0497	11.8786	.0842
40............	21.7245	259.0565	.0039	.0460	11.9246	.0839
41............	23.4625	280.7810	.0036	.0426	11.9672	.0836
42............	25.3395	304.2435	.0033	.0395	12.0067	.0833
43............	27.3666	329.5830	.0030	.0365	12.0432	.0830
44............	29.5560	356.9496	.0028	.0338	12.0771	.0828
45............	31.9204	386.5056	.0026	.0313	12.1084	.0826
46............	34.4741	418.4261	.0024	.0290	12.1374	.0824
47............	37.2320	452.9002	.0022	.0269	12.1643	.0822
48............	40.2106	490.1322	.0020	.0249	12.1891	.0820
49............	43.4274	530.3427	.0019	.0230	12.2122	.0819
50............	46.9016	573.7702	.0017	.0213	12.2335	.0817

Capitalization Tables: Compounded Annually, Nominal Rate 9.0 Percent

Periods	Amount of One	Amount of One per Period	Sinking Fund	Present Worth of One	Present Worth of One per Period	Partial Payment
1............	1.0900	1.0000	1.0000	.9174	.9174	1.0900
2............	1.1881	2.0900	.4785	.8417	1.7591	.5685
3............	1.2950	3.2781	.3051	.7722	2.5313	.3951
4............	1.4116	4.5731	.2187	.7084	3.2397	.3087
5............	1.5386	5.9847	.1671	.6499	3.8897	.2571
6............	1.6771	7.5233	.1329	.5963	4.4859	.2229
7............	1.8280	9.2004	.1087	.5470	5.0330	.1987
8............	1.9926	11.0285	.0907	.5019	5.5348	.1807
9............	2.1719	13.0210	.0768	.4604	5.9952	.1668
10............	2.3674	15.1929	.0658	.4224	6.4177	.1558
11............	2.5804	17.5603	.0569	.3875	6.8052	.1469
12............	2.8127	20.1407	.0497	.3555	7.1607	.1397
13............	3.0658	22.9534	.0436	.3262	7.4869	.1336
14............	3.3417	26.0192	.0384	.2992	7.7862	.1284
15............	3.6425	29.3609	.0341	.2745	8.0607	.1241
16............	3.9703	33.0034	.0303	.2519	8.3126	.1203
17............	4.3276	36.9737	.0270	.2311	8.5436	.1170
18............	4.7171	41.3013	.0242	.2120	8.7556	.1142
19............	5.1417	46.0185	.0217	.1945	8.9501	.1117
20............	5.6044	51.1601	.0195	.1784	9.1285	.1095
21............	6.1088	56.7645	.0176	.1637	9.2922	.1076
22............	6.6586	62.8733	.0159	.1502	9.4424	.1059
23............	7.2579	69.5319	.0144	.1378	9.5802	.1042
24............	7.9111	76.7898	.0130	.1264	9.7066	.1030
25............	8.6231	84.7009	.0118	.1160	9.8226	.1018
26............	9.3992	93.3240	.0107	.1064	9.9290	.1007
27............	10.2451	102.7231	.0097	.0976	10.0266	.0997
28............	11.1671	112.9682	.0089	.0895	10.1161	.0989
29............	12.1722	124.1354	.0081	.0822	10.1983	.0981
30............	13.2677	136.3075	.0073	.0754	10.2737	.0973
31............	14.4618	149.5752	.0067	.0691	10.3428	.0967
32............	15.7633	164.0370	.0061	.0634	10.4062	.0961
33............	17.1820	179.8003	.0056	.0582	10.4644	.0956
34............	18.7284	196.9823	.0051	.0532	10.5178	.0951
35............	20.4140	215.7108	.0046	.0490	10.5668	.0946
36............	22.2512	236.1247	.0042	.0449	10.6118	.0942
37............	24.2538	258.3759	.0039	.0412	10.6530	.0939
38............	26.4367	282.6298	.0035	.0378	10.6908	.0935
39............	28.8160	309.0665	.0032	.0347	10.7255	.0932
40............	31.4094	337.8824	.0030	.0318	10.7574	.0930
41............	34.2363	369.2919	.0027	.0292	10.7864	.0927
42............	37.3175	403.5281	.0025	.0268	10.8134	.0925
43............	40.6761	440.8457	.0023	.0246	10.8380	.0923
44............	44.3370	481.5218	.0021	.0226	10.8605	.0921
45............	48.3273	525.8587	.0019	.0207	10.8812	.0919
46............	52.6767	574.1860	.0017	.0190	10.9002	.0917
47............	57.4176	626.8628	.0016	.0174	10.9176	.0916
48............	62.5852	684.2804	.0015	.0160	10.9336	.0915
49............	68.2179	746.8656	.0013	.0147	10.9482	.0913
50............	74.3575	815.0836	.0012	.0134	10.9617	.0912

Capitalization Tables: Compounded Annually, Nominal Rate 10.0 Percent

Periods	Amount of One	Amount of One per Period	Sinking Fund	Present Worth of One	Present Worth of One per Period	Partial Payment
1...........	1.1000	1.0000	1.0000	.9091	.9091	1.1000
2...........	1.2100	2.1000	.4762	.8204	1.7355	.5762
3...........	1.3310	3.3100	.3021	.7513	2.4869	.4021
4...........	1.4641	4.6410	.2155	.6830	3.1699	.3155
5...........	1.6105	6.1051	.1638	.6209	3.7908	.2638
6...........	1.7716	7.7156	.1296	.5645	4.3553	.2296
7...........	1.9487	9.4872	.1054	.5132	4.8684	.2054
8...........	2.1436	11.4359	.0874	.4665	5.3349	.1874
9...........	2.3579	13.5795	.0736	.4241	5.7590	.1736
10...........	2.5937	15.9374	.0627	.3855	6.1446	.1627
11...........	2.8531	18.5312	.0540	.3505	6.4951	.1540
12...........	3.1384	21.3843	.0468	.3186	6.8137	.1468
13...........	3.4523	24.5227	.0408	.2897	7.1034	.1408
14...........	3.7975	27.9750	.0357	.2633	7.3667	.1357
15...........	4.1772	31.7725	.0315	.2392	7.6061	.1315
16...........	4.5950	35.9497	.0278	.2176	7.8237	.1278
17...........	5.0545	40.5447	.0247	.1978	8.0216	.1247
18...........	5.5599	45.5992	.0219	.1799	8.2014	.1219
19...........	6.1159	51.1591	.0195	.1635	8.3649	.1195
20...........	6.7275	57.2750	.0175	.1486	8.5136	.1175
21...........	7.4002	64.0025	.0156	.1351	8.6487	.1156
22...........	8.1403	71.4027	.0140	.1228	8.7715	.1140
23...........	8.9543	79.5430	.0126	.1117	8.8832	.1125
24...........	9.8497	88.4973	.0113	.1015	8.9847	.1113
25...........	10.8347	98.3471	.0102	.0923	9.0770	.1102
26...........	11.9182	109.1818	.0092	.0839	9.1609	.1092
27...........	13.1100	121.0999	.0083	.0763	9.2372	.1083
28...........	14.4210	134.2099	.0075	.0693	9.3066	.1075
29...........	15.8631	148.6309	.0067	.0630	9.3696	.1067
30...........	17.4494	164.4940	.0061	.0573	9.4269	.1061
31...........	19.1943	181.9434	.0055	.0521	9.4790	.1055
32...........	21.1138	201.1378	.0050	.0474	9.5264	.1050
33...........	23.2252	222.2515	.0045	.0431	9.5694	.1045
34...........	25.5477	245.4767	.0041	.0391	9.6086	.1041
35...........	28.1024	271.0244	.0037	.0356	9.6442	.1037
36...........	30.9127	299.1268	.0033	.0323	9.6765	.1033
37...........	34.0039	330.0395	.0030	.0294	9.7059	.1030
38...........	37.4043	364.0434	.0027	.0267	9.7327	.1027
39...........	41.1448	401.4478	.0025	.0243	9.7570	.1025
40...........	45.2593	442.5926	.0023	.0221	9.7791	.1023
41...........	49.7852	487.8518	.0020	.0201	9.7991	.1020
42...........	54.7637	537.6370	.0019	.0183	9.8174	.1019
43...........	60.2401	592.4007	.0017	.0166	9.8340	.1017
44...........	66.2641	652.6408	.0015	.0151	9.8491	.1015
45...........	72.8905	718.9048	.0014	.0137	9.8628	.1014
46...........	80.1795	791.7953	.0013	.0125	9.8753	.1013
47...........	88.1975	871.9749	.0011	.0113	9.8866	.1011
48...........	97.0172	960.1723	.0010	.0103	9.8969	.1010
49...........	106.7190	1057.1896	.0009	.0094	9.9063	.1009
50...........	117.3909	1163.9085	.0009	.0085	9.9148	.1009

Periods	Amount of One	Amount of One per Period	Sinking Fund	Present Worth of One	Present Worth of One per Period	Partial Payment
1...........	1.1100	1.0000	1.0000	.9009	.9009	1.1100
2...........	1.2321	2.1100	.4739	.8116	1.7125	.5839
3...........	1.3676	3.3421	.2992	.7312	2.4437	.4092
4...........	1.5181	4.7097	.2123	.6587	3.1024	.3223
5...........	1.6851	6.2278	.1606	.5935	3.6959	.2706
6...........	1.8704	7.9129	.1264	.5346	4.2305	.2364
7...........	2.0762	9.7833	.1022	.4817	4.7122	.2122
8...........	2.3045	11.8594	.0843	.4339	5.1461	.1943
9...........	2.5580	14.1640	.0706	.3909	5.5370	.1806
10...........	2.8394	16.7220	.0598	.3522	5.8892	.1698
11...........	3.1518	19.5614	.0511	.3173	6.2065	.1611
12...........	3.4985	22.7132	.0440	.2858	6.4924	.1540
13...........	3.8833	26.2116	.0382	.2575	6.7499	.1482
14...........	4.3104	30.0949	.0332	.2320	6.9819	.1432
15...........	4.7846	34.4054	.0291	.2090	7.1909	.1391
16...........	5.3109	39.1899	.0255	.1883	7.3792	.1355
17...........	5.8951	44.5008	.0225	.1696	7.5488	.1325
18...........	6.5436	50.3959	.0198	.1528	7.7016	.1298
19...........	7.2633	56.9395	.0176	.1377	7.8393	.1276
20...........	8.0623	64.2028	.0156	.1240	7.9633	.1256
21...........	8.9492	72.2651	.0138	.1117	8.0751	.1238
22...........	9.9336	81.2143	.0123	.1007	8.1757	.1223
23...........	11.0263	91.1479	.0110	.0907	8.2664	.1209
24...........	12.2392	102.1742	.0098	.0817	8.3481	.1198
25...........	13.5855	114.4133	.0087	.0736	8.4217	.1187
26...........	15.0799	127.9988	.0078	.0563	8.4881	.1178
27...........	16.7386	143.0786	.0070	.0597	8.5478	.1170
28...........	18.5799	159.8173	.0063	.0538	8.6016	.1163
29...........	20.6237	178.3972	.0056	.0485	8.6501	.1156
30...........	22.8923	199.0209	.0050	.0437	8.6938	.1150
31...........	25.4104	221.9132	.0045	.0394	8.7331	.1145
32...........	28.2056	247.3236	.0040	.0355	8.7686	.1140
33...........	31.3082	275.5292	.0036	.0319	8.8005	.1136
34...........	34.7521	306.8374	.0033	.0288	8.8293	.1133
35...........	38.5749	341.5896	.0029	.0259	8.8552	.1129
36...........	42.8181	380.1644	.0026	.0234	8.8786	.1126
37...........	47.5281	422.9825	.0024	.0210	8.8996	.1124
38...........	52.7562	470.5106	.0021	.0190	8.9186	.1121
39...........	58.5593	523.2667	.0019	.0171	8.9357	.1119
40...........	65.0009	581.8261	.0017	.0154	8.9511	1117
41...........	72.1510	646.8269	.0015	.0139	8.9649	.1115
42...........	80.0876	718.9779	.0014	.0125	8.9774	.1114
43...........	88.8972	799.0655	.0013	.0112	8.9886	.1113
44...........	98.6759	887.9627	.0011	.0101	8.9988	.1111
45...........	109.5302	986.6386	.0010	.0091	9.0079	.1110
46...........	121.5786	1096.1688	.0009	.0082	9.0161	.1109
47...........	134.9522	1217.7474	.0008	.0074	9.0235	.1108
48...........	149.7970	1352.6996	.0007	.0067	9.0302	.1107
49...........	166.2746	1502.4965	.0007	.0060	9.0362	.1107
50...........	184.5648	1668.7712	.0006	.0054	9.0417	.1106

Capitalization Tables: Compounded Annually, Nominal Rate 12.0 Percent

Periods	Amount of One	Amount of One per Period	Sinking Fund	Present Worth of One	Present Worth of One per Period	Partial Payment
1..........	1.1200	1.0000	1.0000	.8927	.8929	1.1200
2..........	1.2544	2.1200	.4717	.7972	1.6901	.5917
3..........	1.4049	3.3744	.2963	.7118	2.4018	.4163
4..........	1.5735	4.7793	.2092	.6355	3.0373	.3292
5..........	1.7623	6.3528	.1574	.5674	3.6048	.2774
6..........	1.9738	8.1152	.1232	.5066	4.1114	.2432
7..........	2.2107	10.0890	.0991	.4523	4.5638	.2191
8..........	2.4760	12.2997	.0813	.4039	4.9676	.2013
9..........	2.7731	14.7757	.0677	.3606	5.3282	.1877
10..........	3.1058	17.5487	.0570	.3220	5.6502	.1770
11..........	3.4785	20.6546	.0484	.2875	5.9377	.1684
12..........	3.8960	24.1331	.0414	.2567	6.1944	.1614
13..........	4.3635	28.0291	.0357	.2292	6.4235	.1557
14..........	4.8871	32.3926	.0309	.2046	6.6282	.1509
15..........	5.4736	37.2797	.0268	.1827	6.8109	.1469
16..........	6.1304	42.7533	.0234	.1631	6.9740	.1434
17..........	6.8660	48.8837	.0205	.1456	7.1196	.1405
18..........	7.6900	55.7497	.0179	.1300	7.2497	.1379
19..........	8.6128	63.4397	.0158	.1161	7.3658	.1358
20..........	9.6463	72.0524	.0139	.1037	7.4694	.1339
21..........	10.8038	81.6987	.0122	.0926	7.5620	.1322
22..........	12.1003	92.5026	.0108	.0826	7.6446	.1308
23..........	13.5523	104.6029	.0096	.0738	7.7184	.1296
24..........	15.1786	118.1552	.0085	.0659	7.7843	.1285
25..........	17.0001	133.3339	.0075	.0588	7.8431	.1275
26..........	19.0401	150.3339	.0067	.0525	7.8957	.1267
27..........	21.3249	169.3740	.0059	.0469	7.9426	.1259
28..........	23.8839	190.6989	.0052	.0419	7.9844	.1252
29..........	26.7499	214.5828	.0047	.0374	8.0218	.1247
30..........	29.9599	241.3327	.0041	.0334	8.0552	.1241
31..........	33.5551	271.2926	.0037	.0298	8.0850	.1237
32..........	37.5817	304.8477	.0033	.0266	8.1116	.1233
33..........	42.0915	342.4294	.0029	.0238	8.1354	.1229
34..........	47.1425	384.5210	.0026	.0212	8.1566	.1226
35..........	52.7996	431.6635	.0023	.0189	8.1755	.1223
36..........	59.1356	484.4631	.0021	.0169	8.1924	.1221
37..........	66.2318	543.5987	.0018	.0151	8.2075	.1218
38..........	74.1797	609.8305	.0016	.0135	8.2210	.1216
39..........	83.0812	684.0102	.0015	.0120	8.2330	.1215
40..........	93.0510	767.0914	.0013	.0107	8.2438	.1213
41..........	104.2171	860.1424	.0012	.0096	8.2534	.1212
42..........	116.7231	964.3595	.0010	.0086	8.2619	.1210
43..........	130.7299	1081.0826	.0009	.0076	8.2696	.1209
44..........	146.4175	1211.8125	.0008	.0068	8.2764	.1208
45..........	163.9876	1358.2300	.0007	.0061	8.2825	.1207
46..........	183.6661	1522.2176	.0007	.0054	8.2880	.1207
47..........	205.7061	1705.8838	.0006	.0049	8.2928	.1206
48..........	230.3908	1911.5898	.0005	.0043	8.2972	.1205
49..........	258.0377	2141.9806	.0005	.0039	8.3010	.1205
50..........	289.0022	2400.0182	.0004	.0035	8.3045	.1204

EXPLANATION OF CAPITALIZATION TABLES

Amount of One (compound interest)

Compound interest is received on a principal sum which is increased by interest earned from preceding periods. The theory underlying compound interest is taken from alternatives of the investor. An investor who lends $1,000 at an annual interest rate of 6 percent would anticipate receiving $1,000 plus $60 interest at the end of the first year. He then, presumably, may invest $1,060 for an additional term, earning the same market rate of interest. Because of this alternative, investors are unwilling to lend money for longer terms unless interest is paid periodically. Though the compounding may be on a monthly, quarterly, or semiannual basis, compound interest is usually converted into an annual rate.

Let the following symbols stand for the variables showing the compound amount of one:

S = Compound amount $(i + P)$
i = Rate of interest per period
P = Principal or amount of money borrowed or invested

The compound amount at the end of the first year would be given by the formula:

$$S_1 = P(1 + i).$$

At the end of the second year, the compound amount would be given by

$$S_2 = S_1(1 + i).$$

This is equivalent to

$$S = P(1 + i)^2.$$

Succeeding periods can be calculated by multiplying the compound amount at the end of each year by $1 + i$. For n number of periods, the general formula would be

$$S = P(1 + i)^n.$$

Amount of One per Period

The compound interest formula serves as the basis of the amount of one-per-period factor. This table is used to value an ordinary annuity— which is defined as an annuity paid at the end of the period. In this context any periodic payment of equal amounts paid over successive periods qualifies as an annuity. The amount of an ordinary annuity is the total of annual payments and interest accumulated in each period.

ORDINARY ANNUITY OF FIVE PERIODS

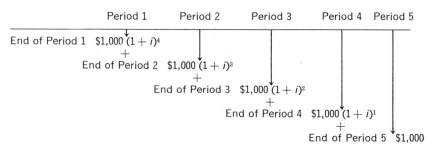

An ordinary annuity of five periods is diagrammed to show the accumulation of interest and an annuity of $1,000 payable for five periods. Note that at the end of the first period, the $1,000 annuity earns interest over four terms. Succeeding payments accumulate interest for a period of one less than the preceding period. The final payment, since it is paid at the end of the fifth term, earns no interest.

Algebraically, an ordinary annuity would be expressed as follows:

$$s_{\overline{n}|} = 1 + (1 + i) + (1 + i)^2 + \ldots + (1 + i)^{n-1}.$$

The accumulation includes the last payment, which draws no interest. The last term in the chart corrects for nonpayment of interest for the last payment. This series describes a geometric progression of n terms, which is represented by:

$$s_{\overline{n}|} = \frac{(1 + i)^n - 1}{(1 + i) - 1}$$

$$= \frac{(1 + i)^n - 1}{i}.$$

Sinking Fund

Sinking fund factors are arranged to show the amount that must be deposited in an interest-bearing fund to recover a given sum. The factor showing the accumulation of one per period shows the amount that one would accumulate, provided that the annuity earned interest over the annuity period. It follows that the accumulation of one per period is closely related to the sinking fund factor. Suppose repayment of a debt requires payment of interest and an annual sum which is to be placed in a sinking fund sufficient to repay the principal. The problem in the latter instance is to find how much of a deposit is required to accumulate to a given sum.

The formula for the sinking fund factor is the reciprocal of the accumulation of one dollar per period, or

$$1/s_{\overline{n}|} = \frac{i}{(1+i)^n - 1} \cdot$$

Present Worth of One

The present value of a future sum, or a reversionary value, is derived from the compound interest formula. Recall that

$$S = P(1 + i)^n$$

Hence the sum, which gives the accumulation of principal and interest, is equal to the principal times the compound interest. To find the future value of a sum or the compound amount(s), solve for P:

$$P = \frac{S}{(1+i)^n} \cdot$$

Present Worth of One per Period

Factors showing the present value of an annuity of one per period are used to give the present worth of the right to a future income. In this respect income from real property may be divided into two portions: (1) income received in perpetuity and (2) income received for a given term. That is, an income of $1,000, representing the economic rent of land, would indicate that the land has a value as capitalized in perpetuity at 6 percent:

$$P = R/i$$
$$\$16,666.67 = \$1,000/.06 .$$

By investing $16,666.67 in land that earns an annual rent of $1,000, 6 percent would be earned on the investment. This is another way of saying that an income of $1,000 capitalized in perpetuity at a discount rate of 6 percent has a present worth of $16,666.67.

But if the $1,000 income is earned for a limited period, the capitalization formula in perpetuity has little relevance. The right to $1,000 payable for five years is clearly not worth $16,666.67. Income for a limited period, therefore, is treated as a series of reversions. The present worth of an income earned at the end of the year for five years is found by adding the discounted values of a future sum paid at the end of each year ($a_{\overline{n}|}$ equals the present value of a future income for n periods).

$$a_{\overline{5}|} = \frac{1}{(1.06)^1} + \frac{1}{(1.06)^2} + \frac{1}{(1.06)^3} + \frac{1}{(1.06)^4} + \frac{1}{(1.06)^5}$$

This formula may be reduced by substituting the present value of a reversion of one dollar for each period:

$$a_{\overline{5}|} = .943396 + .889996 + .839619 + .792094 + .747258 + = \$4.212364.$$

Thus it is fairly clear that the present worth of rights to an income of a limited period is treated as the sum of reversionary values. In the last example, providing a 6 percent discount is appropriate, an investor would pay $4.212364 today for the right to an income of one dollar payable at the end of each year for five years.

It is more convenient to calculate the present value of a future income for a limited period by the formula derived from the sum of present values of a reversion. In the preceding formula, let v, v^2, v^3, ... v^n represent the present values of a reversion. Then,

$$a_{\overline{n}|} = v + v^2 + \ldots v^n .$$

Since this is the formula for the sum of a geometric progression, the formula then takes the form:

$$a_{\overline{n}|} = \frac{v(1 - v)^n}{(1 - v)} = \frac{1 - v^n}{1/v - 1} .$$

Substitute i for v

$$a_{\overline{n}|} = \frac{1 - (1 + i)^{-n}}{i}$$

$$a_{\overline{n}|} = \frac{1 - \dfrac{1}{(1 + i)^n}}{i} .$$

Partial Payment (Installment of One)

Installment-of-one factors or partial payment tables indicate the partial payments necessary to amortize a loan. Mortgages with constant-level payments provide that a portion of the payment constitutes interest on the outstanding principal, with the remaining portion of the payment applying to repayment of principal. Under this plan the loan principal represents the present worth of a series of annuities of equal payments. If $4.21 represents the present worth of the right to an income of one dollar per year for five years, assuming 6 percent interest, it follows that an annual constant-level payment of $1 would be required to amortize a loan of $4.21 over five years, discounted at 6 percent interest.

Installment-of-one factors give factors that are the reciprocal of present value of one-per-period factors. The installment of one required to amortize a loan over five periods, at 6 percent interest, would be given by the following formula:

$$\text{Installment to amortize } \$1 = \frac{1}{a_{\overline{n}|}}$$

Solving for $a_{\overline{n}|}$:

$$a_{\overline{5}|} = \frac{1 - \frac{.1}{(1.06)^5}}{.06}$$

$$= \frac{1 - \frac{1}{1.338226}}{.06}$$

$$= \frac{1 - .747258}{.06}$$

$$= 4.21236$$

$$1/a_{\overline{5}|} = \frac{1}{4.12136}$$

$$\rightarrow .237396$$

The installment of one, .2373936, is the payment necessary to amortize a loan of $1 over five periods, with an interest rate of 6 percent.

glossary

Abstract of title. A summary of recorded documents affecting title.

Abstractor liability. Liability in which the abstractor makes no judgment over the condition of the title; the abstractor is responsible for negligence in overlooking recorded documents or transcribing information incorrectly.

Acceleration clauses. The right of a lender to foreclose on the full amount of the principal in the event of borrower default.

Accredited Management Organization. A designation issued to qualified management firms by the Institute of Real Estate Management.

Acquisition cost. The settlement costs and down payment required for the purchase of a single-family dwelling.

Action and sale. The right to foreclose by filing a suit for foreclosure. If default is proven, the court issues a decree authorizing sale.

Adjusted valuation. A term, usually describing value for property tax purposes, meaning market value.

Agglomeration. Economies referring to the lower cost of production that results from locating in an urban area.

Air rights. The right to use space above the land surface.

Allocation commitment. A statement that a permanent lender will purchase, within a specified period of months, a certain volume of mortgages at a given price at a specific location.

Allodial system. A system of land tenure providing for private ownership without payment of money or services to other persons.

American Institute of Real Estate Appraisers. An organization of designated appraisers (MAI) affiliated with the National Association of Realtors®.

American Society of Real Estate Counselors. An affiliate of the National Association of Realtors®.

Amortized mortgage. A mortgage providing for the repayment of principal over a mortgage term.

Annuity capitalization. The capitalization of net income by present worth of one-per-period tables.

Assessed value. The value placed on property for property tax purposes.

Assumption fee. A charge levied against a buyer of property who agrees to assume an existing loan.

Average rate of return. A comparison of the net income and property value divided by the number of years for which the investment was held.

Avigation easement. The right to restrict use of land at a prescribed height and distance from airport runways for air navigation purposes.

Band of investment. A method of estimating the market rate of capitalization.

Bargain and sale deed. A deed conveying the land, and not an interest in the land with no warranties of title.

Base line. The east-west line associated with each principal meridian.

Bilateral contract. A promise that is exchanged for a promise.

Binder. A receipt of the buyer's deposit pending final closing or disposition of the offer.

Blanket mortgage. A mortgage covering more than one parcel of real estate.

Building codes. Local ordinances which ensure buildings used by the public are safe by regulating the type of construction, materials used, and standards of construction.

Building residual capitalization. A method of capitalizing net operating income by capitalizing income allocated to the building.

Bulk and height restrictions. Regulations of a zoning code that restrict building bulk and height.

Business income. Income of a nonresident foreign alien defined as income connected with a U.S. business and subject to the same federal income tax laws that apply to U.S. taxpayers.

Bylaws. Rules governing the organization and authority of a group such as a condominium association.

Capital gain. Property appreciation providing for sale at a gain subject to capital gain taxes, in contrast to a capital loss.

Capital recapture. An allowance for recapture of invested capital in buildings.

Capitalization in perpetuity. A method of capitalizing income by dividing net income by the capitalization rate.

Capitalization rate. A rate of discount that converts income to a capital value, including capital recapture.

Carrying cost. The cost of holding vacant land pending sale.

Cash flow. The amount of net income remaining after mortgage payments and net income taxes.

Certificate of title. An opinion on the marketability of title executed by an attorney who studies an abstract.

Certified Property Manager. A designation issued to qualified persons by the Institute of Real Estate Management.

Chattel. Personal property.

Coastal zones. An area subject to the Coastal Zone Management Act of 1972.

Common element. A portion of a condominium property not included in a unit.

Common expenses. Expenses for which condominium unit owners are liable to the association.

Community property. An estate created by statute which treats property acquired by either spouse during marriage as community property, belonging to both parties as co-owners.

Community shopping center. A center with a junior department store or a variety store as the main tenant, generally including 120,000 to 200,000 square feet of gross leasable area.

Competent party. Parties legally competent to enter a contract.

Concurrent ownership. Joint ownership by two or more persons.

Condominium declaration. A document which commits property to a condominium form of ownership.

Condominium ownership. Ownership of a unit giving exclusive possession and use, with an undivided interest in the common element.

Condominium unit. A part of the condominium property which is subject to private ownership, such as an apartment unit.

Consequential damages. Damages resulting from an eminent domain taking; usually referring to damages to property not part of the taking.

Consideration. Receipt of a benefit or sacrifice by either one or both of the contracting parties.

Construction mortgages. Loans to finance new building construction.

Constructive notice. The act of recording a document in public records which substitute for actual notice.

Constructive value. A hypothetical value considered as if the idealized conditions of pure competition prevailed.

Consumer price index. An index showing the change in consumer prices in selected urban areas.

Consummate dower interest. An interest held by a widow holding dower rights on the death of the husband.

Contract default. Failure of either party to comply with a contract.

Contract for sale. A deposit receipt describing details of sale that control final title transfer.

Contract rent. The actual rent collected according to either oral or written contracts.

Cooperative ownership. Ownership of a cooperative share, with a proprietary lease granting use and occupancy of an apartment unit.

Cooperative shareholder. A purchaser of a cooperative apartment who holds a share in a cooperative nonprofit corporation.

Coordinate grids. Coordinate grids established by the National Ocean Survey, Department of Commerce, as part of the state plane coordinate system of land descriptions.

Correction deed. A deed issued to correct errors in legal descriptions or other errors or omissions.

Cost approach. A method of valuation based on an estimate of the building cost of construction, the building depreciation, and land value.

Council on Environmental Quality. Three members appointed by the President with the advice and consent of the Senate, as required under the National Environmental Policy Act.

Covenant. A promise by one party to another ensuring certain performance or nonperformance of certain acts or a promise that certain conditions do or do not exist.

Covenant against encumbrances. Promise of the grantor to protect the buyer from any lien or debt against the property known or unknown to the buyer and seller at the time of conveyance and which is not reported in the deed.

Covenant of further assurance. A promise of the grantor to obtain any further documents necessary to give the buyer title as stated in the warranty deed.

Covenant of quiet enjoyment. The grantor warrants peaceful use of the property, free of claims of other persons lawfully claiming a superior title.

Covenant of seizin. A promise that the grantor has valid title at the time of deed execution.

Covenant of warranty. A promise by the grantor to defend title against claims of a person contesting title, even after execution of the deed.

Curtesy. A life estate held by the husband in all real estate owned by the wife during marriage.

Debt service. Repayment of principal and mortgage interest.

Debt service ratio. Net operating income divided by annual mortgage payments.

Deed. A written instrument that conveys an interest in real estate.

Deed restrictions. Restrictions imposed by the owner on the use of the property conveyed.

Deferred income. Income deferred to later periods.

Deficiency judgment. The right of the lender to collect against personal assets of the borrower if proceeds from a foreclosure sale are insufficient to satisfy the mortgage debt.

Delivery and acceptance. The mutual intent to convey title at the time the deed is delivered by the grantor and accepted by the grantee.

Depreciation. The loss in value from any cause.

Discount point. One point equals 1 percent; discount points refer to the percentage discount lenders require for mortgages issued below market interest rates.

Dominant estate. The interest of a person benefited by an easement appurtenant.

Double declining depreciation. A method of depreciating property on the declining balance at double straight-line rates.

Dower. The interest of a surviving wife in land acquired by the husband during marriage.

Earnest money contract. A document that serves as a receipt of the earnest money deposit, including an agreement controlling the closing of the sale.

Easement appurtenant. The right to use property for a specific purpose which runs with the land.

Easement in gross. An easement that is personal and does not run with the land.

Economic life. The estimated useful economic life of a property, which may be less than the physical life.

Economic obsolescence. The loss in value from forces external to the property appraised.

Economic rent. Current market rent that would be realized at the date of appraisal.

Economics of alternative plans. A recommendation by a real estate manager on a program of modernization, rehabilitation, or conversion to some other property use.

Effective gross income. Gross possible income, less an allowance for vacancy and bad debts.

Eminent domain. The right of government to take property in the public interest upon payment of just compensation.

Entitlement to use strategy. A program that describes an internal policy to process land development, required because so many agencies must approve a new project.

Entry and possession. A method of foreclosing which allows the lender to take possession peaceably, recording and publishing the entry, with details.

Environmental impact statement. A statement of the impact of a proposed project subject to the National Environmental Policy Act.

Equity of redemption. The right of the mortgagor to recover the property mortgaged upon payment of the remaining debt to the lender.

Escheat. The right of the state to acquire title of a deceased person who dies without a will or legal heirs.

Escrow agent. An agent who operates under a written agreement stating the terms and conditions under which title is to be transferred.

Escrow deposit. Payments collected with monthly mortgage payments into an account maintained by the lender for the payment of annual property taxes and insurance.

Estate for years. Leasehold estates that continue for a definite period of time.

Estates not of inheritance. Estates that continue only during the life of the person whose life determines the duration of the estate.

Estates of inheritance. Estates that give an owner rights which prevail over his or her time and which pass to heirs.

Evidence. A requirement that parties to a contract must evidence their willingness to contract by words or acts.

Exclusive agency. An agency which allows the seller to sell his own property without payment of a commission and prohibits the seller from listing the property with another broker.

Exclusive right to sell. A listing that grants an exclusive right to sell the property during the listing term. The seller may not sell his own property without paying a commission during the term of the exclusive right to sell.

Executor deed. A deed in which the executor operates under direction of the court; the full sales price is stated, and the executor warrants title only against his acts.

Express contract. Contracts in which the parties to the contract declare terms, conditions, and their intent, by written or oral statements.

Fair Housing Law. The National Fair Housing Act of 1968 prohibits refusal to sell or rent because of race, color, religion, sex, or national origin.

Farm and Land Institute. An affiliate of the National Association of Realtors®.

Farm Home Administration. An organization authorized to make direct loans to farmers and others for terms of up to 40 years.

Farm Real Estate Index. An index of farm values prepared by the Department of Agriculture.

Federal Home Loan Bank Board. The supervisory agency regulating federally chartered savings and loan associations.

Federal Home Loan Mortgage Corporation. An agency which purchases Veterans Administration guaranteed loans, conventional loans, and FHA-insured mortgages.

Federal Land Bank. An agency which grants loans on 65 percent of "normal" farm values.

Federal National Mortgage Association. A privately owned government-regulated corporation which buys and sells mortgages in the secondary mortgage market.

Federal Savings and Loan Insurance Corporation. The agency that insures deposits of member savings and loan associations.

Fee simple absolute. Title conveyed over the life of the owner, which could be inherited without restriction.

Fee simple determinable. A fee simple estate that terminates upon the occurrence of a known event.

Fee subject to condition subsequent. An interest that continues until the owner takes permanent action to repossess the premises.

Feudal system. A system of land tenure requiring payment or services to a superior.

Fiduciary. A relationship formed when good conscience requires one party to act at all times for the sole benefit and interest of another.

Final plat. A subdivision approved for recording.

Financial risks. The risk borne by a land investor who receives no assurance that the investment capital will be recovered.

Fixed rent leases. Leases that provide for a fixed rent over the term of the lease.

Fixtures. An article installed or attached to land or a building in a permanent way so that it becomes part of the real estate.

Flexible-payment mortgages. Mortgages that allow payments of less than the level amortized mortgage.

Flowage easement. The right to flood and maintain property for flood control purposes.

Footloose industries. Industries that produce highly valuable, low-weight products and that have the widest range of site selection alternatives.

Foreclosure. A legal remedy to collect a debt secured by a mortgage on property.

Freehold estate. An interest in land.

Functional obsolescence. The loss in value from a decrease in functional utility.

General partner. A partner who has the right to execute deeds, mortgages, or other real estate conveyances and to perform other management functions.

Government National Mortgage Association. A government-owned corporation which buys and sells mortgages on the secondary mortgage market to support subsidized housing programs.

Graduated leases. A lease in which the rent is graduated in steps, either upward or downward, over the term of the lease.

Grantee. The party acquiring an interest, the buyer.

Grantor. The party conveying real estate, the seller.

Gross income multiplier. A ratio that expresses the relation between gross income and sales price.

Gross leasable area. Total floor area designed for tenant occupancy and exclusive use, including basements, mezzanines, and upper floors, measured from the center line of partitions and from outside walls.

Gross national product. The market value of all goods and services produced in the United States in one year.

Gross possible income. A term used by apartment house managers defined as the gross income earned assuming all apartments have been rented, including an imputed rent for apartments occupied by employees.

Head right system. A means of acquiring land in colonial America which rewarded land to persons responsible for a new migrant.

Homestead right. A formal life contract that gives limited protection of the family home from creditors.

Housing code. Local ordinances enacted to maintain minimum housing standards.

Housing filtering. The process in which original housing occupants move and are replaced by lower income households.

Implicit price deflator. A price series prepared by the Department of Commerce to report gross national product in constant dollars.

Implied contract. A contract by agreement evidenced by acts and conduct.

Improvement clauses. Clauses dealing with land improvements in a long-term lease.

Inchoate dower interest. The anticipated interest the wife has in land of the husband, which cannot be defeated by the husband or by will.

Income approach. A method of valuation based on the concept that market value is equal to the present worth of discounted future incomes.

Indicated value. A value indicated by one of the three valuation approaches.

Industrial performance standards. Regulations that control the performance of industries.

Inflationary rate. The estimated future inflationary rate which foreign investors consider as part of the rate of return.

Inharmonious land uses. Land uses incompatible with surrounding land uses.

Installment land contract. An agreement in which the seller promises to deliver title when the installment payments are completed and if the buyer has observed other purchase terms.

Institute of Real Estate Management. An affiliate of the National Association of Realtors®.

Insurable value. The value of destructible portions of property subject to loss in the case of fire or other catastrophies.

Interest rate. The rate of return on investment which does not include an allowance for capital recovery.

International Real Estate Federation. An affiliate of the National Association of Realtors® for members specializing in international real estate sales.

Interstate Land Sales Full Disclosure Act. A federal law enacted August 1, 1968, directed to preventing fraud, misrepresentation, and deceit in the sale of subdivision lots over interstate boundaries.

Investment feasibility. A study defined as the reasonable likelihood of satisfying investment objectives.

Irretrievable. A land use project in which certain resources will be exhausted and unrecoverable.

Joint tenancy. Ownership of real estate by two or more parties, with the right of survivorship created by the four unities necessary to a joint tenancy.

Joint venture. A joint investment by two organizations.

Junior mortgages. A mortgage subordinate to a prior mortgage.

Just compensation. Payment made for the taking of private property in the public interest, usually defined as equivalent to market value.

Just valuation. A term, usually describing value for property tax purposes, meaning market value.

Land residual capitalization. A method of capitalizing net operating income by capitalizing the income allocated to land.

Land use districts. Districts established by zoning ordinances that regulate land use by districts.

Land use regulations. Restrictions on land use.

Late payment charge. A charge levied by the mortgage lender for delinquent mortgage payments.

Leased fee. An interest held by the lessor.

Leased fee interest. The interest of the lessor.

Leasehold estate. An interest held by the tenant or lessee.

Legal description. A method of describing property, showing boundaries and property lines with absolute certainty.

Less than freehold estate. A partial interest in an estate, such as a lease or easement.

Lessee. A tenant who holds a leasehold interest.

Level-payment amortization. Mortgages in which payments are constant, with the amounts accruing to principal and interest varying with each payment.

Lien states. States that allow the mortgage borrower to hold title and remain in possession until the lender exercises the right to foreclose on a defaulted mortgage.

Life estate. Ownership of property conveyed only during the lifetime of some person.

Life tenant. A party that holds an ordinary life estate interest.

Limited common elements. Common elements which are reserved for the use of certain units, to the exclusion of other units.

Limited-growth policies. A method of restricting population growth by enacting restrictive land use controls.

Limited partners. A partner with limited liability and no voice in management.

Limiting conditions. A statement qualifying an appraisal report and limiting its interpretation and use by the client.

Liquid asset holdings. A term referring to the amount of money available for a housing down payment and the amount available for closing costs.

Liquidity. The ability to convert an asset to cash with a minimum loss.

Listing agreement. A contract employing a real estate broker.

Loan policy. A title insurance policy issued for an amount equal to the outstanding principal balance of the loan.

Long-term leases. Generally a lease of 15 years or more.

Management agreement. An agreement between a real property managing agent and the property owner.

Market approach. The process of analyzing sales of similar and recently sold properties to derive an indication of the most probable sales price.

Market value. The highest price in terms of money which a property will bring in a competitive and open market under all conditions requisite to a fair sale, the buyer and seller each acting prudently, knowledgeably, and assuming the price is not affected by undue stimulus.

Master deed. Comparable to a condominium declaration in some states.

Master plan. Sometimes called the comprehensive or general plan. A statement of community goals covering the physical development of a community with respect to social, economic, and political objectives.

Megalopolis. A term used by Jean Gottmann to describe the northeastern seaboard as a continuous urban area, from the Atlantic Ocean to the Appalachian foothills and from southern New Hampshire to northern Virginia.

Metes and bounds description. A method of identifying a land area by describing boundary directions and their turning points.

Modernization. The replacement of equipment that is wearing out or that is functionally obsolete.

Monthly gross income multiplier. The ratio that establishes the relation between monthly housing rent and single-family dwelling prices.

Monument. An object that marks a point on the earth's surface used in a metes and bounds description.

Mortgage assignments. The right of the lender to assign or sell a mortgage to a third party without consent of the borrower.

Mortgage banker. A company that serves as mortgage loan correspondent to life insurance companies, mutual savings banks, pension funds, and others, and a company that services mortgage loans.

Mortgage broker. An agent that arranges for purchase and sale of mortgage loans but does not service mortgages.

Mortgage constant. The annual mortgage and principal payment expressed as a percent of the original mortgage.

Mortgage covenants. Promises of the borrower and lender included as part of the mortgage.

Mortgage equity capitalization. A method of estimating value according to the return on equity and the expected capital gain or loss realized at the end of the projected investment period.

Mortgage foreclosure. The right of the lender to foreclose on property offered as security for a loan.

Mortgage package. A block of mortgages assembled to meet requirements of a secondary mortgage market lender.

Mortgagee. The lender.

Mortgagor. The borrower.

Multiple listing. A listing that combines features of the open listing and the exclusive right-to-sell agreement.

Mutual mortgage insurance. The housing loan insurance program administered by the Federal Housing Administration.

Narrative appraisal report. A formal written document which contains the estimate of value, the effective date of the appraisal, the certificate and signature of the appraiser, the purpose of the appraisal, and other essential elements of an appraisal report, as required by professional appraisal organizations.

National Association of Realtors®. Formerly the National Association of Real Estate boards, an organization of members who hold membership in local real estate boards. Only members may use the copyrighted term, Realtor®.

Negotiable order-of-withdrawal accounts (NOW). Checking accounts administered by savings and loan associations.

Neighborhood. A community of homogeneous groups of inhabitants or land uses.

Neighborhood analysis. An analysis by a real property manager advising owners on the long-range desirability of a specific location.

Neighborhood shopping center. A shopping center specializing in convenience goods—food, drug and sundries.

Net ground leases. Land leased for building purposes.

Net household formation. The change in the number of households, including single households of single retirees, divorcees, and unmarried singles.

Net listing. A listing in which the seller establishes a minimum acceptable net price.

Net operating income. Effective gross income less operating expenses before depreciation and capital recovery.

Net rentable area. The inside dimensions of office space rented to tenants, measured to the center wall and inside partitions.

Net sales proceeds. The amount realized on a real estate sale after paying the remaining mortgage balance and capital gain taxes.

Nonconforming use. A use that does not conform to land uses permitted by the zoning code.

Open-end mortgage. A mortgage that permits the borrower to secure additional money on the mortgage after part of the original loan has been repaid.

Open listing. A listing in which the seller has the right to list property with competing brokers or to sell the property personally, without liability for a commission.

Option contract. An agreement that gives the buyer the right to purchase property at a fixed price within a given time, in return for consideration.

Ordinary life estate. An estate giving all rights of use, enjoyment, and possession to some person for the life of the person receiving the estate or some other person.

Organized industrial districts. An area subdivided and especially adapted to industrial purposes.

Overall rate of return. The ratio between the annual net operating income and the sales price, including capital recapture.

Owner's policy. A title insurance policy issued for an amount equal to the value of the land and existing improvements at the date of the policy.

Ownership in severalty. Ownership of real estate by one individual.

Package mortgages. A mortgage that includes personal property as part of the security.

Partially amortized mortgages. A mortgage providing for partial amortization and a lump sum payment of the remaining principal at the date of maturity.

Participation mortgage. A mortgage giving several lenders a share in a single mortgage.

Pass-through securities. Securities which are backed by a pool of mortgages insured by federal agencies or guaranteed by the Veterans Administration.

Periodic tenancy. Leases that continue until one of the parties to the lease gives notice of termination.

Personal property. Movable items that are not permanently affixed to land or building.

Physical depreciation. The loss in value from normal wear and tear, action of the elements and catastrophic events.

Physical real property inventory. A description by a real estate manager of interior and exterior building conditions from the standpoint of tenant needs.

Planned industrial park. The assembly of land, under one continuing control, to provide facilities for business and industry consistent with a master plan and restrictions.

Planned unit development. A zoning regulation that gives developers flexibility in arranging space for maximum utility.

Point of beginning. The start of a metes and bound description.

Police power. The inherent right of government to regulate private property for the public interest, convenience, and necessity.

Power of sale. A right granted to a lender to sell the property in the event of mortgage default.

Preliminary plan. A subdivision plan submitted to the local planning office for conditional approval.

Prepayment penalties. A penalty levied by the lender for early payment of the mortgage.

Prepayment privileges. The right to prepay a mortgage loan before maturity without penalty.

Present worth of one. The present worth of $1 postponed to a future date, discounted at a stated interest rate.

Present worth of one per period. The present worth of an annual income of $1 per period, discounted at a given interest rate.

Price index leases. Leases in which the rent is subject to change, according to a specific price index.

Primary mortgage market. The market for mortgage loans between mortgage lenders and borrowers.

Principal meridians. Designated survey lines running north and south which govern legal descriptions in 30 states.

Private mortgage insurance. Companies which insure mortgages on the basis of the degree of risk assumed.

Progressively inclusive districts. The practice of allowing land uses of preceding districts to be used in each successive district.

Promissory note. Evidence of a personal debt.

Property brief. A written description of the property, with photographs, maps, detailed floor plans, and financial data normally included in a professional narrative appraisal report.

Property conversion. A change to a new use because the current use is no longer profitable.

Property report. A report of information on subdivision lots subject to the Interstate Land Sales Full Disclosure Act.

Property residual capitalization. A method of capitalizing net operating income from land and buildings.

Proprietary lease. A lease giving a cooperative apartment owner exclusive rights of use and occupancy of a specific apartment.

Public domain. Public land administered by a federal agency.

Purchase money mortgage. A mortgage given to a seller as part of the purchase price.

Quantity survey. A list of the cost of building materials and the labor required for construction.

Quitclaim deed. A deed conveying only the interest of the grantor in the real estate described.

Ranges. Six-mile-wide areas running north and south, parallel with a principal meridian.

Rate of return analysis. A calculation relating net operating income to the capital investment.

Ratio of net income to operating costs. A common ratio used to evaluate investment feasibility of a commercial property.

Real estate. Land and its attachments.

Real estate agency. A licensed person who acts as agent to sell or lease a property or perform other acts for the principal.

Real estate contract. A voluntary agreement between two or more competent parties who, for a consideration, agree to do or refrain from doing some particular legal act.

Real estate investment trust. A corporation authorized to invest in real estate with exemption from federal corporate taxes which may be passed on to shareholders.

Real estate license laws. State laws that regulate activities of persons performing a real estate service.

Real estate principal. A party who hires a real estate agent.

Real estate prospect. A potential buyer of property listed for sale, with no agent-principal relationship with the broker.

Real Estate Securities and Syndication Institute. An affiliate of the National Association of Realtors®.

Real estate syndicate. An organization formed for gain from an interest in real property, including its sale, exchange, trade, or development.

Real property. A term referring to the legal rights associated with land ownership.

Realtor®. A designation referring to a member of the National Association of Realtors®, a copyrighted designation.

Realtors® National Marketing Institute. An affiliate organization of the National Association of Realtors®, formerly the National Association of Real Estate Brokers.

Recorded subdivision. A subdivision recorded in public records showing the precise location of lots and blocks.

Regional shopping center. A shopping center with at least one main department store of not less than 100,000 square feet.

Regulation Q. A regulation of the Federal Reserve System which establishes maximum interest rates paid by commercial banks on deposits.

Rehabilitation. Restoration of a building to like-new condition, in which the present use is maintained.

Release clause. A clause in a proprietary lease providing for termination of the lease of a tenant-shareholder.

Remainder. An interest in the fee simple estate acquired after termination of an ordinary life estate.

Remainderman. A party that holds a remainder interest.

Replacement cost. The cost of a building serving the same utility as the property appraised.

Reproduction cost. The cost of reproducing a building identical to the property under valuation.

Resident councils. An organization of tenants to improve resident relations.

Resident manager. The on-site property manager responsible for daily operations.

Retrofitting. Methods of remodeling a dwelling to reduce energy costs.

Return on equity. The net income earned on actual capital invested—an equity interest.

Revaluation leases. A lease in which the rent is subject to reappraisal at specified times.

Reversionary right. The right of the owner of a leased fee to possession at the end of the lease.

Risks of the market. Risks caused by unpredictable changes in the economy or local factors that change land use.

Sale adjustment. Adjustments in the sale price to account for differences between the property sold and the property appraised.

Sale-leaseback. A property sale and immediate lease given by the buyer to the seller.

Sale proceeds. The net sales price realized from a real estate sale after retiring outstanding loans and paying capital gain taxes.

Second mortgage. A mortgage subordinate to a first mortgage.

Secondary mortgage market. Institutions that purchase and sell mortgages from other financial institutions and not directly from the borrower.

Section. Approximately one square mile as described by a U.S. rectangular survey.

Security deeds. A substitute for a warranty deed and mortgage.

Servient estate. The interest of a person granting an easement appurtenant.

Settlement booklet. A booklet which lenders, subject to federal regulation, are required to give the borrower at the time application is made for a mortgage or within the following three days.

Settlement statement. A statement required by the Real Estate Settlement Procedures Act that the lender must give the borrower at the time of closing.

Sheriff's deed. A deed issued on foreclosure of a mortgage and public sale.

Society of Industrial Realtors®. An affiliate of the National Association of Realtors®. Members hold the designation SIR: specializing in industrial real estate.

Solar energy home. Dwellings that are fitted with solar equipment to reduce fuel costs.

Special warranty deed. A deed that restricts the seller's warranties to title for defects occurring after the seller acquired title.

Spendable income. Annual net operating income less mortgage principal and interest payments.

Spot zoning. Zoning that conflicts with the preferred zoning recommended by the land use plan.

Standard Metropolitan Statistical Area. A county or group of contiguous counties which include at least one city of 50,000 population.

Standby purchase commitment. An emergency commitment providing for above-market mortgage terms.

State plane coordinate system. A method of describing land according to a system of coordinate grids for each state; identified by longitude and latitude.

Statement of record. A statement that must be filed with the Secretary of Housing and Urban Development for lots subject to the Interstate Land Sales Full Disclosure Act.

Statutory right of redemption. The right to redeem property after a foreclosure sale.

Straight-line capitalization. The capitalization of net income in perpetuity.

Straight-line depreciation. Depreciation of a constant annual percent of building value.

Strict foreclosure. Foreclosure in which title vests in the lender when the court issues a decree terminating rights of the borrower.

Subdivision controls. Local ordinances that require subdivision approval by local agencies.

Subject property. A term used to describe the property under appraisal.

Subject to mortgages. The acceptance of an existing mortgage by a purchaser who makes no personal promise to repay the debt.

Sum of the year's digits. A method of depreciation in which the number of years is totaled to establish the denominator and the numerator is the maximum number of years, decreasing one year each period.

Syndicate offering. An offering that includes a pro forma operating income statement and other facts of a syndicate.

Take-out commitment. A binding letter of agreement from a permanent lender to a mortgage banker in which the lender agrees to purchase a group of mortgages before a stated time at a given price.

Tandem plan. A secondary mortgage market plan that combines operations of GNMA and FNMA for sponsors of nonprofit housing projects.

Tax base. The total value of property assessments in a local taxing district.

Tax capitalization. The effect of shifting nonuniform property tax assessments to buyers in the form of higher or lower market prices.

Tax levy. The amount of the annual tax rate, usually expressed in mills, a tenth of a cent.

Tax mill. One tenth of a cent.

Tax shelter. A taxable loss that may be used to reduce taxable income earned from other sources.

Taxation. The right to tax private property according to constitutional and statutory law.

Tenancy at sufferance. An interest of a tenant who enters the premises lawfully under an existing lease and who holds over without permission of the owner at the termination of the lease.

Tenancy at will. An estate created lawfully with the consent of the owner and tenant that may be terminated at the will of either party.

Tenancy in common. Two or more owners holding an undivided interest without the right of survivorship.

Tenant displacement. Displacement of tenants caused by conversion of property to an alternative use.

Tenants by the entirety. An estate created by statute that treats ownership by husband and wife as ownership by one person.

Term mortgages. A mortgage providing for no amortization of principal over the mortgage term.

Title insurance. Title insurance that protects against loss or damages arising from past events, issued only to qualified title risks.

Title states. States that provide for the borrower to transfer title to the lender under a long-term mortgage.

Torrens Land Title Registration. A system of title registration requiring that county court recorders act as registrars of title.

Township. Survey lines running in an east-west direction at six-mile intervals from the base line. A township also refers to a 36-square-mile area.

Trade market area. The area from which a shopping center may be expected to attract customers.

Trust deed. A trust deed secures a promissory note and requires a third-party arrangement in which the borrower is the trustor, the lender the beneficiary, and a third party the trustee.

Truth in Lending Act. An act to encourage competition among financial institutions by informing consumers of the cost of credit and permitting consumers to compare various credit terms available.

Unearned fees. Fees that Section 8 of the Real Estate Settlement Procedures Act prohibits as incident to or a part of a real estate settlement service.

Unenforceable contract. A contract valid between the parties but unenforceable if either party elects not to perform.

Unilateral contract. A promise exchanged for an act.

Unit in place. The estimated combined costs of material and labor to construct a unit of material.

Units of comparison. A method of basing gross possible income on relative terms, depending on the property appraised.

Urbanized areas. A Census Bureau definition consisting of a central city or cities and surrounding closely settled territory.

Utility value. The power of a good to create satisfaction or decrease dissatisfaction.

Vacancy and bad debt allowance. A deduction from gross possible income which results in an estimate of effective gross income.

Valid contract. A contract that satisfies all legal requirements.

Valuation process. The orderly analysis and presentation of facts to estimate market value.

Value. The power to command other goods in exchange.

Variable payment mortgages. Amortization of a mortgage calling for a constant payment to principal.

Variable rate mortgages. A mortgage in which the mortgage interest may be changed according to changes in a price index.

Void contract. A contract that has no legal effect.

Voidable contract. Contracts that may be enforced or rejected at the option of one of the parties.

Warranty deed. A deed conveying an interest in real estate generally including five covenants or promises of the grantor.

Womens Council of Realtors®. An affiliate of the National Association of Realtors®.

Wraparound mortgages. A second mortgage that includes an existing mortgage.

Zoning code. Local ordinances establishing land use districts, building height and bulk controls, and density regulations.

Zoning variance. A relaxation of the terms of the zoning ordinance where the variance will not be contrary to the public interest.

Index

This book has been set in 10 and 9 point Times Roman, leaded 2 points. Chapter numbers are 72 point Caslon Foundry and chapter titles are 24 point (large) Helvetica. The size of the type page is 27 picas (plus 3 picas for heads extending in margin) by 46½ picas.